Interpreting American History

INTERPRETING

American

Conversations with Historians

Drawings from life by Gail Garraty

History

John A. Garraty

The Macmillan Company / Collier-Macmillan Limited, London

First Printing

Library of Congress catalog card number: 70–97761

The Macmillan Company

Collier-Macmillan Canada, Ltd., Toronto, Ontario

Printed in the United States of America

The most important part of history is really a series of problems. . . . The way to penetrate beneath the petty superficialities and come to grips with historical realities is to propound one incisive question after another, until the past ceases to look like a smooth record and becomes instead a rough and puzzling set of difficulties.

ALLAN NEVINS, *The Gateway to History*

The past is, by definition, a datum which nothing in the future will change. But the knowledge of the past is something progressive which is constantly transforming and perfecting itself.

MARC BLOCH, *The Historian's Craft*

Introduction

Ⓗ ISTORY is made up of facts, but also of opinions; it is not only, as Leopold von Ranke put it, "what actually happened," but also what people who know what happened think about past events. Facts are often difficult to track down and verify, but once located they are immutable and permanently available. Opinions are easily formed, but are as evanescent as ice in August. Of course, historical opinions are based on facts if they are any good at all, and although nearly all of them are subject eventually to modification if not outright rejection, those that retain their plausibility longest are those developed in minds steeped in knowledge of the past. Good historians have always possessed a high degree of intelligence and imagination (essential elements for the formation of sound opinions), but they have also been masters of enormous amounts of factual information collected over years of patient study. This is what raises their considered opinions to the level of what are called interpretations—complex attempts to order many facts in such a way as to form consistent and thus persuasive explanations of some segment of the past.

This book is principally concerned with historical interpretations. It represents my attempt to find out what twenty-nine important specialists think about American history. The historians I have talked with mention thousands of facts, but employ them primarily to explain and justify their opinions, that is, to interpret history. The result makes up a history of the United States from its colonial beginnings to the present, but this is not the volume to turn to to learn the terms of the charter of the London Company of Virginia, the Sherman Antitrust Act, or the Yalta agreement, although these facts are discussed in its pages. It is, rather, a search for the *meaning* of American history to our own day.

All of these historians are productive scholars and thus their interpretations of their subjects of special interest are readily available. But by the very character of historical writing their published ideas appear in contexts determined by themselves and in response chiefly to their own concerns and judgments. Since historical interpretations tend to raise as many questions as they answer, the published works of these men have often led other historians to new opinions of their own, and these, in turn, have sometimes caused the original writers to modify or refine their views. In many cases the historians have not yet published these second thoughts; in some, perhaps, they had not even formulated their responses to the new interpretations. My second purpose, therefore, was to discover what the historians thought about the impact of their own work on other scholars, to obtain their current judgments on the questions they have written about and pondered over throughout their careers.

My method of investigation, being rather unorthodox, requires description. Having obtained the cooperation of each historian, I sent him a long list of questions related to his particular field of interest. He had the opportunity to reject or modify the questions and to add others he wanted to deal with. Then we spent a day together discussing the questions in the presence of a tape recorder. The reason for this procedure was not, as it might seem, to stimulate debate. It would have been presumptuous of me to engage in a contest or argument with historians of this calibre about subjects where their knowledge exceeds my own. My intent, rather, was to compel the expert to respond to his own thoughts, to trigger his enthusiasm for his subject, to encourage him to clarify and expand his ideas and to relate them to other ideas. Thus the prepared list of questions served only as a framework. The answers invariably brought other questions to my mind, and these often led the historian to ask (and answer) new questions of his own. However, my own role was not passive. I came to each interview well prepared and did not hesitate to challenge the experts when their remarks seemed to contradict or ignore facts or interpretations with which I was familiar. But always my purpose was to discover and record the views of the specialist; occasionally I might push or prod him, but he always had the last word.

After each session was over, the tape was transcribed, producing a manuscript of about a hundred pages on the average. This material I then reduced to the length of a chapter by selecting the most interesting and significant exchanges, by excising repetitious material, and by eliminating the excess verbiage that always insinuates itself into conversation. The manuscript was then retyped and sent to the historian for review and further revisions; these ranged from small changes in phraseology and the correction of minor errors of fact to extensive alterations and additions in cases where the historian had further thoughts or where new ideas occurred to him. Thus, while the interviews appear here as direct discourse, they must not be taken as literal transcriptions of "what actually happened." They are in a sense interpretations of these facts, the combined opinions of the experts and myself about what we said. My object has been to preserve the flavor and informal spirit of the interviews but to enhance the transmission of thought by making the material more precise and concise. Both the tapes and the original typescripts are on deposit in the Oral History Collection at Columbia University, where scholars interested in the facts may consult them freely.

Collectively, these interviews provide an authoritative overview of American history and of contemporary historical scholarship. Yet of course, a different group of historians, dealing with the same questions, would have answered many of them quite differently. In deciding whom to interview I sought the "best man" in each field and with only two or three exceptions I obtained the cooperation of my first choice. But anyone familiar with the historical profession could put together a distinguished list without including many of my selections. Moreover, most of the men interviewed are middle-aged and a few are in their seventies. They represent the present-day historical establishment. As a group they hold chairs in the best universities, have headed the major professional associations, have won all the most coveted fellowships and awards, including nine Pulitzer prizes. Undoubtedly their common experience of having lived and done most of their work in the second third of the twentieth century has, along with success and honor, colored and perhaps limited their understanding of the American past. Most of them belong to what may loosely be called the "consensus school" of historical writing, a school which tends to minimize the past conflicts in the American experience and to stress the shared values that the great majority of Americans have held.

Obviously the younger radical scholars of the New Left (and some of the older Marxist and Beardian historians) would take issue with many of the interpretations described on the following pages. I considered including some historians of these persuasions in my list, but to have done so would have meant either sacrificing consistency of approach or greatly increasing the length of the book. Instead, I asked most of the historians interviewed to evaluate the work of the new radical scholars, and I believe their responses are among the most interesting passages in the discussions. Most of my historians are quite sympathetic to what the New Left is attempting, although they find their work full of serious flaws. Their comments do not do full justice to the New Left approach, but I leave to some other historian that task. I commend to him my general approach, and suggest he ask the New Left scholars the question: "What is your opinion of the so-called consensus school of American history?"

I am deeply indebted to many persons for help in preparing this book. First of all, of course, I wish to thank the historians themselves, both for their time and in many cases for opening their homes to me and my wife and entertaining us royally. One of the many benefits that I have obtained from the project has been the new friendships I have made. I also wish to thank David Tiffany, Jay Carroll, and Joseph Falzone of The Macmillan Company for invaluable editorial assistance and advice, and

Ene Sirvet and Romaine Wasserman for their careful typing of the manuscript. Finally I am deeply grateful to my wife Gail. Her portraits of the historians, drawn from life during the interviews, introduce each chapter and speak for themselves, but her contribution has been larger than this and more pervasive. Her presence at the interviews provided the historians with an intelligent and interested but nonprofessional audience. It made them, I am sure, more expansive and at the same time less likely to take too much for granted and thus to speak more directly to the large audience at which this book is aimed. Beyond this, of course, her company lightened the burdens of travel and added greatly to the enjoyment of the entire experience. It is my hope that this enjoyment has by some alchemy been injected into the book and that through the book it will reach those who read the following pages.

John A. Garraty
Columbia University

Contents

Part I

Part II

Interpreting American History

Part I

Sigmund Diamond

The European Basis of American Civilization

ALTHOUGH he is currently a professor of sociology at
Columbia University, Sigmund Diamond was trained as
a historian; most of his published work has involved
applying sociological insights to the study of the past. In
his *The Reputation of the American Businessman* (1955),
he analyzed the obituary notices of six famous tycoons,
ranging from the early nineteenth-century financier,
Stephen Girard, to John D. Rockefeller and Henry Ford,
and showed how these stilted and pietistic sources could
be used to throw light on the social and economic attitudes of the times. In a series of brilliant articles, he has
discussed the social ideas of the founders of the English
and French colonies, and described how actual conditions
in the New World shaped the development of colonial
institutions in ways the founders had never anticipated.
He has also published an important collection of source
materials on late nineteenth-century history, *The Nation
Transformed* (1963). In this discussion Professor Diamond
focuses on the transfer of institutions from Europe to
America in the early colonial period.

John A. Garraty Professor Diamond, if Europeans actually reached the New World as early as the eleventh century, why did they do so little about it at the time, and why was knowledge of their discoveries lost?

Sigmund Diamond If it's true that nothing is so powerful as an idea that has met its time, it's also the case that nothing is quite so futile as a discovery before its time. The early discovery of America proved fruitless because the Europeans did not know what to make of it; they did not have the techniques and facilities to make something of it. America could not really be "discovered" until the means for maintaining a system of regular communication between the homeland and the colonies was perfected, until techniques of navigation and seamanship of a sufficient degree of sophistication had evolved. Then, also, it was necessary to have an economy of a sufficient degree of development so as to be able to maintain the kind of effort that was necessary to engage in colonization, and it was necessary also to have an economy of a sufficient degree of sophistication and organization to make profitable use of whatever resources the colonies might provide.

The third thing that was missing, one of great importance, was the development of national states powerful enough to organize and mobilize the political and military as well as the economic resources necessary to make colonization a reality.

J.A.G. Will you summarize the situation in Western Europe at the time of Columbus, and explain why his discoveries—which, after all, did not amount to very much in themselves—led to the direct and continuous development of both North and South America?

S.D. The relationship between the timing of Columbus' discoveries and the general economic situation of Western Europe at the end of the fifteenth century is an old story. The search for new trade routes to the Orient, in order to avoid the competition of the Italian cities which had dominated the trade with the Orient and the Eastern Mediterranean, was very important. That was one of the factors that was lacking in the eleventh and twelfth centuries.

J.A.G. But after all, Columbus didn't find what he was looking for, a new route to the Orient.

S.D. But even though he didn't find what he was looking for, he did find something. Then the problem was: How could you make the most advantageous use of what was found? There was, on the part not only of the Spaniards, but of the French and the English too, at a slightly later time, a considerable period characterized by trial and error, by experimentation to see to what uses the discoveries could be put. It was not as if, once having been discovered, the New World was instantaneously found to be both desirable and also profitable. There was a long and very difficult period of trying a wide variety of techniques of exploitation and utilization until the colonizing powers hit upon some mode of social and economic organization that would make colonization worthwhile.

J.A.G. After Columbus had found this large area of land, previously unknown, was its development primarily a result of the situation in Europe or of the attractions which the area itself possessed for the Europeans?

S.D. The forces were essentially, I think, at the outset propulsive. It was an explosion from the inside out. The combination of "rightness"—political development combined with economic and technological advances—led to this extraordinary explosive European expansionism.

The attractions of the New World were different by section, and for different groups of people, too. Although, even at a relatively early period, there was for many Europeans an Edenic quality about the New World, it must not be forgotten that no matter how utopian the image, the New World was fraught with unbelievable hardships and dangers. Even more threatening was the fact that no one really knew what to expect. The unknown always has great terrors, and this was a situation in which people were confronted in real fact with the unknown. In order to make them face those fears, there had to be some very powerful impulses pushing them in that direction.

J.A.G. Howard Mumford Jones in his book *O Brave New World* comments on the question that you have now raised. He points out that both Europeans and actual settlers were often ambivalent in their attitudes toward America, some seeing it as an Eden, as you put it, others as "hell on earth." Were these divergent views based on the particular experiences and knowledge of the individuals who held them, or was the New World merely a kind of screen on which individuals projected their underlying views of life?

S.D. I hope you won't force me to say that it was either one or the other. It was both. The fact is that the lack of knowledge was extraordinary and the degree of misinformation unbelievable. Colonists did not know the areas into which they were moving; they had no basis for comparison. There was also an extraordinary amount of lying. I once had occasion to investigate a myth which circulated widely in the sixteenth and early seventeenth centuries—the myth of the city of Norumbega, a glittering city of Kublai Khan, with palaces and pleasure domes, somewhere on the banks of the Penobscot River. It's located in many of the maps of the period, and there is no doubt that, as a myth, it exerted extraordinary power in leading men to explore the area. Of course, it never existed, but that didn't prevent some people from claiming that they had been there and from writing glowing accounts which whetted the appetites of others to try to find it.

But there's another factor, too. Much of North America consisted of empty space. It was possible, in the words of Michael Drayton, to create a society "where none before hath stood." This provided an opportunity (which has seldom occurred in the history of mankind) to escape from history, to begin from scratch. This acted as an extraordinary impetus to social thought; it became possible to speculate in a very real way about creating a better social order, to think about a society all of whose institutions are "the right ones." This explains the important utopian component in early writing about the Americas.

J.A.G.   But men had devised many ideal societies before they found empty America.

S.D.   They had *talked* about ideal societies; Plato had even drawn up a code of laws for one. There had even been occasions when it was possible to put these plans into effect, and by colonization. This is one of the reasons why I'm particularly interested in colonization. Where a group of people are placed where they don't have to accommodate themselves to already existing societies, they can begin with a clean slate. Then, theoretically, they do not have to make compromises with situations that already exist and they can live in such a way as to eliminate those aspects of their own society which they have found wanting.

Plato's code of laws was for a Greek colony. The same thing happened not infrequently during the Middle Ages, as the frontier of Europe expanded to the East. The forms of settlement and land tenure were considerably different in the newly colonized areas from what they were in already established areas. In part, this was because of the belief that, since they were beginning at the beginning, they could plan more rationally, and in part, because to attract people to new areas it was necessary to make certain kinds of concessions.

J.A.G.   Does that explain why Sir Thomas More placed his famous Utopia in the New World?

S.D.   I don't know, but that's not the only symbolic connection that could be made between *Utopia* and the New World. When Sir Humphrey Gilbert went down with his ship while returning from Newfoundland to England, he was seen standing on the deck, a book in his hand, and his last words were supposed to have been, "It is as near to Heaven by sea as by land," which is an almost direct quotation from More's *Utopia*. I don't know if the story is true, but it is very appropriate. There is certainly a relationship between Utopian thought and colonization. Exploration and colonization provided, it seems to me, an extraordinary stimulus to social thought in general. So long as a person or a society knows only one way of doing things, there is nothing problematic about "that way." It frequently happens that there isn't even a word for "that way." But as soon as an alternative is seen to exist, then that which has always been taken for granted suddenly becomes problematic. Men ask, "Why do *we* do it this way, and *they* do it another way?" They then have to decide which is the better way.

One of the consequences of exploration was that it made men aware that other people behaved differently from the way they behaved. An anthropological element entered European thought, and it had very subtle and in some ways humanizing consequences.

J.A.G. I wish you would explain that a little more fully. It seems to me that the experience that Western European nations had with the native populations they came in contact with did not change their values at all. In fact, I've always been impressed by their extreme ethnocentricity, their assumption that what was different was either morally wrong, or, from a practical point of view, stupid. The heartless way in which they treated the native populations of North and South America is only one example of this.

S.D. It's probably a good idea to make sure we understand exactly what we mean. To say that experience with other peoples changed the values of Western Europeans in certain respects is one kind of statement. To say that it created the possibility for some people to look at things in a different way is another. Then there is the question: Irrespective of what it did to values, what consequences did it have for policy?

With respect to policy, you're quite right, policy tended to be ethnocentric. But there are some startling exceptions. For a period at least, in French Canada, the policy was anything but ethnocentric. French policy with respect to the Indians in the early seventeenth century was based on an Aristotelian view of human nature which found all men innately the same. The French recognized the legal and political equality of the Indian, and they encouraged intermarriage. They recognized that there were differences between Frenchmen and Indians, but these differences were, in the Aristotelian sense, "accidents." The Indians were pagans, for example, but they could be converted. The Indians didn't wear the same kinds of clothes that the French did, but this, too, could be easily changed. Little Indian girls could be taught to embroider even as little French girls were taught to embroider. The Indians could be taught French. The Indian policy of the French government was not based on notions of Indian inferiority—quite the contrary.

But policies varied from country to country, and from time to time. Different groups in the mother country might have different points of view concerning policy toward the natives. This was precisely the situation in French Canada, where there were at least three distinctively different points of view toward the Indians: one embodied by the Church; another by the Crown; and the third by the fur-trade interests.

J.A.G. With all due allowances for the Canadian case, wouldn't you agree that the tendency was certainly in the other direction?

S.D. Not entirely. A similar point of view was taken by some Spaniards, who opposed the brutal exploitation and extermination of Indians. I don't say that humaneness became the dominant point of view. But I do say that experience with different kinds of people, living in very different ways, and with very different beliefs, created for Frenchmen, Spaniards, and Englishmen problems of understanding both society and human nature that they had never had before. In some cases, their perplexity led to a more humane view of life, and a more cosmopolitan view. Whether this was translated into policy is a different question. Most of the time it was not. But at least policy was formulated on the basis of a conflict of views, not by the automatic and unquestioning acceptance of a traditional view.

J.A.G. Is it possible to strike a balance about the fate of the first generation in any newly settled area? Were the hardships and losses involved in founding new settlements greater than the benefits?

S.D. It was very difficult for the first colonists; there's no doubt about that. There was a high degree of disappointment and dissatisfaction, partly because anticipation was so high that reality couldn't have measured up to the glittering expectations with which so many embarked on these ventures. Beyond that, life was very difficult. Settlers were simply not equipped, on the most elementary physical and technical level, to handle the practical, day-to-day problems that they had to face. The reality was at such variance from the expectation that people were doomed to disappointment. Letters written by the Virginia settlers in the early seventeenth century to members of their families refer to the concept of psychosomatic illness, although of course they don't use the term: "Our people do grow diseased both of their body and of their minds by having this country too much overpraised to them."

J.A.G. In speaking of the motives of colonizers, it seems to me important to distinguish between the motives of the governments that were behind colonization, of the organizers of particular enterprises, and finally of the actual settlers who crossed the Atlantic. Why did the ruler of Spain, France, and England want colonies in North and South America?

S.D. The history of colonization in the New World has emphasized to an extraordinary degree the question of motives. Did the original settlers come to Virginia to establish, as was once said, a First Republic? Did the original settlers of Massachusetts Bay or Plymouth come in search of religious freedom?

Their motivation is important, obviously. But it's not the only point of importance in discussing colonization, and before answering your question I would like to say what the other matter of importance was. What were the forms of social organization which could be developed in order to harness and mobilize the energies of the settlers? Obviously this question is not unrelated to motivation, because forms of organization designed to harness the energies of the colonists will depend to some degree on what the founders think the motives of the settlers are.

The range of motives which led people to participate in colonizing ventures was very wide indeed. Some who joined the service of the Virginia Company were footloose and fancy free, seeking roughneck and daredevil adventure. Others, of very much the same social class in England, came, as they put it, to repair their decayed estates. One of the problems which the leaders of colonization enterprises had to solve was, what forms of organization would capture men with a wide array of motives? How could you get people who were interested in venturing their purses but not their bodies to participate in the same venture with people who had no money but were willing to risk their bodies? And how could you appeal to a king who might not really be concerned in any significant way with colonization, but who didn't want, say, the Spaniards to steal a march on him?

The importance of colonies for European monarchs must be seen within the matrix of views, common all over Western Europe in the sixteenth and seventeenth centuries, that we call "mercantilist." These assumed a close relationship between political power and economic power, and saw colonies as both political and economic organizations. Rivalry was intense. In the course of my own research I have come across many dispatches written by spies in the service of the king of France, informing him what the Spanish government was doing in the way of colonization, and warning him that if he did not want the king of Spain to beat him to the punch, he had better take cognizance of this development.

The earliest known map of the English colony at Jamestown exists in, of all places, the Royal Spanish Archives at Simancas. It was drawn by an Irish Catholic sailor on an English ship, who was a spy in the service of the king of Spain. He was caught, but not until after he had smuggled his map to the Spanish ambassador in London. In the Vatican archives there is a letter written by an English Jesuit warning the Pope of the departure of a ship from England to North America loaded with Protestants. The ship was the *Mayflower*.

In the nations which were involved in colonization, religious motivations were of considerable importance, too—not only the idea of the general conversion of the heathen to Christianity, but also conflicts between Protestants and Catholics, as in the case I just mentioned of the Jesuit who warned the Society for the Propagation of the Faith of the departure of English Protestants to the New World.

There is no doubt that the whole colonizing thrust of sixteenth-century Spain can be seen as a continuation of the Spanish idea of crusade, symbolizing the importance of the religious motive and also of the national motive. The idea of crusade in Spain had an intensity deeper and greater than in other Western European countries. After all, it was only in 1492 that the reconquest of Christian Spain from the Moors was finally accomplished. The "reconquest" of Spain and the conquest of the New World were seen as separate from one another only in the way in which one chapter of a book is separate from another. The Spanish national state was forged on the anvil of a national and religious war against the infidel, and Spanish exploration and colonization were seen as a further development of the process.

In the case of entrepreneurs, the British and Dutch especially, colonization was a business enterprise. Colonies might enhance state power and the glory of God, but it should be undertaken in such places, in such forms, and for such purposes as would return a profit to the investors.

J.A.G. How did the founders go about the task of attracting settlers with a variety of motives? Did the conception of the New World as *tabula rasa* lead them to believe that new kinds of societies could actually be created?

S.D. Well, let's begin with the particular problems faced by the leaders of colonizing ventures. Some of these, of course, were endemic, enduring problems of human relations and social organization. The way they attempted to solve these problems was distinctively in the mode of the sixteenth and seventeenth century, but the problems were common to all systems of social relations. As a result, there is a constant tension in early colonization between those things which are attempted to be done out of a sense of desirability—what would it be *good* to do?— and those done of necessity—what *must* be done to solve our problems? Not always are these the same. When they conflict, there is great poignancy and even sometimes tragedy in the story of colonization.

The history of English, French, Dutch, and Swedish colonization in the New World (I deliberately exclude Spanish colonization for the moment) shows that one of the primary requisites for successful colonization was the raising of money to finance the venture. In all of these cases, colonization was not undertaken by the state, at least not at the start. Colonizing efforts were for the most part carried out as an aspect of private investment. The state had its interest in these ventures and might interfere in one way or another, but the impetus came from private investment.

Thus, one of the indispensable tasks was to devise forms of social organization which could enlist the purses of the people with money to invest. Various inducements had to be offered. In general, the major inducements were the possibility of profit through the acquisition of land, and privileges with respect to the trade which it was confidently and widely expected would soon flourish.

Another problem was adjusting expectations to reality. In a good many cases in early seventeenth-century English colonization, and sometimes French colonization, the original expectations of the leaders turned out to be very wide of the mark. The original forms of economic activity designed to earn the profits to pay off the investment turned out to be simply impossible in many cases, because the resources out of which it was expected that the profit would be made did not exist. The two great models that dazzled the minds of Englishmen in the period were the extraordinary success of the Spaniards in Mexico and Peru, where silver and gold had been found in profusion, and the mighty British East India Company. Perhaps they should have known that there were great differences between the situations they faced and those encountered by the Spaniards and the British East India Company. There was no gold and silver in Virginia or in New England, and no large indigenous population to be mobilized into a labor force. Efforts to use the Indians, who were few in number to begin with, failed. The East India Company exploited an area which had a highly developed economy; the possibility of establishing lucrative trades existed. With whom were the people in Massachusetts, Virginia, North and South Carolina, and Canada expected to trade? They thought that if only they could penetrate behind the screen of forests to westward they would find the glittering cities of Kublai Khan, so close did they think they were to the coast of China. That myth, incidentally, died very hard indeed. Jean Nicolet, founder of the city of Trois Rivieres on the St. Lawrence, a great *coureur de bois* and fur trapper, as late as the middle of the seventeenth century went annually on an expedition to the Great Lakes to tap additional sources of furs. He always took with him robes of silk and damask to don in case he came across a party of Chinese mandarins.

Eventually, it became clear that they were not that close to China. As a consequence, their original goals could not be achieved; they were forced to change their minds about the purposes of colonization. In case after case, they went through a series of experiments to find commodities which could be produced cheaply and in sufficient quantity, and sold at a high enough price in the markets of Europe to provide them with the profits to pay a return on the investment of their shareholders.

Changed goals meant transformed social organizations; these were, in effect, organizations suited to settled agricultural communities. The types of person needed for the tasks characteristic of agricultural life differ from those needed to dig for gold. The requirements became greater in both a quantitative and a qualitative sense. A larger labor force was needed, but also a force of sober, stable workmen—not roughneck cut-throats who intended to stay only for a year or two and then go back to Europe with their pockets bulging.

How to get such people? Obviously, it was necessary to offer certain incentives or inducements.

These were particular sixteenth- or seventeenth-century problems, but as I have said, there were also persistent problems of social organization and human relations. One was the problem of maintaining order, of creating a social system within which men will carry out their assigned tasks in an orderly fashion. Stated in this abstract way this is clearly a problem that all societies—not only those of the sixteenth and seventeenth centuries—have to face.

Another enduring problem, particularly acute in the colonial situation, was the problem of motivation: how to get people *willingly* to carry out the tasks that they are expected to carry out. I stress "willingly," but perhaps that's saying a bit too much. Of course, there are forms of social organization in which this problem is solved by coercion. I suppose in every society it is solved by some mixture of coerciveness and willingness. But there's a great difference in how much of each, and *vive la différence!* Seventeenth-century colonizers made extraordinary efforts, some of them very sophisticated, to get men to carry out their assignments, to behave as they were supposed to behave, not because some authority was holding a pistol to their heads but because it was the right way to behave.

What created extraordinary problems for early colonizers and what produced the extraordinarily rapid social change that took place in the original colonies was the fundamental incompatibility between the solutions that were devised to solve these problems of order and motivation. What was done in order to solve the problem of motivation made it impossible to solve the problem of order in the way intended. Something had to give, and what gave was the founders' theories of social organization. It was easier to sacrifice preconceived ideas of order than to sacrifice motivation, which was essential to the recruitment of a labor force. After all, without labor, the whole venture would have collapsed.

J.A.G. Would you illustrate this point?

S.D. The example that I will choose is Virginia. The leaders of the Virginia enterprise faced first the problem of order. "Order," to seventeenth-century Englishmen, meant acting in accordance with one's position in society. In a famous speech in *Troilus and Cressida*, Shakespeare makes Ulysses say, "Take but degree away, untune that string, and hark what discord follows." Just as "disorder" in the universe of nature meant that the elements were out of tune with one another, social disorder meant that the elements of society were not acting in accordance with the position into which, for whatever reasons, each had been put. Disorder might result when the lower ranks of society acted as if they were kings, or, again citing Shakespeare, as in *King Lear,* when a king forgets that he's a king and abdicates.

The social organization that the leaders of the Virginia enterprise developed was the joint stock company, a group of people who invested either sums of money or their labor. The price of a share of stock was fixed at the cost of transporting one worker from England to Virginia. At the outset, the founders intended to establish a trading post more than a colony; they were going to hunt for gold and silver (as the Spanish had) and trade with the local population (as the East India Company merchants were doing).

In a way, the enterprise has to be looked at not as a colony, or even a political territorial unit, but as a certain form of property. Virginia was, in 1607, the *property* of a joint stock company known as the Virginia Company of London. The colonists were less officials and citizens than they were employees in one or another position within the table of organization of the Company. It's as if the General Motors Corporation were to get hold of an island someplace and establish a factory on it; those who would be transported there to run the enterprise would be less citizens of a political unit than employees of the General Motors Corporation.

The leaders of the Virginia enterprise developed a table of organization in which every person leaving England to go to Virginia had a particular position. Of course, the term "table of organization" is an anachronism when applied to the seventeenth century; nobody then used it. But the concept is not at all anachronistic. The leaders assumed that order and stability would be maintained in Jamestown, that the Company would exercise the authority necessary to achieve its objectives. Each man would be attached to a particular position, and he would behave in the way appropriate to his position within the social structure. The governor would act in the way it was defined that a governor ought to act, and so on all the way down. The degree to which people were conscious of this pattern varied from time to time, but the more I examine the historical record, the more convinced I become that they were more, not less, conscious of it. In at least one case in the history of Virginia, every position in the colony was named, and next to the name was the description of the behavior that was prescribed as appropriate for it.

The form of social organization devised for Virginia is identical with the model of what contemporary sociologists would call "a formal organization," in which, within the frame of reference of the organization, each man has a particular status, and in which all of his behavior was supposed to flow from the necessities and opportunities that were imposed upon and open to that particular status.

When it became apparent, however, that the Virginians were not going to find gold and silver, they had to convert themselves into some kind of agricultural settlement producing a staple for export to Europe. This required a labor force far greater in quantity and far better in quality. It was one thing to create a table of organization, but as the personnel director of any corporation will tell you, it's another thing to get bodies to fill that table of organization. Thus, in order to solve the second of the two persistent problems of social organization, motivation, they had to offer a series of concessions to induce people to accept the positions that the Virginia Company allotted to them in the "revised" table of organization.

These concessions varied from time to time. The most important in my view, was offering the possibility of promotion within the system by establishing the institution of indentured servitude. Those who accepted a very inferior position in the system for a certain number of years knew automatically that, having survived the period of indenture, they would be promoted to a better position within the organization. They would be given land. In effect, the possibility of promotion to a superior position was used as the bait to get people to accept the burdens of an inferior position in society.

In a way, this is similar to the common practice in contemporary American industry known as "automatic progression." A man hired, let us say, as a milling machine operator, class D, is at the end of six months automatically promoted to class C, with 10 cents or 15 cents an hour more, and eventually to class B and class A. The incentive used to get workers to accept the disadvantages of an inferior salary is the promise of automatic promotion. In a society, we don't call this automatic progression; we call it social mobility. Indentured servitude was a built-in guarantee of social mobility for everybody who survived the five- or seven-year period of indenture.

So indentured servitude became a mechanism to recruit a labor force and motivate it to work with discipline and diligence. The possibility of being promoted to a higher status, that of landowner, provided the incentive to get people to accept an inferior position in the society.

However, as soon as a person became a landowner, his position in the society was no longer what it had been when he first came into the system; he no longer behaved in accordance with the expectations of the leaders of the Company, and with the appropriate degree of discipline. For example, he wanted to sell the tobacco he grew on his land for the best price he could obtain from any ship captain. The Company expected him, as a dutiful employee, to sell his tobacco to the Company magazine at the price the Company fixed. The effect of the concession that had been granted was to give him a new status, and the behavior that flowed from his new status differed from the expected behavior of an employee of the Company. A social basis, so to speak, of disobedience was created.

But other concessions were offered, too, and these had the consequence of increasing the number of statuses that people in Virgina had, thus further complicating their behavior. At the earliest stage in the history of Virginia, virtually the entire population consisted of males. But the Company, desirous of increasing the satisfactions of people living in Virginia, and also anxious to cut labor costs by having at least part of the labor force produced and brought up in Virginia rather than being imported from England, began to ship women to Virginia to be distributed among the more loyal and hard-working employees of the Company as wives. This was actually undertaken as a business venture by a subsidiary of the Virginia Company.

Now consider the consequences of this importation of women. The employee-turned-landowner was now also a husband, and soon a father too. He no longer lived in a barracks inhabited only by other single males. The rigid, military discipline instituted by the Company became impossible. Whatever compulsion he felt to behave in a particular way might follow more from his status as father and husband than from his status as employee.

Another concession that was offered by the Company was the rights of various categories of the population to the consulted in an assembly called by the Governor. The point of this was not to involve the population in the process of law-making, not to share authority with the Company in any way. The purpose was to establish another link in the chain of command, so that the Governor would have a forum at which he could tell the colonists what they were expected to do. However, because of long-standing English traditions of the relationship of political authority to property-holding, it soon became the right of these colonists first to petition for redress of grievances and then to do more than that. Thus, a concession introduced in the interest of efficiency created another status for men which the Company never anticipated, complicating the relationship between employees and higher authorities within the Company.

Each new status created a new relationship, and these relationships didn't always impel people to act in the same way. Instead of a single relationship which connected everybody in Virginia to everybody else in Virginia (the relationship envisaged by the original table of organization of the Company), a whole network of relationships was soon established, some of which were complementary, but others contradictory. This network of relationships resulted from the very actions the Company felt itself forced to perform to get people into the single relationship of the table of organization of the Company. A network of interlocking, sometimes contradictory relationships in which each person occupies a multiplicity of statuses, his behavior being the product of all of his statuses—not simply of one of them—seems to me to be more characteristic of a society than of a formal organization. Thus, Virginia was transformed from a formal organization into a society. What the Company did to solve the problem of motivation made it impossible for it to solve the problem of order as it had intended, and the form of organization then had to change.

J.A.G.   In what way was indentured servitude different from the old system of apprenticeship?

S.D.   In the first place, I do not rest my entire argument about social mobility on the institution of indentured servitude. I stressed indentured servitude to show that even though men were brought to the New World in the most inferior positions, they had the opportunity to move upward. As to the relationship between indentured servitude and apprenticeship, there were obviously certain points of similarity but there were also important differences. Apprenticeship resulted in a person's learning a skill, but indentured servitude resulted in something much much more drastic—the servant was promoted to a higher place in society, he became a landowner.

In the seventeenth century, the consequences of landownership were enormous indeed, and not only economic. Landownership carried with it legal and political rights, and also the right to command social respect. Apprenticeship did not lead to the same political and social consequences. It was, to be sure, a way up the occupational ladder, but indentured servitude was a way up the social ladder. So much was this the case in the North American colonies that I would say that it was one of the most important facts of all American history. The possibility of rising in the world was used as the most important mechanism by which to break people loose from Old World roots.

J.A.G.   Was social mobility the bait, or economic mobility? Wasn't social mobility subordinate in the minds of the recruited to the economic mobility that came with the ownership of land?

S.D.   Probably, but the two things are so inextricably intertwined that one can't really speak of one without the other. I'm impressed by a number of cases in which social mobility was clearly articulated. For example, in French Canada in the seventeenth century, the government sought to recruit an agricultural population, to be fixed on the land, in order to supply food for the French West Indian sugar islands. To this end, laws were enacted providing incentives to the *habitants* of French Canada to raise wheat and cattle, and rather high taxes were imposed on the raising of horses to provide an incentive for the raising of other livestock.

Despite these incentives and restraints, the Canadians continued to raise horses, and apparently enjoyed themselves hugely racing up and down the countryside. Why did they do this? I don't mean to sound very mystical, but it was almost as if they recognized the social meaning of the relationship between *cheval* and *chevalerie*. The higher orders of society were those who rode horses. The possession of a horse and the ability to ride one were signs of social status. When those who in the past had seen other men ride now could own horses, they raised horses with a vengeance. A similar situation existed in some of the Spanish colonies, where the social meaning of a horse sometimes led men, as in Canada, to engage in "uneconomic" behavior. Given the general situation of the sixteenth and seventeenth centuries, social and economic mobility proceeded hand in hand.

J.A.G. Were the founders of the Virginia Company aware of the social consequences of the indentured servant system in the beginning?

S.D. I don't think they were, and that is where, for them, the tragedy and poignancy lay. They saw that economic improvement would lure people into the labor force, but assumed that these people would continue to behave as they had in the past. But of course, they behaved as it was *possible* for them to behave, a very different matter.

Social and also political consequences followed economic concessions. What the Company did to solve one set of problems created another set, which could not be solved within the established framework.

That was the founders' misfortune, but it was America's great fortune. They could not solve the problem of order, they could not create the social stability they wanted. Had they persisted in attempting to do so, either they could not have recruited the labor force they needed, or the settlers would have rebelled against the restraints imposed on them.

As it was, men recruited on the basis of a certain set of psychological assumptions were put into a social system based upon a set of social assumptions which were contradictory to the psychological assumptions. The theory of motivation subscribed to by the founders was essentially an egoistic one; self-interest was counted upon to recruit the settlers. But the social organization in which these people were being put at the outset at least provided very little room for the play of economic self-interest. This severe and highly disciplined social organization had to be loosened up to give freer play to self-interest. In every case, social organizations characterized at the outset by severe discipline broke down. In my view, social revolutions of great importance occurred in the seventeenth century in all of the North American colonies. This was the social cost that the founders paid to recruit a voluntary labor force.

J.A.G. The word "voluntary" in your last sentence encourages me to ask how you account for slavery in this equation? Wouldn't slavery have been the logical answer to the problem of obtaining an ordered, controlled labor force?

S.D.   Slavery was used when it became apparent that the cost of producing certain commodities could be reduced by the use of slaves. But the English had not had any direct experience with slavery; it took considerable time for them to see its possibilities, and by that time the revolution I spoke of had been completed.

The situation in the Spanish colonies was different. At least in Mexico and Peru, the Spaniards did not have to offer concessions or inducements to recruit a labor force. Their problem was how to develop a social organization and forms of social control to mobilize and exploit an already existing native labor force. The Spaniards didn't have to pay as high a price for labor, to put it in blunt economic terms, as the French and English did. Thus, certain important aspects of freedom in North America can be explained as part of the price that had to be paid to recruit a voluntary labor force.

J.A.G.   Would you comment on the political aspects of this "price"? When the House of Burgesses was established in Virginia, for example, was this seen even by the colonists as a concession? Or was it seen simply as as an institution to deal with a practical problem?

S.D.   Well, even if I were to agree, as to a very large extent I do, that the reason for the creation of representative political institutions was overwhelmingly practical, this does not negate the possibility that the long-run consequences were very different from those intended. For example, there is no doubt that the great function of the English Parliament has been to impose limitations on the exercise of arbitrary power by the king. But Parliament was created not by the opponents of kings, but by the kings themselves. Parliaments in the beginning were the highest expression of royal authority, and were called into session by the king to tell his subjects what he expected of them. But institutions, once created, can be adapted for purposes quite different from those intended by their creators.

J.A.G.   But that's exactly my point! Isn't there a great difference, psychologically and socially, between setting up a system which gives people land and which willy-nilly changes their social status and their social expectations, and a system which, having done that, associates political power with the ownership of land? Did the creation of the House of Burgesses have the same effect on the colonists as the granting of land did?

S.D.   I think they were aware that it gave them rights and powers they had not had before, and they proceeded to make use of them. They did not, by virtue of the creation of representative institutions, suddenly become revolutionaries. But it now became possible, for example, to petition for redress of grievances, which indicates the possibility of taking certain kinds of initiatives in the political sphere. I have gone through many documents relating to the British colonies and a great many relating to the French in Canada. There are certain striking contrasts. The sheer number of pieces of paper relating to the one colony of Canada, which had no more than about 70,000 or 75,000 people, is almost as large as those relating to all of the British colonies, indicating that the degree of administrative oversight of French Canada was far greater than that of the British American colonies. Moreover, two classes of documents are not uncommon in the case of the British colonies, and are notable by their absence in the French case: one is petitions for redress of grievances; the other, documents revealing evidence of grassroots organization for the solution of local problems. In the French case, the most trivial problem—a dispute about a man's cow that strayed into the backyard of another colonist and ate his hay—might have to be decided in the Ministry of Colonies in Paris. The thrust of French policy was to discourage local organization for the solution of local problems, in startling contrast to English practice.

J.A.G.   How did the French deal with the problem of recruiting labor for their Canadian colony?

S.D.   The French were never as willing as the English to pay as high a price for a labor force, and the fact of the matter is they never succeeded in recruiting a large population. Some concessions, indeed, were made. The *habitants* in French Canada had considerably more in the way of economic possibilities open to them than the peasants in France itself. On the other hand, the key personnel involved in the establishment of French society in Canada were the *seignieurs*, and a *seignieur* in Canada had far less power and authority than a *seignieur* in France. The French never offered much inducement to get the labor force that they wanted. In a way, they were very Cartesian about it; they tried to do by rationality what the English did with money. They tried to shave costs by devising all kinds of schemes to increase the labor supply without offering what had to be done to get people to come.

There are in the French Archives a good many reports which are marvelous for the social ingenuity and careful planning they reveal. To take one example: an official in the Ministry of Colonies wrote to Colbert about the need to build a larger population in Canada. He pointed out that the government had to bear the cost of transporting settlers, and that since the mode of recruitment involved whole families, the cost included shipping many people who did not enter the labor force. Wouldn't it be better, he asked, to send only single males, active, hardworking, strong? After, say, a year, when they had become inured to the climate and the conditions of life, the government could, on a business basis, ship single women who could be distributed among them as wives. This new labor force would be paid for by the husbands, not by the government. Instead of paying the cost of shipping children over, the children would be born in Canada. To some degree, of course, this was done, but never on a very large scale.

J.A.G. Wouldn't the indentured servant system have solved this problem for the French as it did for the English in Virginia? Why were the French unable to see the advantage of this system?

S.D. I don't know. They were unwilling to pay the price that had to be paid in terms of improved conditions to recruit a large labor force. There was also a serious problem of "leakage" in the Canadian situation. To get people to behave within certain limits, one must eliminate alternative ways of behaving. Yet even French peasants in Canada could engage, against the government's violent objection, in the fur trade. The fur trade was a very serious drain on the labor supply, and it encouraged ways of behaving which compromised the government's objective of building a settled, disciplined, docile, peasantlike labor force on the land.

J.A.G. Did the harsh climatic conditions of Canada hinder recruitment too?

S.D. I think so. It has often been pointed out that Frenchmen were much less willing to migrate than Englishmen. There are some rather plaintive reports in the French documents which say, "No Frenchman wants to get beyond the sound of his own church bell." But, aside from this reluctance, there were other places Frenchmen could go which were more attractive. The weather in Guadeloupe and Martinique is better, after all, than in Canada, and Guadeloupe and Martinique were profitable sugar-growing regions.

J.A.G. How did the Spanish government recruit settlers for its colonies in America?

S.D. The Spaniards never had to offer enormous concessions to recruit labor because there were, in certain parts of the Spanish Empire at least, large existing populations whose labor could be exploited. But they did have to offer inducements to get men to take charge of the enterprises to recruit such people, so land grants and grants of authority over labor forces were made. And once control over land and labor were offered, it became impossible for these people to consider themselves merely as servants in the employ of a higher authority. They began to act as they felt their needs dictated, rather than simply as instrumentalities of a remote government in Spain.

J.A.G. To what extent did Europeans in America learn from the Indians? Can American civilization be described as the adaptation of one culture to another, and were there any significant differences in this respect between the experiences of the French, the British, and the Spaniards in the New World?

S.D.   Some adaptations, of course, are obvious, such as the influence of the Indians in bringing the attention of the white man to certain kinds of products and techniques. There are other questions about which we know a lot less. In a way, all of the areas in which Europeans interacted with a local native population can be seen as a zone of fracture as well as a point of contact. These fractures had very different consequences for the different groups involved. The policies that were formulated to heal these fractures also differed, and thus the consequences for people in one of these zones of fracture are very different than in another.

It has been remarked, for example, that in Mexico there was a catastrophic decline in the Indian population after the Spanish Conquest. Not all of this was the result of war or of the local population's falling victim to diseases that the white man brought in. Anthropologists have often observed the deep anomy or *malaise* which sometimes takes over a population when it has been utterly defeated, psychologically crushed, by contact with a more advanced society. One of the consequences is a state of such deep despair as to result in a withdrawal really from life. This aspect of contact between the white man and the native populations in the New World needs more study than it has received, and it seems to me that we are in a position to study it because it is now possible to look at historical events in the light of experiences and theories that have been developed in other comparable situations in the modern world.

But obviously this terrible apathy did not overcome all Indian populations. What were the variables which will account for the presence of apathy in some cases and not in others? Was it something about the social structure of group A, as compared with group B, or about the value system of one as compared with another? Or was a matter of different policies applied by the Europeans?

What forms of resistance did the Indians employ of a nonmilitary, nonpolitical kind? Particularly in Latin America, there are any number of interesting examples of survival over a long period of certain aspects of indigenous social structure, family structure, and beliefs.

The reciprocal effects of Catholicism and native religious beliefs in Latin America, for example, make an extraordinarily important story. After all, Latin American Catholicism is a very different kind of Catholicism from, let us say, Irish Catholicism. Very often the Catholic church, like other conquering and missionizing churches, established churches in places which were already sacred to the local population. This was a way of identifying the new religion with the old so as to maximize the likelihood of acceptance of the new. But in a subtle way the new also was changed by its identification with the old.

There is another aspect of the question that I referred to earlier in another connection: the great stimulus that contact with other peoples gives to thought about oneself. There is nothing so important, it seems to me, in stirring the imagination as the realization that what one has always taken for granted is not the only way in which life can be lived and society organized.

J.A.G. Do you think that the anomy you mentioned worked in the other direction in the earliest days of colonization? I've always been impressed by the enormous death rate among the early colonists in Virginia and some other settlements. Do you think that the same sense of loneliness, defeat, and discouragement that wiped out such a large part of the Indian population in Mexico affected white settlers?

S.D. It's entirely probable. It is certainly true that there were physical reasons to account for the high death rate: yellow fever and malaria and cholera, as well as sheer starvation. But the immensity, the loneliness, the sheer isolation must have been an extraordinary strain on most people, tearing them loose from all the certainties that provide guidance and a sense of direction for life. The situation was made even worse by the fact that for so many of the first participants, things were so much less good than they had expected them to be, and the gap between expectation and reality was made even worse by the fact that the reality was so immense, so lonely, so isolating, so fraught with the dangers of the unknown. Under those circumstances it would not be surprising if many men simply gave up.

J.A.G. Does your line of argument about colonial societies not serve to document the thesis of Frederick Jackson Turner that the frontier (or perhaps we should say the New World environment) "explains" American civilization?

S.D. I hadn't thought so, despite the fact that I have great respect for Turner's work. There may be certain points of similarity between Turner's thesis and some of the things that I have been saying, but I come at the subject from a very different perspective. I'm not looking for an explanation of American uniqueness. Indeed, one of the consequences of my work, for me at any rate, has been to show that some of the important conditions of American society have counterparts in many other areas of the world.

Marc Bloch, writing about the fact that new and better tenurial conditions often had to be offered to get people in the Middle Ages to cultivate lands that had been wasted by flood or war or fire, says that poverty was the mother of liberty. James Westfall Thompson, writing about the difference in conditions and patterns of land tenure east and west of the Elbe River in Germany, noted the greater degree of peasant freedom east of the Elbe as the consequence of the better conditions that were offered to induce men to migrate to the newly conquered eastern territories. What I'm trying to do is understand some of the social mechanisms that are involved in the process of labor recruitment and what some of the social and political consequences of those mechanisms are. If the social and political consequences of these mechanisms help explain American liberty, I'm delighted. But what I'm particularly interested in is discovering what accounts for the discrepancy between the plan and the outcome. This is different from what Turner was trying to explain.

J.A.G. It seems to me that your work provides perhaps a broader understanding of the same thing that Turner was trying to account for: that a society is in part shaped by the particular environment in which it evolves.

S.D. Society is shaped by the interaction between people and their environment.

J.A.G. You several times referred to freedom as characteristic of the new American societies. If one interprets "freedom" in political terms, one can use the word "democracy" as a synonym; do you think that the American environment fostered the development of democratic institutions?

S.D. I'm not so sure that I would equate freedom and democracy. I would rather argue that certain habits, certain institutions, were established which loosened up all kinds of restraints and rigidities in American society. What makes American society democratic is the degree to which, over time, new kinds of people were accepted into the political and social process. I am not unaware of the fact that there has been for some time a debate among historians over how democratic colonial societies were. What I'm saying is that the democracy of the United States is the result of changes that took place throughout the course of American history. They did not happen once and for all time in the seventeenth century.

J.A.G. Is it possible to generalize about the impact of the New World on Europeans? Are there any characteristically American social institutions that are common to all parts of North and South America?

S.D. There has certainly been a social *problem* which is common to all parts of North and South America—the contacts and conflicts of people of different races. It is a common thread of American history, although this is not to say that there has been any uniformity in the ways in which it has been attacked. And the experience of the Americans with the race problem has raised the level of consciousness of the entire world to its importance as a problem of human relations and of social organization.

J.A.G. Did the settlement and development of America have any universal effects on European society and social institutions?

S.D. The Americas have been peopled by migration, chiefly migration from Europe. The consequences of this migration for Europe must have been extraordinary. I say "must have been," because while it is possible to speak in detail of some of the aspects of the question, a great deal of work needs to be done on the problem. What were the consequences for European society of this unbelievable migration? Certain governments worry today about what is called the "brain drain." What a drain of brains and also of human energy the peopling of the New World represented for Europe! Yet loss of this population may have been Europe's good fortune. Emigration drained off a large population which, if it had stayed, might have made European society even more obstreperous and rebellious.

J.A.G.   It must also have produced social mobility in Europe, must it not?

S.D.   Surely. It's also true that the development of America created an elaborate and intricate network of economic relations between the Americas and Europe which had enormous consequences for the economic development of particular European countries. The relationship between waves of migration and fluctuations in business cycles, and the export of capital from European countries is clear, and had large consequences for *European* development.

One of my students, for example, is now doing a doctoral thesis on Italian immigrants who returned to Italy. His work raises a host of interesting problems. What is the difference between those immigrants and those who stayed in America? What were the consequences of their return for *Italy*? Did they return as innovators by virtue of their novel experience in the New World? Or were they simply reabsorbed by the old institutions? What did the local people think of the ones who had gone away? Did they look upon them, as sometimes happens in traditional societies, as "wise men" who could interpret the world for them? Or were they regarded with suspicion and hostility? Of course, there were some bedrock economic consequences of the fact that many immigrants returned. Many survived in the Old World on savings and pensions accumulated in America, and in some sections of Italy these sums made no small contribution to the local economy.

J.A.G.   What are the chief unanswered questions about the interaction of Europeans in the New World that historians today should examine?

S.D.   Anything which would add to our knowledge of the shape and character of social organization would be important. Then there is the question: Given the necessity to change forms of social organization, how did the leaders of colonizing ventures respond? Did they perceive that change was necessary? Why do some see this before others? Why did some never see it at all?

Among those who perceived the necessity for social changes, how did they act? How far were they willing to move? What are the variables that account for differences in response? Is it a matter of their personal intellectual and emotional equipment, or are there certain kinds of institutions which were more easily adapted and adaptable than others? Comparative research will permit us to ask more significant questions and perhaps come up with more meaningful answers. A single isolated case can disprove a hypothesis, but it can never prove a point.

From a methodological point of view, we very badly need more comparative studies of colonization. To study something comparatively does not necessarily mean that two or more things have to be identical, or that the same institution has to exist in the different cases examined. That is one form of comparative history, and very important, but it is not the only one. Slavery existed in Brazil, in Virginia, in Cuba, and one can study slavery comparatively in Brazil and Virginia and Cuba. But another kind of comparative history rests upon asking a systematic question about more than one place. For example, in any system of social stratification, the position a person occupies in one dimension of the system may be very different from the position he occupies in another aspect of the system, and the evaluation that the society makes of those positions may be very different indeed. A person may be ranked high in the occupational structure of society, for example, but low in the religious structure. The consequences of these variations have been the subject of a good deal of study. One view holds that where there is a "status discrepancy," the person tries to equalize them by raising the inferior status. The effects of this kind of behavior on political activity have also been studied in contemporary society, and there is some reason to believe that such persons tend to be more radical than others. The phenomenon studied in these investigations—status discrepancy—existed in the colonial world as well as in the contemporary world, and it should be investigated in both contexts.

This is a mode of comparative research that I would very much like to see applied to early American history. Aside from the light it might throw on the past, it would permit an interplay between theory and history which I think would be of enormous importance. Theoretical knowledge established by modern social science can be brought to bear on particular historical situations, and at the same time historical knowledge can be employed to test the accuracy and universality of sociological generalizations.

J.A.G.   What are the half-dozen books that you would recommend to persons interested in the subject we have been discussing? In each case, would you indicate what the particular contribution of the volume is?

S.D.   Charles M. Andrews, *The Colonial Period of American History* (4 vols., 1934–38), remains the magisterial book on the subject. Wesley Frank Craven, *The Southern Colonies in the Seventeenth Century* (1949), is the best regional study of the period. The writings of Perry Miller opened up whole new fields of historical scholarships; see, for example, his *Errand into the Wilderness* (1956). Howard Mumford Jones, *O Strange New World* (1964), shows the relevance for the colonial period of literary and intellectual history. Daniel J. Boorstin, *The Americans: The Colonial Experience* (1958), is recent, exciting, and opinionated. Clarence L. Ver Steeg, *The Formative Years* (1964), is a most useful recent summary of the period.

Jack P. Greene

Colonial Institutions

J̲ACK P. GREENE, Professor of History at Johns Hopkins
University, is primarily interested in colonial political
institutions. His book, *Quest for Power: The Lower Houses
of Assembly in Southern Royal Colonies* (1963) is a pioneering study of the means used by local political leaders
to gain and hold power vis-à-vis the representatives of the
crown. Professor Greene has also edited the *Diary of
Landon Carter* (1965), a major source for the understanding of eighteenth-century plantation agriculture and of
Southern social organization, and a number of other volumes, including *The Ambiguity of the American Revolution* (1968), a collection of essays interpreting the
Revolution. In this interview he discusses the development
of social, political, and economic institutions in the colonies
during the seventeenth and eighteenth centuries.

John A. Garraty Professor Greene, the colonial period of American history is so vast as to defy easy characterization. Can you subdivide it and explain the criteria on which the divisions are made?

Jack P. Greene The range of criteria which might be used to divide the colonial era into periods are infinite, and whatever criteria are chosen by an individual scholar will depend of course upon his particular sense of what are the most important and enduring themes about the area and the special angle of vision which that sense gives him.

My own feeling is that the most useful (because it is the most basic) breakdown would be in terms of the changing character of colonial society. Such a division is extremely difficult, however, because colonies and regions were settled at different times and developed at widely varying rates, so that they moved through similar stages of development at different times. Nevertheless, colonial social development can be roughly broken down into two phases. The first phase was characterized by relatively inchoate kinds of society. Because they lacked real functional integration, because social and political leadership was not beyond dispute, and because the organization of the economy was still in doubt, societies during this stage were extraordinarily brittle and unstable. During the second phase, by contrast, society was much more coherent and infinitely more stable, as the lines of social and political authority had become clearer, the structure of the economy had been settled, and a considerable degree of social integration had been achieved.

Although most areas had moved from the first to the second of these stages by the early decades of the eighteenth century, and although it does therefore make some sense to say that the first phase corresponds generally with the seventeenth century and the second with the eighteenth century, it is always necessary to keep in mind that some areas— such as Tidewater Virginia—had already reached the second stage by the last decades of the seventeenth century, while other areas—backcountry Carolina or New Hampshire—did not move into the second phase until after the middle of the eighteenth century.

J.A.G. Let's start in the beginning. Why did the English become interested in colonies in the first place?

J.P.G. The initial interest of the English in colonies can be considered under the two general headings: the example of Spain, and the peculiar thrust of English domestic development during the sixteenth and early seventeenth centuries. Spain had obviously made such a good thing of colonization, especially with the stunning discoveries of the great caches of gold and silver in Mexico and Peru, that every other Western European nation wanted to emulate it.

J.A.G. If British interest in colonization was partially a response to the success of the Spaniards, can you explain the long delay between the beginning of Spanish colonization in the New World and the first English settlements? The Spanish economy was certainly not more advanced than England's.

J.P.G. Of course not. The Spanish venture depended initially upon heroic efforts by a relatively small number of people, efforts very similar to those made by earlier Spaniards in driving the Moors out of Spain. Once they had conquered the great native empires in Mexico, Peru, and Central America, once they had obtained access to and control over the rich stores of gold, silver, and jewels in those regions, they had the economic wherewithal to sustain a vast colonial effort, and during the initial decades of settlement the Spanish colonies were self-sustaining to an extent that the English colonies never were. If John Cabot had discovered another Mexico in 1497 instead of Newfoundland or Nova Scotia and had returned to England laden with gold and silver, the English would probably have founded colonies much earlier.

But Spain also had another important advantage. It had been unified in the late fifteenth and early sixteenth centuries, whereas England was distracted by domestic problems throughout most of the sixteenth century. Henry VII was involved in trying to consolidate the authority of the Tudor monarchy, while Henry VIII and his successors were absorbed with the problems of the Reformation and the unstable political and social situation that followed. These domestic problems diverted energy and attention from overseas expansion and colonization until the last half of the reign of Elizabeth I.

J.A.G. You are implying, then, that the example of Spain was not by itself a sufficient explanation for the development of English interest in colonization?

J.P.G. Yes. Although it provided a powerful stimulus to ambitious Englishmen interested in glory and gold, the example of Spain was far less important than certain economic and social developments within England, developments which both made possible and encouraged English colonizing activities. For England, the years 1480 to 1660 were years of profound change, in which a fundamental shift took place from the still largely feudal society of the fifteenth century to the fully developed market society of the seventeenth. Increasingly, during the sixteenth century, Englishmen, spurred on by the promise of ever greater profits, began to produce goods for the market or to participate in some phase of the marketing process. The direction of English economic life began to move outward. English traders expanded their activities all over the world—to the Levant, northern Russia, the Baltic, and even down the African coast. This push outward inevitably carried them into the American orbit.

More than that, however, these developments contributed to the colonizing process both by providing incentives, resources, and tools such as the joint-stock trading company) which encouraged investors to back colonial enterprises, and by contributing to the creation of conditions in England which encouraged Englishmen of all ranks to consider settling, at least temporarily, in the colonies. The shift to a market society created severe social and psychological strains. Traditional social arrangements seemed to be breaking down as a result of new expanded economic opportunities. Rapid horizontal and vertical mobility, the relative decline of older elites whose power rested upon land and their displacement by newer groups whose fortunes depended on business, the rapid rise of lawyers whose services were required to handle a growing volume of land sales and commercial transactions, the volatile character of mercantile life—all of these evidences of rapid and fundamental social change resulted in an unsettledness that almost certainly made it easier for men to overcome their traditional attachments to place and their reluctance to forsake the known for the unknown and perhaps even predisposed them to move.

J.A.G. That is very interesting. Are you suggesting that these social and economic changes you describe produced more geographic mobility within England, as well as the movement to America?

J.P.G. Apparently, though we still do not have sufficient evidence to say with much precision just how great an increase in geographical or horizontal mobility there actually was. Certainly, contemporaries thought there was a great increase in both kinds of mobility, however.

J.A.G. Did not the Reformation also contribute to this unsettledness?

J.P.G. Of course. By breaking up the monasteries, Henry VIII and his advisors stimulated a considerable redistribution of land and much social movement. Even more important, the Reformation caused extraordinary intellectual and religious ferment. Combined with the disorientation induced by the rapid social changes, this ferment predisposed people to look around for certainty and to be preoccupied with the problem of social and religious order. The extreme popularity during the Elizabethan and Jacobean periods of the ancient idea that there was a grand order in the universe established by God and that every individual had a settled place in that order was one form of response to these conditions. Another was the urge, represented by all of the different species of Puritanism, to discover a purer church and to use that church as a model for establishing a more orderly, less corrupt, and more coherent social and political order.

Some of the formulas that were proposed to settle social conditions and to purify the church could be undertaken at home. But when men began to dream about the creation of a purer society they naturally thought about going to virgin America to create it.

J.A.G.   Are you implying that English colonization of America was basically utopian in character?

J.P.G.   Only partly. Once colonization came to be considered seriously during the last decades of the sixteenth century, the men most interested —people like Richard Hakluyt, Sir Humphrey Gilbert, and Sir Walter Raleigh—articulated a comprehensive rationale for founding colonies. Occasionally utopian in impulse, the writings of such men were largely promotional and tended to put primary emphasis upon more mundane benefits that could be expected to derive from colonies: individual profit, national glory, the advancement of Protestantism, and the rescue of at least part of America from popery.

Yet among many writers and potential settlers there was a pronounced ambivalence about the New World. For every paean to the promises of the New World, there was a warning about its dangers. This ambivalence is perhaps best seen in *The Tempest*, where Shakespeare juxtaposes English civilization, represented by Prospero, against the barbarism of remote, uncultivated places, exemplified by Caliban. The tension between these two symbolic figures is revelatory of the contradictory perceptions Englishmen had of the New World. There was great hope that it might be converted into a new Eden, but there was also widespread fear that the wilderness would prove uncongenial to English culture and would so undermine the power of traditional values and institutions as to reduce the English settlers to the savage level of the Indians.

J.A.G.   Was there any strain within this ambivalent perception that was stronger than the others?

J.P.G.   Although there is no way to discover what motives were uppermost in the minds of the vast majority of colonists, there can be little doubt that the central thrust of the English colonizing movement was economic. Even those Puritans who came to New England largely for religious and social reasons also, in many cases, had strong material aspirations. As I indicated earlier, there had been a tremendous release of economic energy and an extraordinary stimulation of economic and social ambition in England on the eve of colonization, and the opportunities presented by the New World—which was so vast that no one group could monopolize all of the resources or pre-empt all social status —provided an outlet for this energy and greatly increased its power. The result was that even those colonists who did not come for ostensibly economic reasons often found it difficult to restrain their material appetites.

However, it would be a mistake to put too much emphasis upon these material aspirations. Religious motives were present everywhere and, among the leaders of the New England colonies, were almost certainly predominant. Besides, in every colony, there was a powerful movement to recreate in the New World an idealized version of English society. This movement to Anglicize the New World was accentuated by the colonial fear of the barbarizing and corrosive effects of the wilderness, and, because it envisioned the imposition of traditional "civilized" restraints upon individuals and groups within colonial society, the movement often ran directly counter to the materialistic impulses of the colonists and took the form of efforts to bridle those impulses through legislation and exhortation.

J.A.G. Is it useful to distinguish between the motives of the founders of the colonies and the mass of the people who came to them and did the fundamental work of colony building?

J.P.G. In general, the colony planners had much more comprehensive and more fully articulated goals, which they invariably set down at the time of colonization. With the individual settlers, on the other hand, the larger objectives of the planners probably—I say "probably," because most of the settlers obviously did not leave much record behind of why they did what they did—were not of central importance. What concerned such people most were the myriad problems presented by their daily lives. Especially in the early years of settlement, simple problems of survival were paramount.

J.A.G. Did the early colonists anticipate accurately what they were going to find in America?

J.P.G. Certainly not in the case of Virginia. It took twenty-five years for that colony to get on its feet, for the settlers to accept it for what it was and to learn how to utilize and to live in that particular environment. But later colonizers probably expected harsher conditions than they actually found.

The other question, which Sigmund Diamond has addressed himself to in several important articles, is to what extent the aspirations and objectives of the colonizers had to be modified in response to conditions encountered in the colonies. The stated objectives of the colony planners in England invariably gave primary consideration to the corporate interests of the colony and looked forward to the achievement of a tightly integrated society in which each segment—and each individual—contributed to the welfare of the whole. But these objectives, at least in their initial forms, were unattainable and were everywhere quickly abandoned. In Virginia, for instance, the Company early found that it could not recruit settlers if it expected them to work for the Company in perpetuity as it had originally planned. To make Virginia attractive to prospective colonists, the Company had to relax the harsh discipline and rigid work-camp style social structure of the early years and offer incentives in the form of easy access to land and participation in the political process. In the wake of these concessions, the control of the

Company over individual settlers became ever more tenuous, and its original objectives virtually impossible to maintain. This pattern was repeated over and over again during the following century.

J.A.G.   Were new kinds of institutions developed in response to the conditions the colonists discovered in America?

J.P.G.   Except for certain modifications in the labor system which occurred during the last half of the seventeenth century, very few new institutions developed in the colonies. The settlers naturally sought to establish the same institutions with which they had been familiar in England. Unavoidably, of course, these institutions did not function in the same way as they had at home, and over a period of time a subtle process of differentiation in both form and content took place. Most important, perhaps, English institutions rarely had the same force and effectiveness in the colonies that they had had in England. Economic opportunity and social mobility tended to erode the authority of these institutions. Their authority was maintained longer in New England, where the inhabitants had a stronger commitment to the values underlying them and where neither economic opportunity nor social mobility was so great. In Virginia and the West Indian colonies, on the other hand, the authority of all institutions was quickly undermined and extremely difficult to maintain during the early decades of settlement as the settlers, engrossed in the pell-mell rush for profits, dispersed themselves over the landscape, displayed little willingness to let the welfare of the whole society interfere with their own individual ambition, and tried to turn all institutions into vehicles for individual advancement.

J.A.G.   Is it possible that the comparatively strong sense of community which marked New England arose from the difficulty of life there and from the fact that men needed one another? May we, therefore, have overemphasized the role of religious ideas in giving New England such a remarkable amount of social cohesion?

J.P.G.   Although the more difficult conditions of life in New England doubtless were an important factor in the emergence and maintenance of a greater sense of community than existed elsewhere, one should not underestimate the powerful role of religious ideas, especially among colony and community leaders. The Puritan leadership in Massachusetts Bay came to America with hopes of creating a new kind of church and a new kind of society, and they enjoyed considerable authority and confidence among the people, who, in comparison with colonists elsewhere, were a relatively homogeneous group. The result was that they were able to impose their ideas—their religious and social goals—upon the colony to a much greater degree than other colony leaders, such as Lord Baltimore in Maryland or the early Quakers in Pennsylvania. No matter how much Baltimore might have liked to make Maryland into a Catholic colony or how much the Quakers wanted to build Pennsylvania exclusively upon the principles of the Society of Friends, they were unable to do so because of the diversity of religious and social groups in their colonies.

The fact that economic opportunity was less in New England than elsewhere was also important, however. People stuck together in small communities during the first century of settlement because they rarely made enough from one crop to expand very much for the next. If it were possible to measure it, the pace of economic growth in New England during the seventeenth century would almost certainly turn out to be much slower than it was in Virginia and infinitely less than it was in the sugar islands.

J.A.G. How have historians' views of New England Puritanism changed over the last generation?

J.P.G. The change has been extraordinary. In 1927, Vernon L. Parrington published the first volume of his *Main Currents of American Thought*. This volume was a superb statement of the standard view of the Puritans that had taken shape over the previous century. According to this view, the Puritans were a drab, morbid people, preoccupied with saving their own souls, busily looking into everybody else's affairs, authoritarian in government and bigoted in religion. Like many others before him, Parrington chastised the Puritans for opposing religious toleration and democracy. In 1932—just five years later—Perry Miller published his *Orthodoxy in Massachusetts*, the first of a brilliant series of studies of American Puritanism in which he presented a much more sympathetic portrait.

The differences between Parrington and Miller primarily arise out of their contrasting perspectives. Parrington viewed the Puritans from the perspective of the 1920's. From that vantage point—which was nearly three hundred years after the initial Puritan settlements—the Puritans looked curiously un-American: they did not permit people free reign over their individual impulses, they tried to stifle individual initiative and deviation, and so on. What Miller tried to do, on the other hand, was to get back inside the Puritans and to try to understand them on their own terms and to measure them against the standards not of later generations but of their own.

Consider the matter of religious toleration. Miller and later historians following his example pointed out that in opposing toleration the Puritans were no different from all other Christian groups in Western Europe at that time. The old charge had been that they had come to America seeking religious freedom and then immediately proceeded to deny it to everyone else. But Miller showed that they came to America not to achieve toleration but to discover the "true" church. As John

Winthrop said, they intended to found a city upon a hill to which people in England could look for inspiration. That city, it was hoped, would provide a model form of church, state, and society, which could be transported back to England and used to rebuild English political, social, and religious institutions along lines more acceptable to God. Precisely because they believed that there was only one true way in religion and that any other was not merely in error but a sinful deviation from God's one way, any idea of toleration was anathema.

J.A.G. In what other ways has our view of the Puritans changed?

J.P.G. We have also recognized that Puritanism in general was not all that different from Anglicanism. This is not to say that there were not important differences over theology, church polity, and other matters of religion, but only that in terms of their social views—their conceptions of human nature, the process and character of historical change, and the proper organization of society—the two groups had a considerable amount in common. For instance, the Puritans began with the notion that all men, except for the very few who were numbered among the elect, were innately sinful, and that, therefore, very strong social and political institutions were needed to restrain this darker side of human nature. The Anglicans operated out of a very similar conception, albeit they may have had a more charitable attitude toward those men who could not seem to cope with their own frailties. But what has impressed recent students is not the differences but the similarities between Puritan social, political, and economic assumptions and those of Anglican and other contemporary English and European Protestant groups.

J.A.G. It seems to me you are saying that the change in the view of the Puritans has only been to argue that everyone else was just as bad.

J.P.G. I did not mean to suggest that. No one any longer seems very interested in whether the Puritans were "bad." It is easy enough to judge groups in the past by present-day norms and to find them deficient. But that defeats the larger purpose of history, which is not to evaluate the past in terms of the present but to understand the present from the perspective of the past, to use the past as a kind of cosmic backdrop, which, by furnishing us with a wide range of contrasts with the present, can enable us to understand our own behavior and our own societies more clearly. To do this requires us to comprehend the past as much as is humanly possible in its own terms. Thus, what we want to know about the Puritans is how they stand up against their contemporaries, not against us, and how successful they were in achieving their own goals, not ours. From this point of view, it becomes clear that in one sense the Puritans far exceeded most of their contemporaries. To the extent that, as Edmund S. Morgan has pointed out, the Puritans tried to develop a perfect society while recognizing the imperfections of man, there was a certain nobility to their enterprise and an element of high tragedy in their failure. No other group of colonists and few Englishmen at the time set their sights so high.

J.A.G. Is there any connection between the increasing respect for the Puritans and our own contemporary disillusionment and pessimism about human nature?

J.P.G. I am sure there is. The burning or gassing of thousands of Jews by the Nazis, the dropping of the bomb at Hiroshima, and the many other human cruelties manifest in the twentieth century have contributed to a much less optimistic view of both human nature and the historical process. We have thus come around to a point of view quite similar to the Puritans and can thereby appreciate them much more than could earlier generations.

J.A.G. In looking generally at religious life in the colonies, is it fair to say that there was a greater degree of religious toleration than in England, and if so, why?

J.P.G. Wherever there were strong competing religious groups—that is, just about everywhere in the colonies except in New England prior to 1720 and in Virginia prior to 1750—each was forced to tolerate the others simply because no one group had sufficient power to compel the others to conform. Although it is difficult in this area to speak comparatively, this situation may well have resulted in more practical and legal toleration than existed in England. It should be pointed out, however, that the Toleration Act of 1689 established a high degree of toleration for Christians in Britain. I doubt, in fact, whether during the eighteenth century there was more legal toleration in most colonies than there was in Britain.

J.A.G. Would you describe the structure of the colonial economy in the seventeenth century?

J.P.G. The economy rested on an agricultural base. Farming was the principal occupation, and not simply subsistence farming. All over the colonies, farmers were to some extent oriented toward producing a surplus for the market, and this orientation meant the early development of market mechanisms complete with a mercantile community to handle the distribution and exchange of colonial products.

There were, of course, important regional variations. New England agriculture was devoted mostly to the production of foodstuffs, while the Chesapeake colonies organized their agricultural activities around the production of a staple crop, tobacco, for which there was great demand in Europe. The tobacco trade was largely handled by English rather than colonial merchants, who channeled the tobacco to markets both in England and on the Continent. In New England, on the other hand, such enterpreneurial functions were handled by a native group of merchants who developed a brisk trade with the West Indies and the European continent as well as with England and the other continental colonies. This trade involved the export of furs, skins, and fish, as well as agricultural products. Thus, the economic capital of Massachusetts was Boston, but the economic capital of Virginia and Maryland was London.

One result of these dissimilar economic orientations was that the status order in the two regions were organized rather differently. In Chesapeake society, the socioeconomic structure was arranged according to whether one had a lot or a little land, but in New England the large merchants stood at the apex of economic society.

J.A.G. What were the major economic problems faced by the colonists?

J.P.G. There were at least three major problems. The first was finding something that was marketable, that could be exchanged for goods or money in England, on the Continent, or in the West Indies. This problem was solved relatively early just about everywhere. Within a generation, or at most two, the colonists had learned how to utilize the resources in their environment, and had worked out an economic structure that changed very little during the following century.

A second problem, in many ways the toughest in the beginning, was labor. Initially, the demand for labor was met largely through the use of indentured servants, and then after 1660 increasingly by African slaves.

A third problem, which was never adequately solved during the colonial period, was how to get enough capital to finance economic expansion and to keep the economy functioning smoothly. Some mercantile groups in Philadelphia, Charleston, New York, Boston, Newport, and other colonial seaports accumulated considerable amounts of capital, though they often invested it in land or other nonliquid resources. Planters and farmers, however, rarely seemed to have had enough specie even to meet the relatively small costs of household purchases. The result in the early days was a heavy reliance upon barter and later upon bills of exchange, promissory notes, and credit. In Virginia and Maryland, the larger planters managed on credit from English merchants, and the smaller producers on credit from the large planters. Older historians used to consider these arrangements as a major source of alienation of the large planters from England and of the smaller producers from the larger, but that is only part of the story. As debtors at all levels were very much aware, the credit represented by their debts was a resource as well as a burden. Without that credit, economic expansion and opportunity would have been greatly restricted.

The need for an internal medium of trade was satisfied largely by the issuance of paper money by the colonial governments. Although there was strong opposition to such issues from British creditors who feared that colonials would try to pay their debts in depreciated paper, and although there was a considerable amount of depreciation in cases where paper issues were not well secured and well managed, many of these issues obtained a considerable amount of stability and functioned to the advantage of all parties.

J.A.G. Could we go back to the second problem you mention, the need for labor? Why did slavery develop in the American colonies, and can you particularly explain why it expanded so rapidly beginning in the closing decades of the seventeenth century?

J.P.G. That question, as Winthrop D. Jordan has pointed out in his important recent book, *White over Black*, is an extraordinarily complicated one. The standard argument, which contains a great deal of truth, is that plantation agriculture had certain labor requirements which could best— "best" in an economic sense—be met by a system of bound labor, and that the Negro was available and was therefore enslaved. A corollary of this argument is that prejudice against the Negro came about as a result of the debasement involved in slavery. But Jordan has argued convincingly that the origins of both slavery and prejudice are considerably more complicated. The Spanish colonies had had slavery for almost a hundred years before it was introduced into the English colonies, and it was a thriving institution in the English West Indian colonies for at least a quarter of a century before it was employed on a large scale by the continental colonies, and these examples clearly predisposed men on the continent to regard and to treat Negroes, especially after they began to come in large numbers, as chattel slaves. Prejudice, as Jordan points out, clearly antedated slavery, and seems to have depended in major part upon the Englishman's association of blackness with evil. This attitude toward the Negro's color interacted with slavery to degrade the Negro and deeply reinforce prejudice against him in the minds of whites.

One can explain the rapid expansion of Negro slavery on the mainland toward the end of the seventeenth century by the simple fact that it turned out to be an excellent labor system in a staple-crop economy. The initial investment was fairly high, but the slaveowner got perpetual work out of slaves, who reproduced themselves and thus continually replenished and added to the owner's labor force.

Essentially, of course, slavery arose as a result of the unwillingness of the white man to content himself with the kind of profits he could make from his own, his family's, or free labor. Slavery was rooted precisely where Black Power advocates suggest prejudice is rooted today —in the white man's avarice and in his fear of allowing any great measure of freedom to such an exploited and obviously different-looking group. This is not to suggest that only white men were avaricious, but the whites were the dominant group in the colonies, and though other black men may have originally been responsible for selling Negroes into slavery in Africa, the whites were responsible for its introduction and perpetuation in the colonies.

J.A.G.   How would you describe the relationship between England and the colonies in the seventeenth century?

J.P.G.   Initially, the relationship was very ambiguous. It was not very clearly defined, because the English had had no similar experiences with such distant possessions. In the beginning, the English looked at the colonies primarily as units for economic production. The relationship was essentially contractual: the crown gave certain things to certain people in return for certain services, although initially not much more than allegiance was required. This essentially commercial relationship was peculiarly appropriate to a market society, and it encouraged the notion among the colonists that a contract had been made with the English government which guaranteed them the right to pursue their own interests in return for their allegiance and a commitment to set up governments closely resembling the government of England.

The English government looked at the colonies from two points of view: What can these colonies contribute to national wealth; and how do they contribute to the national prestige?

J.A.G.   When did the English begin to see the colonies as a kind of a branch of the English government, and begin to think of establishing a general colonial administration?

J.P.G.   When the crown took over the Virginia colony in 1624, it was for the first time thrust into the position of having to administer the day-to-day life of a colony. But there was only one crown colony until 1660. In the early seventeenth century, the term "the Empire" had quite a different connotation from what it has today. It meant pretty much the same as "dominion": the colonies were part of the king's domain, under his rule. But exactly what kind of status they occupied within the Empire was not very clear prior to 1660, and became so only gradually thereafter.

J.A.G.   If the English viewed the colonies primarily in economic terms, what kind of control did they place on colonial economic activity?

J.P.G.   They began to place controls on aspects of colonial economic life as soon as any element began to loom importantly in the English economy. The first regulations were in relation to tobacco; in 1621, the imperial government required that all tobacco be shipped to England. Later it encouraged tobacco production in Virginia and Maryland by prohibiting the growth of tobacco in England. But there was no general attempt to set up a system of economic regulation until the value of the colonies had become very clear, in the 1640's and 1650's. When the Dutch began during the English civil war to engross a large part of the colonies' carrying trade, English merchants got very upset and demanded some kind of regulation. The early Navigation Acts of 1650 and 1651 were not very effective, but the system was regularized in 1660 and then expanded in 1663 and 1673 in an effort to establish a national monopoly of colonial production. No foreign vessels were allowed to trade at colonial ports, certain categories of goods had to be sent to England before they could be shipped anywhere else, and goods going to the colonies from foreign countries had first to pass through England.

J.A.G. To what extent did this system of regulation result from practical ideas of what was economically profitable for England, and to what extent was it based on economic theory—that is, the theory of mercantilism?

J.P.G. The theory, in my view, was a response to the particular need. Insofar as mercantilism implied only that the state had the right to regulate any aspect of economic life, it was a very old idea, deeply ingrained in English habits. But as a set of doctrines about the desirability of national self-sufficiency, of a national monopoly of all trade and resources in the colonies, it grew up in the seventeenth century. It was a theory related to the notion of scarcity, to the idea that resources, capacity for production, and buying power in the world were limited, and that a nation should get as much of them as possible so that other nations would get as little as possible.

Mercantilism, like capitalism, was really a label for describing a whole series of ideas which came into being and continued to operate precisely because they seemed to be accurately descriptive of the conditions out of which they emerged. Once they were conceived of as a system, they acquired a life of their own and controlled the way men looked at economic arrangements.

J.A.G. It seems to me that the emphasis on mercantilism as a theory tends to distort contemporary realities by suggesting that colonial developments were inspired by the state, whereas colonial developments were primarily inspired by individuals for personal motives. The state simply supervised and responded to their actions. Is that correct?

J.P.G. I think so.

J.A.G. Did the economic regulations imposed by the British hamper colonial economic growth in the seventeenth and early eighteenth centuries?

J.P.G. That is an especially difficult question. No thorough study over time has been made, and there is no clear consensus among historians. My own impression is that they did not, though they might have, had they been strictly enforced. In fact, however, they were never so enforced prior to the eve of the American Revolution. I should add, of course, that there is no doubt that imperial economic regulations did affect the development of the colonial economy by encouraging production of some items and discouraging the production of others, though the acts of encouragement seem to have had a much greater influence than the acts of discouragement.

J.A.G. Is it possible to be more precise? For example, if you were in the port of Boston or New York or Philadelphia in, say, 1690, would you be likely to see a Dutch or a French ship in the harbor?

J.P.G. In 1690 probably not, but in 1681 or 1682 you might very well have seen a Dutch ship in a harbor, or in a remote cove down the coast. Apparently there was considerable trading with the Dutch and French even as late as that. Smuggling and the evasion of duties, however, were probably more common forms of violation.

J.A.G. How did the British system of regulating colonial trade affect private British interests?

J.P.G. The dominant power in this situation was the mercantile groups in Britain. Colonials were forced to accommodate their interests to those of powerful British interests. It is true that in a great many cases their interests were the same, but, when they were not, the decision of the British government was always in favor of the British merchants.

J.A.G. How would you characterize the internal political life of the colonies in the seventeenth century?

J.P.G. Over the past twenty years, historians have come to describe colonial politics as chaotic, even convulsive. Colonial governments seem to have been often in turmoil: colonists expelled governors, rebelled against properly constituted authority, and engaged in internecine strife as they vied among themselves for power and access to primary sources of wealth and status. Political instability, according to this view, derived out of the release of economic and social ambition in the New World and the collision among rival interests in pursuit of their ambition.

This conception explains a considerable amount of colonial political life; it may, however, have been somewhat overstressed. Given the character of life in the colonies, given the lack of a settled social structure, the absence of clear lines of political authority, and the diversity of the settlers, what was probably more remarkable than the brittle quality of colonial public life was the extraordinary amount of stability that was actually achieved after the first few generations of settlement. This stability was especially manifest in the localities where the vast bulk of political activity took place—in the towns in New England and in the counties, municipalities, and parishes elsewhere. There were personal feuds, sectarian clashes, and economic rivalries in every locality, but the striking feature of colonial public life on this level, especially by the early decades of the eighteenth century, is the extent to which the agencies of local government were able to maintain order, enforce laws, and solve local problems to the satisfaction of the vast bulk of the free inhabitants—to perform, in short, with an effectiveness that very nearly equaled that of their counterparts in Britain.

Similarly, on the provincial level, there was a lot of disorder and upheaval, but nowhere, after the early years, was disorder the normal state of politics for long periods of time. My point is simply that government was not merely a vehicle for the realization of individual or group ambitions but also a way to achieve a much more fundamental psychological need: the need for order, which though common to all peoples may have been even stronger in the unsettled and unsettling environment of the New World than it was in older established societies. Governments were not yet conceived primarily as instruments through which people could express themselves but as agencies whose paramount task was to restrain the antisocial passions of imperfect men so that they could live together peacefully if not always harmoniously. This deep-seated drive for order acted as a countervailing force against the disintegrative tendencies in colonial politics.

J.A.G. When and why did the English begin to devise political institutions for controlling the colonies, as distinct from economic regulations?

J.P.G. They began to see the need for some sort of political control very early. But only in the 1660's, after they had realized that the Navigation Act system was at least partially a failure, did they seriously try to establish political uniformity in the colonies. The later Stuart monarchs, Charles II and James II, had a very different conception of the colonies from earlier monarchs. They saw them not only as units for economic production but also as political entities, part of the king's dominions. The first effective central governing agency was the Lords of Trade, a committee of the Privy Council established in 1675. That committee adopted a series of policies. The first was to try to convert all the private colonies into royal colonies on the grounds that the private colonies had too many privileges, too many exemptions from central control. The second policy was to tighten up administration by making policy much more specific and precise.

The Lords also attempted to restrict the power of the colonial assemblies—those local representative institutions which had emerged in response to a variety of local pressures during the early years of each colony and had become both a critical element in the legislative process and the primary agency through which dominant local interests expressed their economic, social, religious, and political aspirations. The Lords of Trade tried to restrict the power of these bodies by applying the principle of Poynings' Law, an old statute which required the crown's prior affirmation to any legislation passed by the Irish parliament, to Virginia and Jamaica. Local interests strongly opposed this effort, and the policy was a failure. But the Lords at least articulated a set of beliefs about the way colonies were to be governed and about the nature of the assemblies.

The third policy was centralization. With the Dominion of New England in 1688–89, crown officials sought not only to centralize the northern colonies into one unit, but to do away with representative government altogether. This experiment was cut short by the Glorious Revolution, however, and the English never again attempted to govern without assemblies.

J.A.G.   If it was official policy after 1660 to convert private colonies into crown colonies, how do you explain the creation of the Carolinas, New York, and Pennsylvania as private colonies after that date?

J.P.G.   The argument against private colonies achieved wide currency only after the Carolina, New Jersey, and New York grants had been issued. As a matter of fact, the New York grant and the Carolina grant were made at the very time the first Royal Commission was sent out to investigate conditions in the colonies. Opposition to private colonies developed over the next decade, and came to be widely accepted in imperial governing circles only after the investigation of the colonies by Edward Randolph, a royal commissioner, in 1675–76.

The Pennsylvania case was special. The elder William Penn had loaned some money to Charles II, and his son used this loan to pry a colony out of the King. There was great opposition to the grant from the Lords of Trade, and, as a result, the Pennsylvania charter was significantly different from earlier private charters. It both required that Penn enforce the Navigation Acts and asserted the jurisdiction of Parliament over the colony, two stipulations not in earlier charters.

J.A.G.   How in general did the Glorious Revolution affect colonial policy?

J.P.G.   Initially, it was not clear how it was going to affect colonial policy. But the issuance of a second charter to Massachusetts Bay in 1691 was an indication that the English were no longer seriously considering doing away with representative institutions. Neither of the other two central goals of the policy of the Lords of Trade was abandoned, however. By the new Navigation Act of 1696, imperial authorities sought to tighten up the navigation system by expanding the administrative network in the colonies, establishing vice-admiralty courts to enforce the Navigation Acts, and asserting Parliament's jurisdiction over colonial matters. Although they did not again attempt to consolidate the colonies into larger and more easily administered units, crown officials repeatedly considered such a step during the eighteenth century.

Perhaps the most significant legacy of the Glorious Revolution was a new attitude toward the role of Parliament in the colonies. Increasingly, after 1689, crown officials generally assumed that any time they could not handle colonial affairs Parliament could be called to the rescue. Both Charles II and James II were reluctant to admit Parliament into any share of the internal governments of the colonies, but William III and his successors operated in a different milieu in which the cooperation of Parliament in most major matters of state was assumed. During the early decades of the eighteenth century, crown officials several times threatened parliamentary intervention in attempting to intimidate recalcitrant colonial assemblies into voting a permanent revenue with which to pay the governor and other local royal officials. The threat was that Parliament would vote such a revenue if the assemblies did not. Parliament never actually did that until 1767 with the Townshend Acts, but the threat revealed that the imperial government had few doubts about the authority of Parliament to tax the colonies.

J.A.G.   If Parliament had such extensive authority over the colonies, at least in theory, what was the constitutional position of the colonial assemblies, and what was their relationship to Parliament?

J.P.G.   The answer is that neither their constitutional position nor their relationship to Parliament was ever entirely clear. Initially, the assemblies resembled the governing bodies of English corporations: they were gatherings of representatives of the stockholders to make bylaws and regulations for their various enterprises. But they had to deal with so many problems which were so similar in character to problems handled by Parliament in England that they very early came to assume that they were the equivalents on the colonial level of Parliament. Especially after 1680, as the emergent colonial elites who dominated the assemblies became more and more intent upon recreating English society in America, the members of the assemblies self-consciously sought to mimic the House of Commons in procedures, forms, and behavior. But English authorities never fully accepted the pretensions of the lower houses. The result was a great divergence between colonial and English attitudes on the legal position of the assemblies. One of the undefined questions was whether the assemblies had exclusive authority over the internal affairs of the colonies or cooperative authority with Parliament. As the constitutional debate over the Stamp Act in 1765–66 revealed, colonists had come to assume that the authority of the assemblies was exclusive, while the British believed the opposite. But this question had never been fully or explicitly canvassed prior to the Stamp Act crisis.

J.A.G.   In general terms, how was life in the colonies in the eighteenth century different from life in the seventeenth?

J.P.G.   There were many differences, most of them the result of the extraordinary expansion that took place in the eighteenth century. There was a rapid acceleration of the economy beginning during the second and third decades of the new century and a corresponding growth in settled territory and in population.

With this great expansion came a number of developments. Commercial towns with populations and amenities equal to those of provincial towns in England developed along the seacoast. Elite groups whose economic dominance and social and political leadership were acknowledged by the rest of society emerged in all of the older settled colonies. The institution of slavery expanded rapidly in the plantation colonies and was accompanied by a change in the nature of indentured servitude. Colonial culture and society became more and more Anglicized as the century went on, and the institutional organization of the colonies became clearer and more firmly established. In short, the expansion of the colonies was accompanied by a sophistication and complexity that made life in the eighteenth-century colonies much different from that in the more rudimentary societies of the seventeenth century. This process was beginning to take place in most of the older colonies in the 1680's and 1690's, but the big change came between the end of Queen Anne's War (a phase of the great European War of the Spanish Succession) in 1713 and 1750.

J.A.G.   Did the structure of the economy change markedly in the eighteenth century?

J.P.G.   About the only structural changes occurred with the addition of new staple products. In South Carolina, for example, the introduction of rice in the 1690's changed the organization of society considerably. Similarly, the development of the naval stores industry in the Carolinas, encouraged by the Navigation Act of 1705 which put bounties on naval stores, was another important addition. Besides these and similar additions, however, there were no substantial changes in the economy such as the introduction of a factory system, the growth of urban areas devoted exclusively to manufacturing, or the reorganization of labor. Urban centers still retained their character as commercial towns, the bulk of the economy was organized around the production of staples or other products extracted from the soil or the sea, and market mechanisms did not change.

One might argue that the beginnings of iron manufacturing, which was by no means insignificant in Pennsylvania and Maryland, represented a new development. But the organization of those enterprises was very much like that of older plantation enterprises. No new techniques of labor relations, management, or marketing were involved, and very little technological advance was made.

J.A.G.   Were British regulations of colonial industry very important?

J.P.G.   British regulations applied to three products—woolens, hats, and iron—and I am not sure how they affected the hat industry because there has been no close study of that topic. But the Iron Act restricted only the *export* of finished iron products, and what finished iron the colonists were producing was for local consumption. The Act did not prohibit the production of crude iron, to which most of the industry was devoted. As for the woolen industry, the inclusion of the colonies in the Woolen Act of 1699 was an afterthought. The Act was really directed against Ireland, and I do not think it had very much effect on the American economy.

J.A.G. Would you describe the character of business relations that developed between Englishmen and colonists during the eighteenth century?

J.P.G. Well, they varied considerably from place to place. As Bernard Bailyn has pointed out, much of the trade in the early days developed within kinship networks. New Englanders started to trade with the West Indies, and they found that sometimes this trade carried them to England. So they began to appoint agents, quite often younger sons of the family, or other relatives, in England and the West Indies. This developed by the end of the seventeenth century into a fairly well-established system of kinship connections radiating out of the home port in the colonies.

The marketing of tobacco, on the other hand, was quite different; it changed dramatically, beginning in the 1730's. Some British importers maintained close family connections with colonial planters, but by the mid-eighteenth century there were many people in the tobacco trade who had at best only distant family connections with Americans, and there developed among the planters an antagonism or suspicion of the merchants. The same was true of the sugar trade. West Indian planters became suspicious of the men who marketed their sugar in England. All kinds of opportunities for fraud existed, and, lacking control over the situation, planters felt at the mercy of these English middlemen. Planter animosity was directed not toward the government or its economic policies but against the British mercantile community. I also suspect that as the colonial economy grew more complex, old family merchant networks tended to break down somewhat and a new, more impersonal kind of business arrangement developed.

J.A.G. Were there any changes in the navigation system during the eighteenth century?

J.P.G. Aside from the development of the bounty system, and the regulation of colonial manufacturing which I have already mentioned, the only important change was the passage of the Molasses Act of 1733, which was an attempt to regulate economic relationships within the Empire in favor of a particular segment of the Empire, the West Indies, by putting a heavy tax on "foreign molasses" imported into the continental colonies.

If the British had looked carefully at trade statistics, they would have realized that the continental colonies were far more valuable than the West Indies because they consumed such an extraordinary amount of British goods. But the old idea that the Caribbean sugar colonies were the real jewels of the Empire because they produced the most valuable staple was so firmly fixed in English minds that whenever they had to make a choice they favored the West Indies. The Molasses Act was the one potentially hurtful piece of legislation in the whole navigation system during the eighteenth century, but because it was not enforced it does not seem to have caused widespread or sustained discontent.

All of these new policies—the encouragement of some products by bounties, the prohibition of manufacturing, and the Molasses Act—fitted in with the framework of mercantilist assumptions as they had been worked out in the seventeenth century. There was no real change in the rationale of the navigation system in the eighteenth century. New policies were adopted, but for old ends.

J.A.G.   What changes occurred in the character of the labor force in the eighteenth century?

J.P.G.   The most important was the extraordinary expansion of slavery. This development had begun in the seventeenth century, but was greatly accelerated in the eighteenth century. The demand for slaves was continual, especially in new areas, in the western parts of Virginia and Maryland, and then in the Carolinas. Slavery even expanded in the northern colonies, especially in the cities.

In areas where there were not large numbers of slaves—in rural Pennsylvania, for instance—indentured servitude maintained the same character it had had all along: servants were primarily undifferentiated workers in agricultural pursuits. But in the cities, where slaves were doing a lot of the old heavy work that servants had formerly done, and on the plantations in the southern colonies, servants tended to be used for more specialized kinds of skilled labor. Many more of the indentured servants in the eighteenth century were of non-English origin, a large proportion of them Germans. But I don't think that these changes in national origins affected the organization of the labor force very much.

J.A.G.   Was there any significant opposition to slavery among the colonists in the eighteenth century?

J.P.G.   As Winthrop Jordan has made clear, what is so extraordinary about the institution of slavery in the eighteenth century is the ease with which people accepted it and used it. That seems to me the most remarkable fact about slavery. Instances of articulate, well-reasoned criticism of slavery are relatively rare before the 1740's. The primary group which opposed slavery, beginning in the 1740's and increasingly thereafter, were the Quakers, who did so largely on religious grounds. But opposition to slavery before the Revolution was limited.

J.A.G.   What was the effect of slavery on slaves? Was slavery in the colonial period any different than in the period just before the Civil War?

J.P.G.   We do not know very much about the effect of slavery upon the slaves. What we do know is that it was never the happy system apologists in the middle of the nineteenth century claimed. On the other hand, the system seems to have been less harsh in the eighteenth century than it later became. Conditions varied from the north to the south; the fewer the slaves in an area, the freer the system seems to have been. In the West Indies, slavery was terribly harsh. The ultimate threat for a slave who would not behave himself in Virginia was that he would be shipped out to Jamaica or Barbados. In Carolina and Georgia, where the ratio of slaves to whites was much larger, slavery was far harsher.

One example of the more lenient treatment in the eighteenth century, at least in Virginia, is revealed by the diary of Landon Carter, a wealthy planter. Carter's diary reveals that the slaves on his plantation lived within a fairly fixed family structure. Carter was always very careful to spell out the relationships of one slave to another: this person is so-and-so's mother, or so-and so's father, or so-and-so's husband. This provides a different picture from that of slavery in the new sections of the South during the 1840's and 1850's. Apparently, by that time in such areas family relationships were neither clearly established nor respected by the slaveowner.

J.A.G.   What effect did slavery appear to have on the slaveholder? Does the Landon Carter diary, for instance, throw light on how slavery affected Carter?

J.P.G.   Slaveowners were not very explicit about this matter, but by reading between the lines in the Carter diary and in a great many others, one can discern several effects of slavery upon slaveholders. Jefferson wrote in his *Notes on Virginia* that the real problem with slavery was not so much what it did to slaves (although he was concerned about that) but what it did to owners. He argued that it made them imperious, even barbarous, because it gave them such unlimited power over other men. A great many others disliked slavery for this reason. Even in South Carolina, where there was very little opposition to slavery, a man like the merchant Henry Laurens, who was active in the slave trade, attacked slavery precisely on these grounds.

Another, more subtle effect, frequently noted by travelers in the eighteenth century, was that in the southern colonies both slaveholders and nonslaveholders displayed an extraordinary reverence for their own independence. Being a slaveholder made Landon Carter much more sensitive to the value of his own freedom. His slaves were perpetual reminders of how terrible the condition of slavery was. When the possibility of "enslavement" by the British government arose before the Revolution, the mere use of this term "slavery" in that connection carried an emotive force that was very strong in the southern colonies.

J.A.G. Could we turn now to the money problem in colonial history, and its relationship to the problem of accumulating capital in a growing economy? Did the colonists ever find a satisfactory solution to this problem before the Revolution?

J.P.G. Not any long-term solution. From time to time, various colonies did in fact have favorable balances of trade; this was the case in South Carolina in the 1750's. Considerable specie came into the New England colonies as a result of their trade with the West Indies, as well as into New York and Philadelphia. But ultimately the colonies relied on credit, most of it from English sources, and upon the paper money issues I previously referred to.

J.A.G. Is it fair to say that British restrictions on colonial paper money were not really the fundamental cause of the shortage of capital, but rather that a growing yet primitive economy with enormous needs for capital could not supply its own needs by any means?

J.P.G. I think that is a fair interpretation. But I would point out that of all the potential economic grievances against the mother country, the policy of prohibiting paper currency, which eventually led to parliamentary prohibition of legal tender issues in New England by an act of 1751, caused most discontent.

J.A.G. Could one say also then that the British prejudice against legal tender was probably dysfunctional from the British point of view?

J.P.G. Yes and no. The fears of British merchants were not groundless. In New England during the 1730's and 1740's and in North Carolina during the French and Indian War, depreciation of colonial paper money was very rapid, and there were some attempts to make sterling debts payable in depreciated currency. On the other hand, there are a number of examples of self-regulated currency systems in the colonies which attained remarkable stability over long periods. What the merchants should have done was to have encouraged Parliament to issue a currency for the colonies.

J.A.G. What were the major changes in the composition and structure of colonial society during the eighteenth century?

J.P.G. Most obviously, as I suggested earlier, there was a remarkable increase in size, diversity, and complexity in just about every aspect of life: population, settled territory, towns, religion, social organization. The diversity was most apparent in the non-English groups who migrated to the colonies—Germans, Scotch Irish, Highland Scots, and other groups—and in the proliferation of religious sects. But the diversity was also directly related to the complexity that came with the increase in size, for the complexity produced a whole new range of economic opportunities in commerce, the professions, and the trades. In commerce, merchants began to specialize, becoming either exporters or importers, concerning themselves with either internal trade or overseas commerce. Among the professions, the law became of great importance. In earlier days, men could go to court and argue their own cases, but as society became more complex so did social and economic relationships, with the results both that the legal system got more and more sophisticated and lawyers had to handle an increasing number of specialized tasks. Although we know much less than we need to know about the development of the law and the legal profession—there are no good, comprehensive studies—it is clear that by the middle decades of the eighteenth century the law was the best route for rapid upward mobility. In the trades, especially in the cities, there was a growing multiplication and specialization, which created new sources of employment for men as free laborers, apprentices, or indentured servants. Whether these new opportunities created sufficient room for upward social mobility to offset the closing up of agricultural opportunity that was obviously occurring in older settled areas by the mid-eighteenth century, whether there was in such areas an over-all increase or decrease in vertical mobility is a matter of great debate at the moment. But there was clearly still considerable opportunity for the ambitious in newly settled areas, and there seems to have been a major rise in horizontal mobility—migration from one place to another—during the middle decades of the eighteenth century, as colonials began to demonstrate a penchant for that restless movement and rootlessness which have subsequently come to be thought of as two of the most important elements in the American character.

Of course, the class structure varied considerably in its specific form from one place to another. More fluid in new areas and in expanding towns, it was less open in older inhabited areas not undergoing any marked economic expansion. The social order continued to be based primarily upon material success, though merchants and planters (the groups who had earlier stood at the top of the prestige order) had to make room for lawyers.

J.A.G. The emphasis that you place on specialization and complexity seems not to have applied to ministers, or to religion. Would you comment more specifically about how social change affected religion in America?

J.P.G. We have traditionally looked at the eighteenth century as a period of considerable secularization. In a general sense, that image is accurate, but most people were still by modern standards extraordinarily pious.

Interest in theology waned, and the Deity may have occupied a less prominent place in the everyday lives of men, but belief remained strong. More significantly, in a heterogeneous society experiencing great social and economic change and constantly expanding, the old religious uniformity could not be maintained. New people with new faiths were coming to America, and along with the extensive religious divisions produced by the Great Awakening in the 1730's and 1740's, this fragmentation greatly altered religious life in the colonies and further stimulated the pressures toward religious toleration that had been present in a number of colonies since the beginnings of settlement. Another change was the continuing decline of the social standing of the clergy. Even in New England, where the clergy was still remarkably influential, young men—John Adams is a good example—who would formerly have gone into the ministry were increasingly turning to the law or commerce.

J.A.G.   What effect did these social changes you have been describing have on politics?

J.P.G.   That depended on the degree of integration in the society of each colony. In societies lacking functional integration, political life tended to be quite fragile anyway, and rapid changes in the eighteenth century only exacerbated this condition. Because most of the societies of the colonies were not yet well integrated, the politics of most colonies was, as Bernard Bailyn has pointed out, unstable, organized around continually shifting factions representing opposing interests, and fiercely competitive. But no single formula will accurately characterize all colonial political systems. A few colonies—Virginia after 1720 and South Carolina after 1745—managed to avoid this kind of intensive factional turmoil altogether. Specifically, in the case of Virginia, society was sufficiently well integrated, the social and political leadership of the large planters so widely acknowledged, and the dominant planter group so homogeneous in interest that the social changes that took place in the colony in the mid-eighteenth century did not lead to factional politics.

J.A.G.   How did the changes of the eighteenth century affect the colonists psychologically? How did change affect their hopes, and also their behavior, in all the areas you have been talking about: religion, politics, cultural life generally?

J.P.G.   From a psychological point of view, the most difficult problem faced by Europeans, even after several generations, was learning how to live with prosperity. Coming out of a society of scarcity, where people actually died of hunger, where whole populations had lived in perpetual poverty not just for one generation but for hundreds of years, they had a hard time learning how to be comfortable with prosperity and the more relaxed form of life it permitted, how not to feel guilty or anxious because they had things so good.

They were able to adjust to prosperity in varying degrees according to the extent of the prosperity. They adjusted most quickly in the West Indies, where a set of values quickly emerged that emphasized acquisitiveness, simply for its own sake. By the end of the seventeenth century, a supremely materialistic society had developed in the Indies. On the continent during the eighteenth century, the colony which best adjusted to prosperity was South Carolina. After 1745, the expansion there had been dizzying. Rice and indigo production and distribution, the slave trade, and the law were so profitable that men starting with very little made enormous fortunes in only one generation. In the 1730's, South Carolinians were just as uncomfortable with prosperity and the extravagance, idleness, and frivolity that seemed to accompany it as men in other colonies. Even as late as the 1760's, men still thought in these terms in Virginia, New England, Pennsylvania, and New York, but not in low-country South Carolina, which by the 1760's was perhaps the place where people were most completely adjusted to what would become during the next century probably the most conspicuous feature of American behavior: unrestrained acquisitiveness and pursuit of individual ambition.

Until quite recently, historians assumed that the Revolutionary generation was committed to social and economic equality, by which they meant social and economic leveling. But no idea was farther from their minds. When they talked about equality in a social or economic sense, they meant no more than that each man should have an equal right to achieve the best material life he could within the limits imposed upon him by his ability, means, and circumstances. Because it was obvious that men were unequal in their abilities, would start on unequal bases, and would achieve varying degrees of success, and because it was also assumed that one of the primary functions of laws, constitutions, and governments was to guarantee that men's property (their material acquisitions) as well as their liberty would be eternally secure, any idea of equality in the sense of social leveling was perforce totally foreign.

From the beginnings of settlement, the day-to-day life of most colonists had been oriented in this way, toward the fulfillment of the economic and social aspirations of individuals. Except for the West Indies and low-country South Carolina after the 1740's, however, there was a marked reluctance to accord full intellectual legitimation to the highly individualistic modes of action this orientation seemed to imply, to develop new values which would correspond to and accurately describe prevailing forms of behavior. Instead, the leaders clung desperately to an older conception that emphasized the organic character of society, the obligation of all individuals to sacrifice their own private interests to those of the public in general, and the antisocial nature of much individualistic behavior.

This conception was an integral part of the intellectual baggage of the earliest settlers, but throughout much of the seventeenth century colonial leaders had watched helplessly as it had been eroded and social order had seemed to give way to social chaos. Toward the end of the century and throughout the rest of the colonial period, emergent elites all over the colonies responded to this condition by trying to superimpose upon colonial society an order very similar to that originally attempted by the founders and still thought to be characteristic of the more settled society of the parent state. Guilty about the unstable, antisocial, and uncultivated character of colonial society, these groups reacted in either or both of two ways. They either looked back to the glorious day of the early founders when men had been more religious, more industrious, more frugal, and more public-spirited, or they looked across the Atlantic to an idealized conception of England for standards to which the colonists should aspire.

One of the main themes of eighteenth-century social development was, in fact, the attempt of the elites to recreate in America a society more closely resembling that of an ideal England. They tried to impose traditional English values upon society, to make colonial political systems conform more closely to that of England, to copy English institutions, and to imitate English patterns in virtually every aspect of cultural life. An obvious manifestation of the frequently observed tendency of provincial societies to seek to model themselves after the metropolis, these mimetic impulses ran very deeply. What is so significant about them is that they represented to a very large degree a rejection of many aspects of colonial life and an attempt to substitute for them an idealized Old World, specifically English, conception of the way New World societies should function. And they were not very successful, despite the fact that, as colonial societies became more complex and more settled during the eighteenth century, they came increasingly to resemble England. But appearances, as elites in the colonies fully understood, were deceiving, and the central question facing them on the eve of the pre-Revolutionary disturbances was whether America's material success might not be a direct measure of its moral and cultural failure.

How far these worries reached down into colonial society is revealed by the Great Awakening which, to a significant degree, constituted a rejection of the materialistic and secular character of American life. Although some groups among the evangelical clergy began during the Awakening to develop a millennial view of America's future, a view that stood in sharp contrast to the pessimistic forebodings of many of the elite, it is significant that their vision of a future in which men with God's help would lead selfless lives and live together in an affectionate union displayed a profound discontent with the present.

J.A.G. But did not the colonists come to see themselves as Americans rather than as transplanted Europeans before the Revolution?

J.P.G. I think they came to see themselves as *British* Americans, not as a separate people with separate values and a different kind of psychology. They were Britons who lived in America, different from the people in Britain, but nonetheless British, and they were very concerned to make that point. The degree to which they had not yet become fully and obviously British was the distance they still had to cover before they could realize the full potential of the colonies and make colonial society complete.

J.A.G. By the middle of the eighteenth century, the word "American" begins to be used. Does not that suggest a sense of similarity among the residents of different colonies which had not existed in earlier periods of time? Where does the word come from, and what does it signify?

J.P.G. It comes from the fact that they all lived in America; it may have been no more than a geographical designation. I do not think that when it was first used it involved an increasing awareness of the cohesiveness or the similarities of the various colonies. What tied Massachusetts and South Carolina and Virginia most closely together prior to 1763 was their common connection with England.

J.A.G. How did these social aspirations, these desires to make the colonies more British, affect colonial attitudes toward Britain in the middle of the eighteenth century?

J.P.G. In general, the colonists were very happy to be British and proud of their connection with Britain. Because it forced them to be concerned with a national (British) problem, the French and Indian War between 1754 and 1763 actually strengthened British patriotism in the colonies. In none of the earlier wars had the colonists contributed so much to an imperial cause or had the theater of action been so much in the colonies. The result was an ever closer identification of colonial interests with those of Britain and an intensification of British patriotism. The great British victories, beginning in 1759, in Canada, the West Indies, and India added enormously to the extent of British territory, and for the colonists it was exhilarating to be a part of what everybody in Britain and the colonies was saying was the greatest empire in history since Rome. From New England to Georgia, colonists took pride in this common achievement, and the significant part they thought they had played in the war both indicated to them that they had finally achieved a position of importance within the British Empire and created expectations that they would play a still greater role in the future. Benjamin Franklin's suggestion at this time that the rapid increase in the population of the colonies might eventually require that the capital be moved from London to Philadelphia revealed the full extent of these expectations.

On the other hand, the war also brought the colonists themselves closer together by forcing them to come to a realization that they had many interests in common. As is well known, a delegation of colonial representatives at the Albany Congress of 1754 proposed a defensive union of the colonies, which was subsequently rejected by local leaders back in the colonial capitols. Traditionally, historians have interpreted this incident as an indication of how disunited the colonies were. But the proper point to make about this episode is not that union was rejected but that it was proposed, that some colonial leaders had so far escaped from limitations of vision imposed upon them by the habitual particularism of the colonies as to be able to see that the colonists had certain common problems that might best be solved by common action.

J.A.G.   Were there any indications before 1763 that the colonies might be about to break free from their English ties? Was the Revolution inevitable, or was it a response to the particular changes in British policy that occurred after the French and Indian War?

J.P.G.   There were no manifest indications that a revolution was going to occur fifteen years later. All signs, as a matter of fact, point in just the opposite direction. There was no major discontent with the Navigation Acts. There was considerable tension between royal officials in London and the colonies and local legislatures, especially during the war, but, because the colonists had been able to achieve a considerable amount of local autonomy vested in their legislatures, there was little basic dissatisfaction with existing political relations between Britain and the colonies. The colonists were full of British patriotism. There seemed to be no reason, in short, why the colonists might not have stayed in the empire indefinitely, or evolved in the way Canada, Australia, and New Zealand later did.

But when one looks beneath the surface, one sees that the colonists were happy with the navigation system only because the parts of it they would have found particularly onerous were not rigidly enforced; that the political relationship was satisfactory only because the English were not making a sustained attempt to enforce certain traditional policies that the colonists regarded as highly objectionable. And one recognizes that the extreme British patriotism of the colonists was dependent upon a conception of their own future role in the empire that was at marked variance with the expectations in Britain. It is also very clear that, since at least 1748, powerful British colonial officials had been intent upon moving in directions that would alter existing economic and political relationships in such a way as to raise colonial resentment and to disappoint colonial expectations.

Through much of the period from 1721 to 1748, relationships between Britain and the colonies were dominated by what Edmund Burke called a policy of "salutary neglect." What Burke meant was that the colonists were permitted an enormous amount of freedom and by and large were allowed to go their own way, except in a few areas in which their behavior impinged adversely upon powerful British interests. None of the old ideals of British colonial policy was actually abandoned during these years, but there had been no systematic attempt to enforce them.

Some of the adverse fruits—adverse from the vantage point of Whitehall—of this policy began to become apparent in the late 1740's. The governors of New York and South Carolina were writing to England constantly, complaining that they had no authority, that they commanded no respect in their colonies, that the assemblies had all the power. A civil war raged in New Jersey. Royal government had broken down almost entirely in New Hampshire and North Carolina. In Bermuda, royal authority had sunk so low that the speaker of the legislature reportedly put a price on the governor's head. Understandably, there was a sense in London that a real crisis had developed in the Empire. Something had to be done. So the Earl of Halifax, an energetic and ambitious man, was made head of the Board of Trade, the chief agency concerned with governing the colonies. He proceeded to try to enforce regulations that had been ignored for twenty or thirty years. Although he encountered a great amount of difficulty in getting official support for many of the more drastic changes he wanted, he used all the powers at his command to try to restore royal authority in every specific situation that he could, until the outbreak of the French and Indian War forced him to abandon his efforts because of the need for colonial cooperation against the French.

Because almost all of his efforts were directed against particular colonies, the colonists as a whole had little sense of the general meaning of his actions. An objectionable instruction to a single governor or disallowance of one or more laws of an individual colony did not seem to portend a general assault upon colonial liberties. In fact, the full meaning of these actions did not become clear for a decade or more. Christopher Gadsden of South Carolina correctly analyzed the situation when he reported that it was not until after delegates from various colonies had gotten together at the Stamp Act Congress that it became clear that all of these seemingly isolated acts were part of a large movement to strengthen royal authority in the colonies, a movement that could only be interpreted by men like Gadsden as a general conspiracy by some figures in the British government to undermine existing colonial constitutions and perhaps eventually to "enslave" the colonies. Only from the perspective of a common grievance such as the Stamp Act, however, could the supposed existence of this conspiracy become clear. Only then, only with the open and explicit re-examination stimulated by the Stamp Act crisis and the events that followed it, did men in the colonies begin to realize that there were certain things about the imperial-colonial relationship that were injurious, or potentially so, for the colonies. Even then, they tended to focus their discontent upon events that occurred after, rather than before, 1763 and to idealize the earlier relationship. My answer to your question is, therefore, that although the essential preconditions for revolt can be found prior to 1763, the revolt was a specific response to British policies undertaken after that date.

J.A.G.   What is your opinion of the so-called "New Left" interpretation of colonial history?

J.P.G.   So far as I know, the New Left has no interpretation of *colonial* history. Staughton Lynd and Jesse Lemisch have written about the Revolution, but no one has really worked on the colonial period.

To the extent that New Left historians are insisting that American historians (like a great many historians of the French Revolution, such as George Rudé and Richard Cobb) should look at the Revolution or society "from below," I think that they are on a profitable track. We have spent so much time in the last twenty years looking at early American history from the point of view of the elite, the dominant groups, that we have tended to ignore other elements in society. It is obviously very important to understand what their attitudes and aspirations were.

J.A.G.   What are the half-dozen or so books that you would recommend to persons interested in the subject we have been discussing? In each case, could you indicate the chief contribution of the volume?

J.P.G.   I would prefer, I think, to talk about historians rather than about books. The only towering figure, the only historian of the very first importance who has thus far produced work of the highest distinction specifically on the colonial period is Perry Miller. Taken together, his many works on American Puritanism have both stimulated a major revolution in the way historians have understood that subject and, vastly more important, demonstrated the potentiality for the understanding of colonial life of intensive investigations of colonial ideas as they were manifested at a variety of levels. It is extremely difficult to make a choice among his several important works, but my own preference is for *The New England Mind: From Colony to Province* (1953), which describes the Puritan response to basic social and economic changes in New England society between the mid-sixteenth century and 1730.

Once you move beyond Miller, there are a number of very good historians. The most important figure in the generation that preceded Miller is of course Charles M. Andrews. Among a massive corpus of excellent work, *The Colonial Period of American History* (1934–37), in four volumes, and *The Colonial Background of the American Revolution* (1924) are of continuing importance. The first three volumes of the former work provide the most comprehensive narrative of the public history of the colonies in the seventeenth century yet available, while Volume IV, along with *The Colonial Background*, constitute the most complete and well-balanced analysis of British commercial and colonial policy.

Among Miller's contemporaries, Louis B. Wright and Carl Bridenbaugh have contributed an amazing number of important pioneer studies in colonial cultural and social history, but the work of Wesley Frank Craven is excelled in quality only by Miller. Craven's *The Southern Colonies in the Seventeenth Century* (1949), which traces the political and socioeconomic history of the colonies from Maryland to South Carolina down to 1689, and his recent *The Colonies in Transition, 1660–1713* (1968), which presents the closest thing we have to a composite political history of any segment of colonial history, are filled with penetrating insights and wise judgments, and will be of lasting significance.

Five men stand out in the generation that followed Miller: Frederick B. Tolles, Edmund S. Morgan, Bernard Bailyn, Daniel J. Boorstin, and Alan Heimert. Tolles has carried the study of cultural history to a new level of sophistication, especially in *Meeting House & Counting House: The Quaker Merchants of Colonial Philadelphia* (1948), a work that employs the intensive study of a single group to illuminate the broader social tensions and cultural trends present in colonial society. The most artful and probably also the most prolific writer of his generation, Morgan has produced several works of major importance on seventeenth-century New England which both amplify and qualify the earlier work of Perry Miller in a number of respects. His *The Puritan Dilemma: The Story of John Winthrop* (1958), is the best introduction to Puritanism during the first generation. Bernard Bailyn's most significant work on the colonial period is *The New England Merchants in the Seventeenth Century* (1955), a work that employed the functional approach of the sociologists to raise our understanding of the socioeconomic and political history of early New England to a new level. In *The Americans: The Colonial Experience* (1958), Daniel J. Boorstin both contributed a provocative general account of colonial development and threw out a multitude of suggestive hypotheses that invite consideration and testing, while Alan Heimert's massive *Religion and the American Mind from the Great Awakening to the Revolution* (1966), despite a number of obvious flaws, is a book of enormous learning that towers over the landscape of eighteenth-century colonial religious history. There are a number of others in this generation whom one would have to mention were he concerned with Revolutionary as well as colonial history, and, indeed, the most important books of both Morgan and Bailyn, respectively, *The Stamp Act Crisis: Prologue to Revolution* (1953), and *The Ideological Origins of the American Revolution* (1967), properly fall within the period of the Revolution.

From a still younger generation, there have been several highly competent works, and it is impossible to mention them all here. I would single out Winthrop D. Jordan's *White over Black: American Attitudes Toward the Negro 1550–1812* (1968), the title of which is accurately descriptive, as the most impressive contribution to colonial history yet published by anyone from this age group.

Bernard Bailyn

The American Revolution

ERNARD BAILYN, Winthrop Professor of History at Harvard University, has ranged over the entire colonial period in his researches. His *New England Merchants in the Seventeenth Century* (1955), by stressing the family ties that bound colonial merchants to English colleagues, threw light on the political history of early America as well as the economic. His *Education in the Forming of American Society* (1960) had equally broad implications for our understanding of family life and of the American character. Currently, he is working on a massive edition of *Pamphlets of the American Revolution*, one volume of which has so far appeared (1965). His *Ideological Origins of the American Revolution* (1967), which won both a Pulitzer and a Bancroft prize, is an expanded version of the introduction to the *Pamphlets*. This book and his *Origins of American Politics* (1968) have forced historians to re-examine the whole question of the causes of the Revolution. In this discussion, Bailyn comments on the major ideas developed in these works and fits the ideology of the Revolution into the larger context of British-American relations during the colonial period.

John A. Garraty   In considering the American Revolution, Professor Bailyn, where does one begin—do the roots of the revolt go far back into colonial history, or was it a relatively sudden upheaval?

Bernard Bailyn   Like any such upheaval, it had immediate causes, but it also had deep roots. My own view is that these roots go back into the early eighteenth century and relate particularly to the way in which social changes had affected the structure of politics. In the perspective of these changes, some of the sudden developments in the 1760's and early 1770's seem logical, almost inevitable. Contemporaries with a sense of history saw this. Thomas Hutchinson, of Massachusetts, the loyalist governor and historian, never doubted that the immediate outbreak was the deliberate work of a conspiratorial clique, but he believed the ultimate cause lay in the growth of American society over the previous century. So I draw back to these social questions of the early eighteenth century that affected the political organization of the British North American colonies as the starting point for any explanation of how the Revolution came about.

J.A.G.   In your recent work you appear to stress the British threat to the political rights of the colonies as the chief cause of the Revolution. Before turning to this subject, however, would you comment on the question of British economic policy before 1763 as a cause of the Revolution?

B.B.   This question of mercantilism and the Navigation Acts as they relate to the causes of the Revolution has an interesting historiographical background. There was a time in the early 1930's when their effect was considered to be crucial. Louis Hacker, in an article called "The First American Revolution," presented a quasi-Marxist interpretation. He argued that the mercantilist system lay at the heart of the causes of the Revolution. This economic system, he said, contained an internal contradiction. At a certain point mercantilistic regulations inevitably created counterforces to themselves, counterforces that would lead to trouble. In constraining the colonial economy, the system developed capital surpluses to a point requiring investment in enterprises that competed with England, especially manufactures. Because colonial expansionism was contrary to the philosophy of the system, such investments would inevitably lead to an explosion. This interpretation was worked out elaborately by formal Marxists, especially by Jack Hardy in a book with the same title as Hacker's article. But more recent writing has pretty well rejected mercantilism as a major cause of the Revolution. The mercantilist regulations did obviously have an effect on the economy, but they were not, it seems to me, a major cause of colonial unrest.

J.A.G.   Could you explain this a little more fully? It's easy to see the mercantilistic system as something that restricted the colonies—that is obviously how the British saw it. How can one argue that the Navigation Acts did not inhibit economic development?

B.B.   I think I can answer this in various ways. The Acts did affect the colonial economy, but how much did they inhibit economic growth? On one point there is, I think, general agreement: the prohibition of trade between the northern colonies and the foreign West Indies. This prohibition inhibited not merely economic growth but, through restraint on markets, equilibrium of the financial system. Had it been enforced, there would have been real economic problems that would no doubt have had political consequences. But the Molasses Act of 1733, which put a high tax on molasses from the foreign West Indies, was not enforced until the character of the regulations shifted in the 1760's. At that point it did become a matter of importance, though still not a crucial one, I think, in the events leading to the Revolution.

Some recent work on this subject goes along the line of econometric analysis. A group of historians at the University of Washington are trying to apply contrary-to-fact hypotheses about economic growth to contrast the actual statistics of colonial commerce with the condition —a hypothetical condition—of freedom from the restrictions of the Navigation Acts in the middle of the eighteenth century. They come up, though by processes that many historians find questionable (how can one quantify the economic value of the protection of the British Navy?)—they come up with the conclusion that the inhibition of economic growth caused by British restrictions was not of great magnitude, but something like an estimated loss of one-half of one per cent of per capita income. This calculation has not been worked out fully, and you have to agree, to begin with, that the econometric technique of hypothesizing what the growth would have been had there not been these regulations and then contrasting it to the existing situation is valid. But I do not think that it will prove much more than that there was a small effect over-all on economic growth. The effect doesn't seem to have been a crucial one. In any case, for the immediate question, the relevant point is this: To what extent was mercantilism an articulated issue during the early revolutionary years? To what extent did informed people speaking for the colonists refer to the system as a grievance, protest against it, and so forth? And my impression is that although it existed as an element in the discussions leading to the Revolution, it was not a significant one.

J.A.G.   Do you think that the average informed colonist had much grasp of mercantilism as a *system*? Do you think that even a merchant who had to deal with the regulations saw mercantilism in the same kind of philosophical way that historians do looking back at it?

B.B.   I don't think they did. They saw it as a group of particular regulations. In fact it is relevant to ask whether even the designers of the
system saw it that way. Mercantilism in its own time was a form of
economic nationalism. The colonists, and I believe the British, saw it as
a way of protecting trade in specific circumstances, particularly by
benefiting the trade, and hence the wealth, of England as opposed to
that of France. As for any systematic understanding of what was involved,
this came later—after the Revolution. In the first place, Adam Smith,
writing *The Wealth of Nations* in 1776, and his followers later, speaking
on behalf of a policy of laissez faire, gave mercantilism a systematic
form it didn't have in practice. Secondly, German economic theorists,
trying to work out their own principles of economic nationalism in the
later-nineteenth century, applied more systematic analysis to these
problems than had been given to them in the seventeenth and eighteenth
centuries. Consequently, when twentieth-century historians began to look
at this problem, they tended to see it through the eyes of Adam Smith
and the German economic nationalists, both of whom had applied theory
where theory didn't exist and given mercantilism a hard, orderly form it
never actually possessed.

But you asked about the colonists specifically in this respect. They
knew that they were contributing to the economic welfare of England
by accepting certain inhibitions of their freedom to act economically.
The crucial areas were the prohibition of direct trade between the
northern colonies and Europe and of the direct sale of certain southern
raw commodities, such as tobacco, outside the Empire. The colonists
did feel these restrictions, but they were not major issues in the discussion of the grievances behind the Revolution.

J.A.G.   If the restrictive aspects of the Navigation Acts seemed to strike
primarily at the northern colonies, how can one explain the fact that in
practice the system seems to have stimulated the northern colonies to
develop a more dynamic economy than that of the southern colonies,
which fitted well into the system (if there was a system!)?

B.B.   Well, the one point of control that might really have damaged the
northern colonies by affecting the balance of payments to England
was the restriction on trade with the foreign West Indies, but as I have
said, that was not enforced. It was not until the late 1760's that the
machinery to enforce this restriction was created, and the *machinery*,
namely the customs inspectors, vice-admiralty courts, and so on, then
became a political grievance. It was associated with other, noneconomic,
problems—political and ideological problems—and became very important.

J.A.G.   Is it possible to look at mercantilism as primarily a political
technique or tactic rather than an economic one?

B.B. I think it's generally thought of now as an aspect of building up a powerful nation-state in a competitive world. The principle was that what one loses oneself is gained by one's competitor—hence the necessity to withhold the benefits of colonial trade from any other nation. In this sense mercantilism was political.

J.A.G. Do you know whether the colonists in general were aware of this aspect of mercantilism before 1763?

B.B. In a very general form, in the sense that they realized that the regulations were strengthening England.

J.A.G. Did they, for example, appreciate the protection that the British Navy provided them against the French and Spanish?

B.B. This became a question. People talked about whether taxation, for example, wasn't really a repayment for the protection offered by Great Britain. I don't believe, if you're talking about the middle of the eighteenth century, that people said, "Look, the Navy is protecting us; we ought to let them restrict our commerce." They thought of mercantilism as a reasonable system of international economic regulation in which they participated. It had abrasive points which they did what they could to alleviate.

J.A.G. Would it be correct to conclude that mercantilism was not a major cause of difficulty with England—that until the changing of the system in the 1760's there was no substantial American complaint?

B.B. Yes, but I think it's more to the point to say that even in the following decade there was little complaint about mercantilism as such, though mention of it was included in certain specific ways in the Declaration of Independence. It was not a major element in the points at issue between England and America up to 1776.

J.A.G. I wonder if I could come back to the first question I asked you? Are you arguing in your books, *The Origins of American Politics* and *The Ideological Origins of the American Revolution*, that the Revolution was the product of the development of American civilization or American nationalism, a sense on the part of the colonists that they had developed a way of life different from the English way?

B.B. I do not mean to say that the immediate causes of the Revolution lay in these social developments. These social developments, and the political consequences derived from them, could have occurred without a revolutionary explosion. There was nothing inevitable about that—no inevitable necessity for the Revolution to take place. What seems to me to have happened is that social changes led to a peculiar construction of Anglo-American politics in the middle of the eighteenth century, which became threatened in the 1760's. These apparent threats roused ideological apprehensions that people responded to very actively. The roots of the Revolution can be traced in this indirect sense to the social changes of the time, but the Revolution was not initiated by these social elements.

J.A.G. Could you in brief scope describe these differences between England and America in the mid-eighteenth century?

B.B. It's very difficult to typify an American and a Briton in the mid-eighteenth century and make the contrast. But by speaking of general conditions and the over-all socioeconomic differences between the two communities, we can isolate certain crucial elements. In the first place, it's certainly true that the scales of social differences in England and America were very different. You just don't have any Blenheim palaces in America; there is no style of life like that of the highest British aristocracy. But this does not mean that American society was unstratified. There was, of course, a stratified society in America, but the scale was different.

J.A.G. A number of Americans, from the upper levels of colonial society, did from time to time go to England. I'm not thinking only of men like Benjamin Franklin, who went in official capacities of one kind or another. How did these upper-class colonists fit into English society? Were they accepted as upper class in England, or were they looked down upon or patronized?

B.B. Well, that's hard to answer in that form. At one point I tried, in collaboration with John Clive, to get at that question by working out a comparison between the condition of an American visiting England and a Scot moving south into England, and we found a very similar response to provincials coming from the west and from the north into the cosmopolitan center. The main question (and I think it more easily answered) is not so much whether they were accepted by the English (they were treated as provincials by the English), but how they responded themselves—what their awareness of this cosmopolitan situation was. That awareness does bear on the Revolution, especially because views of England become crucial at a certain point in the 1760's. Americans in eighteenth-century England felt very much outside, awed by English society and its great expressions, and by British institutions, which they identified with very much. Even those who reacted negatively to the corruption of English life as they saw it, men like young John Dickinson of Delaware, who went to London in 1754 to study law, at the same time were deeply awed by what they found there, and they associated themselves with this society.

But mid-eighteenth-century views of English society are just now being investigated, both by American and English historians. We don't know enough about them yet. What I see from the American side is a mingling of attitudes in a peculiarly ambiguous way. You see the balance of it clearly only in such rare documents as the letters John Dickinson wrote home to his parents from London in the election year of 1754. Dickinson was a great admirer of England, as most Americans were. As a lawyer-in-training he was deeply impressed by legal institutions, by the judiciary, and so forth. But he was appalled by what he saw of the election of 1754, by what went on in English politics, and he thought it was a corrupt system. Yet he thought himself very much a part of the English life and he loved it. It's an ambiguous attitude.

The crucial question is at what point and for what reason did the ambiguity of the image of English society shift into a clearly negative or clearly positive one for Americans. The change takes place during the revolutionary years, in my opinion. In the mid-eighteenth century there was a mingling of these negative and positive views. One of the interesting things we don't know about this yet is whether that was not also true of England itself. There is evidence that the English, although they were the greatest self-congratulatory race of the eighteenth century, also felt that there were things deeply wrong with their society, and there is evidence, such as the great circulation of tracts like Dr. John Brown's gloomy *Estimate of the Manners and Principles of the Times,* which indicates that large numbers of English people felt, as Americans did, that there was something wrong with the society, despite its greatness.

J.A.G.   While you were talking, I was thinking of the work of your Harvard colleague, Howard Mumford Jones, and his emphasis on how, after the discovery of the New World, there was quite an ambivalent attitude toward America, not only in Europe but also among colonists. Some looked at America as a garden of Eden, but others perceived it as a howling wilderness full of dangers and hardships. Does that ambivalence disappear by the eighteenth century?

B.B.   That's a very good point to bring in as a corrective to what I've just said, but I would prefer to put it in a somewhat different way. The eighteenth-century "continental naturalists," Georges de Buffon, for example, systematically argued that sophisticated forms of life regressed in the New World, that the wilderness environment created a regression from the highest attainments of European civilization. British officials in America considered American social and political organizations primitive. Americans did not entirely disagree, but they took, in general, a positive view, dramatically expressed somewhat later at a famous dinner party in Paris where the theories of the continental naturalists were being debated. Franklin asked the company to rise. When the guests measured one another's height with their eyes, it was obvious to all that the Americans were taller and physically more vigorous. But you asked whether there wasn't a negative view of American life. I think there was, particularly on the part of crown officials, but it penetrated into the American community to some extent too. I think, though, that it was a minor and secondary element that burned itself out in the Revolution.

J.A.G. In your analysis of the writings of Americans about their political system during the developing controversy with England, you point out how profoundly suspicious they were of power and that they saw political power as a threat to liberty. What does this suggest about their view of human nature? Is it consistent with the idea that men of the enlightenment were congenital optimists?

B.B. When I went through the literature of the early revolutionary period, the thing that struck me most in a way I was least prepared for was the degree to which the writers were apprehensive about human nature. They felt that a fragile balance existed between those elements of rationality and of coherence and good will in man, on the one hand, and the deep malevolence of human nature, on the other. This dark view is found not merely in the *Federalist Papers*—that I knew—but in the thought of an earlier generation. I was prepared to find this in the *Federalist Papers*, but it has a deep background. Political thinkers early in the period, indeed throughout the century, saw the negative elements of the lust for power and the unreliability of virtue as the dominant force in human affairs. But they believed that enough rationality remained in men so that they could reform the political system in the hope that a better life would be attained.

J.A.G. Are you saying that they had a pessimistic view of human nature, but they also thought of America as a better world? I don't want to put words in your mouth, but are you suggesting that they believed that America was a kind of Utopia, and also that men, in general, were selfish and had to be subjected to checks and balances?

B.B. I would simply say that it's a mingled view in which the pessimistic strains are very strong. Social conditions in most communities they knew of had been such as to bring out all those dark propensities of human nature, and not allow the favorable ones to dominate. The favorable aspects of human nature did exist, they believed, and under certain conditions could dominate. And they hoped to be able to capitalize on this potentiality, because American conditions were favorable, and because reform along particular lines would permit these better elements of human nature to dominate.

J.A.G. You spoke of the "mixed" feelings that Americans had about English society. What particularly offended them? Was English society really corrupt?

B.B. Their comments focus on two kinds of objective problems in England, real things that actually were taking place, which they cast in moral and ideological terms. In the first place, there was a constitutional problem in mid-eighteenth-century England the solution of which they interpreted as corrupt and responded to very negatively, namely, the Walpolian system. The informal control of the House of Commons by the ministry, which Walpole had initiated and elaborated to secure himself in power and to overcome the earlier instability of English politics, they believed to be a corruption of the English constitution and a deeply evil political condition. This was what John Dickinson mainly reacted against in 1754. He saw the ministerial control (bribery, the rotten-borough system, and so forth) and was appalled. Such critics feared that a deliberate break-down of the famous balance of powers between interests in the English constitution was in progress. They condemned it as corrupt, and in this they shared the views of both left and right opposition in England. Both Bolingbroke on the right, and on the left, the libertarian would-be re-formers of the early eighteenth century, opposed Walpole and the Walpolian system.

In the second place, American critics were horrified by the condition of London at this time. London was the seat of government and by far the largest and richest single community in England. Colonial critics were struck by the squalor and vice that existed there. But more important, they saw a mass population that was degraded politically below what independent people should be. They felt that certain kinds of economic qualifications were necessary for a rational participation in politics, and they saw that the mass of London's population did not have them. As a consequence the people were highly susceptible to bribery and corruption and all the other evil influences that the.leaders of the community could exert. Thus, if you ask, "What is the reality behind American feelings?" in these two senses there was reality behind them. The colonists saw a threat in the "disbalanced" constitution that Walpole had worked out after the 1730's, and they saw, especially in the London population, but elsewhere too, the kind of mass degradation that might soften public resistance to authoritarianism.

J.A.G. Did colonial critics view the gross social and economic differences in English society as a form of corruption? It seems to me that the answer to this question will throw a great deal of light on the question of whether or not social differences between America and the mother country were really very important as a cause of the break between the two societies.

B.B. They still lived in a very deferential society. They were still assuming that a good society could be one that in our terms is very highly stratified.

J.A.G. In other words, the fact that there were so many poor people in England did not bother them?

B.B. The issue was not whether the mass of English people were poor— not simply that the condition of their lives was unhappy. It wasn't that so much, as the political meaning of poverty that provided for eighteenth-century critics a source of corruption in the community. This, the Americans said, could be extremely dangerous to the liberties of the people. They believed that liberty could be compatible with high social stratification, but that stratification became a threat to liberty and political freedom at the point at which the people were so degraded that they could not resist the blandishments of demagogues or would-be totalitarians.

J.A.G. Would you summarize the course of events after 1763 that led Americans to believe that a deliberate conspiracy was afoot in Britain to subvert the constitution and destroy liberty, both in America and in the mother country?

B.B. Most of these events—from the Sugar and Stamp Acts through the Coercive Acts—are well known. What needs to be stressed is the growth of the belief that behind these particular events a pattern was emerging. Events played on sensitive issues in the ideological framework of the time and became highly meaningful.

For example, the new Parliamentary regulations of commerce produced objective economic problems and dangers, but they also involved new crown appointments in America, which were seen by many colonists as agents for a kind of regulation of government that had not existed before and that fitted a pattern of deliberate malevolence against the operation of the balanced constitution in America. One way in which a balanced constitution could be corrupted was to place people beholden to the ruling powers in regulatory positions. As a second example, new taxes, which obviously were, from the colonial taxpayers' perspective, problems in themselves in that they indicated the existence of a theoretically limitless power over their property, also fitted an ideological pattern that bred fear and suspicion. The taxes would reduce the population economically and hence also reduce their capacity to resist further political encroachments by a dominant or would-be-dominant group. Further, the colonists argued, the taxation of America would allow the ministry in England to gain complete control of the House of Commons by gifts that would not be dependent on the control of the House itself, namely gifts of offices and of monies derived from the colonies.

The enlarged jurisdiction of admiralty courts also seemed to fall into the pattern. The corruption of the impartiality of justice was one aspect of the question. Another was the attempt to transfer the source of judges' salaries from the colonial assemblies to the Crown. Finally, the introduction of an armed force, in New York earlier, but particularly in Boston in 1768, invoked the old fear of standing armies so prevalent in the late seventeenth century, and fitted a pattern of deliberate "design."

In short, a build-up of apprehension from these new enactments gradually developed in the 60's and early 70's. The main question in American minds was one of motive. Why were these things done? Was it merely that misinformation had been supplied to the ministry? If so, who was doing the misinforming, and why? Or were the ministers deliberately trying to create a different political system?

In my way of thinking about this, one of the most sensitive and revealing figures is Governor Thomas Hutchinson, of Massachusetts, who was seen as an arch-conspiratorial figure, deliberately misinforming the ministry so that they would carry out policies favorable to himself and his group. In 1773 Josiah Quincy went to England in part to try to counteract the misinformation that Hutchinson was presumably giving to the ministry. After 1774, when Hutchinson himself went to England and stayed there, American radicals considered him one of the main powers directing this series of threatening actions. The question, I suppose, that they were asking themselves all the time was whether or not the ministers were deliberate conspirators for their own selfish purposes. The way to understand this question is not so much to enumerate a series of grievances, but to recognize that the configuration of these problematic enactments added up at a certain point in colonial minds to a deliberate attack on the preexisting situation of colonial autonomy that seemed to them to have guaranteed their liberty.

J.A.G.   Was Thomas Hutchinson a significant figure in colonial thinking outside Massachusetts?

B.B.   He was very important, although primarily in Massachusetts until 1773, when two things happened. First, his speech on political theory delivered to the Massachusetts Assembly was published, together with the responses of the House and Council, and it had a wide circulation. Second, and more important, his letters written to England in 1768–69 were secretly obtained, sent to America through Franklin's intervention, and published. The universal importance attributed in America to these quite innocuous letters is astonishing, and very revealing. Their publication was a huge event. People became convinced who never had been before that a malevolent, concerted force was at work against them. Hutchinson had feared exactly some such development, because the letters of his predecessor, Governor Francis Barnard, had been published similarly in 1769, and he had known what effect such publications could have on an ideologically sensitive population. He warned his correspondents again and again in the years before 1773 to keep his letters secret. But when what he feared actually happened even he was amazed at the effect it had. There is no better indication of the ideological saturation of the colonists' minds than their inflamed reaction to these letters. In any case, it was at that point, in 1773, that Hutchinson became a national figure.

J.A.G.   Was there really a conspiracy?

B.B.   No. There was no deliberate conspiracy, in the terms the colonists claimed. But there were elements of change that created the impression, and that really did create upsetting objective modifications of the existing situation. In the first place, there was an effort, starting in the early 1760's, to rationalize the imperial regulation system in ways that had never been carried out before. Imperial relations before 1763 were highly irrational. In formal, legal terms it was a system that didn't work. It has been described, and I think very well, as a kind of coral reef that had grown up over many years: very hard and jagged, randomly put together, full of myriads of pockets of private influence, and almost impossible to remold into a smooth, rational organization. Repeatedly, from the early eighteenth century on, efforts at reform had been made, the most serious by Lord Halifax, as president of the Board of Trade in the 1750's. But nothing had happened, for reasons that can be explained in terms of English politics in that period.

What took place under George III was the effort finally to rationalize the imperial system, to bring it together under concerted controls. This effort culminated in 1768 with the creation of a third Secretary of State, for the colonies, holding most of the strings of regulation. Previously, authority over the colonies had spilled out over a great number of sectors of the British government. The Navy had a piece, the Army had a piece, the Secretary of State for the Southern Department had a piece, the Board of Trade had a piece, and so forth. After 1768, particularly, something like a true imperial bureaucracy began to emerge in the centralization of authority in the colonial secretary's hands.

Colonists were responding to this change, which made deep alterations in the conditions of life—favorable conditions—that had existed before. The change was made deliberately, and in that sense I think it suggests a positive answer to your question. There are now a number of studies that make clear the degree to which the effort to rationalize the imperial regulation system did contribute objectively to changes that could be interpreted in this conspiratorial sense. These studies of Anglo-American politics in the mid-eighteenth century show how the old system had worked. Stanley Katz' recent book on New York, for example, is a deep penetration into Anglo-American policies of a sort that has not been made before. Two books deal with the post-1763 situation, and the change that took place then: Thomas Barrows' study of the customs service before and after 1763, and Michael Kammen's study of the colonial agents. The agents supplied a sensitive point of contact between the Americans and England up to 1765, but then, Kammen shows, the system collapsed after the Stamp Act.

There were also the changes that took place in English domestic politics after the accession of George III. The old system that had favored the colonies was rejected. George III replaced the old ministry with his own men, starting catastrophically with Lord Bute. The shift in the ministerial organization, first under Bute, and finally, after 1770, under Lord North, contributed to the belief that the system was being deliberately overturned. One gets a reflection in certain Anglo-American correspondences of how these domestic changes in England were interpreted by colonists in ideological terms. There is a correspondence on English domestic politics, for example, between Andrew Eliot, the Boston minister, and Thomas Hollis, the libertarian philanthropist, in London, which makes it perfectly clear that changes taking place under George III for domestic political purposes played into this American sense of conspiracy.

J.A.G. Would it be possible to argue that the need for centralization, for rationalization of the system, was a response to American conditions? By the 1760's America was really becoming a unit in a sense that it never was before, when the colonies were separated from one another by large areas of undeveloped land. In other words, could one interpret the British attempt to rationalize and centralize control over the colonies as merely a stage in the growth of central government in the country? Later stages would be the colonial committees of correspondence, the Continental Congress, the Articles of Confederation, and finally the Constitution.

B.B. Well, none of the changes that I'm talking about was such as to bring the colonies together into a political unit. Quite the contrary, they sought to relate the colonies to London in a rational fashion.

J.A.G. There was a central commissioner for the customs to administer the whole area as a unit. Isn't that a form of central government?

B.B. Yes, but it's a question of where it resides. What the British were trying to do was to center control in London.

J.A.G. You see, what I'm asking is this: Were there not two separate questions involved: the *structure* of control, and who runs it?

B.B. Perhaps the Revolution as a whole is entirely a question about who runs the system. Later American history, too, centers on the question of how centralized the controls should be. For example, the conflict over the reform of the Articles of Confederation certainly could be seen in these terms. By the middle of the eighteenth century, as the colonies grew and became more internally complex, they began to rub against one another the wrong way. There's some need for dealing with *American* colonies, as distinct from Massachusetts, Virginia, and South Carolina, and in this sense centralization was inevitable. I'd answer this question two ways. In the first place No, and in the second place Yes. On the "No" side, in 1754 the Albany Congress—

J.A.G.   That's a good example of what I mean!

B.B.   But everybody rejected that. Nobody wanted it except Franklin and maybe Governor William Shirley of Massachusetts. Hutchinson, who was sympathetically involved himself, later pointed out how universally the proposed centralization was rejected. No substantial interest was sympathetic, neither the colonial assemblies nor London wanted it. Nobody acted, but even if it had formally been acted upon, the answer in political terms would have been No.

J.A.G.   Yet a few very farsighted people were favorable to it. Franklin certainly was.

B.B.   A few, yes, but there was so little sympathy with this idea that it got nowhere. But on the "Yes" side, I would put it this way: I think many of the developments that took place in Canada in the early nineteenth century could very well have taken place to the south, had there not been the explosion. The Revolution was not inevitable. There could have been a slow bringing together of common American interests in some form or other, perhaps not in the form of an elaborate constitution, but in some form. Then, too, some kind of articulation of a federal relationship between America and England might have developed. But one can also argue that only the American Revolution made it possible for Canada to evolve as it did. It seems to me that there didn't have to be an explosion. Had there not been an explosion, I do agree with you to the extent of saying that probably some effort to bring together common American interests would have been made.

J.A.G.   What I really was suggesting was that the pressure for control of economic affairs that you were describing seemed to rise out of English dissatisfaction with the inefficiencies of the earlier system. Perhaps the inefficiencies became unbearable as colonial life became more complex and interrelated.

B.B.   Well, when the British appointed a third Secretary of State for the colonies, Edmund Burke's explanation was that the existing two secretaries of state were doing nothing and the third was appointed to help them! He thought it was just a form of political patronage aimed at building up the king's interest. And, in fact, if you analyze in detail why the appointment of a third secretary came when it did you discover the immediate reason to lie in the political exigencies of that year. But the change had a more general justification, and broad effects. If you ask, "Why did they rationalize colonial administration when for three generations they had not rationalized it?," I would answer that the impetus was toward the gaining of a revenue, and thereafter, the desire to control the situation better because of the upheavals that were induced by the effort to get a revenue.

J.A.G.   Much of the political controversy that developed after 1760 seems to have resulted from a difference of opinion between Britain and the colonies about the meaning of a few key words, in particular *representation, constitution, rights,* and *sovereignty.* Would you define these words as they were used in Great Britain?

B.B.   I think that the controversies centered not so much on words as words, but on situations represented by these words and understandings of them. Assumptions had grown up about the meaning of these words and the political reality they represented, assumptions which had not been thought through. Beginning in the 1760's, these concepts come into focus and were discussed as important problems for the first time. Views were articulated that had not been articulated before. Take *representation,* for example. The universal American assumption had not been that proper representation was one man, one vote, or that a representative assembly was a mirror image of the electorate. It was more commonly assumed, rather, that interests, broadly construed, were represented and that those persons were elected to speak for those major interests of the community who could speak best, and wisely decide about them. The controversy with Great Britain, however, evoked views of representation that come closer to what we consider actual representation, and these were clearly incompatible with the British concept of virtual representation.

The meaning of *constitution* before this period was "something constituted." What was constituted was the mode of operation of the government (which included the common law and the judicial system) animated by certain principles. It was the operation of the inherited political system and the animation of its principles that was assumed to be the constitution. What happened during the crisis was that the animating principles became more and more important to Americans. The constitution was thought of more and more as a set of principles, and finally as a written expression of those principles by which form and correction could be given to the everyday action of the government.

What comes closest to explaining the explosion is the controversy over the meaning *sovereignty,* which from the late sixteenth century had been conceived of by Englishmen as a unitary source of power and control that had to be absolute within any given political system. If America was part of the English political community in any sense, there had to be an absolute sovereign power within it, a power which was felt to lie in Parliament, or more correctly, the king-in-Parliament. The Americans made efforts, highly imaginative ones, to devise federalist ideas and apply them to the imperial situation. When, in his famous speech to the Massachusetts Assembly in January 1773, Thomas Hutchinson drew out the platitudes of the time into a systematic statement about the necessity of a singular, absolute controlling power in the political system, and challenged his opponents in Massachusetts on that point, they began to give up the attempt to articulate a federal system and in the end came to agree with him. "If he wants to draw conclusions, then he can draw the conclusion of absolute control or absolute independence," they said, and they knew what they would choose if forced to make a choice.

The wisest heads of the time did not think through this problem of dividing sovereignty into graduated levels of control in a federal system. Like Burke, they said, in effect, "Let the principle stand but don't act on it." Only later, when people started thinking about the relations of the American states to the national government, was that even partially accomplished. There has never, of course, been a complete resolution of this problem in American life.

J.A.G. This controversy over the character of sovereignty, as you describe it, makes the Americans the innovators, attempting to develop new ideas. But couldn't one argue that the innovators at this time were the British? In practice, hadn't there been a division of sovereignty in America from the days of the first colonists?

B.B. Yes, but not in point of theory.

J.A.G. But which comes first, the theory or the practice? Wasn't the theory an attempt to rationalize the practice?

B.B. The division of sovereignty had not been developed through design, but by inadvertence. Because of the failure in England to set up effective administrative machinery, there had grown up an ad hoc division of sovereignty between the local colonial groups and the British power. An attempt to define the principles of federalism to express this situation was begun by Americans first in the late 1760's. It was continued later when discontent under the Articles of Confederation led to the drafting of the federal Constitution. Had they been worked out sooner, and had the British accepted them, there would have been no Revolution. What was involved in all of this was not mere verbal hairsplitting or abstract theorizing but a struggle for power. Federalism has continued to be that.

J.A.G. Where did the colonists get the idea that representatives stood for specific regions, rather than the state as a whole? Was there an English origin to that idea?

B.B. There was, very much so, in the parliaments of the medieval period. But the Americans weren't trying to go back to the actual representation of the thirteenth century. The concept that representatives were acting for a limited constituency as lawyers would act, pleading the case for the local constituency, was not universal in colonial assemblies. It came up at times of political controversy in some places, but not always. For the most part, people were relaxed about this, and didn't instruct their representatives. But there was certainly more instructing of representatives in the colonies than in England, and at critical moments there was a general sense that representatives were "mirrors of their constituency," as John Adams put it later.

J.A.G.   Was there a consistent pattern of establishing residence requirements for legislators?

B.B.   It was widespread, I think for the same reason that it happened in early English constitutional history, the feeling that the controlling body of the unit to which representatives are being sent is an alien one. Colonists could not be sure that the royal authorities would respond automatically to the interests of the community. They might be too compliant to external and not necessarily sympathetic pressures. If the colonies had been autonomous communities in which the leaders controlled the whole system, confidence in the leaders might have made the practice unnecessary.

J.A.G.   Would you explain the historical controversy about the supposed difference in American thought between internal and external taxation by Parliament?

B.B.   There is a general question involved. The argument over external and internal taxation, or external and internal government, was actually one form of a series of American efforts to find a line of division that could be drawn within a system of government. They looked for a line somewhere in what traditionalists said was a monolithic kind of power. They were fumbling around, and the most common way they got at this was somehow to distinguish things external to the immediate community from things internal to the immediate community. The taxation question was one specification of this line of division, but it wasn't a successful one, and this was quickly realized. Professor Edmund S. Morgan is quite right in saying that the argument that the colonists should allow England to impose external taxation, but not internal taxation was never a dominant colonial position. Some people did say that, but they quickly got off this line of reasoning because they saw its weakness. It was an illogical argument, and they abandoned it within a year or two. More persistent was the attempt to describe external government and internal government, rather than external taxation and internal taxation. That attempt to divide sovereignty persisted right up to 1776. It's not a question of whether the difference between internal and external taxation was a crucial or persistent point of argument. It wasn't. It was merely one form of a more general effort to draw a distinction.

J.A.G.   Much has been written about whether or not the Revolution was a profound social upheaval. Some historians argue that there were few important social changes. Others, pointing, for example, to the fact that there were far more *émigrés* in proportion to the population than in

France during the French Revolution, claim that it was a major social upheaval. In your own work you state that no one "deliberately worked for the destruction or even the substantial alteration of the order of society." But you also speak of "the contagion of liberty," and present a great deal of evidence of social change. Would you comment generally on the Revolution as a social movement?

B.B.   There was a great deal of social change throughout the Revolutionary period. But you have to distinguish intent from consequences: what was intended as part of the effort of the revolutionary movement, and what happened as a consequence of it. There are two kinds of very obvious social changes, it seems to me, that result from the Revolution. The first flows from the fact that it was a long and disruptive war, the second from the fact that it was a revolutionary movement that displaced a number of people, many of whom had been in leadership positions. The war and the displacements that followed led to rapid social changes. Also, the war itself stimulated the economy in certain ways that had not been operating before, in ways that favored certain "new" groups.

New leadership groups in the society and in the economy rose in each of the major port centers. It was at this time that the nineteenth-century controlling families of Boston came in from the North Shore areas—the Appletons, the Cabots, and so forth—who were not leading mercantile figures before. Because of the war situation, they moved very quickly into positions of leadership in the economy, and subsequently in the society.

J.A.G.   Why? That is, did they simply replace Tory merchants who went to Nova Scotia or England?

B.B.   The situation can be explained in this way: The war years put a premium on certain kinds of abilities. The situation before had led to control by a group with contacts in England. During the Revolution, new criteria for economic dominance emerged. In the first place, a merchant had to be able to obtain agricultural produce directly from the countryside, in order to supply the urban population and the Army. In the second place, he had to be close politically to the new political leaders, or at least in contact with them. Thirdly, he had to be unencumbered by the preexisting situation. Certain of the old controlling merchants had deep involvements with England that tied them up. They couldn't move fast to capitalize on the new situation. People such as the Cabots on the North Shore, who had immediate access to the produce of the adjoining areas, could obtain supplies quickly. They were politically uninvolved with the previous regime, and had no economic encumbrances that could keep them from quickly capitalizing on the shifting situation. Therefore, and it happened in every port center, new people moved in this way and important social changes took place. Along the Connecticut River, for example, families that had not been the dominant merchants, like the Wadsworths and the Trumbulls, suddenly became important. The Wadsworths were in an excellent political situation and could control the produce of the Connecticut Valley. They got control of the Army commissariat, and once they got those orders for the Army, they established themselves. One could define a profile of the group in the most advantageous situation, and it was not, most often, the group that had control of the economy before. Therefore, social changes resulted.

But beyond this, there were also a series of social consequences from the broadening libertarian spirit of this period. Unlike so many revolutions that have taken place in the twentieth century, the Revolution was not undertaken out of discontent with the structure of society. Rather, it was an effort to preserve a free way of life, threatened, the colonists thought, by a new form of political dominance. If you ask what was the cause of the Revolution in general terms, I'd say it was that—the effort to preserve what seemed to be the freest way of life known. Actually the British system of government was felt to be the freest in the Western world, and the American was a more favorable aspect of it. The purpose spread, however, beyond that of preserving it. There emerged in this crisis a deep antiauthoritarian idealism that worked itself out in different ways and that had profound social consequences, some of which we are just realizing now in the middle of the twentieth century. These ways include an attack on the association of the state with religion, and an increase in public participation in politics. Under the ideological pressures of the revolutionary period, the British system of government appeared to Americans to be unjust, though there was no other place I can think of in the Western world in which it would have been so considered at that time. Similarly, the underrepresentation that characterized the western districts of certain colonies seemed, during the revolutionary situation, suddenly iniquitous. It wouldn't have seemed so in any other country in the Western world. In some of the estates along the Hudson tenancy came to be considered a grievance and this view led to the redistribution of loyalist properties.

J.A.G.   I'm not sure I understand. Are you suggesting that the loyalists' property was confiscated and, in fact, given to tenants?

B.B.   No. It's a question of what provisions were made for the resale of it, and further, what was the redistribution pattern that resulted.

J.A.G.   Are you suggesting that there was probably a decline in tenancy after 1775? Are you saying that the idea of being a tenant came into bad odor, and that was a social change, or that there was a significant decline in the number of people who were tenants because of the Revolution?

B.B.   We don't know all the details, but we do know that people on estates, where they were tenants, felt justified in opposing the conditions of their tenancy, and in certain areas—though I don't think this is the crucial point—they got independent control of the land they worked because of the loyalist exodus. More generally, in the situation of broadening liberalism that this crisis generated, men felt justified in moving in certain directions that led to social change.

One can spell this out, certainly, in church-state relations, and in other ways, as J. Franklin Jameson pointed to in his book, *The American Revolution Considered as a Social Movement*. Some of what has been written about social change I think exaggerated, but what I think is *not* exaggerated is that consequences did flow from the revolutionary principles of the time.

To sum up, the American Revolution was not a great social upheaval in traditional post-French Revolutionary terms. But I think it did build up pressures against traditional relationships throughout society that ultimately led to social changes.

J.A.G.   Had these changes not been partially accomplished before the Revolution?

B.B.   Yes, they had been. The traditional relation between the church and state, for example, had been drawn to such a fine point that it was hardly discernible in some of the colonies. Tradition was probably strongest in New England, and so remained until later, but I think the later change resulted from the impetus supplied in this period. One can certainly see the effect of that impetus in some of the theories that were worked out; on the one hand, by the secular enlightenment theorists such as Madison and Jefferson, and on the other hand, by certain evangelical preachers.

I suppose the question is, "What does all of this add up to?" I think it adds up to considerable social change.

J.A.G.   Would you apply what you have just been saying to the attitudes of the Americans toward Negroes, to the slavery problem?

B.B.   The inconsistency between the plans for liberty that were being made and the status of the large Negro population was seen during the Revolution. And there were some who attempted to alleviate this situation and get rid of this anomaly during the revolutionary period. The political condition that so many Americans held themselves to be threatened with by the new regulations in England was one of slavery. This mere duplication of the word in the two situations was important. Efforts were made in certain areas, in the North particularly, to do something about slavery, and some changes, secondary, minor ones, were made. But generally the discrepancy between the claim for liberty in the political sense for most of the population and the condition of the Negroes, in the South particularly, was not removed. Nonetheless, slavery was seen by many people, North and South, to be a tragic anomaly in the revolutionary movement, and I think that a line can be drawn from their discontent about the fact of slavery, and the later changes that were made. But it is correct to say that the Revolution itself did not involve a popular, nationwide effort to erase the institution.

J.A.G.   Was the revolutionaries' concern for the fate of the American Negro only a product of logic or analogy? Did they merely recognize that it was inconsistent to talk about their own fear of being made slaves without protesting also the treatment that the actual slaves in America were getting? Or was there a real humanitarian element in their feelings about slavery?

B.B.   I don't think the relationship between the slavery the Americans thought they were threatened with from England and the condition of the Negro was simply that of a verbal analogy and I don't think it's merely the spill-over of the verbal cognates that was involved. I think in both instances they were talking about the same thing, namely, a situation in which a person is deprived of his ability to act and is in the possession of another with respect to some actions that he wishes to take. They felt themselves threatened with possession by others with respect to certain things they wanted to control for themselves. Chattel slavery was only a deepened expression, the ultimate expression, of that. It's a question of how completely another will is imposed on one against one's own will. Some limited groups in the population, such as the Quakers, did respond to Negro slavery in humanitarian terms, but not very many.

J.A.G.   In the light of what you have been saying, what are your feelings about Carl Becker's famous aphorism in his *History of Political Parties in the Province of New York* that the American Revolution was not simply a question of home rule but also of who should rule at home? Does this relate to what you have said about social change?

B.B.   I think it's related in a way, but not in the sense that a class struggle was going on in the background of the separation movement which developed further under the Articles of Confederation. Social and political changes did lead to disputes between groups in control, and disputes among individuals and groups for control. Revolution erupted in the first place to preserve what was considered to be very favorable political and social conditions for this American part of the British population. It broadened after that into many areas and some can be construed in Becker's terms, but I don't think that they are primary ones for understanding the revolutionary impulse. In certain communities new groups disputed with the groups that had power. The 1780's is the point where this is best exemplified. In Virginia, political controversy erupted between Patrick Henry's group and Jefferson's and others. But the displacement was relatively slight. At one point, for example, the new revolutionary assembly was simply the old House of Burgesses retitled.

In the course of the subsequent decade there were contests over who should control politics under the new dispensation. In Massachusetts, where there was considerable displacement, a three-way battle broke out in the mid-1780's over who should rule at home, if you want to put it in those terms. And in other colonies also there were contests over control.

J.A.G. But implicit in Becker's idea of who shall rule at home, I think, is a struggle of submerged groups seeking to command authority that they couldn't get under British power. Did that happen?

B.B. I don't think the conflicts should be construed in that sense at all. In a highly unstable political situation in which leadership groups in any case are not clearly defined, contests for power had some social dimensions, but they are not describable within class terms.

J.A.G. To what extent were the colonies "democratic" before the Revolution? More specifically, what is your judgment of the thesis of Professor Robert E. Brown about middle-class democracy, the argument that nearly everyone could vote who wanted to vote?

B.B. I think Brown's is an anachronistic point of view. He does two things in his book on Massachusetts (the book on Virginia is more diffuse). In the first place, he tries quantitatively to establish who held the franchise in Massachusetts. I think he did accomplish something in that, despite some important technical errors in his method. He showed how broad, relative to other, more traditional, societies, the franchise was.

But his second effort was to say something of a broad interpretative nature about American society: that it was democratic at the time. It seems to be very confused as stated by Brown, and anachronistic as interpreted by some others. The word *democracy* applied to eighteenth-century communities is just an anachronism, if *democracy* means a kind of egalitarianism applied to both social and political life. Brown himself provided one of the most interesting leads to this fact in pointing out that the potential franchise was much broader than the franchise as actually used.

The most interesting question to come out of this interpretation is this: Accepting the fact, however qualified on technical points, that there was a relatively broad franchise, at what point, and for what reasons does this franchise become politically operative: And does pressure build up for still further broadening? In the middle of the eighteenth century it was not politically operative; nobody was pressing for a still further broadening of the franchise. It was not a live issue through the early revolutionary years either. Many fewer people were using the franchise than had access to it. Yet at a later point it became an active issue. Efforts were made further to broaden it, and to make use of what the franchise could mean for political purposes. At what point and for what reasons? I don't think we have clear answers to that. In Paul Goodman's book on the Republican party in Massachusetts in the early nineteenth century, the way in which political party controversies led people to capitalize on the potentiality of this political force is very nicely put. But in the middle of the eighteenth century, that issue was inert. It was a deferential society. It was a stratified society. And it was a society in which it was assumed that social leadership and political leadership would continue to be identified.

J.A.G.   Doesn't Brown contribute something (in addition to showing that most people could vote) to undermine the old point of view about Massachusetts politics before the Revolution?

B.B.   What he has written is a contribution to questioning what Beard and others writing in the early twentieth century described as an established aristocracy of Eastern merchants and planters opposed by Western debtor, agrarian, populist, groups. These historians described eighteenth-century politics as the struggle between those two elements. In fact, American politics in the middle of the eighteenth century was a highly contentious, unstable kind of politics, but it is not describable as a conflict of establishment groups against the striving, oppressed populace. I think to some degree Brown has contributed to disproving that older theory.

J.A.G.   Do you believe that the recent work of so-called "New Left" historians has added to our understanding of the revolutionary era?

B.B.   As I understand it, the New Left historians are attempting to show that there are revolutionary origins for the patterns of conflict they now see in mid-twentieth-century American life. They see the conflict of the 1760's and 1770's as a deeply radical revolutionary movement that was suppressed subsequently, in the course of the Revolution, by counter-revolutionary force. In this sense they go back to Beard and far beyond him. I do not think the Revolution can be described as a struggle in American life like that occurring in the middle of the twentieth century.

I don't think there was a major effort to create participatory democracy during the revolutionary years. I don't think slaveholders had to suppress a nascent liberation movement. But I do think there can be some benefits from what the New Left historians are attempting to do, if they work this out right. In the first place, new information will surely emerge from their work. It may run against what they hope to prove, but nevertheless, it can be useful. For example, study of the composition of some of the revolutionary crowds, following the pattern of investigations of mobs in England and France, should yield some useful social data. In the second place, their work is generating interest in a different kind of a problem from what they set out to discuss. They are attempting to show the involvement in the revolutionary movement of the oppressed and repressed part of the American population. It seems to me that the specific relationships they are looking for will be extremely hard to establish, but it is a subject, taken by itself without reference to the Revolution, that we know very little about. We have little social data about the condition of life of the poor. A very important contribution could be made there. Aubrey C. Land, of the University of Georgia, for years has been investigating the condition of the poor on the small plantations of Maryland. His data show that a large part of the population that we know very little about lived under very bad conditions. But Land also shows the limited degree to which people thought in political terms about the problems of their lives. The New Left historians can contribute to this kind of work, although they will not like some of what they discover. They're asking, in other words, a new kind of question. They construe it wrongly, but it is an interesting question.

J.A.G. Turning now to the Revolution itself. Can one estimate very accurately what contribution Tom Paine's famous pamphlet *Common Sense* made toward convincing people that a total break with Great Britain was necessary?

B.B. We don't have the advantage, if it is an advantage, of public-opinion polling to establish how people felt in the period from January to July 1776. But Paine's pamphlet was a shocker, a sensation. It did shake people's thinking. First, because it condemned the British constitution as a whole. American thinking had continued to rest on the idea that it was a proper arrangement, though it had been corrupted. They believed the constitution, per se, was a good thing. Paine said it was an evil thing, that the idea of the balanced strata of the constitution—the Crown, the aristocracy, and the democracy balanced—was a misconception. What had been good about it, he argued, was the degree to which the single vital element, the democracy, had survived the impositions of the two other elements. For ordinary British thought of the middle of the eighteenth century, this was a shocking notion, but I think the colonists were drifting in that direction because of their conviction of the corruption of British politics in America. Paine's vivid rhetorical exposition of his theme crystallized people's thought, and led them into the conviction that they should move toward a republic perhaps faster than they would otherwise have done. *Common Sense* was a condemnation of the institution of monarchy and consequently an imputation of bad motives on the part of the Crown. It was also a brilliant rhetorical production, a brilliant pamphlet by any measure, and I think that the mere vividness of the portrayal of these not-altogether-unheard-of ideas, contributed to the effect of the pamphlet.

J.A.G.   But Paine wasn't the first pamphleteer to attack monarchy. Didn't Jefferson say some fairly strong things about the institution in his *Summary View of the Rights of British America* in 1774? Can you say that the government established in America as a result of the Revolution really reflects the political and social ideas of Tom Paine?

B.B.   No, but I would generalize beyond that single pamphlet. In the first place, the pamphlet, as a constructive argument for what should be done, was not acted upon. In fact, many of the critical points in it were repudiated immediately by people like John Adams, who thought it was a terrible book by a terrible man. But I think it contributed to the conviction that the best form of government was a republic and that it was possible to move in that direction. John Adams repudiated *Common Sense,* but nevertheless he was one of the idealists of this period who looked forward to a new *epocha,* as he kept calling it, in which people could work out new ideas in government. I think it is also true that Paine's argument was carried forward in the constitutional writings of the revolutionary period.

Of course, Americans also clung to the basic principle of the British constitution, which Paine repudiated, the idea of a balance of forces within the constitution. They continued to believe in this, which they quite consciously understood to be the basic principle of the British constitution, despite Paine.

J.A.G.   Yet in American history, there have been other writings of similar impact that didn't produce profound results. I think, for instance, of Edward Bellamy's *Looking Backward* in the 1880's, which was an attack on laissez-faire capitalism. It was equally dramatic, forcefully presented, read by everybody in the society. It dealt with contemporary problems. And yet one cannot argue that it had much effect on events. Haven't we perhaps made too much of Paine as an influence?

B.B.   I think what differentiates *Common Sense* from Bellamy's *Looking Backward* was that it played into deep discontents with the working of the existing constitution, and it played into the feeling a great many people had that they could, realistically, go beyond that constitution to new forms. I don't think there was a similar situation in Bellamy's case.

J.A.G.   It has been customary to say (I believe John Adams was the original source) that during the Revolution about a third of the people were patriots, about a third loyalists, and the rest more or less indifferent. Do you agree?

B.B.   I don't, and I don't think it's a very profitable question to pursue, put in those terms. We have no data that would allow an answer in those strict terms. The interesting and answerable question is not "How many people were for one side or the other side?" but "What was the pattern within these groups?" "What part of what groups were drawn in what direction?" Within the clergy, for example, the Anglicans in the North were loyalist to a large extent, but the Anglican clergy in the South was mostly patriot.

J.A.G.   But, if we can investigate particular groups in a systematic way, can we not then bring the data together and have some rough answer to the over-all question?

B.B.   I don't think we can get an answer in quantitative terms. One can ask, and this has been a traditional question for two generations of historians, "What did the merchants do?" The merchants divided. The interesting question is not what the merchant group did as a whole. That was what Arthur M. Schlesinger tried to answer in *The Colonial Merchant and the American Revolution*, published half a century ago, and I think his response was very important in its time. He saw them split up to a certain point, but then generally siding with the anti-revolutionary position to safeguard their class interests. I think the important thing is that the group divided everywhere. It is erroneous to describe the merchants as a coherent class that saw its interest and clung to it in a uniform way. The significant question is what the division within the merchant group was and why there was a division. In other words, it is the inner patterns that will be most useful, rather than the majority head counts in the groups.

J.A.G.   Well, I'm not entirely satisfied with your answer. If you said, "We cannot find the answer to this question, and therefore we'd just be wasting time speculating on it," I would understand. But it certainly seems to me that it has profound meaning for any understanding of the Revolution to know how widely it was supported. Was it a small clique that put the Revolution over?

B.B.   There was a widespread sympathy, not so much for fighting a tough war, but for the principles that were being stated by the revolutionary leadership. One *can* ask, "What evidence do we have that people were sympathetic to these ideas?" In New England, for example, there are rough ways of measuring public opinion. The unselfconscious portrayals of their views that people put into newspapers and private correspondence, and sermons that we know found a sympathetic response in the congregations, help us to gauge opinion.

J.A.G.   Admitting that one can't say exactly, how much weight should be given to John Adams' estimate?

B.B.   Well, Adams said all sorts of things. This was one of his statements made many years later. On the importance of quantitative data about public opinion, I agree with you to this extent: You have to ask the question, "Were ideas of the leadership generally accepted by the population, or were they impositions by a small conspiratorial group?"

J.A.G.   Suppose the Revolution had been crushed. What would have happened to the revolutionary leaders? Would they have been hanged?

B.B.   There was a discussion of this subject in England before 1776. Could the government extend the Act of Henry VIII on treason to America and get a dozen or so ringleaders over to England, give them exemplary trials, and crush the movement in this way? What would have happened if General Gage had wiped out the New England Army in the battle of Bunker Hill and thereafter captured the American leaders? No one can say with certainty. Beyond that, if the Revolution had failed, would we still be British? And would the seat of the British Empire have eventually been moved to America, as was envisioned by a number of people after the conquest of Canada in the Seven Years' War?

J.A.G.   What are the half-dozen books that you would recommend to persons interested in the subject we have been discussing? In each case, would you indicate what the particular contribution of the volume is?

B.B.   For a detailed narrative of the political events leading to the Revolution, see Lawrence H. Gipson, *The British Empire Before the Revolution*, vols. IX–XII (1956–1965), which is sympathetic to the British point of view; for a briefer treatment by the same author, see his *Coming of the Revolution* (1954). Merrill Jensen has covered the same ground in his recent *The Founding of a Nation* (1968), and has dealt with the events of the postwar period in *The New Nation* (1950). On the inner history of British politics and the Revolutionary crisis, see Bernard Donoughue, *British Politics and the American Revolution: The Path to War, 1773–75* (1964), and Michael G. Kammen, *A Rope of Sand: The Colonial Agents, British Politics, and the American Revolution* (1968). Two of the critical events in the colonies are treated in Edmund and H. M. Morgan, *The Stamp Act Crisis* (1953) and Benjamin W. Labaree, *The Boston Tea Party* (1964).

On the ideological background of the Revolution and the motivations of those who made the Revolution, see Bernard Bailyn, *The Ideological Origins of the American Revolution* (1967); for the role of these ideas and attitudes in the post-Independence period, see Gordon S. Wood, *The Creation of the American Republic, 1776–1787* (1969). On the military events of the war, see Willard Wallace, *Appeal to Arms* (1951) and Eric Robson, *The American Revolution* (1955). On the commercial and some of the social developments, see Robert East, *Business Enterprise in the American Revolutionary Era* (1938). The standard work on diplomacy is Samuel F. Bemis, *The Diplomacy of the American Revolution* (1935; 2d ed., 1957), which should be supplemented with Richard Morris' *The Peacemakers* (1965).

Henry Steele Commager

American Nationalism

H ENRY STEELE COMMAGER, Professor of History at Amherst, is both an important scholar and a well-known public lecturer. Like the great eighteenth-century figures he so admires, he is a man of wide-ranging interests and a prolific writer. His biography of the abolitionist Theodore Parker (1936) has become a classic, and his *American Mind* (1951) is a major analysis of intellectual trends in the late nineteenth and early twentieth centuries. He has also written on constitutional history, civil liberties, the Civil War, historiography, and a dozen other subjects. His *Documents of American History* (known to generations of students as "Commager's Documents") has passed through seven editions, and his *Growth of the American Republic*, written with Samuel Eliot Morison, has long been a leading textbook. The subject of this discussion, the development of American nationalism and the shaping of the American character, has been of continuing concern to him throughout his career.

John A. Garraty Professor Commager, in what way is American nationalism different from other types of nationalism?

Henry Steele Commager American nationalism has some claim to being unique, for it can be said of all other nations that they grew out of a long historical past. But the American was quite literally *made*. Some scholars trace the germs of nationalism back into the ancient world—to the city-states of Greece, for example, or to Rome. Others date it from the late medieval period. More commonly, historians tend to date modern nationalism from the French Revolution. But the American people, in Lincoln's words, were the first people to "bring forth a new nation."

In fact, the United States was the first modern national state; it was the first nation *to be made*. We've become accustomed to that since World War II; something over sixty nations have come into existence, some of them quite artificial. The United States was not a wholly artificial creation, but it was very literally a creation. Americans were the first people to form themselves into a national organization, and quite deliberately to construct the machinery, the institutions, even the spirit and the philosophy of nationalism.

The eighteenth century was not on the whole a century of self-conscious nationalism, but rather of cosmopolitanism. Self-conscious nationalism came to Europe chiefly with the French Revolution. (In France, revolution produced it; elsewhere it resulted from national resistance to revolution.) But even in the French Revolution there was a great deal of what might be called antinationalism. Goethe, by preference, spoke French and greeted the returning defeated remnants of the Prussian army after the battle of Leipzig with French decorations on his bosom. Frederick the Great spoke French, and no king of Denmark knew Danish until the nineteenth century. Scholars, scientists, men of learning, philosophers, and, of course, aristocrats, moved easily from country to country all through the eighteenth century even in time of war. In the midst of the Napoleonic Wars, it was possible for the English chemist Sir Humphry Davy to go to France and receive the Gold Medal of the French Academy; it was as if Robert Oppenheimer, the nuclear physicist, had gone to Berlin in 1944 to get a medal from the German Academy.

Nationalism as a self-conscious thing, deliberately created, deliberately fostered, was very largely an American phenomenon, and because it happened in modern times and not in the dim past of Charlemagne's Gaul or Alfred's England, we know pretty much how it happened. The Revolutionary was an extraordinarily articulate generation, and, as if in anticipation of our current interest, it provided us with a body of data on how to go about creating nationalism. The new nation makers ought to study the American phenomenon: they would learn how to make do with what you have and how to provide for ingredients that are not there.

J.A.G.   When did the English colonists in America begin to think of themselves not as a political nation but as a cultural group—as Americans?

H.S.C.   This is a difficult question. Historians have exhausted themselves trying to determine the antecedents of American nationalism. In all likelihood, it was not before the 1770's that Americans thought of themselves as a distinct people. There are some stray suggestions in the 1750's and 60's, the kind of thing Homer had in mind when he wrote of the dream of the shadow of smoke. Colonists then began to use the word "American," and some of the early almanacs suggested the term. But one can always find antecedents for anything. Not until the 1770's, and not really until the Revolution and the post-Revolutionary age, did Americans cease to think of themselves as British (or as Virginians and Yankees and Pennsylvanians) and see themselves in continental terms. It did not happen all at once. Virginians spoke of Virginia as "my country" as late as the 1840's, and so did South Carolinians. Loyalty to locality persisted down to the Civil War, and loyalty to region has persisted in to our own time. That loyalty, however, came to be more and more attenuated, except in the South. It became a literary or psychological phenomenon rather than a real emotion.

A convenient place to start the study of American nationalism is 1774. Beginning with the meeting of the Continental Congress and the various declarations and assertions that we were United Colonies, a New World orientation occurred, not right away to a national sentiment, but very often merely to local and regional sentiments. The transformation of those into nationalism has been a very gradual process. Indeed, it would be an exaggeration to say that it is wholly completed even now. In the South, an emotional attachment to the Confederacy lingers on, not as a serious commitment, but as a term of defiance. It's impossible to date the creation of a sentiment of nationalism precisely, but a practical working date is the Declaration of Independence.

J.A.G.   If we study colonial history, we see New World conditions making extraordinary changes in people's thinking and their ways of living. Why did it take such a long time for the concept of the uniqueness of America to be absorbed by the people themselves?

H.S.C.   It didn't take a long time historically. It took a good deal longer for the Spanish colonials to think of themselves as distinct from Spain. It took rather longer for the French inhabitants of Quebec to think of themselves as unique.

On the whole, the English colonists in America arrived at national characteristics rather quicker than most colonials do. The process of Americanization was rapid. It does not, however, follow that the processes of amalgamation and unification were equally rapid. It was much easier to think of yourself as a Connecticut or Massachusetts man, as distinct from being an Englishman, than to think of yourself as an American as distinct from being either an Englishman or a man of Massachusetts. Only when the Revolution brought people of all the colonies together in a common cause, forced them to cooperate politically, to fight together, to think together, was there a real advance in what might be called an American sentiment as distinct from merely a non-English or anti-English sentiment.

J.A.G. Do you think that the structure of government imposed upon the colonies by the English delayed the development of nationalism?

H.S.C. I think the English thought of the colonies as a unit, and did not in any way try to fragment the American colonies. The fragmentation was largely a geographical and economic phenomenon. English colonial administration was, after all, centralized in the Privy Council and in Parliament, and applied universally to all the American colonies. But the Revolutionary reaction to England was a general reaction rather than a specific one. When committees of correspondence were set up in Virginia they were promptly matched by committees of correspondence in Massachusetts. Americans mostly spoke the same language, and they possessed a fairly unified body of ideas and values. Jefferson writes like Hamilton; Adams thinks like John Jay and James Wilson. The common vocabulary of the Revolutionary leaders is one of the most fascinating phenomena of the eighteenth century. It's quite possible for the writing of Jefferson to be taken for Hamilton's. "The sacred rights of mankind are not to be rummaged for among old parchments or musty records. They are written, as with a sunbeam, in the whole *volume* of human nature, by the hand of the Divinity itself, and can never be erased or obscured by mortal power." That's pure Jeffersonianism. But it was Hamilton who wrote it.

Or consider the controversy that has existed for so long over the authorship of certain of the *Federalist Papers*. Imagine a controversy over the authorship of a common body of papers written by Adlai Stevenson, Dwight Eisenhower, and Richard Nixon. It is inconceivable that anyone would wonder who wrote which.

But to get back to the ingredients of nationalism in America, there is pretty general agreement that nationalism requires, first, a common territory; second, a common religion; third, a common language; fourth, a common government; fifth, a common body of history and of traditions. Of these, the new United States had only two or three, and did not have those in any satisfactory fashion. It had, after a fashion, a common territory, but the territory seemed too big, and far too disparate. Indeed, Europeans took for granted that the United States could not be a single nation. They had been brought up on Montesquieu's notion, that a despotism could be large, a monarchy could be a moderate size, but a republic had to be small. Almost everyone assumed that the new nation would break up into a number of parts. Even in America there was a good deal of talk about a New England, a Middle States, and a Southern confederation. Gouverneur Morris, for example, thought it fantastic to suppose that one hundred years later this vast territory would be one nation. Elbridge Gerry said the same thing, as did many others. Never before had there been so large a republic.

The general notion was that the United States couldn't control so much territory. The first question any student of American nationalism must ask himself is why the United States didn't go the way of Latin America. On the surface, Spanish America had more ingredients for unification than the United States. There was a single language there, not a half-dozen languages as in America; everyone was a Catholic; the Spanish colonial administration far more effectively controlled the mechanics of government and trade. And yet Latin American broke into some twenty-two different countries, and the United States remained one. This is one of the spectacular phenomena of history, not only of previous history, but of today. On the whole, nationalism is fragmenting. Nationalism in Europe has gone from the general to the particular. It has broken up previous nations in the Old World. Nationalism is fragmenting Africa and Asia; it has fragmented Latin America. Only in the United States has it led from the particular to the general. This gives a unique and extraordinary interest to the American experiment.

It must be said that we had a common language, although there were large numbers of Germans and smaller groups of Celts and others who did not speak English. Why English remained the common, indeed the universal tongue is, when we contemplate the fact that over fifty percent of the American people today are of non-British stock, one of the great mysteries of history.

However, there was no common bond of religion. It was assumed, and is still assumed in most countries, that one of the essential ingredients in nationalism is a common religion. Nearly every state in Europe to this day still has a national church. Arab nationalism is religious, Jewish nationalism is religious, much of the nationalism of Asia is still predominantly religious. But religion never played a part in American nationalism. We were the first country to get along without an established church. How Americans managed to hold together without an established church is another wonder of history. Almost all Europeans who considered the phenomenon assumed that either a national church would be created or depravity would set in and the nation would go to pieces morally.

The greatest of American nationalistic achievements was the creation, almost overnight, of a history. The country began without a common past, without tradition, almost without history. Scholars who have considered the nature of nationalism have all concluded that this is the most important of all its ingredients. They have defined nations in terms of common pasts—with common triumphs, common defeats, common glory, common tragedy. This is what eventually brought Italy together as one nation and what eventually animated the nationalism of the Germans. It was this kind of nationalism to which Hitler appealed in so tragic a fashion, and this is what animated the nationalism of the Bohemians, the Irish, the Norwegians, and other people. To this day every French child grows up near a Place de Napoléon or a Place de la Concorde or something of that kind. He sees everywhere the evidence of ancient times. Joan of Arc is as close to him, perhaps, as De Gaulle. And think how a London child is exposed, almost from birth, to the memories of a thousand years past—of literature, royalty, empire, battles.

But in America all this was lacking. What the Americans did was to make do with what they had. With extraordinary, spectacular speed and success they conjured up the Pilgrim Fathers and John Smith and the Indian Wars, and brought them, as it were, into the consciousness of the people. This was partly achieved by the propagandists and historians, the Noah Websters and Parson Weemses—people of that kind. Heroes of the Revolution were surrounded by an aura comparable to that of such antique giants as King Alfred, Joan of Arc, even of Romulus and Remus. One can see the process in the deification of Washington. Washington was an American god even as a young man. John Adams (who was jealous of everybody) said as early as 1775 that Washington was a man of such greatness that he made every king in Europe look like a valet. Parson Weems, who was an expert on the matter because he was a parson, described Washington's entry into heaven with all of the Americans there rushing up to greet him and to deify him. It was accepted by that generation that Washington was unique—as indeed he was, you know. Even before they were dead, the Founding Fathers entered Valhalla. There's a fascinating letter from Thomas Jefferson to Madison, written in Paris in 1787, commenting on the plans of the Federal Convention to write a new Constitution. Much is to be said for a new constitution, he remarked, but on the whole wouldn't it be "better to amend that venerable old fabric, the Articles of Confederation" which had existed for six years! Things become venerable in America that fast.

Americans did another thing that's absolutely fascinating. They substituted the future for the past. If we didn't have a past to look back on, we had a future to look forward to, and that in turn led to the deliberate repudiation of the past—the past was bad, the past was corrupt, the past had nothing to teach us—and also to the realization that we had for the first time in history an opportunity to make a different society. Jefferson was absolutely right when he said America had an opportunity unique in the whole of recorded history to show what man could do if he started fresh, with everything in his favor. There's a marvelous passage in James Fenimore Cooper's *Notions of an American*. I can't quote it exactly, but Cadwalader, speaking to a traveling German baron, points to a map of America and says: "Look at this vast territory. You in the Old World have only the past to look back on. As you traverse the plains of Hellas you are reminded at every step of melancholy tragedies—the glories are two thousand years away. But we of America know that everything that man has imagined can come to pass. This is the significance of the West."

J.A.G.   Are you not neglecting one aspect of American nationalism? I am thinking of Franklin's famous aphorism: "We must all hang together or we will hang separately." To what extent was nationalism forced upon Americans by the need for common defense during the Revolution?

H.S.C.   That is precisely what created a national state. They had to do it. Yet it wasn't always clear to everyone. Virginia fought a private war; the so-called "conquest of the Northwest" by George Rogers Clark was a Virginia enterprise, not a United States conquest. And there was much confusion and difficulty involving state and national diplomatic and financial negotiations abroad. But what is fascinating is that Americans developed the resourcefulness and wisdom to solve the problem of organizing a nation in the midst of war and crisis, one of the greatest achievements of modern political history. The Americans of the Revolutionary generation proved themselves the most creative statesmen in modern history, perhaps in all history. They established institutions that have had a more lasting influence than any established anywhere else.

We've been living on that capital ever since. All our political and constitutional institutions were created in the eighteenth century. Of these, perhaps most important was federalism, a new form of nationalism and the only form which could possibly have worked. Had the Americans set up a consolidated national government, it would have come apart in their hands. The people didn't revolt against George III and Parliament in order to duplicate the British system. The wonder is that they got as centralized and consolidated a government as they did, considering the long history of local attachments and local self-government in America.

Alexander Hamilton was almost the only important American who wanted a consolidated government, which would have been necessary if the nation were going to be ruled by an effective, enlightened despot. (Hamilton would have been a very good despot, by the way. He would have been the best enlightened despot of his time.) But other Americans knew instinctively that they must allow a very wide latitude to local attachments and local administration. And they worked out a most remarkable solution, federalism. Federalism was very ancient, but there had never before been a successful federal system. The federations of ancient Greece were not true federations; there was no federation in the Roman Empire. The confederations, such as they were, of the city-states of medieval Italy were not modern federalisms, nor was the Hanseatic League, nor the Swiss Confederation.

The only possible antecedent to American federalism was the British Empire. It operated very much as a federal empire, but in theory it was consolidated government. The Declaratory Act of 1766, in which the Parliament solemnly announced that it had the right to bind the colonies in all cases whatsoever, was simply nonsense. It wasn't true, of course, but it was the British theory and they stuck by it. The difference between the doctrinaire British mind and the American pragmatic mind of that time comes out marvelously in the debate between Governor Thomas Hutchinson and John and Samuel Adams. Hutchinson, thinking he'd read a lesson to these foolish Americans, said: "It is impossible that there should be more than one government in one and the same state." To which the Adamses made a marvelous reply: "We submit to your Excellency that there are in fact fourteen—one in Westminster and thirteen in America, and if they interfere not with one another, what prevents them from going their own way and working happily together?"

If the British had had enough sense to realize they had a federal system which was working very well, the government in Westminster managing general matters like war and commerce, the colonies managing local affairs, the Empire might well have stuck together.

J.A.G. Are you saying that the British created federalism, then rejected it, whereupon the Americans reconstructed it?

H.S.C. No. British federalism lacked the quintessential element. The essential element of federalism is a separation of powers between local and general governments, which the British had pretty well effected. The quintessential element the Americans worked out: the sanctions behind federalism. If you trace through the Federal Convention the probings and discussions and soul-searchings of the delegates as they tried to solve this insoluble problem, you will illuminate a great deal of history, including contemporary history and the problem of sanctions in the United Nations. What happens when the constituent parts of a federal system don't abide by the agreement? What had always been done from the beginning of time was to march an army into the offending region, seize a weapon and kill somebody. This was the original plan of the Federal Convention; Edmund Randolph's plan gave the national government the power to coerce the states. But gradually it became clear that to resort to force was to decree perpetual civil war. So the Founders, as one of them put it, "substituted the benign magistracy of the law for the awful sanctions of the sword."

They worked out sanctions which were enormously ingenious. The first was dual citizenship. Every American was a citizen of the state and of the nation. Secondly, the federal government was made to operate through law on each individual citizen, not through force on the states. If the citizens in Pennsylvania do not obey a federal law, you don't declare war on Pennsylvania, you arrest the people who are breaking the law and try them. Lincoln, with enormous good sense, insisted that the Civil War wasn't a war: large numbers of *individuals* were out of their proper relation with the Union, and they were individually liable; the Army was a vast *posse comitatus* sent in to put down treason and rebellion. This approach enabled Lincoln to do what Congress later failed to do, because Congress was blind to the legal distinction. Lincoln could end the war by an act of amnesty, which took care of individuals. The question didn't come up, "How do you get the states back into the Union?" They *were* in.

Now this is the system Americans discovered: dual citizenship, and a government that could operate directly on the citizens *through the courts*. For the first time in history, a system was created which depended for its effective operation on the integrity, wisdom, and effectiveness of the courts. So that more than any other government in history, ours is a government of law. That is why so much of American nationalism is told in terms of judicial history, of Supreme Court decisions. Almost every issue of state versus nation has been fought out in the courts. Of course, if the courts fail—as they failed, for example, in the Dred Scott case—all hell breaks loose. And if the government is so weak that it cannot, or so pusillanimous that it will not, enforce a court decision, as with *Brown* v. *Topeka*, the School Desegregation case, then the system breaks down.

Americans didn't borrow this idea from the British. They did borrow the division of authority, and, on the whole, carried on what the British had developed over a century and a half in the division between local and centralized political activities and powers in America, but this system of sanctions was original.

J.A.G. How did it happen that the judiciary played this role only in the United States, and why did the Founding Fathers come to this particular solution to the problem of federalism?

H.S.C. It is not clear that the Founding Fathers realized the role that the judiciary would play. Judicial review wasn't spelled out in the Constitution, though the best students have concluded that the majority of the members of the Convention assumed that the judiciary would play this role. There were a number of antecedents. There was the famous case of *Bayard* v. *Singleton* in North Carolina, where Justice Iredell laid down the principles of judicial review, and the case of *Trevett* v. *Wheaton*, and others. But it is absolutely certain that the Founding Fathers had no notion of the potentialities of this weapon. We've ascribed enormous wisdom and vision to the Founding Fathers, but they couldn't anticipate everything. For example, one of the things we're very much concerned with is the danger that presidential elections will not be decided by the Electoral College and will be thrown into the House of Representatives. The Founding Fathers assumed that elections would usually go to the House of Representatives. Madison said they would go there nine times out of ten, George Mason estimated 49 times out of 50.

The Founding Fathers couldn't have realized the large role the judiciary would play, but they had enough instinct or hunch, if you will, to create a government where it was possible for it to develop. They built better than they knew, or perhaps they knew what they were doing but didn't realize how significant their action was.

As to why this system hasn't developed elsewhere, this is one of the most tantalizing questions, I think, in comparative history. A number of countries have copied some features of judicial review (Canada, Germany, Brazil), but nowhere does it operate as in America. The Germans, for example, in their new Constitution, set up a special court for judicial review of federal problems. Unless I'm mistaken, only one case has come before it since this new constitution was established. The simplest explanation, a deceptively simple one, is that we set up a federal system, and in a federal system, unlike in a national system, there has to be a neutral arbiter. Almost all cases of judicial review concern challenges to state legislation in the federal courts, not federal legislation. Justice Oliver Wendell Holmes once remarked that he did not believe the United States would come to an end if the Supreme Court lost its power to review acts of Congress, but that he did not see how the nation could last twenty-four hours if the Court were deprived of its power to review the laws and acts of states. Without a common interpretation of the laws and the administrative acts of states, the Union would go to pieces.

The function of the Supreme Court has been to harmonize the federal system. That is still its great and absolutely essential function. But we have to go farther and ask: "Why did the Americans accept it?" And this leads to a still larger question: "Why has the judiciary played so large a role in American history?" It has not played a comparable role in the history of other countries. Those familiar with Montesquieu constantly observe that he distinguished separation of powers in Britain. Well, he did after a fashion, but he paid no attention to the judiciary. Montesquieu separated the powers of the executive and the legislative branches, and argued that the judiciary was really of no great importance. Even John Adams, who wrote what is to this day one of the most elaborate defenses of the Constitution, in celebrating the principle of balance in America, amazingly left out the judiciary. We sometimes forget that John Adams was Chief Justice of Massachusetts; he never served, but he was appointed to that position. And he was a distinguished lawyer. Yet it didn't occur to him that the judiciary would play any role in maintaining the balance of power in the states or in the United States.

So we have to ask how it happened then that the American people came to accept this extraordinary role of the judiciary, as they swiftly did. Tocqueville noted in his great *Democracy in America* that the judiciary, even by 1835, had become the aristocracy of America, and that sooner or later almost all great issues were submitted to the courts. The answer is that the American judiciary was truly independent. The judiciary was set apart; it was given tenure for life. No Supreme Court judge has been successfully impeached. By great good fortune, the judiciary has attracted from the beginning men of the highest caliber. Notwithstanding the animadversions of our Wallaces and Russells and Thurmonds, and others of this ilk, the Supreme Court is to this day the most admired, the most esteemed, and the most trusted institution in American life. If you ask whether people trust the presidency, often the answer is No. If you ask whether they trust the Congress, a deafening negative comes up. But if you ask whether they trust the Court, almost everybody says they do.

J.A.G.   There are two other aspects of the federal system that I would like to ask you about. One is the presidency. Was not this office, as defined in the Constitution, as unique as the federal structure itself?

H.S.C.   Quite, but you beg the question. There were antecedents—above all, the state governorships—and in all likelihood, the presidency was modeled closely on the governorships of Connecticut and New York. But nowhere else in the Western world was there an *elected* head of state. All other heads of state held their positions by hereditary right or had jostled themselves into office through military power or something of that kind. The fact is that the Founding Fathers wandered in a wilderness when they came to set up the presidency. It is interesting to look statistically at the debates in the Federal Convention; more time was devoted to the executive than to any other aspect of the Constitution. Members changed their minds frequently. They didn't quite know what they were doing. About the presidency there was a kind of schizophrenia in the Convention. On the one hand, there was deep distrust of the executive, an instinct almost everywhere—perfectly natural after their experience with George III and certain royal governors—to create a weak executive and a strong legislature. But by what now seems another example of providential intervention in the affairs of America, George Washington was President of the Constitutional Convention, and the delegates all knew that he would be the first President. The Presidency was in a way modeled on Washington. You couldn't be too critical about presidential power when you were looking at Mr. Washington.

J.A.G. But while the Founders deified Washington in his own lifetime, I don't think they thought he was immortal. Your argument here seems inconsistent. The general suspicion of executive power was modified by the fact that Washington was the obvious first choice, but what of the future?

H.S.C. It's not inconsistent in the light of human nature. As you and I both know from attending faculty meetings, when everyone admires the president of the university we may look ahead to a time when he will be succeeded by somebody else, but it's very difficult to be too critical of the presidential office. But it is quite true that the Founding Fathers looked to the future, and Article II on the presidency is filled with ambiguity. This executive article is the vaguest of all the articles. "The Executive Power shall be vested in a President." Now, heavens alive!, what does that mean?

Well, *I* know what it means. The executive powers are those powers successfully exercised by Presidents! Washington used the executive power very broadly and very firmly and got away with a great deal, and thus precedents were established. Presidents *make* the executive power. A weak President like Buchanan is responsible for a decline in executive power, a strong one like Lincoln advances executive power.

Americans have become increasingly accustomed to a strong executive, in part because they don't really trust Congress very much, and in part because a country as large as the United States has to have a common symbol. Most people don't know who their congressman is. (They may know the names of their senators, though there's no reason why they should in many states.) But everyone knows who the President is. The President is a bit of everything. He's a symbol of the nation, the chief executive, the commander-in-chief, the conductor of foreign relations, the head of his party—he's a dozen different things. So we have become accustomed to, though not always resigned to, the broad interpretation of executive power.

J.A.G.   My other question about the Constitution is: Why were the Founders so suspicious of government if the people are sovereign?

H.S.C.   That is not difficult to answer. The best example of it is Tom Paine's famous observation that government, like dress, is a badge of lost innocence. Almost everyone was afraid of government because they were afraid of human nature. The widely accepted precept of eighteenth-century philosophy was that all men were corrupt. In America, the doctrine of the depravity of man was strengthened by Puritan theology. There was a pessimism in the Enlightenment, along with an ardent strain of optimism, and this pessimism lingered on for a long time. Cecelia Kenyon has described it in a fascinating study of the Anti-Federalists, which she called *Men of Little Faith*. Those who opposed the Constitution most, opposed it on the ground that it put too much power in the hands of everybody, including themselves. The Patrick Henrys and others who declaimed against it conjured up the dreadful circumstances that would arise when Congress had control of a ten-mile square District of Columbia, and had established a tyranny over the inhabitants like that of Nero and Caligula in ancient Rome. Such men believed that the highest statesmanship was to contrive as many limitations on power as the ingenuity and wit of man could contrive. Even John Adams, no Anti-Federalist he, boasted that there were thirteen different checks and balances in the Constitution of Massachusetts. That's what his three-volume *Defense of the Constitutions* was about. He ransacked history to prove that all men would abuse their power.

On the other hand, Jefferson knew just as much history as John Adams. He, too, knew that men had abused power. But he said, "We're different. The past doesn't count. It's the future that counts." Adams didn't think we were different. He said all men are the same—corrupt, jealous, envious; filled with passion, lust, greed, and self-interest.

J.A.G.   Given this underlying suspicion of human nature and fear of tyrannical authority, why has there been a steady increase in the powers of government?

H.S.C.   There was less ground to distrust human nature in the 1780's when the leaders of the country were men like Washington and Jefferson and Adams, than there is in our day, when perhaps public men are not so commonly virtuous. But, as you say, the power of government has grown. The explanation is elementary. Circumstances of modern life in a technological society require governmental action, the growth of a welfare state. Nothing has worked more effectively for a strong government than wars, and we've engaged in a great number of them. War always centralizes government and enhances its authority.

The American mind is still schizophrenic about this matter, however. The same elements in America that denounce big government day and night—chiefly the Southern states-rights elements—are also those that want a bigger and stronger military system. What they're supporting, of course, is an expanding central government. We should not be surprised that the Founding Fathers did not foresee everything, when we see that the current Fathers hardly foresee anything.

J.A.G. To what extent was American culture in the pre-Civil-War era influenced by nationalism?

H.S.C. Inspired rather than influenced. The inspiration was there because the yearning was there. From the very beginning Americans said, "We are an independent nation. We should therefore have an independent culture." And they racked their brains to find an American language. It is probably a canard that it was once proposed that Hebrew should be the national language, but it is illuminating that it should be a canard. "We are independent; we must have our own law," Americans said. They couldn't have their own law; their law was the English common law, and its modifications had little to do with nationalism and everything to do with circumstances.

There was a desire to have national painting, national music, national art, national drama. But alas, the Americans didn't have the ability to give substance to these desires; American culture remained derivative through most of the nineteenth century. Hemingway was quite right, in a sense, when he said that American literature started with *Huckleberry Finn*. Maybe it started with Walt Whitman, but that is a minor matter. The great American painters of the early period worked in the classical tradition. Benjamin West was trained in Italy. When someone took him to see the Apollo Belvedere, he looked at it and said, "My God, how like a Mohawk Indian." John Singleton Copley ended up as an English painter (and the father of a Chief Justice of England). It cannot be said that the American painters were any different really from Reynolds or Gainsborough or Romney.

Much the same can be said of our early architecture. Jefferson borrowed his conception of Monticello from Palladio, via a whole series of architectural books. The New England builders all worked out of English books. Bulfinch was deeply steeped in English tradition. Tastes shifted from Palladio to Greek revival, from Greek revival to Gothic, and so on. We didn't begin to get an architecture of our own until we developed the skyscraper, which was a calamity.

It's very difficult for a country to manufacture a new culture. Science is cosmopolitan; philosophy is cosmopolitan. The yearning for a national culture was a phenomenon of romanticism, and romanticism, which has misled us in so many things, misled us in this as well. For, of course, it wasn't only the Americans who wanted a national culture; the Germans, the Norwegians, the Italians were all determined to have one.

Our cultural story is almost entirely a story of borrowing, and to some degree of transforming. In the 1840's and 1850's there were fifty American sculptors and painters in Florence and Rome. Later they shifted to France, some went to Düsseldorf, which, like the skyscraper, was a great calamity, ending up with Washington crossing the Rhine, in Emmanuel Leutze's dreadful painting. On the whole, Americans were enormously successful at borrowing, but not very successful at transforming. They did best when they merely used the materials they had to put together. It's no wonder that the architectural historian Lewis Mumford emphasizes the building of the Brooklyn Bridge and the Eads Bridge over the Mississippi. It's no wonder that Emerson was enthusiastic about the clipper ship. Where Americans had to meet practical problems of how to use science and technology to deal with issues that couldn't be avoided, they fell back on their own resources and produced things that were often of a distinctive character.

In things like education, or like libraries, where Americans had to meet problems that did not exist in the Old World, they called on their ingenuity and they usually did very well. They invented the college, for example. There are no colleges anywhere else in the world; there are universities, not colleges, and the college has played a very interesting role in American history. Where Americans have had to meet practical problems rather than aesthetic problems, they have been able to be inventive and original.

J.A.G.   May we turn now to the subject of American sectionalism? To what extent was the Confederate States of America an expression of sectionalism and to what extent was it an expression of Southern nationalism?

H.S.C.   It's not always easy to distinguish between those two things. A good deal of what might be regarded as sectionalism in, for example, Russia, might be called nationalism in the Ukraine or Lithuania or Latvia. I suppose one might use the word "sectionalism" to describe the old Austro-Hungarian Empire which broke up into four or five separate states. I'm inclined to think that, on the whole, the South had more of the ingredients of nationalism in 1860 than the United States had in 1776. If we go back to the various ingredients of nationalism (common territory, common race, language, and religion, common economic interests, a sense of a common past—things of that kind), the South came closer to being a unit than the original United States did.

The South too had ingredients far more unifying than those of the North. Its white population in 1860 was about 98 percent Anglo-Saxon. It was almost entirely Protestant. The Anglican church was not established, but it might as well have been; most "gentlemen" were Anglicans, certainly in the Deep South, and the Anglican establishment was also part of the political establishment and the cultural establishment and the plantation establishment. The ruling classes throughout the South knew one another and understood one another, and intermarried with one another as in England and France; thus the South had far closer political unity than the North did. It had far more economic unity in the plantation system, and it had the most unifying factor of all, its commitment to Negro slavery. Though there were only some 354,000 slaveholders, almost the whole of the South was held together by a common commitment to white supremacy.

The South had other features of nationalism more common to the Old World than to the New. Numerous institutions, professional, social, and otherwise, held the ruling classes together. The South, for example, was military-minded. Members of the upper classes went into the Army in the South, but not in the North. Even many of the leading "Northern" generals during the Civil War were Southerners. Winfield Scott was born in Virginia, so was George Thomas, and Admiral Farragut was born in Tennessee.

The South was bound together by what we might call its professional attitudes. The thing to be was a planter, or a lawyer, or a clergyman. There was an interlocking directorate of the ruling classes from one end of the South to the other. It is no wonder, therefore, that the South found it relatively easy to organize as a nation. What is astonishing, what proved to be fatal, was that the South organized a nation on the irretrievably antinational basis of particularism—the basis of states rights. States rights worked very well for destroying the Union but very badly indeed for creating a new nation. One of the reasons the South lost was precisely its belief in states rights, the operation of particularism state by state, and even county by county. A psychology of distrust of effective power pervaded the Southern mind.

One of the tantalizing questions we'll never be able to answer is: Would Southern nationalism have lasted had it not been for the war? My own feeling is that Southern nationalism was defeated by states rights and localism, and also by slavery, which prevented foreign intervention and encouraged localism and individualism to a degree that is hard to imagine. But the Confederacy was one of the interesting attempts at nationalism, a failed nationalism, and deserves a great deal more attention than it has received. One of the oddities of American historiography is that hardly anyone has written on Southern nationalism from the point of view of its institutions or lack of institutions. No one has investigated the reasons for the failure of some institutions to develop, or traced the holdovers of Southern nationalism in the postwar years. The South has kept its sectional identity longer than any section. Because it fought for a "cause," and that "cause" was lost, the South has used the psychology and the sentiment of the lost cause to foster and perpetuate a kind of romantic nationalism. The Southern nationalist psychology aided in the subordination of the Negro, while the need to keep the Negro subordinate aided in the perpetuation of romantic nationalism.

Southern nationalism is to be understood, as the whole South is to be understood, not so much in American terms, as in European terms. The South was (indeed, still is) in many respects the most European part of America. It had a stratified class system, it romanticized the church and glorified the military. It had a romantic attachment to the past, and to the picturesque, and to legendary things. The essence of romanticism was to adore the Middle Ages, to adore chivalry, to adore crumbling palaces, to adore legends and myths. Romanticism looked backward everywhere except in the North.

The Southern emphasis on chivalry, the tendency to speak of "Southrons," and the passion for the novels of Sir Walter Scott, the emphasis on race, all reflect a romantic view of life. The Southerners developed to a ridiculous degree the theory that they represented the great Mediterranean-French-Norman tradition that had come over to Virginia, while New England represented the awful Germanic, Anglo-Saxon peasant tradition. The Anglo-Saxons had always been the peasants, the yokels, while the Normans were the conquerors and the horsemen. Therefore the pure blue blood of the ancient world flowed in Southern veins. All this nonsense was part of the romanticism that we connect with people like Chateaubriand, and it reeks of racism. Although there is some of it in the chapter on race in Emerson's *English Traits,* there was very little of it in the North, partly because there were too many racial ingredients in the northern population. But since the South had what might be called racial purity (leaving the Negro out of the picture), it was possible there to develop this curious racist romanticism.

J.A.G. Were not most of the characteristics of Southern nationalism as you've described them existent in the eighteenth-century South?

H.S.C. I don't think so. On the whole, the leaders of the eighteenth-century South were deeply rooted in the Enlightenment. They were cosmopolitans. Jefferson and Madison and Wythe and the Pinckneys lived in a cosmopolitan world, a world of reason. There were romantic ingredients in Jefferson, as there were in Voltaire, for example, but primarily he was a child of the Age of Reason.

J.A.G. Were not the Southerners among the Founding Fathers acutely aware of their southernness and of Southern interests, such as slavery? Are they better described as nationalists or as *Southern* nationalists?

H.S.C. It's very difficult to generalize about Southern leaders. The prominent ones wanted to get rid of slavery, but as Winthrop Jordan has made clear in *White Over Black*, the rank and file were committed to slavery. In critical moments the South opted for slavery and not for freedom, notwithstanding the attitude of Jefferson, Washington, Madison, Patrick Henry, and various others. Southerners were confronted—we must be somewhat sympathetic here—with practical problems. Patrick Henry put it well in one of his letters. He would like to get rid of slavery, he said, but what could he do? His wife couldn't go in the kitchen and cook. How do you raise crops? One must use the labor that is there. If you free that labor, what do you do then? Southerners thought that if freed, the Negroes would all either starve to death or be back on their hands as dependents. That didn't turn out to be true, but they thought it would be true.

J.A.G. Would you explain the coexistence in the South of both nationalism and a belief in states rights?

H.S.C. I'm something of a dissenter on this question. I don't think Southerners genuinely believed in states rights. They deluded themselves that they believed passionately in states rights, but what they actually believed in was Southern nationalism. "In Dixieland we take our stand" rather than in South Carolina or Virginia.

The emphasis on states rights was at first a strategic one. Then, as is so often the case, strategy took over thought. States rights was a device, and perhaps the only device, that slave power had to protect itself. The slave power, and I use that word in a rather old-fashioned sense, was the largest single interest in the country, but it was weak, inescapably vulnerable. Slavery existed by virtue of municipal law only. It did not exist in the eyes of international law. Such protection as the federal Constitution gave it was practically nothing.

Slavery had to depend, therefore, on the states. Slavery went against what early became a fundamental principle of American constitutionalism: that major interests looked to the national government for aid and support. In the very nature of things, slavery was bound to be outvoted sooner or later. The North was growing faster; there was no chance of slavery going into the North or the West. After six years of southern efforts to dominate "Bleeding Kansas," there were only three slaves in the whole territory. It was a beleaguered institution. Only by closing ranks around the sole constitutional principle which gave it any hope of holding its own could it protect itself. This remains true as a strategic principle down to the present. Southerners now think they can control the Negro situation and maintain segregation in the schools by state dominance. They don't really object to national *support* of schools. They don't object to national support of anything so long as it doesn't result in interference with local control.

So I think the whole states-rights argument has about it an air of unreality and hypocrisy. I don't mean that this was conscious. Many of us have beliefs that aren't really genuine; we just think they're genuine. We think individualism is genuine. We think laissez faire is genuine. We don't really want it. Big business bemoans government interference. It would be horrified if the government, for example, did away with patent laws.

J.A.G. But can we really dismiss Southern states rights as hypocrisy?

H.S.C. Not at all! I don't believe in hypocrisy as an historical ingredient. People are everywhere under compelling psychological pressure to rationalize their conduct; they have to believe that they are sincere. I said that those who subscribed to the idea believed it. A great many Southern whites *believe* today that Negroes are inferior to whites. When they say "God is white," they really believe it. "Of course, God is white," they insist. "He made Adam in His image, and Adam was white." (After all, every painting of Adam and Eve depicts them as white!) If a whole society believes something strongly enough, most people accept it as a matter of course. One might ask: "How deeply did those who fought over their Protestant or Catholic faiths really believe them?" Hardly any were theological students; only one out of a hundred understood the theological issues. But they went to war and died for these issues all the same. We are loyal to things not because we have investigated them and come to the conclusion that they're best, but because we're part of them. A student is loyal to Columbia or Amherst, not because he has made a survey of all colleges and concluded that these are the best, but because it's *his* college and that's the end of it.

Southerners stood for their state because that's what they'd been brought up to do. But the roots of their psychology were not local, but regional. The Confederacy was larger than any country in Europe except Russia. The forces that created the Southern sense of identity were national, or in the American context, sectional.

J.A.G. I'd like to question you about Northern nationalism. Northerners were willing to fight a civil war to preserve the nation. How can their opposition to the extension of slavery be explained in the light of the fact that the chances of slavery expanding its frontiers were very small? Were not the vast majority of Northerners unsympathetic to Negroes? Why were they unwilling to let the South have its "peculiar institution"?

H.S.C. Almost all Northerners were willing to let the South have its institutions, but not to expand them.

J.A.G. Then the issue over which the war was fought was artificial.

H.S.C. It was in one sense artificial. History shows that people often fight and die for artificial issues. I wonder if the issue was any more artificial than the issue of Communism raised in the 1950's by Senator Joseph McCarthy. If you believe passionately in something and think that it's threatened, it ceases to be an artificial issue, and reason is powerless to deal with it. The South suffered from a kind of paranoia about the North, and a good many Northerners suffered from a comparable paranoia about slavery.

Furthermore, I'm not sure the North was ready to fight in 1861. Being ready to fight is not the same thing as allowing yourself to drift into a war. Were we ready to fight in Vietnam? Had the question, "Will you fight?" been put to a vote in the summer of 1860, almost everyone would have said "Certainly not," just as the country apparently voted against fighting in Vietnam in 1964. But once the issue of the Union was at stake, the country was prepared to fight. And it is not at all certain that slavery would have been ended had the South not persisted in its folly. It's interesting how few concessions Northern states were prepared to make to Negro rights. The inhabitants of Oregon, almost all of whom came from the North, were antislavery, but the Oregon Constitution of 1859 forbade free Negroes to come into the state. Slavery was wicked, most Northerners believed, but of course, the Negroes were not equals. This kind of logic, or illogic, was a commonplace, and no more surprising than the illogic we now employ in our own conduct in foreign affairs throughout the globe.

J.A.G. Looking at the whole sweep of American history from independence to the end of the Civil War, do you think that the unified nationalism which developed was, on balance, a good thing or a bad thing?

H.S.C. There are so many "ifs" in that question that it is very difficult to deal with, quite aside from the ifs about what we mean by "good" and "bad." I'm not sure there ever was any alternative. If you ask, "Does civilization do better in small organizations or in larger ones?" I would be forced to say "small ones." One of the sobering considerations of history is that by whatever tests of civilization we apply, all great civilizations have developed in small countries of states—Judea, Athens, the Roman Republic, Florence, Venice, the Low Countries, Elizabethan England, Weimar, Denmark. Even in our own history it would be difficult to reject the statement that the greatest era of statesmanship was the eighteenth century, that eighteenth-century Virginia with a white population of less than 300,000 produced more and greater statesmen than the whole country has ever since. It's a nice question whether bigness is not in itself inimical to a high degree of civilization. Even if we interpret civilization not in high cultural terms, but in terms of whether babies die or not, whether the water is pure, and things of that kind, I think most objective students would say that Sweden and Denmark and Holland and Switzerland are the most civilized countries in the world today. Life is safe, people are taken care of and educated, and cultural standards are high.

But what would have happened if nationalism hadn't occurred? Would it have been possible to have five or ten countries on this great continent? Clearly it *was* possible. Europe has eighteen or twenty countries, each with a flourishing civilization. The forces of modern science and technology, however, are inimical to local civilizations. Time was when every town in Italy had its own architecture, its own culture, its own philosophy, its own gastronomy. We might argue that one of the tests of a civilization is the gastronomical and wine test, that France, with four hundred wines and three hundred cheeses, is much more civilized than the United States with about ten wines and three cheeses. But in all probability France will succumb to Coca cola and the supermarket. Maybe localism is a thing of the past. And it remains to be seen whether a large country can have a great civilization. The question is wide open so far as the United States is concerned.

J.A.G.   If modern technology and all the tendencies of modern society make nationalism illogical, why does it persist?

H.S.C.   You might as well ask why racism flourishes in the face of scientific evidence that there are no real differences between the races, or why Protestantism or Catholicism remain separate when the differences between them can be detected only by theologians. Such things are deeply rooted in the psychology of man. When you're raised to believe in the superiority of your own country, it's very difficult to rid yourself of the belief. There are, of course, practical advantages to national organization, and out of these, loyalties develop. There's no reason in and of itself why other institutions should not attract comparable loyalties, but so far they have not. I'm not at all sure they'd be any better.

J.A.G.   How about loyalty to humanity?

H.S.C.   I suppose it's too vague, and without a sufficient body of day-by-day mechanisms bringing it home to people. It requires an enormous degree of sophistication to think in terms of mankind. We're prepared to let a million people starve in Asia or Africa, but our hearts would be wrung if we knew of one child in our own locality that was starving. We're prepared to drop napalm on Vietnamese children, but we would swoon of agony if we saw a child burn in our own country. We are so contrived that we can take in only what is close to us. If we ever learn to feel comparable anguish of spirit for all people, we will have reached the point where it will make very little difference what form our institutions take.

J.A.G. What are the half-dozen books that you would recommend to persons interested in the subject we have been discussing? In each case, would you indicate briefly what the particular contribution of the volume is?

H.S.C. The best single book on the nature and history of nationalism is Hans Kohn's *Idea of Nationalism* (1944). Kohn has published, too, *American Nationalism* (1957), a series of lectures, elaborated and documented with his customary thoroughness. Boyd Shafer has given us in *Nationalism, Myth and Reality* (1955), not so much a history as an interpretation of the impact of nationalism on the eighteenth and nineteenth centuries. Carleton Hayes, *Essays on Nationalism* (1937) analyzes the relationship of nationalism with religion, militarism, war, and culture, and raises in urgent fashion the question whether nationalism has been, on the whole, more a curse or a blessing. Sir Ernest Barker, *National Character* (1927), is a magisterial study of the roots of nationalism and the national sprit in the ancient world and of the various expressions which it adopted in more modern times. Louis Snyder has given us two original studies: *The Meaning of Nationalism* (1954), a series of penetrating essays on the meaning, sentiment, and character of nationalism, and on some of its economic and political manifestations. Breaking new ground is his *The New Nationalism* (1968), a comparative study of the nationalisms that have emerged so abruptly in the twentieth century with those of earlier years. Salo Baron's *Modern Nationalism and Religion* (1947), traces the relationship between nationalism and Jewish, Catholic, and Protestant religions with deep insight and profound learning. Two books illuminate the cultural history of American nationalism: V. L. Parrington's great *Main Currents of American Thought: The Romantic Revolution* (1927) and Benjamin Spender's *The Quest for Nationality: An American Literary Campaign* (1957), which covers the literary manifestations of nationalism down to the end of the nineteenth century.

Richard B. Morris

The Confederation and the Constitution

RICHARD B. MORRIS, Gouverneur Morris Professor of
History at Columbia, specializes in early American legal
and diplomatic history. His *Government and Labor in
Early America* (1946) was a pioneering study of wages,
working conditions, and the legal status of wage earners
and bound servants in the colonial period. His *The Peacemakers* (1967), which won a Bancroft prize, is a definitive
account of the peace treaty ending the Revolution. He is
coeditor with Henry Steele Commager of the multivolume
New American Nation series, and editor of the *Encyclo-
pedia of American History* (1953). Currently, he is working
on an edition of the papers of John Jay, first Chief Justice
of the Supreme Court. In the discussion which follows,
Morris offers his views on a wide range of questions
related to the history of the early years of the Republic,
a period which, despite the great volume of historical writing it has inspired, remains full of controversial issues.

John A. Garraty Professor Morris, Bernard Bailyn, in his study of the political controversies leading to the Revolution, suggests that the basic principles of government applied by Americans in framing both state governments and the government of the United States—principles such as the separation of powers, the idea of a written constitution, and the division of sovereignty between local and central authority—were worked out well before 1776. Do you agree with him?

Richard B. Morris Bailyn's statement is generally true, but it seems to me that several seminal ideas were not worked out before 1776. The very notion of constitutionalism, the ideal of government stemming from the people, and the notion of framing a constitution not by a legislature but by a convention specially elected for that purpose, as well as the principle of submitting a constitution to popular referendum (as was done in the case of the Massachusetts Constitution), were principles of the first importance. No precedent for them can be found in the period before 1776.

The era of the Revolution was also a time when much more emphasis was placed on bills of rights and on civil rights than in the colonial period. Colonial charters had few references to rights. Some refer to religious toleration and so forth. Early seventeenth-century charters contained rudimentary bills of rights, but in the course of imperial charter-giving, the idea of civil rights more or less disappeared. Colonists *assumed* that they had the English civil rights which are found in the Bill of Rights and the Petition of Rights; the rights were not spelled out. Even the freedom of the press, traditionally said to have been won by the acquittal of Peter Zenger, editor of the New York *Weekly Journal*, who was charged with seditious libel for having printed political criticism in 1735, was accepted in only a limited sense in the colonies.

J.A.G. Wasn't spelling out the "rights of Englishmen" what the whole argument with Britain was about between 1763 and the Revolution?

R.B.M. One could say that the American Revolution was an attempt by the patriots to get back to the English Constitution of 1689, while the British were attempting to fit the colonies into the gradually emerging constitution of the eighteenth century. I would say, however, that the colonies were trying to move toward what would later be called commonwealth status. They were nudging the Empire into what the British did, for example, in Canada in the nineteenth century. So the Americans were not really moving back to 1689. They were attempting to develop a new scheme for the sharing of imperial responsibility.

J.A.G. Having won independence and set up their own government, why were the colonists so concerned about protecting themselves against government through bills of rights?

R.B.M. The explanation lies in the events that triggered the Revolution, the retrospective look the colonists took at their past. They attributed all the troubles to big government, the big government of the Empire: the recent harsh enforcement of the revenue laws, the royal flunkies sent over as governors and judges, the disallowance of colonial laws by the Privy Council. They were trying to get away from super government and executive power. The Declaration of Independence put the blame upon the *King;* essentially it was an attack on monarchy, and that meant executive power.

J.A.G. Was it more a revolution against centralization than against control imposed by an alien authority?

R.B.M. The Revolution contained two elements. It was democratic in a sense that it was a popular uprising. The patriotic parties represented a large number of people, probably a majority. At the same time, the colonists were attempting to win back the kind of local autonomy they had won during the period of salutary neglect prior to 1750.

J.A.G. Did the first state constitutions merely provide a new legal basis for pre-existing colonial governments, or did they embody significant political changes?

R.B.M. The answer depends upon which constitutional structures you're examining. In Connecticut and Rhode Island they merely continued their old charters. The other states all adopted new constitutions, beginning in 1776 with South Carolina and Virginia. These constitutions all had interesting innovations. They conformed to colonial constitutional experience, but they also took into account public opinion about the causes of the Revolution. Of course, all had a working constitutional structure to start with: a governor (Pennsylvania excepted), a legislature, and a judiciary. But some very profound changes were made in the powers of each branch, particularly those of the governor, which were watered down and weakened. New York state, for example, created a Council of Appointments which shared the appointing power with the governor, and a Council of Revision which shared the veto power. This fear of a strong executive was widespread and shared by all patriots. Conservatives—John Jay, Robert R. Livingston, Gouverneur Morris—wrote the New York Constitution of 1777, but they reflected the popular view.

The other principal difference involved the bills of rights. Having separated themselves from the British system, Americans no longer had to fear imperial review of judicial cases, or the disallowance of legislation. But they felt that their personal security had been rendered unsafe by things that happened after 1763, and therefore they laid down other principles of civil liberty, which, in turn, were embodied in the first ten Amendments to the U. S. Constitution.

J.A.G. I can understand why colonists would want to have bills of rights which would protect them against Great Britain. But why were they so concerned to protect themselves against their own government?

R.B.M. Because they feared what would happen when power accumulated in any one man or any group. Theirs was a pessimistic view of human nature; all the Revolutionary figures shared it. They felt that human beings could not be trusted with too much power. For this reason they made the terms of governors very short. The terms of legislature were very short in some cases also; the continual turnover of government officers was very much on their minds, and they were concerned about things like nepotism. Limitations on power, I would say, was the central constitutional principle that comes out of the American Revolution.

J.A.G. Given the political and military situation in 1781, and considering the strength of American local loyalties, was the first national government established under the Articles of Confederation as strong and effective an instrument as one might reasonably have hoped for?

R.B.M. It probably was as strong as one could have hoped for at that time, yes. It went as far as the people were willing to go without learning some very hard lessons.

J.A.G. In what specific ways did the Articles of Confederation reflect anti-British prejudices?

R.B.M. Anti-British prejudices were reflected in the relative weakness of the Congress, if one sees Congress as the equivalent of Parliament. The Articles didn't give Congress the power to tax, because Americans had not wanted Parliament to have the power to tax them. This attitude also explains the failure to give Congress the power to control interstate commerce, which grew out of colonial experience with the Navigation Acts.

J.A.G. On balance, did the government established under the Articles of Confederation handle adequately the task of supervising the war effort? Could the victory over Britain have been achieved sooner and at less cost if the federal government had been stronger?

R.B.M. To be technical, there wasn't any Confederation, merely the Continental Congress until 1781, by which time the Revolution had been substantially won. But there was very little difference, of course, between the Congress and the Confederation. What the new government did between 1781 and 1783 was to create an organizational structure to deal with foreign relations and finance, and with a modest degree of effectiveness. It set up a Secretary of Foreign Affairs and a Superintendent of Finance, and I think both of those operations were important. But probably the American Revolution would have taken about the same course whether or not there had been a Confederation government. The people who won the war, George Washington and the troops, would have done everything the same way whether the Confederation government or Congress was in power. Again, I don't think that the Confederation government is entitled to much credit for obtaining the peace treaty ending the Revolution. It was in power too short a time to be credited with either winning the war or gaining the peace.

J.A.G.   Would you comment generally on the Peace of Paris ending the war?

R.B.M.   The Peace of Paris was in a way a tribute to the fact that a revolution had taken place. For the first time in modern history, a great empire was forced to recognize the independence of colonies. The most important provision of the treaty was the one which recognized the United States of America. It was also remarkable that the American commissioners were able to get a viable state. The question was whether there was going to be a country hemmed in by the Appalachians. It's true that the boundary lines were very fuzzy, but considering the inaccurate maps of the time, the fuzziness was unavoidable. Further, without supplying a timetable, the treaty provided for the evacuation of the British troops on American soil. In sum, the treaty acknowledged the full sovereignty of America and its freedom from outside military interference.

J.A.G.   In your book *The Peacemakers*, which deals with the complex negotiations leading to the signing of the Peace of Paris, I was particularly interested in the way you were able to distinguish the roles played by the individual negotiators both on the American and on the British side. Would you describe the contributions of the leading figures?

R.B.M.   Benjamin Franklin's total accomplishment as a diplomat has probably never been equaled in American history since that time. Franklin symbolized to Europeans what was considered the best in the American way of life; he had a talent for public relations which ingratiated him with the French court and with French intellectuals and with the French masses, a talent which no other American diplomat has manifested in the same degree. His major role was to keep France mollified during the war, and to get financial assistance for the United States. That was more important than obtaining an actual military alliance. Franklin was not much concerned about the military alliance; the French wanted it much more than he did. Franklin sought financial aid, and got it even when the French were dissatisfied with the way the peace negotiations were going.

France's aim in the war was to separate the American colonies from England, and thus reduce the prestige of the British Empire. Therefore the French *had* to continue the war to complete victory; they *had* to supply aid to America. But there is some question whether anyone other than Franklin could have gotten such aid as effectively. Franklin was the only American, except for Washington, who had real prestige abroad. At the same time, Franklin fully appreciated the importance of French aid. He leaned over backwards to "sell" the French point of view to the other American peace commissioners.

Franklin was also the commander of American fighting forces overseas; all privateers operating in European waters were under his control. And he secretly directed American propaganda in Europe, having his own printing press in the basement of his house at Passy, whence an enormous amount of propaganda was poured out. The Revolution was probably the first war in modern times in which propaganda played such an important role. It was important to America to win the intellectuals to its side, because the intellectuals of that day had the ears of European monarchs such as Frederick the Great of Prussia and Catherine the Great of Russia. Their voices helped to neutralize the sympathies of the despotic powers which would normally have been in the direction of George III.

J.A.G. Did Franklin's prestige have any influence on the British, who, after all, were negotiating the treaty?

R.B.M. Franklin was the archenemy of the North ministry. But when the Rockingham-Shelburne ministry came to power in March, 1782, former friends of Franklin, many of whom had kept up correspondence with him during the war, rose in influence. Lord Shelburne, an enlightened intellectual with rather radical views despite his aristocratic background, respected Franklin immensely. The new British leaders felt they could deal with Franklin, whereas they did not know John Jay and John Adams, the other commissioners, personally. When the new ministry picked the British peace commissioners, they chose men who knew Franklin personally, like Richard Oswald, and the intermediary, Benjamin Vaughan, a radical intellectual who had been a close confidant of Shelburne and who had been in constant correspondence with Franklin. Indeed, Vaughan was the first editor of Franklin's papers, which were published in England in 1777, during the Revolution! In other words, the British named persons who would be palatable to the Americans, who would "speak their language," and who at the same time would be trusted by the new government in Britain.

J.A.G. Would you comment on John Adams' role in formulating the Peace of Paris?

R.B.M. John Adams came into the Paris negotiations rather late. He was there for only a little over a month. He had been in Holland and arrived in response to letters from John Jay, who needed help because Franklin was not in good health. Franklin had a very serious attack of kidney stones in Paris, and he may also have had a slight stroke. He was not, therefore, capable of the physical effort needed to resist the pressures of the French, nor was he psychologically prepared to thwart his French admirers. He never liked to growl, anyway.

Adams, of course, was the ideal man to start a row. He enjoyed a contest, and was congenitally suspicious of the French court to begin with. His principal role was in connection with the fisheries and the payment of prewar debts. Before Adams' arrival, neither Franklin nor Jay had the slightest intention of recognizing the debts due to British merchants, but Adams, without consultation, said at his first conference, with Oswald: "Of course, honorable men must pay their debts." Thus he cut the ground from under Jay and Franklin.

J.A.G.   Was that an example of bad communications among the commissioners, or did Adams in effect just overrule his colleagues?

R.B.M.   At the beginning, there was very bad communication. Jay had to use almost the point of a gun to get Adams to pay a visit to Franklin. Adams was terribly jealous of Franklin, and felt that he had been undercutting him everywhere. But Adams was a headstrong person; he often moved too fast without thinking, overwhelmed by his own eloquence. He blurted out his concession about the debts, and no one can say whether he regretted it or not. My own feeling is that it was wise for the Americans to agree to pay the debts. The debts had nothing to do with the American Revolution, and if the Americans hoped to get back into trade relations with the British and develop a sound national credit they would have to honor their obligations. But of course the debtors in America didn't like it.

J.A.G.   How did Adams contribute to the solution of the fisheries problem?

R.B.M.   Adams greatly magnified his role in the fisheries controversy; most of the points that he made were already being insisted upon by Jay, who made it very clear that the United States wanted not only the right to fish off the Grand Banks but also the right to dry fish on the coast of Newfoundland. But Adams was very thorough. He gathered together all the American ship captains in Holland or in France, and asked them for full details: the time of the year the fleets went to the Banks, the problems of inshore fishing, and so on. With this information he was prepared to argue why it was so important that the Americans should obtain inshore fishing rights—which was critical, because the New Englanders could reach the fisheries each season before the French and English. The drying privilege was necessary because of the lack of refrigeration; it was essential to have the right to temporary occupancy of unoccupied beaches to dry the catch. Adams, having gathered this data, was able to overwhelm his colleagues and the British with his technical knowledge.

J.A.G.   Would you comment now on John Jay's role?

R.B.M. John Jay is a controversial figure in the history of American diplomacy, from the time of the peacemaking to his negotiation of the Jay Treaty of 1794. He was the central figure at the Paris conference. Early pro-Franklin historians, like Jared Sparks, believed that Jay, because of his egotism and vanity, had unnecessarily insisted on independence as a precondition of entering into negotiations, and that this was a mistake. They felt that if the negotiations had been entered into quickly, America would have been able to get Franklin's original demands, which included all of Canada. Jay was a lawyer, and he thought as a lawyer. He believed that British recognition of independence was vital. The details of territorial settlements were relatively minor in comparison. Certainly, that has been the argument of revolutionary states in our own day.

As to his not insisting on getting Lower Canada, I think it was better to take a natural boundary—the Great Lakes. Furthermore, if he had obtained the 45th parallel as the boundary, ultimately it would have meant the 45th parallel all the way to the Pacific. By accepting the Lakes boundary, the United States ultimately got the 49th parallel west of the Lakes. So while we lost upper Ontario, we eventually got the Mesabi Range iron deposits and all of the great Northwest.

J.A.G. Why were the British willing to make peace on terms so favorable to the new United States?

R.B.M. We must distinguish between the British people generally and the Earl of Shelburne. The Earl was one of the most inscrutable men in history. He makes a typical "enigmatic" Russian or Chinese seem very open and clear. What his motivations were I guess will never be completely known. Deep down he was friendly to America, but at the same time he was an imperialist. When the chips were down, he would support America as against France. He was trying to get the best deal he could: first, to try to keep the United States within the Empire; second, to get the French and Spaniards out of the war. He suggested a separate peace between France and England, leaving Americans out in the cold. France was fighting for two different reasons, for American independence and to get Gibraltar for Spain. France had changed the character of the war by its alliance with Spain; of that there was no question. Of course, Shelburne knew this, and was eager to drive a wedge between the French and the Americans. At the same time, I think he knew that American independence had to be recognized. But he didn't dare tell that to George III, who suffered a profound psychological block on the score of American independence. The colonies were his children; he would go into a tantrum when the idea of independence was broached.

Moreover, public opinion in England, based on military evidence available in 1782, was not prepared for the disastrous defeat that American independence represented. Shelburne was deluged with mail saying: "Stand fast like a true Briton," and so forth. He had a tricky problem, because he was a man without a party and didn't know how to build one. He was not personally much liked. His parliamentary position was very shaky. So he had to operate deviously. He tried to drive a wedge between the United States and France by conducting elaborate negotiations with the French diplomats, which greatly alarmed the Americans. This led Jay to accept a compromise terminology on the preconditions of recognition of the United States, and as soon as Shelburne had that, he convinced the ministry of the advantages of recognizing the United States and starting quickly with peace talks in order to separate America from the French and Spaniards.

J.A.G.　How did Shelburne persuade the British public, and particularly George III, to accept American independence?

R.B.M.　He held a long series of conferences in which he tried to show that the concessions which the Americans were willing to make regarding the debts and the property of Loyalists were very substantial. And he held out to George III the expectation of a formal alliance between the United States and England. I don't think George III really understood what independence was going to mean. When he actually announced it to Parliament at the end of the preliminary negotiations, he choked on the word.

We must remember also that nobody knew what was going on. The treaty was absolutely secret. When its terms were published, it was a bombshell. The Shelburne ministry was overthrown. But the treaty had to be ratified anyhow. Obviously it was too late to back away. Sentiment in the country was for peace. After all, the British got out of the war with a certain amount of prestige. They had smashed the French Navy in the West Indies; they had defeated the French in India; they had crushed the French and Spaniards at Gibraltar. All they lost were thirteen little colonies.

J.A.G.　How did the ending of the war affect the problems faced by the American government?

R.B.M.　The ending of the war left the new government with perfectly enormous problems. Take the mere question of the ravaged areas of British occupation. New York City, for example, was almost a complete wreck. There had been two major fires in the lower part of the city, and no rebuilding had taken place. The British had used many houses for barracks. In the countryside, farms had been burned, orchards destroyed, and so on. A number of towns had been burned. On the frontier, there was considerable devastation.

Then there was the question of the evacuation of troops. To get the enemy off American soil was a difficult problem. The British ordered

Canadian authorities not to remove their troops from the western forts.

J.A.G.   Was there any delay in the removal of British troops east of the Appalachians?

R.B.M.   Only in the interior, as in up-state New York; otherwise the removals were made on schedule.

J.A.G.   Approximately how many British soldiers were there in the former colonies at the time of the signing of the peace treaty?

R.B.M.   Perhaps 15,000 or 18,000 men, a very sizable army—much larger, by the way, than the American army in the field.

J.A.G.   Were the years between 1783 and 1789 really a "critical period"?

R.B.M.   Well, this is a loaded question. When the historian John Fiske gave the period that name late in the nineteenth century, he was trying to show that a strong national government was absolutely essential. On the other hand, he was using words which had been used by the Founding Fathers themselves; quite a number of them had said it was a critical period. Fiske did not invent the term.

I would say it was critical for the creation of a viable union, but not in terms of the ability of the four million Americans of that day to function in some way. The average person was concerned with the bread-and-butter questions—soldiers getting back to their families and farms, merchants rebuilding trade. The *states* were concerned about stabilizing their financial houses. The larger picture was seen only by statesmen, who had to deal with questions of central taxation or possibly trade regulations, and who recognized the necessity of a strong national government.

J.A.G.   What were the national problems that informed persons of that time considered "critical"?

R.B.M.   The problems were of two kinds. The first may have been over-emphasized: the domestic economic and fiscal difficulties. These were serious because, in the postwar period, pent-up demand burst forth for goods unavailable during the Revolution and British manufacturers dumped goods in America at bargain prices. The effect of this dumping was to damage badly domestic manufactures and to overextend lines of credit. Americans were buying more than they could afford. The government was powerless to prevent this dumping of the goods because there was no national tariff. The British government, of course, encouraged this because it wanted to re-establish its dominance of American trade.

J.A.G.   Did British merchants dump goods in America for strategic, political, or economic reasons in order to control the American market? Or was there a glut in England because of the cutting off of trade with America for so long?

R.B.M.   There were lots of goods in British warehouses, and they were thinking of long-range economic patterns. The British government was not officially involved in dumping. Lord Sheffield, in his famous report, opposed a reciprocal trade agreement with the Americans, on the theory that they would have to buy from England because English goods were cheaper than anybody else's. After July, 1783, British orders in council virtually re-established the colonial system, but with the United States outside. America was excluded from the West Indian trade. The Americans had expected to get all the benefits of being in the British Empire without any of the detriments. One of the benefits was the right to trade with the British West Indies, but they were barred from that trade, a serious blow.

The economic situation was tied up with the fiscal situation. In general, the states assumed the responsibility for putting their own fiscal houses in order without turning to the Continental Congress. This involved heavy taxation at a time of declining commodity prices, so that in certain rural areas—Massachusetts is a good example—there was a good deal of unrest. Court records in Massachusetts in the two years preceding Shays' Rebellion reveal a massive rise in mortgage foreclosures and the sale of debtors into servitude, even the jailing of debtors. Farmers were losing their land all over the state. Some states, on the other hand, seemed to do much better than others. New York, for example, apparently flourished during the 1780's, which probably explains why New York was less inclined to give commercial power to the federal government. When American leaders wrote to one another they tended to say that conditions were awful, but when they wrote to foreigners, they took a different tack. Compare Jefferson's letters to his local friends with the kind of letters he was sending abroad, or Franklin's.

There is another factor which complicates the picture, a very important one. Those historians who have claimed that there was great prosperity in the critical period base their argument upon volume of business activity. They neglect the fact that this was a period of enormous population growth. Between 1783 and 1789 the population rose from two and a half million to four million! Naturally, gross figures for production and trade rose sharply, but not necessarily the standard of living.

J.A.G.   Where did the immigrants of these years come from?

R.B.M.   From England, Scotland, and Ireland, and to some extent from Germany; the classic pattern with somewhat more Irish immigration than before.

J.A.G.   That's very interesting. The entire history of immigration suggests that foreigners came to America in good times. Isn't this an indication that the economy was flourishing at that time?

R.B.M.   Everything is comparative. Economic opportunity seemed much better than in Europe. But this was also a pent-up immigration. There had been an enormous immigration to America between 1763 and 1775. Enormous. This influx stopped when the Revolution broke out. Thousands of Europeans were waiting to come in once peace was restored. They were not worried about commodity prices, or the fact that certain businessmen were losing money. People, after all, were starving in parts of Scotland and Ireland. What difference did it make if there was a "depression" in America? They thought of America as a land of opportunity.

J.A.G. Isn't it remarkable that large numbers of English subjects, immediately after the termination of the Revolution, would go to settle down permanently in a country that had just been their enemy?

R.B.M. I'm glad you said "English subjects" rather than Englishmen, because most of these immigrants were Scots or Irish, and considered themselves separate nationalities. One could also make a case that the American Revolution was an English civil war; there was important opposition to the war in England—working-class people in London who supported John Wilkes, and a peace group somewhat like the elements opposing the Vietnamese War in our own time. The Revolution was one of the most unpopular wars the English ever fought. Of their 60,000 soldiers in America, 30,000 were German mercenaries. This was a tribute, I think, to the inability of the English to get enough native-born troops to fight against the Americans.

But to return to the character of the "critical period," there were other serious problems: the inability of the central government effectively to control the frontiers, to get the British out of the West, to create territorial governments for those areas. All sorts of secessionist schemes were in the air, plots and counterplots. The real focus in the Confederation period should be on these great problems of foreign affairs. Could we win the respect of foreign nations? They were convinced that the United States had no long-range future, that it would fall apart, that they could then come in and pick up the pieces.

The United States had not the strength to conduct foreign affairs effectively. Take the projected reciprocal trade treaty with Great Britain. John Adams was a very intelligent, tenacious person, and yet he got nowhere at all with the British. Parliament was committed to the policy of Lord Sheffield: that England didn't have to make any concessions to America in order to dominate American trade. Parliament was also under pressure from two powerful lobbies—the Scottish and English merchants demanding payment of pre-Revolutionary debts, and Loyalist groups which were demanding compensation for confiscated property in America. Of course, as a matter of conscience the British felt an obligation to the Loyalists. It is significant that after the peace was signed, there probably was considerably more confiscation by the states of Loyalists' property than occurred before. Therefore the British would make no trade treaty with America.

Conflict with Spain in the American West was another critical problem. We were "given" by the British all territory east of the Mississippi, but this was a bilateral agreement between England and the United States. Spain had not relinquished its claim to territories between the Mississippi and the Appalachians. The boundary of west Florida was also in dispute, as was the right of navigation on the Mississippi. To Westerners, the Mississippi was a lifeline of commerce. It was very important to press for free navigation of the river. Secretary for Foreign Affairs John Jay engaged in long negotiations with the Spanish without success. At last, in desperation, he finally recommended to Congress that we forbear for a limited period from pressing for free navigation. His explanation was that we did not have the military power to engage in a war with Spain. Thus, the nation failed completely in negotiations with Spain.

Finally, the United States found itself in the humiliating position of having to buy off Morocco, Algiers, and Tripoli to end their bandit raids on American commerce in the Mediterranean. In all these respects, American weakness in foreign affairs was very serious, but most serious of all was our inability to get the British to leave the western posts. These "western" posts were not so far west. British troops were stationed on Lake Champlain, on Lake Oswego, all along the northern edge of New York state. So long as the British remained, settlement of western New York and of the Northwest Territory could not proceed at a rapid pace.

So, to a considerable extent, I would say the Confederation period was "critical." But to the extent that the *states* were able to function—providing a reasonable degree of law and order and getting their fiscal affairs in balance—it was a constructive period. It was the national government which was in a crisis, rather than the state governments.

J.A.G. Could a stronger national government have had any more influence on British trade policy than the one that existed, or on British policy with regard to the western posts, or on the Spanish refusal to accept the American interpretation of the southwest boundary?

R.B.M. The answer to that is Yes and No. After 1789, the national government couldn't do anything about the West Indian trade, but it was able to get the British soldiers removed from the posts and make a treaty with Spain.

J.A.G. Why couldn't the weaker government have done so? What constitutional weakness did the government under the Articles of Confederation have that inhibited it in foreign relations?

R.B.M. The major weakness was that it lacked retaliatory power in commercial conflicts. It could not retaliate against foreign nations commercially, because each state had control of its own trade. Of course, the lack of taxing power also meant that it was impossible to maintain a strong army and navy as a force in the international balance of power.

J.A.G.   Can the movement for strengthening the central government be explained entirely in terms of these particular problems, or does it also reflect the growth of American nationalism at the grass-roots level?

R.B.M.   The ultimate acceptance of the Constitution was due to the fact that most people were agreed that there should be, as it were, a hoop for the barrel. How strong the hoop should be, people weren't agreed upon. But even the anti-Federalists agreed to give the taxing power to the federal government and to allow it to control interstate commerce. This was a reflection of nationalism. You find it expressed by people like Noah Webster in this period, and especially by George Washington.

Nationalism in America was, however, to some extent consciously created by leaders. Only in part was it a grass-roots movement. It certainly did not submerge loyalties to the states completely. But the Constitution could not have been ratified if people hadn't had some sense of national mission or destiny—if they hadn't considered themselves Americans. Undoubtedly, many more people considered themselves Americans in 1787 than in 1777.

J.A.G.   Both the Constitution and the men who drafted it have been deluged with praise by historians. What is there about the Constitution, aside from the fact that it has endured so long, that makes it such a remarkable document?

R.B.M.   I think you have stated the main reason—its endurance. This question is very difficult and complicated. One can say that the Constitution is quite extraordinary in that it did *not* represent any broad philosophical principles, but was a patchwork of compromises. Take the power of the presidency and the term of the President. Some people wanted the President to serve for six years without being eligible for re-election; others wanted the President to serve for life; others advocated a term of two or three years. So they compromised. They did the same thing, of course, on the question of the equality of the states, as expressed in the Great Compromise creating the House of Representatives and the Senate. These were patchworks. When the Philadelphia convention started, nobody had the entire Constitution in mind. The Madison and Randolph plans were the closest thing to what happened, but they were far from the final document. The flexibility of the Constitution is another important reason for its success. It contained enough of a reserve of national power to enable resourceful leaders to expand the functions of the federal government when it became necessary (and popular) to do so.

This is the greatness of the Constitution: It is a flexible instrument, skillfully worded. And it is also remarkable in that it was produced at phenomenal speed. All the conflicting issues were settled in four months, and the writing of the Constitution by the committee on style was accomplished in two days! That seems absolutely extraordinary, because the phraseology of the Constitution is so magnificent.

J.A.G.   Can you explain why a nation of three or four million persons whose culture was provincial and derivative, a nation which turned out relatively little that was original or even first-rate in any of the arts, was able to produce in a single generation so many great statesmen?

R.B.M.   You've put your finger on the greatness of the period between 1775 and 1800. In part, the explanation lies in the British tradition that politics was the proper business of every gentleman, that public service was an obligation of every educated man. Office-holding entailed great prestige. Consider, for example, the careers of John Adams and John Jay. These men *never* practiced their profession of law after the beginning of the Revolution, although Adams lived until 1826 and Jay until 1829. They never engaged in any livelihood other than the public service. Washington refused to accept any salary for serving as general.

This commitment to putting public interest above private concern was very important. There were, of course, many who tried to profit from the war. Robert Morris or Benjamin Franklin were somewhat fuzzy on this question of conflict of interest. But even they regarded public service as the highest achievement and made many sacrifices in order to engage in it. Franklin retired from business at forty, and lived on for over four decades, devoting himself largely to public affairs. He could afford to do so, but most of the men in public life were not men of great wealth.

There was a very Roman quality about the Founding Fathers, which disappeared very rapidly in the nineteenth century. With the democratization of politics, of course, we lost this ability to attract the very best people to public life. The great minds are seldom found in government service today.

J.A.G.   Then there really were no more great men per capita in America in that era, but more of those of outstanding ability and character went into politics?

R.B.M.   Yes, I think so. Furthermore, probably the American colonies had the highest level of literacy in the whole world at that time. And the eighteenth century was a very political century. Everybody in America talked politics. European travelers were flabbergasted by the fact that ordinary colonials could talk about politics intelligently. This was not the case in England or France at that period.

In any event, this was a very crucial advantage. Whatever else contributed, the character of the new nation was determined by the quality of its leadership. Whether we were going to be a first-rate country or a second-rate country depended on who was running it, what ideas they had, and to what extent talented men were willing to go into public affairs. The opportunities for amassing wealth were so great that one could have excused men of talent if they had not devoted themselves to the public service.

J.A.G.   Who in particular among the delegates to the Constitutional Convention were most influential in shaping the Constitution?

R.B.M.   The Constitution emerged chiefly out of the Virginia Plan, which was drawn up by James Madison and Edward Randolph. Randolph, however, played an ambiguous role: after he put through his inventive plan, he refused to sign the Constitution. Of course, one might say that that was merely because he was a Randolph; all the Randolphs were eccentrics. But it was also because he heard that Patrick Henry back in Virginia was raising the devil, and he was afraid that maybe he'd be doing something very unpopular.

Madison played a crucial role not only in his advocacy of the Virginia Plan but also in the discussions that went on all through the Convention. William Paterson of New Jersey was also important. While his New Jersey Plan was nothing but a "souped-up" version of the Articles of Confederation, it did represent the voice of the small states, which had to be placated if the new system was to work. Since the Founders wanted to get the states to agree to a federal system, they tried, perhaps too hard, to avoid the use of the word "national" in the Constitution. To a large extent, whatever national tone there is and whatever emphasis on popular sovereignty comes through, were supplied by James Wilson. And we owe a good deal to the work of Gouverneur Morris on the Committee on Style. Lastly, it seems to me that the conscience of the Convention was expressed by George Mason of Virginia. His was the voice at Philadelphia attacking slavery. You may ask, "What does the Constitution say about slavery?" Not much. Yet it remained for a Southerner to attack slavery in the strongest terms it was ever attacked in a public place up to that time. And his was a very important contribution: the clause on the slave trade. Technically, it forbade Congress to interfere with the trade for twenty years, but in effect it put on record the fact that after twenty years the trade would be abolished.

I would not, certainly, include Alexander Hamilton. His famous speech of June 18 was so extreme, almost monarchist in character, that it had no weight at all with the delegates.

J.A.G.   What about Washington and Franklin?

R.B.M.   Your point is well made. Without Washington I don't think they would have had a Constitution. Washington represented the national interest; his image had a great deal to do with persuading people to accept a strong presidency. They didn't care too much about how the President was elected, because they felt that Washington was certain to be the first President. The Electoral College was merely a patchwork. But without Washington there would have been an impasse over the issue of the Electoral College. Franklin was a great symbol of the past, a man of diplomacy and conciliation. Because he was also felt to be somewhat to the left, somewhat closer to the people, his acceptance of the Constitution was very significant. Thus advocates could go to the people and say, "The oldest of the Founding Fathers has accepted the Constitution. The Commander-in-Chief of the Armies favors the Constitution." This was a selling point, I'm sure, in all the private debates on ratification. "What are you worrying about?" supporters could say. "Washington's going to be the first President."

J.A.G.   Was Washington a great President?

R.B.M.   Beyond question he was a great President, for several reasons. First, I think because he was a symbol of consensus. Everyone agreed to Washington.

J.A.G.   Excuse me. That would almost make Eisenhower a great President.

R.B.M.   That wasn't the same kind of consensus; a lot of people voted for Adlai Stevenson. But of course there was far more to Washington than merely his being a symbol of consensus. He was a symbol of respect for office. The presidents of the Continental Congress were, in the main, men of no special consequence. The office of President had to be made into a dignified office which would command popular allegiance, and only someone like Washington could have done it.

J.A.G.   Are you saying that Washington was a great President simply because he was Washington?

R.B.M.   No. Washington was also a great President because of the manner and dignity of his behavior, and because he created under his administration a very important *unwritten* Constitution. Under the Constitution, the President can make treaties with the "advice and consent" of the Senate. But when Washington called on the Senate for "advice" and it refused to give it, he developed the practice of merely submitting treaties to the Senate for ratification. Thus he established the principle that the President makes the treaties and has them ratified by the Senate. This actually changed the Constitution.

J.A.G.   But most historians hold that a strong President is one who uses the executive powers broadly and decisively. It is difficult for me to see how this applies to Washington. Wasn't he overly concerned about not interfering with the prerogatives of the legislative branch of the government?

R.B.M. You must remember that everyone was wedded at that time to the notion of separation of powers. Washington had great respect for this principle. When he refused to turn over executive papers to Congress, he stood on the ground of separation of powers. From that point on, Congress was unable to hold the executive branch to direct accountability. In addition, we owe to Washington the innovation of the cabinet, something which was not recognized as such in the Constitution. The heads of departments were supposed to consult with one another and consult with the President. Originally, Washington's heads of departments consulted with him individually. Next, they began to write letters to one another. Then he had them consult collectively, and finally he brought them together as the cabinet, which has become part of the unwritten Constitution.

Furthermore, for generations our entire foreign policy was founded on Washington's Farewell Address, on the notion that the nation should steer clear of permanent alliances with foreign powers, without abandoning the possibilities of occasional alliances in emergencies. This idea certainly controlled American policy right down to World War I and beyond. The country could have fallen apart, it seems to me, in 1793–94, because of the division of opinion on the French Revolution. Washington held it together.

J.A.G. Did Washington make *any* mistakes? Can't you find anything to criticize in the way he ran the United States?

R.B.M. I think he probably overemphasized the dignity of his office. He was in personality rather cold and aloof, and overconcerned about his prestige as head of state in a republic. His formal levees had almost a monarchical character. But he was trying to set up a new state, and this was how he conceived his task. Subsequent Presidents, from Jefferson on, moved away from the very formal, almost regal behavior.

Possibly, Washington exaggerated the importance of the Whisky Rebellion. The confrontation of the United States Army with a few "rebels," with the President himself commanding the forces in the field, was possibly a mistake. Let us say he overreacted. But the general feeling was that the country was weak, torn by faction. Perhaps the presence of the President of the United States would bring about an acceptance of law and order. This, of course, is what happened: The Whisky rebels didn't resist when they were confronted with the presidential forces.

I don't think myself that Washington made any major blunder. His mistakes were trivial ones, largely due to the innovating character of the office. His tendency to lean more heavily on Hamilton than other members of the cabinet, and to accept Hamilton as a kind of a prime minister, may have been a mistake, but that was eventually corrected.

Hamilton himself conceived of the office of Secretary of the Treasury as similar to the First Lord of the Treasury in England, who was the head of the cabinet.

J.A.G.   Most students would agree that being a successful President involves being also a successful political leader, a partisan politician. Would you comment on Washington's political role?

R.B.M.   This is our view today, that the President is also the head of his party. But no one in 1789 held that view, because no one advocated a party system. Washington felt that parties would divide the country. He was consistent in seeing himself not as the head of a party, but of the nation. The "other fellows" had the party. I think this attitude had a profound effect on the Federalists; it explains a lot of the mistakes John Adams made in not developing an effective machine of his own, and allowing the Federalist leadership to fall into the hands of others. The idea that the President should be a party leader who must mold opinion and use patronage for partisan purposes did not evolve until the time of Jefferson.

J.A.G.   Doesn't that suggest a weakness in Washington? During Washington's administration, parties formed. The whole history of the United States was influenced by this fact. Yet you point out that Washington wished to remain above party, outside the party system.

R.B.M.   Washington's mistake was the mistake of all the leading Federalists. They did not recognize that the party system would be permanent. They knew that there was another party, but they felt that it would be beaten, and that their party was the *national* party. Their conception of politics was unrealistic in terms of what happened after 1798, but not in terms of the first six or eight years of American history.

J.A.G.   During the 1790's, were Jefferson and Hamilton really as much at odds with each other as each apparently believed?

R.B.M.   Their differences were more of personality than of principle. This is clear when we consider what Jefferson did when he became President. He applied a broad Hamiltonian construction to the Constitution in the Louisiana Purchase, and in imposing the Embargo in 1807. His fiscal policies, while they emphasized retrenchment, were merely modifications of Hamilton's; there was no overt repudiation of Hamilton's policies by Jefferson. The differences were in tone rather than substance, although I think the tone was very important.

On foreign policy they did disagree, although I think over policies more than principles. Jefferson was concerned about monarchical tendencies in America; he felt, therefore, more enthusiasm for the French Revolution than the Federalists. (Everybody in America favored the French Revolution when it first broke out.) But after the execution of King Louis XVI and the Terror, the differences become very sharp.

J.A.G. Was there any rational basis for the divisions which were produced in America by the French Revolution? For example, wasn't the Reign of Terror just a matter of internal French politics?

R.B.M. Only in part. The radicalization of the Revolution led the crowned heads of Europe to try to overthrow the new French government. In defense, the French sought to spread revolutionary doctrines abroad, and the Revolution became an imperialist threat to the peace of the rest of the world.

J.A.G. Americans were divided about the radical changes that were made internally in France. But were any real American interests threatened by these changes?

R.B.M. The United States was bound by treaty to defend the French West Indies, and there was also a question of whether we should, under the treaty, allow the French to equip privateers in American ports. That would have involved the nation in a world war. So it was a very big issue.

J.A.G. But isn't it true that those Americans who became anti-French did so largely because of the social changes that resulted from the Revolution, and because of the Terror? Did these really matter? If France had gone to war with England without having had a social revolution, the question of our defending the West Indies would surely have come up. Such a war was certainly possible, even likely, given the long history of Anglo-French conflict in the seventeenth and eighteenth centuries.

R.B.M. My feeling is that if France had gone to war with England without the French Revolution, the United States would have adopted the same principle of neutrality, but the emotional issue would have been played down. You are correct, however, to the extent that some Americans were willing to follow the French regardless of their twists and turns of policy because of their admiration for the Revolution, while others opposed France because they considered the Revolution abominable. After 1793, the Federalists felt that the French, because they were atheistic or communistic or whatever, were a danger to other nations.

At the same time, the Federalists were concerned about specific national interests. Washington and Jay, for example, were extremely levelheaded. They wanted the United States to keep out of the war. This meant they *had* to be pro-English, because the English didn't expect America to go into the war on their side. It was the French who sought American participation. The French interfered in American domestic politics, possibly even tried to overthrow the government. This aroused national sentiments and affronted American nationalism. The fact that there were people in the country who supported France raised the possibility that France could drive a wedge between American citizens and the government.

J.A.G.   To come back to Jefferson and Hamilton. In your opinion, which of these men had the soundest grasp of America's problems in that period?

R.B.M.   If you mean the immediate problems of the country, I think Jefferson was very fuzzy-minded. He lacked administrative talents as Secretary of State. He had no meaningful national program in the 1790's other than enlightened opposition. But when Jefferson accepted the responsibilities of office, he became a very effective President. He accomplished a considerable amount, and his failures were largely caused by events beyond the influence of any President of that time.

J.A.G.   Can you explain how men who have consistently demonstrated such a high regard for liberty and such a great fear of arbitrary government could have passed the Alien and Sedition Acts of 1798 and employed the Sedition Acts so ruthlessly during the presidential campaign of 1800?

R.B.M.   Well, we can consider this from two points of view. These revolutionary leaders had had their revolution. Everything was now "right." They didn't want anyone to spoil it. Only Jefferson, of all the revolutionary leaders, said a new revolution was necessary every twenty years, and he probably intended the remark as a joke. The Federalists didn't want another revolution, especially a *French* revolution. They thought that the radical foreigners who were coming into the country were trying to overthrow the "good" government they had created by the sweat of their brows. Thus old American revolutionaries were as opposed to revolutionary agitation as the present-day government in the Soviet Union is opposed to agitators in Red Square.

The second explanation is hysteria. Men overreacted to the dangers of invasion and subversion in the United States. A wave of chauvinism, nativism, and hysteria, plus the belief that the American government was libertarian and therefore no one had a right to overthrow it, explain the Alien and Sedition Acts. But one must also distinguish between the Pickering type of Federalist, the hotheaded extremists, and more levelheaded men like John Adams, who were much more temperate.

J.A.G.   How did the extreme partisan spirit associated with the Alien and Sedition Acts spring up so suddenly in a society that had so highly valued the Roman view of the role of the statesman and the public interest?

R.B.M.   The deterioration of the world situation which increasingly set off alarm bells after 1792—the meddling of Citizen Genet in American internal affairs, the Jay Treaty with Great Britain, and then the XYZ Affair, with its exaggerated tales of bribery—were all considered tremendous affronts to national honor. The young state was very proud. We were as touchy about national dignity as the citizens of, say, Guatemala, are today. Conservatives felt that the French were attempting to drag us into a world war, and at the same time affronting national honor and attempting to appeal over the head of the President to the people. Any American who appeared to countenance this subversion seemed virtually a traitor.

J.A.G. Was this foreign political controversy, and the unbridled criticism that was associated with it, the beginning of the end of the Golden Age of American statesmanship? In other words, did the rise of partisan politics lead to the decline of politics as an attractive career for outstanding people?

R.B.M. I think so, although most historians would more likely argue that the decline occurred in the Jacksonian period. But somewhere between 1797 and 1828 the appeal of government service slackened for men of wealth and status. Many of the old Federalists had had their fill of politics. These people had been in the public service from 1774 to the election of Jefferson in 1800; then they were thrown out on their ears. They felt that the country was very ungrateful. They'd gone through a lot of turmoil, been subject to libel and slander. Hamilton was hit on the head with a stone; John Jay burned in effigy. Such men were very thin-skinned; they were not used to "taking it" the way that politicians are expected to take it today. John Adams, after he was defeated in 1800, never thought of coming back. I think the decline of the Federalist party was due more to the fact that the Federalist leaders lost the will to fight than to the reasons that are generally used to explain it, such as that it was an old-fashioned, discredited party in a new era.

J.A.G. Yet the great figures of the Revolutionary period would have passed from the scene in any case. Did the new, bitter political partisanship discourage the outstanding men of the next generation from making politics a career?

R.B.M. I think so. I believe the killing of Hamilton in the duel with Aaron Burr, attributable to intemperate actions during an election campaign, was particularly unfortunate. Hamilton was a relatively young man who was snuffed out in midcareer. The horror and waste of it had considerable influence among the nation's elite.

J.A.G. John Adams has been justly praised for refusing to be stampeded into war with France in 1799. But why had a man of as much intelligence and force as Adams allowed control of policy to be taken out of his hands as President?

R.B.M. Adams had no conception of the President as a political leader; he didn't realize that a President must make policy in his own house first, be in command of his own cabinet. Despite all his sophistication, Adams was a political innocent. He invited his enemies to stay in the cabinet without even knowing they were his enemies. When he finally realized it, his wrath was unbounded and he kicked them all out. But it took him an awful long time. In those days, removing important officials was not considered proper. Since he had been Washington's successor, cabinet members, technically speaking, were his supporters, although in reality they opposed him. But I don't think Adams would have made these errors fifteen years later, if he had been President then.

J.A.G.   Would you assess the Federalists' contribution during the period 1789 to 1800?

R.B.M.   The Federalists made the nation. The entire fiscal program on which the credit of the United States was constructed was built under the Federalists. They gave the United States a breathing spell by keeping out of the European wars of their day. That was an enormous achievement.

J.A.G.   What were their weaknesses as a group?

R.B.M.   They didn't understand that the party system was emerging; they didn't build up party support from the grass roots. They felt that political organization was beneath them, that it was wrong to try to manipulate opinion. A leader should stand on the issues as an individual, not as a partisan. This approach, of course, proved totally ineffectual against the operations of Jefferson and Madison and the political machine that they created.

In the second place, the Federalists, having done their job, really had nothing more to offer. They had become more and more removed from the people. There was, by 1800, a need for a President who was closer to the common man and closer to common aspirations. The Federalists had an elitist view of government—not necessarily an undemocratic view, but certainly one not democratic in the same sense as Jefferson's and Madison's.

J.A.G.   What has been the impact of the so-called "New Left" interpretation of history on our understanding of this period?

R.B.M.   Curiously, not very great. New Left historians have attempted to get the common man into the American Revolution, to assess the role of mobs in shaping events. This work has not been of earth-shaking significance, but it adds another dimension to our knowledge. Secondly, there is the emphasis of the New Left on the issue of slavery. They claim to have discovered a sharper racial controversy at the time of the Constitutional Convention than I believe actually existed. Staughton Lynd argues that the Constitution represented a compromise on slavery. He relates, for example, the adoption of the Northwest Ordinance banning slavery from the land north of the Ohio to the various compromises of the Constitution made almost at the same time. By inference, he concludes that the North allowed the South to have slavery in the territory south of the Ohio in exchange. But he's not supported by the historical record, either in the debates or in private correspondence.

His argument is not entirely implausible, but I think he oversimplifies the matter. I still feel that the Upper South was prepared for the gradual abolition of slavery. The opposition to the slave trade at the Constitutional Convention was led by Virginians. If there had been a poll on the abolition of slavery in 1787, I think most of the Founding Fathers would have voted Yes, although they would have put off the effective date to some future time.

The New Left historians have also focused attention on the Negro in the American Revolution—the fact that Negroes fought on the patriots' side, and the less well-known fact that most Negroes were probably Tories. But I don't think the New Left has so far come up with a special interpretation of the Federalist period. I shall be interested in seeing what they make of it, for it seems to me that party issues were so polarized that they should find the Federalist period a happy hunting ground.

J.A.G. What are the half-dozen or so books that you would recommend to persons interested in the subject we have been discussing? In each case, would you indicate what the particular contribution of the volume is?

R.B.M. First of all, one would mention J. Franklin Jameson's *The American Revolution Considered as a Social Movement*. A series of provocative lectures, published in 1926, Jameson's book argues the thesis that the Revolution produced a greater democracy and social change, much of which transpired in what is technically called the post-Revolutionary years. This thesis has been re-examined, most recently in my *The American Revolution Reconsidered* (1967).

Secondly, in order to come to grips with the thesis advanced back in 1883 by John Fiske that the Confederation years constituted a "critical period," one must consider the reappraisal offered by two works of Merrill Jensen, *The Articles of Confederation* (1940) and *The New Nation* (1950), along with E. James Ferguson's *The Power of the Purse: a History of American Public Finance, 1776–1790* (1961). These relatively recent works suggest that the period was by no means chaotic, and that the states were taking constructive measures to assure fiscal stability.

As regards the framing of the Constitution, one must indubitably examine Charles A. Beard's challenging *An Economic Interpretation of the Constitution* (1913) with its depiction of the Founding Fathers as motivated by economic interests. Beard has been taken to task by Robert E. Brown, *Charles Beard and the Constitution* (1956), and at many points refuted by Forrest McDonald, *We the People: the Economic Origins of the Constitution* (1958), a study in depth of the interests of all who voted in the ratifying conventions in the several states.

Still the most original and illuminating pieces of research shedding exhaustive light on the diplomacy of the Confederation and Federalist periods are Samuel Flagg Bemis' *Jay's Treaty* (1923) and *Pinckney's Treaty* (1926), although Alexander De Conde's *Entangling Alliance* (1958) and *The Quasi War* (1965) add depth to our understanding of Franco-American relations in the administrations of Washington and Adams.

One could cite innumerable monographs covering this period, but the starting point henceforth for all students of these years will be the monumental publication projects devoted to the Founding Fathers, notably Julian Boyd's edition of *The Jefferson Papers* and the Syrett and Cooke edition of *The Hamilton Papers*. The editions of the Madison and Adams papers still do not run down far into the Confederation years, but they also give promise of providing an added dimension to our knowledge of the period. Lastly, one should mention the forthcoming edition of the papers of John Jay.

Richard Hofstadter

The Development of Political Parties

RICHARD HOFSTADTER, De Witt Clinton Professor of History at Columbia, has taken as his field the whole range of American political and intellectual history. Repeatedly, his books have caused historians to re-examine and modify their views of important issues; probably no living historian has won so many prizes for his work. Both his *Age of Reform*, a study of Populism and Progressivism (1955) and his *Anti-Intellectualism in American Life* (1963) won Pulitzer prizes. His *American Political Tradition* (1948), a series of essays on the great political leaders of the United States from the Founding Fathers to Franklin Roosevelt, was one of the first books to develop what has come to be called the "consensus" interpretation of American history. He has also written on the history of higher education and on American historiography, and is widely known as an essayist and lecturer. Currently, he is completing a study of the early history of political parties.

John A. Garraty Professor Hofstadter, it is clear from their writings that the Founding Fathers did not envisage the development of political parties, and that they considered rigid partisan alignments a threat to republican government. Why was this so?

Richard Hofstadter They had inherited this idea from the English; indeed, it was standard in Anglo-American thought in the eighteenth century. The English had had a good deal of experience with political parties, some of which, particularly in the seventeenth century, had been traumatic. The English thinkers of the early eighteenth century looked back on what they sometimes called the era of "the Great Parties" as a period of violence, of attainder for treason, of a troubled body politic. They sought instead a political order in which national unity and national harmony would prevail. Interestingly enough, this idea prevailed across a very wide political spectrum in eighteenth-century England. It was a view taken by Tory thinkers like Bolingbroke (who was very influential in America) and also by Whig dissenters (who were even more influential than Bolingbroke).

Distaste for parties also seemed to fit with their own experience. The rudimentary parties of the colonial period were sometimes very troublesome and productive of political chaos. It was common on both sides of the Atlantic to believe that parties were tools of unrestrained special interests, that they resulted in an unnecessary and dysfunctional amount of discord, and that they therefore threatened republican government. Either the disorder that they would create would lead to the rise of a tyrant, or some single interest would, by control of a party, dominate all the other interests.

J.A.G. Had the colonists' own experience with partisan politics actually been dysfunctional?

R.H. Except in New York and Pennsylvania, where rudimentary two-party systems were beginning to emerge toward the end of the colonial period, Americans hadn't had much experience with partisan politics in the modern sense, though there was a fair amount of troubled factionalism over *ad hoc* issues from time to time in all the colonies. Party government had not developed for a number of reasons. One was that there was no need for a highly developed party structure because it was not necessary to appeal to a large electorate. Party structures appear when what we might call the doorbell-ringing aspect of the party system emerges. With a very small electorate such as existed in the colonial period, the voters could be reached without elaborate structures. Colonial America was led by what some political theorists have called "notables," men who attracted a following because of what they *were*, and not because they took a particular stand on a consistent series of issues. Under these circumstances, parties could hardly get beyond the rudimentary stage of family factions and shifting *ad hoc* alliances. But there was another very important reason why party systems did not develop very much in the colonies, and that was the nature of the political conflicts that took place. Most conflicts occurred between the assemblies and the royal governors, and these fights had a tendency to unify the leading colonial factions. Hence they put a damper on divisions within the electorate.

J.A.G.   Does this explain why certain kinds of people became Tories during the Revolution?

R.H.   Of course, the governors always had their factions. But quite aside from attitudes toward this or that governor, loyalty to England was still strong as late as 1774 in a large range of the population. Also, various groups had material reasons to be loyal: certain types of merchants, members of the Anglican church, persons closely related to officialdom, and so on. Others, from force of habit, or out of settled conviction, felt that even though they sympathized with colonial grievances, striking for independence was going too far, and might endanger both property and liberty.

J.A.G.   You suggested that colonial factions never became rigid because they tended to coalesce behind the assembly against the governor. But wouldn't the royal authority, because of the patronage and influence it controlled, be able to attract large numbers of what in modern terminology we might call "fellow travelers"?

R.H.   Oh yes, in those days they were called the "court party." But it is also important to keep in mind that in an age which predates mass participation in politics, there were not many issues that required month-by-month and year-by-year discussion, or that parties and politicians take some kind of a stand. The issues were relatively limited; government consisted more of administration and less of politics in the eighteenth century than is true today.

J.A.G.   Why did the two-party system in American politics evolve so rapidly after Independence? Was it produced by the events of that particular time, or by the character of the new Constitution?

R.H.   A pattern of partisan division first emerged out of the issues posed by the Revolution, and became sharper and permanent with the issues posed by the Constitution. Although it was meant to create an institutional system which would check and control parties, in fact the Constitution stimulated the development of parties. National partisan division appeared first, of course, over resistance to Britain. Next came the fight over the Constitution itself in 1787–88, and then the rather rudimentary party division that was precipitated by Hamilton's financial system, which was an attempt to stabilize the new government and implement the Constitution.

J.A.G. Is it possible to generalize about the socioeconomic character of the Federalist and Republican parties in the 1790's?

R.H. I suppose it's always possible to generalize. Certainly, the Hamiltonian system had a great deal more appeal to mercantile elements, speculators, and others with liquid capital than it did to small farmers and to planters; that rather glib and old-fashioned generalization still holds up fairly well. Beyond that, I wouldn't care to generalize. Although we think of Virginia as being Antifederalist, even in the late 1790's when party divisions were most acute, about one-third of the Virginia Assembly was Federalist. In South Carolina, a similar situation existed. It has been suggested that those small farmers who were most involved in domestic and overseas trade tended to be more sympathetic to Federalism than the subsistence farmers. This was probably true enough. And of course there were regional political loyalties. New England had a special complex of attitudes and a different political culture from that of the southern states.

J.A.G. This is a particularly important question. If parties formed where none had existed before, people must have had reasons for joining one or the other; it could not have been, as it so often is in our own time, a matter of habit or family tradition. What made a person become a Federalist rather than an Antifederalist, or Republican?

R.H. Nobody was born a Federalist or a Republican in that generation; men had to find their allegiances, and I believe the determining influence, aside from the simple socioeconomic attributions that I have just stated, were their interests and their social position, feelings about authority and about economy, or frugality in government. Everyone who knows anything about the Revolution understands how strong was the popular feeling against taxation. This feeling constantly rumbled under the surface of American politics, and it was one of the things that split the Federalist party in the late 1790's. The Federalists' interest in a large Navy and Army became a great rallying point for Republicanism, chiefly because of the cost involved. Economy was central to Jefferson's program. Remember that he promised a "frugal" government, in his first inaugural address, not merely a wise one.

The question of authority goes back even further, because it relates to issues that were brewing all over the Western world in the eighteenth century. How far could a people go in stripping kingly and aristocratic government of prerogatives? How far toward republicanism, and even toward democracy (though that word wasn't used so much then), without risking the danger of anarchy? One can easily exaggerate the philosophical differences on the proper limits of authority between the average Federalist and the average Republican. All of them were Whigs; all believed in republican government, that government must rest on the consent of the governed, that there had to be a strong, popularly elected assembly in any "balanced" government. But they tended to differ on what might be called the spiritual intangibles in the political culture. There was a difference both in philosophy and in tone between the two parties. People with a bent toward authority found Federalism more comfortable. Those who felt that they were the carriers or inheritors of the Revolutionary republican impulse found themselves at home in the Republican party.

J.A.G. Do those generalizations apply equally to the two great figures of these parties—Hamilton and Jefferson? Have the differences between these two been exaggerated?

R.H. Not between them, but I think that the difference between their parties has been exaggerated. Hamilton was, I think, a somewhat unstable political thinker. At times, he seemed like a sort of moderately right-wing American Whig, and at other times he acted very much as Jefferson pictured him—a man completely infatuated with the English system, who was plotting to restore monarchy. Certainly, Hamilton felt that the national government had gone too far to the left. He even spoke of the Constitution a few years before his death as a "frail and worthless fabric." And there was always a faction of high Federalists who stood at least as far to the right as Hamilton. But there was also a large body of moderate Federalists. Despite the shrillness of the rhetoric of their leaders on the general problems of the structure of republican government, the two parties stood closer together than Hamilton and Jefferson themselves did.

What made the differences between the parties unnegotiable was not the structure of the Constitution, but the French Revolution and the events which followed it. In 1793, after all of the Hamiltonian measures had been either adopted or rejected, William Branch Giles of Virginia, the floor leader of the Jeffersonians, introduced a set of resolutions to repudiate Hamilton's conduct as Secretary of the Treasury, and he did not get nearly the full support of the Republican members of Congress. Some of the older historians in the Progressive tradition, such as Charles A. Beard, exaggerated the divisions by paying more attention to the rhetoric that attended the debates than to the actual votes. But in 1793, with the outbreak of the wars of the French Revolution, it became necessary to make foreign policy choices between the two great powers in Europe, France and England. What had thus far been a negotiable series of differences, of philosophy, of regional temperament, of economic interest, then became inflamed by issues that had both serious economic dimensions, and also grave ideological implications. Many Republicans remained sympathetic to what they considered the fundamental republican implications of the French Revolution, while the Federalists saw in the "excesses" of the Revolution an anarchy that presaged tyranny. The rise of Bonaparte confirmed their fear that the French Revolution was following the old classical political cycle, ending in tyranny, that had been laid down by Aristotle.

Thus three different kinds of forces converged: differences of economic interest that had already been made manifest by the Hamiltonian system; differences in foreign policy posed by the necessity of making choices between British and French commercial policies in wartime; and immensely inflammatory ideological issues.

J.A.G. Was there any significant group in America that really approved of the Terror, for example, or of the more extreme social reforms imposed under Robespierre in France?

R.H. No.

J.A.G. Then the pro-French point of view of Americans, seen ideologically, was emotional rather than logical?

R.H. Yes. And of course its intensity among the Republicans after a certain point was exaggerated by the Federalists. When the Federalists considered Jefferson an insane Francophile, Jefferson was perfectly capable of writing to one of his friends, in effect, we must clear ourselves from both European combatants and stand on our own ground as much as we can.

J.A.G. When we use the word "party" to describe Federalists and Republicans, are we really talking about organizations even remotely like modern political parties?

R.H. Remotely, certainly, particularly in the case of the Jeffersonians, who saw themselves as having a large popular constituency. The Federalists were accustomed to thinking of parties in the old-fashioned sense, with leadership resting on deference to men from the leading families—the mercantile and planter upper class. Being in possession of the government from the beginning, they did not develop the same kind of party structure that the Jeffersonians, being a party of opposition, rapidly began to create. The Federalists were a transition between the old colonial politics of leadership of notables and the modern party. The Republicans come much closer to the modern popular party with its elaborate structure in state and nation. Of course, as David Fisher has shown in *The Revolution of American Conservatism*, after their defeat in 1800, the Federalists began to realize how deficient they'd been in the development of a party organization and tried to copy the Jeffersonians, but they were too late.

J.A.G. You've several times mentioned "deferential politics." What do you mean by that term?

R.H. Deferential politics describes a social situation where leadership falls to people because they are notables, very often because of the kind of families they come from. It is a situation in which those who have the suffrage tend to vote for such men mainly because of who they are, not what they stand for. Deferential politics exists most comfortably where vital issues do not arise in the body politic, where there is a governing class with a sense of responsibility, and where political relations can be carried on face to face—where a leader can go out and meet with his constituency, and by his cordiality, his entertainment, his *noblesse*, command their deference. It breaks down, of course, when class antagonisms are acute, when the governing class is irresponsible, when social development removes face-to-face contacts, and when issues have to be decided as issues and not in terms of which men you have trust in.

J.A.G.   But haven't most political leaders in all periods of American history been drawn from the upper class, from men who command deference?

R.H.   There has always been a mixture of deference and issue politics in our society. Indeed, deference politics is coming back to some degree. The twentieth century has created a kind of well-to-do, second- or third-generation leader with inherited wealth, a feeling of *noblesse oblige*, and a glamorous reputation. The Harrimans, the Rockefellers, and the Kennedys are obvious examples. But there are also politicians who succeed not because the public defers to them, but because they defer to the public—men like Humphrey and Nixon fall into that category.

J.A.G.   If we are re-entering a deferential age, does television help explain why?

R.H.   Yes. Television creates a sense of personal relationship, and opens more opportunities for glamour to make itself felt.

J.A.G.   But doesn't the concept of deferential politics in the early national period create the false impression that it was replaced by a mass-democracy politics in the age of Jackson? Even then, the "common man" seldom ran for political office.

R.H.   No, he didn't. I think there are three basic reasons why one votes for a particular man. One is the deferential basis I've already defined; another is partisan identification; and the third is identification with issues. There's always a mixture of these going on in political life. But as time passed in the nineteenth century, with the development of machinery to reach a mass electorate, leadership in politics fell to people who were willing to make a full-time job of it: men who didn't have businesses to run and large fortunes either to manage or enjoy, small men coming out of the middle class, men who did not think it undignified to make placatory gestures and indulge in a kind of communion with the public. A Martin Van Buren did not think it was beneath him to seek popular support; a John Quincy Adams did.

J.A.G. Did the so-called "Jeffersonian Revolution" of 1800 change the character of the parties and the way campaigns were conducted?

R.H. Certainly, the character of political parties changed. The Jeffersonian party began to invade New England, and soon even reached the point where it could elect a governor of Massachusetts. It became a true national party, while the Federalists became a sectional party. But the most revolutionary thing about the Revolution of 1800 was that it was not a revolution. A transfer of power from one *popular* party to another here occurred for the first time in history, to my knowledge, without any upheaval. Of course there had been transfers of power in the English experience, but these did not involve popular parties in the American sense. This was a great step in the development of democracy. The chief of state was changed by popular vote, and neither side resorted to violence or secession.

J.A.G. What produced the Era of Good Feelings?

R.H. Two things, I think, produced the so-called Era of Good Feelings. One simply was the fact that one of the two parties had succeeded in knocking the other out of business. The other was a change in the nature of the issues. The parties had originally come into being over differences on the Hamiltonian system. These were intensified by the European wars. But the Hamiltonian system had been accepted by long usage, and the wars in Europe finally ended in 1815. Thus both the foreign and domestic issues disappeared after 1815 and American politics underwent an enormous adjustment while searching for new issues and new alignments.

J.A.G. What was unique about Jacksonian democracy? Do you see the Jacksonian Democratic party primarily as a political organization, or as a response to social changes in the United States? In other words, were the Jacksonians merely shrewd politicians who developed new techniques for interesting and organizing voters, or were they reformers concerned with rousing public interest in political affairs in order to effect social and economic changes?

R.H. There were so many kinds of Jacksonians that I'm reluctant to generalize about them. Also, I see no necessary alternative or disjunction between their being shrewd politicians with new techniques and at the same time reformers concerned with bringing about social and economic changes. Many of the Jacksonians were genuinely afraid of aggrandized power symbolized in the Second Bank of the United States, and they mobilized with great sincerity to attack the Bank. A lot of them were concerned about aggrandized federal power in general. Being admirers of Jackson, they didn't fear power in the President but in large expenditures by the federal government. But certainly, most of the Jacksonians who achieved national prominence were true politicians interested in developing the new techniques that had grown out of the partisan warfare of the previous generation.

J.A.G.   A number of recent writers have suggested that for some Jacksonians politics was a new, very exciting game rather than a way in which a public-spirited citizen could contribute to the working out of the national destiny. Was Jacksonian politics simply a new way of being a politician, rather than a new way of dealing with social and economic questions?

R.H.   It is correct to say that the Jacksonians began to see politics as a kind of game: they were quite articulate about this. But they didn't see it as a game without advantage to the public. They thought of the vocation of political leadership as a profitable occupation that earned its way, so to speak, by serving the public interest, and the contest of parties as of value to democracy. They reasoned that men who ran parties and who even sometimes surrendered their individual judgment in the interest of party solidarity were performing a valuable civic function, by providing instrumentalities through which citizens could be educated about political issues and through which they could express themselves.

Some historians find the Jacksonian Democrats always on the more democratic side of issues, but the question of how much more democratic or reforming the Democrats were than the Whigs is still open. Democrats tended to be interested in certain kinds of reforms—what we might call populistic reforms, of which the antibank issue was a perfect example. But there was a lot of interest in reform in the 1830's, and many humane social issues like antislavery and the abolition of imprisonment for debt were supported by many Whigs as well as Democrats.

J.A.G.   Did the Jacksonians really lower the tone of American politics? Did their techniques tend to drive intelligent and high-minded men out of political life?

R.H.   I think that they opened up political leadership to men of middle-class origins, and that men of aristocratic personal habits and convictions tended more and more to find politics distasteful. Tocqueville reports this, for example, in *Democracy in America*. But while the tone of politics in some respects deteriorated, we must not overstress the importance of tone as opposed to the gains that were being made. This new breed of politician had a solid grasp of the kind of machinery that was necessary, with all its faults, to democratic political life.

J.A.G.   Did Jackson and his followers invent the spoils system?

R.H.   No, but they invented the conscious and articulate defense of it. Washington appointed men to office who happened to agree with him. Since there were no clearly developed parties, no one could say that he was distributing spoils, but he certainly hoped to run the new government with men who had favored its being called into being in the first place, a not unreasonable strategy. Under Jefferson, there was a considerable turnover of personnel, and the Jeffersonians candidly admitted that they had to have a certain proportion of the public officers to maintain themselves as a party. The rhetoric of popular American history has often exaggerated the extent to which Jackson threw people out of office; his incursions weren't as great as they've sometimes been pictured. But the Jacksonians insisted that the spoils system was a good thing in itself. They believed that public offices should be so simplified and rationalized that the ordinary citizen would be capable of filling most of them, and that both democracy and efficiency would be served under this kind of system. They were wrong on the count of efficiency, but there is a lot to be said on their side so far as the element of democracy is concerned. If a party is a functional instrument of government, then it has to have loaves and fishes to keep itself going. The Jacksonians said this very candidly.

J.A.G. After about 1840, what were the differences between the Democrats and the Whigs?

R.H. So far as the style of party rhetoric and organization was concerned, the Whigs caught up with the Democrats in a way that the Federalists had failed to catch up with the Republicans after 1800. Indeed, in 1840 the Whigs got a step ahead of the Democrats in the famous "Tippecanoe and Tyler too" campaign, with their log cabins and parades and hard cider and so on. They developed political showmanship well beyond what the Democrats had been able to do, at least on a national scale. Of course, the Whig party still appealed more to the upper crust, and both North and South Whigs differed from Democrats philosophically in favoring the diffusion of political power. They looked askance at centralized leadership in the presidency, even taking their name from the Whig opponents of royal tyranny in England in the eighteenth century. The Whig party remained more than the Democratic the party of protective tariffs, and it was distinguishable from its enemy on other issues.

J.A.G. Can you explain the persistence, after 1836, of the Whig belief in a weak executive? It's easy to see it as a response to Jackson's particular temperament and power, but how could it have survived when all of the experience of the United States before 1840 and after has shown how important a strong executive is to effective government?

R.H. The Whigs were really following the line of the Jeffersonians. Belief that an excessively strong executive was a menace to the country was thoroughly American. It took the form under the Articles of Confederation of a plural executive, and the resistance to a powerful executive at the Constitutional Convention was counteracted only by the enormous authority and prestige of George Washington. People on both sides of the political fence were worried when the Constitution was adopted that the President would combine the functions of being leader of the national government and leader of a party. This was considered to be a danger by most of the Founding Fathers.

What happened to the presidency under Jackson was that a tremendously arbitrary and self-willed man had to confront two important crises—nullification and the Bank issue. This combination brought out the full latent power of the office. But it is worth noticing that, while one may say that the Democrats have inherited from Jefferson and Jackson a preference for a strong President, there were really few strong Presidents after Jackson. The machinery of American politics conspired to keep the executive fairly weak, except in crises, and most Americans seemed to think that this was a good idea. Looking back with the experience of Presidents like Jackson and Lincoln and Wilson and the two Roosevelts in mind, we may think that the strong President is the good President, but put yourself in the place of a man of the 1830's and I think you can understand the Whig fondness for a relatively weak executive.

J.A.G. Perhaps I can make my point better by avoiding the words "weak" and "strong." Why did the Whig party tend to pick presidential candidates who had relatively little political experience, who were not associated with issues, and who could presumably be manipulated by the politicians? I do not think this tendency existed in the Democratic party.

R.H. It was certainly characteristic of the Whigs, but if you put aside Jackson, who was an extraordinary man in an extraordinary situation, wasn't it also true of the Democrats? Even Polk, who was strong-willed, and who got his way because he was able to precipitate a war crisis, was certainly not nominated with the expectation that he would be a powerful President. Remember the slogan that was raised by his opponents in the 1844 campaign: "Who is James K. Polk?" He was a seasoned and experienced politician, but he had never made any particular mark for himself.

J.A.G. On balance, does Jackson rate inclusion in a list of great Presidents? What were his virtues and defects as a statesman and political leader?

R.H. Well, I'm not one of Jackson's greatest admirers. In the Bank controversy, for example, I don't think he understood what he was dealing with and made himself the tool of forces that were, at best, not particularly constructive. It is obvious that he had the qualities of great leadership; whether he put them to good use is the question. He shows up best in the Nullification crisis, where he attacked South Carolina's resistance to federal authority, even though he had considerable sympathy for the states'-rights position, when it threatened the government of which he was the sworn custodian. He opposed dissident force, yet was amenable to substantive measures which appeased the dissidents.

J.A.G. John C. Calhoun is generally regarded as a political thinker of some stature, at least by American standards. What is your opinion of him as a politician?

R.H. Calhoun had a hard row to hoe as a politician. As everyone knows, politics is the art of the possible, but Calhoun, as time went on, addressed himself increasingly to the impossible. He can be criticized for that, but it is somewhat unfair to judge a man for not realizing what is impossible. He had great ability as an administrator, but I personally believe that his stature as a political thinker has been overrated. As a politician, he was not particularly adroit, even granting that what he was trying to do—defend the interests of a minority (the South) and also become President—was impossible. He was deficient in the arts of appeasement and negotiation, arts which any politician who wants to become an intersectional or interclass leader must possess. He became increasingly narrow in his views, and seems not to have thought through the implications of this for his personal career, though he did think through the implications for the South.

J.A.G. Can any case be made for some of his ideas—for example, the concepts of Nullification and the Concurrent Majority—as practical solutions to early nineteenth-century sectional problems?

R.H. I don't think so. The idea of the Concurrent Majority was really an argument for a minority veto, and I don't really see how a large nation could function on that basis. In a complex, pluralistic society, a minority has the power to persuade, to convert, to make alliances and coalitions to achieve its goals. That is about all a minority should be encouraged to think feasible.

J.A.G. But what about Nullification? Given a federal system, given a nation which in Calhoun's day really didn't have a national economy in the modern sense, can it not be argued that a system which allowed a state to have its own set of rules within a particular area was fair and reasonable? After all, Nullification would always involve a specific measure. Is it not possible to see Nullification as a way to preserve harmony in a decentralized society?

R.H. How could one state nullify a tariff law and expect it to be enforced in all the others? It seems to me that Nullification would not work in just those areas where it was likely to be invoked.

J.A.G. Consider the tariff. If South Carolina had been allowed to nullify the tariff on cotton textiles, this would not have permitted textiles to enter the rest of the United States without paying the duties. Theoretically at least, under Calhoun's system, if cotton textiles were imported into Charleston and then reshipped to New York or the West, they would fall under the provisions of the tariff law as soon as they crossed the South Carolina border.

R.H.   Nullification may have been feasible as an economic proposition, but I suppose that if it was accepted as a governing principle, other states would have nullified other federal measures and the national government would have collapsed.

J.A.G.   To what extent did partisan political rivalry contribute to the breakup of the Union in 1861? Did it play a major role in leading to secession, or did it perhaps delay secession?

R.H.   I would say that the existence of intersectional parties delayed secession. The Union did not break up until both major parties had divided and until the presidency came into the hands of a political leader who was the head of a purely sectional party. There is no point in blaming political rivalry for the breakup of the Union. The very genuine conflict over moral and economic issues which neither party was capable of solving produced the Civil War.

Partisan political rivalry became a divisive factor because issues emerged that the political culture was not capable of resolving. In judging party systems, we often fail to distinguish between the weaknesses of the party systems and those of the culture as a whole. I think the party system was the strongest element in American political life before the Civil War. It ought not to be blamed for the breakdown of national institutions. One could make out a very good case for the argument that the United States has been well governed only during relatively brief stretches of its history. But I do not think this was because the two-party system is inadequate. Rather, the difficulty has been that we have had a lot of extremely serious problems—slavery and racial prejudice, the task of developing a huge continent, coping with the great nations of Europe, the whole business of absorbing thirty-five million immigrants. These problems would tax any political culture. We've failed to perform with great distinction, but my disposition is to defend the party system, whether under two parties or more, and partisan rivalry as being structurally essential to a good working democracy.

J.A.G.   What were the effects of the Civil War on the political system, and on the character of political parties?

R.H.   First of all, the parties developed new constituencies. The Democrats relied on the solid South, certain urban pockets, and commercial interests that favored low tariffs; the Republicans on northern farmers, most manufacturing interests, and the Negro. But I don't think that the fundamental character of the party system as opposed to party alignments was profoundly affected by the war. Obviously, the Thirteenth, Fourteenth, and Fifteenth Amendments produced a drastic shift in the direction of national power. But the nation continued, in the main, to elect weak executives, and the two parties maintained a very close balance of power. Politics continued to be fairly excitable, but became very low key so far as issues were concerned. The Civil War had a traumatic effect upon the public attitude toward political conflict. The election of 1876 was in effect stolen by the Republicans, yet consider the relative public calm in which that tremendously controversial issue was worked out. The voters knew that not much was really at stake between Hayes and Tilden, between the Democrats and the Republicans. They'd had a surfeit of political conflict.

The postwar era certainly was not a time we can look back at with admiration for the tone and character of political life. But it was not a period of singularly low competence as compared with the 1850's, or with the period from 1805 to 1812, which was marked by incredible fumbling and governmental incompetence. As I said, there have been lots of low points in our political history. The corruption of the 1870's and 1880's was no doubt harmful, but many more harmful things have happened.

One other point should be made. Despite the close balance between the parties nationally, large areas of the country did not really have a two-party system. Many states were either overwhelmingly Republican or overwhelmingly Democratic. Whatever the merits of two-party government are, they were lacking in most of the South, in New England, and elsewhere. Many of the serious failings of the political system in this period resulted not from having too much of party rivalry, but too little.

J.A.G.   Did the reform of the civil service and the modification of the spoils system after 1883 affect the organization of parties and the conduct of political affairs?

R.H.   I doubt that civil-service reform affected the organization of the parties very profoundly. A considerable number of federal posts were liberated from partisan control, but plenty were left to provide party workers with offices. It has been said that when the parties were deprived of the spoils, they became increasingly dependent upon the largesse of big businessmen and corporations and that this led to business control of political organizations. I'm doubtful about that. The number of great corporations and of millionaires proliferated enormously after the Civil War, and it was this development, not the civil-service system, that caused the influence of business in politics to grow.

One of the most notable aspects of civil-service reform was that it was not of much concern to men who sought major changes in American society. It was the issue of an educated, high-minded stratum of the public that felt that certain values (order, efficiency, economy in government) were being flouted. It was a very narrow issue, without much mass appeal. It took the assassination of President Garfield to get the Civil Service Law passed.

J.A.G. Can you explain, then, why the politicians responded with such vituperation to the concept of civil-service reform?

R.H. Some of them were pretty coarse fellows; they reacted to challenges to doing things their way. It was a conflict over values and roles, really, rather than over any fundamental problem. Just as Mugwump gentlemen felt that intelligence and merit were being by-passed by the spoils system, so the politicians felt that they were being looked down on by overeducated, "effeminate" types. It's a rather interesting controversy because of the way in which personal values got projected into a political argument, but I don't thilnk it really touched the fundamental problems of the period.

J.A.G. The late nineteenth century was certainly a time when the office of the President was at a relatively low point in power and prestige. Then, beginning with Theodore Roosevelt, a very significant percentage of the Presidents were strong and powerful leaders. Can you explain why this change occurred?

R.H. This is a very interesting phenomenon. I've already touched on the fact that we have had few executives of really outstanding prestige and power. You can exhaust them without using up the fingers of one hand before the end of the nineteenth century, and then, suddenly, came a whole string of them. Two tendencies were at work here. The President is the only figure in our national government who has, by the very nature of his office, a national constituency. Under the modern welfare state, the federal government has taken over an increasing number of functions of great import for the nation as a whole. Strong Presidents like Wilson and Theodore Roosevelt came in, not surprisingly, in the Progressive era when government began to deal increasingly with issues of sweeping significance. Furthermore, the weak executive was a product of national insulation. With the development of America as a world power, foreign relations became far more important, and the chief executive, who must of necessity call the tune in foreign affairs, gained ascendancy by way of his strategic position. Most recently, because of the Vietnam experience particularly, liberals are worrying about the possibility that the presidency is getting too strong. This is a new note, a response to twentieth-century conditions.

J.A.G. Looking at political history from the ratification of the Constitution to the beginning of the twentieth century, was political partisanship a constructive force in the national life?

R.H. I think it was, on balance, a force for good. Obviously, political partisanship can create false issues, develop dysfunctional rivalries, make social trouble. But in a democratic political system, the point at which the common man exerts influence in government is when he votes, and he votes with meaning when he has parties to choose between. Along with the party rivalry comes misrepresentation, exaggeration, distortion; but at the same time, the parties find issues and put them in a form in which citizens can pass on them. The job of leaders is to refine the macroscopic judgments of the public into reasonable policies. It's hard to see how this function can be performed without parties.

There is no doubt that American parties have tended to blur issues. Whether this is a good thing or a bad thing depends on the particular issue. Slavery was a different kind of issue from the protective tariff. The demand for sharpness and clarity in the posing of issues can be overstressed. Surely, a different kind of a party system might have exacerbated social conflicts more than ours has. The parties should not be viewed from two perspectives at once. We should not charge them with stirring up hostility in the body politic by their rhetorical excesses, and on the other hand say that they blunt and soften issues in the effort to achieve a wide following. Remember also that the American party system contains lesser planets, the third parties that sometimes come into being and go into orbit about the major ones. They perform a valuable function in taking issues that the major parties have fudged and, by focusing attention on them, forcing the hand of one or both of the major parties.

What our parties characteristically do is to feel their way toward a consensus on issues. Take social security, for example. That issue was agitated for a long, long time by a limited stratum of reformers. Finally, much too late from the standpoint of the suffering that was caused by the delay, the Democrats took it up in the 1930's and enacted it into law. Now it has become a basic aspect of our way of living: only a very small number of people question it. To make a large change like social security requires an overwhelming majority. An innovation adopted by a narrow margin is likely to be divisive.

A constitutional consensus, which has to do with basic rules of doing the nation's business, has to exist at all times if you're going to have a stable political order. A policy consensus is something that the parties, by their seesaw operations, gradually arrive at. But parties do differ. They may not differ as night from day, but some of the issues they pose are clear enough to enable a thinking citizen to make a rational choice between them at most points in history.

J.AG. What was distinctively American about the American political system, and what was merely an American reflection of the trend toward democracy and republicanism that was characteristic of all Western society in the nineteenth century?

R.H. Your word "reflection" helps to get at the answer to this question. America was the *avant garde* in the development of political democracy, and in a double sense. First, in the development of mass suffrage. A very high proportion of the adult male population was voting in the 1820's and 1830's, whereas mass participation in politics wasn't realized in England until the late 1860's and 1870's. The same thing was true of the development of the party system. In spite of the example of the Whigs and Tories of England in the eighteenth century, the Americans developed the first popular parties. Once this wide public had to be reached, machinery to reach them had to be developed. America was also in the *avant garde* in developing the egalitarian sentiments which provided a moral or temperamental *ambiance* for the suffrage. Of course, all the Europeans were thoroughly aware of this; sometimes they marveled at it, and sometimes they intensely disliked it.

J.A.G. What are the half-dozen or so books that you would recommend to persons interested in the subject we have been discussing? In each case would you indicate briefly what the particular contribution of the volume is?

R.H. Histories of the various parties are too numerous to mention here, although, oddly enough, neither of the two major parties has had a general history that could be called definitive. A good general discussion of parties may be found in Austin Ranney and Wilmoore Kendall, *Democracy and the American Party System* (1956). There are many illuminating essays on modern and contemporary parties in Norman L. Zucker, ed., *The American Party Process* (1968). The first party system, from the Revolution to 1809, is the subject of William N. Chambers, *Political Parties in a New Nation* (1963). Richard P. McCormick traces the formation of parties in the Jackson era, and provides a great deal of detail on party development in the states in *The Second American Party System* (1966). William N. Chambers and Walter D. Burnham, eds., *The American Party Systems* (1967) is a set of important essays on the development and the functions of parties in the United States. Robert A. Dahl, ed., *Political Oppositions in Western Democracies* (1966), puts the American pattern in a comparative perspective.

Stuart Bruchey

Economic Growth and Change to 1860

$\mathbb{S}$TUART W. BRUCHEY, Allan Nevins Professor of History at Columbia, is noted for his broad grasp of American economic history in the pre-Civil War era. His *Roots of American Economic Growth* (1965) is a synthesis of a great mass of highly technical monographic material on economic history, while his *Robert Oliver: Merchant of Baltimore* (1956) is a detailed study based on Oliver's business records. He has edited *Cotton and the Growth of the American Economy* (1967) and other collections of documents. He serves also as general editor of the Allan Nevins reprint series in economic history, published by the Columbia University Press. The discussion ranges over the whole course of American economic development from the early colonial period to the Civil War, and calls special attention to the great variety of new insights that economic historians have arrived at in recent years.

John A. Garraty   Professor Bruchey, it is frequently said that from the earliest colonial times America was a land of economic opportunity. But we also know that from the beginning, life in the colonies was hard and everyone was dependent economically on England. Was colonial America really a land of opportunity?

Stuart Bruchey   There is an element of truth and an element of boosterism in that statement. To take the latter first, people whose interest it was to attract settlers naturally spoke in sanguine terms about the life to be expected here, but on the other hand, the element of truth ought not to be overlooked either. In some very cunning passages in his *Wealth of Nations*, Adam Smith refers to that element of truth. Whenever there is a paucity of settlers in a new land of abundant resources conditions favor the settlers. Their opportunities for a life of plenty are much superior to those of populations that press against a scarcity of land.

We have to recognize, however, that this was not immediately so. Although the Virginia Company had sent out 5,000 settlers by 1625, in that year only some 400 remained alive. Life was not easy in the beginning. Efforts had been made to find commercial crops, which could be exchanged for manufactures and other goods that were not available in the colonies.

By the 1660's, the economy was solidly established. I recall reading a sermon that the Reverend John Higginson gave in Boston at that time, in which he said that the people were far better off than they had any right to expect to be. With the expanded cultivation of commercial crops, particularly of tobacco in the South, and with the growth of fishing in the North, and the hunting of fur-bearing animals and whales, there occurred an expansion and diversification of economic activity which added greatly to the rude sufficiency of the early years.

Although one must remember the differences between the experiences of some people in some parts of the colonies and other people in other parts, in general the first century was one of experiment: in governmental forms, in accommodation with the Indians, in learning to use the native crops of America. As time passed one would expect that growing familiarity, growing adjustment, would make for a situation of increasing ease. Certainly, by the late 1690's a New England merchant like Colonel William Pepperell enjoyed a great deal more than mere self-sufficiency. And by 1743 we find Benjamin Franklin observing, in his call for the formation of the American Philosophical Society, that the first stage of founding or settling new colonies was now pretty well past and that in all of the provinces many persons lived in circumstances that set them at ease.

J.A.G. Could such prosperity have been maintained without the constant infusion of new capital from England?

S.B. This is a subject we know relatively little about. In the seventeenth century, settlers were inclined to bring considerable capital with them. But those who stayed behind also provided important capital in the form of credit for goods.

J.A.G. If at any time during the first century and a half of America's development an iron curtain had been dropped down the middle of the Atlantic between Europe and America, could the economy of America have prospered?

S.B. What you're really asking is the extent to which American prosperity depended upon foreign trade, and particularly trade with England. So far as the colonies were able to enjoy levels of living superior to the rude necessities provided by self-sufficient farming, they did so through trade. European commerce made a very important contribution to growth. Douglas North and his student Gary Walton have studied productivity change in shipping during the colonial period. Important productivity gains were realized, largely because of the increased security against piracy (which made it possible to dismantle the guns that ships used to carry). With that great stress on the structure relieved, it was possible to build larger vessels, and this increased the load factor—the proportion of freight in relation to dead weight. So that there was an increase of productivity here. Shippers could also dispense with soldiers on board vessels, and this reduced costs. The second factor contributing to increased productivity was the widening of markets, which made it possible for vessels to make more trips each year than they previously had been able to make.

J.A.G. Is it possible to conceive of colonial economic growth in anything like the terms we associate with the late nineteenth or even the early nineteenth century?

S.B. Growth certainly took place, but its sources differed, at least in part, from those of the later periods you mention.

J.A.G. Were there no substantial technological improvements in shipping, for instance?

S.B. No. Apparently not.

J.A.G. Granted that the economy grew larger, did it grow more intensively? Was there any substantial improvement in the efficiency of the individual argricultural worker?

S.B. Let me try to answer that question in general terms by talking about the problem of economic growth. The statistics upon which reliable estimates of per capita income can be based really date from about 1869, and sketchy evidence makes it possible to extrapolate, so to speak, estimates back to 1834. The economist Paul David has pushed the lamp of learning farther against the darkness and gone back to 1800, in a series of what he calls "controlled conjectures."

But when it comes to the eighteenth century (to say nothing of the seventeenth), we have problems of a different order. Although fragmentary statistics have survived, they are so scattered, so piecemeal, that they do not serve as an adequate proxy for the total value of goods and services produced. Furthermore, since a great deal of economic activity took place within the home and was for use rather than for market sale, the problem of estimating production is a very difficult one.

There have been some rather brave Promethean efforts to estimate the rate of growth in the eighteenth century. George Taylor has gone on record as estimating that the rate of growth from about 1720 to the end of the colonial period may have been as much as 1 percent a year.

J.A.G. A rate of growth of 1 percent seems rather slow for an area where so many new people were settling and where the amount of land under cultivation was increasing.

S.B. You can double the beginning total in less than a century by proceeding at the rate of 1 percent. It seems very small, yet its cumulative effects were quite impressive. From about 1840 to 1960, the average annual rate of growth was 1⅝ percent. So that when Taylor hypothesizes a 1-percent rate of growth, at an earlier period, he is really not talking about a very small sum.

J.A.G. Will you describe the character of the American economy in the middle of the eighteenth century?

S.B. It was overwhelmingly an agricultural economy of course, even as late as 1790. Almost nine out of every ten people were still engaged in farming activity. In New England, in addition to self-sufficent farming, there was a great deal of fishing, and even some tobacco growing. Livestock, particularly horses, and hogs, were raised, but these were relatively small in comparison with the importance of fishing, and, of course, trading.

The middle colonies were largely engaged in grain production, and the South was committed mainly to the growth of tobacco and indigo, although naval stores and hides also figure among the exports of that region. In general, the products of the South were very much wanted by England, and they were enumerated, that is to say, listed among those goods which could be shipped only to the mother country. The problem of paying for British manufactures was therefore quite simplified for Southerners. Often, the very vessel that came from England with manufactured goods loaded tobacco on board for the return trip. So far as the New England colonies were concerned, however, roundabout trade had to be engaged in if those colonies were to obtain British goods. They lacked commodities to exchange directly in the way that the South could make direct exchange. And so their task was to engage in trade.

J.A.G.   Do you mean that the New Englanders were essentially middle-men carrying other people's products from one place to another?

S.B.   Well, no. They carried some of their own, fish and lumber, for example, and they carried rum which they had themselves distilled from the molasses imported from the West Indies. They sold the rum in Africa, exchanging it for slaves, which they took to the West Indies. From the West Indies they brought back molasses, sugar, and bills of exchange. This "triangular trade" is much emphasized in most text-books. Actually, there were many angles of the trade, and coastal trade was also very important. It was a kind of shuttling trade between ports.

J.A.G.   Is the traditional distinction between the middle colonies and the New England colonies of much real significance?

S.B.   The middle colonies were the breadbasket of British America, but conditions in the middle colonies were similar to those in New England in that, as a rule, their products were not wanted in England. Grains were no more wanted in England than fish. In this sense, both areas confronted a similar problem of exchanging the products of their region for those which were wanted in England.

J.A.G.   How did these differences within the economies of the colonies affect social structure?

S.B.   I think economy and society are intimately related. Although the whole question of colonial social structure is one we know far too little about, it's certainly a fascinating area for investigation. The work of Aubrey C. Land is particularly important in this connection. Land discovered that the laws of Maryland required a probating of the personal estate of every freeman at his death. He examined these records from 1690 to about 1760, and classified the freemen of Maryland in accordance with the valuation given their personal property. He found that in the decade 1690–1700 approximately 74 percent owned personal property valued at less than £100. Those owning property valued at between £100 and £500 amounted to 22 percent of the population, and those who owned property worth more than £1,000 made up only about 1½ percent. The economic elite, in the early period, was a very small proportion of the total. Interestingly enough, in the period 1730–1740, which is the cut-off date for his published results so far, the 74 percent had declined to 55 percent; the 22 percent in the category of the £100 to £500 increased to 36 percent, and there was approximately a doubling to about 3.6 percent in the very wealthy group. Although Land's study ignores landed property, being merely an evaluation of personal property, it indicates the increasing well-being of the majority of the people in Maryland.

One of the things that emerged from Land's study is particularly important in expanding our understanding of the lives of the wealthier planters. He found them not only engaged in the growing of tobacco, but also engaged in money lending, in mining, in manufacturing, in multiple activities. Older views had tended to treat the planters as essentially not interested in the market. But Land finds them very much interested in increasing their income through diversified forms of economic activity. There was surely a maritime gentry in Maryland; it was comparable to the maritime gentries that Carl Bridenbaugh discovered in many of the ports which he wrote about in his studies of colonial cities. Of course you also find a rural gentry, for example, the Blands and the Lees—one could call the roll for some time in Virginia. The great question remaining is whether or not the number of people at the opposite end of the scale could rise easily from the lower levels of well-being to higher levels. For the Revolutionary period, the recent studies of Jackson Turner Main are very valuable, but we have not had comparable quantitative studies of the colonial period.

J.A.G. Is it possible to generalize about the social effects of the economic differences which developed in the colonies, especially the differences between the northern group and the southern?

S.B. It's very difficult to generalize about social structure, not only in the colonial period but in later periods.

Our thoughts about social structure in the early nineteenth century, for example, are coated over with the easy generalities of Tocqueville, who left us a picture of an egalitarian society, one of small distance between man and man. It's very difficult to disabuse popular opinion of this view. We have traditionally seen the colonial social system as one in which an aristocracy dominated the political and economic life of both the seaboard and the rural areas. But the work of Robert E. Brown has made an important contribution, in that it calls attention to a basic set of differentiating circumstances in the country that made it unlike the situation of Europe. Again I return to the difference of the land/man ratio. People had a greater opportunity to rise than they had in Europe, and therefore the European social categories were less meaningful when transplanted to this side of the Atlantic.

On the other hand, we don't yet have the quantitative studies of immigrant lists, of taxes, of wills, and of other sources to enable us to say with precision what percentage of a given group rose from one level to another level. There was a seaboard elite, mannered, elegant, wealthy, although we are not talking in terms of millionaires. Samuel

Eliot Morison, in his *Maritime History of Massachusetts,* tells us that Thomas Boylston, with $400,000, was the wealthiest colonist. There was a wealthy gentry, urban and rural, and they can be named and identified in all of the colonies. There was also an urban poor. Poorhouses existed in the early eighteenth century, perhaps before. My own tentative persuasion in this matter is that regardless of how many poor people lived in the cities, the cities themselves accommodated a relatively small part of the total population. Thus the amount of poverty in the country must have been comparatively limited.

J.A.G. You haven't said anything about slavery. Ignoring for a moment at least the moral aspects of the subject, did the existence of slavery have any effect on regional social and economic conditions? For example, was the Southern slave seen simply as an economic man, in a different economic position from the small New England farmer?

S.B. Oh, of course, without question. The difficulty here is that most historians have not emphasized the presence of the slave as an element of colonial society. Slaves have been thought of in terms of capital investment, and the problem of whether or not an egalitarian or deferential social structure existed in the colonial period has been attacked not in terms of the acknowledged deference of slaves to their masters, but of the poor, or less influential, whites to the well-to-do elite.

J.A.G. When Aubrey Land writes that in the 1690's 74 percent of the people he was studying had less than £100 of personal property, was he including the slaves of Maryland?

S.B. No, only the estates of freemen were assessed.

J.A.G. Did Land, in arriving at his conclusions, include the value of the slaves as property?

S.B. Yes, only landed property was excluded.

J.A.G. What would have happened to the American economy if there hadn't been a revolution? If the colonies had submitted to British policies after 1763, would they have suffered economically?

S.B. This is a fascinating question and one that historians can't avoid. It has two aspects. One has to do with whether or not the British Acts of Trade and Navigation imposed costly burdens upon the American economy which the Revolution removed, thus permitting a more free and rapid development. The second has to do with whether or not acts of the *American* government contributed to a subsequently higher rate of growth in a way which would have been impossible without sovereign power to enact this legislation.

Some years ago, Lawrence Harper attempted to discover whether or not the British Acts of Trade were burdensome. He concluded they were, and established both upper and lower estimates of the amount of that burden. The upper limit was $7,000,000 and the lower one $2,500,000.

To reach these figures, he took into account, for example, the cost involved in the requirement that tobacco be shipped to the British Isles rather than directly to the Continent. This prevented the tobacco growers from realizing income. He pointed out that even his lower estimate, admittedly a small sum in comparison with modern-day budgets, came to within 16¢ per capita of meeting all the costs of the federal government in the last six years of Washington's administration.

Recently, the economic historian Robert Paul Thomas has made a comparable quantitative estimate of the burden of British legislation, and has come up with a figure very close to the lower estimate of Harper. Thomas, however, emphasized the smallness of his figure, which, he said, amounted to about 54¢ of each $100 of per-capita income in the colonies; in other words, had the Navigation Acts not been on the statute books, the rate of growth would have been only one-half of 1 percent a year more rapid than it was.

But both of these efforts are inadequate, because the relationship between the colonies and the mother country had numerous aspects involving costs and benefits which are very difficult to assign quantitative values to. For example, the security provided by the British fleet had to be provided by American arms and vessels after independence. The value of free trade with the mother country and the British West Indies and all the other benefits of membership in the British Empire were surrendered after independence.

When we come to the positive side of the question, we are on even more fragile and difficult ground. To begin with, the annual rate of growth in this country from about 1790 to 1860 probably averaged about 1.3 percent; the economy did not develop at a more rapid rate following independence, not even in association with the undeniable industrialization and urbanization that ensued, particularly during and after the 1820's. Therefore, if we do not have statistically viable evidence of more rapid growth in the sixty or seventy years following independence, is it not pretty hard to maintain that independence made a positive contribution? Yet I would maintain it. Independence made possible legal actions which probably would not have been possible before. Only a half-dozen business corporations were created during the entire colonial period, yet, between independence and 1800, more than three hundred were chartered. It is my hypothesis that the growth in the economy alone could not account for such a vast increase in a mere seventeen years. The shift from the executive to the legislative arm of government explains these corporate charters; legislatures, being much more sensitive to community desires, enacted these charters. It is interesting, for example, that fully two-thirds of them provided for improved transportation, a vital necessity in most regions. Most charters issued before the Civil War were quasi- public in nature, and created corporations involved in furnishing transportation—turnpikes, canals, bridges, and so on.

Now these are forms of social overhead capital investment. I have a strong feeling that generations which foot the bills for such investments themselves forego rising standards of living, but make it possible for subsequent generations to enjoy them. Just as innovations beginning at a particular point in time and in a particular sector of the economy must work their way from industry to industry, firm to firm, and region to region, before they can achieve their effects, so the building up of the social overhead of an economy requires time before economic activity so generated can produce its effect. If canals are built, it takes time for people to use them, to go out and settle new areas, get them into production, and ship their surplus produce back over the canal to market. And if one multiplies these lapses by the numbers of canals and turnpikes and railroads, one can understand why the enjoyment of the benefits of social overhead capital is delayed.

Therefore, despite the length of time that elapsed between the enactment of the legislation made possible by independence and the increase in the rate of economic growth, the importance of legal freedom must not be discounted. Furthermore, the period between independence in 1783 and 1860 seems to us now very long, largely because the period between 1860 and the present is comparable in length. When we back off from this period and view it in greater perspective, as we would a comparable period during the Middle Ages, I suspect the hypothesis will seem more reasonable.

Corporations, of course, are created by state action; at the level of the federal government also, very important legislation was passed. A Constitution which forbade the states to place obstacles in the way of the free movement of people and goods and capital from state to state did not create a national market, but provided the legal foundations for that market and probably prevented America from breaking up into a number of national states, with tariff walls and other obstacles to the free movement of goods and people and capital. It would have been very difficult for industry to enjoy the benefits of large-scale production without a national market. The American "common market" of the nineteenth century was one of the outstanding reasons for the economic growth of the nation.

J.A.G. Was the so-called "critical period" actually a time of serious economic trouble?

S.B. In the 1880's John Fiske fastened that sobriquet upon the 1780's. Without question, he drastically exaggerated the extent of the discontent and the degree of the economic malaise. He wrote "without fear and without research," but, if he grew a popcorn from a kernel of truth, the decade did indeed have serious economic problems. The only question really is whether or not they add up to a justification for the calling of the Constitutional Convention. That is the unspoken issue behind current historical investigation of the economy of the United States in the 1780's. Some authorities, such as Merrill Jensen, disagree with John Fiske, and argue that the economy was getting along very well in the early "experimental" period, and that under the Articles of Confederation the new government confronted its problems effectively.

The most recent work on the economy of the 1780's by Gordon Bjork seeks to reconstruct a series of trade figures for all the states. His general conclusion, which reinforces Jensen's position, is that 1784–85 were years of depression, but that by 1787 the economy was out of the doldrums and well on its way to the wave of prosperity that washed the new Constitution into wide acceptability.

Albert Fishlow, in a telling criticism, argues that Bjork exaggerated the gains made by American tobacco planters that resulted from their ability to sell directly in European markets, and that this led him to exaggerate the general improvement. But when this modification is taken into account, it seems that things weren't quite as bad as Fiske claimed. The economy was going through an experimental stage. The real question in my mind is the adequacy of the economic nexus in an effort to account for the movement for the Constitution. I think the movement was very complex, involving many more elements than the economic, and that the historian had better fully take them into account.

J.A.G.   Given the fact that so much of the resentment which led to the Revolution resulted from the attempts of the British to establish more stringent controls over the colonial economy, would it be reasonable to have expected the Americans to establish a more powerful central government, with more power over the economic activities of its people at that particular time?

S.B.   I think that if a poll had been taken, the widespread resentment of executive authority and the Acts of Parliament would have been sufficient to rule out a central government with greater power than that provided by the Articles of Confederation. The animosity toward control by a distant government was such that the power to tax and the power to regulate foreign and interstate commerce were not surrendered. I find little reason, in the few years intervening between the adoption of the Articles and the adoption of the Constitution, to believe that any fundamental shift in American sentiment would have occurred had it not been for the initiative exercised by an elite leadership. That initiative, motivated in part by the desire of people like Hamilton for a strong national government that could cut a figure in the arena of world politics, in part by states which had not done very well as independent sovereign entities in the 1780's, and in part by individuals who wanted to strut on a wider and more important stage than allowed them by the state, put the Constitution over.

J.A.G. Would you discuss Hamilton's economic concepts and explain how his policies fitted the needs of the American economy?

S.B. The basic motivation of Hamilton was neomercantilist; he wanted a strong, prosperous, diversified economy in which political independence would find its roots. To achieve these ends he sought to restore the national credit, which had fallen so low that American federal bonds were worth only about twenty cents on the dollar.

J.A.G. Was the parlous state of the national credit in the early 1780's a product of the political structure under the Articles of Confederation, or can it better be explained as a result of the heavy expenditures and of the dislocations that the war produced?

S.B. The great size of the debt in 1783 resulted from the inability of the government under the Articles to raise money by taxation. It had to borrow to pay soldiers and purchase supplies. What else would have led to the decline in the market value of these promises-to-pay—the bonds were essentially IOU's—but a loss of confidence on the part of the American people in the ability of the government to redeem these promises?

J.A.G. Now you sound like John Fiske, whom you just said did not correctly interpret the period!

S.B. I said there were elements of truth in Fiske, and this is one of the elements. Another element of truth that one may still find in Fiske, although I see no particular reason for going to him for one's support, is that the British government very clearly recongnized the inability of the thirteen states to adopt a single Navigation Act, or a single tariff that would be equally applicable in all ports. Britain, therefore, made no maritime or commercial concessions to the United States.

J.A.G. Getting back to Hamilton, you mentioned his awareness of how important it was to re-establish the federal credit. Would you like to go on with that subject?

S.B. Yes. He believed that if the debt were not paid off, foreigners would be far more reluctant to lend money in the future. And he believed that America's development would depend to a considerable extent on importations of capital. The federal assumption of state debts and the other measures adopted, including the chartering of the First Bank of the United States by Congress, made a positive contribution, and not only in the amount of capital that directly and immediately came to the United States for investment in shares of the Bank and in the bonds of the federal government. Many foreigners failed to distinguish between the excellent credit of the federal government and the credit of the states, and bought state government bonds, which enabled the states to invest in canal companies, turnpike companies, and railroad companies.

J.A.G. You have emphasized how important the development of more efficient internal transportation was to the economic prosperity of the nation. Was Hamilton particularly concerned with these internal improvements?

S.B. I rather think not. Hamilton was a good deal less concerned than was Jefferson's Secretary of the Treasury, Albert Gallatin, for example. Hamilton wanted to discourage the westward movement. He wanted to confine capital and labor to cities in order to stimulate the development of manufactures.

J.A.G. Does that suggest that Jefferson had a deeper insight into the economic future of the United States than Hamilton?

S.B. I think Jefferson acted more wisely than he knew. He very much distrusted and disapproved of almost the entire paraphernalia of commercial capitalism: banks, manufactures, and cities, which he regarded as affecting the health of the society the way human sores affect the human body.

J.A.G. He did believe in internal development of the nation.

S.B. He did as President, but in his private preferences, I believe he continued to disapprove of economic development. As President, he recognized the necessity for bowing to the will of the people, as he heard that will. "Not my will but theirs be done," he specifically said at one time. And since increasing majorities were won by him in every Congress while he was President, he had every reason to believe that the will of the people was behind his program, and wanted the things which he, Jefferson, in his heart, I think did not want.

J.A.G. We know that Hamilton's bank served in some ways the function of a central bank. Did Hamilton understand what was happening, and was the bank used efficiently and intelligently for this purpose?

S.B. I'm quite confident that Hamilton was not a central banker in any sense of the word. He opposed setting up branches. As he told the cashier of the Bank of New York, "Don't think I was asked about the branches and said 'No.' I simply was not asked." He thought branches would be difficult to control from the central board in Philadelphia, and that the local branches would make investments that might imperil the well-being of the institution as a whole. He also had confidence in state banking institutions as alternatives to the issuance of paper money by state governments. He was afraid that there would be no limit to the workings of the printing press when states issued paper money, but with private institutions it would be to the interest of the men who invested capital in them to see that issues were not so great as to place their investments in jeopardy. Unwise loans would not be made, and the quantity of notes issued would not be too great. Hamilton looked upon banks as devices for issuing that amount of currency that would suit the actual needs of the business community, without producing currency inflation.

J.A.G. Did he understand how a powerful central bank could regulate the policies of other banks?

S.B. I think not. Hamilton's high regard for soundly managed, stable state banks made it very difficult for him to see the First Bank of the United States as a peculiar instrument for the achievement of a stable currency.

J.A.G. There has been a great deal of discussion by historians about the concept of take-off in economic growth. Would you explain what the phrase means?

S.B. The phrase is W. W. Rostow's, and it stems from an essay written by him in the 1950's on the stages of economic growth. Rostow's assumption was that there were five stages in the development of an economy: the traditional stage, the preconditions to take-off, the take-off itself, the drive to maturity, and the age of high mass consumption. What launched the take-off, in Rostow's view, was a sharp increase—approximately a doubling—of the rate of capital investment.

The first comment to be made is that Simon Kuznets, the acknowledged father of National Income Accounting, has examined the growth experience of a dozen modern European, Asiatic, and American states and found not a single instance in which there was a doubling of the rate of capital investment as required by the Rostowian concept.

In the second place, many historians naturally reacted with suspicion to the idea of discrete stages, recognizing as they would the prevalence and overlapping of more than one stage at a given moment. While appreciating the desirability of intellectual constructs of some kind for the purposes of systematic thought, they found Rostow's far too similar for comfort to the stages adopted by German economic historians in the nineteenth century. There's a kind of logical irreversibility that's implied in stage constructs of development which, again, doesn't fit very well the stubborn facts of history.

At any rate, the Rostowian idea is no longer taken seriously. It was attacked vigorously by Kuznets; the attack was picked up by Robert Fogel and by Albert Fishlow, and more recently by Paul David, and I would say that the last nail has been driven into its coffin. It's very similar, I might say parenthetically, to the Toynbean concept of the Industrial Revolution as a sudden and dramatic change from a traditional society in which happy children play on the greensward in a pure atmosphere to the next morning, so to speak, when the factories are belching forth their black smoke, polluting the atmosphere and corrupting the lives of women and children. We know as historians that change takes place gradually. Perhaps the happiest attempt to reach an accommodation with the Rostowian concept and at the same time express the reservations of historians was Phyllis Deane's work on English economic history in which she referred to the "significant discontinuities" which sometimes occur in the seamless web of history. Which is a way of saying that the web is always seamless, except sometimes.

J.A.G. How did the economy change in the first half of the nineteenth century?

S.B. Transportation made regional specialization possible, made division of labor possible, and also accounted for a shift in the locus of economic activity. The development of first the steamboats on the western rivers, and then of canals, and then of railroads, made it possible for each of the three major sections of the nation, north, east, and west, to specialize in the production of a particular kind or category of goods.

I don't want to overexaggerate the degree of the specialization, but in general the northeast was the manufacturing area, the south the producer of industrial raw materials, particularly cotton, and the west the area that produced food. Now what made it possible to specialize was, first, steamboats on the western rivers, and then canals, and then railroads. Prior to the appearance of steamboats in 1816 on the Mississippi, traffic was possible as a rule only downriver. Flatboats were loaded with produce for the port of New Orleans. Shipments upstream, against the current, were expensive even for light and valuable merchandise.

The steamboat vastly changed this situation. It shifted the terms of trade in favor of the western farmer; his products were able to command a larger quantity of imported merchandise. This encouraged settlement in the west and the commercialization of agriculture.

As far as manufacturing is concerned, the textile industries were the first really to be subjected to factory forms of organization; probably the Boston Manufacturing Company founded in 1813 in Waltham, Massachusetts, was the first in the textile industry in the country. In the 1820's and 1830's, the factory system was introduced into iron manufacturing, and by the time of the Civil War, at least some of the significant prerequisites of factory development were present in the boot and shoe industry. There was, in other words, a progression, rapid in some industries, less rapid in others.

Only in the 1850's, however, did a really important development of manufacturing corporations appear. More corporations were chartered in that decade than in all prior years. Far more railroad track was laid in that decade than in any previous decade. A vigorous expansion in foreign trade occurred. My candidate for "take-off," although I object to the term and the concept, would be the 1850's—which is not very far, of course, from W. W. Rostow's idea of 1843–60. (No one denies that the economy expanded more rapidly at some times than at others, but Rostow's idea that there was a sudden change of character as well as degree, marking off a "traditional" economy from one which "takes off" into a modern economy, I find objectionable.)

J.A.G. I'd like to question you further about the changes that occurred in manufacturing. Is it possible to generalize about the impact of technology on manufacturing before 1860?

S.B. I think one has to look at particular industries at particular times.

J.A.G. There are no generalizations?

S.B. I would make generalizations in much the way the English economic historian John Clapham did. He surrounded them with a curvature of reservations to emphasize the inadequacy of any blanket statement to cover so many protruding particulars. Steam engines made their appearance quite early, but as late as 1869 half of the power used in the textile industry was developed by water wheels. It takes time for new technology to permeate the economy; the effects of an innovation cannot be discerned immediately. The substitution of metallic machinery for wooden machinery took time, because of the reluctance of men who had made investments in older types of machines to discard them for more costly substitutes, even if they were superior. The idea of America as the land of eager entrepreneurs ready to scrap old investment, in favor of innovating new capital goods, promising greater rewards, is incorrect, as Paul Strassmann has shown in *Risk and Technological Innovation.*

J.A.G. You're raising, it seems to me, a very basic question about historical interpretation. What is significant in history? In this case, is the time that a new thing first appears significant, or is it only significant when it becomes universal and everybody uses it? To argue that the introduction of the factory system of production was not important before 1860 because in 1869 or even in 1880 there was still a great deal of production that wasn't organized around the factory, certainly seems subject to argument.

S.B. I would not argue that it was not significant. The question of significance depends upon the kind of question asked. If one were to argue that without the advent of the factory at some point in time and place, it could never have permeated the economy, that is a perfectly viable argument. But if one is concerned not with the indispensable prerequisites for later growth, but with the fact of growth itself, then one can argue that what matters is the extent to which an innovation has permeated an economy.

J.A.G. Were the social effects of industrialization in the United States similar to those which were produced earlier by the industrialization of England?

S.B.   I think not. *All* we know about the English industrial proletariat points to very unhappy immediate results of industrialization, and only *some* of what we know about the results of industrialization in this country points in that direction. The low pay and the long hours worked by factory laborers, particularly immigrants, is an unsavory story which cannot be washed away by any kind of comparison. But the land/man ratio in this country must be taken into account. Industrialization, when it did occur, did not have the consequences that it had in Western Europe. I don't think there was an industrial proletariat in the same sense. Labor continued to think of itself as only temporarily in that class. Workers had a kind of entrepreneurial cast of mind; they envisaged themselves at some future date as owners of small businesses.

The wage data of the ante-bellum period are very fragmentary, very scattered, but they seem to indicate very strongly that productivity gains in manufacturing were not passed on in the form of higher wages. Despite that, any comparison between the industrial workers of this country and Europe appears favorable to industrial workers here. High returns in agriculture furnished a floor beneath which industrial wages were not likely to sink. These high returns meant that many immigrants went directly to the west rather than settle in industrial cities.

J.A.G.   Were industrial laborers better off than their counterparts in England and on the Continent? Did the so-called modified safety valve force wages up?

S.B.   There is no evidence that it did. We need more studies like Stephan Thernstrom's work on unskilled laborers in Newburyport, Massachusetts, in the period 1850–80. If we had comparable studies for the earlier period, we would be able to assess the extent to which the utopian notion of easy social mobility was really true. All we actually have is the rhetoric of people like Tocqueville, Francis Grund, Charles Dickens, and other travelers. One of the contributions that the new economic historians are making is precisely in this area. They're pointing to the inadequacies of what Thomas C. Cochran has called the tyranny of persuasive rhetoric. Quantitative studies need to be substituted for that tyranny if we are ever to know if it indeed was possible for industrial workers to move from one occupation to another, and better their conditions. One thing that suggests that it was possible is that the level of technology was not very demanding in the ante-bellum period. Men could master the requirements of new occupations far more easily than is true now. The extent to which they did, in fact, is a historical problem that remains for investigation.

J.A.G.   Was American agriculture in 1860 very different from what it was in 1790? Was the average farm larger or smaller? Had mechanization affected agriculture? Was scientific knowledge being applied to farms? What was the so-called agricultural revolution of the pre-Civil War era?

S.B.   The concept of revolution is one that needs constantly to be assessed and evaluated. Historians tend to analyze into untenable tidbits such concepts as Renaissance, revolution, and the other great categories by which we organize the stuff of history, and then, bowing to the inevitable, they accept and try again to pump some meaningful content into them. I think this is true of the Industrial Revolution and of the Agricultural Revolution.

To address myself directly to agricultural change, I find relatively little evidence of a permeation of farmer practices by concepts of scientific agriculture in this period. There was plenty of interest on the part of agricultural reformers in improving livestock and plant life, rotating crops, and fertilizing soils, but a great deal of opposition on the part of dirt farmers. The opposition did not stem from ignorance or from the kind of peasant traditionalism that one associates with the Middle Ages, but from the availability of cheap land. It was cheaper to buy new land than to try to renovate land that had been worn out. And since labor was also scarce, to work farms more intensely was equally costly. So that the increased demand for agricultural commodities was filled by the westward movement of farmers to new land, and by mechanization. The westward movement, seen in these terms, was a redisposition of agricultural resources to enable the agricultural sector to cope with expanding demand. It resulted from the inability of a labor-scarce and capital-scarce nation to replenish worn-out soils economically.

As for mechanization, the steel moldboard plow of John Deere was not a mechanized implement, but it was a very important innovation. The iron plows previously used often shattered against the tough prairie sod, or rocks beneath the surface. True, agricultural machines (mechanized threshers, harvesters, drills, corn pressers, and things of that sort, and cotton gins in the South) were widely adopted in the period from 1855 to 1865. Thus the "first agricultural revolution" really occurred between 1850 and 1870. (The second, incidentally, was associated with World War II.) Mechanization, meaning not merely the first appearance of these new implements but their wide-scale adoption, came in this period.

J.A.G.   If I may quibble about a small point, is it correct to call the cotton gin an agricultural machine? Isn't a gin really the machine that is used in the first stage of the manufacture of cloth?

S.B.   It would all depend upon one's preference, but I think it belongs more closely to the growing of cotton than to the manufacture of cloth. It's used on the plantation. It's used prior to the baling process.

J.A.G. To use a "counter-factual" argument, wouldn't it have been possible to ship the cotton to the centers of cloth production before the seeds were removed and gin it then?

S.B. Had it been shipped with the seeds in, the cost would have been greater because of the increased weight.

J.A.G. One could say with equal logic that if farmers had had a household method of weaving the cotton into cloth, shipping costs would have been even lower than they were in fact. It seems to me more reasonable to consider the cotton gin as a technological improvement in the manufacturing of cloth which had an enormous stimulating effect on the production of cotton, just the way the spinning jenny had a similar effect somewhat earlier.

S.B. Well, I think it's one closer to agriculture than to manufacturing, but as I said, it is a matter of definition.

J.A.G. Would it be correct to say that the entire United States was one national market by 1860?

S.B. I would say that the national market was constantly in need of being re-created. In a sense there was a national market in the eighteenth century, when most settlements were close to the seaboard and it was possible for areas of supply to furnish goods required by areas of demand, through seaboard communications. But when westward settlement got underway, particularly in the 1790's, and then again after the War of 1812, this national market was disrupted and needed to be re-created. This was accomplished, I think, between 1840 and 1860, when a kind of regional specialization and division of labor developed, a regional interdependence. In that sense there was a national market. But then again, following the 1860's, a further extension of western settlement occurred, with the consequence that the national market had to be re-created once again, as it was by about 1900. This concept of achievement, disruption, and re-creation well suits the continued movement to the west that is peculiar to our national experience. On the other hand, if by national market one means an economy with a single price level for labor or for bills of exchange or for interest, then beyond question there was no national market at all during the entire nineteenth century.

J.A.G. What role did the government—local, state, and federal—play in stimulating economic growth during the period up to 1860?

S.B. There was a period in our history when it was a favorite belief of businessmen and others that the role of government in American development was minimal, that what made the country prosperous was the free action of enterprising businessmen. Actually, I believe the opposite was the case. From very early in our colonial experience down to the establishment of the Atomic Energy Commission, government was a pioneer in the investment process. During the colonial period, as Richard B. Morris has shown in *Government and Labor in Early America*, local governments took action to encourage scarce supplies of capital to produce needed public utilities—grist mills, for example. Tax exemptions, grants of land, and other forms of aid and encouragement were extended to induce private individuals to provide needed public services. Hamilton, in his Report on Manufactures, offered bounties and awards and premiums to investors in machinery to displace scarce labor. The same policy was followed by the states all during the ante-bellum period, and by local communities thereafter.

In the late 1940's, the Council for Research in Economic History sponsored a series of studies of the role of the state: a study of Massachusetts by Oscar and Mary Handlin, another of Georgia by Milton Heath, one of Missouri by James N. Primm, one of Pennsylvania by Louis Hartz. The economist Carter Goodrich and his students also have made extensive studies of other states. This research proves conclusively that it was neither private enterprise nor public enterprise, but "mixed enterprise," public and private interests joining hands, that built the turnpikes, canals, railroads, and other forms of social overhead capital of the ante-bellum period. In some instances, private individuals alone did so, as in the case of most turnpikes. In other instances, states made the entire contribution, as in the case of the Erie Canal, which was paid for to the last penny by the state of New York.

Let us consider the specific case of Virginia. Virginia in 1816 appointed a committee of the legislature to study the internal-improvement needs of the state. The committee urged the government to provide these internal improvements, otherwise labor and capital might move to some adjacent state. The Virginia legislature proceeded to set up a Board of Internal Improvements, consisting of the governor, the attorney general, the treasurer, and ten citizens representing the major geographic areas of the state. Under this system, private individuals could suggest particular projects; these were then examined from the point of view of their engineering feasibility by a chief engineer who reported to the Board of Public Works. If his report was favorable, the Board as a rule made the project a state-financed project. The state government thereupon appropriated 40 percent of the capital cost, and the corporation set up to conduct the work provided the rest. As a result of this system, a number of railroads, turnpikes, plank roads, and bridge companies were developed in Virginia. And the story of Virginia could be multiplied by that of most states. It exemplifies the way states joined with private individuals organized into corporations to provide internal improvements.

The federal government also made important contributions. It built the Cumberland Road; it conducted engineering surveys through the Army's Corps of Engineers; it granted tariff rebates on imported railroad iron; it donated important quantities of land from the public domain to encourage internal improvements. The Internal Improvements Act of 1841, the Swamplands Act of 1850, the Illinois Land Grant Bill of 1850, and other federal legislation granted land to states for the purpose of encouraging internal improvements.

J.A.G. Were the political controversies that raged throughout the pre-Civil War period over public assistance to internal improvements and the tariff, which also affected the economy, economic conflicts, rather than philosophical arguments about the proper role of government in economic affairs?

S.B. Oh, yes. There was no philosophical objection to state aid. Mostly it reflected sectional discords, often resulting from economic changes. For example, John C. Calhoun of South Carolina, the leader of the "pro-federal funds" school of thought in 1816, migrated in the 1820's to the opposite position when Southerners became convinced that these improvements would, in all likelihood, benefit the North more than the South.

J.A.G. Would you name the half-dozen books in American economic history that you consider to be outstanding? Please explain your choices.

S.B. My half-dozen all-time favorites, listed in alphabetical order to spare the feelings of the living, are: Victor S. Clark, *History of Manufactures in the United States* (1928); Thomas C. Cochran and William Miller, *The Age of Enterprise* (1942); Albert Fishlow, *American Railroads and the Growth of the Antebellum Economy* (1965); Lewis C. Gray, *History of Agriculture in the Southern States to 1860* (1933); Fritz Redlich, *The Molding of American Banking* (1951) and George R. Taylor, *The Transportation Revolution* (1951).

Two of these books, Clark's and Gray's, were published in the 1920's and early 1930's. Both are monumental works of scholarship, products of a lifetime of labor and reflection that will doubtless long remain indispensable. Taylor's panoramic treatment of the ante-bellum period, although omitting agriculture because of the inclusion of that subject in another volume in a series, summarizes the whole range of critical scholarship in a work of enduring value. Cochran and Miller, while published more than twenty-five years ago, is a wide-ranging testament to the conviction of both men that in the study of the economic past economics is not enough. Redlich's work in banking was a pioneering masterpiece. It was he who "discovered" Nicholas Biddle as central banker; his treatment of the rise of investment banking in the United States remains unequaled.

I have saved Fishlow for the end. By far the youngest of the group, Fishlow is a "new" economic historian—that is to say, a scholar trained as an economist to employ the tools of statistical inference and economic theory in reconstructing economic history. I think his book is the finest product of the "new" economic history thus far to appear.

Despite my inclusion of Fishlow in the list, these selections make it clear that my own training as an historian places me in the camp of the "old" economic history. At the same time, I am quick to acknowledge the great value of much of the work being done with the use of the newer quantitative and theoretical techniques. Theory is essential if facts are to be explained; but without facts there is nothing to explain.

Stanley M. Elkins

Slavery

STANLEY M. ELKINS, Professor of History at Smith College, is best known for his *Slavery: A Problem in American Institutional and Intellectual Life* (1959), a book which has been responsible for an enormous amount of controversy, and which therefore has led to much further study of the so-called "peculiar institution." In the following discussion, Professor Elkins, among other things, explains how this new work has influenced his own views. In addition to his work on slavery, Elkins, with Eric L. McKitrick, has written a number of provocative essays on such subjects as the influence of the frontier on political institutions and the Founding Fathers. He and McKitrick are currently working on a reinterpretation of the early national period of American history.

John A. Garraty Professor Elkins, none of the European nations which colonized the New World possessed any substantial number of slaves. Yet their colonies developed slave societies in one form or another. What was the general attitude toward slavery in Western Europe in the sixteenth and seventeenth centuries?

Stanley M. Elkins Historians have until recently assumed that European slavery was a thing of the past, that it ended well before the sixteenth century. But the work of David Davis has uncovered the continuity in Western thought on the subject. The colonizing Europeans knew all about slavery, and the slave institutions which developed both in Latin America and in North America reflected European values and precedents.

However, I feel that the character and quality of slave institutions in the New World had a unique rigidity; they carried the logic of absolute ownership to extremes. Furthermore, Davis argues that the slave institutions of Latin America were not significantly different from those of North America. I'm still impressed by the *tabula rasa* quality of slavery in Virginia. These colonists actually manufactured an institution in which the dominant facts were the property value of the slave and the absolute power of the master. The attitudes which emerged out of this institution by the middle of the eighteenth century strike me as extraordinarily monolithic; they had a quality that goes with a new society. And I'm still impressed by the limitations that were placed on slavery in Latin America: limitations of law, of religion, and of conscience on the part of the slaveowner.

I'm forced to admit that a simple dichotomy between Latin America and North America won't hold up. The situation was very complex. But in Latin America, if for any reason a slave had any natural bargaining power (if he was, for example, a skilled worker), this bargaining power was enhanced by the Catholic church. Skilled workers were co-opted into religious brotherhoods in Havana and given an education. Given the opportunity, the church tried to ease the impact of slavery—above all, to encourage emancipation and to guarantee stature as a citizen and as a human being to the manumitted slave. This, I think, was missing in North America, and even in the English West Indies. A laissez-faire attitude toward slavery was typical of British America. Although not as decisive as I believed when I wrote my book, *Slavery*, I still consider this the central fact shaping British-American slavery.

J.A.G. But why was there slavery of any kind in either Latin America or British America when the institutions of the mother countries really didn't allow for slavery?

S.M.E. One reason was the tremendous ambition and enterprise of the settlers. The colonists were an expression of the West's emergence into the modern age. A fortune made in Spanish America or English America could be translated into a position in society. One of the central facts of life in the New World was the possibility of striking it rich, of moving ahead dramatically. This produced tremendous temptations. Resources were plentiful; land, especially, existed in unimaginable abundance. The one thing men lacked was labor. In a setting like this, colonists seized upon whatever labor force they could get their hands on. For a number of good reasons, the most efficient available labor was African.

J.A.G.   On the one hand we tend to think of the New World as dignifying labor because of its shortage, yet on the other hand the shortage leads to slavery. Can you explain this paradox?

S.M.E.   The paradox is understandable. The shortage of labor is central. If the employer has to bargain, then the laborer has the advantage. If he does not have to bargain with the worker, then the very fact that labor is in such demand places an enormous premium on absolute control.

J.A.G.   Would this explain the difference between Latin American and North American slavery? Did the South American slave have greater bargaining power?

S.M.E.   In some instances, the South American slave had more bargaining power. Consider Havana, one of the largest colonial cities in the Western Hemisphere. It was a major rendezvous for the annual Spanish fleet, with a corresponding need for all sorts of skills and services. The Spanish tradition that white men did not work if they could avoid it meant that the bulk of skilled trades in Havana were monopolized by black men. The church and the crown helped the skilled slave to improve his dignity as a human being in society. One thing built on the other. But, apparently, a black plantation laborer (say in Brazil) wasn't a great deal better off than his counterpart in North America. The power of the church operating by itself was probably not very great, but given a certain environment, as in Havana, it was quite dramatic.

J.A.G.   Does the fact that the European colonists were coexisting with technologically primitive native populations explain their resort to slavery? They certainly looked on the Indians as childlike, inferior creatures. Could this have conditioned them to make slaves of fellow human beings?

S.M.E.   I think not. The Indian was very difficult to enslave in North America. It was too easy for him to slip off into the forest. Also, the tribes of the East Coast had very little experience with agriculture. An Indian from a hunting tribe, where only the women engaged in agriculture, usually preferred death to agricultural work, which he considered totally humiliating.

For the African, the situation was entirely different. Take a shipload of African blacks arriving in Virginia. They come from different tribes; they're in a state of shock; they don't speak the language. You manage them by giving them very simple tasks and very simple rewards and punishments. In a setting like this, the poor Africans look terribly primitive, crude, and stupid. After all, later Americans could even convince themselves that nineteenth-century Western European immigrants were naturally stupid. Strangeness and foreignness are easily translated into "these people are, by their nature, not very bright."

J.A.G.   The Indian always appeared in stereotype as crafty, if nothing else.

S.M.E.   Yes, because the American Indian had the advantage of being a native. He was on his home ground. On the eve of King Philip's War, the general conviction in Massachusetts Bay was that the Indians were no match for the white community. Then, in a matter of about two weeks, the colonists discovered that they were no match for the Indian in fighting in the forest. After this tremendous psychological shock, the Indian was viewed as shrewd and crafty and vicious, but never stupid. The American soldier's image of the Vietcong reflects the same attitude. "You may hate Charlie's guts," the G.I. says, "but he's got them and he's no fool." No one describes him as stupid. If you've tried your best and you're not able to overcome someone, and he's stupid, obviously you're more stupid. The fact of the matter was that the Virginians did succeed in dominating the blacks.

J.A.G.   Then why did slavery develop so slowly in Virginia and Maryland?

S.M.E.   In the beginning, the most efficient laborer was the indentured servant. He could speak English, he was well motivated; if he worked for six or seven years, he received his freedom and could eventually become an independent farmer. Slaves, on the other hand, seemed dangerous; they were foreign, exotic, expensive. Only sufficient examples of the successful use of blacks could change this view. Some were imported very early. What their original status was is an open question; some were treated as indentured servants, but apparently others were not. But over time it became clear that native-born blacks made good workers, and they did not have to be liberated after a given number of years. Gradually, the colonists discovered that by using a few native-born blacks as drivers, they could work out techniques for exploiting large numbers of African-born blacks. But the big importations didn't begin until the very end of the seventeenth century and the beginning of the eighteenth century.

J.A.G.   What are the roots of abolitionism in America?

S.M.E.   The first real pressures to abolish slavery came with the Revolution. Being concerned about the rights of man, the colonists had to try to account for men in the community who had no rights. Since slavery was not especially profitable at that time in many areas, some Americans began to push the rights-of-man argument to its logical conclusion. One of the tragic figures in this regard in America was Jefferson. He was never really able to come to terms with slavery. He resolved his doubts by concluding that black men were so different that they could not be integrated into American society. There are some wonderful passages in his *Notes on Virginia* in which Jefferson speculates on the character of the black man. He twists and turns, but eventually comes to the conclusion that the Negro is different. He never quite says why.

Jefferson was one of the most socially imaginative and creative figures of the eighteenth century. President Kennedy's well-known remark to a White House gathering of Nobel Prize winners was scarcely an exaggeration. He called the group "the greatest collection of intellects that had dined in the White House since Jefferson dined alone." Jefferson excelled at analyzing the character of society, yet, when he dealt with the question of slavery, he was amazingly unimaginative. He might have encouraged manumission, or some form of sharecropping; there were all sorts of possibilities for getting around the economic problems of emancipation. He might have concocted a plan for educating the blacks. But somehow, on this subject Jefferson's social imagination was paralyzed. He could not imagine an integrated society.

J.A.G. But there were a substantial number of free Negroes in America in Jefferson's day. Did this free black community cause a great deal of social conflict?

S.M.E. Much less than the whites did. This is what I mean by Jefferson's lack of social imagination. Some free Negroes caused trouble, but what would it have taken to make them productive members of the community? Land, a place in society, the possibility of fulfilling ambition. Southerners appeared to be determined to fail in dealing with the Negro. Theirs was a self-fulfilling prophecy; by insisting that the blacks were inferior, they made them inferior.

In the stratified society of Latin America, integration seemed a less serious problem. In America, with its fluid society, freedom was an absolute. Once you're free there's no way to check you; talk of manumitting slaves leads to the famous Southern rhetorical question: "Would you like a Negro to sit at your dinner table or marry your daughter?" Such a thought never entered the head of an upper-class Spanish colonist. The number of people of any color who could aspire to sit at his table or marry his daughter was small indeed.

A number of Americans, almost without exception men of aristocratic temperament (Alexander Hamilton is an example), were not impressed with the idea of the supposed inferiority of Negroes. Henry Laurens of South Carolina, son of a prominent slaveowner, argued for the enlistment of slaves in the Continental Army during the Revolution. Men like Laurens were convinced that slaves would make good soldiers because they were obedient, not-very-bright men who would do as they were told. The aristocratic temper of these people, who viewed their fellow whites as in the main rather stupid, made them much more generous and easy-going in their treatment of slaves. In a stratified society with strong aristocratic attitudes, there is no need to define the Negro as hopelessly inferior, because the greater portion of society is inferior in varying degrees. However, the idea that all men are equal creates a terrible tendency to draw the line, and then logic compels the conclusion that Negroes are not really men.

J.A.G.   How was slavery abolished in the Northern states?

S.M.E.   There was pressure from abolitionist societies, revolutionary libertarian sentiment, and a growing religious feeling against the evil of slavery. Combined with the fact that slavery was not economically very advantageous in the North, these pressures led to emancipation laws in the late eighteenth and early nineteenth centuries. After emancipation, the Northern Negro's situation improved dramatically until the great influx of immigrants in the 1840's. Then the black man lost out. First the immigrants won many of the skilled jobs that Negroes had held, and then, gradually, Negroes lost their political rights, at least in many Northern states.

J.A.G.   Did the invention of the cotton gin have as great an impact on slavery as is usually attributed to it?

S.M.E.   The classic interpretation is: Eli Whitney invented the cotton gin, and slavery was fixed on the United States for another full generation. Like most legends, this one contains an element of truth. There was a large expanse of virgin land which, after the War of 1812, was available in areas like Alabama and Mississippi, and a labor force that was not being used efficiently in the older slave states. Industrial developments in England made it possible to produce large amounts of cheap cotton cloth, assuming the raw material was available. Finally, the species of cotton that would grow in the South was hard to separate from its seeds. Well, Whitney invented a machine that could separate it, and this machine broke a barrier. The variables I've mentioned then began to interact on one another.

The dynamic force in the situation was not unlike that which fixed slavery on the New World. There were fortunes to be made or recouped in cotton on fresh western land. Here was a chance for Virginians and South Carolinians to use their excess labor force. Together with the constant expansion of the British demand for cotton, this created an economically dynamic situation which did help fix slavery on the country until the Civil War. The gin alone was not responsible, but it symbolizes and dramatizes the tremendous economic expansion that took place.

J.A.G.   But considering the impasse that Jefferson and his generation found themselves in, isn't it doubtful that the institution would have become any less "unstuck" even if there had not been this economic expansion?

S.M.E.   I don't know. If slavery had been economically unprofitable, there would have at least been a temptation to experiment with other possibilities. Faced with the alternatives of bankruptcy or of loosening the system, I think Americans would have loosened the system. But Jefferson's doubts about the possibility of black men and white men living together on any other basis than master and slave coincided with the economic needs of an expanding plantation agriculture.

J.A.G.   Did Southern agriculture shape slavery, or did slavery shape Southern agriculture?

S.M.E.   Southern planters often argued that the kind of agriculture they engaged in was necessitated by the limitations of their labor force, but I think that agriculture shaped slavery. Gang labor seemed to be the most efficient way to produce cotton, sugar, and rice. If it had been more efficient to operate in another way, economic pressure would have been decisive and slavery might have worked out rather differently. Yet men tend to do what they're doing. If everybody assumed that the only way to work blacks was in gangs, few would be tempted to experiment.

J.A.G.   Would you describe the so-called Great Debate on slavery that occurred in Virginia around 1830?

S.M.E.   On the surface, the Great Debate appeared to be the last surge of old Virginian abolitionism. Ironically, it was Jefferson's grandson, Thomas Jefferson Randolph, who pressed for some form of emancipation. But the debate was initiated by Nat Turner's bloody slave uprising. Virginians were wrestling with fears roused by the growing black population of the state, and the one thing that they could not resolve was the same question that Jefferson couldn't resolve: What are we going to do with the blacks if we emancipate them?

The emancipators were doomed from the beginning, because they didn't have a program. All they could propose was large-scale colonization sending the blacks back to Africa—and that was not a viable solution. What actually happened was that Virginian slaves were sold to planters in the expanding cotton areas in the Deep South. Once the concentration of Negro population began to drop off, emancipation became a dead issue.

In a way, I would think that Thomas Jefferson doomed the Great Debate. If he had been able to think through the problem of what to do with the free blacks, Randolph would have had a platform on which to stand.

J.A.G.   Why was the issue of slavery in the territories so bitterly fought when it was clear that the regions in question were not really suited for slavery?

S.M.E.   Slavery was an ideological and moral question. The American living north of the Mason-Dixon line was anxious to resolve the problem of slavery, but reluctant to accept the black man as a full-fledged member of the community. By opposing the expansion of slavery, he was able to resolve this conflict. He could say to himself that he opposed slavery and salve his conscience with the comforting thought that, once restricted, slavery would eventually disappear. At the same time, it enabled him to keep the blacks out of his own area. This sounds cynical, but I don't think Northerners saw it cynically. Particularly in the Midwest, many persons had left the South to get away from slavery, and they didn't want it to follow them into the areas where they and their descendants hoped to go. They weren't challenging slavery where it already existed, and they did not want to live in an interracial community.

J.A.G.   Is not this the attitude held by many Northerners today?

S.M.E.   I don't think that is quite fair. There are Northerners certainly who feel this way, but many others want to integrate the blacks into white society.

J.A.G.   Considering slavery in the territories from the Southern point of view, why did Southerners insist on the right to bring slaves into an area where in fact slavery could not exist?

S.M.E.   They were an intensely ideological people. Concerned about the future of slavery, they were determined to make the North accept slavery as a positive good. Just as the North had to restrict slavery to demonstrate that it would eventually disappear, the South had to insist on its right to expand to demonstrate that it would exist forever. It is erroneous to consider this a practical question. Stephen A. Douglas made that mistake in the Kansas-Nebraska bill fiasco. Ideological issues can be very real.

J.A.G.   In the early nineteenth century, slavery was apparently a thriving institution in Southern cities. Yet on the eve of the Civil War it seems to have been rapidly declining in urban areas. Why was this so?

S.M.E.   Richard Wade has argued persuasively that Southerners recognized that slavery would not thrive in the cities, and indeed that the cities represented a positive threat to its security. They were not able to work out a system of slavery sufficiently flexible to take into account the opportunities that the city provided for the slave. City life produced slaves who were independent, who had special competencies—who could, in other words, take care of themselves. This kind of black individual threatened the dominant planter ethos, the notion of the totally dependent slave. All sorts of political pressures were brought to bear to restrict the independence of the slave in the city and to limit his numbers. The dominant political forces of the South were determined that there must be no cracks in the system, and the city was a crack. The maintenance of slavery as a simple system of total dependence and absolute control was more important to the South than the development of its cities.

J.A.G. Well, how do you account for the exceptions? A number of free Negroes in the South, and even some slaves, achieved a great deal of independence and responsibility within this extremely rigid system. Why were they tolerated?

S.M.E. In part because they were few in number, and in part because they were useful. The *theory* of the system required the slave to be stupid and irresponsible. However, an intelligent slave who was responsible and literate was very valuable to his master. As long as there weren't too many exceptions and as long as the exceptions were not used to challenge the rule, they could be tolerated.

J.A.G. Were the interests of nonslaveowning Southern farmers, a very large proportion of the Southern population, antithetical to the interests of the slaveowners?

S.M.E. The question is, "How does a man see his interests?" A white mechanic might argue that it would be to his advantage to combine with black mechanics in a common front against employers, but that argument would be wildly abstract. His desire was to *eliminate* black mechanics. A white cotton farmer who owned no slaves was caught in a complex bind. Basically, he wished that everybody who grew cotton would be like him. He certainly didn't like competing with slave labor, but he didn't want the slaves freed either. He was torn in his attitudes toward the planter. He respected his wealth, and hoped perhaps someday to buy slaves and join the planter class. But he knew instinctively that slave labor was depressing the Southern economy.

J.A.G. You said in discussing the colonial period that there was little significant abolitionist feeling in America. Why did abolitionism develop in the United States after the Revolution?

S.M.E. There was a growing recognition in Western society of the immorality of slavery. It was part of a general religious revival which produced an intense concern with the personal sinfulness of the slave system, and a conviction that good men were morally bound to do something about it. I have been impressed by the extent to which the leaders of the antislavery movement were the descendants of ministers and magistrates.

Initially, most abolitionists shared the general prejudices of nineteenth-century America, which were strongly racist. But many of them overcame these prejudices, and pressed for rights for the black man in the North as well as in the South. The abolitionists were driven point by point to recognize what Jefferson would not recognize, that emancipation had to be accompanied by something approaching full equality, certainly full civil equality.

When I first began to study the history of slavery, I was annoyed by what I thought was a lack of humanity on the part of abolitionists. They seemed more interested in smashing slavery and smashing the Southerners (punishing sinners, if you will) than in doing something concrete for the black man. But they moved steadily in the direction of full equality. And whatever their motives, in the last analysis you can only judge them on what they accomplished. However, if you assume that abolitionists are necessarily attractive people personally, you're in for a big disappointment.

J.A.G. The abolitionists of the 1840's seemed totally impervious to the practical difficulties involved. It's difficult to see them as genuinely trying to solve the problem.

S.M.E. The abolitionists had to confront equally powerful Southern intransigencies.

J.A.G. Is not the modern Black Power movement very similar to the abolitionist movement in its uncompromising demands?

S.M.E. An argument can be made that the abolitionists were dealing with a situation in which the forces opposing them were uncompromising; any willingness to compromise, any flexibility would have gained them nothing. I'm not entirely certain that that argument is correct. Dealing with the problem piecemeal might conceivably have helped to subvert the system. American slavery was rigid, but it was also fragile.

But in any case, the militant advocates of Black Power are *not* faced with an unyielding opposition. They're faced instead with a community which is anxious to compromise, to deal concretely with the race problem. Unfortunately, when the Black Power advocates define the entire white community as totally uncompromising, unyielding, corrupt, and racist, and act on that basis, after a while that community may begin to take the shape of their nightmares.

J.A.G. Was slavery the primary cause of the Civil War?

S.M.E. Slavery was *the* cause of the Civil War. The issues between the North and the South were all negotiable, with the exception of slavery. Revisionist historians like Avery Craven, writing in the 1930's and 1940's, believed that the issue wasn't real. It was an ideological issue, but as I've said, ideological issues are anything but unreal. The "real" issue was the kind of society the United States would be.

J.A.G. But President Abraham Lincoln said flatly in 1861 that the war was not being fought to abolish slavery. If slavery caused the war, and if the war resulted in the abolition of slavery, why did Lincoln insist that the fight was over secession?

S.M.E. From the point of view of an outsider, let's say an interested Englishman, there was great hypocrisy in the Civil War. The Republican party opposed the extension of slavery into an area where any extension of slavery was unlikely. Lincoln called for war, but insisted that slavery had nothing to do with it. Even the Emancipation Proclamation was, from the point of view of such an observer, a very questionable document; it emancipated no slaves within the reach of the Union forces, but only those behind the Confederate lines.

But the Northern public realized from the very beginning that slavery was the central issue. The Union was merely the issue on which Lincoln could organize the largest coalition. For the Northern people, one of the central facts was the experience of the war. Once the North became deeply involved in the war, and once it recognized that slavery was a major support for the Confederacy, there was overwhelming pressure for cutting down the war-making power of the Confederacy. The best way to do this was by chipping away at its labor pool of black slaves.

Over the course of the war the North drew a new line, not between black and white, but between blue and gray. The South was the enemy, of course, but eventually the black man became a friend, in the very real sense that he fought on the Union side. When this truth began to penetrate the Northern consciousness, the foundation of the radicals' reconstruction policies was laid. The North, by the end of the war, felt committed to the black man: to protecting him, and to giving him political rights so that he could protect himself.

I don't think there were a handful of Americans on the eve of the Civil War who could imagine a black man fighting for his own freedom. By the end of the war, about 190,000 black men had served in the Union Army.

J.A.G. Aside from the obvious effect of the Thirteenth Amendment, how extensively did the Civil War influence the lives of American Negroes after 1865?

S.M.E. The war itself had a profound impact. Emancipation was a gradual thing. It began as early as 1861. Throughout the history of American slavery, the possibility of escaping from the authority of the master was very remote. The legend of the Underground Railroad is in part true, but it helped very few people. The Civil War made the possibility of escape a reality. By the late summer of 1861, if a slave could get behind the Union lines he was a free man. If he could slip down to a river and paddle out to one of the blockading vessels off the southern coast, he was free. This placed a premium on initiative and courage and independence. The war, in other words, created a competing authority, the Yankee Army. And gradually the news spread that in many instances it was stronger than the Confederate Army. But above all, the war provided an impetus for changing the Negro from a dependent to an independent person. Instead of calling the conflict "The Civil War," or, as they say in the South, "The War Between the States," I think it should be called "The Great War of Liberation." In the eyes of the black community, it shattered the slave system. It offered an opportunity not merely for initiative, but to play the kind of heroic roles that were practically out of the question for Negroes in the prewar period.

The war also gave the blacks a moral claim on the North; they had fought in the Union Army. The combination of their liberation and the claim that they had on the Northern conscience set the stage for Reconstruction. I think it gave them the experience and self-reliance to play an independent political role, and it provided a moral claim which persuaded the Northern electorate to support legislation guaranteeing black men the right to vote and a whole range of civil rights. The Civil War amounted to much more than the Thirteenth Amendment. It was an experience of emancipation, of *self*-emancipation for many Negroes, and an experience of emancipation from prejudice for much of the North—not complete emancipation, alas, but at least a move in that direction.

The personality and character of the typical southern-born black man in the late 1860's was dramatically different from what it had been in the late 1850's, and the attitude of the typical Northerner (and perhaps of many Southerners) in the late 1860's was also different from what it had been earlier.

J.A.G.   What evidence is there that the war affected the attitudes of white Southerners toward the Negro?

S.M.E.   The South had to face a number of hard facts in the course of the Civil War. First, the fact that their slaves were not loyal. The notion that they would remain loyal no matter what disappeared quickly. This demonstrated that the system was, in the last analysis, based on force. Then there was the belief that the slave was totally incapable of independent action. Countless escapes destroyed this illusion. The Southerners had been convinced that the black man couldn't conceivably fight for his own freedom. Experience demonstrated that this was not so. One of the great ironies of the Civil War was Robert E. Lee's request to the Confederate Congress that it enlist slaves in the Confederate Army. The very notion of blacks in the Army would have been considered madness in 1861. After the 54th Massachusetts' unsuccessful attack on Battery Wagner, the Confederate officers looked at the black prisoners who had been taken with incredulity. *Brave* blacks! They just couldn't be real. And despite the fact that the Confederates had promised to execute Negroes found with arms, these men were treated rather well, perhaps in part from fear of retaliation against Southern prisoners, but in part, I think, from grudging recognition that they were not what they had thought they were.

In this connection, I've always felt that the Civil War generation in the South was probably more open-minded about the capacities of the black man than the generation that grew up in the Progressive era. There people had lived through a revolution, and all their theories about the natural inferiority and limitations of the slave hadn't coincided with the facts. They developed a flexibility which was not inherited by their sons. Perhaps it is reappearing again in their grandsons, but I think the Southerners who grew up in the first decades of the twentieth century were far more rigid than those who lived through the Civil War and Reconstruction.

A number of young historians are trying to demonstrate that slaves were brave, self-reliant, and heroic. Hence, for example, their attack on William Styron's fictional portrait of Nat Turner, the instigator of the most important pre-Civil War slave rebellion. These young historians are missing a great opportunity by not devoting more attention to the Civil War and Reconstruction in their search for heroes. American slavery was so rigid that the range of opportunity it offered for heroic action was of necessity limited. But conditions changed dramatically in the war.

Young black scholars in particular could bring something quite special to this subject, a special sensitivity rising from their own experiences of what liberation means. What did service in the Union Army mean to a slave? How did the political activity that was opened to Negroes by Reconstruction affect them? What was it like to organize people who had no political experience? Answers to these questions would make far more impact on American thinking than waging war on William Styron over his fictional rendition of Nat Turner.

J.A.G.   If institutions and cultural values affected slavery, how did slavery affect other institutions?

S.M.E.   That's a question that concerned Thomas Jefferson. One of his criticisms of slavery was that it had a bad effect on the moral character of the young whites. In recent years, the historian Eugene Genovese has argued that the Southern planters attempted to create a feudal society, a nonbourgeois culture, in the South. I have some reservations about this idea, but it is undeniable that slavery created a unique and special social pattern in America. It gave the planter tremendous power over human beings, and also considerable responsibility for them. This style of life was very satisfying for many Southerners, although probably more so for men than women.

In any case, the quality of Southern life was inevitably affected by slavery. The institution limited the economic opportunities of nearly everyone. Almost the only way to rise was by acquiring slaves. The range of activities so common in the North and West, such as opportunity to develop a small business, was much smaller in the South.

J.A.G.   Did slavery corrupt white Southerners by giving them more power than they were emotionally capable of handling?

S.M.E.   Clearly, slavery gave people power if they wanted to use it, or if they wanted to abuse it. In the last analysis, the inhibitions on the use of power were internal. If the man was a sadist and his plantation was somewhat isolated, there was practically no limit on what he could do. The overwhelming majority were not sadists; the impact of slavery on them was to create a sense of responsibility as well as one of power. The danger for them was the feeling of benevolent omnipotence that resulted; the planter tended to view himself as somehow a greater man than he was in fact. This could have some very attractive results—a kind of gentility and security was characteristic of many Southerners. On the other hand, it could also produce smugness and inefficiency. The extraordinary difficulty that the Confederate government had in finding efficient administrators was not unconnected with the plantation culture. Being accustomed to having his own way isn't the best training for an efficient administrator.

J.A.G.   What is your view of the theory that because of slavery Southerners suffered from a massive guilty conscience?

S.M.E.   I don't quite know, but one thing is clear: once slavery was gone, nobody really mourned for it. There was a lot of nostalgic writing about the Old South, but no one suggested restoring slavery. Beyond that, it is true that men like Robert E. Lee were hostile to slavery and felt guilty about it. On the other hand, I think that the success of the proslavery argument before the war in convincing whites of the justice of the institution cannot be discounted. One of the most persuasive arguments was that the black man was incapable of taking care of himself; that it was the responsibility of the white man to look after him. Probably, most Southerners were able to resolve their guilt by stressing the paternalism of the system. It was possible for Southerners to picture themselves as humane, Christian planters responsible for the material and spiritual welfare of their "families," the black and the white members alike.

J.A.G.   What was the effect, psychologically and socially, of slavery on the slave? Would you describe the "concentration-camp analogy" developed in your book, *Slavery*, and indicate if the criticisms that some other historians have made of your analysis of the slave personality have led you to modify your opinions?

S.M.E. The concentration-camp analogy was, I still think, a good idea, but an idea with a limited purpose. Let me give you the context. The problem I was investigating was posed by Kenneth Stampp's comment in the introduction of his book *The Peculiar Institution* that the Negro was, after all, only a white man with a black skin. In emphasizing the essential equality of men, liberal American historians like Stampp were playing down the impact of a culture, of a society, on men's behavior. Stampp was doing what the abolitionists often did: describing slavery as a terribly coercive and restrictive institution, and then assuming that the products of slavery were like free, white, Anglo-Saxon Americans. This struck me as both incorrect and unjust. Therefore, I tried to demonstrate that there had been situations in which complex Europeans had been reduced to terrible dependence, which had a profound effect on their personalities. I chose the concentration-camp analogy because it was dramatic, because it was fresh in our memories, and because it got around the problem of race.

My purposes were limited. What I wanted to do was to show that granted sufficient power you could do terrible things to personality. The problem with the analogy was that it was a little too vivid. The tendency was to take it literally. A number of critics insisted that I was calling the Southern plantation a concentration camp, which was sheer nonsense. Others accused me of arguing that slavery wasn't really so bad, because if slavery was like a concentration camp, the Negro personality would have been much more crushed than it was. I found myself being attacked by supporters of the pro-Southern historian Ulrich B. Phillips, and by those who adopted a strong liberal position on racial equality.

Now, over the years, I've been stuck with the concentration-camp analogy, but I'm perfectly willing to live with it. In recent years there have been some quite sophisticated criticisms of the idea, the most sophisticated one being that, as analogies go it was too dramatic, that it might be better to make an analogy with prisons or mental hospitals— institutions which are closer to the plantation in that their *aim* is not the destruction of personality.

I think Americans are very reluctant to accept the notion that social institutions affect personality. They don't like to believe that power can change people. Americans haven't always thought this way; the Founding Fathers took the notion pretty much for granted, which explains why they were so suspicious of power. But somewhere around the 1830's or 1840's the romantic idea developed that men cannot be corrupted by society, by institutions—by anything. Thus the frightening thing about the concentration-camp analogy was the notion that, granted sufficient power, men can be changed against their wills.

J.A.G. What light does this interpretation throw on the controversy over the degree to which American slaves were rebellious?

S.M.E. The historian Eugene Genovese has an interesting answer to this question. Under a slave system, he argues, a tremendous amount of aggression has to be repressed. If the structure of power in the community remains intact, the slave can exist as a very dependent and irresponsible, and even a loyal and faithful servant. But suddenly the repression can crack and turn the slave (Genovese uses Haiti as the example) into a wild, explosive revolutionary.

My own view is that the system was very coercive, but any human arrangement is imperfect. Being imperfect, slavery allowed many to escape its full impact—that is, to vent the aggressions that the system theoretically would not tolerate. Such men could develop complex enough personalities to rebel.

The difficulty in understanding the Nat Turner uprising is that it does not fit into any simple formula. If you take the Denmark Vesey uprising, the pattern seems to be fairly clear cut. These were urban slaves with a maximum amount of independence, not closely supervised by their masters. Many of them were skilled workers. They had their own social life. But Nat Turner and his followers do not fit into this pattern.

The number of slave rebellions, however, was limited. This did not mean that slaves were happy, but that both rationally and subconsciously they knew the system was too powerful to challenge. Therefore, they internalized their aggressions, or channeled them into safe modes of expression. For example, I think the legendary stupidity of slaves that planters always talked about was a perfect device for expressing aggression. One thing a slave could do was never quite learn what he was supposed to. The breaking of tools, the abuse of animals, were indications of aggression.

J.A.G. The so-called New Left historians have criticized older historians for having failed to provide them with what they call a "usable past." In part, their argument rests on the way historians have treated the history of the black man in America. What is your opinion both of their complaints and of their own attempts to provide us with a usable past?

S.M.E. The problem of providing Americans, black and white, with a "usable past," is a very tricky one. If Negroes want the kind of usable past that Parson Weems offered—a black George Washington chopping down a cherry tree and throwing a silver dollar across the Rappahannock—this can be provided. We can trot any number of black heroes across the stage. But I don't think this is really a "usable past." A true usable past for the Negro would be a re-creation of the life of the black community under slavery, during the Civil War and Reconstruction, and in the latter part of the nineteenth century. The kind of past the black American needs is the sort that has been given to the immigrant in history. The black experience has not yet become a part of our general culture, but it can so become if historians do their job. However, the kind of past that many of the New Left historians—some black and some white—have been asking for would be as phony and as stereotyped as that provided for immigrants a generation ago. You know—Chaim Solomon helped to finance the Revolution, and so forth and so on. "Pick your ethnic group and we will explain what a great role it played in the crucial years of American history." Nobody really took this kind of history seriously, or not for very long. To ask historians to provide the Negro with this kind of usable past would be like the Russians ordering artists and writers to produce art that will foster revolutionary morale. Without exception, the result will be stereotypes, and about as exciting as social realism in Russian art.

What is most important in writing the history of the Negro is that standards be maintained: the standards of good critical history and imaginative literature. There must not be a double standard: we must judge this "art" the same way we judge any other art. Given time, and I do not think it will take a great deal of time, the black experience is going to be part of the general American experience.

J.A.G. Is it possible for historians ever to know what it was like to be a slave, given the inarticulateness and the illiteracy of the overwhelming majority of slaves?

S.M.E. The era of slavery will be the most difficult to write about, but the Civil War and Reconstruction eras, and of course more recent times, present increasingly less difficult problems. There's a mine of material, and once we get a clear sense of the later period, our ability to project back to ante-bellum days is going to increase.

J.A.G. Are there any records of the experience of being a slave, other than those of the very small handful who escaped, and those of exceptional ability who learned to write?

S.M.E. Some black historians, Vincent Harding for example, have argued that there are records—folklore, songs, religious traditions—that can be used effectively by imaginative researchers. I don't think we will ever be able to re-create the life of the slave the way we can re-create the life of the immigrants. On the other hand, I think we can get a lot more mileage out of the material we've got. How much information do we have about the life of Egyptian peasants three thousand years ago? The average ancient historian roars with laughter when we complain about the scarcity of material. We must attack the subject with the kind of patience that the historian of ancient times employs as a matter of course. I would hazard the guess that there's more there than any of us realize, and also that we'll know a great deal more about slavery ten years from now than we do now.

J.A.G. What are the half-dozen or so books that you would recommend to persons interested in the subject we have been discussing? In each case, would you indicate briefly what the particular contribution of the volume is?

S.M.E. Ulrich Phillips, *American Negro Slavery* (1918). Phillips presents a very benign picture of slavery, and his treatment of the Negro is maddeningly condescending, but this was *the* basic book on the subject for well over a generation, and it is difficult to fully appreciate the books written during the last fifteen years without some knowledge of the work of Phillips.

Kenneth Stampp, *The Peculiar Institution* (1956). Utterly rejecting Phillips' assumptions about the essentially paternalistic character of American slavery, Stampp stressed the brutality and exploitation which underlay the entire system.

Frank Tannenbaum, *Slave and Citizen* (1948). Tannenbaum's brilliant comparison of the slave system of North America and Latin America helped launch a major argument over the precise character of slavery in the Western Hemisphere. Although a number of Tannenbaum's assertions have been questioned, this is still one of the most challenging books on the subject.

Eugene Genovese, *The Political Economy of Slavery* (1964). Genovese's analysis of the slaveholding South is the most imaginative piece of Marxist scholarship in our generation. Taking the Southerners at their word, he argues that the ante-bellum South was indeed a separate civilization, a pre-capitalist culture which was both unwilling and unable to adjust to the liberal, democratic, capitalistic values that increasingly were coming to dominate the rest of the nation.

Richard Wade, *Slavery in the Cities* (1964). A specialized study, but one that provides a unique insight into one of the basic dilemmas of the ante-bellum South. How do you retain control over slaves in an urban environment?

David Brian Davis, *The Problem of Slavery in Western Culture* (1968). A sweeping survey of Western attitudes toward slavery from ancient times down to the nineteenth century. Davis deals with the problem of slavery in the broadest possible context, and concludes that its central characteristics were rooted deep in Western civilization.

Winthrop Jordan, *White Over Black: American Attitudes Toward the Negro, 1550–1812* (1968). One of the few truly definitive books on the relationship of slavery and race. Jordan traces the development of racial attitudes in the North American colonies, and carefully considers the role which they played in defining the place of the Negro in American society.

Russel B. Nye

Thought and Culture: 1775–1860

RUSSEL B. NYE, Distinguished Professor of English at Michigan State University and former President of the American Studies Association, is an authority on American intellectual history. His *George Bancroft: Brahmin Rebel* (1945) won a Pulitzer prize, and his *Cultural Life of the New Nation* (1960) is the standard work on the United States intellectual currents before the Civil War. His other books include a study of *Midwestern Progressive Politics* (1948), a biography of *William Lloyd Garrison* (1956), *Fettered Freedom: Civil Liberties and the Antislavery Controversy* (1947), and several volumes of essays. Professor Nye discusses social and cultural trends in the United States from the Revolution to the Civil War.

John A. Garraty Professor Nye, looking at American civilization broadly, at the time of the American Revolution was it merely a provincial European civilization? For example, was the so-called "American Enlightenment" different from the European Enlightenment?

Russel B. Nye It seems to me that there are three salient facts about the American Enlightenment. It came late, it was eclectic, and it was American. The Enlightenment in Europe and in England probably reached its height in the late seventeenth and early eighteenth centuries, a full generation or more before Americans grasped its ideas. Americans of the late eighteenth century—men like Thomas Jefferson, Thomas Paine, Benjamin Franklin, Joel Barlow, Philip Freneau, John Adams, and Alexander Hamilton—worked with ideas that were half a century old. Americans were still quoting Locke when Rousseau was writing; they were using the English Revolution of 1688 to justify their own revolution almost a century later. And the Enlightenment remained an operative force in American culture until the 1820's, long after the romantic movement in England had reached its climax.

The American Enlightenment was a hodgepodge of ideas, British, French, and others. When a British idea—say, the right of revolution—appealed to Americans, they chose it; when French ideas attracted them —for example, the ideas of the goodness of human nature and the beneficence of the universe—they used those. So if the American Enlightenment was a system of contradictions, it was also a very useful system. One characteristic of the Enlightenment in America was the tendency of Americans to copy what the French and a few British radicals were doing. The British Enlightenment was predominantly a conservative movement; Americans tended to espouse ideas from it that British devotees were, at best, not very sure of.

Of course, there were conservative and radical elements within the movement in America, too. Take President Timothy Dwight of Yale, for example—I'd call him a conservative Enlightenment revolutionary. He had a strong belief in the continuity of institutions, in property rights, and in the sanctity of contracts, but he also had a great deal of hope for, if not complete faith in, the ability of human nature to govern itself wisely. On the other hand, a radical like the poet Philip Freneau was a kind of Frenchified revolutionary: anti-institutional, much less concerned with property rights than with human rights, a worshiper of Reason, with a capital "R."

The third important thing about the American Enlightenment was that it was *here*, in a different kind of political and social environment, in the midst of institutions and ideas that differed from those of Britain and the rest of Europe. It had a very strong nationalistic context. The ideal of the Enlightenment in Britain and Europe was to be a citizen of the world. A rational, enlightened man was supposed to be above nationalistic sentiments. The fraternity of enlightened, rational men, whether they were French, or British, or whatever, considered themselves part of an international society.

But in this new, self-conscious, deeply nationalistic society, a society searching for its own identity, men of the American Enlightenment were convinced that theirs was a separate and distinct kind of civilization, with a future of its own. Thus, the Enlightenment idea of universality, when transferred into a society where class lines were indistinct and fluctuating, where power was shifting toward the middle class, became a very different thing. Ours was a nationalistic Enlightenment, which is almost a contradiction in terms in the eighteenth century.

J.A.G. Can you explain how a society which produced so many outstanding statesmen and political thinkers in the Revolutionary generation developed only second-rate writers and artists?

R.B.N. American colonial culture was, of course, quite naturally colonial; its models were British and the standard of achievement that dominated it were British-derived. An American poet or painter or writer could find success only in London, and if he were London-approved. Even after the Revolution, American authors, in order to gain critical recognition or approval, sometimes pretended to be English. James Fenimore Cooper started a rumor that the pseudonymous author of his own first novel was really an Englishman. Benjamin West, Copley, Vanderlin, and Stuart all felt that they had to go to Europe if they were going to be true painters.

Until Americans could free themselves from this kind of thinking and do things in their own way for an American public and in an American frame of reference, first-rate cultural achievements were unlikely. Looking at it from another angle, however, one might say that American cultural achievements were really better than one might expect. In the late eighteenth century, the occupations most challenging to a young man seeking to make his way in life would be politics, law, and business, not painting, poetry, or any of the gentler pursuits. John Quincy Adams, who liked to write poetry, and wasn't a bad poet at that, put it well when he said it was extremely difficult to be a man of business and a man of rhyme. I often wonder what kind of pictures Jefferson would have painted, for example, had he lived at a different place or time, or what kind of poetry Alexander Hamilton, who was a sensitive, perceptive (and, I think, romantic) man, might have written under different conditions.

J.A.G. If the provinciality of American colonial life inhibited the development of a native art and literature, how did the rise of nationalism after the Revolution affect these pursuits?

R.B.N. Nationalism was *the* major influence, probably. It led to an aggressive, widespread, and urgent demand for a native culture, a specifically *American* literature, that dealt with American materials and presented them to American audiences. Critics demanded, "Let us have an American Shakespeare, an American Milton, an American Addison," and everybody who could write tried to do it. Nathaniel Appleton said, just after the Revolution, "We are called upon to sing a new song, the song that neither we nor our fathers were ever able to sing before." The period after the Revolution was filled with such exhortations. A new great nation ought to produce a new great art to prove its greatness, Americans felt.

Demands like this encouraged many people to produce art, some of it very bad. Critics tended to praise or condemn art depending on whether or not it was national. So nationalism had both good and bad effects; but, in the long run, the good outweighed the bad. The demand forced Americans to reshape their critical standards. What kind of art do we want? Granted that it should be nationalistic, what should we accept, what should we reject? What should we do with this whole great new area, the American experience? Nationalism forced Americans to look at and define themselves, as well as their art. The intellectual energy expended on these questions led to new ideas, new critical standards. I think this was intensely important in determining the shape of American culture. For all creative persons, the central problem was how to be a good artist and also an American.

J.A.G. Did the new emphasis on *American* art affect popular taste? Did people stop reading British novelists?

R.B.N. They continued to read British novelists; there was no copyright law, and they read British novels by the reams, and attended British and European plays. But a young American playwright would choose a popular British or German play and translate it into American terms— that is, write an imitation of it. Novelists took the British sentimental epistolary novel of the time and wrote their own versions of it. But there was an American quality in much of this work. Royall Tyler modeled *The Contrast* (1787) on Sheridan's *The Rivals*. It's quite derivative of Sheridan, so Tyler did not write "the first American play" in a strict sense. What he did was put in a real American character, Jonathan the Yankee, and contrast American and European manners. And the play begins and ends with a great exhortation to the audience about patriotism.

J.A.G. What was the impact of the work and ideas of Noah Webster on American culture?

R.B.N. The greatest impact of Webster was exactly in this field of cultural nationalism, of which he was one of the great proponents. "America must be as independent in literature as she is in politics," he said. He saw this as a declaration of cultural independence that should go along with the declaration of political independence. His contributions to language and lexicography, of course, were his best-known achievements. His famous speller of 1783 sold upwards of 75 million copies within a few generations and shaped American spelling and pronunciation for all time to come. His monumental dictionary of 1828 had a similarly profound impact. Linguistic nationalism was just part of his effect. He championed an American system of education. He labored long and hard for the passage of a copyright law to protect American writers from foreign competition. He prepared the first American revised version of the Bible, and as a magazine editor, critic, and essayist he also stressed nationalism.

He asked people constantly to be conscious of themselves and their culture and their values, even their language—to be self-conscious, self-critical, self-aware. He did this aggressively, sometimes abrasively, and sometimes uncritically, but he did it.

J.A.G.   At the beginning of the nineteenth century, the United States was still predominantly rural and agricultural. Did it have a rural culture— that is, one that was dominated by rural attitudes and values?

R.B.N.   Society was predominantly rural in 1800, yet I don't think that American culture was dominated by a rural attitude. There is an interesting dichotomy in the late eighteenth and early nineteenth centuries between theory and practice. Americans were heir to the myth of agrarianism. They were heirs of Rousseau and the English tradition of country life, but at the same time an urban culture developed rapidly in New York, Boston, Charleston, Baltimore, and other towns. Americans pretended that the rural life was best, but they were living in cities and developing an elite urban culture. American poets lived in cities and wrote lovingly of the joys of country living.

Of course, Jefferson traced many of Europe's ills to the city. But I think this was partly an intellectual pose rather than his actual belief. There is a long American tradition of hating the city, from Jefferson right down to Frank Lloyd Wright. The city has always been the home of the intellectual, who can't live without it but who has been its most vocal critic. It is interesting to note that Jefferson's architecture was anything but rural, being a highly sophisticated continuation of a highly urbanized tradition, just as Frank Lloyd Wright's was.

In the light of recent work in urban social history, we can question now the oft-repeated statement that until the mid-nineteenth century American culture was predominantly rural-oriented. The United States in the 1780's was only about 3 percent urban in population, but the fact that the nation had a large rural population doesn't necessarily mean that it was rural-dominated. Carl Bridenbaugh pointed out some time ago that five urban centers—Boston, Newport, New York, Philadelphia, and Charleston—dominated American culture by about 1770. No matter how rural the mass of the population was, these were the centers of culture. Eighteenth-century America was much like eighteenth-century England in this respect, where cultural life was focused in London. Among the Founding Fathers, only Washington and Madison could really be called "country gentlemen."

J.A.G. Not Jefferson?

R.B.N. I don't see Jefferson as a real country gentleman. He was certainly no farmer; he was a highly sophisticated cosmopolitan who happened not to live in an urban setting. The Adamses, Hancock, Franklin, Hamilton—they were all city-bred products, and city-oriented. Furthermore, even for country gentlemen the custom was to be educated somewhere else—in England or on the Continent by preference. And they brought back with them the values of a highly sophisticated, urban civilization.

Late colonial and early republican social, political, and cultural life were focused on urban centers. Yet, for a number of reasons the rural agrarian way of life has always had more articulate spokesmen than the urban way, and thus we may have overemphasized the rural-agrarian aspect of American culture.

J.A.G. But how did the growth of cities change American culture?

R.B.N. First of all, the movement from country to city, combined with a much swifter growth of population in urban centers, drastically changed the nature of the American population. While nonurban population grew two-and-one-half times larger in the early nineteenth century, urban population was increasing about seven times. This urbanization influenced American life by causing a rethinking of social and community relationships. City living tended to isolate people in groups. The poor lived here, the rich there, one ethnic group here, another there. There was a business section and a residential section. As cities grew larger and larger, the problem of establishing workable relationships among groups became much more knotty, relationships on every level from social and economic to political and intellectual much more complicated. Yet answers were needed quickly.

The traditional virtues of self-reliance and individualism did not apply directly or exactly to city life. The city had many problems that required group action, intergroup action, and, indeed, social action. So the rise of urban culture called into question the American belief in individualism.

In the second place, urbanization produced the beginnings of a mass society—large concentrations of people subject to more or less the same influences—at the same time that the mass media began to emerge. Thus the conditions for creating mass culture appeared in the American city. Improved presses, improved communications, better roads—all these things began in the early nineteenth century. The newspaper and the magazine have to have concentrations of people in order to exist. The theater is a peculiarly urban type of art; you can't have a theater in an open field. The novelist seeking to sell his books needs a concentrated mass market. Therefore, the growth of urban civilization was a prerequisite to the growth of a mass culture.

An urban civilization was also a prerequisite to an elite culture. The cities attract the very wealthy, the discriminating, the highly educated —that is, the demanding kind of elite audience necessary for so-called high art as opposed to popular or mass art. The patrons of poets and musicians, the purchasers of paintings and sculpture live in cities. Art galleries and symphony orchestras, theaters and specialized libraries are possible only in an urban setting. All these things developed in early nineteenth-century American cities.

The city also encouraged cultural diversification and individuality. This may seen a paradox, but I believe it is true. In smaller communities, standards of taste and behavior are likely to be set by small groups. Everybody understands what they are, and departures from the standards set by these groups are rather noticeable in a small town, and quite easily controlled. But a large and diverse city tolerates, even encourages, differences. The city is filled with many groups pursuing their own interests in their own way. No over-all set of rules governs them all. So the rise of cities encouraged intellectual and artistic and social diversification in ways that smaller, nonurban communities did not.

The social organization of cities became more complex, too. Individuals, again paradoxically, had a greater opportunity for self-development. It is hard to imagine Walt Whitman, for example, writing *Leaves of Grass* in a back-country New England community. He needed the city's individuality and diversity, and of course the sustenance that he drew from it. He might have been a poet had he lived on a farm, but he wouldn't have been the Whitman we know.

The growth of urban America fostered a kind of cultural behavioral individualism, in somewhat the same way that the frontier may have fostered social and economic individualism. One kind of individualism is city-produced, the other kind frontier-produced. I suppose this is a kind of Turnerian theory of cultural urbanism. A somewhat different point has been developed by David Weimer, the idea that the city has provided artists and writers with a continuing metaphor for the interpretation of American experience. Weimer's book, *The City as Metaphor*, is a good analysis of this idea. Morton and Lucia White's *The Intellectual Versus the City* is another provocative approach. The love-hate relationship that Americans have had with the city from the very beginning, their ambivalence toward urban life, the pervasiveness of the rural myth even today in a nation which is primarily urban, has provided motive power for a good deal of American thinking. Simply by existing, the city has had a great cultural impact because it has led us to question certain rural values that don't work there.

J.A.G. Do you think that the agrarian myth, as it is commonly referred to, was produced by the decline of agrarian life? Is it purely a romanticization of the past?

R.B.N. To a great extent, but I think it was a romanticization even when the nation was rural. Take even a man like Crèvecoeur. Who was he? A French aristocrat; his *Letters from an American Farmer* (1782) are a highly romantic Rousseauistic view of what nature and man ought to be like. Of course he was a gentleman farmer of some means who married a wealthy Tory lady and who named his estate in French country fashion. Agrarianism was a myth even to Crèvecoeur; indeed, he was one of the originators of the myth.

J.A.G. Was that true of Jefferson, when he wrote that "those who labor in the earth are the chosen people of God"?

R.B.N. I think so. The attitude has existed since the late eighteenth century. It is one of the great reasons for the appeal, for example, of something like Whittier's "Snowbound," which was, incidentally, one of the most popular poems of the nineteenth century—popular with all sorts of people who'd never been close to a New England snowbound farm. A generation that had moved to the city was nostalgic for an America that did not exist. In our own day, New York apartment-dwellers set up barbecues on their balconies nineteen stories up; they are living a kind of agrarian myth.

J.A.G. Are there any realistic descriptions of rural life in the eighteenth or early nineteenth century comparable, for example, to the writer Hamlin Garland's description of the crudeness and difficulties of agricultural life in the post-Civil War years in books like *A Son of the Middle Border?*

R.B.N. I really don't know of any. There were, of course, highly urban and sophisticated artists, writers like Oliver Wendell Holmes, Sr., William Cullen Bryant, the Knickerbocker group, but I can't think of any writer who really said, "Look, rural life is not all that it's cracked up to be. Farm work is hard and crude and dirty and you don't make very much money." Instead, the nostalgic remembrance of a kind of existence that probably never did exist is pervasive through the period.

J.A.G. How did the influx of non-English immigrants between 1790 and 1860 affect American society and culture?

R.B.N. Obviously, this influx caused many social, political, economic, and religious changes and problems. This has been detailed in a good many places. What I'd rather talk about are the cultural issues and problems, using the term "cultural" rather broadly.

The large numbers of immigrants as well as their non-English origins brought up for the first time the problem of Americanization, of assimilation. An earlier American society didn't find it difficult to tolerate a few immigrants of different stocks, even if they weren't assimilated. But beginning in the nineteenth century, large numbers of people who had different languages and cultures and religions and values came in, and the nation had to try to figure out how to handle them.

J.A.G. Wasn't this a political problem rather than a cultural one? Many Scotch-Irish migrated to Pennsylvania in the eighteenth century. In proportion to the population, that immigration was very heavy. Yet, in a colonial society that had not developed a sense of its own nationality, their sociocultural differences didn't seem very important.

R.B.N. There is certainly a parallel between nationalism and cultural assimilation. The immigrants had to be assimilated somehow into the American political system. In culture, as in politics, as in society, nineteenth-century citizens came back to this same question: "What is an American?" If these newcomers are going to be Americans, then what precisely *are* they going to be, and how are we going to make them be it? The idea of the melting pot arose clear back in the eighteenth century. The ideal was the assimilated immigrant. That meant one thing when one dealt, as Crèvecoeur did, with a Scottish Protestant farmer in 1790. It meant quite a different thing when applied to an Irish Catholic unskilled laborer or factory hand in 1840. So the problems, "What is an American?" and "How is one made?" first became serious in the early nineteenth century, and these were problems of immigration and naturalization policies, methods of acculturation, the question of whether or not the immigrant retains his values or loses them, and of whether he changes his language. What arises is the melting-pot concept of culture as opposed to the mosaic concept of culture. (Another, less elegant metaphor is the "melting pot" versus the "beef stew.")

A second result of this flood of immigrants was to make American culture uniquely heterogeneous. No other modern culture is so utterly and thoroughly composed of borrowed elements. By the mid-nineteenth century it was perfectly clear that American culture meant cultural multiplicity, a society open to the ideas and cultures of many other nations. We could have kept the immigrants out, but we didn't. We continued the "Open Door" policy until the twentieth century. The decision not to close the door was crucial. It was made before 1850, I think consciously. All the heterogeneous masses of immigrants brought contributions with them, and that early-nineteenth-century decision to have a society of cultural multiplicity guaranteed, I believe, a kind of

receptivity to American culture. In other words, it made Americans willing to receive, as few other cultures are, contributions from elsewhere.
It also assured a pragmatic or practical approach to foreign ideas and
customs. Americans choose those that they need and reject those they
don't need. Receptivity and practicality or pragmatism are very much
a part of the American character, and they date from the early nineteenth
century. We choose what's useful to us. We'll choose a European art
form if it's useful; we'll accept certain contributions, let's say, from
Jewish, Italian, or Catholic immigrants that fit, and reject others . . .
this kind of thing.

    This attitude helps explain the dynamic nature of American culture
and society in the nineteenth century. I don't mean that American
culture is simply a conglomerate mixture of all these contributions. Far
from that. But the influx of immigrants gave Americans the opportunity
to select those aspects from other cultures that were relevant and useful
to the national culture.

J.A.G.   Would you discuss the changes that occurred in education, religion, philosophy, and political ideology in America between, roughly,
1790 and the 1840's?

R.B.N.   Changes in almost all areas of thought in this period seem to
group themselves about one common factor that characterizes the early
nineteenth century, that is, the emphasis on the importance of the individual: on his ability to identify his problems and to solve them; on
the necessity of providing the individual with the political, intellectual,
spiritual, and social means to develop himself to the fullest; on the belief that the individual must realize all his potential. This element unites
what at first glance seems to be a confused and disparate kind of age.
It's the element that unites Emerson and Jackson, William Lloyd Garrison and Horace Mann. These men and dozens of others in one way or
another would have agreed that the chief end of society is to provide the
individual with unlimited opportunity for self-development—what Emerson called in one of his beautifully turned phrases, "the infinitude of the
private man." Jackson could never have stated this as well as Emerson,
but the Jacksonian political philosophy, if we can call it a philosophy,
was rooted in exactly the same kind of belief.

    There is a difference between the nineteenth-century belief in the
individual and the eighteenth-century belief. Jefferson was a great be-
liever in the individual; he saw man as a piece of a social unit, a part
of the aggregate. There is a strong social aspect in the eighteenth-century
concept of the individual. Now nineteenth-century thinkers took a view
of the individual that was characteristically romantic. The individual
was separate, free-standing—an independent unit. His social connections
were less significant. Thoreau, who repudiated society, is a good example

of the romantic individual in action here. Jefferson would never have repudiated society in the way that Thoreau did.

How did one go about developing the individual? Chiefly through broadening the base of education, getting more children into school. Education was aimed at the development of the individual. It might have all sorts of social consequences, but the main point was to educate the individual. And the social reformers of the period were simply finding ways by which institutional hindrances could be removed from individual development. It might be through a food fad, like vegetarianism, or through liberation in dress, like bloomers. It might be by establishing a utopia in which the individual could come to full fruition, like in Brook Farm or any of the other utopian communities of the time, which all aimed at liberating the individual.

J.A.G.   These were communal forms of individualism?

R.B.N.   That's right. It's a great paradox—one entered a communal society, put himself under a communal discipline, in order to develop his individuality. This is the key to understanding the Oneida community and many of the others. Oneida is particularly interesting in this connection because there individual talents were employed for the social good. The man who made mousetraps well could make the best mousetraps in the world if he developed himself individually, that was the theory—but then, of course, he was also part of the society.

Abolitionism, the whole argument over civil liberties, was aimed at freeing the individual. This seems to me the factor that binds all the reform movements together. The key to the dynamics of the period was the belief that the individual had the power to make correct decisions and to transform his society by making these decisions. Take the sum total of these individual decisions, translate them into social, political, and economic terms, and you improve life for everybody. That was what Emerson meant when he said, "Society is like a wave." The wave itself advances and the individual particles which are part of the wave advance too. It's a nice metaphor.

The central theme of all the changes was man's faith in his progress. It was a terribly self-assured age. The Shaker seeress and mystic Paulina Bates said: "The present age is commencing the most extraordinary and momentous era that ever took place on earth." That's a pretty broad statement, but not uncommon for the period. This is what they felt. Americans believed that, if they could liberate the power of the individual (and they were sure they could), they could redirect and reform their lives and their society. That was why a hard-headed Yankee workingman would join a utopian community, what sent Boston ladies to work in madhouses, what sent Unitarian ministers into the hurly-burly of the abolition movement. Remove the obstacles from a man's path, give him an education and the vote, teach him habits of thrift, organize labor unions, improve the schools, wear sensible clothing. Some attempts to free the individual were far out on the fringes. Many reformers were fanatics. But they were all making serious attempts to make the individual count. James Russell Lowell said that this was an idea "of the most deadly explosiveness."

J.A.G. Literary historians usually refer to the first half of the century as the Romantic Age. What was specifically romantic about the best literature of the period?

R.B.N. Exactly what romanticism is is hard to establish. Beginning about the middle of the eighteenth century, thinkers revived interest in a body of ideas that had been relatively neglected for a century and a half. These ideas which caused people to question some of the attitudes of the Age of Reason and Enlightenment were called "romanticism." It's not a terribly good term, and does not describe a unified system, but a kind of climate of opinion.

The romantic view rested on three general concepts. One was the idea of organism (things were conceived of as wholes with their own internal laws of development and governance). This was true of both men and societies. If society and its institutions were organic units, they could be studied as other organic units were studied. If they had internal laws of governance, these could be discovered. This idea opened the way for a new, confident approach to man and to society.

The second concept was the idea of dynamics, of motion and growth. Everything is in flux, progressive probably, but in any event moving. Beliefs, institutions, concepts—all of these being fluid are capable of being manipulated and adapted. This is quite different from the approach of the Enlightenment, which saw things as fixed and stable. If societies can be changed and if they move, they can move toward the better.

The third concept of romanticism was the idea of diversity, that differences of opinion, culture, taste, and societies and characters are valuable. To the Age of Reason, rationalism meant a kind of conformity; there were rational standards to which things conformed. To the Romantic Age, consensus was much less important than individual diversity. Diversity to the romantic was "natural" because he saw it in nature. This, of course, reinforced individualism, belief in the value of being different. The American admiration of a man like Byron reflects this perfectly.

J.A.G. If diversity and a sense of the dynamic character of life are elements common to all romantics, what is distinctive about American romanticism as compared with European?

R.B.N. In America, these romantic values seemed to be validated by experience. The land itself revealed tremendous diversity. Belief in progress was easy where everything was growing bigger. This was the generation that had successfully prosecuted a revolution against the world's greatest military and naval power and won it. It was embarked on building a new society. The standards of the Old World didn't mean anything any more. Romanticism had a great deal of meaning in the American environment.

But there were differences between American romanticism and that of England and Europe. Partly it was a matter of emphasis. American romanticism emphasized certain things and played down certain others. For example, in America, romanticism never had quite the same political emphasis that it had in Europe and England. We had already had a political revolution; ours was an "achieved democracy." American romantics could turn their energies toward social and humanitarian goals, at liberating man generally and perfecting him. Rather than going into politics, they concerned themselves with the temperance movement, or educational reform, or women's rights.

America also had a strong Puritan, Protestant Reformation tradition which controlled the manners and morals of the Romantic Age in a way that was not the case in England. It is hard to imagine Emerson, for example, with a French mistress, or Longfellow going to fight in a Greek war. There was little rebelliousness in American romanticism, partly because of the Puritan "backlog." Some of the younger Americans played at this game. There is a wonderful picture of Whittier as a young man, with a Byronic tie and a soulful look and long hair. He said later on, "I fear I was a gay young Quaker." A lot of young Americans played this Byronic game, but with them it was only a game.

Then the American romantic had a different relationship with nature —Nature with a capital "N." American romantic poets, for example, had a much more direct relationship with nature than did British or European romantics. They stressed the visual, auditory, and tactile relationship of a person to nature in a way which, it seems to me, the British and European did not. Philip Freneau's poems on the West Indies abound with images of color and taste and temperature. Emerson said that in nature he became "a transparent eyeball," melting into his surroundings. Thoreau spoke of almost physically swimming in natural sensations, and once said jokingly that he ate the bark of trees and muskrats raw. This was his way of expressing this direct sensory contact with nature. William Cullen Bryant's almost personal emotional relationship with trees runs through his poetry, and a similar relationship pervades the work of the Hudson River painters, too. I suppose American romantics regarded nature not as watchers or spectators but as participants. They not only observed nature, they felt it. In the pictures of Niagara Falls done in the European tradition the view is from above, a vista which shows people in the foreground and the falls "over there." An American paints Niagara Falls down at eye level; you see the falls right there in front of you, you can almost hear the noise.

J.A.G.   Do you think this is related to democracy? Did Europeans still think of nature as being a matter for peasants?

R.B.N.   That may well be part of it. Part of it, of course, is that Americans had contact with nature of a kind that Europeans didn't have. They saw nature in the raw. Compare an American landscape with a carefully barbered and tailored eighteenth-century garden. Niagara Falls probably scared early travelers to death. There is a difference in the quality of the response to nature, of the intensity of the reaction.

There were also aspects of romanticism in which Americans had really not much interest. In a country where feudalism and traditionalism and political privilege were nonexistent, they didn't need to be attacked. The American did not have to be a rebel or an iconoclast; he had fewer enemies, and a much more fluid society to which to move. America produced a Thoreau but not a Marx, a Longfellow but not a Byron.

J.A.G.   Can the sudden appearance in the period from the middle 1830's to the middle 50's of such first-rate American writers as Poe, Hawthorne, Melville, and Whitman be explained in environmental terms? Was there a general flowering of American culture at this time?

R.B.N.   I'm not sure that anybody can explain why any particular period produces more or better literature or culture than another; we don't know enough about creativity to know what sparks it. Certainly, there was an unusual burst of literary activity in the mid-nineteenth century, what F. O. Matthiessen called an "American Renaissance." The growth of population between 1790 and 1830 had doubled the size of the reading public. This was a highly literate public too, as was not the case in Europe. Especially on the eastern seaboard, it was a population relatively cosmopolitan in outlook; though the country was still predominantly rural, it wasn't insular or provincial. There were urban centers of wealth and of elite taste, with strong commercial and intellectual connections with Europe and with Asia. It was also a society open to new influences and ideas, but with a very strong sense of its own past and its own future.

The country had dared a good many things, and most of them had worked. The characteristic of the period which strikes me most is its confidence in itself. Americans believed they had the ability to do what they wanted, and do it better than anyone else. In 1826, when Americans looked ahead at the second half century of independence, they overflowed with optimism. Fourth of July orators emphasized not only the power and the wealth but also the morality and the cultural accomplishments of the people.

By the 1850's, I think American society had found ways of joining powerful opposing intellectual and emotional forces without destroying the energy and vitality of these forces. A peaceful coexistence reigned, for example, between nationalism and cosmopolitanism, between traditionalism and innovation, between popular culture and an elite taste, between faith in progress and a kind of cautious conservatism. Intellectually and culturally, in the early part of the nineteenth century, the American people first developed this great ability to reconcile incompatibles, to harness in some way the energy of ideas which are opposed to each other. The American Renaissance produced an Emerson who saw the light and a Melville who saw the dark. They existed together, and both, of course, made great contributions. Longfellow urged men to have a heart for any faith, and Hawthorne refused to trust the heart at all. Both were able to interpret and to use the American human experience in quite different ways.

J.A.G.   What was particularly American about the work of the great literary figures of this period?

R.B.N.   American literature had many qualities in common with British and European literature, qualities common to all romantic literature, for American writers were part of the same romantic movement that swept the Western world. But it does seem that reading an American author (or seeing an American painting) involved something more than qualities of style. First of all, American literature had to be useful; it had to have a point or purpose. The idea of art as play was never American, nor was the idea of art as a separate entity, something removed, or even of "art for art's sake." Beginning with the Bay Psalm Book (1640) itself, Americans believed that art ought to have connections with some action, some idea, some principle. The Bay Psalm Book was designed to put the Psalms into a form that could be sung or recited by the congregation, as is made very clear in its preface. The Puritans wrote a lot of poetry, but with a functional purpose. They wrote elegies and exhortatory poems and things like that. The fact that Longfellow was the most popular poet in America is a good example of this because Longfellow had a strong sense of purposefulness. Poe had it too, in quite a different way. American art, with some notable exceptions, has been essentially one of hopefulness and confirmation. There is a strong, dark strain in writers like Melville and Hawthorne, but the stronger strain of the period is that of Emerson and Longfellow, Thoreau, Bryant, Lowell, and Whittier, and a host of lesser lights. I can't think of any really popular American writer of the period whose attitude was one of negation and doubt and despair. Remember that interest in Melville's *Moby Dick* dates from our own time and not from the nineteenth century.

There was also in the literature of the period a kind of self-assurance and independence. American writers were willing to break the rules, to be "untraditional." Sometimes they didn't even know the rules, but more often they didn't care whether the rules were there or not. Benjamin West, for example, changed the course of English painting because, as an American, he didn't know the European studio tradition and saw things differently. Thoreau and Whitman exhibited the same aggressive individualism. Whitman said, in effect, "I don't care what the rules are, I'll do it my way."

Then the American artist had a directness and simplicity, possibly even a naïveté, though he was by no means unsophisticated in all cases. Americans never took kindly to ornamentation and display. A characteristic of American prose style all the way from Cotton Mather to Franklin, to Thoreau and Emerson, right down to Hemingway, was the avoidance of ornamentation, of display for its own sake. I suppose this is part of American functionalism; the integration of parts to purpose was cultural as well as mechanical. Let me use another example of this kind of directness or naïveté or simplicity. John Smibert in the seventeenth century was an English portraitist who by London standards was third rate. He was a great success in the colonies because his direct and honest reportorial style was exactly what Americans liked.

J.A.G.   When did America begin to have an organized popular culture, and in what ways was the popular culture of the American Renaissance distinctive from the high culture of the period?

R.B.N.   You can't have popular culture unless you have a lot of people; the emergence of a popular culture was obviously tied to the emergence of a mass society. I think the terms "popular culture" and "mass culture" are interchangeable, though I realize that some students try to make a distinction.

The great population growth of the early nineteenth century laid the basis for the emergence of a popular culture. Along with this came technological advances which made it possible to supply that great population with cheap books, magazines, and newspapers. The perfection of new and cheaper paper-making techniques, of stereotyping, electrotyping, cast printing all occurred early in the century. Improved book binding machines were introduced shortly after the War of 1812, and in the 1830's came the cylinder press. Attach a cylinder press to a steam engine, and you have a publishing *industry*. In art, improvements in engraving and the development of the chromolithograph and of machinery for the reproduction of pictures took place quickly. Thus, in the early nineteenth century a mass cultural market appeared along with the technological means of supplying it. Writers to supply it appeared too: popular poets, popular artists, popular novelists. Mrs. Lydia Sigourney, the sweet singer of Hartford, published fifty-six books, two thousand articles, and contributed to three hundred magazines. She was a phenomenon of popular culture. Longfellow, I suppose, was the greatest of them all. His publishing record was fantastic. His books of poetry appeared in first printings of 150,000 to 200,000 copies. His birthday was celebrated as a national holiday; and of course he was (and still is) the only American poet memorialized in Westminster Abbey. Then there was Joseph Holt Ingraham, the first of the great American hack writers. Every boy knew Joseph Holt Ingraham; he wrote I don't know how many novels. This type of literature simply couldn't exist before; neither a public nor the means of producing or distributing it had existed.

The effects of this outburst of popular culture are quite clear. Most of all, cultural standards were no longer set by an elite but by the middle class. Culture was democratized.

J.A.G. Do you think that the development of a mass culture tended to raise the standards and improve the tastes of the mass?

R.B.N. Popular art is first of all aimed at a market. It is not a naive or unsophisticated creation at all. Obviously, the popular artist has got to be popular; he writes for the market place.

J.A.G. But Longfellow, though not a really great writer, was certainly not a hack grinding out poems for a "market." Were not many of the very best writers of this period also popular? Melville's *Moby Dick* was not widely read until later, but his earlier writings, which were not trashy, reached a wide audience. And what about Hawthorne?

R.B.N. Longfellow is an interesting case in point because there are two Longfellows. As Norman Holmes Pearson put it, "There was a Longfellow who wrote for Harvard yard, and there was a Longfellow who wrote for the people, and they both exist." Longfellow was a poet of tremendous sophistication and skill. On the other hand, he was popular because he had an almost uncanny ability to put the basic ideas of the American people into not-too-complicated verse. There is the Longfellow of "The Golden Legend," and the Longfellow of "The Village Blacksmith." He certainly wrote a lot of poor poetry in response to "public needs." As for Hawthorne, he was never a tenth as popular as Susan Warren or some of the other female novelists he called a "mob of scribbling women."

J.A.G. Would you compare the writers of the 1840's and 1850's with the leading literary figures of the previous generation, such as Washington Irving and James Fenimore Cooper?

R.B.N. This was the second generation of American writers. None of them had colonial roots; all were products of a half century of strong nationalistic feelings and of the American version of romanticism. Their chief difference from the generation of Irving, Cooper, Freneau, Barlow,

and Charles Brockden Brown was their self-confidence and their awareness of themselves as Americans.

Irving spent more than twenty years of his life abroad, and was in
many ways a European romantic. Of all his short fiction pieces, only
seven have American backgrounds, and of these we remember only
"Rip Van Winkle" and "Sleepy Hollow." The *Sketchbook*, for example,
is much more British than is commonly thought, both in manner and
subject matter. Both Fenimore Cooper and Charles Brockden Brown
were in a good many ways European-style novelists. The next generation
never rejected Europe, it *used* it. It was part of their heritage that they
could choose and use. Emerson said, "We have listened too long to the
courtly muses of Europe. We will walk on our own feet; we will work
with our own hands; we will speak our own minds."

A second difference was that this second generation of writers participated to a much greater extent in the life of the period. Longfellow, of
course, stayed more or less aloof from his times. It is surprising how
much you can read of Longfellow without ever knowing that there was
an abolition movement, a Mexican war, a Civil War, or a westward movement. But in general, Emerson, Thoreau, Whittier, the various Chan-
nings, historians like George Bancroft, scholars and critics like Edward
Everett—all the men whom Emerson called the "Young Americans" in
1844—were involved in affairs in a way that their predecessors were not.

J.A.G. Would you contrast the culture of the North with that of the
South on the eve of the Civil War? Can the differences be explained
entirely by slavery?

R.B.N. By 1860, the North and the South and the West had become
separate cultural entities; there was a self-conscious awareness of regional cultural difference. People had a lot more in common, of course,
than in contrast, but each section assumed a separate identity which the
people acted out, quite self-consciously, creating a myth of a North and
South and West which was partly founded on fancy but nevertheless
existed. Each of the regions was searching for a place within the national
identity.

Out of this mixture of half-truths, wishful thinking, and realistic
observation of differences, stereotypes emerged. The West was rough
and ready and independent, and maybe crude, but nevertheless energetic
and vital. The North was busy and materialistic and aggressive and
practical. The South was aristocratic and gay and chivalric. These generalizations were rooted in fancy as much as in fact, and perhaps more
so, but the point is that Americans believed they were true, and began
to *act* as if they were true. We still have this same sense of these regional
identities.

The stereotypes of *Cavalier and Yankee* have been analyzed by
William Taylor, and John William Ward's study, *Andrew Jackson:*

Symbol for an Age, is a work in the same vein. The concept of a North, South, and West began to pervade, for example, the magazines of the time: the democratic West, the machine-shop North, and the magnolia-scented South. These images had perhaps some basis in actual cultural differences, but as symbols they were also of great importance in determining the social-cultural climate.

But at the same time the North and South had much in common: a very strong sense of history and tradition, as seen in a New England novelist like Hawthorne; and a very strong sense of place, of identification with a locale. Both sections also had strong Protestant Reformation roots. Southern Anglicanism was conservative Anglicanism, and the great influx of Scotch-Irish into the South contributed a Calvinistic strain similar to the Puritanism of New England. In short, northern and southern Americans were identifiable; the Yankee and the prewar Southerner had clear images of themselves and of each other. Naturally, different values were bound to develop over a century and a half of separate experience. Southern culture before the Civil War had what John Crowe Ransom called "a sense of ceremonial style," a kind of formality based on a recognition of the nuances of a situation, a way of making occasions out of things, a feeling for an ornamental quality in life. I don't think that existed, then or now, in the Northern or Western approach to life. Northerners had manners, but that's not quite the same thing. They had manners but not ritual, celebrations but not ceremonials. Northerners self-consciously admitted to a kind of practical and pragmatic and utilitarian approach to things. The "Yankee" approach was, of course, despised by the South; the figure of the shrewd Yankee trader was not amusing to Southerners; it threatened their whole way of life.

Northern culture, and Western culture too, had a public aspect which the Southern never had. Southern life tended to be private, restricted. For example, a Southern gentleman might write poetry and essays. But he would publish them under a pseudonym. Or his poetry might be circulated privately for his friends. You left your poetry to your family, you didn't publish it. A gentleman simply didn't expose his thoughts in public. There are still Southern families who preserve the poetry some great-grandfather wrote, and some of it is very good poetry. This is no longer true, of course, in the twentieth century. The Southern writer today can hardly be restrained from telling all, and making a business of it. But Southern culture, even though it was private in the ante-bellum period, was not introspective. Southerners weren't given very much to self-analysis; they were not much interested in defining things or exploring life.

J.A.G.   Was there a connection between that and slavery? Was there a parallel between their banning abolitionist literature and their refusal to look inside their own hearts?

R.B.N. Possibly one can tie it to their sense of guilt about slavery. But Southerners never did analyze themselves, even in the seventeenth century, when slavery was not yet an issue. I don't think that by any stretch of the imagination there could have been an Emerson in the South. You could have had a Southern Addison, but I don't think you could have had a Southern Emerson. It seems to me that the prewar South was similar to Revolutionary France. It had something of the same flourish, something of the same easy confident feeling of superiority, a kind of *après moi le déluge* psychology. Allen Tate said once that the prewar Southerner was Cicero distilled by Castiglione, the Renaissance expert on courtly manners. I'd say that the Northerner was by Plato out of Calvin. Henry Adams was a classmate at Harvard of Robert E. Lee's son. In his *Education*, Adams says that Lee never had an idea in his life, but that he lived beautifully.

J.A.G. In the decades before the Civil War Southerners bitterly resented the "invasion" of the region by Northern commerce and industry. Was there a similar resentment of Northern culture? Did the South feel that it was becoming a cultural colony of the North?

R.B.N. Oh, yes. There was a great demand for Southern poets and artists, and for Southern magazines to publish Southern materials. Unfortunately, there wasn't really enough public to support this kind of thing. Southern writers who tried to live by their pens practically starved to death.

J.A.G. Looking at American culture broadly, was it less provincial and derivative in 1860 than at the time of the Revolution?

R.B.N. I think it was. In the beginning, the problem for the United States was to achieve cultural independence without cultural isolation; by 1860, the United States had not only gained a good deal of confidence in its values and goals, but it had also learned how to be independent without being isolated, how to select, how to adapt, how to absorb things from the rest of the world without being dominated by the rest of the world.

By about 1830, Americans no longer felt that they had to reject or accept England and Europe. They'd found a way to steer a course between insular nationalism on the one hand and a loose and diffusive cosmopolitanism on the other. Longfellow made the point very well when he wrote that nationality was a good thing, but that nationality within universality was even better. It was easy for the post-Revolutionary generation to declare its cultural independence, but having done this the problem was how to determine what to reject and what to retain.

First, Americans had to avoid what Webster called a "servile imitation" of foreign cultural models. Note the qualifying adjective. Americans could imitate but not be slaves, not be tied to European culture. European and British models should be used as a way of releasing native creative powers. No American artist should give up the inspiration he might derive from Milton or Shakespeare or give up the great British and continental traditions in drama or painting.

Secondly, Americans felt they must reject anything foreign that was immoral or dangerous to American values and principles, or unacceptable in the American situation. The poet Joel Barlow said that Americans ought to avoid ideas that had degraded mankind in other countries.

Thirdly, again to quote Barlow, American culture should accept that which is "true and useful." Take that which has a function in American life; by this pragmatic test what he called "vile foreign trash" could be kept out. It was not enough to abstain from imitating or to set up barriers against the wrong kind of cultural import. Americans must have a positive criterion for choice. In 1832, fairly early in his career, Longfellow used two words which also apply. He urged American poets, and by extension other American artists, to be "native and original." That, of course, was what people tried to do, and they did it rather well. They took what they needed and used it. Emerson took Kant and Carlyle and Plato and Swedenborg and the *Bhagavad-Gita* and he produced something native and American—transcendentalism. George Bancroft took European historical theory and method, and wrote a distinctively American history. Rip Van Winkle is a German legend that Washington Irving transferred to the Catskills. These Americans weren't at all afraid to borrow, and what they borrowed they made their own.

J.A.G. Were middle-class Americans of the mid-nineteenth century Victorian in their social and moral attitudes in the same sense that Englishmen of that age were?

R.B.N. To define "Victorianism" is not an easy task. If it means a set of manners and attitudes that emphasize prescriptive morality, a kind of overheated sentimentalism, a tendency to overindulge in emotionalism, and an exaggerated formality in social relationships, then the answer is no doubt "Yes, American society was Victorian." But, as always, this is only true with reservations.

In nineteenth-century America, as in England, there was a very strong underground current of sexuality and vulgarity, not by any means confined to the lower classes. In the first half of the nineteenth century there was, for example, an obscene burlesque, common in beer gardens and honky-tonks and low-class theaters (known as "slabs" or "dumps") from the Bowery to San Francisco. This kind of entertainment had its prose equivalents too, and almost as open and as obvious as in England.

Human nature in the United States was much the same as it was anywhere else.

On the other hand, if "Victorian" designates a set of intellectual qualities, we have to look at the term in a somewhat different way. The Victorian Age was by no means a neat period. The identifiable qualities of the Victorian cultural and intellectual milieu were a belief in progress, Evangelicalism in religion, utilitarianism, a deep concern for morals and manners, a search for harmony amid tensions, and a kind of energetic exuberance.

As Matthew Arnold, Charles Dickens, Mrs. Trollope, and other British visitors make clear, the British didn't think that American Victorianism was like British Victorianism. And conditions in America were different; its culture was derived from a different set of social and religious and artistic conceptions. American Victorian society was much more aggressively middle-class and democratic, much more fluid, less tightly compartmentalized. American literary men of the period were more morally concerned. Their work was more directly involved with religious and behavioral issues. American writing was controlled a lot more closely than British by social and moral standards, especially at the popular level. It was this kind of Victorian literature that Whitman and Twain and James and Howells rebelled against later on.

But my own preference would be not to use the term "Victorian" in reference to American society and culture at all. Even the Victorians were not quite sure when the Victorian Age began and ended. In literature I can't find any way, either by context or chronology, to get Emerson and Thoreau and Poe and Whitman and James and Twain and Emily Dickinson and Henry Adams all under one "Victorian" tent.

J.A.G. Was American civilization in 1860 closer to the civilization of 1760 than to the civilization of 1960?

R.B.N. I don't think so. Certainly, the American of 1860 looked out at quite a different world from that of the American of 1760. Too much lay between: the Revolution; a new government; the recognition of national identity; great shifts in patterns of living, thinking, and communicating; and great differences in society and population. I doubt if men from 1860 and 1760 would have been able to talk to one another with any real understanding.

Of course, between 1860 and 1960 another great gulf exists: the Civil War and two World Wars; Darwin; Freud; a completely different kind of economic structure; a different kind of politics; the communications revolution. But I think that the American of 1960 would have had less trouble communicating with the American of about 1880 or 1890. He could talk to men of that age; that is where the roots of our world lie, rather than in the age of Emerson and Jackson.

J.A.G. Would an American of 1850 have been more at home in the year 1800 or in the year 1900?

R.B.N. He'd be more at home in 1800. Here we can identify changes specifically. Developments in communications and transportation and education and science, and the traumatic experience of the Civil War had a tremendous effect on the late nineteenth century.

J.A.G. What are the major unanswered questions that historians should ask about the subject we have been discussing?

R.B.N. I'd like to know more about the underside of nineteenth-century life, the life that didn't get into the books and isn't on the records. And I'd like to know more about the popular culture of the period, about the best-selling novelists, the popular heroes, and this kind of thing. The information exists, but I don't think we've really studied it. What was the reason for the popularity of Mrs. Lydia Sigourney's novels? Or for that matter, for Longfellow's popularity? I also wish we knew more about the conflict that went on from about 1840 to 1870 between romanticism and pragmatism, and that so clearly led to the emergence of a different kind of culture. What happened to the ideas of 1840 when they confronted the realities of 1880? What happened to the subjective view of the world as it ought to be when it confronted the objective view of the world as it is? That is very much a nineteenth-century question, the differences highlighted by Emerson's Oversoul and Henry Adams' dynamo. Leo Marx has dealt with this question in his book, *The Machine in the Garden*, but he's just opened up the discussion.

Another thing that I wish we knew more about is how the nineteenth century responded to its many crises—crises brought on by war, by science, by industrialism, by urbanization. The range and the quality of the response of the nineteenth century to its crises has never been adequately studied. The responses in literature and in religion need investigation. How was history used as a way of solving, or at least understanding, crises? Then, too, it would be fascinating to study anniversaries and commemorations. We're very historically conscious as a people. I'd like to take 1826 and 1876 and 1926 and then 1976 and see how what people said on these occasions changed. These were times of stocktaking, when men look forward and backward. What did the newspapers say in 1901 about the nineteenth century? What did they say about the future? Historians have made studies of the great world's fairs, and these are quite interesting, but other kinds of comparative studies would be equally fascinating. I was fascinated myself by comparing the Canadian "Expo '67" with the Philadelphia Exposition of 1876. Both commemorated one hundred years of national independence, but a different hundred years, and almost one hundred years apart.

Another thing worth investigation is the relationship of business with cultural life. Business history and cultural history have existed separately, but there must have been interpenetrations. What was the role of the businessman in nineteenth-century culture? (I don't mean merely the rich men who bought Old Masters and founded libraries, but the whole business ethic.) This aspect of cultural history hasn't been explored. Literary people tend to see all this through the eyes of unsympathetic observers. They look at nineteenth-century industrialism through the eyes of Thoreau, who didn't like it. We read Thoreau and Melville and Emerson and others who say, "Away with material things"—and tend to accept this as what people believed. All sorts of cultured people hailed business, industry, and technology as the hope of the future.

These are some of the things which I think we historians should investigate.

J.A.G. What are the half-dozen or so books that you would recommend to persons interested in the subject we have been discussing? In each case, would you indicate what the particular contribution of the volume is?

R.B.N. F. O. Matthiessen, *American Renaissance* (1941) gives a broad but penetrating assessment of the major literary figures of the earlier nineteenth century.

Leo Marx's *The Machine in the Garden* (1967) is a provocative discussion of the conflict in early nineteenth-century America between a developing technology and the agrarian ideal.

Howard Mumford Jones's *O Strange New World: American Culture, The Formative Years* (1964) is a brilliant study of how over the first century and a half the Americans used, adapted, and absorbed European ideas to create their own culture.

William R. Taylor, in *Cavalier and Yankee* (1961) studies the origins and development of these cultural images, which had great effects on the relations between the two sections.

Daniel Boorstin, in *The Americans: The National Experience* (1965), discusses what the author calls "the years of self-discovery," between the Revolution and the Civil War, in an unusually engrossing and perceptive way.

Richard Beale Davis, in *Intellectual Life in Jefferson's Virginia* (1964), provides the beginning chapter of what is much needed—that is, a cultural-intellectual history of the South.

Neil Harris, in *The Artist in American Society: The Formative Years, 1790–1860* (1966) studies the emergence of the American artist, his position in and his attitudes toward American social and cultural life, from the Republic to the opening of the Civil War.

George Dangerfield

The United States in World Affairs: 1790–1860

GEORGE DANGERFIELD, who is currently Professor of History at the University of California at Santa Barbara, first attracted the attention of readers of history with his study of *The Strange Death of Liberal England* (1935). Since then he has concentrated on American history in the early national period. His *Era of Good Feelings* (1952) won both a Pulitzer and a Bancroft prize. He has also written a biography of *Chancellor Robert R. Livingston of New York* (1960), and *The Awakening of American Nationalism: 1815–1828* (1965), a volume in the New American Nation series. In all his work he has combined sharp historical insights and a brilliant literary style, qualities which come through clearly in this interview on aspects of the foreign relations of the United States between the Revolution and the Civil War.

John A. Garraty   Mr. Dangerfield, in the popular mind American foreign policy after the ratification of the Constitution is usually associated with the idea of isolationism, with Washington's warning against "permanent" alliances and Jefferson's against "entangling" ones. Were Washington and Jefferson actually isolationists?

George Dangerfield   No, I don't think they were actually. It's hard to apply the word "isolationist" in this stage of American history, because the government was looking for some kind of identity in the world, not trying to escape from it. I don't think one can use the word "isolationist" at all about Washington. He knew that his business was to symbolize the nation—nobody else could have done it as well, if at all—so it was a very fortunate thing that he was there. When he got the government going, he became not isolationist so much as just cautious. His Farewell Address reveals that he had a simple, quite conventional idea of America as potentially a great country. It wasn't at all an isolationist document. If you take from it its obvious relation to the coming election as a piece of propaganda for keeping the Federalists in power, which it certainly was, the rest seems to say, "When we're strong enough, we can do what we please."

J.A.G.   Was there a difference between Washington's position and Jefferson's? They disagreed about tactics, certainly.

G.D.   I don't think Jefferson ever could be called an isolationist. In a letter to a Dutch friend he once wrote: "I wish to stand, with respect to Europe, precisely on the footing of China," but that was years earlier, sometime in the 1780's. We take so much of our knowledge of Jefferson from his letters that we get into trouble. A letter writer contradicts himself constantly because he is usually expressing a mood and not a conviction, and writing to different people on the spur of the moment. This was particularly true of Jefferson. He was a most incautious letter writer, consequently a writer of lovely letters. Sometimes he seems an isolationist, and sometimes he took a broad world view.

J.A.G.   But if you consider those two famous phrases, Washington's "no permanent alliances" and Jefferson's "no entangling alliances" (and both come not from casual letters but from important state papers), is it not correct to say that Jefferson's is the more isolationist?

G.D.   That's a matter of semantics, isn't it? A permanent alliance does, in a sense, entangle, and an entangling alliance is apt to be as permanent as any other.

J.A.G.   But I think there are overtones in the phrases. "No permanent alliances" could mean one agreement with a nation one day and another one with another nation another day—in other words, being very involved in international affairs. But the word "entangling" suggests a dislike of alliances.

G.D.   That could be. But I don't think so. Jefferson had a very subtle and complicated mind; he was much more a child of the Enlightenment than Washington. The Enlightenment never did really explain how you were going to make things happen institutionally. Jefferson envisioned a world where America would be the shining example and would attract people like some kind of moral magnet. When we are strong enough and secure enough, he believed, we will be a kind of moral beacon to the rest of the world. Eventually, he realized that it wasn't going to happen. While he died a happy man in terms of his personal life, knowing that he had done some really remarkable things, he died with his whole political philosophy in ruins.

J.A.G.   Could you explain what you mean by that?

G.D.   In 1820—he was referring to the Missouri Compromise which he rightly construed as fatal—he wrote, "my only consolation is that I live not to weep over it," and in 1825 he summed it all up in his famous statement predicting the rise of a new aristocratic government, founded on banking institutions and moneyed corporations, "under the guise and cloak of their favored branches of manufacture, commerce and navigation riding and ruling over the plundered ploughman and beggared yeomanry." Six months later he was dead.

J.A.G.   How did this affect his sense of America's place in the world?

G.D.   The last statement may have been to some extent rhetorical: the first I think was not. But anyhow, and in spite of all this, as you can see in his later letters to John Adams, he never seems entirely to have lost his faith in an exemplary America. He was a beautiful human being but not the easiest to understand.

J.A.G.   Did Washington lack this sense of mission? Or was he merely less articulate than Jefferson?

G.D.   I think they were alike in having a passion for peace. But Washington was looking at the question with a rather simple mind. He was for peace because the nation was too weak to fight a war. To Jefferson, peace was "our passion." That conviction lies behind the Embargo, along with a rather shrewd conception of commercial advantage. I once called the Embargo a mixture of commercialism and the Sermon on the Mount. But Jefferson's feeling about peace did not prevent him from acting as forcefully as Washington in carrying out his policy. His enforcement of the Embargo involved as brutal use of the powers of government as Washington's overawing the Whisky rebels with a large army. Washington's feeling for central power was far stronger than Jefferson's, but when the chips were down they both behaved like American Presidents; if force had to be used they used it.

J.A.G.   Would you comment on the development of American nationalism during the Washington-Adams period?

G.D. I don't think it was a period of burgeoning nationalism; I see no tremendously strong feeling of nationalism, at the time, say, of the Philadelphia Convention. The Constitution was ratified in spite of parochial battles, of course, and the whole Hamiltonian program was anything but conservative in this sense. When faced with the French Revolution, however (in 1793, for example), public opinion split the national spirit almost in two. One could hardly describe the Americans as nationalist, depending as they did on one foreign country or another for their political identity. Are you pro-English or pro-French? There was the split, and it was a desperate split. Just as the American Revolution—an event that shook the world—brought on the French, so the French Revolution shook America almost to bits. It turned Washington, incidentally, into an angry man and no democrat, always supposing that he'd ever been one.

J.A.G. It has often been noted that Jefferson's actual foreign policy was far different from the one he outlined when he became President. What were the contradictions and how can they be explained?

G.D. We should make a very clear distinction between what he said in opposition and what he did when in power.

J.A.G. But in 1801, after he became President, Jefferson said that the United States already had enough land to last for a thousand generations, and two years later he doubled the size of the United States by purchasing Louisiana territory.

G.D. Oh yes, but in the case of the Louisiana Purchase it is clear that he he hadn't expected it. He did not really change his policy. He had, it seems to me, persistently pursued his notion that peace was our passion.

J.A.G. If peace was his passion, why did he suggest, when he contemplated the possibility that France would not sell New Orleans, that the United States might "marry ourselves to the British fleet and nation" to obtain that city?

G.D. Again, it was a specific situation he was confronting. He said, in effect, "if we're forced to, we'll do it, but we'll do it with great reluctance." His policy did not change. He said much the same thing to Monroe, before the Doctrine was formulated.

J.A.G. Well, would you explain the larger political and economic circumstances that made the acquisition of Louisiana so important to the Jeffersonians?

G.D. The economic ones, involving the navigation of the Mississippi, are self-evident, but the political ones are more complex. Before the Seven Years' War, France thought that having Canada and Louisiana she could continue to constrict the British North American colonies into the area east of the Alleghenies. They could exist there forever, the French didn't care. But in that war they lost Canada and Louisiana. It was a frightful defeat. When the American Revolution broke out and they allied themselves with the colonies, recovering these possessions was one of the things they had in mind, and they partially succeeded, at least in getting the colonies free from Great Britain, although they couldn't get Canada or Louisiana themselves. Now here was Napoleon; from what he'd already done it must have been apparent to Jefferson that he had hopes of restoring French power in North America. Jefferson could see what a dangerous man Napoleon was after the retrocession of Louisiana to France by Spain. He hadn't then lost Santo Domingo, his fleet hadn't been smashed at Trafalgar. There was real terror in the hearts of Jefferson and Madison lest this new force be established on the west bank of the Mississippi, and in New Orleans, where it could ruthlessly close the river. On the other hand, as the historian Henry Adams said, when Spain was in control the area had the attraction for Americans that a whale has for its captors—the attraction of something huge but helpless. Yet even Spain was rather disturbing; there was always a danger when a foreign element controlled the west bank, it seems to me. But Jefferson thought he could get New Orleans from Spain if he had to, even when the Spanish closed the port temporarily. He was not afraid of the Spanish because he felt they could be driven out, not that he wanted to exercise that kind of force.

But the terrible Napoleonic dream of retaking Santo Domingo that made Louisiana important to France as a future source of foodstuffs . . .

J.A.G.   Was Jefferson aware of Napoleon's plans? Did he see the relationship between Santo Domingo and Louisiana?

G.D.   Presumably he did; it must have been obvious. Louisiana would be a perfect place to grow food for the West Indies.

J.A.G.   The only thing that seems weak to me about your argument is that Jefferson wanted only New Orleans. He did not appear to fear French control of the rest of that huge Louisiana region.

G.D.   A French Louisiana without New Orleans wouldn't have been nearly the threat that it would have been with New Orleans. But you have a point. When Jefferson and Madison wrote the instructions to Livingston governing his negotiations with Napoleon, they specified that he was *not* to ask for the west bank, only New Orleans. But they felt uneasy, nonetheless, at the thought of the French around them. The French had beaten Europe already; they were a cocky, tempestuous people.

J.A.G.   Would you comment on Jefferson's handling of the negotiations that led to the Louisiana Purchase?

G.D.   I think they were brilliant. He and Madison made a wonderful team, and Robert R. Livingston in Paris carried out their policy admirably— and small thanks he got for it. First Jefferson told Livingston to inform the French of American opposition to the retrocession of Louisiana to France in the strongest possible terms. Livingston did so most firmly, telling the French, in effect, "We aren't as quietist as you think. We will *act.*" The one thing Napoleon feared was British *rapprochement* with America. That would ruin his imperial notions altogether. Jefferson also talked to Louis André Pichon, the French Chargé d'affaires, in Washington, a very astute and a sensitive fellow. To Pichon, Jefferson played down the whole business. Westerners were upset, but he doubted it would come to anything. But then Pichon talked to Madison, and Madison tried to frighten him. It was touch and go whether or not Westerners would be restrained from invading Louisiana, Madison said.

J.A.G. Was this not just bad communication between Jefferson and Madison?

G.D. No, I think it was done deliberately to keep Pichon wobbling. He really got scared—he didn't know what was going to happen. They played this mystery carefully—one never knew whether it would be peace or war with those two fellows! They had no money, no soldiers, no fleet, no anything—but they had intelligence and style. As diplomats, they were unbeatable when they really got going. They sent Livingston to Paris because he was a francophile (he hated the English) and an aristocrat, a man calculated to be acceptable in consular circles. But they also sent James Monroe, who was known as a ferocious republican. Monroe was not popular in France; he was not liked by Bonaparte.

J.A.G. I wonder if this subtlety wasn't lost on Napoleon.

G.D. It could easily have been. I don't think he gave a hoot. But he may have been influenced by one very able paper that Livingston wrote: "Is it advantageous to France to take possession of Louisiana?" Later on, in a note addressed to Joseph Bonaparte, Livingston asked boldly, "Why don't you sell the United States all of Louisiana above the Arkansas?" That was contrary to Livingston's instructions but he said it anyway, arguing that the territory would make a marvelous buffer between the French in Louisiana and the British in Canada. Joseph undoubtedly passed this on to his brother.

I think that made some difference. I can't prove it, because there is no evidence that Napoleon ever thought about anything that way. I also think, by the way, that when he finally declared war on Britain, Napoleon did so because he had lost interest in Louisiana.

J.A.G. It's usually argued that Napoleon was willing to sell Louisiana because he was determined to fight England and might have difficulty holding it. Are you suggesting that because he saw that his Louisiana adventure was not going to work out, he decided to turn instead on England?

G.D. I think he vacillated among various plans for conquering the whole

Western world. Supposing by some extraordinary chance he had conquered England. It would have made him master of Western Europe, with Russia at his feet. He could then have taken Louisiana back in two minutes. With the British at his feet I don't see how anybody could have kept him out of the New World. Treaties meant nothing to him. He wasn't a man who kept faith, with nations or with individuals.

J.A.G.   It's very interesting, isn't it, how the European powers, totally lacking in sympathy for the United States, repeatedly made the most generous kinds of diplomatic agreements with them: for example, the peace treaty after the Revolution, so generous that it mystified the French; and this Louisiana arrangement, which gave America an empire for practically nothing.

G.D.   I suppose what the European powers really thought was that while America was the country of the future, that future was so very distant that America couldn't bother them.

J.A.G.   If Jefferson really had a "passion" for peace, why did he involve the United States in the war with the Barbary pirates? Was any important national interest at stake?

G.D.   It doesn't seem in character, does it? Perhaps he felt it had become unendurable for a small nation to receive insults that larger nations could laugh off. The great powers could say, "All right, we'll pay these fellows off." But the pride of a small, beginning nation was injured by having to pay tribute to protect its commerce. Yet I've never really discovered the reasons. Perhaps the insults had gone on too long.

J.A.G.   What is your opinion of Jefferson's response to English and French violations of American neutral rights after the resumption of the war in 1803?

G.D.   His policy of "peaceful coercion" worked well until 1807; the nation's commerce prospered, and war was avoided. But the moment things got really tough after the British Orders in Council and Napoleon's Berlin and Milan Decrees, I don't see what choice Jefferson had except an embargo or war. It seems so to me. When he chose the Embargo, he did what to my mind was a very noble thing. He did it very quickly, but he'd obviously had it in his mind a long time.

J.A.G.   Many historians have criticized Jefferson for not having built up the Army and Navy in order to bring pressure on the belligerents to respect American rights on the seas. I gather that you don't agree with this interpretation.

G.D.   I think the Embargo reflected the feeling of an idealist who said, in effect, "We can fight back without drawing a drop of blood." The Embargo almost succeeded—I realize some historians will say, "that's rubbish"—but the British economy was extremely hard hit. The British could ship goods to American ports, but since exporting was prohibited, the ships had to leave in ballast, so it was not worth their while. What saved them from economic catastrophe was the opening up of big markets in South America, which Jefferson could not have foreseen. Even so, Britain really felt the pinch, and if the Embargo could have been maintained another year, I think she would have had to repeal the Orders in Council. She needed American markets in the worst way. Where Jefferson made his mistake was in misunderstanding the character of his own countrymen, thinking that they had the same dream of peace by example that he had. He asked them to endure a period of austerity for a principle, and they refused. They could have endured it, of course, with their agrarian economy, but they would not. Still, it was a noble experiment, at least until Jefferson had to use powers of government that no President had used before to enforce it.

J.A.G. Is it not baffling that Jefferson, the apostle of liberty, rode roughshod over civil rights in this matter?

G.D. I think he did so because he was a fanatic about the idea that peace can be taught, that the ways of peace can be introduced into a corrupt world.

J.A.G. Aren't you also leaving Napoleon out of the picture in your analysis? If the British had repealed the Orders in Council, they would have played into the hands of their enemy.

G.D. I think they would have done it nonetheless. They could have got along without those orders. As it was, there were leaks in the blockade all over Europe—through Holland, through Russia, through Spain. Indeed, as Madison noted in his War Message, they systematically forced their own goods through their own blockade.

J.A.G. Then can you explain why the British were so disrespectful of American neutral rights? If they had allowed a little more leeway to American commerce with the Continent, the trouble would have been avoided.

G.D. It was probably stupidity. The British often behaved stupidly toward the Americans, whom they didn't exactly love. They misunderstood the American character; they thought that the United States would give in and allow its carrying trade to be controlled by English policy entirely. They despised the Americans, in some odd way of their own, and at the same time they were afraid of them. They could see as no other nation could the future of the United States—its fantastic carrying trade and its extraordinary sailors. But they believed Americans were altogether too commercial-minded to be willing to fight. So they kept those famous Orders in Council—trade on our terms, or you shall have none. It was a mad and foolish policy, to which Jefferson responded, in effect, "We will simply withdraw our merchant fleets."

J.A.G. Was Madison's policy different in any substantial way from Jefferson's when he became President?

G.D. I used to think that Madison came floating in to the presidency on the wreckage of the Embargo and continued to drift—that the Nonintercourse Act and Macon's Bill No. 2 reflected the bankruptcy of his ideas. Some historians, however, now feel that on the contrary he was moving very much toward war with Great Britain.

J.A.G. Surely the Nonintercourse Act and Macon's Bill No. 2 lacked the moral grandeur and simplicity of the Embargo, but can they not be seen as realistic compromises with the same principle of applying economic pressure but standing firm for the idea of peace?

G.D. Except that Macon's Bill No. 2 favored England. Once American ships were allowed to leave harbor, the British would benefit because they had the naval power to stop goods from getting to France.

That's the way I used to read these Acts, but it is possible that Madison was really gratified by Napoleon's fake repeal of the Berlin and Milan Decrees, and used it for all it was worth to bring on war with Great Britain. A number of good Republicans felt that if things went on as they were, with England enforcing the Orders in Council and impressing American seamen in such a brutal fashion, when the European war was over, no matter who won it, all the powers would turn on the United States. Republicanism, which was unpopular all over Europe, would then be extinguished. That belief may have animated Madison; it certainly did some Republicans. In his own quiet way, perhaps he felt a war with England was necessary. He'd even suggested fighting what would have been an absurd triangular war against both England and France.

J.A.G. Did Jefferson approve of Madison's policies? I ask because you said earlier that Jefferson knew that a victorious Napoleon would represent a very grave danger to the United States. By siding with Napoleon in the war against Britain, was not the United States taking an even greater risk?

G.D. Yes, he did. But I believe he thought Napoleon the lesser of two evils. Insults had been heaped on American ships and sailors both by France and by England, but the French insults were less extreme, less pressing, and, being usually perpetrated under the umbrella of French municipal law, presumably more legal.

J.A.G. Impressment was a very grave insult, but would a victorious Britain have represented as grave a threat to the United States as a victorious Napoleon?

G.D. No, but that's hindsight. There were people in England who argued, "Let's crush them and get them back again." Enlightened statesmen like Lord Castlereagh were not such fools as to want to take over again the management of people as difficult as the Americans, but no one could be sure that their view would prevail. Many Americans thought that the British were really out to clobber them, and if this were so the British could have done it much better than the French, because they had a much more powerful navy.

J.A.G. Would you comment on the complex historical controversy that has evolved over the years about the causes of the War of 1812?

G.D. It's a circular controversy. The original "Patriotic" construction was that we went to war because our honor had been stained by British violations of freedom of the seas. Henry Adams accepted this reasoning but employed a more subtle argument. Adopting a Comptian approach, he said that every society passed through theological, metaphysical, and scientific or positive stages. The War of 1812 represented the end of America's metaphysical stage. Knowing that the world was at war, Jefferson should have seen that the chances of profitable neutral trade existing unscathed were very slight. He should built a strong fleet instead of those wretched gunboats which always scurried up the streams at the approach of an enemy or turned over and sank in every stiff breeze. Instead he economized, paring down on military outlays. That was the metaphysical stage.

However, according to Henry Adams, the war ended that by showing that the American people had advanced into the next, or positive stage. You remember his extraordinary accounts of naval battles? He gives the exact weight of the metal the American vessels threw, the size of their crews, and so on, and he turns this into a proof that the Americans were both scientifically and morally superior to the British. The war was necessary to prove that the United States had passed out of one stage and into the next, Adams wrote. He made Jeffersonian metaphysics appear absolutely clownish, and then he described the battles of Lundy's Lane or Chippawa as heroic situations in which the new spirit of America came through.

It's an extraordinary argument he uses, a little Spencerian but mostly Comptist—very odd. However, he saw the war definitely as involving the national honor or, if you prefer, the scientific character of American society.

This view prevailed until A. L. Burt, after a very close examination of the whole British system on the high seas and its effects on America, deduced that impressment forced America to fight because it produced both intolerable economic effects and was an affront to the national honor. The Orders in Council were not significant because merchants were reasonably happy so long as the profits of one successful voyage were greater than the losses sustained by many British seizures.

Then historians began to stress the Western character of the war.

Louis Hacker argued that frontiersmen favored war because they wanted the rich Canadian lands to the north. Julius Pratt denied this, pointing out that there was much land going begging on the frontier so questioning why they should want lots of land. I tend to support Hacker in this argument. It seems to me that where land was in question, frontiersmen didn't consider whether they had too much "at home" or not. Getting rid of the Indian "menace," which was clearly over the border in Canada, also affected Western opinion. Indian troubles were undoubtedly English-inspired, though not just before the War of 1812. They were carefully holding off, they didn't at that time want to stir America to war.

Pratt saw the war party as an alliance between the West and the South. The South would help the West put an end to the Indian menace by seizing Canada and in turn get Western backing for taking Florida. Next, George Rogers Taylor, a wonderful historian, put the war down to the economic depression in the West. Frontiersmen were convinced that they couldn't get rid of their produce at a profit because England had denied them a competitive market, Taylor claimed. And so it goes. Lately, historians, such as Bradford Perkins in his brilliant *Prologue to War*, seem to be coming back to the old notion of national honor. All these causes existed, including the desire for Canadian farmland, but together they don't amount to a complete explanation of why the war occurred.

J.A.G.   This historiographical evolution is a particularly famous one, but the pattern is universal. Why does this happen? If, as you say, Henry Adams got pretty close to the truth in the 1880's, why have historians gone through all these convolutions?

G.D.   There seems to be an absolute necessity for each generation to overthrow its predecessor. After all, any young historian who has a gift for research, who doesn't cook his evidence, and who keeps his hypotheses within reasonable scientific limits, if he's bright enough can "overthrow" any earlier interpretation. And I think that is constructive. History is, after all, a set of intellectually enchanting abstractions. It bears very little relation to your sordid reality. Historians like to overthrow for the sake of producing a new thing which is enchanting; it's like higher mathematics, where an argument can be beautiful even if it's wrong. Also as knowledge accumulates, historical methodology gets more and more precise, and in a way more beautiful. In other words, history is enriched by each of these revolutions.

J.A.G.   Does this mean that history at its most fundamental level is meaningless; that events occur without regard for causes?

G.D.   I'm inclined to think that if you get right down to it, yes. Of course, as historians we can't work with that hypothesis. You can't work with absurdism. Probably our work is absurd, but if you admit that you cease to be an historian.

J.A.G. How could the War of 1812, in which American arms performed so badly and which had no official result other than the restoration of peace, have resulted in what you have called "the awakening of American nationalism"?

G.D. Perhaps I should have said "the reawakening." Clearly, something dormant was aroused by the mere fact of coming through the war. From the Americans' point of view, they had taken on the most powerful naval force the world had ever known, and survived the contest. Of course, the battle of New Orleans, which wasn't really relevant, added to this sense of having done the job. There was a feeling of relief that the beastly business was over and hadn't cost too much, in men or money. Furthermore, although at first men like Clay and Calhoun were convinced that the peace was only an armistice, it soon became clear that the British wouldn't come back again. Of course, we can't be sure just how much this sense of nationalism was inspired by the land boom and the cotton boom that followed the war. But it was there. People seemed to feel more like a nation, more nationalistic—if one can define nationalism as a belief in the existence of some common experience and a desire to live together in the future. One of the signs of this nationalism was the vote of the South for the protective Tariff of 1816, which certainly didn't help the South in any way. Apparently, Southerners felt that the Northern manufacturers deserved something now that the war was over and that they were faced with sharp British competition.

J.A.G. Southerners adopted Washington's theory that what was good for one part of the country was good for the whole country?

G.D. Yes. I have never felt that the argument that Southerners expected soon to be making their own manufactures was very persuasive.

J.A.G. You have called the Transcontinental Treaty of 1819 with Spain "one of the outstanding achievements of American nationalism." Superficially, the treaty was primarily concerned with the acquisition of Florida, a relatively minor piece of real estate. Why was the treaty so important?

G.D. I wouldn't call Florida a minor piece of real estate, but its importance had nothing to do with its value as real estate. The treaty cleared the Gulf Coast of foreign powers. But John Quincy Adams, who negotiated the treaty as Secretary of State, wasn't so concerned with getting Spain out of the way because he felt certain that sooner or later Spain would have to go. What he was after, I think, was keeping England down. He was looking at the Columbia River basin in the far-off Oregon country. He wanted to draw the Spanish boundary all the way to the Pacific and as far south as possible, and he did so. He was a very far-sighted man.

J.A.G.   Why did Adams consider that eliminating Spain from the Northwest was so important?

G.D.   He wanted to draw a line that would put a northern limit to Spanish claims, and incidentally show that the United States had a claim from that line northward. To have a line was terribly important, particularly a line to the Pacific—this was his idea; no one of his day except John Quincy Adams had the imagination and daring to draw that line. It provided a base from which the United States could aim north, beyond the Columbia River. He kept trying to get Britain off the continent, or at least north of the line of 54 degrees North Latitude. He was a continentalist, unlike Jefferson, who thought at most of a colony across the Rockies. Old John Quincy Adams didn't care about the land itself. As far as he knew, the whole area was a damned desert. But he was going to get to the Pacific. This was vision, I think, of a most extraordinary kind.

J.A.G.   How did the British feel about the Transcontinental Treaty?

G.D.   They didn't mind too much; in fact, they put pressure on the King of Spain to ratify it. They wanted peace with America because they wanted access to American markets.

J.A.G.   This reinforces what you just said about Adams' brilliance. If the Transcontinental Treaty was directed against Great Britain, he was striking at the British and they didn't even know it.

G.D.   No, because I think they preferred to have the United States there. The way the British yielded in the Treaty of Ghent prefigured their willingness to submit to American expansion. The profits they could make from an expanding America were terrific.

J.A.G.   The British should have adopted this policy in 1783, or perhaps in 1775.

G.D.   William Pitt wanted to. He was defeated in Parliament, but at least he had the idea.

J.A.G.   Most historians agree that Adams was a brilliant Secretary of State. Why was he such a disastrous failure as a President?

G.D.   John Quincy Adams was a diplomatic genius. When he became Secretary of State, America had emerged finally from the shadows of its colonial past and become a real nation, but it was still fighting for a respected place among the family of nations. There wasn't a government in Europe, including the Swiss republic, that didn't think a republic of the American kind was a menace to peace. Adams was fighting against what he considered to be a corrupt European diplomacy, and he wanted the powers to view the United States as a tough country. Good manners didn't matter, because if Americans displayed good manners, Europeans would have sneered at them anyway.

But as President he didn't understand the nature of American politics. He'd been away too much on foreign assignments. He didn't realize, or didn't wish to realize, that politics is a ruthless game. He didn't kick people out as he should have. He could be ruthless as a Secretary of State because he knew foreign policy inside out; he was the most experienced diplomat in the whole of America. But when it came to domestic politics he was pretty well at sea, at least while he was President.

J.A.G. What was Adams' role in the formulation of the Monroe Doctrine?

G.D. I believe that Adams, without ever thinking that the occasion was going to arise, had been making plans for such a "doctrine" for a long time. As with the Transcontinental Treaty, he was trying to restrict the British in the Western Hemisphere. He saw the policy as a rebuff to Canning, the British Foreign Minister. President Monroe originally was willing to go along with Canning on a joint statement guaranteeing the independence of the new South American republics. But Adams argued that the United States should have a policy of its own instead of "coming in like a cockboat to the British man of war." From the very beginning he insisted there was not the slightest danger of the Holly Alliance or France attempting to overthrow the new South American republics and restoring Spain's colonial empire; that was just as impossible as for "the Chimborazo to sink below the ocean."

J.A.G. Was Adams thinking at this time exclusively of the negative aspects of the Monroe Doctrine—that is, of keeping the European powers out of the Americas?

G.D. He was thinking of the Northwest, the Oregon country. He was a continentalist and wasn't interested in South America. After he became President, at the time of the Panama Congress of 1826, he moved toward "the spirit of Monroe," as that fine historian Samuel F. Bemis has put it. But when he was Secretary of State, he was following his father's line that the Latin Americans were a pretty worthless people.

J.A.G. What was President Monroe's "spirit" with regard to the Doctrine?

G.D. Monroe's position was very different. He was the last of the old Republicans. He wanted to include everything in the statement, even the kitchen sink! He even proposed praising the Greeks for their fight for independence. He wished to say, in effect, "Look, we are the most exemplary country in the world. We want to prove to the world that we believe in democracy and republicanism." But Adams restrained him, pointing out that such a statement would infuriate the Russians and make enemies all around. What Monroe felt was the good old Virginia magic. Adams took it out, and to my mind with that the old Virginia Republicanism vanished from the Doctrine altogether.

J.A.G.   But Canning certainly was thinking about Latin America. The origin of the whole question lay in South America. Are you saying that Adams simply took it out of that context and put it in another?

G.D.   Except for one important thing. Somewhere along the line, Cuba came into the picture very clearly. Canning was practically asking for a commitment that neither England nor America would ever take over Cuba. Adams had always wanted Cuba, and felt that sooner or later, by the law of political gravity it was bound to fall into American hands. He was not going to make any deal about Cuba with Canning.

J.A.G.   Did Adams consider the Monroe Doctrine the enormously significant policy statement that it later became?

G.D.   He thought the noncolonization principle very important, because that was specifically aimed at the British. They were most likely to colonize the Northwest coast. It was, by the way, the noncolonization idea that really made the British furious.

J.A.G.   Did the British, or any European power, take the Doctrine seriously in 1823?

G.D.   The continental European powers dismissed it as bluster, and the British didn't think it had any operative value, but it was a kind of challenge. How did the Americans dare to say that the continent was no longer open to colonization when the whole Oregon country was open?

J.A.G.   If most of the world ignored it, why is the Doctrine considered so important? For that matter, did Monroe and Adams consider it vital? After all, the policy was announced merely as an afterthought in a long, dull Message to Congress.

G.D.   You have to look at it in the context of the Navigation Laws of 1817, 1818, and 1820, which hit back at the British navigation laws after the Napoleonic Wars. The British trade regulations had not been enforced during the wars; many ports were kept open to American vessels by proclamation. When the wars were over, the British clamped down, and they didn't expect the Americans to hit back. So far as the British were concerned, the Americans could engage in direct trade with England but not with the English colonies in America. The Americans retaliated by forbidding British ships from coming from West Indian ports into America with West Indian produce. These laws were made stiffer and stiffer, but instead of fighting back, the British, in their American Trade Act of 1832, practically established a system of reciprocity.

However, concessions only made the United States more demanding; Americans even claimed equal rights with British ships within the British Empire. Not even preferential duties should be imposed, they insisted, which was of course ridiculous in those days. Up to the promulgation of the Doctrine itself, America had attacked the British navigation laws very successfully by condemnations against British shipping in

American ports, which the British had tolerated because they needed American markets for their manufactures. In England itself there was a movement to repeal the navigation laws, pressed by business interests who were beginning to see free trade as the only answer for an industrial country. "Conquer the world with free trade" was their motto. So the British were giving away and the Americans were pressing them hard. The Monroe Doctrine came as a culmination to this pressure.

J.A.G. Are you suggesting that concern for Latin America was not the true origin of Canning's original proposal for an accommodation with the United States?

G.D. Yes; at any rate not entirely. The original proposal also fitted into the British policy of backing down under American pressure. They'd realized since 1820 that they needed desperately a more or less tariff-free American market. Canning's suggestion, to my mind, was partly touched off by the feeling that Great Britain should make friends with the Americans on the ground that it pays to make friends with profitable customers. Lord Liverpool said in 1820 that the Americans were the only people who could act in terms of unrestricted world trade. Other nations had old habits and a great crust or cake of laws, hard to get rid of. British policy was an instinctive reaction on the part of a burgeoning industrial nation to make friends with the United States.

Adams was shortsighted in this instance. He was a neomercantilist, a high-tariff man. He wanted an isolated, independent America which took everything and gave nothing.

J.A.G. But free trade with the West Indies did not come until the 1830's.

G.D. That's correct. It was during the Jackson administration, and it was obtained by absolutely denying the policy of Adams. But the Monroe Doctrine helped make it possible by reminding the British, "We can hit back—we do not need you."

J.A.G. Did Adams envisage at this time the later importance of the Doctrine as justifying the United States acting as a kind of policeman for the Western Hemisphere?

G.D. No, and I don't think Monroe did either. It was merely, it seems to me, a statement of independence.

J.A.G. Would you comment now on Andrew Jackson's place in history? Was he really a great man or only a great personality?

G.D. That's a vague question but a good one. He wasn't a great statesman, clearly, but he was a great man in the sense that he was a unifier. Jacksonian democracy itself was a kind of mediator between the sections, not a divisive force. But while Jackson was a unifier, he was not a centralizer. The Jacksonian party was a states rights party. For example, as Jackson demonstrated in his veto of the Maysville road bill, he did not believe in a strong federal effort to construct internal improvements. He was a unifying force in that the people saw him as a symbol of the nation, like Washington. He believed in the Union but saw no conflict between the Union and states' rights, no reason why the states shouldn't have a great measure of autonomy so long as they didn't take too hopelessly sectional an attitude.

Nor do I think that Jackson was a reformer. In the 1828 election, some of the stodgiest Federalist types in New England voted for Jackson because they felt that the Adams administration had been too innovative, too much in favor of big government. Many Federalists voted for Jackson because they thought he was going to lead them back into a much purer world than the world inhabited by people like Adams and Clay.

J.A.G.   You're making Jackson the conservative and John Quincy Adams the radical! Are you saying that he was popular because he lacked the vision and sense of national purpose that Adams had?

G.D.   I would qualify that to the extent that I don't think many people thought Adams had much vision. They thought of him as a consolidator, a centralist. But Jackson, while he certainly appeared to be leading the nation back into the pure world of the Founding Fathers, was a symbol of the economy of waste, of what I call democratic nationalism—the idea of a nation composed of individuals dedicated to getting ahead, with a government that spent its time removing obstacles like monopolies from their course. Economic nationalists, such as Adams, believed in a primitive form of social planning, which of course would have required a considerable amount of centralization and restraint.

J.A.G.   But surely the men of that day looked at Jackson as the new man, and Adams as the tie with the great statesmen of the founding generation. Are you suggesting that the opposite is true, that Adams was the "new" man?

G.D.   Yes, or at least the dangerous man to defenders of old ways. Whether to call him "new" is debatable, because the centralizing idea had been there from the very beginning. Hamilton was a centralizer, and Madison has been called a mercantilist.

J.A.G.   In this context, where would you put Henry Clay?

G.D.   Henry Clay was very much in the centralizing tradition. His American System of national internal improvements, national banking, and a protective tariff on manufactures would have required centralization and planning. But the American people weren't ready for it. They had a tremendous domain waiting for them to exploit, and Clay seemed to be telling them to go cautiously.

J.A.G.   But wasn't the American System really adopted? The country built internal improvements, and relatively high tariffs were passed from time to time.

G.D.   Yes, but it was done on a piecemeal basis, by fits and starts, and it wasn't carefully planned.

J.A.G.   Turning now to the annexation of Texas, why was Jackson so reluctant to take Texas into the Union while he was President?

G.D.   He was reluctant only while he was President. He still saw himself as a mediator, a unifier, a national figure. He did not want to divide the country. He saw annexation as a very troublesome issue because of the slavery question. He had no personal objection to slavery in Texas, but he knew there would be vehement opposition in the North (to say nothing of Mexico), so he didn't want to bring Texas in at that time.

Later on, of course, he was all for it. Why not, sitting out in the Hermitage in retirement? Jacksonian democracy, as a mediating forth, didn't outlast Jackson very long.

J.A.G.   John C. Calhoun, of course, felt very differently about Texas. But can you explain why Calhoun was so reluctant to go to war with Mexico over Texas in 1845 and 1846?

G.D.   He had at least two reasons. He was a very conservative man in some ways and a very moral man. We look at his radical side and forget what a conservative he. was in many, many ways. He thought that to send troops across a border, which was by no means assuredly a Texan border, was outrageous. He felt that no President had a right to start a war on such flimsy grounds. Furthermore, he did not want to connect slavery with an aggressive war. He was well aware that to do so might be the beginning of the end of the Union. I believe that a lot of other conservative leaders in the South were against the Mexican War for the same reason.

J.A.G.   On the surface, the Mexican War seemed to be another triumph for American nationalism. It was a swift and decisive military victory that resulted in a further expansion of the national territory. Yet, the results of the war were extremely divisive. Why was this so?

G.D.   The Mexican War was a definite aggressive act that seemed out of character to quite a number of Americans. The concept of Manifest Destiny was not basically aggressive; its adherents were simply saying, "Sooner or later we're going to have the whole continent." But when expansion was accomplished by provoking a war and, incidentally, by a very flagrant misuse of the Monroe Doctrine (to say "foreign countries are meddling in your affairs and therefore we are going to attack *you*," is to turn the Monroe Doctrine upside down), it was patently aggressive and it divided the country.

J.A.G.   When you discussed Calhoun's position, you said he shied away from war with Mexico because he realized that it would stir up a hornets' nest, because of slavery. Now you suggest that it was the immorality of the attack on a small nation that caused the division. Would you clarify this point?

G.D.   Because it was an immoral war, all that Calhoun had foreseen had come to pass. Northerners attached it to slavery. "This is a bad war, an aggressive war," they said. "And why? Because it's a proslavery war."

J.A.G.   Was Manifest Destiny as unaggressive as you suggest? During the Oregon controversy, men demanded "Fifty-four forty or fight," did they not? Much of the rhetoric of Manifest Destiny seemed to consider war to be a proper instrument of national policy.

G.D.   I don't think any responsible persons tied it to war. As I see it, the psychology of expansionism was: "Yes, Manifest Destiny will be very clear one of these days. We're bound to go to California. Nothing can stop us." The stress was on the word "destiny."

J.A.G.   What about "Fifty-four forty or fight"?

G.D.   Consider how quickly that slogan was dropped. I doubt if most of the American people ever knew what fifty-four forty meant; they settled readily enough for the line of forty-nine degrees. President Polk was never blamed for the compromise.

J.A.G.   Everything that you have said in the· course of our discussion, beginning with the Louisiana Purchase and running down through the Monroe Doctrine and culminating with the career of Jackson, with his emphasis on national unity, reflects the growth and strengthening of American nationalism at home and the acceptance of American national existence by the great powers of Europe. Yet a short generation after the events you have described, the Union was disrupted by the Civil War and the European powers were again seeking ways of destroying the United States. Is there any explanation of this sudden reversal other than the disruptive force of slavery?

G.D.   We have here, of course, one of the great tragedies of the Western world. I don't know that any of us will ever be able to gauge how much European liberalism (to say nothing of American) suffered from this terrible upheaval. I would assume that nothing else but slavery could have been responsible for the break. I mean slavery with all its implications—such as Southern hallucinations about the dire effects of Northern propaganda, and such as Northern racism. Was it possible that the North, when it vetoed slavery expansion, was really trying to keep the black man in his place—his place being bondage in the South? I don't in any case believe the tariff system could have done it—that was clearly susceptible to compromise, which after all is the genius of all political democracies. No lasting compromise with slavery was possible. But I would take the question of nationalism out of the discussion. In the Civil War two different nations faced each other, each with its own mystique.

The real nurse of slavery was the Industrial Revolution. The South's infatuation with the idea of King Cotton (the belief that Europe couldn't get along without American cotton because its textile industry was so vital to its prosperity) had the effect of hardening political arteries. Without the Industrial Revolution, slavery might have bowed out of its own accord. The Industrial Revolution was responsible for the flourishing of American slavery. But I don't see how we can escape the fact that slavery was the thing which divided the country.

J.A.G. What are the half-dozen books that you would recommend to persons interested in the subject we have been discussing? In each case, would you indicate what the particular contribution of the volume is?

G.D. Samuel Flagg Bemis, *John Quincy Adams and the Foundations of American Foreign Policy* (1949) offers a deep and, I would say, an indispensable investigation of the ideas, aims, and achievements of a master diplomat. For a rich and none too reverent view of Washington's foreign policy I would suggest Alexander DeConde, *Entangling Alliance* (1958). Marshall Smelser, *The Democratic Republic, 1801–1815* (1969) gives in a brief space a remarkably succinct and stimulating account of the administrations of Jefferson and Madison. (Henry Adams, *A History of the United States during the Administrations of Jefferson and Madison* [1889–91], in nine volumes, which Smelser claims can now be studied only as a literary masterpiece, is, in my opinion, still valuable as history.) Bradford Perkins, *Castlereagh and Adams* (1964)—a third volume in a most distinguished trilogy—presents a beautifully researched account of Anglo-American relations from the end of the War of 1812 until the formulation of the Monroe Doctrine.

The Jacksonians are a continuing mystery, but much can be learned from a reading of Arthur M. Schlesinger's grand *The Age of Jackson* (1945), which shows them, on the whole, as reformers and anticapitalists, and of Richard Hofstadter's *The American Political Experience and the Men Who Made It* (1948), which, in a most persuasive essay, weds the movement to the interests of the small capitalist. The movement is odd enough and hospitable enough to entertain both interpretations without undue discomfort. And finally, for the Mexican War I would suggest Frederick Merk's *The Monroe Doctrine and American Expansionism, 1843–1849* (1966), a fine account of the fears, suspicions, and appetites of the Polk administration.

Ray A. Billington

Westward Expansion and the Frontier Thesis

R AY A. BILLINGTON, the nation's leading authority on the
history of the frontier, is Senior Research Associate at the
Huntington Library in San Marino, California, and former President of the Organization of American Historians, the American Studies Association, and the Western
History Association. In addition to his standard text,
Westward Expansion (1960), he has written *The Protestant
Crusade: 1800–1860* (1938), *The Far Western Frontier:
1830–1860* (1956), and a number of other books. He is
currently engaged in writing a biography of the father
of the frontier interpretation of history, Frederick Jackson
Turner. Both the westward expansion of the nation and
the Turner theory are analyzed by Professor Billington
in this discussion.

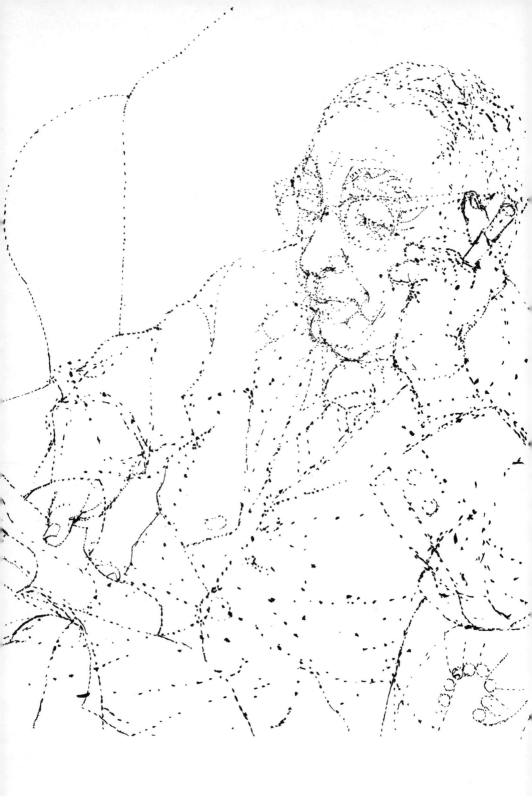

John A. Garraty In early nineteenth-century America, was there such a thing as a "Western type," or were Westerners merely those persons who were living in the western districts of the United States at any particular stage of national development?

Ray A. Billington I would not be true to my profession if I did not insist that there was a Western type, but I "insist" with many modifications. We gain our knowledge of types, Western or any other, by observations made at the time. These observations come from Westerners themselves, and from travelers. Virtually all insist that one passes a cultural fault at the edge of the frontier, a cultural fault as observable as a geographical fault is to a scientist. But I'm always suspicious of these accounts, especially those of travelers. They were always fascinated by the few Westerners on the fringe of the settlements who were seeking to escape society. These so-called backwoodsmen, or squatters, were disreputable characters and far from typical. Yet they are painted as typical by travelers. The real question is, "Was the small farmer who moved west different from those who stayed behind?" and my answer is, "I'm not sure."

Of course it's easy to exaggerate the differences, but it seems to me that there was some slight difference, at least. Those who were willing to trade security for the chance of betterment, with all of the gambles involved (the uncertainties and dangers, the discomforts of life on the frontier) were different from the type of person who stayed in the East. The Westerner was inclined to be more daring, more ambitious, somewhat less bound by tradition; he had a touch of the rebel.

J.A.G. But couldn't one say that all Americans were Westerners in this sense? Everybody who came to America was moving west from Europe, and if some kind of segregation process was going on, didn't it affect Europeans coming to America in the first place?

R.A.B. Very definitely. The first "West" was in the East. The settlers of Jamestown, Plymouth, Massachusetts Bay, and New York had far more risk and faced far more uncertainties in crossing the Atlantic than anyone moving to a later frontier.

J.A.G. How, then, does moving west create a special type of *American?*

R.A.B. The same process operated in successive Wests, with a skimming off in each case of those with a greater spirit of adventure or greater hope of gain. The effect is easy to exaggerate, but it seems to me it existed. The travelers could not have been universally wrong.

J.A.G. Is it possible to generalize about why so many persons have gone west throughout American history?

R.A.B. Human nature is naturally acquisitive; natural man in a free-enterprise society hopes to better himself. Again, however, we have to differentiate between individuals of different cultural backgrounds. The

Spanish came to the Americas in the sixteenth century and they were frontiersmen, but they reacted differently than did the Anglo-American frontiersmen. They came from a Spain that was just emerging from feudalism, where the capitalistic philosophy had not been thoroughly engrained in the culture. They came with a tradition of absolutism. And so they responded differently to the opportunity of the frontier than the English did. The English came a century later, when the feudal heritage was disappearing, absolutism in church and state declining, and the capitalistic philosophy dominating the economic behavior of all classes.

The frontier nevertheless did provide a whole series of opportunities for self-betterment in the successive Wests. True, there were still adequate resources in the Easts. It was a matter of degree. Some men had an instinct for the greater chance. Travelers described, for example, abandoned farms in Ohio in the 1840's, when that country was just beginning to be developed. A few adventurous souls decided they had to go on someplace else. One migrant reported, "This is a land of plenty but we're proceeding to a land of abundance." Given that situation— the chance of betterment on successive frontiers—it's easy to understand the numbers that went west. Today, if you could move from one block to another in a city and possibly increase your income from $10,000 to $20,000, a good many would take the chance. But others would not; they would decide they liked their house, their neighbors, the stability of being where they were.

I don't want to suggest that the hope for gain was the sole motive that drove people to frontiers. Psychologists talk about deficiency motivation and abundancy motivation. There were some who moved to escape dangers and anxieties and discomforts. Some were unhappy with the political climate, with their jobs, with their lack of success. But the abundancy factor seems to me far more important.

J.A.G.   Have there been any differences between the motives of European immigrants and native-born Americans in going west?

R.A.B.   Basically I suspect that the motives were the same: self-betterment, adventure, escape, with a combination of abundancy and deficiency motivation present in each person in varying degrees. But there were national differences, and differences over time between the frontier movement of the eighteenth century and that of the nineteenth century. In the eighteenth century, the frontier was near at hand. It was far easier for persons to move. In the nineteenth century, with the frontiers more distant and more expensive to reach, economic factors intervened. Most Irish immigrants did not have the economic resources to move west. Furthermore, their social impulses were more cohesive; they liked to stay with their own group. On a peasant farm in Ireland one lived near his church, near society. This was not the case in the American Middle West of the 1840's. Cultural traditions operated. Immigrant groups (or native groups for that matter) tended to move into areas where persons from their community had previously gone. The historian Dorothy Johannson has worked out a very interesting theory, sociologically based, on the differences between modern Oregon and Washington. Because of the prior movement into Oregon of more adventurous sorts, those who went over the Oregon Trail before 1846, a pattern of adventuresomeness was established. In Washington, where the migration came later and life was more stabilized, a less adventuresome type predominated. And Johannson argues that the differences are still noticeable today.

Of course, movements of peoples also depend upon the availability of knowledge: upon advertising by real-estate salesmen, shipping companies, railroad companies, and so on. In the nineteenth century these companies were advertising heavily in certain parts of Europe and not in others. Ireland got very little of this advertising, the Scandinavian and German countries a great deal. On the other hand, ethnic groups responded in different ways to different frontier environments. The Irish and the French seemed to be inclined to cling to their own ways, to adjust less readily. Why, I just don't know.

J.A.G.   Was it actually easier for a settler to move to Kentucky in 1790 than to move to North Dakota in 1890?

R.A.B.   It depends on what you mean by "easier." From the point of view of physical difficulty, it was about the same. But from the point of view of establishing a farm, it was far easier to do so in Kentucky than it was in North Dakota. Financially, for one thing; in the Dakotas frontiersmen had to buy land, usually from a speculator, whereas in Kentucky many squatted on the land and simply appropriated it. One could get to North Dakota faster from New York in 1890 if one had the railroad fare, but you had to have the railroad fare. You had to have money—along with the ability to endure the North Dakota winters!

J.A.G.   It took between seventy-five and one hundred fifty years for settlement to reach the Appalachian Mountains after the first colonists arrived in America, and as late as the 1770's there were only a relative handful of Americans living beyond the Appalachians. Yet, fifty years later the frontier had crossed the Mississippi, and by the time of the Civil War, Oregon, California, and Texas were states in the Union. Were the Appalachians a serious barrier to the westward movement? And why was the movement so rapid after the Revolution?

R.A.B.   The Appalachians were not a barrier. It's true they were hard to cross. There were only four passes through the mountains: the Mohawk, the Pittsburgh route, the Cumberland Gap, and the one around the southern end. But the Rocky Mountains were far more difficult to cross than the Appalachians and with only South Pass leading beyond. I don't think the mountains were really an important factor. No geographical barrier was too powerful to be penetrated if the urge for expansion was running strong. The Appalachians would have been passed over in no time if there had been sufficient urge.

There were many reasons for the westward surge after the Revolution. One was the pressure of population. Population had been growing of course through the colonial period, but at a relatively slow rate. Overcrowding was not a major problem in the 1770's, excepting in certain portions of New England. But after the Revolution, the natural increase in population accelerated, and after about 1830 immigration began to flood in from abroad. Successive Wests fed themselves, populationwise. Each new West came into competition with the East immediately behind it. The Easts found it difficult to compete with these new Wests, because the soils were fresher. This led to the development of the urban trend in the successive Easts, and the driving out of Easterners to the new Wests. A classic example, of course, is the rural decay of New England after the opening of the Erie Canal.

Another obvious cause of westward expansion was the improvement of transportation. In the colonial period, rivers provided the chief access to markets. After the Revolution, the steamboat and the canal reduced the cost of moving goods and made it far easier to develop the trans-Appalachian region. Then, too, the role of the government has to be considered. The British, unsympathetic for the most part to American expansion and influenced by two powerful pressure groups, the fur-trading interests and the humanitarians wanting to protect the Indians, offered a certain amount of opposition to expansion. This was not the case after the Revolution. Furthermore, as the successive Wests were settled, political power gradually shifted to them, and they used this power to obtain legislation beneficial to the West. The whole liberalization of the land disposal system, culminating in the Homestead Act, illustrates this, as does the steady removal of the Indians. You can't imagine Parliament acting, as did Andrew Jackson, in the expelling of the five civilized tribes of the Old South.

All these factors produced a sort of momentum. The frontier fed on itself. As it expanded, it created pressures that led to further expansion.

J.A.G. Much of American political history between 1800 and 1860 is commonly analyzed in sectional terms. Was there actually a Western interest in the sense that there were Northern and Southern interests in this period?

R.A.B. That is an extremely difficult question. The traditional view, of course, is that the West did vote as a bloc on such issues as land policy, the United States Bank, tariffs, and internal improvements. This view holds that the West was the unstable element in the three sections, swinging back and forth between North and South, trading votes on the tariff for votes on land policy, and the like. But this is a highly unsophisticated form of analysis. It seems to me that to answer this question properly one must achieve a balance somehow between geographic factors, political motivations, and a variety of other things. Recently, new techniques based on computer analysis have been applied to the problem but with inconclusive results. More study is necessary. My impression is that sectional divisions were of some importance, but not nearly as important as Frederick Jackson Turner thought them to be. There was a Western interest, but it was based upon idealism as well as materialistic interests. And local issues, subsectional divisions, party loyalties, and individual leaders operated at times to destroy any unified, geographic force in shaping the opinion of peoples.

Turner, bless him, went too far in this direction. To me, reading the letters that he wrote in his latter years, it's a tragedy to see how much reliance he placed upon the section to explain political behavior. To him it was *the* interpretation, far more important than the frontier. The maps that he drew up to illustrate sectional voting are unbelievably complex, impossible to translate onto a page of a book. He tried to get too much on them, to show these various factors operating.

J.A.G. Did not the West itself divide North and South, especially where slavery was concerned?

R.A.B. That's right. And not only over slavery. The tariff, land policy, and internal improvements often divided Westerners. When Turner talked about the West he was talking about the Old Northwest, not about the Southwest.

J.A.G. Well, would you discuss now the role of the West in some of the important political controversies of the early nineteenth century? First of all, the purchase of Louisiana?

R.A.B. The West was still very sparsely populated and not important as a political force in 1803. In negotiating for Louisiana, Jefferson was responding to historic forces rather than to political forces.

J.A.G. His policy is usually discussed in political terms.

R.A.B. In a sense this is correct, because Jefferson knew perfectly well that any closing of the port of New Orleans was going to lead to turmoil in the West and, possibly, separatism. The whole history of the navigation of the Mississippi, from the days of the abortive Jay-Guardoqui Treaty of 1785 on, had shown perfectly well that the West was willing to take almost any steps in order to keep the Mississippi River open. So there was in this sense a Western pressure. But I don't think it was a politically exerted pressure to which he had to respond.

J.A.G. How do you view the role of the West in causing the War of 1812?

R.A.B. There has been a revolution in the interpretation of this question recently, with the older view coming under attack that the West wanted war because of land hunger, the Indian menace, the economic depression in the Ohio Valley. If you read the congressional debates you certainly can find ample evidence that these motives existed. But recently, Bradford Perkins, Reginald Horsman, Norman R. Brown, and other historians who've been working on the problem, have developed a far more sophisticated approach and have certainly done a far better job on vote analysis. They show that there was no solid Western phalanx, and that the Western pressures were insufficient to cause war even if the section had been solid. There was great sentiment for war in the South, and even in the middle states. Further, the basic demand of the West was not for Canada, but for defending the national honor and preserving the freedom of the seas. It was nationalism speaking rather than anything else. The West was a strongly nationalistic region; it depended upon the national government. Above all, I don't think that the West was primarily responsible for the war.

J.A.G. Turner rested his argument that there were distinct Western interests in politics very strongly on the tariff controversies of the period after the War of 1812. How do you feel about that?

R.A.B. I don't think we can form any positive judgment; we must wait for a more sophisticated study of the sectional controversy. For the most part, we base our assumptions on Western solidity for protection on congressional debates, a very faulty way to test public opinion. Probably the West was protectionist, having been sold on the home-market idea after Waterloo, when Europe began again to produce most of its own foodstuffs. There was also a constant feeling that the West should develop its own industries so as to be less dependent on transportation.

J.A.G. Was there a Western position in the financial controversies revolving around the Second Bank of the United States?

R.A.B. This again I find almost impossible to determine. I don't think that the Bank was nearly as much a sectional issue as the tariff. Opinion in the West was divided, with the divisions on political and class lines. Many speculators were opposed to Biddle's operation of the Bank because he was checking the inflationary tendencies of the state banks. But there was a strong hard-money element too.

J.A.G. Perhaps we're wrong in trying to find a rational explanation for the West's position on such a complex subject as banking and finance.

R.A.B. All questions of this sort are generally beyond the comprehension of the average individual, who is inclined to follow his leaders. Many Westerners backed Jackson, whether their true interests were for hard money or soft. His veto message said that the Bank was a monster, and therefore it was a monster.

J.A.G. Do you consider Jackson as primarily a Western leader?

R.A.B. A Western leader in what sense? He represented one group in the West, but by no means all western people, it seems to me. And yet he was obviously an idol of the West in the sense that as a military hero, a man who had "fit the Injuns," he had captured the hearts if not the minds of westerners.

J.A.G. It seems to me that everything you are saying points in the same direction: the enormous force of nationalism functioning psychologically on the successive waves of western expansion.

R.A.B. I think that is right.

J.A.G. What about the Mexican War? Was there a Western position on the Mexican War?

R.A.B. Here again I think it's impossible to answer with any degree of sureness. Someday soon someone will write a good modern study of the Mexican War. But certainly the West was responsible for the Mexican War in that expansion brought on the war. If it hadn't been for western expansion, there wouldn't have been restless American pioneers in Texas; there wouldn't have been a Texas Revolution; there wouldn't have been a Nueces River controversy over the boundary with Mexico, there wouldn't have been the settlement of California, and so on. But perhaps there would have been no war if there hadn't been the threat of France and England in California and in Texas and in Oregon, as Frederick Merk has shown in his *Monroe Doctrine and American Expansion*. Merk's argument that expansion was necessary to secure the national interests is convincing to me. Again we come right back to nationalism.

J.A.G. If Westerners were confirmed nationalists, how can you explain the persistent secessionist psychology of the West—such movements as the attempt to set up the state of Franklin in Kentucky, and James Wilkinson's conspiracy to make the Southwest Spanish.

R.A.B. In such cases, Westerners were pulling Eastern leaders by the nose, in my opinion. Now, Wilkinson—nobody will ever know *his* motives. But the great mass of Kentuckians and Tennesseeans had no genuine interest in trading the security they had under American rule for the tutelage of Spain.

J.A.G. Weren't the first Americans in Texas perfectly willing to become Mexicans?

R.A.B. Perhaps. But they were extremely disappointed when they could not trade their Mexican status for American status immediately after the Texas Revolution. They wanted to come into the United States. They were strongly nationalistic.

J.A.G. What was meant in the 1840's by the term "manifest destiny"? Was there anything in the concept that was really new?

R.A.B. Thomas Jefferson and others of his era thought of the United States as a "standing monument and example." The perfection of American institutions seemed such that inevitably monarchies would crumble throughout the world, and republicanism would be established everywhere. This was the belief until about the 1840's. There was no need to do anything about this. It was going to happen automatically. But in the 1840's men began to doubt. Monarchy was not crumbling; indeed, it appeared to be threatening our very existence, in Texas, in Oregon, in California. The "expanding area of freedom" concept was not sufficient for that particular day; a new aggressiveness developed. It seems to me that manifest destiny was simply a matter of changing techniques rather than a new philosophy.

If one reads the speeches and the newspaper reports of the day, one finds no hint of imperialism in this concept. The United States was going to elevate the Mexican peons and lift the yoke of monarchy from the backs of the Canadians. You tell this to students today and they laugh. They won't believe it. But I am convinced that it was the case. Not many persons responded to the call of manifest destiny. Only about five thousand went to Oregon in the 1840's, about one thousand to California. Manifest destiny as a moving force was not very important, but as a psychological force it had great significance.

J.A.G. Was there a Western position on slavery?

R.A.B. I don't think so. The West was too varied. Southern Illinois and southern Indiana were settled primarily by Southerners. But some who came there liked slavery, and others were fleeing from slavery. However, there are two factors that substantiate *to a degree* the argument that there was a Western position on slavery.

One was the abolitionism of the Old Northwest. That region was not a center of radical abolition of the type advocated by William Lloyd Garrison, but rather of the gradualism of Theodore Dwight Weld. It had strong religious overtones, and fitted in well with the revivalistic emotional religion that was popular on successive frontiers. Secondly, an economic factor existed. Most Westerners were always looking ahead to the next frontier. Farmers in Illinois were looking to Iowa. Farmers in Iowa were thinking about going to Kansas or Nebraska. They wanted to keep these as free territories. They believed, rightly or wrongly, that it was impossible for free labor to compete with slavery, that if slavery was permitted in those areas, the normal migration on which they depended would be impossible.

J.A.G. But serious controversy over slavery in the territories did not occur until most of the territory that was suitable for a slave economy had already been taken into the Union. Why did it become an issue when it no longer mattered?

R.A.B. People didn't know this. In their eyes, Kansas was as likely a slave territory as Louisiana.

J.A.G. But in the debates that led to the compromise of 1850, the point was made repeatedly. Senator Stephen A. Douglas certainly took that position.

R.A.B. That's right, but many people were not convinced that it was true. An emotional factor was involved: You're not going to be convinced against your will.

J.A.G. What about the idea of popular sovereignty? Did the concept of allowing local residents quickly to establish their own government have any advantages to settlers in territories, or was it just a political slogan?

R.A.B. The Westerners thought that it did. Popular sovereignty was strongly supported in the West, and not simply as a device for settling the slavery issue. They wanted to control their local institutions. This was part of the whole democratic philosophy of the frontier.

J.A.G. Did the improvement in communications with the Atlantic seaboard between 1820 and 1860 affect Western attitudes significantly?

R.A.B. It did, in two respects. The economic impact was considerable; new trade routes led to greater prosperity. But more than this, as Carter Goodrich and others have shown, there was a tendency for industries to cluster around transportation routes. Better transportation sped the urbanization of the West. This meant a breaking down of provincialism, closer ties with the East and with Europe. The changes wrought in the structure of society and culture had a great effect on Western opinion. Then there were obvious political effects. The shifting of trade routes from West-South, down the Mississippi River, to East-West, produced a corresponding shift in the Old Northwest's basic allegiance, and surely influenced the section's actions when the Civil War broke out.

J.A.G. Did the rapid breaking down of self-sufficiency and isolation on each new frontier because of improvements in transportation affect the "Western character"?

R.A.B. In a sense, yes, but on the other hand, it also accentuated the Western character by creating greater opportunity. The go-ahead spirit, the get-rich-quick philosophy was accentuated.

J.A.G. But it must have de-emphasized differences between East and West.

R.A.B. That is true. Our whole history is one of the lessening emphasis upon difference. That's why the younger critics of the Turner thesis refuse to admit there is a Turner thesis. They see no difference. But I can still see a difference when I compare California to the East; Los Angeles is different from New York.

J.A.G. Would you define that most confusing term, "the frontier"?

R.A.B. I suppose I should start by talking about Frederick Jackson Turner. He has been more sharply criticized for his failure to define the term "frontier" properly than for any other reason. He used the term at a time when it had had no exact definition; it was just coming into the dictionaries in its modern connotation. Previously it meant "a barrier," as a frontier between nations. Secondly, I don't think that the term as used by Turner lent itself to exact definition. He used it in various ways, depending upon the context. It could be a line, it could be a migrating zone, it could be the area of a certain population density. To his own generation, certainly, the context explained the meaning. In some of his later correspondence he talked about this, and said, in effect, "My readers understood me. Why should I go further in trying to define this elusive word?" But if we must define the word, it is necessary to recognize two different usages: the frontier as place, and the frontier as process.

To define a frontier as place, it is necessary to recognize basically the changed man/land ratio in a West as compared to an East. Gertrude Stein once said that "In America there is more land where nobody is than there is land where anybody is. That's what makes America what it is." In Europe, even in the seventeenth century, there were a great many people and very little land. In America, there was a great deal of land and very few people. And this distinction, varying in intensity, designates the frontier in history.

The frontier as place has to be defined in relativistic terms. There were few people in Ohio in 1840 by modern standards, but there were fewer people in Missouri or Iowa. The frontier as a place is a geographic region in which a low land/man ratio and unexploited natural resources provide an exceptional opportunity for the small propertied individual to better himself.

The idea of the frontier as process is based on the assumption that life on a geographic frontier alters man's behavior and thought patterns. These variations vary in turn with the ethnic and cultural background of the newcomers. I would define frontier as process as the way the socioeconomic and political behavior of men is altered by an environment in which a low land/man ratio and untapped natural resources provide unusual opportunity for individual self-advancement.

When defined this way, the frontier is not a line, but rather a broad zone, moving erratically in time and in place. Obviously, this varies a great deal from our modern use of the term. We speak of frontiers of space, frontiers of science, and so forth. The essence of a frontier as I've defined it is the exploitability of unused natural resources by small propertied individuals. In this sense, the age of the frontier in America is gone, never to return. We have been adjusting gradually through the twentieth century to a closed-space existence, and many of our social problems are partly the result of the psychological readjustment that has become necessary in this changed physical situation.

J.A.G.   Would you summarize Turner's interpretation of the role of the West, or of the frontier, used in both these senses, in American history?

R.A.B.   I find it difficult to do so, partly because Turner himself did not exactly define his understanding of the West. Of course he spoke in exaggerated and poetic terms of the influence of free land. In the first place, there was no free land in the traditional sense; land was cheaper than elsewhere, but there was some price fixed to it. Turner was also inclined to speak of land per se, rather than of mineral resources, forest resources, all of the forms in which natural resources were available. Turner always called his course "The History of the West." He first gave it at the University of Wisconsin in the 1890's, and his last course at Harvard in 1923–24 was still called "The History of the West." (I inherited a course in "The History of the West" when I came to Northwestern, and a student violently complained after the end of the first quarter, saying he'd taken a course in the History of the West and had only gotten up to the Appalachians.) Turner never recognized that a History of the Frontier and a History of the West were two different concepts completely.

Nevertheless, Turner did believe that free land lured men westward and altered them and their institutions. He believed that frontiering endowed them with certain traits, which he distinguished as American: an exaggerated belief in democracy, a type of individualism, nationalism, mobility, coarseness and strength, a practical and inventive turn of mind, a masterful grasp of material things, a lack of artistic sensibility, a restless nervous energy, the exuberance that comes from freedom. Such was his concept. He popularized it, but he didn't test it. Actually, I think Turner lost interest in the frontier shortly after he read his famous 1893 paper. He dedicated virtually all of his life to a study of the sectional concept and sectional problems. According to his friends, he always carried a piece of paper with him, and when he read about a congressional vote in the newspaper, he would quickly map that vote, showing the sectional division on the issue.

To me it's tragic that he spent so much time on the sectional concept at a time when sectionalism was dying. Nationalism was superseding sectionalism, but he felt that sectionalism was going to be the great force of the future. It amazes me the correspondence he had with influential men of his day—Felix Frankfurter, Harold Laski, people of this sort. They considered his sectional work the greatest thing in the world. We were going to do away with state boundaries in favor of section divisions. This was Turner's real interest, and so he never developed the frontier hypothesis as it should have been developed.

Turner is frequently attacked as being a monocausationalist. The frontier explained everything. But as I indicated, the section was more important to him than the frontier. Furthermore, his interest was not in any one aspect of American history. I suppose nobody of his generation and few people since then, with the exception of Allan Nevins, have had such a grasp of *all* American history. He left thirty-four letter filing cases, crammed with notes and clippings, starting with Columbus and going all the way to Herbert Hoover. That was his interest. He didn't believe that there was any one key to American history. In late life he denied that "the frontier phenomenon was the one key to American history. It was *a* key, and a neglected one." He specialized in the frontier and sectionalism because he felt they had been neglected.

J.A.G.   It has been argued by a number of historians that all Turner's ideas about the frontier were derived from the work of earlier writers. Is that a fair statement?

R.A.B.   Yes and no. He did select ideas from dozens of different writers, but he mixed them up in his own mind and produced a concept that was entirely fresh and original. It is possible to trace the reading he was doing at the time he developed this concept. There are a whole series of additional filing drawers in his papers, and one of those drawers contains notes on the reading he was doing when he developed his frontier concept. I have reread all that he read at the time: census documents, statistical abstracts, travel accounts by the score. He read a whole series of theoretical writers—economists, political economists, and the like. Lee Benson has done a brilliant job of "proving" that the Italian political economist Achille Loria was really the author of the frontier thesis. But the notes that Turner took from Loria do not refer to the part that Benson said influenced him at all. This is not to say, of course, that Turner was not influenced by the book. The English political scientist Walter Bagehot's *Physics and Politics* also attracted Turner's attention; his copy of that book is heavily underlined. Turner's phrase, "breaking the cake of custom," he took literally from Bagehot. He went through dozens of different things. As he read, he jotted down notes such as: "America, the most mechanical of nations. Why? Frontier experiences?" Or, "West —influence on America. Breaker of custom." So in this sense, he did gather together and forge into one concept the writings of many individuals. When Theodore Roosevelt read Turner's 1893 essay, he congratulated him on putting into definite shape ideas that had been "floating around rather loosely." This seems like a funny statement, but actually it is true.

Turner's contribution was to recognize the relationship of a variety of ideas and to blend them into a new concept. Interestingly enough, he missed the one writer who would have been most influential of all, E. L. Godkin, whose essay on "Aristocratic Opinions of American Democracy" was published in the *North American Review* in 1865, which is to me the best statement of the frontier thesis before the time of Turner. When it was called to his attention long afterward, he laughed, and said, "Godkin has stolen my thunder." The historian Edward Channing of Harvard often began his seminar by opening a drawer and pulling out this pamphlet and saying, "Here, gentlemen, here is where Turner got his ideas from," and slamming it back into the drawer again. Turner and Channing did not like each other. It probably was Godkin's essay he was pulling out, but nobody will ever know.

J.A.G. In what sense, if any, did the frontier serve as a "safety valve" moderating the lot of the poor, and raising living standards in America?

R.A.B. This, of course, has been the most disputed point in all the controversy over the frontier hypothesis. The frontier safety valve is part of our folklore. The idea was expressed as early as the seventeenth century. Economists today would agree that the frontier operated as a safety valve, but not in the classic sense. Few wage earners left eastern factories to become western farmers. They didn't have the money, and they didn't have the skills. Turner recognized this; his files contain a sheaf of notes two inches thick on the cost of moving west in the 1850's. He came to the same conclusions that Clarence H. Danhof did in his articles on the subject, which were great tools of the antisafety-valvers.

One can understand the true workings of the safety valve only by viewing the effect of the total frontier on the total economy of the nation. Any movement of peoples from east to west, whether of wage earners or of farm laborers, relieved pressure on the eastern labor market and pushed wages up. Secondly, we must understand that the frontier was a broad zone. Migration continued to parts of each frontier over a good many years. The exploitation of frontier resources was a peeling off of a series of slabs, with the firstcomers getting a very small slab, the nextcomers, with higher technological development and greater capital, getting a larger slab, and so forth.

An obvious example would be the mining frontier. Firstcomers, using a washing pan and a cradle, skimmed off a little of the surface gold from the streams. Then they developed a sluice box which allowed a greater concentration of labor on a particular area. Then they began digging shafts down to bedrock, and damming rivers, and thus took off the pay dirt from the whole bottom of the river. Finally, the big corporations sank shafts thousands of feet into bedrock, applying great capital expenditures and modern technological devices to get all the wealth out.

The same development took place in forestry and in agriculture, over the course of many years, with a constant attraction of labor from east to west to take part in this successive exploitation. This meant not only a drainage away from the eastern labor market, but also an increase in per-capita income as western resources were translated into capital and fed into the national economy. The result was a building up of wages and a lowering of the prices of consumer goods. American workers did not, of course, achieve the perfect standard of living. There were still strikes and much discontent. But they did have a higher standard of living than that of most countries of the world of that day with correspondingly less social unrest.

There was also a sociopsychological safety valve. Through the nineteenth century at least, the average worker *believed* that he could escape to the frontier even though he could not. "Come a depression, I will go west. I will buy a farm. I will grow rich." The man who believed that he was a potential capitalist, even though he was not a capitalist, had less incentive to protest. So I believe there was a safety valve, not in the traditional sense of escape from factory to farm, but in the impact of the frontier upon the national economy.

J.A.G.　How did frontier society differ from the society of older regions?

R.A.B.　There were differences of degree, if not of kind. The frontier social order was patterned on those of the successive Easts. Every pioneer envisaged the creation of exactly the type of society that he had left behind. Man is a creature of tradition, after all, and changes his customs and institutions reluctantly and slowly. But in the different social atmosphere of the frontier communities I think some changes did occur.

Basic, of course, was the greater opportunity for advancement that existed. This was due to the presence of unexploited natural resources, which meant that the small propertied individual had a better chance to win affluence. The less rigidly stratified social structure that existed in pioneer communities was another key difference. Class lines existed everywhere, but they were not as tightly drawn as in eastern communities. Vertical mobility was possible to a degree that it was not in the various Easts. The ambitious could improve themselves, not only economically but socially. This fact, I think, altered behavioral patterns. It stimulated the growth of social democracy in contrast with political democracy. All men were potential millionaires, therefore all men should be treated as equals.

Opportunity also encouraged physical mobility. Men moved about to better themselves; there was less attachment to place. Greater opportunity bred wastefulness; exploitation rather than conservation was the quickest way to wealth. The frontiersman was a little more inclined to improvise. He was forced to be inventive by nature, because he faced unusual situations in a new land.

You ask also, "Have these traits persisted," and again, the answer is Yes and No. All have been weakened to a degree by the passing of the agrarian environment and the emergence of an urban-industrial one. But men infected with that "go-ahead" spirit, with the belief that opportunity lay ahead, remained infected. A child bred in that tradition was far more likely to believe in it than a person bred in a more static society. A child who was moved frequently from place to place by his parents would have less attachment to a place himself. The social atmosphere of the frontier did persist down into the twentieth century, and we are still to a degree governed by that atmosphere. Other traits have not eroded away—social democracy, for example. Servants are still hard to find in this country; the easy familiarity of the taxi driver with his customer is another indication of this. Social mobility remains high. Elite groups open their ranks more readily to the newcomer. We have a "throw-away" philosophy as far as material goods are concerned. Physical mobility is still high. We still are hard-working people; we don't have the leisurely luncheon or the siesta. We do now have the "coffee break," but it is a revolution in American life. It's something very recent in our development, a product of the affluence of industrialization, just as hard work was a product of the frontier.

J.A.G. Your argument is a relative one, but some of the comments that you made almost parenthetically bother me a little. For instance, you see the West as a dynamic, open society. Wasn't the East equally dynamic and open, in perhaps different ways?

R.A.B. I don't think it was equally so. It was dynamic and open, and far more so than England or France, but it is a matter of increased openness, increased plasticity of society as you move West. New York was an open society compared with London, but Buffalo was an open society compared with New York.

J.A.G. Do you think that the openness of Buffalo, say, in the 1840's, was a product of that area having been a frontier?

R.A.B. To a slight degree, yes. A tradition had been established in the beginning, and it persisted. But far more responsible was the economic opportunity, the opportunity for self-betterment, that existed.

J.A.G. How could the typical westerner be both an individualist and a conformist, both very materialistic and at the same time extremely charitable and public-spirited?

R.A.B. "Individualism," as we employ the term in "rugged American individualism," certainly does not imply rebellion against convention. Americans are among the most conformist peoples in the Western world. We are inclined to follow the herd; there is a monotonous uniformity in our towns (as travelers have pointed out). This conforms to the frontier tradition. Conformity and cooperation were essential to survival in pioneer communities. Cooperative enterprise was necessary for defense, house building, and barn raising. But in the economic realm, the frontiersman personified the philosophy of individualism as we use the term. In no other environment was every man so near to being a capitalist. Nowhere was a stake in society more easily obtained. So Westerners became acutely aware of the sanctity of private property. Even though they had little themselves, they were going to have some, and they were determined to guard their right to use property for their own purposes. They might favor regulatory measures that would interfere with free use of capital, but only to prevent individuals from being injured by social predators. They were unalterably opposed to government "interference."

The frontiersman was not a theorist; he was thoroughly inconsistent in his social and economic philosophy. But pragmatically he held that private property was above the reach of the social order. There are obviously two forms of American individualism at the present time. One is a relative lack of respect for the law; we are inclined, as a people, to do what we want to do when law is involved. The other is a resentment of regulatory measures. The greatest outcries against the New Deal occurred when the government interfered with private enterprise. Some Southerners expressed the same view when they raised the umbrella of states rights to prevent government interference with the racial situation, but what they basically were talking about was not states rights, but individual rights—the right of the individual to associate with whom he pleased.

J.A.G. How could frontiersmen be so materialistic and also so wasteful of material goods?

R.A.B. They could gain more material goods by being wasteful. They destroyed forest resources because the tree was their enemy. It had to be cut down. By ruthlessly cutting down trees they could bring land into production. They could hurry the process of accumulating wealth by wasteful techniques. The conflict between materialism and public-spiritedness is somewhat more difficult to explain. Physical needs always transcend cultural needs in a new society. The tendency for the frontiersman was to work endlessly for immediate gain and to neglect the cultural aspects of civilization. But after the initial frontier stage, men pursued wealth not for wealth's sake solely, but as a symbol of their elevated status. Americans have traditionally felt inferior to Europeans, and Westerners have traditionally felt inferior to Easterners. I was brought up in the Middle West. I saw this feeling in Detroit, where money meant not simply affluence but a chance to build a museum that would be better than New York's Metropolitan, a zoo that would be better than the Bronx Zoo. This has been the motivating force of Western public-spiritedness. Frontiersmen looked up to the areas they had left behind, and wanted to copy them as rapidly as possible in all their cultural aspects.

J.A.G. Were frontiersmen more committed to democracy than other Americans?

R.A.B. I think they were. The frontier served as a leveling force by lessening the difference between individuals. The rich became richer, but the poor became rich; there was less of an economic gulf between classes. New societies also altered the power structure by reducing stratification. A new community had to develop its own leadership group.

These situations encouraged experimentation, usually in a way that meant greater freedom and self-expression for the people. The frontiers, from the seventeenth century on, displayed a trend toward greater control of government by the people. The trend was not universal, and frontiersmen did not invent new democratic institutions. Western state constitutions were basically scissors-and-paste jobs based on Eastern constitutions, but the trend was toward the more democratic features of older constitutions: shorter terms for governors and longer terms for legislators; more direct popular elections; manhood suffrage; eventually initiative, referendum, and recall.

European travelers all through the nineteenth century found the "I'm as good as you are and sometimes a damn sight better" spirit in every West. Why be servile to a man who was temporarily above you, when you expect to be a landowner yourself sometime? This spirit, fanned by the plastic nature of frontier society, persists to the present day. Class lines are hardening; social stratification is gaining ground in this country, but it is less rigid in the West than in older communities. Los Angeles society is highly stratified, but compared with that of Boston, it's an open society. It is far easier to get into the California Club of Los Angeles than into the Chicago Club, which, in turn, is easier to enter than the Somerset Club of Boston. The further west one goes, the more open the society.

Of course, everywhere in the Western world industrialization and the managerial revolution are making social escalation easier. Our society offers tremendous opportunities for self-advancement. The shift from a blue collar to a white collar is relatively easy.

J.A.G. If frontier life made people believe that one man is as good as another, why have the sons of frontiersmen so often opposed giving equal opportunity to the urban masses who flocked into these regions with industrialization?

R.A.B. This is human selfishness, isn't it? Regardless of social forces, men cling to a political structure that gives them power.

J.A.G. One of the most interesting chapters in your book *America's Frontier Heritage,* but also, I think, one of the most difficult, deals with the economic impact of the frontier. Would you explain how the frontier speeded economic growth, aside from the obvious fact that expansion added to the economic resources of the nation?

R.A.B. What I was trying to do in that chapter was to fit into the broader frontier story David M. Potter's explanation of Americans as *people of plenty,* a very impressive theory, but one that would not have applied to this country had there not been a frontier. I was also trying to utilize the theories of sequential growth developed by modern economists. We have to think of a dual geographic frontier—a zone where exploitive techniques are being applied to virgin natural resources, and, secondly, an area behind this immediate frontier, a subfrontier where a thickening of the population makes possible a division of labor, more advanced technology, and the importation of larger sums of capital for the intensive utilization of these same resources. The principal national economic impact of the frontier came when the subfrontier was developed. This is the point that David Potter makes so strongly, and he's perfectly right in doing so.

The initial exploitation encouraged the importation of capital, essential, of course, in the development of any new region. We must think of the United States as an underdeveloped country in the nineteenth century. The exploitation of the geographic frontier usually attracted relatively little Eastern or European capital. (The mining frontier and the cattle frontier in the 1870's and 1880's are exceptions.) Behind this frontier in areas where the population was thickening, transportation outlets were being provided. There, a combination of resources, labor, and markets provided an admirable opportunity for the investor, with less risk to his capital than on the initial frontier. Into the subfrontier flowed capital from the east. This meant, in turn, technological improvement, the use of machinery necessary to extract and process natural resources. Take as an example the movement of the plantation frontier westward into Alabama and Mississippi in the 1840's and 1850's. The initial development was never undertaken by the plantation owner, but rather by the small farmer. After the soils had been tested, the region proven, then the plantation owner came in with his capital; he consolidated small farms, and built his plantation. The flow of capital under these conditions had a second effect: It allowed the sequential utilization of more and more resources as labor and technological skills were applied. Finally, this process begins to realize local funds for further investment. Capital in the form of profits is used for further exploitation through still further technological advance. Industries develop, and gradually economic diversification takes place.

This process did *not* operate on the frontier. But my point is that there would have been no subfrontier had there not first been a frontier. The sequential growth that David Potter made so much of could not have taken place without a frontier.

J.A.G.   Why haven't modern underdeveloped areas in Africa and Latin America responded to their frontiers in this way?

R.A.B.   Sequential exploitation of resources depends on three ingredients: manpower, capital, and technological know-how. The first two ingredients are available to a degree to the underdeveloped nations of today. But I do not think that technological know-how is as readily available as as it was in this country. Our frontiers were occupied by men who had been reared in a tradition of technological change and improvement. They were a product of the commercial and industrial revolutions of England. In America, too, the incentive values of capitalism operated as they do not in many of the underdeveloped countries of the present time.

More important, in today's underdeveloped countries, the surface resources have been used for centuries. This is especially the case in Africa and India, where the soils have been mined for generations with primitive techniques that led to soil depletion. The initial frontier development has to be made by agriculture, but in these countries the mining of the soil has reduced the marginal productivity of labor in agriculture to near zero. There is little chance to begin the cycle of sequential growth so typical of the American experience. In many parts of the world we, the Western nations, are trying to impose an industrial structure on societies that have no agricultural base for it.

J.A.G.   Did the United States in the first half of the nineteenth century have a more socially and economically mobile society than in later periods?

R.A.B.   The important thing to me is not to compare frontier mobility with today, but to compare it with mobility in Europe at that time, where there was no frontier. And fragmentary evidence suggests that the rate of mobility in this country was far greater.

J.A.G. But was there as much economic and social mobility in a frontier district before 1860 as people of that time thought?

R.A.B. No. I would certainly say there were not, but they were greater relatively on the frontier than elsewhere.

J.A.G. Granting everything you've said about the impact of the frontier, are you certain that "frontier" is the best term to use to describe the phenomena you've been discussing? Could one not argue, for example, that the central force in creating American conditions was the favorable man/land ratio, which operated on all sections of the nation at all periods of time?

R.A.B. I would thoroughly agree. I am by no means satisfied with the term "frontier" to picture the broad social processes triggered by the westward advance. That term has become too much associated with Turner's ill-defined phraseology. If we could devise another, more descriptive term, it would be a boon to us "frontier" historians, and would free us from the blood-and-thunder school that capitalizes upon the romance of the frontier. But until we have devised such a term, I find "frontier" sufficiently descriptive of the process. But you're perfectly right. We must see the United States in the eighteenth and nineteenth centuries as an area of declining population density as one moves from east to west, starting in Europe and going out to the extreme edge of settlement.

But changes were most dramatic in areas where the man/land ratio was lowest—near the actual physical frontier. Secondly, if there had been no frontier, there would have been no gradation from east to west. If America had been like Australia, with an arid interior blocking expansion, or like Canada, where the Laurentian Plateau diverted the westward movement southward, or like Africa, where an earlier civilization had skimmed off the surface wealth, we would not have had the pattern of growth that we have had.

J.A.G. What are the chief unanswered questions about western development before the Civil War and about the role of the frontier in American history?

R.A.B. This is a subject dear to my heart, but I'm not going to talk directly to your question. I'm not going to say, "Here is a problem that needs to be solved." We've talked about these problems all through our conversation. The frontier school of history has been in eclipse for a generation now, partly because we have committed many sins. We have been too tempted to popularize. We have tried to compete with the dime novel, with the Western film, with "Gunsmoke." Now, it's easy to understand this temptation. We're interested in selling books, and one way to sell books is to cater to that market. We have stressed the "glamorous" elements of Western history, and written about cowboys and Indians, about gun fighters and mountain men. We've preferred to make Wyatt Earp a hero rather than devoting ourselves to serious research on Western history. And the result is that Western history is legitimately looked down upon by a good many younger historians.

How can this be changed? First of all, I hope Western historians will pay less attention to the pioneers and more to the modern West. The story of the frontier has been retold far more than it deserves to be. Think of the words wasted on the Oregon Trail, over which only five thousand people moved before 1853. The Donner party has had more ink spilled over it than many significant events in history. Think of Custer and the battle of the Little Big Horn. Fewer than three hundred men were killed, and yet it's been more written about than World War I. Think of the way we've glorified the despicable Western bad men— punks like Billy the Kid and other misfits. We need studies of western migration in the late nineteenth century, of urban growth in the West, of the economic impact of transportation. We need to study the development of industries in the West. Andrew Rolle's study of Italians in the West, *The Upraised,* a challenge to Oscar Handlin's thesis of the immigrants as "uprooted," typifies what can be done.

I hope also that future students will place less emphasis on narrative history and begin to probe the socioeconomic foundations of Western society. How did the Western economy emerge? What was the extent of capital flow? Where did the capital originate? What were the technological changes and innovations that the Western scene inspired? We need to pay less attention to the routes of explorers. Historians spend a lifetime trying to decide whether an explorer went up one side of a river or the other. They spend months in the desert, retracing a trail to find out whether Frémont went here or there. Now this is unimportant; it's glamorous and romantic, and it's one of the little stones in the great mosaic of history, but the serious student should not squander his time on such things. We need instead to determine the nature of the society that developed in the wake of the first settlers. We need to apply sociological theories to the migration process. We should forget the military exploits of the Army, and concentrate on the economic impact of the Army on the American West: how it inspired the early trade routes; the flow of capital from the Army into towns; how urban communities concentrated around early forts. We need careful studies of railroad building. Richard Overton's new book on the Burlington Line is one of the few great studies that's been done. The Union Pacific still awaits its history. Robert Athearn is working on such a volume, but hundreds of books could be written from the archives of the Union Pacific Railroad.

Another area of investigation would be the statistical study of the West. This is a dull, time-consuming job. But somebody has to do it.

We won't know how and why the West was occupied until statistical evidence is made available. Merle Curti showed how to do this in his work on Trempeleau County in Wisconsin. We've got to have thousands of such studies—or at least hundreds—before we can generalize. Where did Westerners come from? What was their economic status when they arrived? How soon did they rise above that economic status? What were their cultural interests?

These are the directions that I think frontier studies should take. I think they're moving in this direction. But one final word. I would hope that scholars would continue to pay attention to testing Turner's frontier hypothesis. In *America's Frontier Heritage* I simply attempted to synthesize the work that has been done, and to apply certain economic and sociological theories to the subject. Many books will have to be written before we can begin to understand whether or not the frontier hypothesis has validity. It's perfectly possible that testing will show that there is no validity to Turner's hypothesis. If so, we can throw it out completely. Fine. As long as we test it. The whole field awaits further exploration and exploitation.

J.A.G.   What are the half-dozen or so books that you would recommend to persons interested in the subject we have been discussing? In each case, would you indicate what the particular contribution of the volume is?

R.A.B.   Any proper understanding of the frontier's role in American history must begin with a reading of Frederick Jackson Turner's seminal essays, particularly his ground-breaking "The Significance of the Frontier in American History" (1893). These are collected in his *The Frontier in American History* (1920), and *The Significance of Sections in American History* (1932). A sympathetic, but at the same time perceptive, analysis of Turner's historical views, presented against the background of his times, is in Richard Hofstadter, *The Progressive Historians* (1968). This same author has collaborated with Seymour M. Lipset in editing *Turner and the Sociology of the Frontier* (1968), a collection of essays by historians and sociologists debating the merits of the frontier thesis. Henry Nash Smith, *Virgin Land* (1950), relates the views of the frontier held by Americans in the eighteenth and nineteenth centuries to the concept of the frontier as developed by Turner and later historians, while Richard C. Wade, *The Urban Frontier* (1959) demonstrates that in the Ohio Valley, at least, cities played a major role in the transit of civilization. An example of the type of study needed to make the frontiering experience meaningful in understanding the modern West is Robert A. Dykstra, *The Cattle Towns* (1968), an intelligent study of the "cow towns" in terms of social and political power structures. No less significant in this respect is Merle Curti, *The Making of an Ameri-*

can Community (1959), which employs mass-data techniques to show that the frontier in Trempeleau County, Wisconsin, was an area of unusual economic and social vertical mobility. The impact of the closing of the era of expansion in the Western world is the theme of Walter P. Webb, *The Great Frontier* (1952), which postulates a vast alteration in economic and social institutions as peoples of the Atlantic basin learn to live within closed space.

Roy F. Nichols

The Causes of the Civil War

Roy F. Nichols has had a long and distinguished career both as a scholar and teacher and as a university administrator, having served as Dean of the Graduate School and Vice Provost at the University of Pennsylvania as well as Professor of History at that institution. He is also a former President of the American Historical Association. In addition to *The Disruption of American Democracy* (1948), which won a Pulitzer prize, he has written the standard biography of President Franklin Pierce (1948), *The Stakes of Power: 1845–1877* (1961), *Religion and American Democracy* (1959), and many other books. In this interview he discusses one of the most controversial issues in American history, the causes of the Civil War.

John A. Garraty Professor Nichols, in your book *The Disruption of American Democracy,* you argue that the Civil War was caused by a weakening of common loyalties and the breaking down of unifying national institutions. When did this process begin? If, in the colonial period, localism was a stronger force than nationalism, and if, in the decade before 1860, nationalism was weakening, when was nationalism *strongest* in the United States?

Roy F. Nichols My feeling is that nationalism was strongest during and immediately after the presidency of Andrew Jackson, and to a certain extent it was a reflection of Jackson's personality. He impressed people as a man of power, and his magnetism was contagious—a sort of personification of whatever he touched. Whenever he dealt with people, they had to take him on his terms. The fact that his opponents were called Whigs is, I think, suggestive, because a Whig was an opponent of kings and tyrants. That the nation more or less assumed that Jackson was someone whom Whigs would oppose, gives a sense of what a dominating character he was.

His enthusiasm for Oregon and Texas reflects his intense nationalism. He wanted these territories as evidence of national power and also, presumably, of his own power. At this time Americans had a "thing," as I believe they call it today, about England and France, who supposedly were plotting to destroy the United States. This idea became a part of American folklore. If I had to select a single point in time, I would say that nationalism was probably strongest in the United States in the year 1846.

J.A.G. Slavery was obviously an extremely important cause of the breaking down of national unity, but what were some of the others? Would you comment on the argument that the development of manufacturing in the North was a major cause of the Civil War?

R.F.N. Emotional attitudes had a great deal to do with the breaking down of national unity. The growth of industrial wealth and the expansion of commercial activity in the North produced in the South a concept of the Yankee as a counterjumper and a moneygrabber. Southerners felt that acceding to Northern manufacturers' demands for protective tariffs would injure their economy, although probably they were wrong. Northern business did a good deal for the South, supplying its wants, not only of goods but of capital. It banked Southern money and in other ways supplied agency services. Yet Southerners resented this, and spoke of Southern wealth being converted into Northern profits. Any injury which the North's economic system did to the South was probably more psychological than material. But more generally, I have no use for economic determinism. I think people get mad for other reasons.

J.A.G. Can you explain why the Southerners saw Northern industrial growth as something which threatened them? Why did they object to depending on Northern manufactured goods?

R.F.N.   There again I have biases, and one of them is that the chief cause of the Civil War was political. People develop what might be called "political attitudes," and one of the most important phases in the developing of a political attitude is feeling that somebody's doing you dirt. A good many Southern politicians found themselves more potent politically when they were fighting enemies. Now, you can't fight your brother as an enemy just by definition; there are fraternal ties. But if you argue that the people with whom you are associating are dangerous, you have a rich source of political antagonism. Southern politicians found it convenient to claim that the South was surrounded by enemies: abolitionists who wanted to steal slave property, bloated capitalists who were profiting from Southern labor.

J.A.G.   Was not the protective tariff a real issue?

R.F.N.   I don't think so, but *they* thought so. I have never found any evidence which seemed to me to indicate that the South had much to fear from the tariff. Of course, high tariffs raised the price of, for example, clothes, and if you have to pay more for something you think you're being cheated. But those in the South who were most exercised about the tariff were quite wealthy. A few cents a yard on cotton would not have ruined them.

J.A.G.   It seems strange, does it not, that since the American economy was becoming more closely knit, the interdependence of the sections did not act as cement for the Union?

R.F.N.   People's judgments are apt to be shaped by their emotions. The fact that the South *thought* it was an injured party probably kept regional interdependence from having a more unifying effect.

J.A.G.   To what extent were genuine constitutional scruples involved in the break between North and South?

R.F.N.   I am afraid I'm cynical enough to believe that constitutional scruples are usually assumed for a nonconstitutional purpose. Southerners believed in their own pretensions. They knew enough Anglo-American history to suspect that their liberties were in danger, that Anglo-Saxon values were being threatened by a strong central government. Northerners, on the other hand, felt themselves at a disadvantage and inferior because what I might call the original "establishment" was Southern—the Virginia dynasty. The new Republican party was a symbol of a Northern political interest fighting for a larger share of power; its psychology was essentially similar to the Southern.

Each side wanted to maintain a balance, not to achieve domination, but when you get a sense of grievance, you begin to find logical reasons for it, usually in the Constitution.

J.A.G. Was any significant Northern group or interest trying to make any basic change in the balance of authority between the central government and the states?

R.F.N. I'd put it this way. The United States and the Constitution were made by Southerners. Four of the first five Presidents were Virginians. The idea seemed to develop that somehow or other the government was run by Southerners. But the North became more enterprising in many ways, economically as well as politically, and there soon developed among Southerners a feeling that the government was too much in the hands of what might be called unfriendly interests, Hamiltonian Federalists, who were seeking to increase the power of the central government. In short, I think that certain Northern politicos resented the power of the Virginia dynasty, but that the Southern fear of a Northern plot to crush state independence was entirely illusory.

J.A.G. Turning now to the slavery question, did very many people in the North actually believe in Negro equality, or even in granting civil rights to Negroes?

R.F.N. The more I study this subject the more I find evidence that most Northerners had the same attitude toward Negroes that they have today: they don't like them. I don't think I have any prejudice, but a great many people do.

J.A.G. If that was true, what was the basis of the Northern dislike of slavery? If Northerners disliked Negroes and thought them inferior, why did they object to slavery?

R.F.N. In our day we have abolished sin. One can go into any number of churches and not hear the word used any more. But in the pre-Civil War period people were sin conscious. Slavery seemed to many Northerners sinful. It is difficult to prove, but I believe that they saw slavery as a sexual sin. Moreover, a system that permits a man to buy and control women stirs up in the minds of many people not only an antipathy for that sort of social arrangement but also a certain amount of envy. One of the reasons Americans of that generation persecuted the Mormons so much was because of the same thing in a different form —polygamy. Not much was written about this issue, but many men in the North were no doubt envious of Southern slaveowners at an unconscious level.

J.A.G. How can this kind of historical generalization be tested? Is there anything that can be done to throw light on a theory that seems plausible but which cannot be proved by conventional means? It is not merely a matter of sexual questions, they are merely the most obvious.

R.F.N. Well, something can be done through what we call oral history.

J.A.G. To a certain extent, that's what we're doing here.

R.F.N. Right. But it seems to me that it should be more general. When my wife, Jeanette P. Nichols, was working on the life of Senator Nelson W. Aldrich, she went all over the country interviewing senators, and she found that after ten minutes she could get them to talk about things that ordinarily they would never have written down.

J.A.G.   But the question is more difficult than that. Is it safe historically to make generalizations about Northern attitudes toward the Negro question in the pre-Civil War period on the basis of what we know or can find out about Northerners' attitudes toward Negroes today?

R.F.N.   Well, of course it isn't safe. Yet nothing that we do historically is safe, because we depend on human documents. If you read a letter, how safe is it to quote it? The author wrote it under certain circumstances. Was he telling the truth or was he not? When do you believe a person? How many people can accurately judge their own reasons for doing things? It seems to me that one of the basic needs in training historians is to give them a good grounding in psychology.

J.A.G.   How can the intense emotional conflicts in Congress over the issues that divided North and South be explained?

R.F.N.   When the Founding Fathers set up the Republic they created an establishment. This establishment had a structure which was not only that defined by the Constitution, but which developed certain characteristics of its own—namely, partisan politics. Very early there developed a rivalry, particularly in Congress, as to who was to control the establishment. You had a small group of political activists shut up in two small rooms, wherein operated the House and the Senate. Then, when the government moved to Washington, living conditions were crude and often uncomfortable. The members of Congress lived together in messes. They legislated all day and spent the rest of their time almost literally in one another's hair. There was nothing to do but talk, think, and act politics, and the result was all the emotional overtones of being rivals together in discomfort. I don't know what the exact effect of living in constant discomfort was, but it was certainly bad. Washington life is so comfortable now. But in those days nobody was ever warm in winter, because the heating systems were not adequate, and most of the summer was a time of obvious discomfort. It is difficult to conceive of what it cost emotionally to be a part of the government in Washington, where there was influenza in winter and malaria in the summer, and hangovers a good deal of the time.

   In any case, the attitudes which developed in the various sectional controversies were not particularly shaped by any keen sense of economic or sociological rivalry. Men's ideas reflected their dislikes and their discomforts, and also the raw struggle for power.

J.A.G.   To what extent was slavery an issue at the Constitutional Convention of 1787?

R.F.N. The Founding Fathers adopted a very cagey attitude about using the word "slavery." They were concerned about the counting of Negroes in determining taxation and representation, and a good deal of thought was devoted to creating circumlocutions to handle those two matters. They were very conscious of slavery and its divisive potentialities, and they never faced it frankly.

J.A.G. The historian Staughton Lynd has suggested that attitudes toward slavery were the central cause of conflict in the Constitutional Convention. Do you think he is correct?

R.F.N. In my opinion, the sectional issue at Philadelphia can be reduced to the difference between "How are you gettin' along this mornin'?" and "How do you-all feel?"

J.A.G. It's as simple as that?

R.F.N. Well, they had different folkways, different attitudes toward life.

J.A.G. This suggests to me that you agree with Lynd, at least in part. Traditionally, historians have looked at the debates over the Constitution in a variety of ways, but more commonly as reflecting economic conflicts, as Charles A. Beard argued, rather than ideological ones.

R.F.N. I would say that the Constitution was a social adjustment. Surely no one sat down and figured it out in dollars and cents. I've always been a great admirer of Charles A. Beard, but when he got an idea he rushed at it. I'm afraid he didn't do his homework.

J.A.G. If sectional balance in Congress was so important to Southerners, why did they agree to the Missouri Compromise? Anyone with the most superficial knowledge of American geography would see that the North gained the lion's share of territory in that settlement.

R.F.N. The answer seems to be that they thought that most of the western territory north of the line 32°30′ was not fit for human habitation. It was another example of what might be called the lack of realism or the lack of knowledge that bedeviled the politicians. They were attempting to solve a "problem" which they had created by their own febrile imaginations.

J.A.G. Apparently the big issues involved in the Compromise of 1850, after the Mexican War, were the extension of slavery into the Mexican cession and the return of fugitive slaves who had escaped to the free states. Did Southerners really think that any significant part of the Southwest was suitable for a slave economy?

R.F.N. Certainly, they had not scientifically examined this question, or made up their minds on the basis of a rational discussion of evidence. They jumped to conclusions shaped by their prejudices. In 1850, people looked at California as a Northern state, but it was actually controlled by the tightest Southern party machine that ever existed. In 1860, it had been possible to take slaves into New Mexico for ten years, and there were twenty-three Negroes there. What speciousness! They were going to make a fight for principle, as a matter of right. But the principle and the right from the standpoint of practical experience was absurd. There are times when I think that if there had been sufficient common sense in the United States, we'd never have had the Civil War.

J.A.G.   What about the fugitive slave issue? How many slaves were escaping from the South before 1850?

R.F.N.   Perhaps two hundred a year at most. But there again it was a power struggle, and an irrational one at that.

J.A.G.   Most historians would agree that the Kansas-Nebraska Act was a disaster, especially from the point of view of anyone interested in muting sectional controversy and speeding the economic development of the nation. They would also agree that Stephen A. Douglas, the author of the Act, was both a clever politician and an exponent of national unity and expansion. How, therefore, can Douglas' behavior in pushing the Kansas-Nebraska Act be explained?

R.F.N.   Douglas' political situation both in Illinois and in the nation at large was driving him to seek formulas of adjustment. His consciousness of the division of the nation, and particularly of the Democratic party, made him realize that he must overcome those divisions if he were to achieve his ambition to be President. He was a realist, impatient with the hypocrisy of many of his opponents; he wanted to get down to cases, to get on with the division of power and the spoils, and to exercise power.

He knew how unrealistic much of the sectional controversy was, and was anxious to reduce unreality. Of course, he was always caught between Illinois and the nation. He had to carry Illinois to get anywhere nationally, but he also had to win influence in Washington. The Senate of the United States at that time was dominated by a very interesting group of men who messed together near the Pension Office. The chairmen of the committees on Foreign Relations, the Judiciary, and Finance, and the President pro tempore of the Senate practically had the legislation of the Senate in their hands. Douglas always wanted to be in that power group. He of course had an important committee assignment, the Committee on Territories, but these four men, Senators Acheson, Butler, Hunter, and Mason rather rubbed his nose in the dirt upon occasion. He didn't belong to the lodge.

Douglas felt that he ought to control this territorial bill, but when Senator Acheson told him, in effect, "You're not going to get this bill through unless you shape it the way we want it," Douglas capitulated, agreeing to incorporate the provision repealing the Missouri Compromise. But he was realistic enough to know what would happen to him in Illinois if he favored unconditionally the repeal of this great charter of freedom. So he seized upon the idea of squatter sovereignty, the principle of allowing local settlers to decide the fate of slavery, which was one of the phoniest concepts that was ever produced by the mind of a politician. That produced one of the most complicated political maneuvers of all time. The result was what could be called the Compromise of 1854: that there would be two territories, Kansas and Nebraska, rather than one; and that the people of the territories were to be masters of their own legislative fate, which meant not only the question of slavery, but also who's going to give the licenses, the franchises, and every other form of patronage and favor. People wanted these favors and, I'm sorry to say, they were willing to pay for them. Whoever got into the first legislature of a territory knew that he was in the money, or, to put it more politely, had the economic opportunities. The issue got into an almost unbelievable tangle. Sometimes I feel I've spent almost half my life trying to understand the Kansas-Nebraska Bill!

J.A.G. Acheson's interest in Kansas being a slave state is clear enough, since it was contiguous with his own state of Missouri. But why was the rest of the South so concerned? Wasn't it clear that slavery would not be an economic force in Kansas?

R.F.N. Well, not that clear. Southerners had an idea that somehow or other they were going to grow hemp there with slave labor. How many people believed this is hard to say, but congressmen certainly talked about it in the debates. This brings up an interesting question, by the way. It is entirely possible that half of the speakers were drunk most of the time when they spoke. Before their remarks were printed in the *Congressional Globe*, they fixed up what the reporter had recorded. So one can never be sure that anything in the *Globe* was ever said. To what extent this official record is a representation of what actually went on, I've never been able to decide. In any case, drunken assemblies are not the best examples of what might be called the work of pure reason.

J.A.G. Can you explain the enormous consumption of alcohol among the American politicians of this period?

R.F.N. Partly the custom of the times, partly tension, but also the peculiar meal hours in Washington. One had a heavy breakfast at nine o'clock, and then, theoretically, one didn't eat anything again until the legislative day was over, about four o'clock in the afternoon. Congressmen had to find some way around this, so they developed what was known as "The-hole-in-the-wall," which was a counter where you could go and get yourself a snort.

J.A.G. Right in the Capitol?

R.F.N. Almost outside the door of the Senate and the House. They rushed out and got a highball or a whisky—and on an empty stomach. Another cause of heavy drinking was the interminable dinners served in Washington. The only way to live through these dinners, at which the food and the guests were always pretty much the same, was to drench yourself. And after dinner, what did they do? Pennsylvania Avenue was lined with gambling halls. Congressmen had nothing to go home to in those days because most of them didn't bring their families to Washington. There were no other forms of entertainment. So many of them frequented the saloons, gambling houses, and also places of worse reputation, of which there were many.

J.A.G.   In the complex, tragic controversy that developed over Kansas, was President Pierce at fault, or was the trouble, once the territory had been opened to slavery, inevitable?

R.F.N.   It was the nation's misfortune to have Pierce in the White House, though at this particular time probably no other type of President would have been possible. He had to meet a personal tragedy which was impossible for him to surmount. He had an invalid wife who was socially what you might say a cut above him. Her people were Lawrences and Appletons, his county farmers. Then, unfortunately, he had a tendency for what might be called alcoholic exaggeration. It wasn't that he drank so much, but he couldn't drink anything without getting high.

J.A.G.   Hadn't he overcome his alcohol problem by the time he became President?

R.F.N.   It had never been solved. The way they had "solved" it was by getting him out of Washington, where he had been a congressman. Mrs. Pierce was determined he should never go back to Washington. He could have gone back as a senator, and Polk wanted him in his cabinet.

But in 1852 the Democratic party found itself hardly able to choose a presidential candidate. One group of Democratic politicians, veterans of the Mexican War, had formed an organization, the Aztec Club. They all hated General Winfield Scott, their former commanding officer, whom the Whigs were playing up for President. The Aztec Club attitude to Scott was, "Over our dead bodies." The group came up with the idea that one of *them* ought to be the Democratic candidate, perhaps Gideon Pillow of Tennessee, or Pierce. They employed a "second choice" strategy: "We know you're for Lewis Cass, we know you're for William Marcy, we know you're for. . . . But supposing he can't get it? Who will be your second choice? Now, we've got a fine, upstanding man who has suffered in the field of battle and so on and so forth." Depending on who was doing the talking, the man was either Pillow or Pierce. Well, that worked. The main contenders killed one another off, and Pierce was nominated.

But there is another part to this story. Pierce had told his wife that he had no interest in the presidency. After he was elected, one of his intimates, Senator Appleby of New Hampshire, was escorting Mrs. Pierce to Washington. She had recently suffered a terrible tragedy. Her third and last son had been killed before her eyes in a railroad accident. The Pierces rationalized this catastrophe on the ground that it was God's will. Had the little boy lived they would have paid too much attention to him and his father could not adequately have taken care of his responsibilities as President.

Well, crushed by this event, she had to go to Washington where she didn't want to be. On the way, Appleby told her—I suppose they had to talk about something—that far from being opposed to running for President, Pierce had worked hard to get nominated. She'd lost her son; now she lost her faith in her husband. When she reached the White House, she went upstairs and locked the bedroom door. That, presumably, was more than Pierce's unstable nervous system could assimilate. Thereafter nothing went right.

J.A.G.   Would you comment on the motives of the judges in the Dred Scott case in deciding to go beyond what was necessary to settle the fate of that one particular slave and make a broad statement about slavery in the territories?

R.F.N.   The Democratic majority of the Court was trying to take the controversy out of politics, chiefly for fear that the Republican justices were seeking to use the case for partisan purposes. The Democrats said, in effect: "If the Republicans are going to make political use of this and try and upset the Democratic party by a Supreme Court decision, we'll go them one better. Squatter sovereignty and free soil are both unconstitutional." In other words, the Republican party platform was unconstitutional. By saying that Stephen A. Douglas' squatter sovereignty was unconstitutional, the Southern Democratic judges also hoped to kill him off as a presidential candidate.

J.A.G.   Your way of interpreting all these controversies suggests that the issues were unrealistic. Was Northern fear of the constitutional principles enunciated in the Dred Scott case unrealistic?

R.F.N.   The decision stimulated the idea of a Southern plot to subvert the Constitution, a plot that did not exist.

J.A.G.   The Dred Scott decision made slavery technically legal even in Oregon Territory. Do you think Northerners really believed that anyone was going to bring slaves into a Northern territory?

R.F.N.   Well, the interesting thing is that a rather strong Democratic party was organized in Oregon. There were many pro-Southern Democrats out there. In 1860, Joseph Lane of Oregon was nominated for Vice President on the Breckinridge Democratic ticket.

J.A.G.   Would you describe your thesis that the chief cause of the breakup up the Union was a collapse of statesmanship, the triumph, that is, of shortsighted, local partisanship, over broad policies aimed at benefiting the whole society?

R.F.N.   We are in a position today, I think, to understand matters as they developed on the eve of the Civil War more readily than at any other period in our history. The collapse of President Lyndon Johnson as a man of power and a directing force resembles the collapse of the Democratic power more than a hundred years ago.

   In 1860, the predominant party had reached the point of experience which had brought on an attack of fatigue. No party stays in power much longer than twenty years under our system. The New Deal, for example, came into existence as a result of the election of 1932 and went out twenty years later. The worst thing that can happen to a democracy is the loss of know-how or statesmanship by those who are presuming to lead the people. But there must also be statesmanship on the part of the led. In other words, the people must be sufficiently acute to recognize and follow statesmanlike leaders. When the politicians achieve such a state of stupidity as developed in 1860, there is no telling what may happen.

J.A.G.   Would you now consider the career of Abraham Lincoln as it fits into this context? In his early years he was pretty much a run-of-the-mill Whig politician. What do you think of the argument that the slavery question and the Kansas-Nebraska controversy transformed Lincoln into a statesman?

R.F.N.   In 1858, Lincoln and Douglas were two Illinois politicians, playing politics the way people on the prairie do. Lincoln, I think, was more honest than Douglas in trying to face up to reality. Squatter sovereignty was a dishonest trick. But I do not feel that Lincoln was transformed into a statesman until some time in 1863, when the troubles that he had been forced to confront made it possible for him to write the Gettysburg Address and the second inaugural. He was a late bloomer in statesmanship; I never thought that Kansas did much for him.

J.A.G.   But doesn't Lincoln's position on the slavery controversy in the Kansas crisis reflect at least partially an awareness of the complexity of the problem?

R.F.N.   When he and Douglas debated, it seems quite obvious that Douglas showed himself a man obtuse to moral principles. Lincoln came forth with some of his best rhetoric, and he demonstrated that Douglas had no appreciation of what might be human dignity. Lincoln appeared as a much more admirable character than Douglas. But then came that awful Republican convention of 1860, and his sordid manipulations to obtain the presidential nomination. His greatness was that he could surmount this selfishness and become, under the pressure of war, a great man.

J.A.G. You have been very critical of Douglas in your comments. Could it not be argued that he was a realist who saw the true interests of the nation? He certainly had no illusions about slavery as a real issue. He justified his position on the Kansas-Nebraska Bill by saying that slavery wasn't going to go into Kansas anyway. If everyone had been like Douglas, there probably wouldn't have been a Civil War, and you have certainly suggested that the war was a tragedy brought on by bad statesmanship.

R.F.N. I evaluate Douglas this way. The squatter sovereignty argument was utterly specious. Yet Douglas destroyed the Democratic party because it wouldn't take it. He was a desperate man, his presidential ambitions threatened, and in order to save himself he tried to persuade the people of the United States to buy a phony project.

J.A.G. You have written that after the Democratic convention of 1860 failed to agree on a candidate for President, the Civil War was probably inevitable. Would you explain why that was so?

R.F.N. It was not so much that Southerners were unwilling to accept the legality of the election, as that they were not willing to accept a Republican—in other words, a Northern President. Therefore, anything that made likely the election of a Northern President, such as the inability of the Democrats to agree, makes secession inevitable. But that does not necessarily mean that the Cival War was inevitable.

J.A.G. Were there any heroes of this tragic crisis? Did any of the political leaders of that time rise above partisanship and emotionalism and propose constructive policies?

R.F.N. Not unless you think of John Crittenden of Kentucky and his compromise, and Douglas and his proposal for a customs union, as heroic. These propositions were constructive but proved not to be appealing. The idea of compromise had been worn out by the settlements of 1820 and 1850. People were tired of compromises. I haven't been able to find any heroes. As I've said, I used to think that Lincoln was a hero, but I don't think that Lincoln had anything to offer in the secession crisis. If you've ever read his speeches as he came from Springfield to Washington for the inauguration, talking about his new whiskers and the like. . . .

J.A.G. If the war somehow had been avoided, what would have happened to slavery?

R.F.N. Well, what's happened to it today? Did the Civil War accomplish anything except the *legal* freeing of the slaves?

J.A.G. Even if that was all it accomplished, it was still a substantial result.

R.F.N. Very much so. But my own feeling is that slavery was a problem that *couldn't* be solved by the people. At times I fear that the racial situation we face today can't be solved. I came through my early training feeling that the Civil War had been a great thing, that it solved the race problem and also the problem of nationalism versus states rights, but I no longer see it that way.

You see, I was born in 1896, at the beginning of the Progressive Era. To have grown up in the Progressive Age was a great disadvantage, because life gave you no sense of reality. When I was a boy, we were discovering sociology; we were going to eliminate crime and race prejudice and so on. We were going to make life easy for all men. By 1918, we'd even done away with war. We had the League of Nations, we had Woodrow Wilson. All things were possible. Then we began to learn that a good deal of this was totally unrealistic. We hadn't fought a war to end wars; the League of Nations had not made the lion and the lamb lie down together; crime and poverty had not been erased. The Ten Commandments of the Progressive Era, the direct primary and all that sort of thing, hadn't made our politics pure. We entered a period of disillusionment. So anybody like myself is a poor person to evaluate the results of the Civil War. We believed so many things that weren't so that we take a dim view of all crusades.

J.A.G. What are the implications of this dark view that you take of the political climate of the 1850's with regard to the standard thesis that historians have developed about the Grant era—the Gilded Age?

R.F.N. I think of that period as a time of moral battle fatigue. The nation had wasted so much of its substance, of life, of spirit, that there was just nothing left.

J.A.G. Was the political immorality of the 1870's any worse than that of the era we've been talking about?

R.F.N. I don't think so. If you study the 1850's, you can find almost any form of human chicanery that you're interested in. But it was never brought together by a Thomas Nast and advertised. I believe we're seldom better or worse in one decade than in another. Human nature has a certain continuity. I won't say of good or evil; it's just behavior.

J.A.G. What are the half-dozen books that you would recommend to persons interested in the subject we have been discussing? In each case, would you indicate what the chief contribution of the volume is?

R.F.N. The fullest modern analysis of the events leading to the Civil War is Allan Nevins' multivolume *Ordeal of the Union* (1947–62), a comprehensive rethinking of the whole question by one of the great scholars of our generation. Thomas J. Pressley, *Americans Interpret Their Civil War* (1954), is a convenient summary of the enormous literature on the subject. Beyond that, I would recommend to students three books by historians who have devoted much effort to the period and who have summarized their ideas in brief compass: Avery Craven's *An Historian and the Civil War* (1964), Richard N. Current's *Lincoln and the First Shot* (1963), and C. Vann Woodward's *The Burden of Southern History* (1950).

T. Harry Williams

The Civil War

T. HARRY WILLIAMS, Boyd Professor of History at Louisiana State University, is both a fine scholar and a talented literary artist, whose books have attracted a wide readership. His *Lincoln and His Generals* (1952) was a Book of the Month Club selection. In addition to the standard life of the Confederate General P. G. T. Beauregard, *Napoleon in Blue* (1955), and a number of other military studies of the Civil War, he has edited the presidential diary of Rutherford B. Hayes, and he has just completed a biography of the notorious Louisiana Senator of the New Deal days, Huey Long. In this discussion, Professor Williams treats both military aspects of the Civil War and also some of the larger issues involved in explaining why the North won the struggle.

John A. Garraty Professor Williams, what is your position on the much-debated question, "Was the Civil War inevitable?"

T. Harry Williams I think it was inevitable, in the sense that some solution had to be found to an issue which had been tearing the country in two for three decades before 1860—the issue of slavery. Either the North had to quit agitating against slavery, or the South had to agree that in some way, at some time, it would get rid of it. Since either possibility seems very remote to me, I think the war was inevitable. The North was not going to give up its belief that slavery was morally wrong and contrary to the spirit of the nineteenth century. The South was not going to give up its "peculiar institution."

The South, given its mentality and culture, could not consent to the abolition of slavery. To do so was not within the capabilities of the men of that time. As I see it, there are some situations in history that *have* to have a tragic solution, and this was one of them. This doesn't mean that the war had to come in 1861. It might conceivably have come later. But there had to be a solution to the slavery problem, and I don't see how it could have been resolved except by force.

J.A.G. Yet only a tiny minority of Northerners demanded the abolition of slavery at any time before the war.

T.H.W. That's true, but the majority opinion in the North was antislavery, in the sense that Lincoln was antislavery. It wanted the institution put on the road to ultimate extinction. In the election of 1860 almost 70 percent of the people voted for either Lincoln or Stephen A. Douglas, who were committed by one formula or another to preventing the expansion of slavery into the national territories. The fact that the majority of Americans wanted to prevent the expansion of slavery is clear evidence that the people were antislavery. This was a fact which the South had to face.

J.A.G. Why did the South secede? Didn't secession involve abandoning the very objectives for which the South was contending—the expansion of slavery into the territories, and the enforcement of the fugitive slave law?

T.H.W. The election of 1860 was the only contest in our history in which the defeated side felt that it could not live with the result. The Southern states passed resolutions when they seceded stating their reasons for leaving the Union. It's significant that these did not stress past grievances. They stated that they were leaving for fear of *future* dangers. What were they afraid of? It's obvious from these documents and from what we know about the Southern mind that they were afraid that sometime, maybe in the very near future, maybe at a more remote date, the hostile majority controlling the national government would in some way interfere with slavery and race relations in the South. Joe

Brown, the Confederate Governor of Georgia, made a speech which many historians have neglected. He stressed that a Republican President would surely appoint a Postmaster who would permit abolitionist literature to be delivered in Southern post offices. For many years, Southern postmasters had had an unofficial agreement with the Post Office Department that they could throw these things in the wastebasket. Now, men like Brown saw cracks in the wall of Southern solidarity.

The leaders of the projected new Southern nation were, of course, acting very shortsightedly. Secession would aggravate the problem of recapturing fugitive slaves, and unless they could effect some kind of agreement with the North on the territories, the West would be closed off to them. Moreover, they would be subjecting themselves to greater antislavery pressure. The South was, except for Brazil and Cuba, the only slave area in the Western world. For thirty years they had been under the disapproval of world opinion. That disapproval was bearable as long as they were part of a larger country, but it would be much harder to bear if the South stood out as a country all by itself. But in the end they seceded in order to break the tension. Men who counseled delay could only offer more of the same; the seceders said, "Secede and it will be different."

J.A.G.   Did Southerners believe that secession could be accomplished peacefully?

T.H.W.   Many of them, perhaps the majority, did. I've always been impressed by the degree to which a legal, constitutional way of thinking permeated the Southern mind. On the eve of the war, General Beauregard was appointed Commandant of the United States Military Academy at West Point. He held the office for only a few days because his superiors, not wanting an avowed secessionist in that post, removed him. He returned to Louisiana, and when Louisiana seceded, he resigned his commission in the United States Army. Shortly thereafter he was appointed commander of the Confederate forces at Charleston, South Carolina. But during this interim he served a demand on the United States Army for his expenses from West Point back to New Orleans! Even when he was at Charleston, commanding a Confederate force, he kept writing to Washington demanding this money, which amounted to about $160. To Beauregard, there was nothing incongruous in this. Southerners were assured by their leaders that there would not be any war because secession was legal, that the North would not compel a people who had acted legally to come back into the Union.

The only Southern state which had any doubts about Northern coercion was Louisiana, because of the Mississippi River. Louisianians thought that the Northwest might demand war on them alone to keep the Mississippi open. Before the Louisiana Secession Convention adjourned, it adopted a resolution addressed to the Northwest, saying, in effect, "Don't worry, you'll always be able to use the Mississippi River." In other states, most of the people believed that secession would be peaceable. Legal issues aside, the attitude was that the North would be glad to see them go, or at least wouldn't want to fight to get them back. After all, there was considerable evidence from Northern newspapers that the North would not fight. Indeed, it took some time for Northern opinion to coalesce on this matter. When the "Star of the West" was fired on as it attempted to enter Charleston harbor to relieve Fort Sumter, there was no great outcry in the North. It wasn't until the Confederates attacked Sumter that Northern opinion hardened.

J.A.G. Given the enormous superiority of the North in manpower and matériel, how could the South have dared to risk secession if it was even possible that secession would lead to war?

T.H.W. To begin with, not many Southerners appreciated the enormous potential of the North to wage modern war. The Civil War was a new experience for the American people, the first big undertaking they had ever been engaged in as an entity. Hardly any leaders on either side realized that the war would be as long and costly as it was. Each side had a tremendous sectional ego, and the South more than the North. Southerners were inclined to think that they would simply overrun those popinjays, those tradespeople of the North.

Secondly, they counted on the reliance of Europe on their cotton. Even some Southerners who appreciated the economic superiority of the North thought that the dependence of England and France on their cotton would force those powerful nations into the war on the Southern side. Actually, I think the South had a reasonable chance to win the war, despite the "superiority" of the North. Economics and production were not as important as they were in the great wars of the twentieth century. The South might have won a military decision up to the year 1863. It resorted to conscription a year earlier than the North and got its manpower into the field faster. Look at the size of the opposing armies in the first two years of the war. Although the Northern armies were usually larger, they were not decisively larger. For example, the two armies were approximately equal in size at First Bull Run and not very much different or perhaps the same at Shiloh, the first great battle in the West. In the seven days before Richmond, the Federal Army numbered perhaps 100,000, the Confederate 85,000—not a decisive majority. So, as I see it, it was possible—*possible*—for the Confederacy to have won a military decision up to the year 1863. Of course, in order to win a military decision, the Confederacy would have had to inflict some kind of a stunning or smashing defeat on a Federal army; and in the Civil War, it was hard for one army to do this to another army, because each side had approximately the same weapons. It was hard for an attacking army to so break up a defending army that it ceased to be an army. The closest approach to such a victory in the entire war was the Battle of Nashville, in which George Thomas defeated General Hood's Confederates. Thomas had great superiority in numbers when he accomplished this feat. But even at Nashville, a part of the Confederate Army got away. Civil War armies did not have the mobility to follow a fleeing foe and crush it.

However, the Confederacy had also a *psychological* chance to win the war. Confederate strategy erred in the first two years of the war in not being more offensive than it was. For example, if the Confederates could have won a major victory on Northern soil, the Union might have given up the struggle. The Confederates did not even have to convince the North that they could not be conquered, only that the game wasn't worth the candle. The North was fighting for restoration of the Union; it had to occupy large areas of Confederate territory. There was always a great temptation for the Northern people to say, "It's not worth it. Let's call the whole thing off." The Northern people came closest to giving up in the summer and autumn of 1864, during the presidential election. Some historians have argued that, if it had not been for the victories of Sherman at Atlanta and Sheridan in the Shenandoah Valley, the Democratic candidate, George B. McClellan, would have been elected and presumably some kind of peace might have followed. However, even if elected, McClellan would not have assumed office until March 4, 1865, and by that time the war would have been over.

One final point. I don't believe that wars are fated to turn out the way that they do turn out. Accident and luck play a large part in any battle. Supposing during the Battle of Gettysburg that a Federal brigade commander on Cemetery Ridge had panicked and pulled his unit out of line. The Confederates might have made a real breakthrough. Then all those statistics about Northern economic superiority would have been meaningless.

J.A.G. You mentioned the Battle of Nashville as being one time when a decisive defeat was administered to a Civil War army. What about the Battle of Antietam? Do you disagree with historians who claim that McClellan could have crushed Lee if he had continued his attack?

T.H.W. If McClellan had delivered another attack, he would probably have driven Lee from the field, but I think Lee would have withdrawn in such order and with such good bluff that McClellan would not have followed his victory up.

J.A.G. Suppose, without achieving a decisive victory over the Union Army, the Confederates had captured a major city such as Washington. Could that have led to a "diplomatic" victory?

T.H.W. Possibly, but I don't believe that the capture of Washington would have done it. There are two strategies in war: the strategy of annihilation, in which the aim is to engage the enemy in a showdown battle and destroy him; and the strategy of exhaustion, in which the aim is to occupy large areas of enemy territory and deprive him of the wherewithal to resist. The occupation of Washington would not have been an example of the strategy of exhaustion, and I doubt that the Confederates could have pulled that off with their resources. The Federals did it later; Sherman's march through Georgia was an example of the strategy of exhaustion.

It has been conjectured that this strategy was in Lee's mind when he invaded Pennsylvania. If he could have occupied *and held* certain key areas, he could have cut off the shipment of coal from the Pennsylvania fields and perhaps forced the abandonment of the blockade. But he would have had to hold that area for a fairly long time, so I don't see that the Confederates could have pulled off the strategy of exhaustion.

J.A.G. Turning back to the period between the election and the beginning of the fighting, would you describe Lincoln's position during this crisis? Why did he finally decide to use force in April of 1861?

T.H.W. According to the American practice of the time, there was no provision for consultation and cooperation between the outgoing and incoming Presidents between the election and the inauguration. Lincoln could do little or nothing until he assumed office. During the campaign, he stated his position hardly at all. He said that his views and the views of the Republican party were outlined in the official party platform, and that if he said anything it would be distorted and the situation made worse. He continued this policy between his election and his inaugural.

Historians have long debated what was in Lincoln's mind during these months. Would he use force to restore the Union after the Southern states seceded, or would he seek a compromise to persuade them to come back into the Union? The evidence is incomplete and inconclusive. I think that Lincoln was prepared from the beginning to use force if he had to. Naturally, he hoped he wouldn't have to. If he could say anything or do anything that would persuade these states to come back, he would do it. If his assurance that he intended no attack upon slavery would serve that purpose, he would give that assurance. But we don't know really how seriously Lincoln took the secession movement. Some historians think that he thought it a bluff, intended to wring concessions from the North. It is suspected that he thought there was a strong Unionist movement in the South, that if he became President and made no overt move, these Unionists would conclude that Southern institutions were not in danger and would then force their governments to return to the Union.

On the other hand, it is possible that he never believed that. Whatever the case, I'm convinced that Lincoln was ready to use force—if it had to be done—to restore the Union. The American experiment in democracy was the big element in all of Lincoln's thinking. He would do anything to preserve what he called the "last best hope of earth." And I think that before he came to Washington he had decided that coercion would have to be used. Some historians have argued that his inaugural address was not a frank statement. Many academicians expect politicians to act the way they think they do, which is always to be frank and open and balanced. Well, a politician can't always act that way. A politician has to be, sometimes, evasive. Naturally, Lincoln did not, in the inaugural, reveal everything that was in his mind. From a political point of view, that would have been stupid. But he outlined with reasonable clarity what his policy would be: the seceded states could, if they wished, come back into the Union, with the assurance that his administration would not interfere with slavery or the Southern way of life. But—and this was his essential point—they could *not* demand concessions as the price of coming back. If they didn't do that, then Lincoln was going to use some kind of force.

J.A.G.   But this interpretation doesn't explain the decision to reinforce Fort Sumter. The federal government had allowed other military posts in the South to be taken over by the Confederates. Why didn't he wait a little longer?

T.H.W.   The military importance of Fort Sumter has been much exaggerated, but because of its location in Charleston harbor, it had become a symbol. If Lincoln abandoned Fort Sumter, would the Northern people have believed that he was determined to uphold the Union? By April, he realized that there was no significant Unionist sentiment in the South and that some kind of a showdown was essential. Lincoln was a great politician; he saw that the tug had to come. So he engaged in a very complicated maneuver, sending a relief expedition with supplies to Sumter, and informing the *South Carolina* government, not the Confederate government, that a relief expedition was on the way and that the troops accompanying it would not be landed if no attempt was made to resist the arrival of the expedition. This put the Confederate government in a tough spot. If they allowed the expedition to land, many of their people would not believe that the Confederate government seriously meant to maintain Southern independence. Yet if they resisted, they would have to make the first overt act of war, fire the first shot. In short, the Confederates would lose something no matter what they did. Lincoln was maneuvering so that if a shot had to be fired, the Confederates would have to fire it.

J.A.G.   Well then, why didn't Lincoln try harder to relieve Fort Sumter?

T.H.W.   Perhaps he should have. If you have to act, the correct, smart, and eventually humane thing to do is to act decisively. Maybe it would even have been better if a crisis had been forced in 1850, when fewer Southern states would have seceded. If a few Southern states had rebelled and been put down, there might never have been a real Civil War. If in the crisis at Sumter everything possible had been thrown in, perhaps the war would have been averted. We don't know.

J.A.G.   How did Northern and Southern leaders, once the fighting began, plan their strategies?

T.H.W.   Neither side had a prepared strategy or plan of war. Obviously, the South didn't have a plan ready because there was no South until 1861; the Northern government might have had a plan, but there was no agency in the military organization charged with the function of studying strategy. There was an agency loosely called the General Staff, but it was made up of the heads of the various Army bureaus. It was not a collective agency; no one on it was charged with planning strategy. So both sides had to prepare plans after the war started. This was not necessarily bad. It's possible to become so committed to a prearranged plan that you don't take account of changing conditions. Germany's Schlieffen Plan of World War I had been drawn up some years beforehand; it should have been modified when the war started, but it wasn't.

The Northern strategy obviously had to be offensive because the North's policy was to restore the Union by force. This could not be done unless Northern armies invaded and occupied large areas of the South. Conversely, the strategy of the South had to be largely defensive, if for no other reason than to repel Northern attacks. However, offense was also a possible policy for the South, since by invading the North and defeating Northern armies it might force the Union to accept secession. The geography of the United States also had a great deal to do with strategy. The Appalachian Mountains split the war into two theaters; it was practically impossible to carry on unified operations on both sides of the mountains.

As the war went on, the United States developed a more complex and sophisticated command system, but the Confederacy did not. The heads of the bureaus in the War Department were given a chairman appointed from the outside, and brought together as a collective agency. And Lincoln, on frequent occasions, advised with them. They were perhaps not the best advisers on field operations, because all of their experience had been as staff officers, but at least they were professional military men. Then, in the summer of 1862, Lincoln appointed Henry W. Halleck General in Chief. On paper, Halleck looked like an ideal choice: he was a student, author of a book on the art of war, and translator of Baron Henri Jomini's highly regarded *Précis de l'Art de la*

Guerre (1838). As Departmental Commander in the western theater, he had won victories. (We know now, of course, that these victories were primarily the result of U. S. Grant's activities, but Halleck got the credit.) However, Halleck didn't like to make decisions, and, as a result, the responsibility for making them fell again on Lincoln until 1864, when a modern command system was at last created. U. S. Grant was appointed General in Chief and charged with formulating strategy for all theaters.

Confederate strategy was dominated by President Davis, who because of his military background fancied himself an expert. Until 1862, Robert E. Lee was General in Chief, but he gave up this post when put in command of the Army in Northern Virginia in 1862. In 1864, President Davis appointed Braxton Bragg, who had failed as a field general in the west, to direct strategy. His real role, however, was merely to give advice when Davis asked for it. In fact, neither Lee nor Bragg devised an overall plan when they were Generals in Chief, perhaps because Davis didn't want them to, or perhaps because they didn't want to think generally about the war. Late in the war, the Confederate Congress, in a bold attempt to restrict Davis' authority, created the formal office of General in Chief, and made clear that Davis must appoint Lee to the post, which he did. It's doubtful that Lee could have commanded a field army and also planned strategy for all theaters, but the war ended before he could even try. It was hard for the Confederates to construct a central command system and to think centrally about the war. As the great authority on the art of war Karl von Clausewitz, says, nations fight wars that reflect their culture and social systems. The Confederacy was founded on the principle of states' rights; it fought a localized or states'-rights war. When General Joe Johnston heard in 1865 that Lee had been appointed General in Chief, he said, "Why does he want to be a mere clerk?" The office of General in Chief is not a clerk's, but Johnston instinctively thought of it as one.

J.A.G.   I know you have a high opinion of Lincoln as a military strategist. Did Lincoln learn his strategy by reading about military affairs, by generalizing on the basis of his experience, or did he have an innate military talent that emerged when he began to think about war?

T.H.W.   During the war, Lincoln read some books on the art of war, and of course he consulted various military men. But I think Lincoln is an outstanding demonstration of the truth of another of Clausewitz's statements: that the primary qualities of a military leader are not education or experience, but mind and character. Lincoln had the mind and character to master the problems of command. War is both simple and complex. It is complex when it comes to moving troops on the battlefield, but it is simple when one looks at a map and decides where and how to fight. A very intelligent man, without previous experience, is perfectly capable of being a good strategist.

J.A.G.   What is your view of George B. McClellan as a general?

T.H.W.   To put it mildly, I have a low opinion of McClellan. In writing military history, authors hardly ever really try to decide what makes generals good, great, or mediocre. What are the standards of evaluation? I think often we tend to make this business too difficult. Obviously, a general has to know something about his profession, the technical side of the business. He presumably has to have some ability in administration if he's commanding a large army. But a general can have these qualifications and still be a failure, as McClellan was.

J.A.G.   Because of a lack of intelligence and character?

T.H.W.   It is a matter primarily of character; intelligence is, of course, a very desirable quality in a general, but character is more basic. It's a hard thing to define, but it involves nerve, courage, resolution—the will to force the enemy and his own army to do what he wants done.

McClellan, I think, lacked this essential element of character. He was intelligent and he knew his job, but he lacked this great quality. Psychoanalysts would have been fascinated by him. He exposed himself in a series of remarkable letters to his wife, which he saw fit to publish. He lived in a world of fantasy and make-believe. He always saw great dangers. The enemy out there was always increasing in size. On the eve of the Seven Days before Richmond, his intelligence reports estimated the size of the Confederate Army at 180,000. This was a gross exaggeration, but McClellan added 20,000 to that number in making his own estimation. The actual number of Confederates was 85,000. Everything that McClellan did in the Seven Days was predicated on the assumption that he faced an enemy twice that size. (War is not what is; it's what is in a general's mind, you see.)

J.A.G.   Why, then, did Lincoln put up with McClellan as long as he did?

T.H.W.   Lincoln chose commanding generals by a kind of rule of thumb: if a man had done well in an independent operation, even a small one, Lincoln assumed he might be able to command an army. McClellan had done well in western Virginia, so Lincoln thought he could command the Army at the Potomac. As to why he put up with McClellan so long, his own answer was, "Who've I got around that's any better?" After the second Battle of Manassas, Lincoln was very critical of McClellan's behavior, and decided that he would not again have field command. But then Lee suddenly invaded Maryland. The Federal Army had to go out to meet him. Lincoln asked General Burnside to take command, but Burnside refused. Who else was there at that point but McClellan? Face it, the Union Army suffered from a paucity of good generals.

J.A.G. Were Southern military leaders as a group much superior to Northern ones?

T.H.W. This is an old line of argument, but one based largely on the war in Virginia, and on the theory that Southern generalship consisted of Robert E. Lee, Stonewall Jackson, and maybe James Longstreet. Lee was one of the two great generals of the war, the other, of course, being Grant. Obviously, the leadership of the Confederate Army in Virginia was superior to that of the Army of the Potomac. But compare the Confederate generals in the western theater, Albert Sidney Johnston, Braxton Bragg, Beauregard, and Joe Johnston, with the Union leaders, Grant, Sherman, Sheridan, and Thomas. The latter far outshone the former.

J.A.G. Is Lee's reputation as a military genius justified by the facts?

T.H.W. I think so, on the whole. Lee had the character which I said was essential to good generalship. But he had weaknesses. For example, he never devised a really adequate staff. In fact, in some respects, Lee was not a modern-minded soldier, probably because he was a product of a conservative culture, a culture that looked backward instead of forward. I think it was harder for Lee to adjust to the new ways of war than it was for Northern generals.

The most notable way in which he failed to adjust to modern war was in his strategic thinking, or his lack thereof. He produced no over-all plan, or perhaps it would be more accurate to say that like other Confederate leaders, he could not grasp the idea that to win the war the South had to adopt a revolutionary point of view. He did not grasp the connection between war and politics. When a Confederate congressman proposed to him that the Confederate capital at Richmond should be moved to a more secure place, Lee refused to discuss the question on the ground that it was a political, not a military issue. But what could be more military than the location and safety of the capital? His lesser weaknesses were also related to his lack of "modernity." Although he had a very good eye for terrain, his use of maps left much to be desired. He did not understand fully the function of railroads in modern war. And very probably he was an indifferent quartermaster.

J.A.G. Did the Civil War generals, Northern and Southern, learn through experience? That is, was the general level of leadership superior in the latter stages of the war to what it was in the beginning?

T.H.W. This was so especially among the Northern generals, largely, I think, because of the character of Northern society, which was more adaptable, more open to change. The Northern government acted in far more revolutionary ways than the so-called "rebel" government; therefore it was easier for Northern generals to conceive of new and revolutionary ways of waging war. Sherman, devising new and more ruthless ways of fighting, is a good illustration of this point. The Southern military leadership, by way of contrast, was, at the end, pretty much what it was when the war started. I don't think that Southern generalship grew as much as Northern generalship did.

J.A.G. Why, especially in the early years of the war, did the Northern armies fare so much better in the western than in the eastern theater?

T.H.W. It was partly because of the ability of particular generals, but more decisive was the fact that in the west, the North had the advantage of sea power on the rivers. The first objective of Northern strategy in the west was to occupy the line of the Mississippi. Many of the important operations in this theater were amphibious operations. Iron gunboats were built as the war progressed on the Mississippi and its tributaries.

J.A.G. Would you comment on the significance of some of the major battles of the war?

T.H.W. Each battle had its significance, sometimes large and sometimes small, sometimes military and sometimes political. First Bull Run had no large military outcome. The Confederates held the field, but didn't have the organization to exploit the victory by advancing on Washington. Actually, the battle had a more beneficial effect on the North than the South, because it knocked some of the nonsense out of the Northern mind that it was going to be a short and easy war. Conversely, it was probably bad for the Confederates, who concluded that Yankees couldn't fight and probably wouldn't fight.

J.A.G. What about the Seven Days before Richmond?

T.H.W. The Seven Days' Battle is interesting in many ways. If McClellan had been a more resolute commander, very possibly the North might have captured Richmond in 1862; his scheme for attacking Richmond from the east along the waterways had many merits. The Seven Days is interesting to military men because it was much like a modern battle. Most Civil War battles lasted only one or two days, after which the defeated side retired and recuperated. Then months might go by before another engagement was attempted. The Seven Days was very much like the long battles of World War I or World War II.

J.A.G. Is there any justice to the argument of the defenders of McClellan that Lincoln and the politicians in Washington interfered with his strategic plan by insisting on keeping too many troops to defend Washington?

T.H.W. This is one of the great controversies of the war. Before McClellan moved his force to the York River, Lincoln had been worried that the Confederates would counter by attacking Washington. McClellan had promised to leave a defending force "in and around Washington." Lincoln naturally understood "in and around" to mean in the city and its environs, but McClellan understood the phrase in the military sense (which was quite correct) to include also the Shenandoah Valley. He left a statement detailing how many troops he had left and where they were, but he counted some troops twice, and played around with the figures pretty loosely. When Lincoln found this out, he quite properly, I think, ordered the detachment of McDowell's Corps of 30,000 men for the defense of the capital. McClellan might have avoided a lot of misunderstanding if he had been frank and open with the President. He might have persuaded Lincoln that the troops in the Shenandoah Valley would deter Lee from moving north. Then he would have had McDowell with him. But McClellan couldn't be frank and open with the President or anyone else.

J.A.G.   What was the significance of the Battle of Shiloh?

T.H.W.   Shiloh was the first great battle in the west. It provided a great strategic opportunity for the Confederates. If they'd been able to smash Grant's army before it was joined by Don Carlos Buell's, they would have been in a very advantageous position. They surprised Grant in the strategic sense, but failed to drive the Union forces from the field. Perhaps the main significance of Shiloh was that Grant learned an important lesson: never to assume that the enemy will do what you expect or want him to do.

J.A.G.   What was the importance of the Second Battle of Bull Run?

T.H.W.   Second Bull Run shows Lee at his best. He wanted very much to smash up a Union army. He knew that it wasn't enough just to repel Northern armies as they came on Richmond because they would merely re-form and return. At Second Bull Run he took a great risk. He saw that McClellan was going to withdraw from below Richmond after the Seven Days, and that General Pope's army was collecting in the Rappahannock-Rapidan triangle. Therefore he ignored McClellan, and sent the bulk of his army rapidly north to fall on Pope. It was a very daring scheme, but he was not quite able to pull it off. He defeated Pope very badly, but did not destroy him.

J.A.G.   What of the Battle of Antietam?

T.H.W.   Antietam is, of course, related to the issuance of the Emancipation Proclamation. It was one of the turning points of the war. In the fall of 1862, the Confederates mounted a two-pronged offensive into Maryland and Kentucky under Lee and Braxton Bragg. Many students consider this the most dangerous moment of the war for the North, because if both offensives had succeeded, European intervention might well have followed.

J.A.G.   Well, how successful was the Emancipation Proclamation in accomplishing its propaganda and morale purposes?

T.H.W.   Very successful, I think. Of course it didn't free a single slave directly, since it applied only to areas still under Confederate control, but when the Union armies occupied large additional areas of the South, the Proclamation did become effective. But its chief value was undoubtedly psychological and symbolic. The war had taken a new turn; the Union was going to be restored, but not as it had been. Undoubtedly, it had a very important influence on the attitude of the English and French governments. After January 1, 1863, no European power would have dared to intervene in the war on the side of the slave power.

J.A.G. What was its effect on the morale of the South? Did knowledge of it encourage slaves to revolt, or to run away to the Union lines, or in other ways to interfere with the Southern war effort?

T.H.W. It didn't encourage the slaves to revolt. This was one of the remarkable facts about the war. The Confederacy was fighting to uphold slavery, yet its slave population remained relatively quiet. But on the other hand, the slaves had, even before the Proclamation, some vague knowledge that the war was about slavery. They came into Northern army camps almost from the first year of the war. Often, particular subordinate commanders would hide these Negroes and send them back to their home towns. For example, Rutherford B. Hayes, later President, sent some Negroes back to his home town in Ohio with instructions to his family to find work for them. But the Proclamation undoubtedly intensified this movement of slaves into the Union lines. As for the effect of emancipation on Southern whites, the direct evidence suggests that it made them more determined, but in the secret hearts of many Southerners it must have brought some foreboding and dread. Would the slaves revolt? Did the Northern government actually have the power and will to put a thing like this over?

J.A.G. Is it possible to weigh accurately the role of the Negro in deciding the outcome of the war?

T.H.W. The impression is often given that the Negroes were pawns in the antislavery struggle. Some white people wanted to abolish slavery; some white people didn't; the helpless Negroes were in the middle. Well, the Negroes had some ideas about this too, and they helped to determine the outcome of the war. The use of Negro troops was authorized by Congress in 1862, and ultimately some 170,000 Negroes served in the armed forces. Emancipation wasn't achieved by white efforts alone.

There has been a great deal of rather strange writing about the performance of Negro troops in the war—to the effect that if they did very well, it proved that Negroes were equals of whites, and if they did badly, they were inferior. What was proved was that Negro troops, like white troops in certain situations, act in certain ways. There are examples of Negro units breaking under fire, and examples of white units doing this too. And examples of Negro troops fighting very bravely. Some Negro units, coming out of slave conditions, at first not being paid equally with white troops, didn't do so well. But what do these facts prove? Very little to my way of thinking. The Negroes acted as you would expect any troops to act.

J.A.G.   Was there much pressure in the South to use slaves as soldiers?

T.H.W.   Midway in the war, at a conference of western generals, Pat Cleburne of Arkansas proposed the use of Negro soldiers. The idea horrified the generals present, but by late 1864 and early 1865 the manpower shortage was so apparent that the Confederate Congress finally acted to use slaves as soldiers. President Davis was authorized to ask the owners of slaves for any number of blacks he deemed necessary. If this number was not forthcoming, he could requisition for their quota of 300,000 slaves for military purposes. Although General Lee and others thought the slaves serving as soldiers should be freed after the war, emancipation was not specifically provided for in the act of Congress, which stated that military service would not alter the status of the slaves without the consent of their owners, or of the state of their residence. However, if the Confederacy had won its independence through the use of a slave army, slavery in the Southern nation would undoubtedly have ended, which would have been an ironic end of the war.

J.A.G.   Was Southern opposition to putting slaves in the army based on the fear of giving them guns?

T.H.W.   No, I don't think they were afraid of what the slaves would do if armed. It was more that they saw the incongruity in using slaves to fight to protect slavery.

J.A.G.   How important in winning the war was the Northern blockade of Southern ports?

T.H.W.   Some historians have come to the conclusion that it was not effective because so many ships were able to evade it. This view overlooks the fact that the ships that got through, being built for speed and deception, had to carry light supplies; they could not carry the heavy equipment that was most needed by the Confederacy. However, the main effect of the blockade was probably psychological. The Confederacy was being squeezed from all sides. On land, the North was pressing forward relentlessly. From the sea, the North was not only blockading the Atlantic coast but also threatening certain points on the Gulf coast. Naval raiding parties struck inland to cut up Confederate railroads. The blockade was another shutting off of the Confederacy from the outside world, and this psychological effect may have provided its greatest impact. Moreover, the fact that the North could impose a blockade on the South was a demonstration of the superior power of the North.

J.A.G.   Could England have broken the blockade if it had decided to try?

T.H.W. Only in the early stages of the war. As the United States Navy increased in size, it came to be a very formidable force indeed. By 1864 and 1865, it is doubtful if a British naval force could have broken the blockade.

J.A.G. Why did Great Britain remain neutral, given its need for Southern cotton and the government's hostility to the United States?

T.H.W. So far as cotton was concerned, the crop of 1860 had been an unusually large one; English cotton manufacturers were overstocked when war started. The Confederate decision to withhold cotton had the effect of raising the price in the English and European markets, enabling textile manufacturers to dispose of this surplus at a higher-than-ordinary price. So during the first year, and possibly the second year, there really was no cotton shortage. But by 1863 English and French textile manufacturers were hurting for cotton.

England, the key nation, did not intervene for several reasons, chiefly its reliance on Northern wheat and the attitude of the working classes. This latter reason, however, has been very much exaggerated. The anti-American feeling of the English upper classes, and possibly also the French upper classes, was not all that strong. It's true that some persons hoped that the American "experiment in democracy" would fail, and some leaders saw diplomatic advantages in a divided America. But there was probably more of a sympathy for the Northern cause in Europe than historians have suspected. The British might conceivably have intervened for reasons of power politics: if there were two Americas, one of them would have to lean on England. But this doesn't mean that Britain wanted to destroy the United States. The guiding factor in the whole situation was the military one. England and France were not going to intervene in the war on the side of the loser. And the military situation never got to the point where they felt they could safely intervene in behalf of the Confederacy.

J.A.G. Were the two battles of Gettysburg and Vicksburg as crucial in determining the Northern victory as they are usually portrayed?

T.H.W. I think so. After Gettysburg and Vicksburg it was unlikely, if not impossible, that the South could have won a military decision. At Gettysburg, Lee's Army of Northern Virginia was bled almost white: Confederate losses, killed and missing, were perhaps 25,000 men, a terrific drain on Southern manpower. Lee was never again able to assume the offensive.

With the fall of Vicksburg and the other Confederate river fortress, Port Hudson, Louisiana, the entire line of the Mississippi River fell under Federal control. The Confederacy was split in two, the three states west of the river isolated. Gettysburg and Vicksburg had a special impact because they came together in one dramatic week in July, 1863. But actually there was a third turning point, the Federal seizure of the Chattanooga

line. Simultaneously with the Federal victories at Gettysburg and Vicksburg, General Rosecrans advanced toward Chattanooga. This went almost unnoticed in the rejoicing over Vicksburg and Gettysburg. The
Confederates evacuated Chattanooga. Forgetting that he hadn't actually
defeated them, Rosecrans rushed in pursuit and was almost smashed up
at Chickamauga, but then managed to retire into the defenses of Chattanooga. Grant replaced Rosecrans with General Thomas, and at the
Battles of Lookout Mountain and Missionary Ridge the Federals drove
the Confederates into Georgia. Chattanooga was a jumping-off place, a
really decisive point. Once the Federals had it, they could divide the Confederacy again by driving either to Mobile, Savannah, or some other point
on the coast. This is what Sherman did in 1864.

J.A.G.   What were Grant's chief attributes as a general? Was he primarily
a great strategist or tactician, or was he primarily a great leader of men?

T.H.W.   To me there were two great generals in the war, Grant and Lee.
They were great because, in addition to their qualities of mind and
experience, they had that indefinable but precious quality—character
or will. Grant was a better strategist than Lee, and Lee the better tactician
of the two. Grant had the ability to think centrally about the whole war,
to produce an over-all plan. I do not think that Lee had this ability,
although he often produced a brilliant plan for a particular battle. He
devised Jackson's Shenandoah Valley campaign of 1862, and the strategy
of the Seven Days, but he was not an over-all strategist for all theaters.

Both Grant and Lee had defects. Probably they did not understand the
impact that modern weapons were having on tactical formations. We're
familiar with criticisms of Grant, that he threw his men on such-and-such
a fortified position and lost heavily. But so did Lee, at Malvern Hill and
at Gettysburg. Of course we criticize them for this and say that they
should have employed more flexible formations. But it was very hard
in the Civil War—indeed, in all wars before World War II and the
communications revolution—to keep control of large forces in a fluid
situation. In the Civil War, they tried to do it with musical signals by
the regimental musicians. You can imagine the difficulties. Soldiers might
not hear the calls, they might hear those of another unit, the enemy
might be using the same signals. It was very hard for generals to keep
control of men out of their sight. There was some hope if they were
close together; that is why close formations were not abandoned, although they often led to heavy losses.

As to Grant's being a leader of men, he was not the kind of leader
that McClellan was. When McClellan appeared on the field, the soldiers
threw up their hats and cheered. Soldiers hardly ever cheered U. S.
Grant. But when he rode by, they said something like, "There goes the
old man." He inspired a quiet confidence and respect.

J.A.G. How can Grant's success be explained in the light of his mediocre career before 1861 and his, to put it mildly, less than completely successful career after 1865?

T.H.W. There are some men who can be great in one specific situation. They are made and geared for one activity. For Grant that was war. He didn't succeed in anything he attempted before 1860; and after 1865, although he was a great hero of the nation, he was an indifferent President and a failure in business. The war awoke in Grant, I think, certain emotions and sensations. He delighted in combat, in the clash of arms. Observers have called Grant apathetic and torpid during the war, but when a battle situation developed, this sleepy-looking little man changed.

J.A.G. Considering the enormous superiority which his army had in the latter stages of the war, does Grant deserve as much credit as he is often given for having finally defeated Lee?

T.H.W. Grant had 120,000 men—perhaps 130,000 finally—to Lee's 60,000. His army was not much larger than Joe Hooker's army during the Chancellorsville campaign. Yet in that operation Lee, with only 60,000 men, defeated Hooker decisively. For a Civil War campaign and for the kind of fighting he intended to do, Grant's numerical superiority did not mean that victory was certain. He faced a veteran army led by a very able antagonist, and he had to attack over very difficult terrain. He could very well have been defeated or turned back, certainly at the beginning, during the confused fighting in the Wilderness. Yet he kept on, to victory.

J.A.G. What was the role of the so-called "political" generals? Was it a serious error on the part of the government to appoint politicians to high command?

T.H.W. The political generals nearly always were Democrats or former Democrats. Lincoln viewed these appointments as investments in national unity. And to unify the Northern people in support of the war was a legitimate way of making war. But the difficulty was that these men commanded troops in battle. Possibly, Lincoln thought that they might be able to master the art of command, but no general from civilian life demonstrated the capacity to command an army in the field. Benjamin F. Butler, for example, was a bungling handler of troops. Nathaniel P. Banks was very aggressive, but rash. But both of them brought important groups of followers to the support of the war.

J.A.G. Did nonprofessional officers contribute much to the success of the Union Army in subordinate posts?

T.H.W. Many generals from civilian life did awfully well in regimental and brigade commands, and sometimes even as divisional and corps commanders. In General Sherman's army in the Georgia campaign of 1864, many of the corps and divisional commands were held by civilians. There simply were not enough West Pointers available to handle the bulk of the regimental and higher unit commands. So there came into the armies a number of civilian officers, who learned their trade after the war started. For example, Rutherford B. Hayes, a man of great intelligence, came into the Army, learned his business as the war went along, became an excellent regimental commander, and before the war was over, was handling commendably still larger units. Another future President, James A. Garfield, rose to be Chief of Staff to General Rosecrans. John A. "Black Jack" Logan was another civilian who did very well during the war. Lincoln once said, talking of the variety of occupations and professions that could be found in a typical Northern regiment, that there was hardly a regiment that might not contain a future President of the United States. Curiously, the regiment which Hayes commanded—the 23rd Ohio—had within it *two* future Presidents: Hayes and McKinley.

J.A.G.   Would you comment on Lincoln's performance as a home-front leader during the war?

T.H.W.   Allan Nevins once wrote that Lincoln's primary task was to preserve a nation, whereas Davis' task was to create a nation. Davis failed, and Lincoln succeeded. Nevins conjectured that one reason why Lincoln succeeded was that he was willing to use revolutionary powers. Possibly, another way of putting it would be to say that Lincoln was a great politician who was not afraid to use power.

There are many examples of Lincoln's willingness to use power. His call for militia to bring the seceding states back into the Union was equivalent to a presidential declaration of war. His proclamation of the blockade, his increase of the regular army without constitutional authorization are similar examples. He once said that he was not so timid or tender that he would be afraid to violate one-tenth of the Constitution in order to save the other nine-tenths. Lincoln's willingness to use power was one secret of his success as a home-front leader. Sometimes in the writings about him one gets the impression that he used these powers because they were there, that anybody in the office would have used them. I'm not sure that this is right. I can think of many men who might have been President who would not have acted with Lincoln's boldness.

Lincoln was also a man of real passion. He believed deeply in democracy. Jefferson Davis believed in the Confederacy with his mind, but I don't think with his heart. He spoke in cold or wooden terms; Lincoln, with warmth and feeling. It is no accident that Lincoln's words are remembered and quoted and that Davis' are forgotten. Lincoln handled so many controversial issues in just the right way. Take the most crucial issue of all—slavery. Should it be abolished during the war as the radical Republicans wished, or should action be delayed until after the war? As a conservative, Lincoln would have preferred gradual action, but he saw that immediate action was necessary. He took it up and molded the antislavery movement during the war at just the right time. Finally, in his speeches and writings, Lincoln tried to lift the Northern cause to the highest possible level. He made the war a crusade for all mankind, for the cause of democracy. He did this best in the Second Inaugural.

J.A.G. I gather that you would not agree with Professor David Donald's argument that Lincoln was essentially a President in the Whig tradition of weak chief executives.

T.H.W. Donald argues that Lincoln did not often try to influence the course of legislation in Congress. He was not a strong President in the Wilsonian or Rooseveltian sense, although there are occasions where he did act decisively—for example, when he made Congress soften the provisions of the Confiscation Act. But it was not then important for the President to influence the course of *legislation*. As Commander in Chief, he used the powers of his office expansively. He took control of the emancipation movement, for example, by using the presidential power of proclamation. It's irrelevant to say that he did not function as some Presidents did in time of peace.

J.A.G. How do you think that Lincoln would have handled Reconstruction if he hadn't been assassinated?

T.H.W. It is undoubtedly a misnomer to call his Proclamation of Amnesty of December, 1863, a "plan," or his final thoughts on the issue of reconstruction. As I see it, that proclamation was a way of making war. If Lincoln could induce a few Southern states to resume their allegiance to the Union by granting them easy terms, that would weaken the will of the remainder to resist. This set in motion certain things that we later associate with Reconstruction: oaths of allegiance, an attitude toward slavery, and so forth. Yet Lincoln did not require that a state formally abolish slavery to re-enter the Union. He merely required that the people recognize the war-time acts of the President and the Congress regarding slavery.

Lincoln realized immediately that, however he had intended it, his plan was occasioning grave doubts among many Republicans. At the end of the war, he was moving toward some new plan of reconstruction. Had he lived, he would have worked out a more detailed plan, undoubtedly one that would have required a greater national protection of the rights of the freedmen.

J.A.G. Did the war change the attitudes of the average Northerner toward Negroes?

T.H.W. Certainly, many Union soldiers came to modify their opinions about the Negro. We have diaries and letters that indicate that contact with runaway slaves and Negro soldiers affected the views of many. How much this affected the civilian population is difficult to determine.

Inevitably, as a result of the war being seen as a crusade for the Union and for emancipation, a spirit of idealism flourished. But I am skeptical as to how long this feeling prevailed after the war.

J.A.G.   Did the North win the Civil War or did the South lose it?

T.H.W.   Several years ago, the Louisiana State University Press published a book which eventually came out under the title *Why the North Won the Civil War*. Before publication, there was a discussion about the title, several editors favoring *Why the South Lost the War*. What are the factors which determined the outcome of the war? From the viewpoint of the Confederacy, the deficiency in manpower eventually became serious, its deficiency in industrial and agricultural production hampered it, its railroad system collapsed when rails and engines were worn out and destroyed. The historian Frank Owsley, on the other hand, contended that the Confederacy died of states' rights, that it was founded on a principle that insured its destruction because a nation devoted to states' rights can't fight a modern war.

But I think that the war was won upon the battlefield by men with guns in their hands who didn't know how it was *supposed* to come out. Historians tend to assume that one side had the total capacity to determine the outcome of the battle. Many Southern writers, for example, in discussing Gettysburg say that Lee wasn't himself, he didn't have Jeb Stuart's cavalry, A. P. Hill was sick, or Stonewall Jackson was dead, and suggest that one or more of these facts explain the result. This view overlooks the fact that over on Cemetery Ridge there were 90,000 Yankee soldiers, who conceivably may have had something to do with determining the outcome of the battle. The North had a stronger economy and a larger population, and these influenced the result, but the ultimate result was determined by the soldiers and the generals. Despite the industrial superiority of the North, the Confederacy still might have won if a few key battles had come out differently.

J.A.G.   What is the place of the Civil War in the history of warfare?

T.H.W.   In some ways, the Civil War was the first "total" war. Evidence of this would include the use of mass armies, the importance of industrial production, and the application of the heavy hand of government on the lives of civilians. It was a war of unlimited objectives; neither side could compromise. The South had to fight for independence or give up. The North had to restore the Union or give up. Yet at the same time, it was also the last of the traditional wars. Soldiers still charged, shoulder to shoulder. Generals still made speeches to their men on the field. Young men, as they fell, still said things like "Tell my father I died for my country." Men on both sides did chivalric, considerate things for men on the other side; the concept that wars were fought by gentlemen still prevailed. In a sense, it was two wars in one, which is perhaps what gives it its fascination. On balance, the Civil War stands as a turning point in the evolution of warfare. Concepts of strategy developed by Napoleon and Jomini were applied and misapplied in this war, and in the end, Grant and Sherman won it by following the modern strategy of exhausting all the enemy's resources.

The war was much studied in later years by European students of war. The Germans were very interested in the use of railroads during the war. Other European military men studied it, looking for proof of the virtues of some particular doctrine. Curiously, when soldiers study doctrine, they often look for an instance in the past that will justify what they want to do in the present or future. For example, the English studied Lee's early campaigns in a period when England seemed to be isolated. Lee's handling of inferior forces, moving swiftly on interior lines, seemed useful to a nation in something of the same position, facing the continental powers. What happened? In World War I, mobility disappeared with the machine gun and other weapons. It became a war of position. The British should have studied the Virginia campaigns of 1864 and 1865, where trench warfare first evolved. They'd studied the wrong battles!

J.A.G.   Was the Civil War a good thing for the American people? Could slavery have possibly been abolished in any other way?

T.H.W.   The Civil War was the great turning point in American history, just as, for example, the critical moment in French history was the French Revolution. The great results of the Civil War were that the concept of nationalism was fixed beyond a doubt in the American mind and that slavery was abolished. These results were accepted as both permanent and good by both the North and the South. The nation took a new course, and if the result had been otherwise, the course would have been different.

Slavery presumably could have been abolished without war, if the slaveowners had ever decided that it was an unprofitable institution. The first great historian of slavery, Ulrich B. Phillips, concluded that by 1860 only a few slaveowners were making substantial profits on their investment. However, the weight of modern opinion is that slavery in the 1850's was thriving. Even when the limits of the expansion of cotton culture were reached, slaves could have been used in other ways. Slave labor was used in the Tredegar Iron Works at Richmond. Slave gangs might have been employed in the factories of a new industrial South. It has even been conjectured that if there had not been a Civil War, gangs of migratory slave workers might have been used in Northern wheat fields.

But even if slavery had not continued to be profitable, would the South actually have abolished it? In addition to being a labor system, it was a white supremacy device. If the South abolished slavery, what would it have put in its place? Southerners could conceive of no way to remove the Negroes from the country and no way to live with them as free men. How long would this have gone on if there hadn't been a civil war? Obviously, not down to the present day. But I don't believe that the South would ever voluntarily have abolished slavery. Freedom had to come by war.

J.A.G.   What are the half-dozen books that you would recommend to persons interested in the subject we have been discussing? In each case, would you indicate what the particular contribution of the volume is?

T.H.W.   It is inhuman to ask a Civil War scholar to name a half-dozen books on the conflict. The literature is so vast and the quality of it is so good that it is difficult to make choices. The best introduction to the subject and an invaluable reference, is J. G. Randall and David Donald's, *The Civil War and Reconstruction* (1961) published in a shorter version as *The Divided Union* (1961). For a good summary of the North at war, I recommend Bruce Catton's, *This Hallowed Ground* (1956), which is stronger on military events than on the political and economic aspects of the war. A balanced account of the South at war is Clement Eaton's, *A History of the Southern Confederacy* (1954). There are a number of good anthologies, and of these one of the best is Henry S. Commager's, *The Blue and the Gray*, in two volumes (1950). For a facet of the war often neglected, the interested reader should consult Benjamin Quarles', *The Negro in the Civil War* (1953). If he wants a good short account of the battles, he should look at R. Ernest and Trevor N. Dupuy's, *A Compact History of the Civil War* (1960).

Clement Eaton

The Confederacy

As is clearly revealed in the following discussion, Professor Clement Eaton of the University of Kentucky is a Southerner, with a deep loyalty to and sympathy for his section, but also a scrupulously objective historian. His many books include *Freedom of Thought in the Old South* (1940), *The Growth of Southern Civilization* (1961), *The Mind of the Old South* (1967), and a *History of the Southern Confederacy* (1954), the subject of the following interview. Professor Eaton is a former President of the Southern Historical Association.

John A. Garraty   Professor Eaton, why did the South secede?

Clement Eaton   The immediate cause was the election of Lincoln. The South was alarmed because the Republican platform described slavery as a great evil, a violation of the spirit of the Declaration of Independence, and insisted that neither Congress, nor a territorial legislature, nor individuals had the right to establish slavery in the territories of the United States. This moral disapprobation was regarded by the South as a great stigma on its basic social institution.

The underlying cause of secession was the fear that the victory of the Republican party threatened the Southern way of life—not immediately, but within the near future. Lincoln's famous speech of 1858 when he was running as a candidate for the Senate—the "house divided" speech—said as much, and it made a great impression on Southern people. He had said that the "divided house" would have to end and that slavery would ultimately be extinguished. This probably was a more extreme statement than Lincoln intended it to be, but it was very threatening. Furthermore, Southerners believed that the real power behind Lincoln was William H. Seward, and Seward had made so many extreme statements that the South was extremely distrustful of him.

We know now that Lincoln was a very pragmatic, modern individual. I am very much impressed with how popular misconceptions affect history. When William H. Russell, the correspondent for *The Times* of London, was in this country, he wrote a fine travel account called *My Diary: North and South.* He interviewed Seward in New York. Seward told him that the Southern people were very different from the Northern people. He said that the society of the South (which incidentally he knew very little about) was based on black labor and idle extravagance. He described tumbled-down old hackney coaches such as had not been seen north of the Potomac for half a century, harnesses that were never cleaned, ungroomed horses, badly furnished houses, bad cookery, imperfect education. He spoke of the North, on the other hand, as a section of the country where "all was life, enterprise, industry and mechanical skill." This was his stereotype. Now, if so intelligent a man had a stereotype of the South such as Seward had, what must have been the view of the average, untutored Northerner?

The stereotype that the South had of Northerners was no more accurate, and I think these misconceptions played a very important part in leading the South to secede.

J.A.G.   Was there any real danger in 1860, supposing that the South had accepted the result of the election, that slavery could have been abolished even in the territories?

C.E.   The Republican platform definitely said that the party would not interfere with the rights of states. And Lincoln made it very clear that his party did not intend to destroy slavery. In fact, he was willing to accept a constitutional amendment to that effect. As to the territories, the Republicans could have done nothing at the moment. The Senate was dominated by Southerners, and even in the House the Republicans did not have a clear majority. So, from a legal, technical point of view, there was no danger. But the South had a great fear of the future. Men do a lot of things because they feel it's too dangerous to stand still.

J.A.G.   How general was the feeling among the people of the South after the election that secession was necessary?

C.E.   We know that John C. Breckinridge, the candidate of the extreme proslavery element, received only 44.7 percent of the popular vote of the slave states. But a most interesting shift occurred between election day, November 6, 1860, and December 20, when South Carolina took the plunge and seceded. I have concluded from a pretty wide study of newspaper editorials that the Southern people were not at all ready to secede in November. They felt that a compromise could be reached, that Northern public opinion might change. But by mid-December views had hardened noticeably.

I should like to emphasize the importance of agitators in the development of the secession movement. We now realize that John Brown's raid on Harpers Ferry at the end of 1859 had a profound effect upon Southern public opinion. The support that Brown obtained from prominent Northern leaders and from the press and from people in general stirred them deeply. But the Southern people were not responsive to the fire-eaters for quite a while; men like Congressmen William L. Yancey of Alabama and Robert Barnwell Rhett of South Carolina really were not popular figures. But between November, 1860, and the secession of South Carolina, there were slave insurrection scares. Newspapers reported that Northern agitators were working with the Negroes, that arms had been sent down, that poison had been discovered in wells. The people were very jittery, very easily susceptible to alarming rumors.

J.A.G.   Was there any truth behind these rumors?

C.E.   I don't think so. It is true there were some Northern Methodist ministers in Texas who might have made statements that were interpreted as incendiary, but the Southern people suspected any Northern politician; they were liable to put the worst construction on anything that he said.

On the other side, Northerners made a very great mistake in thinking that the South was bluffing *all* the time and that they would never secede. Lincoln himself held that feeling. He thought there was a Unionist majority in the South that could overcome the secession movement if properly managed. But the southern Unionists were not absolute Unionists. They were Unionists *provided Southern rights could be pro-*

tected, but if Southern rights were sacrificed, they would no longer be Unionists.

I've often thought of writing a book about the role of honor in Southern life. Of course a high sense of honor is not peculiar to the South; the Japanese have an exaggerated sense of honor, for example. But prewar Southerners had a sense of honor that went far and beyond common sense, an honor that not only applied to individuals but also to the region. The feeling became general that it would be dishonorable to accept anything less than equality in the Union, and they interpreted equality to mean the right of every individual to carry his personal property wherever he wanted to. Since slaves were personal property, they believed they had a right to take them into the Western territories. Today we might think that this was an abstraction of no practical value, but people often are motivated by abstractions.

Nor can we completely discount the influence of leaders. I was brought up on the teaching of Professor Arthur M. Schlesinger, Sr. I was very much impressed as a young graduate student by his description of the power of social forces, his argument that individuals could modify movements only in detail, could not really change great trends. I agree only partly with that today. We have de-emphasized the importance of individuals too much. Shortly after the Civil War John William De Forest, a Northern writer, wrote an excellent book, *A Union Officer in the Reconstruction*. He was impressed by the fact that in every little Southern community there was some leading man, whom De Forest compared to the big monkey around which all the other little monkeys gathered. This central figure would state his opinions blodly and authoritatively, and ignorant country people looked up to him as the interpreter of life. Such leaders, scattered throughout the South, must have strongly affected public opinion. Southerners were not as a whole readers; they didn't read the newspapers as Northerners did.

I think that one ought to pay a lot of attention to South Carolina, not only because South Carolina led off the secession movement but also because of the wide influence of South Carolina in the Southern states. Many of the leading advocates of secession had emigrated from South Carolina—to Mississippi, to Alabama, to Texas. The South Carolina conservative mind had a wide influence. Virginia had a wide influence in the golden period of Southern history, with Jefferson, Madison, the lawyer George Mason, and that group. Virginia ideas were moderate, very much a part of the American Enlightenment. But with the rise of King Cotton, South Carolina took the leadership. You can hardly name a great Virginian after 1830.

The typical South Carolinian had an unusually conservative point of view, based partly on the fact of great plantations, I think. Although they gave lip service to the Declaration of Independence, the leaders of the state really believed that the intelligent, well-born, wealthy people should rule. The diary of Mary Chesnut, wife of the planter-politician James Chesnut, provides a wonderful view of the South Carolina mind. Her comments on individuals show how unimportant the common people were in South Carolina. And South Carolina was the only state that did not elect the Presidential electors by popular vote; indeed, the governor was not elected by the people but by the legislature.

There is much evidence of the changing state of feeling in this critical period after the 1860 election in South Carolina. Right after the election, the fiery federal judge Andrew Magrath resigned and became a great hero. Very shortly after that, Senator James Chesnut resigned, with similar results. Then Senator James H. Hammond followed suit. As a young man, Hammond had felt that South Carolina should secede, but as he grew older he began to realize that the state would be helpless without the support of the rest of the South. The nullification crisis taught him a lesson. In 1860 he opposed immediate secession, but he resigned because of the contagion of example. He later regretted it, and said he had played the fool in resigning.

In many parts of the South the large planters favored caution. Their property was at stake; they wanted to see what Lincoln would do. It is also clear that many of the businessmen in the cities were opposed to secession, even in South Carolina, although others were ardent secessionists—men like Joseph Anderson, President of the Tredegar Iron Works in Richmond, and William Gregg, the great textile pioneer.

One cannot discount the fact that Lincoln was very silent during the critical period after he was elected. He refused to give the South any assurance of his future policies. He resisted the appeal of Alexander H. Stephens to issue a statement, also of George D. Prentice, the powerful editor of the *Louisville Journal*, and of other conservative Southern Unionists. Then, too, the failure of the Crittenden Compromise, which would have recognized slavery in territories south of 36°30′, caused thousands of Southerners to lose heart and to think that secession was inevitable. One of the most interesting aspects of the secession movement was that it was pushed through so quickly and so hastily. Most historians feel that, if there could have been a delay, the cooperationists —the group which favored consulting the other Southern states—would have had an opportunity to bring their influence to bear and there might have been a cooperative movement, and the secession movement might have been headed off. Of course, the Southern people never had a chance to vote directly on whether they should secede or not. Only the state of Texas submitted the ordinance of secession to a popular vote. (Virginia did also, but long after any real opportunity existed to express a negative opinion.)

J.A.G. Do you think that there was much chance that the secession ordinances might have been rejected in some of the Southern states?

C.E. Yes, in the key state of Georgia, for example: the cooperationists had some excellent leaders in Georgia, men like A. H. Stephens and Herschel Johnson; and in Louisiana, which lost very important advantages in joining the Confederacy. They lost the federal sugar subsidy. Furthermore, New Orleans was full of Northern men, merchants and businessmen.

J.A.G. Was there any opposition to secession afterwards? Was there a group in the South during the Civil War comparable to the Northern Copperheads?

C.E. Once the die was cast, once the decision was made, practically all the people, except in the mountainous areas, accepted it and became loyal Confederates. There was that feeling that a man was a traitor to his state unless he did join in after the people had made the decision.

J.A.G. Did Southerners believe that peaceful secession was possible?

C.E. One of the big talking points of secession leaders was that secession would not result in war. They thought that Northern people were very mercenary, that money guided them, that they were prosperous as things were and wouldn't want to fight. The Confederates sent commissioners to Washington and offered what they thought was a very reasonable basis of separation. The provisional government at Montgomery opened up the Mississippi and New Orleans to Northern commerce. It proposed an equitable distribution of the national debt. Of course Southerners believed also that secession was a legal right. George Pickett, the Confederate cavalry leader at Gettysburg, reported that he was taught at West Point that secession was legal. Some realists like James L. Petigru, the South Carolina lawyer, who was a Unionist, foresaw that a war would result. But even to this day I don't see why they could not have made a peaceful arrangement. I know that that is against the nationalistic interpretation of history that is very common today. But the Southerners believed that they were fighting for democracy, as much as did Northerners. They thought the issue was self-determination, that they shouldn't be held in a union they hated, that they ought to have the right to form their own government.

Now I don't think Union is a sacred thing myself, although I'm glad the South was defeated, which I know was in the best interest of both sections. But I do not look upon Union as something as sacred as democracy. Two societies could have existed on this continent, just as Canada exists with America.

J.A.G. Didn't Lincoln deal with this question effectively when he tied resistance to secession to democracy?

C.E. Yes. His argument was that the United States had a mission: to demonstrate to the world that a democratic government could not be destroyed by any disgruntled group wishing to break away. The secessionists should have waited certainly until after Lincoln had taken office and had given some indication of what his policies would be.

J.A.G. I was raising the question of the morality of seceding immediately after being defeated in an election. The Southern leaders had gone to the people of the country and lost. No one questioned the legality of Lincoln's election. Weren't they on weak ground, saying, in effect, "We lost, so we won't go along with the result"?

C.E. Their argument was that Lincoln got virtually all of his votes north of the Mason-Dixon line, that it was really a sectional victory rather than a democratic victory.

J.A.G. Given the enormous superiority of the North in population and material wealth, how could the Confederate states have dared to risk the possibility of war?

C.E. The South was indeed weak economically. The eleven Southern states that seceded produced only about 10 percent of the nation's manufactured goods. They had one-third of the railroad mileage and practically no shipping at all. Just looking at the cold statistics, it would seem absolutely absurd to fight. The Southerners of course counted on "King Cotton diplomacy," the belief that Europe would come to their aid because they supplied three-fourths of the cotton used in France and England. They assumed that those countries would recognize the Confederacy and probably break the blockade.

Southerners also had a low conception of Northerners, as a mercenary "race" unaccustomed to arms. They believed in the spiritual advantage of fighting for the homeland, a truth that has been demonstrated again and again. They also discounted economic forces. They thought that Southern soldiers would prove very superior to Northern ones. Then, too, many thought that secession would be peaceable. But above all, we must see them as a provincial-minded people who did not realize the strength of the North, or of economics.

Of course, the South could have won the war. No one knows, for example, what would have happened at Gettysburg if Stonewall Jackson had not been killed at Chancellorsville, or if Lee's battle plan had not fallen into the hands of McClellan before Antietam. There was always a possibility that the South could win, or that the North would get discouraged and give up the struggle. We know that the North in the winter of 1863–64 was terribly discouraged; the Peace Democrats and Copperheads were arguing for a negotiated peace.

J.A.G. In what ways was the Confederate constitution and the government which it established different from the government of the United States?

C.E. Alexander H. Stephens, who had a profound influence upon the drawing up of the Confederate constitution, was an admirer of the federal Constitution, and thought that the Confederacy should adopt it as it was. And the Whig party, which was very powerful in the South, had no real quarrel with the Constitution. But the Southerners thought of the Constitution as it was originally established in 1789. The constitution that they did draw up contained several innovations: for example, the President was to be elected for a six-year term and be ineligible for re-election. Giving the President the power of vetoing separate items in appropriation bills was another important change, as was the clause making the amendment process easier. Instead of three-fourths of the states, amendments were to require only two-thirds. Of course, it also guaranteed slavery and states' rights and prohibited *protective* tariffs. Yet it did not definitely state the right of secession. Probably the Confederates assumed that the right of secession was implied just as they thought it was implied in the old Constitution. Essentially, the Confederates were very conservative, keeping most of the Constitution of the United States.

J.A.G. Did the Confederate constitution protect states' rights in ways that the federal Constitution had not?

C.E. Only by spelling states' rights out more clearly.

J.A.G. Did Southerners really believe in states' rights, or Southern rights? Was there, in other words, a great concern for states' rights *within the Confederacy?*

C.E. States' rights, although still held firmly, it seems to me were gradually converted into Southern rights. But the idea of states' rights was unquestionably a defense mechanism, used by minorities in the North as well as in the South. I do think that Southerners had a greater love for locality; they were more provincial. And states' rights fitted the economic interests of an agrarian people.

J.A.G. Can you explain why the Confederacy failed to develop a two-party system?

C.E. During the secession movement there was a strong desire to present a united front. It was perfectly natural that the provisional government established at Montgomery would be nonpartisan. Jefferson Davis was elected President with scarcely any opposition whatsoever. Many old Whigs and many Unionists suppressed all partisanship and out of patriotism supported the government.

But opposition developed, primarily because of the centralizing policies of the Davis administration. It would have been better if the

Confederacy had developed a two-party system and channeled criticism toward issues rather than personalities, but it turned out differently. The opposition criticized Davis and demanded a reorganization of the cabinet, and a real organized opposition simply didn't develop. During a war period, on the other hand, it is difficult to form a real two-party system.

J.A.G.   Did Confederate leaders have a military strategy at the beginning of the war, or did they merely react to Northern attacks?

C.E.   There were two points of view, and the one that prevailed was that held by Jefferson Davis. Davis realized that the South was much the weaker section of the country. He thought, therefore, that the best policy was the defensive policy. He also advocated a policy of dispersal: he scattered troops all around the perimeter of the Confederacy, instead of concentrating them in strong armies. He took this position partly because public opinion in the different states demanded it, and partly because, like most West Point graduates, he subscribed to the theories of Baron Jomini whose study of Napoleon's campaigns was highly regarded in military circles. Jomini wrote that the prime duty of an army was to hold territory, and to maneuver so as not to have to fight battles to the death.

Davis had a rigid and conservative mind. He divided the theaters of war into departments, and insisted that troops from one department should not be moved into another. When one of the ablest of the Confederate Secretaries of War, George Washington Randolph, a grandson of Jefferson, tried to order troops from west of the Mississippi River across in order to aid General Pemberton in the defense of Vicksburg, Davis countermanded the order and lectured him severely about departmental "autonomy."

Certain generals favored taking the offensive, the most prominent being Beauregard, Stonewall Jackson, and the Irish-born Patrick Cleburne, "the Stonewall Jackson of the West." So did the Georgia politician Robert Toombs. Had he been elected President—and he was perhaps the best qualified man in the Confederacy in spite of his hot temper and his proneness to get drunk from time to time—the South would have fought an offensive war. There was a good opportunity to take the offensive after the first battle of Bull Run, not immediately, but in the month following, when the North was off balance and had not really organized its forces. If the Confederates had followed Beauregard's advice, concentrated their troops, they might have captured Washington, which might have ended the war.

The South did depart from the defensive policy on three important occasions. In the fall of 1862, General Braxton Bragg invaded Kentucky. He ought to have won a great victory, but he let the Union army slip by him and seize Louisville with its control of the Louisville and Nashville Railroad, which was a key supply route for the federal armies. The second occasion was Lee's invasion of Maryland, which also might well have succeeded if his orders had not been captured, although he was also hampered by the tremendous amount of straggling in his army in that campaign. Lee's defeat at Antietam was probably more important than Gettysburg in the actual defeat of the South. The third offensive was the invasion of Pennsylvania, culminating at Gettysburg. The Confederate cabinet argued about permitting that at great length. Many leaders felt troops should be diverted to the support of Vicksburg, which was in serious danger.

J.A.G. Was Southern military leadership in the field superior to that of the North?

C.E. Military leadership depends partly on training, and the South had only about one-fourth of the graduates of West Point. So, from the point of view of training, the North was definitely superior. But it is interesting to note that some of the best Southern generals had the poorest records at West Point. Lee, of course, was second in his class, and there are others with good records, but James Longstreet was third from the bottom of his class, and Pickett, who led the famous charge, was right at the bottom of his class scholastically. (That might have something to do with his failure!) In the eastern theater of the war, the Southern generals were definitely superior until the very end, when Grant took over the Union command. In the western theater, however, the South was extremely unfortunate, notably in the case of Braxton Bragg, who really was the dominant influence in that region, and there was little excuse for the vital loss of New Orleans early in the war.

Northern generals had the advantage of good staffs. Lee had twenty-two men on his staff, and none of them of general grade, whereas Grant had about one hundred fifty, including many major generals and brigadier generals. That was a great weakness of the Confederates. The Southern generals had another failing: they believed in fighting a gentleman's war. There were a few exceptions such as Stonewall Jackson and Patrick Cleburne, but in general they wanted to fight along chivalric lines. They had no conception of total war and didn't like to entrench their soldiers until toward the end of the struggle.

Grant was free of this illusion. To Grant, war was a matter of common sense, of using your forces ruthlessly, and making your objective the destruction of the enemy. The Confederate leaders lacked the instinct for the jugular.

One point that Douglas Southall Freeman made in his writing about the war was that there was a tremendous mortality among the officers of the Confederacy partly because of this chivalric idea. They felt they must lead their troops, get out there and get shot. Even the very top generals on some occasions led charges. Even Lee wanted to do so, and so did Albert Sidney Johnson. The Northern generals were not quite so chivalric; they had more sense. As the war went on, there was an enormous attrition among Southern officers.

J.A.G.   How did the Confederate government face up to the task of mobilizing its resources and manpower?

C.E.   Not very well. Davis was so much concerned with the military direction of the war that he neglected encouraging the development of manufactures. He did not exercise any great control over the transportation system or over blockade running, and it was not until 1863 that the Confederate government had a centralized purchasing agent in Europe to buy arms. Blockade running and the bringing in of resources were pretty much left to individuals until 1864, when Colonel Thomas Baine was placed in charge. The blockade was run for the profit of foreigners who had invested capital in the business.

The South frankly lacked good businessmen. Southerners have never properly valued the businessman. In my boyhood, I remember my mother's regret that her sister had married a merchant who had three stores. She felt that demeaned our family. The lack of really good business heads contrasted sharply with the North. The North had Tom Scott, President of the Pennsylvania Railroad, as Assistant Secretary of War, and another very efficient businessman, Montgomery Meigs, who was Chief of the Quartermaster Corps. By way of contrast, the Confederate Assistant Secretary of War was Albert T. Bledsoe, Professor of Mathematics at the University of Virginia, a man absolutely controlled by abstractions—a ridiculous thing. In the North, two of the ablest businessmen, Herman Haupt and Daniel McCallum, organized the railroad system efficiently. The South could certainly have used some good businessmen in developing their manufactures and their transportation system.

J.A.G.   Why didn't the South use slaves as soldiers? After all, a soldier is a kind of a slave, of whom unquestioning obedience is demanded.

C.E.   They ultimately came to that conclusion, when things got desperate. One of the things that the South has been rightly criticized for by modern historians is that it did not to any extent conscript slaves for war purposes, or even for industrial and economic purposes. The Confederates conscripted men, but they regarded slaves as property and left the control of slavery to individual masters. Southerners suffered from a great misconception as to the nature of the Negro. They thought they knew the Negro, but they didn't. They thought the Negro cowardly, inefficient, stupid, incapable of action without the direction of the white man.

Now the North enrolled over 170,000 Negroes in the Army, and they proved very brave soldiers, under white officers it is true. Anyone who reads Thomas Lee Higginson's *Life in a Black Regiment* will certainly be convinced of the great ability of the Negro as a soldier. He needed leadership because of his depressed rearing and background. And, as the war went on, the South decided that they must use the Negroes. Some of the most intelligent of the leaders, such as Judah P. Benjamin, the Secretary of State, argued for the use of Negro slaves. Davis at first strongly opposed this, in the end strongly favored it.

J.A.G. Was there any fear that if the slaves had guns they would rebel?

C.E. There were several cases of plots, but no actual rebellions took place during the war, and I frankly don't believe that Southerners felt that it would be dangerous to arm the slaves in groups under white officers.

J.A.G. What were Jefferson Davis' strengths and weaknesses as President, compared with Lincoln's?

C.E. When Jefferson Davis was chosen, I think the vast majority of people thought that he was the ideal President. He had been an officer in the Mexican War; he had been one of the ablest Secretaries of War this country has had; he had been an outstanding Senator. So he started off under the most favorable auspices. (I probably would have voted for him for President of the Confederacy if I had been alive then.)

His weaknesses became apparent as the war went on, but first I should mention his virtues. He was a tremendous worker, wholly dedicated to the Confederacy. He worked long hours at night—too long, for his frail health. He possessed great industry and dedication to the cause, and he was a man of the highest honor. He also had a lot of military knowledge, but it was military knowledge of a past war, the Mexican War. His defects begin to appear when the Confederacy began to fall on bad days, and then we see him as really inadequate to his job. He was a poor judge of men, and he played favorites. General Braxton Bragg had already clearly proved that he was not suited to military command, but Davis kept him on—even promoted him—and brought him to Richmond.

Then his pride was such that he quarreled with some of the leading generals; Generals Joseph Johnston and Beauregard both hated him. He could not get cooperation from them. And then, too, there was a "credibility gap" between Davis and the people. Davis had a fine opportunity to inspire the people, but he was so busy with military affairs that he failed to do so. When he did speak to the people, he spoke in abstractions and platitudes. He was very aloof, a reserved man, a cool man who couldn't get along with the leaders of Congress. He tended to bog down in details. And he had a supersensitivity that caused him to take affront, to be insulted by things that an ordinary man would ignore.

Lincoln was much the superior. He had the wonderful ability of self-effacement that Jefferson Davis didn't have, as was shown in his relations with generals like McClellan, who actually insulted him, and Hooker, who constantly criticized him, and with many politicians. As far as I can understand, Lincoln simply never got angry.

J.A.G.   Was this necessarily a good thing? He was certainly self-effacing when confronted with the insults of McClellan. Wouldn't a little of Jefferson Davis' domineering quality toward generals have been more effective, in this instance at least?

C.E.   I would agree with you on that. Lincoln was a very loose administrator. He was great in his ideas and great where Davis failed, in appealing to the people and presenting noble ideals in his speeches. When we think of Lincoln, we think of that beautiful ending of his first inaugural, of the Gettysburg Address, of his second inaugural. Although he appeared very melancholy and probably was, he had a great outlet of humor and folksiness, which established a bond with ordinary men.

Some military historians think that Lincoln was a better strategist than any of his generals, but Lincoln himself was very humble about it; after Grant's Vicksburg campaign he wrote him a letter saying, "I was wrong. I thought that instead of going south, you should have attacked in a different direction." Lincoln did make mistakes, but his general concept of strategy was much better than Jefferson Davis'.

J.A.G.   Would you comment on the objectives and effectiveness of Confederate diplomacy?

C.E.   Most Confederate leaders believed that cotton was so important to the European economy that England and France would break the Northern blockade to get it. But the government sent over inept ambassadors at first. However, it probably wouldn't have made much difference if the ablest men had been sent. The thing that determined European diplomacy was that it was to the interest of Europe to be neutral. In England, the upper classes had great sympathy for the South, but Queen Victoria and Prince Albert favored the North. An extremely able man, Henry Hotze, a Swiss who'd settled in Alabama, was sent to England in 1862. Hotze, a journalist, founded a Confederate magazine called *The Index*. Working very shrewdly, he paid leading British journalists for articles. He also furnished reliable information to the British press. One of his propaganda strokes was to publish in *The Index* an appeal of several hundred Christian clergymen, in which these clergymen showed that the South was a very Christian nation, that all the leading men were good Christians, that slavery was sanctioned by the Bible and was a very humane institution.

The Confederacy was represented in Paris by John Slidell, one of the ablest diplomats of his era. Slidell had great success in winning the confidence of Emperor Napoleon III and the banking firm of the Baron Erlanger. The Erlangers, rather than the Confederacy, proposed a loan of $25 million to the South. But their terms were so stiff that Secretary Benjamin scaled it down to $15 million. The bonds at first sold well, but in 1863, when Confederate military fortunes were low, they began to drop, and the Erlangers persuaded Slidell to buttress the market by buying back $7½ million. In the end, the Confederacy got only about $2½ million out of the $15 million, and the Erlangers made a killing.

As to why England didn't support the Confederacy, in the first place, the textile workers of Lancashire, convinced that the North represented the democratic cause in opposition to slavery, supported the Union. Furthermore, Lord Derby, leader of the Conservative party, did not favor intervening. He was influenced partly by Queen Victoria, but I think that the British were influenced by the fact that they were making very good profits out of the war. The merchant marine of the United States was destroyed by Confederate commerce raiders, for example. Also, as Norman Graebner has shown, Russia had a very important influence on both England and France. Russia was the only friend that the North had in Europe. She refused to support a scheme for mediation proposed by Napoleon III. Russia feared England and backed the United States as a counterforce.

I'd like to add a word about United States diplomacy. William H. Seward was a very aggressive Secretary of State. He had a very able representative in Great Britain, Charles Francis Adams. Seward continually treatened war with either England or France if they received Confederate Commissioners, or recognized the Confederacy. England did not want war, and Seward was able to convince the government that he would really fight. He was also successful, through Adams, in stopping the British from building the Laird ironclad rams that probably could have broken the blockade. He also did very well in dealing with France. France was sympathetic with the Confederacy, partly because it hoped to build a French empire in Mexico. But French policy, unsupported by a strong navy, depended entirely on the cooperation of England, and this it never obtained.

J.A.G. We know that Confederate finance was inept and that there was runaway inflation in the South. Would you describe how the Confederates attempted to pay for the war? Was there any practicable alternative to inflation?

C.E. The alternative would have been to ship a large supply of cotton in the first year of the war, when the blockade was ineffective; but to do that the South had to have merchant vessels, and it had practically none. There were some who advocated establishing a great supply of cotton—"white gold," it was called—to buy munitions. Alexander H. Stephens proposed a grandiose plan that was impractical. Secretary of the Treasury Christopher Memminger favored the idea—one of the few good points about Memminger. But most Southerners suffered from the delusion known as King Cotton Diplomacy. They held back their cotton on the theory that doing so would force European intervention. The Confederate Congress did not pass a law prohibiting the export of cotton. Vigilance committees were formed to prevent the exportation of cotton, and state laws were passed. And so the South lost an opportunity to send cotton abroad to serve as security for loans, or to purchase matériel.

How did the Confederacy finance the war? It has been estimated that it had only $27 million worth of specie, yet for four years it kept an army of between 600,000 and 800,000 men in the field. During the first year, when patriotism was flaming high, the Confederacy sold bonds for gold and silver. The government also got a considerable sum from the sequestration of Northern property in the South.

After the South was drained of gold and silver, the government obtained what was called a produce loan. Planters could sell their cotton, sugar, and tobacco to the government for bonds. But apparently this was mismanaged; much of the supplies were destroyed. The produce loan was a failure. Then the Confederate Congress was extremely reluctant to tax the people; it has been estimated that only 1 percent of the revenue collected was raised by taxation, whereas the North raised close to a third of its needs by taxation. This fact alone is a glaring condemnation of Confederate policy. Most of the Confederate bills were paid by printing Treasury notes with no metallic backing. These were promises of payment two years after the end of the war. A billion and a half dollars of paper money was issued, by the Confederate government, and by the states, and also by corporations such as railroads. The strange thing is that this paper didn't depreciate nearly as rapidly as one would expect until after Gettysburg, when there was a precipitous drop. Toward the end of the war, the ratio between Confederate money and gold was probably 200 to 1—the greatest inflation that this country has ever had, with the possible exception of the American Revolution. This might have been mitigated by a realistic system of taxation, but the Congress wouldn't do it.

J.A.G. Did Northern currency circulate in the South during the war?
C.E. Southerners were glad to get it. Even Confederate soldiers were sometimes paid in federal greenbacks, obtained by illegal trade through the lines. One of the things the North did that was pretty unscrupulous was to print Confederate paper money, which was easy to counterfeit.

J.A.G. What happened to the typical Southern rural community during the war?

C.E. Life went along fairly normally on plantations except near the front. The slaves kept working, but it was necessary to appease them a little bit. William Gilmore Simms, the novelist, reported that he had to give his slaves molasses to keep them working. And they worked less because they didn't have any real supervision. The important change, I think, was on the small farms. So many men were drafted that women had to handle things themselves. The community of plain people were the ones that suffered, rather than the plantation owners. In most instances, life went along normally for the first two years: the children went to school; the Negroes worked well. But when Northern armies began to come in, the situation changed. Many slaves fled to the Union lines; armies tore up fences and took livestock. But the interior South was not greatly affected. People had plenty of food as a rule, until late in the war.

J.A.G. How did the Confederacy attempt to make up for its lack of manufactured goods?

C.E. The Confederate government concentrated on the manufacture of war materials; it did very well in this area. The great Tredegar Iron Works at Richmond flourished. At Selma, Alabama, a naval ordnance plant manufactured cannon and iron plate for warships, and at Augusta, Georgia, Colonel G. W. Rains established a powder factory. Some of the states, such as North Carolina, obtained materials by operating state-owned blockade runners and by developing cotton mills. However, one thing that was a great deterrent to establishing manufacturing was the belief that the war would be short and that it wouldn't be worthwhile to invest money in building factories. And of course the lack of capital was an enormous disadvantage.

J.A.G. A great deal has been written about the suppression of civil liberties in the North during the Civil War. Did comparable repression take place in the Confederacy?

C.E. No. About three hundred newspapers were suppressed in the North. In addition, about 15,000 people were arrested, denied the writ of *habeas corpus* and imprisoned. Although Lincoln talked a lot about democracy, he was a very pragmatic man and used any device that would advance the Union cause. Jefferson Davis, on the other hand, strongly protected civil liberties. No papers were suppressed by the Confederate government. Parson Brownlow's paper, *The Knoxville Whig*, was suppressed by state authority, with much justification. Then there were a few insignificant instances of suppression by public pressure. For example, James Honeycutt, who later became a scalawag and radical leader, had his paper, *The Christian Banner*, suppressed in

Virginia by mob action, and there were several instances of that. But Fremantle, in his *Journal,* which I regard as an extremely good source, said in 1863 that he was amazed at the degree of the freedom of the press that was allowed. Fremantle spoke especially of *The Chattanooga Rebel,* which was edited by Henry Watterson, later famous for his *Louisville Courier-Journal. The Chattanooga Rebel* attacked General Bragg's inefficiency bitterly; it was really a disloyal paper. The Confederacy did pass a law prohibiting the publishing of news about the movement of troops, but it did not suppress opinion.

J.A.G. Was there no substantial group of Southerners comparable to the Copperheads of the North?

C.E. Well, yes. In the Appalachian region there were secret organizations such as the Heroes of America. These were rather ignorant Unionist groups. Alexander H. Stephens bought up a paper, *The Augusta Constitutionalist,* in which he developed antiwar sentiment, and William Holden, editor of *The North Carolina Standard,* used his paper for the same purpose. But I'm really proud of the fact that the South seems to have believed truly in freedom of the press.

J.A.G. Can you generalize about the social effects of the war in the South? Were there any changes that were independent of the fact that the South was defeated?

C.E. The ante-bellum South, especially in the rich agricultural regions, had a rather aristocratic social structure; the aristocratic class looked down upon the lower classes. During the war, that aristocratic social structure began to give way. The Army contained all different types together. In Kate Stone's autobiography of life on a Louisiana plantation, *Brockenburn,* she describes her interest in a handsome young overseer. Socially he was not of her class, so she had to forget him. But she noted that in her brother's company, in which he was a private, one of his officers was a butcher, another an overseer. There was an intermingling of classes in the common cause. The social structure bent a good deal during the war.

Then, of course, the position of women changed very considerably. In *Life in the South from the Commencement of the War by a Blockaded British Citizen,* Katherine C. Hopley noted significant changes in the life of Southern women. Many of them took charge of plantations, some very successfully. Before the war, the father had often been the disciplinarian of the family; now the mother becomes the disciplinarian. Katherine Hopley also observed, by the way, that on the Milton plantation in Florida, where she was a tutoress, Mrs. Milton whipped and flogged the children much more than she did the slaves. Many women went into enterprises that they never would have thought of if the war hadn't occurred. Some worked in government offices, others in cutting out clothes for the Ordnance Department. And of course the teaching profession was pretty much monopolized by women, although another effect of the war was the virtual destruction of the weak school system. Many private academies closed down and never reopened. There had been a beginning of public education in Kentucky and North Carolina, which was sharply curtailed.

J.A.G. Did the war change the white Southerners' opinion of slavery at all?

C.E. A very interesting movement to ameliorate the condition of the slave took place, which might have continued and accomplished good results even if the South had won. Men like Calvin Wiley, superintendent of public schools in North Carolina, and the Reverend James Lyon of Mississippi advocated teaching the slaves to read and write, and making the marriage relation sacred. They also proposed laws in all the states prohibiting the selling of children under ten years of age away from their parents. There was definitely a movement to ameliorate slavery during the war.

J.A.G. Would you comment of the state of Southern morale? Did the great outburst of local patriotism you mentioned continue throughout the conflict?

C.E. It began to decline when the first Conscription Act was passed. One of the great evils of the Conscription Act was the exemption provision, which enabled a man to escape military duty by paying $500. The wealthy often took advantage of that, until the practice was abolished in 1863. More important, the second Conscription Act of October 1862 provided that one slaveowner or overseer for every twenty slaves would be exempted from military service in order to supervise the slaves. Actually, few took advantage of the law and were exempted. In South Carolina, only 401 did so, in Alabama, only 150. Yet the law was a symbol of privilege, and was regarded as a great injustice; it made it look like a rich man's war and a poor man's fight. Actually, it could be justified by the need to keep the plantation economy going.

Another cause of declining morale undoubtedly was the speculation that occurred. There was a vast amount of speculation, although much more in the North than in the South. Men made fortunes in blockade running and by selling scarce goods at high prices. Furthermore, poor families on farms were often not well provided for. Bushwhackers, outlaws, and deserters attacked them, and the women wrote letters to their men in the Army begging them to come home. Also the newspapers weakened morale. Anti-Davis papers were so extreme and bitter that they undoubtedly caused disaffection, as is clearly seen in the amount of desertion in the Confederate Army. About one in every seven soldiers deserted from the Confederate Army. Those who deserted were princi-

pally men from the mountain areas, which had originally opposed secession. Confederate officers, however, were extremely lenient toward
deserters and men who were absent without leave.

Another factor eroding morale was the political in-fighting that
occurred in the Confederacy among state governments. And then peoples'
morale always seems to decline when their economic status goes down.
(One of the reasons why morale was relatively high in the North was
that economic conditions were good.) But the basic reason was the defeat
of the Confederate armies. After 1863, any thoughtful observer could
see that the contest was pretty hopeless, although I don't believe the
average Southerner quite realized the significance of Gettysburg and
Vicksburg. After the election of Lincoln in 1864, which ruled out a
negotiated peace, the morale of the common people began to sink
very, very decidedly.

J.A.G.   How did the South react to Lincoln's Emancipation Proclamation?

C.E.   Southerners regarded it as an encouragement to servile insurrection.
They reacted violently. I believe the Southern people actually thought
slavery was all right. They had come a pretty long way from the days
of Thomas Jefferson and the liberal Southern critics of the peculiar institution. They had been converted by proslavery propaganda and the
arguments of their ministers and editors. My grandfathers on both
sides owned slaves. They were both fine men, good Christians, and I
can't conceive of them continuing to hold slaves unless they believed
slavery was justifiable. Maybe they would agree in principle that slavery
was evil, but as a practical proposition, they felt that slavery had to be
maintained.

J.A.G.   Do we know anything about how slaves felt about the Civil War,
both before the Emancipation Proclamation and after?

C.E.   Although the slaves on many plantations seemed to be happy and
contented, I think that nearly every slave would have preferred to be
free; Southerners were rationalizing when they said that slaves didn't
want freedom. In wartime, by the grapevine, slaves learned what the
war was all about. The striking thing is that when the Federal armies
got into an area and there was an easy chance to escape, the Negroes
ran away in droves. That in itself, it seems to me, explains how the slaves
felt.

Of course their idea of freedom was rather naive. They thought it
meant freedom from work. But they also knew that freedom meant an
end to being flogged, and to the fear of separation of families. Katherine
Hopley talked with slaves in Richmond, and she found out always
hanging over them was the possibility that they would lose their sons or
daughters or wives in the slave trade.

J.A.G.   How, as historians, can we find out how slaves felt about anything?

C.E. I have often wondered at our rashness, our audacity, in trying to explain how slaves felt. We have *some* evidence—for example, the diary of a free Negro barber of Natchez, which provides one realistic view of the life of a free Negro. I have also come across a brief fragment of autobiography of a Negro in Richmond, and we have a few slave letters. But in general they were a mute race, and seldom had a chance really to express their inner thoughts. The Negro was inclined to tell an interviewer what the person wanted to hear. When Fanny Kemble went down to the Pierce Butler plantation in Georgia, the Negroes just told her all kinds of horrible things that had happened. Yet some years later her daughter went back to the plantation and had a very different story to tell, a much more realistic story. The difficulties in finding out what the Negroes felt are very great. The most articulate ones would be like the black militants of today. Men like Frederick Douglass, who escaped to the North and had their narratives edited by abolitionists, painted the darkest pictures that can be imagined.

J.A.G. What effect did the war have on the price of slaves?

C.E. Prices held up surprisingly well until 1863. After that there was a drift downward, but slaves still continued to be quite valuable.

J.A.G. That's very interesting, because in ante-bellum times the value of slaves was closely related to the value of cotton. I should have thought that with the great diminution in the production of cotton the need for slaves would have gone down.

C.E. That's a cogent observation, but nevertheless slaves continued to be held as an investment, and for prestige. The Negroes remained useful in growing food crops and as domestic servants, and some worked in munitions plants. They repaired railroads, too.

J.A.G. Do we know anything about the internal slave trade during the war?

C.E. There was quite a movement of slaves from the seacoast and the dangerous areas. Whole plantation crews were moved to Texas, for example. But I don't think that the internal slave trade flourished as it had before the war.

J.A.G. On balance—and this is perhaps an unfair question—do you think the Confederacy was defeated by the North or by its own mistakes?

C.E. It seems to me that the North was bound to win a long war. This war had continued four years; I don't see how the South could have won it. Its economy was deteriorating, its railroads were shot to pieces, its ports were blockaded. It was simply a question of superior power of the North, plus the fact that the North had developed two remarkable generals, Grant and Sherman, who were better than the Southern generals.

J.A.G. Do you consider Grant a superior general to Lee?

C.E.　That is a most difficult question, and I fear my Southern prejudices would enter into any judgment. But looking at it in a hard, realistic way, I believe that Grant's military policy was more effective than Lee's. He was more modern in his point of view; he pursued his objectives with relentless determination. We usually think of Grant as using a bludgeon of great power and Lee as using a rapier of great skill. If Lee had had all the arms and forces that Grant had, and Grant had had the forces of Lee, it's quite likely that Lee would have beaten him. But I base my opinion of Grant's superiority primarily on his modern ideas of warfare, which in the end had to prevail.

J.A.G.　Would you summarize the actual losses of the South as a result of the war, without regard for the burdens imposed on the section after Appomattox by the North?

C.E.　Instead of the usual assessment based on material losses, I should like to begin with the intangibles, which of course are extremely hard to document. I think the Southerners, being a very religious people, thought in the beginning that God was on their side. As time went on, they began to doubt that, and toward the end they began to feel that possibly slavery was a great evil and that God had willed that they should lose. That meant a great lose of pride, yet perhaps also the development of a different sense of values: I think they then realized that Yankee efficiency shouldn't be looked down upon and discounted. Another loss developed from the fact that a whole generation grew up lacking the cultural advantages that their fathers had had; the leadership of the South was much weakened as a result. I count that as one of the most important of the losses.

Then, too, the Civil War stopped the literary development of the South for a period of about twenty years, until the rise of the local color school. It also, of course, affected the standard of living of many people. Cotton production did not get back to its 1860 level until 1879, sugar until 1890. Livestock was enormously depleted, and of course many homes were destroyed and fences wrecked. The cities seemed to recover very much more rapidly than rural areas. But the South was basically rural; the effect upon the society as a whole was pretty largely determined by the effect on the rural population.

J.A.G.　What are the chief unanswered questions that future historians are likely to ask about the history of the Confederacy?

C.E.　I think that future historians will want to make comparisons. Southern historians have been too provincial; they have only looked within their own borders. Future historians will look at societies that might have similarities or differences, in Europe and also in the North. They will also be much more interested in what was happening to the common people during the war, the families out on the farms. And they will study the attitudes of people toward war; no one, for example, has made any investigation of the conscientious objector. The draft laws exempted Dunkers, and Mennonites, and Quakers, but not conscientious objectors. I think we also need more study of the role of women in the Confederacy. But above all, I think, as we retreat from this period in time, that historians will not, as I have, have deep emotional feelings about certain things, and can therefore be cool and objective. Sometimes when I lecture, when I come to Pickett's charge at the battle of Gettysburg, for example, my voice clouds up. I feel very, very ashamed. I can't explain it at all. But I have this emotional feeling; I guess it comes partly from the fact that my grandfather on my mother's side was a major in Wade Hampton's cavalry. He fought all four years through the war. The family tradition is that, after the war was over, he never wanted to talk about it, and on his way back to South Carolina he took his officer's sword from its scabbard and threw it on the battlefield as a symbolic gesture.

When you're a Southerner you're to a certain extent indoctrinated during childhood. It's not that way in the North. As William Faulkner has pointed out, history lives in the South. One of my memories as a very small boy is of an uncle who had entered the Army as a little drummer boy. I used to see him, with his long gray beard, long gray hair, and fine features—he was a great hero to me.

J.A.G. Professor Eaton, I wonder if it is true, as you seem to feel, that being emotionally involved in what you're writing about is a disadvantage to an historian? Doesn't emotional involvement help both in writing and teaching history to make the student aware of the reality of the subject?

C.E. I would agree that absolutely passionless history is uninteresting. But to be a true historian one must see the past in perspective, and not interpret things in terms of the present, as the New Left apparently does, or be as affected by personal memories as I sometimes am. At the same time, one must have a certain historical imagination, and this may create a certain amount of emotion. So your point, I think, is well taken.

J.A.G. What are the half-dozen or so books that you would recommend to persons interested in the subject we have been discussing? In each case, would you indicate what the particular contribution of the volume is?

C.E. E. M. Coulter's *The Confederate States of America, 1861–1865* (1950), is the most comprehensive volume on the Confederacy; while David Donald (ed.), *Why the North Won the Civil War* (1960) is a collection of essays by experts analyzing the strengths and weaknesses of the two sides. On the military, D. S. Freeman's *R. E. Lee: A Biography* (1934–35, in four volumes), and his *Lee's Lieutenants: A Study in Command* (1942–44, in three volumes) are brilliantly written and based upon a profound study of the sources, although pro-Southern in viewpoint.

R. S. Henry's *The Story of the Confederacy* (1936) is a well-written and sound one-volume military history. B. I. Wiley, *The Life of Johnny Reb, the Common Soldier of the Confederacy* (1943) is a delightful account, enlivened with much humor, and Wiley's *Southern Negroes, 1861–1865* (1965) destroys many old stereotypes. F. L. Owsley, *King Cotton Diplomacy* (1959) is the standard account of the Confederate government's foreign relations.

David Donald

Reconstruction

David Donald is Harry C. Black Professor of American History at Johns Hopkins University. Among his many books are *Lincoln's Herndon* (1948), a biography of Lincoln's law partner, *Lincoln Reconsidered* (1961), a collection of his scholarly papers, and *Charles Sumner and the Coming of the Civil War* (1960), which won a Pulitzer prize. He is coauthor with the late J. H. Randall of a standard textbook, *The Civil War and Reconstruction* (1961). Currently, he is finishing his life of Sumner and serving as Director of the Institute of Southern History at Johns Hopkins. Professor Donald discusses the era of Reconstruction in its various political, economic, and social aspects.

John A. Garraty Professor Donald, when historians speak of the era of "Reconstruction," what exactly do they mean?

David Donald By long usage, the term refers to the period 1865–77. "Reconstruction" involves principally the binding up of the nation's wounds at the end of the Civil War. Usually the focus is first on Washington, on Congressional legislation, and then on actions within the South—how the Confederate States formally re-entered the Union, how a new social system began to develop there, and how by 1877 Southern governments passed back into what is called "Home Rule" or control of the native whites.

This is the conventional way of approaching the subject. I don't think it is a very satisfactory way; the period has a broader significance. My own thinking about this has been influenced by the greatest of the Reconstruction historians, William A. Dunning, who wrote of Reconstruction as a national problem. These years have great meaning, not just in Southern history but in our national history. In at least three major ways the whole country was affected by Reconstruction. First of all, basic social changes occurred: the Thirteenth, Fourteenth, and Fifteenth Amendments, together with Congressional laws implementing them, meant that Negro slaves were freed, made citizens, given the right to vote, made more or less equal participants in American society. Comparable to this enormous change was the declining status of the Southern whites.

Second, Reconstruction was marked by enormous economic changes. During these years came the real emergence of modern industrial capitalism in America: the rise of big business, the first trusts, the consolidation of the railroads, the first modern labor unions. There was also a long, debilitating depression.

Thirdly, there was a political transformation. The Republican party became *the* national party, and the South, which had been the dominant force in American political life before the Civil War, was now subordinate to the North.

I don't like the dates that are normally associated with Reconstruction. Most of the things I think Reconstruction historians ought to be interested in started a good deal earlier than 1865. For instance, the history of emancipation begins at least with the Emancipation Proclamation in 1862. The creation of new governments for the Southern states also began during the war, with the military regimes that Lincoln set up in Louisiana, Tennessee, and Arkansas, and tried to establish in North Carolina and Florida. The socially revolutionary possibilities of Reconstruction were evident as early as the wartime division of lands at Port Royal, which Willie Lee Rose described so well in *Rehearsal for Reconstruction*. What happened in New Orleans under the government set up there under General Banks during the war is another part of Reconstruction; many of the patterns typical of postwar Reconstruction were established there. Changes in Washington, D.C., during the years 1862–65 were also of very great importance. What happened there was an omen of what was going to happen in the Scuth as a whole after 1865.

J.A.G.   Could you elaborate on that last point a little bit? I'm not sure I understand.

D.D.   During the war, Washington, D.C., provides a fascinating case study of race relations. In 1860, it had a free Negro population of about nine thousand and about two thousand slaves. These made up roughly one-fifth of the total population. As the war progressed, fugitive slaves came in from Virginia and Maryland. When compensated emancipation was passed for the District of Columbia in early 1862, more and more such people flocked in, perhaps as many as forty thousand. The city had all the economic problems that came with the newly freed population. The Negroes didn't have anything to do; they had no family ties, no roots. Something had to be done about housing and maintaining them. Then there were legal problems. Until 1860, the free Negroes of Washington were controlled by Black Codes, laws borrowed from Maryland and Virginia. A Negro, for example, could only get a license to conduct a business from a pushcart or a wagon; it was illegal for any Negro in the District to have a store, because he couldn't get a license to do so. Emancipation wiped away the Black Code. Then, for the first time, the problem of what to do with these freedmen, now members of civil society, erupted. Did they have the right to vote, hold office, run businesses, and attend schools? All these issues pressed for settlement in Washington before 1865, and the solutions achieved served as precedents for the social reorganization of the conquered Confederacy. There were, for example, a few integrated schools in the District. Washington Negroes voted with great zeal and, on the whole, with intelligence and discernment. Some exceedingly interesting legal cases, precursors of the later civil rights cases, were decided in Washington. When Negro doctors trained in the North came to Washington to practice, they had to force the white-controlled medical association to give them hospital privileges. Cases of discrimination in public carriers (wounded Negro soldiers coming back from the front, for example, were made to ride outside in the rain and snow because of the Jim Crow rules and regulations) were discussed, argued, legislated about well before the end of the Civil War.

Thus precedents governing later practice in the South had, in the Sea Islands of South Carolina and Georgia, in Louisiana, in the District of Columbia and other places, been set well before 1865. I would be very unhappy writing a book about Reconstruction if I could start only in 1865.

J.A.G. What about the terminal date, 1877? Was the South actually "reconstructed" by 1877?

D.D. Most Southern states had undergone the entire transformation well before 1877. By "entire transformation" I mean the process of establishing provisional governments, replacing them with radical regimes under the Congressional legislation of 1867, and then overthrowing these governments and re-establishing conservative ones. The dates would vary considerably from state to state, but only three—Florida, South Carolina, and Louisiana—still had radical regimes in 1877. Certainly, 1877 doesn't apply at all to the economic reconstruction, the broad social changes, or the constitutional developments which give the period its national significance. Nor was there a discernible change in political patterns in that year. If I had to select a terminal date for a book, I might have to settle for 1877, but, like Rembert Patrick, I would add a long chapter, running at least down to the 1890's, dealing with race relations and ultimate disfranchisement of the Negro.

J.A.G. Do you think that the assassination of Lincoln had a major effect on the course of post-Civil War history?

D.D. So many questions about Reconstruction are "if" questions. About this one I think I must say Yes and No. Let me explain. I say No in the long-range sense. I am not convinced that any form of reconstruction could have worked out very much differently from what actually happened.

Suppose, for example, really draconian measures had been adopted—the exiling of all Confederate leaders, the disfranchisement of all whites who had participated in the rebellion, the enfranchisement of all Negroes, and the granting of forty acres and a mule to each of them. Would it have worked? I've had doubts about this for a long time. This kind of welfare program would have required an army of bureaucrats as large as the Department of Agriculture today in order to patrol the South and ensure that independent ownership would work. Yet this was the era of Ulysses S. Grant. I just cannot imagine that such a program, administered by William W. Belknap, John A. Rawlins, or any other of the Grant toadies and sycophants, could have been effectual. Assuredly, much of the land given to the Negroes would have been lost to them within a single generation. Most had no experience in independent farming; almost none had any capital; and they didn't know about marketing procedures. Very probably forty acres was not a viable economic unit in the South in any case. I'll make a guess: Within a generation, three-fourths of such independent farmers would have forfeited or been swindled out of their landholdings. Real economic and political power was destined to be vested in the Southern whites, barring some kind of fervent Northern missionary effort to make over the society, a kind of drive that Americans have never been able to sustain over a long period of time. If Lincoln's policy had been adopted, or Andrew Johnson's, Thaddeus Stevens', or Charles Sumner's, then, probably, all would have worked out pretty much the same in the end.

J.A.G.   If Lincoln hadn't been killed, he probably would not have imposed a draconian solution on the South. Given the enormous prestige that Lincoln had at the end of the war, would not whatever policy he proposed have been more likely to be accepted? Would not, therefore, the bitterness that grew out of Reconstruction have been muted if he had remained alive?

D.D.   In the short run, I think Lincoln's assassination *did* make a difference. He did have enormous prestige as the victorious war President who had just been triumphantly re-elected, with a Congress that on the whole was more amenable to his wishes than any Congress he had had up until this point. The question, then, really becomes, "What would Lincoln really have wanted? What was Lincoln's plan of Reconstruction?"

J.A.G.   What were his plans?

D.D.   We don't know much, but from a number of things that he did we can infer what he *might* have done after the war. Immediately after the outbreak of the war he decided to hold Maryland, Missouri, and Kentucky by using troops—in effect, to guarantee governments that were favorable to the Union. Then in 1862 he appointed Andrew Johnson Military Governor of Tennessee when that state was taken by Union forces. The President had no constitutional power to appoint a military governor; he simply assumed the right under the war powers. Johnson, in turn, assumed that the war powers of the President attached to him as Governor and ruled with a high hand, disfranchising those who would not agree to certain terms and dictating how Tennessee was to be restored. A third precedent of Lincoln's was his famous 10-percent plan announced in 1863, which promised that when as few as 10 percent of the 1860 voters in any Southern state showed themselves again loyal, they could elect local officers, congressmen, and senators.

Here were three very different Lincolnian programs. The differences, I think, ought to be emphasized, for they show a good deal of flexibility on Lincoln's part—a willingness to try different things at different times for different areas of the South. To no one of them was he immovably attached. Just before his death, for instance, he was trying hard to secure the readmission of Louisiana, which had set up a government under the 10-percent plan—one which, as Louisiana governments go, was fairly decent. There was a knock-down-and-drag-out fight in Congress about this. Summer took the lead in blocking it with a kind of filibuster. Lincoln was balked. Where would he have gone from there? Nobody really knows. Sumner wrote a very significant letter to Francis Lieber while this controversy was going on, explaining how he had urged upon Lincoln "the duty of harmony between Congress and the Executive," and had proposed that Louisiana be admitted under its present government providing that Lincoln agree to a broad "Reconstruction Bill for all the other states, giving the electoral franchise to 'all citizens,' without distinction of color." Whether Lincoln really agreed to this we don't know, but in his last public address, four nights before he died, he said he had new plans in the making.

Almost certainly he would have tried to conciliate Sumner and Stevens. Whether he would have gone all the way to endorsing immediate universal suffrage I greatly doubt. Some historians, wishing to make Lincoln the father of the present civil rights movement, have decided that he was, deep down inside, in favor of immediately enfranchising the former slaves. More probably he would have backed some kind of qualified suffrage. He had already urged privately that Negroes who had served in the Union Army, and perhaps those who paid certain taxes or met certain educational requirements, be allowed to vote in the Southern states.

What, then, could Lincoln have expected the political future of the South to be? If I am right in thinking that he did not favor the massive enfranchisement of the freedmen, he must have known that political power in the South would remain in the hands of the whites. There was a clear danger that these states, once readmitted to the Union, would follow their former Confederate leaders, join hands with the Peace Democrats of the North, and sweep the Republicans from power. Yet Lincoln, an ardent Republican, did not favor massive disfranchisement of rebels in the conquered South. Since the President was an astute politician, I conclude that he must have had some strategy in mind to prevent the certain defeat of his own party, and watching what he did in the states where Reconstruction processes were begun, reading his letters carefully, remembering his pre-Civil War record, noticing how he operated politically in Washington, I think it likely that he may have hoped that the former Whigs of the South would provide a reliable Unionist element in the section. If Reconstruction put them into power, and if the Confederate leadership was discredited, and if *some* Negroes were enfranchised, a viable Republican organization in the South could be created to work with the Republicans of the North to prevent the restoration of Southern Democratic dominance.

J.A.G.   Isn't that what President Hayes tried to do in 1877?

D.D.   Well, that is what C. Vann Woodward argues Hayes' policy was, though I am obliged to say that little was done to implement it. To arrive at this policy required no great brilliance on Hayes' part, nor on Lincoln's. There were really only three possible Republican strategies toward the South, all of which were tried between 1865 and 1877. One was the politics of moderation that I think was Lincoln's and that Mr. Woodward says was Hayes', the hope that somehow or other by relatively moderate steps enough white loyal Unionism in the South could be developed so that the Republicans would gain control in that section. John Bingham of Ohio was the most articulate and intelligent spokesman for this point of view. The advocates of this policy tended to come more from the Middle West than from New England.

Another strategy was the policy of the Radicals, who hoped to disfranchise enough Confederates and enfranchise enough Negroes to give Republicans control of the South. The Radicals never entirely succeeded, but this was clearly a viable way of assuring Republican continuity in power.

The third strategy had mostly been neglected by historians until John and La Wanda Cox pointed out its significance. This was the policy that William H. Seward, the Secretary of State, and his close friend, Thurlow Weed, editor of the *Albany Evening Journal*, devised. In a certain sense it was the policy that President Andrew Johnson, in his bumbling way, tried to pursue. It stemmed from the creation in the North during the war of a Union party, composed of moderate Republicans and Democrats. (Remember that Lincoln in 1864 ran on the Union, not the Republican, ticket.) If this bipartisan coalition of the Center could be maintained after the war, both the Radical Republicans and the Peace Democrats would be politically impotent. As Southern states sought readmission to the Union, Seward thought that they would repudiate the Confederate leadership which had brought them only defeat, and would naturally gravitate toward this massive Union coalition.

J.A.G.   If Lincoln had lived, wouldn't his prestige, and the extraordinary quality of compassion which he showed toward the South, have made any of these strategies workable?

D.D.   Assuming that Lincoln would have rejected the Radical approach, the problem is what his effect would have been not on Southern but on Northern opinion. Neither the Bingham proposal nor the Seward proposal required any drastic social readjustments in the South beyond the abolition of slavery. Could Lincoln have sold either of these programs to the Northern population? I feel very sure that he couldn't have sold Seward's plan. Immediately after Appomattox, Northerners saw Southerners as enemies of civilization, people who had tortured Union soldiers, who had made drinking cups of the skulls of Union soldiers found on the battlefield. Whether he could have sold them on the middle-of-the-road position of Bingham I don't know. It would have been difficult, especially in view of the fact that a large element in his party was exceedingly articulate, vociferous, and pretty well organized against this very plan. If one had had some way of muzzling men like Salmon P. Chase, Charles Sumner, and Thaddeus Stevens, it might have been possible. These men had been sounding the alarm that freedom was in danger since the 1840's. They were not likely to relax and say that Lincoln could be trusted to settle the Southern question. Sumner, after all, fought the President to a standstill over Louisiana Reconstruction just a few weeks before his assassination.

J.A.G. Could we turn now to Andrew Johnson's approach to Reconstruction? Where did he go wrong? His administration was a disaster.

D.D. I consider Andrew Johnson one of the most baffling figures in American history. I don't understand him; I don't think anybody understands him. There was a curious opaque quality about the man. I'm always dubious about metaphors, but there are dark patches in the sky at night through which you can't see the stars which you know to be on the other side. Andrew Johnson was such a great opaque body, and nobody knows what went on within his mind. I try to read everything I can about Johnson (I'm now wading through his collected *Papers*), but I know almost nothing about his mental processes. You have to speculate about his motives, almost as wildly as if you saw an ant running across the ground in one direction rather than another direction and you tried to figure out what its purpose was. In other words, any statement about Johnson has to be viewed with a healthy skepticism.

What did he do that went so badly wrong? His weakness derived partly from his view of the constitutional limitations of his office. The only consistent thread I find in his writings is his feeling that the Constitution is a sacred document, the full, complete law, which must never be transcended. He shared none of Lincoln's views about loose construction of the Constitution. Yet many of Johnson's acts were at least as unconstitutional as Lincoln's. To appoint a provisional governor for North Carolina, or to demand that the conquered states ratify the Thirteenth Amendment were not powers conferred upon the President by the Constitution. Johnson seems to have thought of himself as acting in these cases under the war powers, which, like Lincoln, he construed broadly. Once the war was over, he thought that kind of exercise of power was illegal. This was unfortunate, for there were many things that Johnson could have done by public statements, by a little judicious pressure, by perhaps a shrewder use of patronage to influence Southern actions. For instance, he could have intervened to secure a more favorable consideration of the Fourteenth Amendment by the Southern states. They might not have adopted it under his pressure, but they wouldn't have turned it down virtually unanimously. Johnson tied his own hands by his strict interpretation of the Constitution.

A second source of Johnson's weakness was his personality. It is, of course, hard to evaluate this factor, for it is easy to fall into circular reasoning: a successful man is a man who has the kind of personality that makes him successful; since Johnson wasn't successful, therefore he had an unfortunate personality. But Johnson had undeniable weaknesses. He tended never openly to disagree, to argue face-to-face with those who held different views. When men said to him that the Southern whites were all disloyal and that the Negroes had to be given the vote, Johnson would sit impassively at his desk, not moving a muscle, and his interviewers left believing that he had agreed to their arguments. Sumner had such an interview; Chase had another. Such men, reporting that Johnson was on the Radical side, were not liars; they misinterpreted his silence.

Silent before his enemies, Johnson was incapable of confiding in his friends. In early 1866, there was a very real possibility that there could be a moderate substitute for the proposed Fourteenth Amendment that would have given certain basic guarantees of citizenship to Negroes but would not have disqualified the former Confederates. Such an amendment could have secured widespread support both in the North, which insisted upon protecting the freedmen, and in the South, which was reluctant to turn against its wartime leadership; it might have provided a viable platform for the political coalition Johnson wanted. Yet he did nothing at all to muster support for the proposal. Self-imposed constitutional restraints and his inability to deal with people on a personal level deprived him of many legitimate sources of power. By definition, his administration was bound to be a failure.

J.A.G.   What do you think of Eric McKitrick's analysis of Johnson as a perennial "outsider"?

D.D.   There is much to be said for McKitrick's judgment that Johnson—like almost every other human being—was his own worst enemy. But I don't agree with McKitrick's view that Johnson was a man who could be happy only on the minority side. After all, he had been Mayor of Greenville, Tennessee, a legislator in Tennessee, Governor of the state, a member of the House of Representatives, a Senator, and Vice President of the United States. I don't think of him as an outsider. He always worked within the established channels of political power.

J.A.G.   Would you define the term "Radical Republican"?

D.D.   This is surely the most obsessive quest among present-day Reconstruction historians. For many years it was assumed that there was a sizable group within the Republican party known as Radicals. Radicals were defined, first of all, in terms of their position on slavery during the war. They urged prompt, uncompensated emancipation. Radicals were also defined in terms of their views on Negro suffrage and economic and social change in the South after the war. To that conception of Radicalism there was added in the 1930's the thesis that behind these attitudes lay the political motive of securing Republican control of the federal government and an economic motive of aiding big business through high tariffs, hard money policies, and land grants to railroads.

The present generation of historians, re-examining this concept of Radicalism, has come up with a series of negatives. It is pretty clear now that one cannot make any close correlation between Republicans' economic views and their attitudes on emancipation, enfranchisement, disqualification of Confederates, or seizure of planter estates. There is no connection, for example, between the voting of senators on the Fifteenth Amendment, and on currency, banking, and tariff bills. Probably, most Radicals were pro-business in the sense that virtually all Americans always have been pro-business. Of course, these congressmen were concerned about keeping their party in power, but I suppose any politician is; so that doesn't tell us very much.

It's very hard even to say exactly who was a member of this Radical group. I'm reminded here of a doctoral oral exam at Columbia. Professor Allan Nevins asked a student, "Now, Mr. ———, do tell us who the Radicals were during Reconstruction." The student thought a minute, and said, "Well, there was Charles Sumner." Professor Nevins said, "Yes, and who else?" And the student said, "Well, there was Charles Sumner and . . ." "Yes," said Professor Nevins, "but who else?" After three more tries, finally Professor Nevins said, "Well, if you're only going to give the name of one Radical, you certainly have picked a good one."

There is a valid point to this story—namely, that when you get beyond Charles Sumner, Thaddeus Stevens, Ben Wade, Zack Chandler, and maybe about four others, your group tends to disappear. Aside from these implacables, congressmen were sometimes Radical and sometimes not. Take Lyman Trumbull, for instance, who was clearly a Radical in 1864–1866 in sponsoring the Freedmen's Bureau and advocating the Civil Rights bill but who by 1868 supported Johnson against impeachment and by 1872 voted for Horace Greeley.

The enormous changes in the membership of Congress with each election make identification of Radicals exceedingly difficult. As many as half the members of any House of Representatives might be freshmen. When half the people are constantly going out one door and half the people coming in another, it becomes difficult to talk of groups.

To add to the complexity of this problem, on certain issues there was very little division among Republicans of any persuasion. All agreed that the Republican party ought to be continued in power, that the Democrats were traitors and shouldn't be allowed to take over. All this is a very circuitous way of saying that it is hard to tell who a Radical was.

J.A.G.   Can one really say that a Radical Republican was a man who believed in Negro equality? The reason I ask is that the men you identify as clearly Radical—Sumner, certainly, and Stevens—believed in Negro equality. But while the Radical position was popular in the North, the mass of Northern voters did not favor a policy of Negro equality at all, in the North or the South.

D.D.   That is a very good observation. It is not fair to generalize from Sumner and Stevens, who had no racial prejudice at all, as to Radicals' attitudes toward the Negro. Probably more representative, at least of the Northwestern group of Radicals, was Ben Wade, who campaigned vigorously for Negro rights but wrote letters from Washington to his wife in Ohio explaining that he wished he could get away since Washington stank of "niggers." It used to be fashionable to say that men like Wade really didn't believe in humanitarian goals, that they defended Negro interests for political advantage. I don't think this is fair. It wasn't really to their advantage to adopt an extreme civil rights position. Indeed, Wade was defeated when he ran for re-election in 1868, partly because he had been too extreme for his constituents.

It remains curious, however, that a number of the most earnest Congressional advocates of Negro rights during the Reconstruction period had a marked aversion to the Negro race or, at best, had a very low opinion of its possibilities for social and intellectual progress. Two things may explain this. The most highly regarded scientists of the day, including Louis Agassiz, a man of international reputation, had decided that the Negro race was so inferior that it was probably not going to survive in freedom. Negroes ought to be protected during what one could think of as the "declining years" of their race.

J.A.G.   Wasn't he in fact an abolitionist before the Civil War?

D.D.   Yes, he was a genuine antislavery man. But rather like Theodore Parker, he thought that the Negroes were going to die off.

Another explanation of racist Radicals is that they were fighting for the removal of the stigma of race from the statute books. Like many civil rights advocates today, they were not operating under any illusion that striking down legal discrimination would necessarily make whites and blacks equal in all respects. But I think that they were genuinely concerned with removing legal disabilities of the freedmen simply as a disinterested act of justice. I don't think that they were using this issue for political advantage.

J.A.G. Just how important were these Radicals in determining the course of Reconstruction?

D.D. I do not think that the Radical faction in Congress ever dominated legislative proceedings. The program of Reconstruction that is commonly called Radical Reconstruction was not a triumph of Radicalism at all. I know that what I am saying runs contrary to accepted views of Reconstruction. We normally talk about Presidential Reconstruction while the Radicals were gathering their forces; and beginning with the Reconstruction Act of 1867, which divided the South into five military districts, we speak of Radical Reconstruction. Yet, when you look at the major legislative decisions of 1867–75, the striking fact is that the people that we can truly identify as Radicals never got their way. The Military Reconstruction Act of 1867, which set the whole pattern of subsequent actions, was not what the Radicals wanted; it was not what Thaddeus Stevens desired, and Charles Sumner fought it bitterly. It was a law much more congenial to John Bingham and to John Sherman. The Fifteenth Amendment was not a Radical act. The Radicals wanted to say that all Negroes should have the vote. As finally adopted, the Amendment said that no state should deprive any citizen of the right to vote because of race, color, or previous condition of servitude. This left loopholes; it was constitutional to deprive people of the vote because of lack of literacy or education. The Civil Rights Act of 1875, enacted as a memorial to Charles Sumner, was gutted before it was passed. Sumner wished strongly that the Act include a prohibition against segregated schools. This was dropped; there is no mention of schools in the Civil Rights Act of 1875. There was, therefore, no Radical Reconstruction in the commonly accepted sense. All major pieces of legislation of the period were much nearer to the Moderate position than the Radical.

J.A.G. Did Southern whites make a serious effort to reconstruct their society after the Civil War in the light of the Thirteenth Amendment?

D.D. I think very few did. The Amendment, after all, simply ratified wartime changes, and Southerners didn't think of it as requiring a drastic redesigning of society. This is what causes me to be seriously troubled by Eric McKitrick's view that, with proper leadership right after the Civil War, there could have been a North-South understanding. Southerners felt they had been asked to make the ultimate concession in freeing the slaves. Almost nobody was prepared to go any further.

J.A.G. Didn't intelligent Southerners see the need to make social adjustments after eliminating slavery?

D.D. These could be taken care of relatively easily, they believed. They expected to do way with the term "slavery" (the word, the legal language) but to keep the Negroes on the same plantations, doing the same kind of work. There is not much evidence that many white Southerners thought that they must construct a new social and economic order.

J.A.G.   Suppose I ask the same question this way. If one begins with the assumption that the Southerners accepted the Thirteenth Amendment, and if it's generally agreed that few Southerners wanted Negro equality, was there no new position at all? Didn't anyone want to do something about Negro education, about legalizing Negro marriages and so on? It would seem to me that even from the point of view of the white majority there would be need for social change without regard to whether they were ready to go all the way to equality.

D.D.   That is correct in the sense that certain kinds of institutional controls which had hitherto been exercised by slaveowners now were exercised by state or local government. For this purpose, the governments that Johnson set up promptly enacted the Black Codes regulating the condition of the freedmen. From the Southern point of view, the laws were extremely generous. They recognized that slaves were free, that they were human beings. But they assumed that, since blacks were not considered to be anywhere near equal to whites, they had to be regulated closely. For instance, Negroes couldn't engage in certain kinds of businesses; they couldn't buy or carry firearms; they might be forced to work under compulsion.

J.A.G.   There was no interest among white Southerners in educating the Negro?

D.D.   Not very much. There was, of course, a great interest on the part of Northerners. Quite a number of them, including my own grandfather, came down feeling very strongly that these new citizens somehow or other had to be trained to be efficient members of the body politic. These newcomers from the North were savagely abused; some were tarred and feathered and driven out by the whites. The idea of teaching reading, writing, and arithmetic to Negroes seemed to most white Southerners like educating cows or horses.

J.A.G.   What can be said about the hopes and the demands of the Negroes themselves?

D.D.   We know all too little about what the Negroes wanted. It's always a difficult historical question—what did the inarticulate masses think? Most Negroes were illiterate. Few kept written records, diaries, or letters. Few edited newspapers or made speeches in Congress. Yet we do have records that are exceedingly revealing. The voluminous Freedmen's Bureau papers in the National Archives are one of the most important sources in Negro history—not the papers of the head of the Bureau and his chief agents, but those of the agents in the field, in Huntsville, Alabama, and Lynchburg, Virginia, and so on. These people wrote about conditions in their areas. Their papers show that most Negroes in the South knew about emancipation well before 1865, and that almost immediately they exhibited an earnest desire for two things— land of their own and education.

Their desire for education was one of the most remarkable and touching aspects of the whole Reconstruction period. It shows, I think, that the Negro was basically trying to assimilate white middle-class values. Not merely did young children flock to the schools of the Freedmen's Bureau and the missionary societies, but adults, after a day's work in the fields, used to get the primer and, sitting on the split log at the back of the school, slowly decipher "A, B; A, B, C. . . ." Negroes made very great progress in literacy during this time, though we don't have any reliable statistical measure.

The desire for land was equally strong, and it too shows something about the bourgeois values that Negro slaves had assimilated. Theirs may have been a singularly inappropriate aspiration. Southern agriculture was primarily big-plantation agriculture; it often was not for small farmers. One might make a living from forty acres of cotton, although, except with care and fertilization, the soil would be exhausted very soon. But forty acres of tobacco was not a viable unit because the crop so rapidly wore out the land, and forty acres of sugar cane would be impossible from the outset.

How much more Negroes wanted is hard to say. There is very little evidence that many were talking in 1865–66 of political equality or the franchise, and even less that many sought social equality—mixed schools, desegregated public transportation facilities, and the like. But there occurred a significant transformation of the Negro community during the early years of Reconstruction. We are just beginning to study the emergence of a very tentative class structure within the Negro population of the South. One of the first things that had to be done was to form the basic social group, the family. Negroes had not been legally married under slavery. Now they had to be, and sometimes there were difficult problems. What did a man do who had a common-law wife and family on Mr. Jones's plantation, but who had been sold off to Mr. Smith's plantation where he acquired another wife and family? Despite the problems, there was an immediate rush to have these common-law marriages legalized.

J.A.G.   Did the pressure for this come from the Negroes?

D.D.   Very much from the Negroes themselves, though doubtless white missionaries and agents of the Freedmen's Bureau used moral suasion. There was also a rush in 1865 to demonstrate physical mobility, in many cases just to see that they did have freedom enough to get off the plantation.

During this hubbub there gradually emerged Negro leaders. We don't know enough about these yet, but relatively few had been free Negroes in the South during the ante-bellum period. Before 1865, free Negroes were a degraded caste in the South, despised by both the slave and the white man. On the other hand, free Negroes who had gone North before the war often came back during the Reconstruction period as "black carpetbaggers" and became leaders.

There was also a growing leadership from within the former slave community, and while we don't know enough about this development, the key, I'm convinced, lies in the Negro churches. Before the Civil War it had been customary to have Negroes and whites in the same church, the Negroes sitting up in the balcony or in the side pews. Now separate Negro churches were formed. A number of Negro political leaders emerged from this religious separatism. Negro preachers had a degree of autonomy that perhaps in Southern Negro communities today is equaled only by the keepers of undertaking establishments. (A significant number of recent Southern civil rights leaders have been morticians.)

There is growing evidence of what one can properly call Radicalism among Negro leaders around 1870. In the 1868 constitutional conventions, Negroes were still on their best behavior, deploring the disfranchisement of ex-Confederates and denying any aspiration for social equality. But later, Negro leaders voiced different attitudes as they engaged in fierce rivalry for political office. By the early 1870's they had had a good deal of experience. They knew where the power, prestige, and money was, and saw no reason why they should be excluded from important offices. As they demanded their share, they increasingly alienated Southern whites, and Northerners too, who had hitherto been using them and were now being pushed aside.

But they did not just demand offices. They asked for certain social changes as well. By the 1870's there were Negroes who protested that it was preposterous for blacks to be thrown off decent railroad cars, while any drunken, ignorant white would be accommodated. There was also a growing demand for integrated schools. From the white point of view, the most dangerous of the Negroes' demands was for a restructuring of the tax system. The question of where the tax burden was going to lie was, in my opinion, the key question in the latter phase of Reconstruction. If there was a heavy tax on land, the white planter might very well find himself in grave difficulties. In the Mississippi Delta, half of the entire land was forfeited for taxes by 1875. Many of the big planters in the Mississippi Delta, who up to that time had been cooperating with the Republicans, thinking, "We don't really care if Negroes vote; we can control them," now suddenly discovered that they had strong racial feelings.

J.A.G. What happened to the land that was forfeited for taxes? Who got it?

D.D. This is a very interesting and quite complicated story. If the land had been divided up in some fashion, the revolution that the Radicals wanted might have occurred, though much of it wasn't land that could have been profitably farmed in small units. But when the conservative state government took over under what is called "home rule," there was a kind of mass forgiveness for most overdue taxes. Other lands that were forfeited were snapped up by speculators.

J.A.G. I'm not quite clear about the implications of your answer. Are you saying that because of Negro political influence the state undertook certain social functions—education, for example—and financed them by putting the burden on landowners? That either the landholder paid the price or, if he was bankrupted by the taxation, the capital for these social improvements came from outside the South in the form of land purchases by railroad interests, or English capitalists, or Northern investors? Does this mean that under governments where Negroes had influence there was an infusion of new capital from outside the South paid for in land?

D.D. Yes, though with some modifications. The amount of capital from outside the South invested in land before 1877 was not great. Much land was about to be forfeited just at the time when these governments were overthrown. When the new conservative Bourbon regimes were established in the South, they "forgave" the debts. Really massive sales of lands in the South, therefore, did not take place.

The significant point, however, is that by the 1870's some Negroes were beginning to see that the budgets of state and local governments could be used as instruments of social change in the South. It is easy to recognize that through the expenditure of its funds a government can choose to favor one group rather than another. Thus the Southern states before the war had expended all their small budget for education to benefit whites; after 1868 tax money went also to Negro schools. We sometimes forget, however, that in selecting the sources of its income a government also has a powerful weapon to alter social structure. To be sure, in the postwar South there were not many sources of revenue; with little commerce or industry, the region could only raise money by taxing its land or its people. The whole subject awaits further study, but it seems clear that Negro leaders by about 1870 strongly opposed poll taxes and favored property taxes. There is also evidence to show that they wanted lighter taxes on small farms and homesteads, which blacks occupied, and heavier taxes on the large plantations, owned by whites.

In a quiet and perhaps not altogether conscious way, then, Southern Negroes were by the 1870's moving to secure for themselves what Radicals like Sumner and Stevens had earlier planned, a reorganization of the economic basis of Southern society. The methods they used were not revolutionary, but if they had been continued for several decades, the results might have been.

J.A.G.   Is there any connection between this Negro economic pressure and the almost coincidental lessening of Northern pressure to make white Southerners conform to the Radicals' conception of what the South should be like?

D.D.   I think so, though this is not easy to trace. Some Northerners voiced complaints about "confiscatory" taxation. But indirect expressions of sympathy were more common, as when the Northern reporter James S. Pike wrote his series of articles, describing South Carolina as "the prostrate state," run by Negroes whom he described as resembling apes and baboons, uncivilized creatures who were squandering the resources of the state.

J.A.G.   Would you comment generally on the character of Negro governments in the South?

D.D.   The first thing to say is that there weren't any Negro governments in the South. In no case was a state controlled by Negroes. There were no Negro governors, though Negroes served as lieutenant governors in Louisiana, Mississippi, and South Carolina. Only in South Carolina was there a Negro justice of the supreme court. Only in South Carolina did blacks dominate both houses of the legislature, and even there their control was short-lived. During the entire Reconstruction period, from the entire South, only two Negroes were elected to the United States Senate, only fifteen to the House of Representatives.

J.A.G.   But isn't that rather a quibble or a contradiction? You've just been arguing very persuasively that Negroes were exercising political power by shaping the tax structure in a way that could have had revolutionary social and economic effects.

D.D.   The emergence of a new kind of Negro political leadership was just beginning to be a threat. At no point were Negroes really able to dominate the governments. I was projecting a trend. Had Reconstruction continued, had federal troops continued to support the regimes, one might have had by 1880 not necessarily an all-black government, but a government that was dominated by the new Negro leadership.

But getting back to the Negro politicans and leaders, they were a mixed bag like any politicians at any time. There were no men of towering accomplishments, and there were many of rather mediocre abilities, but there were also some men of considerable distinction. Take, for example, Hiram Revels of Mississippi, the first Negro Senator, who sat, ironically enough, in the seat vacated by Jefferson Davis. He was a man of moderate ability but nonetheless of solid competence. Blanche K.

Bruce of Mississippi, the other Negro United States Senator, was an effective speaker and a skilled politician, well thought of by the white community as well as by Negroes. His record as Senator was respectable if not better.

If you move down the scale from these national figures, you have to deal with virtually anonymous people. But this was not because they were Negroes but because of the nature of the political offices they held. Who knows now, for example, who his local justice of the peace is or who represents him in the city council or state legislature? And the same was true in the 1870's. A survey made by Vernon Wharton of officeholders in Mississippi shows that the Negro sheriffs were on the whole about like their white counterparts, of about average respectability, competence, and honesty.

We must recognize, though, that there were scoundrels among Negro officeholders—just as there were, and are, scoundrels among white officeholders. I think it's safe to say that anybody in Louisiana politics at that time was probably corrupt. Anybody who had anything to do with the government of Vicksburg, Mississippi, whether white, black, mulatto, or Indian, was almost assuredly corrupt. The machine that the black Republicans established in Savannah, Georgia, would have made New York's Boss Tweed blush with shame.

J.A.G. Were the South's economic problems really ones of reconstruction, that is, of repairing the damage that the war had done?

D.D. This is an exceedingly interesting question. Not long ago, John Kenneth Galbraith, in one of those brief, brilliant essays of his, pointed out that the collapse of Southern finances during the Confederacy period was an index not just of poor fiscal management but of the general economic weakness of the area. He may very well be right, and it follows that the economic difficulties of the postwar South were not so much the product of Reconstruction or even of the Civil War, but of the prewar system. Exactly how to factor out these elements when dealing with the economic rebuilding of the South, I don't know. What limitations on Southern economic growth should be attributed to the antebellum period, what to the destruction wrought by the war, what to the social unrest of Reconstruction? These are very difficult things to separate.

J.A.G. Even assuming that there were inadequacies in the economic organization of the South up to 1860, I'm troubled by the fact that it took at least twenty years after the war for the South to get back to where it had been in 1860. How can that be explained?

D.D. Probably, plantation slavery was a more efficient labor system than sharecropping and renting. But sharecropping was the favored labor system in the postwar period.

J.A.G.   Why was it preferred?

D.D.   With freedom came the problem of how labor was to be paid. One answer, of course, was to pay wages. But the planters had little cash. To pay wages to a sizable labor force for an entire year until the crop was sold was too much of a drain. Moreover, the Negroes, after the first few months, displayed a remarkable hostility to the wage system, which they felt made them totally at the disposal of the man who was hiring them. Wage labor, therefore, became increasingly rare.

Two other forms became more acceptable, renting and sharecropping. Under rental, the Negro tilled the land for a season, and out of the proceeds paid a fixed amount to the owner. Under sharecropping arrangements, the owner provided the tools, the mules, the seed, and perhaps the fertilizer. He received perhaps half of the total crop and the cropper the rest. The actual shares varied considerably. Usually Negroes preferred to rent, because that system gave them greater control over the land and their own labor. Planters mostly preferred the sharecropping system because it allowed them to dictate what should be planted and where. Of course, the planter usually won out. He had the economic resources and the Negro hadn't.

I suspect that sharecropping was less efficient than the gang labor of slavery days. To a degree, the sharecropper was master of his own time. Of course he had to produce something or he wouldn't be a sharecropper the next year, but he now had bourgeois aspirations. He thought that his wife should not have to work in the fields day in and day out; he wanted his children to go to school; he felt he ought to have a weekly day of rest, even a vacation. The number of days that he and his family actually spent in the field was probably less than under slavery. Moreover, the driver or the overseer no longer threatened him. The owner might come out once or twice a day, and say, "Sam, you're not making much headway; you'd better get that grass out before the rains come." But once the owner turned his back the cropper could slow down if he wanted to. I believe that not until the 1880's was the *individual* record for cotton picking as high as it had been before the war. And not until 1879 did the total production of cotton reach the pre-Civil War level.

J.A.G.   You would argue, I gather, that the sharecropping system was pretty reasonable, given the attitudes of the white majority and the educational and social status of the Negro.

D.D.   I think so. The real problem was not so much sharecropping, but two other developments that coincided with it. One was the depression of the 1870's. Sharecropping in a time of prosperity might conceivably have produced savings, so that some families could have scraped together enough to put a down payment on a little farm of their own. Simultaneously, it was an era when the government was backing away from direct intervention in the economy. If the government had been willing to guarantee or underwrite mortgages, it might have been possible to inject some mobility into the sharecropping system. But government negativism plus depression constructed a box from which there was no exit.

J.A.G. Is that entirely true? Didn't some Negroes make their way from sharecropping to independent land ownership?

D.D. Of course some did. This is roughly like saying, however, that there were Negroes who made their way out of slavery in the ante-bellum period. They were so rare that they are decidedly atypical. In 1880, between 1 and 5 percent of the land in the various Southern states was owned by Negroes, but the Negroes constituted as much as half of the population in some of these states. The few Negroes who did become property owners, moreover, often could afford to buy land of only marginal worth. A student of mine has made a study of one of the parishes of Louisiana from 1860 to 1880. Negroes purchase sizable tracts of land, but most of their holdings were cut-over pine barrens in the hills, land so poor that no white man really wanted it.

J.A.G. We have been talking for some time about Southern social and economic developments. Earlier, you stated that you thought of the Reconstruction era in national terms. How are these changes in the South related to broader national changes?

D.D. This is one of the most difficult problems confronting the historian of Reconstruction, and it may explain why no fully satisfactory general history of the era has yet been written. Of course, when one is dealing with Congressional legislation concerning the South and the freedmen, there is a direct connection with events in the South. But many of the most pressing national issues of the period seem very loosely related to changes in the South. Take, for instance, the resumption of specie payments, the subject of protracted debate in Congress and throughout the North. One would think that we should be able to find some connection between a congressman's views on this question and his attitudes toward the South, but, as Irwin Unger's careful study, *The Greenback Era*, has demonstrated, there is little significant relationship between the two. It is as though one were dealing with entirely separate sets of variables. Foreign policy issues of the Reconstruction period seem similarly unrelated to the Southern developments we have been discussing.

J.A.G. Do you think that this is the most serious difficulty confronting the historian who tries to write a comprehensive account of the Reconstruction era?

D.D. Yes, though there is one other almost equally difficult. Being of a liberal persuasion, most recent historians have tended to look favorably upon Republican efforts in the South in behalf of the Negro. They are disposed to praise, sometimes to overpraise, the achievements of the carpetbag-scalawag-Negro regimes and to minimize their failings. The same historians, however, tend to deplore most other Republican actions —the looting of the public lands, the handouts to railroads, the protective tariffs, the financial policies that benefited creditors, and the like. The historian of the Reconstruction period may find himself split: he favors Republican Radicalism in the South but opposes it in the North.

J.A.G.   Why did the federal government eventually give up trying to "Reconstruct" the South?

D.D.   Simply because it found the task impossible. By 1876, the North had tried to reshape the South by cajolery, by conciliation, and by coercion. Nothing seemed to work. After nearly a decade, most Southern whites seemed unrepentant. Though there were a good number of scalawags, Southern white Unionists had never emerged in the numbers that Republican moderates had anticipated, and by the mid-70's they were fleeing from the Republican party as Negroes began to play a more powerful role. Though Southern blacks had made some progress, they seemed unable to hold their own, either politically or economically, without support from the federal Army; but, given that support, they were beginning to raise dangerous questions about the distribution of property and about racial segregation, questions that as yet applied largely to the South but might soon have serious implications for Northerners.

Earlier, Radical Republicans might have welcomed these developments as a challenge to promote further change in the South, but by 1876 most of the great Radical leaders had died or had disappeared from the Washington scene. The new Republican politicians were not, for the most part, veterans of the antislavery crusade, and they did not have the same moral stake in protecting the rights of Negroes. Whatever their personal wishes, moreover, they did not have the power long to continue unpopular and expensive programs for reorganizing the South. The Democratic party was resurgent. In 1874, it elected a majority of the members of the House of Representatives; and in 1876 it nearly elected a President.

J.A.G.   What is the significance of President Hayes' withdrawal of the troops? We know that very few troops were really involved.

D.D.   I think it was symbolically important. Only a handful of troops were involved, but their presence signified to Southern whites that the federal government still kept an eye on their doings. In withdrawing those troops Hayes was saying, "From now on, you white people in the South run things in your own way."

J.A.G.   In connection with the compromise of 1876–77, would you comment on the complex explanation of this settlement advanced by the historian C. Vann Woodward in his book *Reunion and Reaction*.

D.D. This is a very important and suggestive book. Woodward attacked the traditional view that the disputed election was a political and constitutional issue settled by a compromise at the Wormley Hotel in Washington between representatives of the Republican candidate for President, Rutherford B. Hayes, and Southern Democrats. If the Southerners permitted Hayes to be counted in as President, the Republicans promised to withdraw the remaining federal troops from the South.

Woodward suggested that this agreement had little importance and that the real settlement involved complex political and economic maneuvers. The political maneuvers had to do with the desire of moderates in the Republican party to build an alliance with conservatives in the South. The hope, as we said earlier, was to reconstitute a North-South coalition like the old Whig party. Behind these political plans, Woodward argues, were powerful economic interests concerned with internal improvements, and especially with building a transcontinental railroad across the South through Texas. This group very badly needed federal appropriations. There was, according to Woodward, a converging of interests—Northern and Southern businessmen, Northern and Southern politicians. They proposed an elaborate solution to the disputed election crisis. On the political level, Hayes was to be installed as President. James A. Garfield was to become the Speaker of the House of Representatives, but a Southerner was to become the Postmaster General, with all the patronage at the disposal of that office. Other appointments in the South were to go to anti-Radical Southern whites. The implication, not clearly spelled out, was that racial matters would be in the hands of white Southerners. On the economic level, Hayes' administration would support legislation for clearing rivers, constructing levees, and building railroads—including the Texas & Pacific.

Woodward is at his best in tracing these very complicated behind-the-scene intrigues. He argues that the Wormley Hotel agreement was a face-saving device. Southern congressmen couldn't go home and explain that they had agreed to let a Republican be counted in as President in return for promises of patronage or pledges to help the Texas & Pacific Railroad. The Wormley conference permitted them to tell their constituents that they had accepted Hayes' election in order to secure "home rule."

Now, *Reunion and Reaction* is an interesting and stimulating book, but I have some fundamental disagreements with it. First of all, it is based on a misconception about the nature of American politics, for it assumes a class, or at least an economic, basis for our major parties. Woodward holds that in the ante-bellum period the distinction between

Whig and Democrat had been not merely a party distinction but a class distinction, that the Whigs were the party of business, the Democrats the party of the people. This view of pre-Civil War history is one that has been discredited by numerous recent studies. Secondly, Woodward's thesis is based upon a misreading of subsequent history. The striking fact is that the bargains which he so elaborately traces were not carried out. It is true, of course, that the Democrats by discontinuing their filibuster allowed the Electoral Commission to choose Hayes as President, but Southerners did not permit Garfield to become Speaker. It is true, too, that Hayes appointed David Key, a Southerner and an ex-Confederate, to his cabinet, but little patronage went to white Southerners and no Republican party was built around those appointments in the South. The economic favors promised to the South never materialized. Not even the Texas & Pacific got its land grant. Southern promises to protect Negro rights were never kept.

In attacking the older view about the Wormley conference, Mr. Woodward speaks of that alleged agreement as constituting one of the strangest bargains in history, because, he says, Southern Democrats traded something they had already agreed to (readiness to allow Hayes to be inaugurated) in return for something they had already received (Hayes' repeated pledges to permit "home rule" in the South). I would say, in turn, that the bargains which Mr. Woodward has traced are surely even more curious, because they were all systematically broken by all parties concerned.

Now this is not to say that I think *Reunion and Reaction* is a poor book. I think it is a very important one. It shows that in the political maneuvers of this time many different things were going on simultaneously, sometimes at cross-purposes, sometimes together. But it is not possible to show that most of these maneuvers actually affected the outcome of the election dispute. The rivalry between Collis P. Huntington and Thomas Scott over the construction of a Southern transcontinental railroad is certainly interesting, as is Scott's demand for federal subsidies in order to build his road. Mr. Woodward has not, however, been able to make a direct connection between this rivalry and these demands with the voting in Congress. Without such a demonstrated connection, much of the behind-the-scenes maneuvering which he so effectively traces is simply irrelevant.

I tend to think that Woodward dismisses rather too easily the Wormley Hotel bargain. It was a very real bargain in the sense that both parties had something to bargain with. The Southern congressmen could have held up the work of the commission by filibustering so that there would have been no declared President by March 4. Hayes also had something at his disposal, for, even without a Congressional appropriation, he could very well have kept the troops in the South. I am rather more in sympathy with traditional accounts of this disputed election than otherwise.

J.A.G.   Is it possible to say who was really "elected" in 1876?

D.D.   No, it is not possible, because one has to ask not merely what votes were cast but also what votes were not cast. If there had been no intimidation, if all voters in the United States had been allowed to vote, almost assuredly Hayes would have been elected, because the Negroes in the South would have voted Republican. If, on the other hand, we assume that only those votes which were cast ought to be counted, Tilden clearly had a majority.

J.A.G.   Would it have been possible to appoint a commission that would have decided any way except on purely partisan terms? Did the Democrats yield on the Presidency because they had more to gain by yielding than the Republicans would have?

D.D.   It was the Southern Democrats who were prepared to yield. They were the ones, after all, who knew what civil strife was all about, they weren't going to be caught in another civil war if they could help it. And yet it's quite possible that there could have been shifts the other way. There is some evidence, for example, that Senator Roscoe Conkling of New York, who disliked Hayes, would not have been altogether unhappy if there had been a Democratic President. But who can say that it really would have made any significant difference, Hayes or Tilden? We're now getting into that group of Presidents who are like Tweedledum and Tweedledee, except that one had a beard and one didn't.

J.A.G.   What is your view of the so-called "New Left" interpretation of the Reconstruction period?

D.D.   The New Left hasn't written much specifically about Reconstruction. Historians of the New Left in a certain sense are inhibited in writing about the subject. The people they most criticize, the historians of consensus, have pretty much the same attitudes on racial issues as the New Leftists. I don't think that they have added significantly to our knowledge of the period.

J.A.G.   What about the current concern for the need to rewrite American history, paying proper attention to the contribution that the Negro has made to American development? Do you think that this trend will affect the writing of the history of Reconstruction?

D.D.   I hope that it will. This was a time when Negroes played a very active and innovative role in American society. The Reconstruction period is something of which Negroes can, on the whole, be proud. This is not to say that the record is an unblemished one; there were tawdry and tarnished Negro as well as white leaders. But there were important black men during these years, men of considerable achievement. If this new interest only produces a "black icing" on American history, a listing of names of assorted lieutenant governors and state librarians to be trotted out as heroes, I don't think we will get very far. If the concern leads to an investigation of *types* of Negro leadership, of directions in which the Negro was going by the end of Reconstruction, of the social patterns emerging among Negroes, of ideas and ideologies, the work could be very profitable.

J.A.G.   What are the major unanswered questions about Reconstruction?

D.D.   Surely, one of the major problems is how to determine the ideas, attitudes, interests, and actions of the Negroes. This was a largely inarticulate group, and in dealing with it the historian must face all the problems that arise in studying any group that has left few written records. What we can say is going to have to be based on inference. From actions we are going to have to judge motives; from statistical data on migrations we are going to have to speculate on why such actions occurred. Yet I think a lot can be done in this direction.

A second need is a careful political history of the Reconstruction period, especially after 1867. Very few historians have ever actually read through the proceedings of Congress during this period. There is no book analyzing what went on in Congress after 1867. The *Congressional Globe*, which became in 1873 the *Congressional Record*, is a source that historians have quoted, but they rarely have systematically studied it. We need also many more biographies dealing with this period, especially a life of Ulysses S. Grant that covers his Presidency in adequate detail.

On a very different level, we need more exploration of the intellectual history of the period—the kind of study that has largely been neglected since Paul Buck's *Road to Reunion*. George Frederickson's *The Inner Civil War* provides a model of the kind of intellectual history that would be exceedingly valuable.

Finally, I should like somebody to do a really magisterial study of the constitutional problems of the Reconstruction period, a work comparable to J. G. Randall's *Constitutional Problems Under Lincoln*.

J.A.G.   What are the half-dozen books that you would recommend to persons interested in the subject we have been discussing? In each case, please indicate what its particular contribution is.

D.D.   It is hard to select so few titles from a body of historical literature that is so rich and in many cases so rewarding to the reader. The most comprehensive bibliography of that literature is contained in J. G. Randall and David Donald, *The Civil War and Reconstruction* (second edition, revised; 1969). But here are my six choices.

1. William A. Dunning, *Reconstruction, Political and Economic, 1865–*

1877 (1907). Though old, this is a comprehensive survey by a master historian. Dunning's biases in favor of the South and against the Negro are here muted, as he places Reconstruction in a national setting.

2. Kenneth M. Stampp, *The Era of Reconstruction, 1865–1877* (1965). This is the most successful synthesis of Revisionist scholarship, friendly to the Radical Republicans and favorable to the Negroes.

3. W. E. B. DuBois, *Black Reconstruction: An Essay toward a History of the Part which Black Folk Played in the Attempt to Reconstruct Democracy in America, 1860–1880* (1935). Massive and discursive, marred by a quasi-Marxist bias, DuBois' book is nevertheless valuable because it points out the achievements of Negroes during Reconstruction and suggests important class relationships among planters, poor whites, and blacks in the South.

4. Howard K. Beale, *The Critical Year: A Study of Andrew Johnson and Reconstruction* (1930). Though severely criticized by later scholars, Beale's work remains a landmark, important both for its rehabilitation of Andrew Johnson and for its discussion of the economic motives of Radical Republicans.

5. Eric L. McKitrick, *Andrew Johnson and Reconstruction* (1960). Along with W. A. Brock's *An American Crisis* (1963) and *Politics, Principle, and Prejudice* (1963), McKitrick's study challenges all of Beale's arguments; it is, in addition, an interesting attempt to apply the insights of the related social-science disciplines to a historical problem.

6. Paul H. Buck, *The Road to Reunion, 1865–1900* (1937). Buck's book remains one of the few studies which, minimizing the political, stresses the intellectual and economic aspects of the period.

Part II

Edward C. Kirkland

Economic Growth and Change: 1865–1890

Mₒₐₑ than a decade ago, Edward C. Kirkland
retired from his position as Professor of History at Bowdoin
College, but he remains one of the most active and forward-looking scholars in the field of American economic
history. His *Industry Comes of Age* (1961) is a brilliant
synthesis of an enormous mass of scholarly research on
late-nineteenth century developments. Since his retirement, he has written a life of Charles Francis Adams, Jr.,
The Patrician at Bay (1965), an important study of business attitudes, *Dream and Thought in the Business Community: 1860–1900* (1956), and has just published a new
revision of his popular economic history textbook, *A
History of American Economic Life* (1969). Of his earlier
productions the most important is *Men, Cities, and Transportation: A Study in New England History, 1820–1900*
(1948). Professor Kirkland is a former President of the
American Association of University Professors, of the Economic History Association, and of the Mississippi Valley
Historical Association, being, as he likes to point out, "the
first easterner to hold the last job." In the following discussion he comments on the changing character of the
American economy between the Civil War and the depression of the 1890's.

John A. Garraty Professor Kirkland, it is an historical truism that the last third of the nineteenth century in the United States was a period of enormous economic growth. How fast, actually, did the economy expand compared with the rate of expansion in earlier times? Could you compare it with pre-Civil War growth, then with growth from 1900 to, say, World War II, and also from the end of World War II to the present?

Edward C. Kirkland Well, this depends on how you measure growth. There has been a very considerable effort made to find a standard that new, old, and decrepit historians can use, and much to my delight they seem to have settled upon what they call Gross National Product. The statisticians don't agree that it's a good measure, but it is something like a population figure—you can use it for purposes of comparison. Gross National Product is the value of all goods and services produced in a given year. It also has a certain vogue because of its chauvinistic advantages. You can compare our Gross National Product with other people's Gross National Product, particularly that of the Russians, and show how we're falling behind the Russians, and all the dominoes are going to fall down somewhere in worship at the shrine of a higher Gross National Product.

Then, also, it's highly useful in measurement for countries that are in the course of development to know whether they are becoming "modern," which is to say industrial and capitalistic. Gross National Product is something that you can put down on a position paper and say: "This country is getting ahead. It's attained a Gross National Product of a certain amount." And then you can compare it with other developing countries. I think these are the reasons for the vogue of the Gross National Product, aside from the fact that it's convenient to have a single standard.

On this basis, the last two decades of the nineteenth century represented a very great forward spurt in American economic history. It might be said also that there was a very great forward spurt just before the American Civil War. Of course, you can always get ahead faster when you start from nothing up to something, than if you start from something up to something else.

So Gross National Product was very rapid in the late nineteenth century and even in the middle nineteenth century. To be meaningful, the Gross National Product should, statisticians seem to feel, be reduced to dollars of constant value in order to do away with changes in valuation due to the rise and fall in the value of the dollar. On this basis, the Gross National Product on a quinquennial basis had a great forward spurt from 1874 to 1893, and another from the late 90's down to about 1908. There was kind of a plateau in the first part of the twentieth century, then a spurt in the 1920's. Most people think of the 20's as a period of pre-

Depression (the period of prohibition, the period when every policy was wrong, every act wrong, and every businessman a crook), but the Gross National Product grew very fast in that decade. Then with the Depression, it sank sharply, but revived spectacularly after World War II. Generally speaking, from about the middle of the nineteenth century to the middle of this century, Gross National Product grew at a rate perhaps never equaled over such an extended period in any country.

J.A.G. Could you describe the reasons for the economic expansion of the period from 1870 to the end of the century?

E.C.K. The cautious answer, and therefore probably the sound one, is, It was a mix. One reason was, of course, as contemporaries put it, that our national problems had been settled; they were out of the way. The nature of our government has been determined; this is a way of referring to the Civil War. And so the field was clear for rapid economic expansion.

The growth of the railroad system in the 1850's was a precondition for this growth. Another reason was the ingenuity and facility that people developed for dealing in larger sums of money, and making more lavish use of credit than they had in a more austere, agricultural civilization. The Civil War cost a lot of money. It was raised in part by selling government securities, and this accustomed the people to a larger and different way of saving and investment. The prospects were glorious. There was adequate population, and by this time a population considerably trained in the mechanical-industrial disciplines. As the growth continued in the late nineteenth century, the populations of Europe were displaced by the attractiveness of American opportunities, and the number of immigrants greatly expanded. The mid-1880's were the peak of immigration until the twentieth century.

J.A.G. How do you feel about the argument—which does seem to be reinforced by statistics—that immigration is a result, rather than a cause, of economic growth? Did the economy grow because large numbers of Europeans were displaced and came here looking for a chance to work, or did the expansive situation in America attract them?

E.C.K. Of course the answer is both, because individuals are more than workers. We're apt, I think, to forget that individuals constitute a market, and in that sense the sheer arrival of people who've got to be fed and who've got to be housed, who've got to be settled somewhere, is an expansive factor, regardless of their labor contributions.

J.A.G. Is it possible to make any generalization about immigrants as a source of capital? We think of immigrants in general as being poor. But when one considers the large numbers who came in the 1880's, for example, do you think that the money that they brought with them amounted collectively to enough to have a stimulating effect on the economy?

E.C.K. It was a factor, but I should think proportionately in this period a minor factor. Certainly it was a very important factor, say, in the colonial period. The Puritans, for example, brought money with them, some of them a good deal of money, and it had an expansive impact at a time when the impact really counted.

There are statistics on how much each immigrant probably brought; these figures are a series of averages and test samples and things of that kind. But probably there was a decline in the amount of money that immigrants brought with them because immigration was shifting from Northern and Western Europe to Southern and Eastern Europe, and the people who came from the latter regions were less well off. The Germans who came before the Civil War came pretty well supplied with money by and large, but the Italians, the Slavs, the Jews who came later were more needy.

J.A.G. Do you feel that the concept of modern economists and economic historians known as "take-off" finds reinforcement in the study of this period?

E.C.K. The idea of "take-off" is the brain child of W. W. Rostow. He's a very ingenious man, but I don't think he's an American Karl Marx. In the first place, he's a sloganeer. "Take-off" is almost the only economic formula, except some from John Maynard Keynes, that has entered popular discourse. There is a drama, an excitement about the phrase that makes people remember it, and forget there were other stages in Rostow's theories. From time to time he has modified his theories, because, of course, he has been very severely criticized. The last statement of his that I've read was to the International Congress of Historians, and it strikes me that he's terribly eclectic, or perhaps "wisely eclectic" is the phrase I should use. He's so tolerant, so broadminded, that one could fit his thesis to almost any structure. When a man finally ends up saying that the process which he describes is not automatic, scientific, technical, and that social changes must occur before it becomes built into a society's outlook, habit, and institutions, there's not much distinctiveness to the theory. When one has said that, one has said everything.

I've sometimes thought all economic historians are going to become historians of education. They are insisting on considering social factors in analyzing economic affairs. A lot of us stupid oafs had once thought of that, but we thought it would take up too much space in our books. But now we're told we left out the most important thing. When you put political, societal, and legal factors to work in explaining growth, you've got everything.

Rostow thinks the take-off in the United States occurred between 1843 and 1860, but those who criticize his theories say that what was taking place in that period was not take-off but "the preconditions to growth":

the growth of banking; the growth of railroads; the Western expansion; the arrival of workers, and so on.

J.A.G. Charles Francis Adams, Jr., whose biography you've written, said in his autobiography that after the Civil War railroads were "the most developing force and the largest field of the day." Now, in a sense, wasn't he suggesting that the railroads had a multiplier effect on the economy, that they caused an economic take-off in the post-Civil War period? Did the railroads play a special key function that spread beyond themselves to affect the economy more generally?

E.C.K. Yes, but so did everything else. And that's precisely the point where Rostow has begun to fray the edges of his theory. The multiplier effect was operating in other innovations and other changes, in addition to railroads—in the iron industry, in the chemical industry, and in many others. Rostow advances another key phrase in his thought—"leading sectors." Well, if I understand such economists as Schumpeter and Wright on this point, and I think I do in a certain crude way, the whole economic advance is the result of advances in one calling, one occupation, one industry after another. As many "experts" said in the late nineteenth century: "What will we do—what will the country do—after the railroads are all built?" And the answer is: Relax; don't worry. There'll be another leading sector, just as accompanying the railroads there was the leading sector of petroleum; following the railroads, the leading sector of electricity; and in this century, the leading sector of the automobile, the leading sector of aviation, and the leading sector of war production.

J.A.G. But what did Charles Francis Adams mean? He decided to focus his own career—he said he was going to and he really did—on the railroads. He had some insight there, didn't he?

E.C.K. Adams had lots of insights, some of them perverse. But no one can deny that the growth of the railroads was an enormous influence. It was a leading sector. But I doubt that it was *the exclusive* leading sector, and if I must call to my support a frail reed, Robert W. Fogel apparently agrees with me in his book *Railroads and Economic Growth*.

J.A.G. I would like you to comment on Fogel's work, by the way.

E.C.K. Oh dear. Well, I suppose you can comment upon a book in many ways. You can comment upon what it says and you can comment on the way it says it.

J.A.G. I would like you to evaluate Fogel's conclusions, and secondly, comment on his particular approach to economic history.

E.C.K. Fogel set out to demonstrate that historians have used the word "indispensable" in describing the role of the railroads in economic growth loosely, overdramatically, and overromantically. And I think he has demonstrated by his book that the word "indispensable" is the wrong word. There were other factors concurrent with the railroads and other factors after the railroads that were enormously important. He considers the multiplier effect of the railroads on the iron industry, and argues that before 1860 the nail industry was more "indispensable" for American advance, because the tonnage of iron going into nails was greater than the tonnage of iron going into railroad cars, rails, and all the paraphernalia that railroads use. This part of his book I think is very sound.

But the trouble is that Fogel is like a man who gets out on a limb and is intoxicated by the dizzying view from it. He throws in all kinds of *obiter dicta* that are difficult to defend by reasoned argument. The railroads were not indispensable, he writes, because canals and wagons could have done what the railroads did, down to roughly 1890. After 1890, the railroads were probably indispensable, but until that date waterways, artificial and natural, and wagon transport could have carried all the commerce of the country.

His weakest point on the purely factual side is that he did not take all the traffic of the railroads into account. He considered only the grain traffic. To say that the railroads were not indispensable because they did not carry grain between eighteen primary centers and primary markets, I think is a limited proof.

But when he goes on to say that the railroads *may* have retarded the introduction of the automobile—that is mere fantasy! The many technological advances embodied in the automobile were not dependent upon the inadequacy of the railroads.

In general, Fogel claims too much. Consider this statement in his *Railroads and Economic Growth* (page 240):

> Many qualitative differences in economic life are of such a nature that their explanation can only be cast in quantitative terms. The counterparts of American entrepreneurship, modern steel plants, railroads, airplanes, IBM computers, coal and other mineral resources, skilled technicians and virtually all the other elements characteristic of a highly industrialized society are also to be found in India. At the same time, individuals who lack pecuniary incentive, who cannot cope with the technical problems of modern industry, who prefer to consume rather than save, who scorn the achievements of modern science, etc., are to be found in both nations. The *qualitative* difference between the developed and the underdeveloped nations is not explained by the presence or absence of qualitative

endowments. Rather it is explained by the difference in the proportions and amounts in which the various qualitative endowments are found in the respective nations.

Well, let's take India. How does one measure and put in a table the capacity to consume rather than save, a scorn for modern science and modern industry, lack of pecuniary incentive? And even if they can be measured, where are the statistics? They don't exist and won't until sometime between now and never.

J.A.G. When Fogel says that if there hadn't been any railroads, the automobile would have been invented sooner, isn't he simply saying, "Necessity is the mother of invention"?

E.C.K. If it's that vague, it's meaningless.

J.A.G. Would you feel that this "counterfactual" approach has no use or no value for historical study?

E.C.K. I would be inclined to believe that it has little value. People of the turn of mind and approach of Fogel hope to make history a science. In science it's valuable to have a control group; then you can isolate the causes and the forces at work. But I don't think it is very valuable to have a control group that you *imagine*, rather than one that exists. This counterfactual trend, I think, is an attempt to remedy the inherent defects of historical thought, if it's to be regarded as a science. I think it is an unsound methodology.

J.A.G. Was the economic expansion that occurred during the late nineteenth century uniform throughout the economy? Especially, I'd like you to discuss the economy of the South. Historians write that Reconstruction slowed the Southern economy down, yet on the other hand they talk about the New South, and the rapid growth of cotton textiles, iron in the Birmingham area, and so on.

E.C.K. The New South in the nineteenth century is, we might say, counterfactual. Economic expansion did occur in the 1880's, when the region began to pick itself up and slough off the effects of the dislocations and destruction of the Civil War, but it was not until World War II, or the period just before, that the South made *real* economic progress. Merely that Henry Grady earlier christened it the New South, does not prove anything. The South lagged.

I don't feel that the South or, for that matter, the West were exploited in this period by the East. The current phrase is, "They were kept in a colonial status." The basis for any such accusation is probably a misunderstanding of what colonialism is and a misunderstanding of what was going on. There was an immense desire to develop the South in northern sections. This should be clear to anyone who goes through the files of the *Commercial and Financial Chronicle*. That paper was full of editorials pointing to the possibilities of the South and the advantages of developing the South.

J.A.G. If the late nineteenth century was a period of very remarkable economic expansion, why did so many contemporaries believe that the era from the mid-1870's at least down to the mid-1890's was a period of depression?

E.C.K. If I understand cycle theory correctly, the cycle theorists believe that in the moving stream of history, "Both good and bad, both depression and prosperity, move along." If at a particular turning point, certain of these factors come to the surface, years of prosperity result; if they turn the other way, the depression factors predominate. So even though there was hardship and unemployment in this period, and the poor had the usual hard time that scripture tells us they had, there were at the same time elements of vitality and life. After all, these were the years when Americans built the steel industry and the petroleum industry. These were also the years when American cities were built. Think of how much construction must have been going on, considering how many people thronged into the cities. The provision of—would it be misleading to call it "social overhead capital"? continued even in bad times. That is the way I reconcile it.

J.A.G. But this is exactly the point I am after! We look at what happened, we see the growth, the vitality of the economy, not only in the 1880's, but in the 1870's. Why did so many informed people who knew what was going on in the economy believe that times were bad? How could they talk about "overproduction" at a time when they must have been selling what they were producing or the economy would not have continued its expansion? Why did contemporary Americans so often feel they were enduring a "Great Depression" when, as you just pointed out, there was so much industrial and urban expansion, when social overhead capital was being created in huge amounts, and when manufacturers like Carnegie and Rockefeller and many others were making very large profits?

E.C.K. I suppose the easy answer is: "What are people's levels of expectation?" or "What are people's levels of recollection?" What is just or unjust, prosperous or depressed, is apt to be determined by what one is accustomed to. This was a period of great change, and people were getting rich—that is, *some* people were getting rich. Others, apparently acting in the same way, were not. Those who were getting rich were pleased and satisfied, and thought the times are good. Those who weren't —well, they felt differently.

J.A.G. Is there any relationship between public attitudes toward the state of the economy in this period and the fact that it was a period of deflation rather than of inflation? In our own times, prosperity seems to be intimately associated with rising prices, but for twenty years at least in the late nineteenth century, prices on the average were going down. Do you think that misled people?

E.C.K. The economists Milton Friedman and Anna Jacobson Schwartz suggest that this was the case in their *Monetary History of the United States.* And the post-Civil War period has always seemed to me to confound the current theory that the money supply must increase by 3 percent every year in order to have economic growth. I once heard an economics professor at Dartmouth College explaining the economic effects of World War I. He was way ahead of me on foreign exchange rates, and he said, "Well, people are wondering why exchange rates don't vary in accordance with the way we economists have pictured them." (He couldn't have used the terms "model," because this was long before the days of "models." Then he added: "All signs fail in dry times." I think he had the best explanation for the way things worked out of the nineteenth century. "All signs fail in dry times."

Let me give you another example. The late Fred Shannon once wrote an immense article that absolutely proves that no farmer could have lived through the 1890's. I mean, he's got all the figures, and his conclusions are unbrokenly pessimistic. But another historian, after reading the article carefully, told me: "I was a child on a midwestern farm in the 1890's and I don't remember any of this. All I know is, my father made money and he sent seven children through college." But that was a qualitative judgment, and we must avoid those, or we'll have an army of new economic historians upon our necks. In other words, I'm not completely satisfied in my own mind about the causes of the contradiction you mention nor, for that matter, the attempt at reconciliation I have made.

J.A.G. Aside from its economic importance, which is perhaps not precisely measurable, can any judgments be made about the railroad industry in the late nineteenth century? I'm interested, for example, in your opinion as to whether the roads were run in the public interest in that period.

E.C.K. The real answer depends upon the determination of public interest. If we mean, by public interest, a reduction in costs of transportation, we have to admit that the railroads were run in the public interest. Not all railroads, necessarily, but by and large, the railroads were run in the public interest. Prices for the carriage of goods fell steadily and drastically. The price of carrying people fell somewhat. I have always been delighted with the publicist Edward Atkinson's designation of Commodore Vanderbilt as "the greatest Communist" in the United States. His argument was: No one else has done more to lower the price of bread in New York City than Commodore Vanderbilt. Atkinson was a ghastly bore, but he had the sense to see the other side of the coin once in a while, and I think in this case he did.

It would be harder to use the test: Did all communities and all regions have adequate railroad service? By and large they had service, and I believe also that most communities of any substantial size were not dependent on a single railroad for marketing their goods. By the way, if wagons were as efficient as Mr. Fogel says, I don't see why farmers who felt that there was no competition didn't lug their grain to some other railroad. There was certainly one within twenty miles, which is Fogel's distance for profitable carriage from most farms.

But not everybody was pleased with the rates, any more than everyone is pleased with the mail rates nowadays. Oil men didn't think that their oil was being carried cheaply enough. And there *was* rate discrimination. But I have been impressed by the naturalness, almost the inevitability, of discrimination, which so often is regarded as malevolent, sinister, or conspiratorial. I was most impressed when I read over the early manuscript records of the Boston and Worcester Railroad. The Board of Directors tried to run the railroad as a law-abiding enterprise. They were presented with a letter from a manufacturer of iron products, which ran, in effect, as follows: "If you will give me this rate on my freight I will locate my factory in Framingham. If you won't, I'll locate it on the Blackstone Canal." And the rate that they had to give him was below the rate they were charging for other shipments.

J.A.G.   Are you saying that discrimination, if it was a problem, was a dual problem? That it was not simply the railroads discriminating against shippers, but also shippers discriminating between railroads and other means of transportation?

E.C.K.   If a general answer must be made, Yes. Personally I believe that railroad charges should be equal between shippers, if the circumstances are identical. But the more I read about railroads, the more understandable rebates and discriminations have become to me, and the more natural they seem to me. I haven't been quite as willing to condemn them out of hand as many did at the time.

J.A.G.   Essentially, are you saying that the controlling interest was where the power lay? Can one make any judgment about where the power lay, overall? In the nineteenth century, were the railroads discriminating against society as a whole?

E.C.K.   Discriminating against society! What's the test? Cheap rates? Frequent service? Careful handling? These the railroads provided. You can't get away from it. And they were advantageous to the growth of the economy, by and large. Critics talked of "grievances" against the railroads. The word is significant, because these grievances were the railroads' imperfections. To my mind, the whole trend of thought and action in American movements for reforming business is the removal of imperfections, the remedy of grievances or abuses. When reformers said that the railroads were discriminating against society, they were referring to imperfections in the operation of the system. They didn't want to change the system, but they wanted to eradicate its abuses. This program runs from the nineteenth century on through Wilson to F.D.R.

J.A.G. Would a government-owned railroad network have been practicable in the late nineteenth century?

E.C.K. When the Union Pacific Railroad was up for sale in the nineties, because it couldn't pay its debts to the government, there was a very large group that said the government should keep this railroad and use it like a yardstick, a measuring rod, for judging the performance of other lines. But considering the general level of political thought in that period, I don't think that this proposed program had any possibility of adoption. I don't think most Americans wanted to change the system. As I said, they wanted to correct the grievances, the imperfections.

J.A.G. Would you discuss the regulation of railroads in the post-Civil War period?

E.C.K. All railroads were subject to control from the beginning, for the means by which they came into existence included statutory control. Railroad charters not only prescribed how much stock should be issued, where the road should run, but in some cases also regulated rates, provided for interchange with other railroads, and so on. Further regulation usually resulted from the imperfections of railroads.

Safety legislation, for instance, almost always followed an accident, and often depended upon the importance of the people who were injured in the accident. So the state came in because of grievances (imperfections), and railroad commissions were thought to be more effective, better informed, and more dispassionate in this role than state legislative committees could possibly be.

The first commissions were established where the railroads were the oldest, in the East. In the 1870's, the railroad commission spread to the Midwest; later to the South. It tended to ossify (as most bureaucratic arrangements do), and also the railroads were continually outrunning the realm of state regulation. They were interstate in character. The resort to federal regulation was made because the scope and nature of the railroad business was national.

A great deal has been made of the distinction between "advisory" railroad commissions and the stricter "regulatory" type. An advisory commission was a weak commission. It held hearings, heard grievances, and then issued judgments, which it could not put into effect. Such commissions performed roles similar to a legislative committee on railroads.

J.A.G. Was it not the rationale of advisory commissions to call the attention of the public to bad situations, so that the public would, through its political arm, the legislature, correct any grievance or problem by law?

E.C.K.   Yes. A Massachusetts railroad commissioner once said that the advisory system could work only in the state of Massachusetts; in no other state in the Union were the people as well read, as well informed, or as interested in public affairs. State chauvinism aside, the advisory system assumed a certain intensity of popular interest. The Massachusetts system produced legislation when there was widespread heartburn or irritation or outrage in the electorate, as was the case after the railroad strike of 1877.

J.A.G.   How effective were the regulatory commissions?

E.C.K.   They were not very successful. They undertook tasks which were too large and too complicated, perhaps in their nature unhandleable, such as the establishing of uniform rates for railroads, whose costs and location and skill (or lack of it) in management all varied.

J.A.G.   Did federal regulation under the Interstate Commerce Act work any better? For example, did the flat prohibition of charging more for long hauls than for short hauls stop that practice?

E.C.K.   That prohibition caused the commissioners more perplexity, I think, than any other provision in the Act. They had to make so many exceptions to secure equity that it's very doubtful if they met the problem. In general, regulation of such complex enterprises was extremely difficult. Now, of course, the I.C.C. "throws" (as Carnegie said of the consolidation of the steel industry) "sheep and goats together and calls them elephants." They allow railroads like the Pennsylvania and the New York Central to combine when they can't make money when competing with each other.

J.A.G.   Would you explain what the historian A. D. Chandler means when he says that the railroads of America were "the nation's first big business"? Did he mean more than merely that they were large?

E.C.K.   Yes, their diversity of operations is also involved. Railroad corporations had to construct the apparatus—the railroad itself—to begin with, and then maintain it. They had track departments, machine shops, sales organizations, complex accounting staffs, and so on. Of course, the mere size was very important. They were the nation's largest employers of labor, and they had the largest capitalization of any corporations in the country for a long time.

J.A.G.   The conventional way of talking about economic change and development, especially, I think, in the late nineteenth century, is to concentrate on production—the expansion of volume of goods produced. Should we instead spend more time studying how businessmen organized this very complex process?

E.C.K.   That is what Chandler has done in *Strategy and Structure,* a very good book, provided you can get over the first seventy pages of definition. All large corporations, even in the nineteenth century, had complex problems only indirectly related to production. They had to raise fixed capital and working capital, for example. Corporation presidents became managers of teams rather than rugged individualists. One of the most astonishing changes in the internal organization of corporations was the new concern they gave to labor relations. Managing workers was no longer a haphazard job for someone of good will or ill will, or for a foreman. It became a job for specialists, people of professional competence. Then, also, corporations had to develop large legal departments.

J.A.G.   You've written extensively about American industrialists and their ideas, as distinct from their productive accomplishments. Is there any justification, in your opinion, for characterizing the late nineteenth-century businessman as a robber baron?

E.C.K.   This is a smear word, like "scab." It's pejorative, and it gives the impression to me of a castle and a deplorable character in armor putting a chain across the Rhine and charging every boat that goes down the river so much toll. That probably was the whimsical picture the coiners and users of the phrase had in mind.

J.A.G.   What is your own view of the typical big businessman of this period?

E.C.K.   Your question is like "Have you stopped beating your wife yet?" I think these people generally—generally, I say—took the short-run view. That was characteristic of them. They saw in the short run how a thing could be done profitably, and they possessed the energy, the force, and the diplomacy to do it. The growth of a big combination was not foreordained or dictated. It was a matter of persuasion and agreement. Consider the people who came into Rockefeller's Standard Oil. The old story is that Rockefeller went around and got rebates, and then sneaked in the back door of his competitors and said, "Look! Aha! You've got to surrender your plant to me at my appraisal or take Standard Oil stock." That's nonsense! He had to be persuasive.

They were aggressive, they were powerful, and I've sometimes thought of elaborating a playful theory that the big businessmen succeeded because they were good-looking.

J.A.G.   I wish you'd explain that one!

E.C.K.   Well, you may remember that John Adams at one time discussed the basis of greatness. One of the sources he included was beauty. I used to wonder how young Andrew Carnegie looked when he was delivering telegrams in Pittsburgh. Then I saw a boyhood picture of him. He was a bright, attractive youngster. And of course he looked pleasant and receivers of telegrams remembered him.

J.A.G.   It certainly is fascinating to speculate upon what made certain individuals so phenomenally successful. It would be very difficult, I should think, to explain either Carnegie or Rockefeller in terms of their mastery of technology.

E.C.K. They had little, and with the exception of Edison, Westinghouse, George Eastman, and Ford, neither did most other big businessmen. Some had sense enough, as did Carnegie, to hire a "chemist." Of course, industry was going to expand anyway, but I dislike the theory that these people merely rode a wave that was going to come whether they got in there and pulled on the oars or not.

J.A.G. Can a case be made for calling the businessman of the late nineteenth century the first "organization man," rather than an individualistic robber baron?

E.C.K. In a sense that was the great contribution of the late nineteenth century business leader. He was interested in devising organizational means to carry out purposes. I suppose Andrew Carnegie is the sport, the deviant that everyone picks to "prove" points that can't be proved any other way. But certainly he always said, and I think genuinely, that if his plants burned down and his workers were dispersed, if he still had his organization he'd soon be back right where he was before. He had a very strong team sense. Rockefeller, while somewhat secretive, was a great taker of advice, a listener. I don't think of him as "going it alone" in the oil industry.

J.A.G. How about the area of public relations? We are all familiar with the statement of W. H. Vanderbilt—"The public be damned." But is it accurate to say that the businessmen of the late nineteenth century were not concerned about how the general public reacted to their behavior?

E.C.K. Vanderbilt really said that, but whether he meant what has been read into it by historians is debatable. According to the story, he was discussing a particular issue about the timing of trains between New York City and Chicago. The schedule had been readjusted and a reporter said, "Well, won't this discomfort the public?" Vanderbilt replied, "The public be damned." What he meant was, there are other problems in running a railroad besides pleasing passengers. And C. P. Clark, the President of the New York, New Haven, & Hartford, once said in a disillusioned tone: "What the public wants to do is travel for nothing, and have its breakfast thrown in." But I do think they were interested in public opinion. They couldn't help it. They were concerned with the market. I've always felt the phrase of Rockefeller's, "We make a cheap oil and it is our pleasure to do so," is not to be used derisively. I think that reflects the market point of view: "We make a cheaper oil than our competitors."

Of course, one is disturbed by the self-righteous note that creeps in to these people when they talk about labor. There is a note of hypocrisy in their claim to be performing a great public service by giving men employment.

J.A.G. This makes, I think, a good transition to a discussion of the fate of workingmen in the late nineteenth century. Did they improve their standard of living?

E.C.K. They moved in the direction of attainment of better conditions. This can be demonstrated statistically. Working hours were very considerably reduced, real wages increased, and we know that prices were going down a great deal. Another factor that leads me to believe that workers were improving their lot was the hard sledding of the union movement. There were a great many favoring factors toward unionism in the late nineteenth century, and I think that the John R. Commons school of labor historians has played these down. Yet the union movement grew slowly.

J.A.G. Is it possible to say anything about social and economic mobility of workingmen?

E.C.K. There are so many tests for social mobility that the economic historian feels most at home in using employment status. Immigrants rarely got very high by this test. The sons of immigrants did. Thus in the coal mines Welsh and English names predominate among foremen, Poles and Slavs among pick and shovel men. Entirely aside from immigrants, it is hard for scholars, where professional career lines are relatively fixed and traditional, to realize what a variety of occupations a workingman passes through as a matter of course. A certain geographical restlessness —compare the American farmer to the European peasant—and the universality of free education contributed to economic mobility.

J.A.G. The late nineteenth century was marked by a great increase in the regulation of individual activity, either by private groups or by the state. How can this tendency be reconciled with the continuing widespread commitment to the ideas of individualism and, at the political level, laissez faire?

E.C.K. Well, what we're really embarking upon with this question is whether an ideology arises out of current or past circumstances. In the latter case it is an inheritance.

J.A.G. That's a good answer.

E.C.K. We cling to our ideals, even though the circumstances to which they are applicable no longer exist. That's what was happening in the late nineteenth century. Take Senator Justin Morrill of Vermont, who repudiated "the idea that nothing should be done by any people through legislation to change or to elevate and increase their industrial power." His particular concept of the way to do this may have been limited, and confined too much to certain interests. But, nonetheless, the conception of public activity to accomplish economic objectives was common in the late nineteenth century.

J.A.G. To conclude, Professor Kirkland, would you name the half-dozen or so historical works to which you would refer persons interested in the subject we have been discussing, and indicate what the special quality of each of these books is?

E.C.K. Matthew Josephson, *The Robber Barons*. A popular and well-written account, almost a period piece, which accepts most myths and rejects crusading. One critic has called it "not socialistic enough."

Allan Nevins, *A Study in Power, John D. Rockefeller, Industrialist and Philanthropist*. Treats the whole man and the times to which he made such marked social and economic contributions.

F. L. Allen, *The Great Pierpont Morgan*. An urbane account of a "gentleman," banker, and a business savior.

Thomas C. Cochran, *Railroad Leaders, 1845–1890, The Business Mind in Action*. A unique treatment in their own words of how a large and significant group of businessmen regarded their duties and practices.

Sidney Fine, *Laissez Faire and the General-Welfare State. A Study of Conflict in American Thought, 1865–1901*. A slightly opinionated rescue operation in behalf of nineteenth-century liberalism, but still a fair and indispensable summary of what alarmed thinkers and nonthinkers and inspired them to reform.

R. W. Fogel, *Railroads and Economic Growth: Essays in Econometric History*. One of the best examples of what can and cannot be done through the quantifying techniques of the "new economic history."

Albert B. Chandler, Jr., *Strategy and Structure*. With ample illustration, makes the useful distinction that "big business" was not wholly big, and explains why.

Robert D. Cross

American Society: 1865–1914

ROBERT D. CROSS, President of Swarthmore College, is an administrator who has not surrendered his concern for teaching and research. He is the author of *The Emergence of Liberal Catholicism in America* (1958), and editor of *The Church and the City* (1966) and of a series of special studies on *Critical Periods of History*. He has also written numbers of scholarly articles on social aspects of religion, urbanization, education, and other topics. Professor Cross discusses American social changes in the decades after the Civil War.

John A. Garraty Professor Cross, looking broadly at American society in the half century between the Civil War and the First World War, what were the major changes that took place?

Robert D. Cross I think I'd start with a few generalizations that we might explore later in more detail. The first thing that a social historian should note are the gross facts of demography. After all, our country grew from about thirty-five million people in 1865 to about one hundred million just before the war—a pretty extraordinary population explosion, and I think it had some important consequences.

Secondly, he should consider some of the consequences of urbanization. He ought to note that the rapid industrialization of America, while greatly increasing the productivity of the average citizen, did not spectacularly augment that citizen's disposable income; the great growth of consumer prosperity had to wait till after the First World War.

The historian ought also take into account the steady decline of parochialism in American life. Partly this occurs as a reflection of the progressive nationalization of political and economic activity; decisions made by Washington-based bureaucrats, or by the New York banking community, or the Chicago Board of Trade came to have an immediate bearing on the daily life of people thousands of miles away. And the farmer who learned the time of day by the passing of the Burlington or Great Northern train, and the local editor who held up his press until the Springfield *Republican* or the New York *Tribune* was delivered, were alike attuning themselves to different rhythms and imperatives than had been impressed upon them earlier. Furthermore, the old isolation from Europe was beginning to break down; not long after writing *Life on the Mississippi* and *Roughing It*, Mark Twain was to celebrate the experience of *Innocents Abroad*.

And then, finally, the social historian ought to say something about secularization—the slow erosion of the traditional religious assumptions about what existence was, and by what norms daily life should be ordered.

J.A.G. Will you describe the demographic changes that you mentioned?

R.D.C. It might be worth while to start with one model we have about the consequences of demographic change. We're all familiar with the argument which David Riesman advanced in *The Lonely Crowd* about types of population distribution. First, he posed a kind of traditional society in which you had very high death rates and very high birth rates. He tried to show the effect of this kind of birth rate/death rate pattern on social and cultural values, working from family patterns to religious values and so forth.

A second type he called "inner-directed," a culture which, he argues, depends more than anything else upon a society which had a very high

birth rate and a very low death rate. We don't need to accept his conclusions; I mention his work simply to suggest why it may be useful
to establish the facts of population distribution.

We don't know an awful lot about birth rates in most of this period
in the nineteenth century. But we do know that life expectancy changed
quite radically. Our best estimate of life expectancy in 1865 would be
about forty years for a live birth; by 1914 it was about fifty-five to
sixty. To put it simply, it means an increasing proportion of people had
lived through a lot of American society, a lot of American culture. This
situation began to create a different kind of stability in society than had
existed previously.

Infant mortality, especially in the last part of the period, dropped
very radically; probably it was about cut in half between the late
nineteenth century and 1914. Thus, between 1865 and 1914, a radical
change in the age distribution pattern in society took place.

These effects, however, were modified by the fact of massive immigration. People don't immigrate to America at randomly distributed
ages. If you assume that twenty or twenty-five million people, mostly
from Western Europe, immigrated in this period, it also would be pretty
clear that at least 75 percent of that figure, maybe more, would be in the
age group eighteen to thirty-nine—that is, people in the family-forming,
child-rearing age. Mass immigration meant that instead of getting a
population with a greater preponderance of older people, you had a
continual infusion of people in what was for them early middle age,
plus huge cohorts of children. So if one takes the average age of an
American in 1914 and compares it with 1865, these would be little
different—somewhere in the early twenties at both dates. But if you
think of the social structure, you've got a more complicated thing. To
return to Riesman's point, when you have people who have been born
and brought up in the culture for a long time and lived with their grandparents and so forth, that may produce his third type, an "other-directed"
society, but that won't be true for immigrants who were brought up in
Europe and whose children are growing up certainly apart from their
grandparents, and maybe apart from any member of their family. To
use Yeats's phrase, America was not a country for old men.

J.A.G.   Are you prepared to make any guesses about what the effects of
these demographic changes were in the United States?

R.D.C.   For one thing, because of the very large number of young people,
and the special type who are children of immigrants, the formal
processes of socialization were stressed much more heavily. You can
hardly imagine a situation more likely to have to emphasize schools or
settlement houses—take those two as examples—to manage the socialization of children. On the other hand, when you get an aging popula-

tion, you're going to have different patterns of care for the wards of society.

In cultural life there will be a group of people who, simply because they were brought up a generation ago, will be defenders of an older culture against the innovations of a younger group. This is a very crude analysis, and it doesn't work for every individual. But I think it applies in large cultural terms. It helps explain the genteel tradition of the late nineteenth century.

The same argument helps explain changes that took place in religious life—a clash between certain kinds of innovations and very desperate conservatism.

J.A.G. Would it be correct to say on the basis of your argument that the native population had one kind of age distribution (more older people and more younger people), whereas the immigrant population lacked at least the older group, and that the absence of an older, more conservative, tradition-oriented element in the immigrant society led immigrants to develop a different type of society and culture from the native-born population?

R.D.C. Right. I think that's very well put, and I think it also helps to explain some of the conflicts in political life between older people with an older kind of politics, and a new group with different kinds of interests. One of the awful difficulties about studying anything as complicated as social and cultural history is that there are always reservations to be made. For example, some of the things I have said about native Americans—the changes in death rates for one—don't apply to the Negro population, and as a group they were as "native" as anybody could be in this period.

J.A.G. Historians tend to look at the differences between immigrants and the native population in terms of cultural conflict and linguistic problems, but you are suggesting that there may have been more fundamental causes for these differences that were demographic.

R.D.C. I can't think of anything more important in the immigrant culture than its age distribution patterns. People didn't usually talk about that except when they talked of immigrants having too many children, but pretty clearly it would have to condition many of the ways in which immigrants acted.

J.A.G. Among the changes taking place in these years, one that you mentioned was "urbanization." Does the term imply anything more complicated than the fact that a larger percentage of the population was living in cities?

R.D.C. I think it does. I think urbanization involves more than the fact that there are more people per square mile in certain areas.

For one thing, in a city there are always a lot of people around whom you don't know. Even in fairly small cities this would tend to be true. I was recently reading a study of a slate-mining town in Vermont. The people of the town were mostly Welsh immigrants. One of their major problems was figuring out who those other Welshmen were. They all seemed to be named Evan Evans, but what Evan Evans? That kind of problem is continually arising in any urban society, and it has all sorts of implications, both for organizational behavior, for politics, and for basic value schemes.

Secondly, by and large in cities, people do not live and work in the same place. It seems to me a most important social-cultural fact that a person goes to work, leaves his family, leaves probably even his neighborhood, goes off and spends a large part of his time away from his family in an experience which they do not share, and then returns, worn out after a long period of work. Such a pattern must affect his attitude toward his work, his attitude toward his family, and his family's attitude toward him. The effect is most dramatic, certainly, in very large cities with internal transportation systems that make it possible to work quite far from one's home, but even in smaller ones the impact is large.

Urban life also exerts a tremendous pressure to develop more specialized forms of institutions. Instead of everything revolving around the church, or grange, or town hall, people have necessarily to join special institutions for special things: a mutual aid society in one place, Sunday worship in another, recreation in a third. The traditional communal life that was characteristic of at least some rural Americans thus disappears. It may be true that the more you look at rural life the less communal it seems, but there is something in the contrast. The effect on family life is particularly obvious. When the father is away at work, and perhaps the mother too, a lot of things like schooling have to be conducted someplace else. The socialization of the child takes place in formal, specialized institutions.

J.A.G.   In our own day, the cities seem to be the centers of most of the social problems of the time. Was this true in the 1880's and 1890's?

R.D.C.   Before we look at the specific problems of the city, I think we have to put them in context, as your question implies. You don't get the impression from reading about the Grangers and the Populists that rural America was exactly a culture without problems. There was a lot of anxiety, a lot of unresolved difficulties, some of which were specific to the rural condition: isolation, the unsupported encounter with nature, which can be pretty tough. And I think it puts urban problems in context to point out that most people who left the country for the city preferred urban problems to the problems they had faced in the countryside.

But the problems that people saw in urban life in the late nineteenth century were newer and more intense, and they attracted a lot more attention. In most cultures, novelty tends either to be extremely attractive or extremely frightening. Consider that catalogue of American concerns, Josiah Strong's *Our Country* (1885). Most of the troubles he saw in America he traced in one way or another to city life. Whether he was talking about intemperance, or Catholicism, or socialism, or anarchism, he thought they stemmed from city conditions. We would not now accept that analysis, but it typified the disposition in that period to see America's problems as urban problems.

Now what do these problems consist of? One that was most visible and probably for most people most real was the problem of housing: how to pile people on top of one another in very constricted areas. The history of urban housing in the late nineteenth and early twentieth centuries is a touching story of men trying to figure out how to increase the density of population on the land without making life absolutely intolerable. Each generation looked back on the attempts of previous generations and thought they must have been conceived by devils. The twentieth century talks about the "old-law" tenements of New York with horror, but these buildings were the result of reform measures, the best thing that architects could figure out to provide decent housing.

But what a truncation of the normal notion of a house or a home those tenements were! They were places to get in out of the rain and keep more or less warm, to sleep, perhaps to cook some food, and in those built after 1880 or 1890 there was probably a toilet somewhere within the building. But beyond that they didn't provide very much.

J.A.G. Of course, the typical rural house was also rather crude.

R.D.C. Right. But you could argue that a balance of outdoor and indoor living was more possible in a log cabin than it was in a six-floor tenement. I would suppose that most Americans usually thought of the good life very much in terms of having a decent place to live. The fact that by and large the city wasn't able to provide such a place gets pretty close to the heart of why people talked about urban problems.

Another difficulty of urban life was that with people living in such close proximity to one another, marginally normal behavior became very much harder to tolerate. A person who gets drunk in the woods gets drunk, but the fellow who gets drunk in a city and falls down in the gutter or staggers through the streets accosting strangers, or being accosted by them, or going home into an overcrowded apartment, becomes a much more serious kind of a problem. Or take the question of mental infirmity. I remember reading one time a remark of Henry Wallace: "We have some people out in the farms in Iowa who would cause a riot if they ever got into a big city." He meant that they were a bit odd, but on the farm their behavior could be tolerated; there was social space around them. They couldn't be tolerated in the city; too many people didn't know them. It would become necessary to start doing things for these people.

We know, of course, that there were rural saloons in the nineteenth century. In some of Faulkner's stories there are marvelous accounts of going over the hill to the little cabins where a man could get royally inebriated. But there was little social concern about this.

J.A.G.   Drunkenness, in a technical sense, is a form of crime. Was there really more crime in the cities, or was it simply that it was more noticeable and more socially disturbing when it occurred?

R.D.C.   I don't think it's possible to answer that question flatly. The crime of drunkenness is an individual's crime against himself. But the juxtaposition of a large number of persons made crime against other persons more possible. The fact that so many different *kinds* of people live in the city may make crime more common, in the sense that certain kinds of crime are more readily committed against people who seem different racially, ethnically, linguistically, and so forth.

But it may be that you get more crime because in the city you begin to get pressures toward a common definition of what crime is. For example, in certain cultures it's perfectly appropriate for a husband to beat his wife if his wife doesn't get the soup ready on time, or even because he feels it would be good for her. But in the cities of the late nineteenth century there is an attempt to establish one pattern of what is crime and what is not crime. A husband beating his wife, although wholly appropriate in certain cultures, becomes a criminal act. Thus, you may get more crime simply by defining crime universally and saying that there is one law and one pattern of behavior.

J.A.G.   The crimes of each special group become the crimes of all, and therefore there are more crimes?

R.D.C.   I don't see how you can have a definition of crime that isn't culturally subjective. In some areas even certain kinds of murder are not crimes. Most crime is culture-defined. A bunch of Irishmen having a good time in a bar *looks* to some people like a criminal occasion because it's a fairly physical affair, a donnybrook, which in Ireland is not really regarded as a wholly criminal activity. But in American terms a donnybrook is a riot and ought to be put down.

J.A.G.   All right, but what, in culturally defined terms, are the differences between your present-day conception of urban problems in the late nineteenth and early twentieth centuries and the conceptions of the people who actually lived in the cities in those days?

R.D.C.   Instead of overcrowding, nineteenth-century people probably talked about filth; instead of drunkenness they would talk about saloons. One thing I haven't mentioned was that very prominent in their view of city life was what was usually called "the social evil," prostitution. From our perspective it would be very hard to argue that there was more sexual promiscuity in this period than there is today. But again, it was more visible (in red light sections), and it was tied up with politics and the police. It therefore became one of those things that every reformer in the late nineteenth century worried about.

And then one should mention political corruption, as it was called. The cities seemed, to contemporaries, to develop a kind of political life that was alien to the ideals that people thought America stood for. It's in this area that the most drastic contrasts exist between the way people at the time regarded urban problems, and the way historians today see them. Without idealizing the urban political arrangements, the machines and the bosses, we today take a much more benign view, seeing these as a kind of functional solution to political difficulties. In large cities the traditional modes of government, with a board of aldermen and a mayor, were slow in responding to urban problems, especially those of the different ethnic groups to be found in cities. And they did not adequately provide individuals with the things one expects from a political order: a certain kind of security; a certain kind of understanding; a certain kind of aid in meeting the basic questions of shelter, and food, and employment.

The corrupt bosses—and unquestionably many were scoundrels and rascals—took the old structures and made them deliver certain kinds of services to people that were not being delivered: helping people get around the housing laws, getting them out from underneath the police, who were enforcing rules perhaps arbitrarily; getting them jobs that they might not have gotten because they didn't know English very well. On the Jewish East Side in New York in the early twentieth century, a reform mayor announced that he was going to enforce all the pushcart ordinances that existed. These ordinances were perfectly appropriate to middle-class society with other systems of food distribution, but the pushcart was the way in which the Lower East Side dealt with the problem of food distribution, and it was also a way of life for people engaged in it. Fortunately, Tammany Hall had the political clout to prevent these ordinances from being enforced—a negative function, but still a function. The reform mayor thought it was terrible that the laws weren't enforced. That can be considered by one side as corruption, and by the other side as a perfectly appropriate function of government.

J.A.G. Aren't you confusing two different aspects of the urban political system? Were contemporary critics of urban government really exercised about the aspect of the machine that provided "give" and adjustment for new people, or were they concerned about the corruption of the system through padding city payrolls, or stealing from the public treasury on the one hand, and on the other hand the misuse of the democratic system, bribing voters and falsifying election returns? If the bosses were performing social functions so effectively, why was it necessary for them to use floaters and ringers in elections? I find it a little difficult to see Boss William Marcy Tweed of New York as a Robin Hood type.

R.D.C. I agree that it's too easy if you romanticize the boss system, but I would still hold to my general point. Some of the voting of floaters and the taking of bribes can be interpreted, refraining from moral judgment for a moment, as an informal way of getting the income to support the kind of crude social service machine I've been talking about, a sort of Tammany Hall equivalent of requiring all office workers to kick in for the Christmas party.

But I want to make a second kind of argument about the urban machine, which I think may be quite important. One of the vital services that the machine performed, for a good many people anyway, was that of making American government seem somehow or other connected with the people of these areas, particularly immigrant people. One of the terrific city problems—and it would be true even for the country kid who came to the city and found it a bewildering experience—was the lack of any feeling of participation. You may say that these people were deceived by the glad-handing of the ward-heeler. But when you ask the question, "How do people come to feel that they are even in a symbolic sense part of the body politic?" I think that this kind of connection was very important. It enabled poor newcomers to feel that the political scene was possible for them. I think the Negro ghettos of the United States today would have a lot healthier situation if they had good political machines.

J.A.G. How successfully did city people of the late nineteenth century deal with urban problems? How successful were they in adjusting to the difficulties of urban life?

R.D.C. Not very successfully. As Lewis Mumford once said, the industrial city of 1890 was an absolute horror. Things were never worse. Which isn't to say that they might not have been still worse if reformers had not done some of the things they did. "Old-law" tenements were an improvement over the barracks and shanties that people had been living in before. But they were still pretty awful.

In some areas there was considerable improvement in the cities, for example in the rationalization of streets and highways, and of other means of communication—mail service, the telephone. Fewer areas were ghettos in the pure sense, really self-contained and without any kind of affiliation with the larger society. Fire protection, water supply, which were real conundrums for people when they got to large cities, were much improved by the late nineteenth century in most cities.

J.A.G. Did the Progressive generation bring significant improvement to urban life?

R.D.C. There was a very considerable change and development. Effective housing legislation was finally passed, not ideal but a great improvement, as illustrated by the "new-law" tenements of New York. The settlement houses provide another example. The striking thing about the settlement houses was that they started not with the perceived moral failings of city residents, but with the desire to provide functional substitutes for the good life which couldn't be lived in the city. They were willing to start with the fact of crowding, the fact of ethnic difference, and so forth, and say: "What kind of a decent life can we help these people live?" The celebrated willingness of Jane Addams to work with a corrupt political boss for the well-being of the Chicago poor was, it seems to me, a different way of dealing with the difficulty. Jane Addams did not admire the bosses, but she felt that they were appropriate people to work with to improve city life. One of the striking social facts of the Progressive era was the recruitment of people of education, wealth, and power to involve themselves in the settlement houses. One of my favorite illustrations is Jacob Schiff, a very prominent and very upper-class banker, who had dinner one night every week at the Educational Alliance on the Lower East Side with anybody who'd come. He'd sit there and try and help out in any way he could.

Yet, despite what I've just said, I have a nagging feeling that the quality of city life was not improved very much by the Progressive generation. To take one simple but vital criterion: Birth registration statistics indicate that if you lived in the Lower East Side of New York, or in a Polish area in Chicago, the mortality rate was still pretty high, at least through the end of World War I.

J.A.G. Is it possible to generalize about what sorts of people were reformers?

R.D.C. They were not utopians; very few had models of a radically different society from anything they'd seen before. In a sense they were rather conservative. They wanted to revive the kinds of human relations that they remembered, or thought had once existed, in America. By and large, they came from upper-middle-class backgrounds, and felt there was no intrinsic reason why America, even urban America, could not somehow or other achieve a benign kind of existence and restore some of the potential decencies in society that urban growth had destroyed.

This was true even of reformers who came out of the ethnic groups.

One of the things that has always interested me most about reformers of the Jewish East Side in New York is that a very large number of them were of socialist background. But when they turned their attention to New York, they seemed to concentrate on changes that might be made directly. They did not call for revolution or even a drastic reshaping of society. During a garment strike, the Russian-born Meyer London, who considered himself a doctrinaire Socialist, ended up negotiating a wage increase for the strikers with the employers. He said that socialism was a fine thing but that he was concerned with improving the lot of the people on strike.

J.A.G. What of the thesis that Progressive reformers were disgruntled members of formerly dominant groups which were losing status?

R.D.C. Obviously, they were people who had the leisure and the standing to engage in activity which was not immediately self-rewarding, but I doubt that most of them did so out of a conscious or unconscious feeling that other elements of society were passing them by. The theory would certainly apply to *some* people, but it doesn't seem to me a helpful way to go about studying reform.

J.A.G. What about the argument that urban political reformers were motivated not really by the wish to improve the democratic system, but by the opposite, a desire to keep the new immigrant groups from taking over power in cities?

R.D.C. If you limit yourself to the "good government" people, that's a fair statement, although I don't think *they* thought they were anti-democratic. Confronted by an apparent choice between the older model of government and the city machine, they either chose the old model or tried to devise new techniques, like commission government, which would provide a more honest system. Very few of them understood the services that the machine performed for people.

I don't know of any reform group that explicitly wanted to take power away from the immigrants. They simply wanted the immigrants to act more intelligently and support the "right" kinds of things. They had a touching but naive faith that if better government proposals were made and if better men stood for office, they would win the support of the immigrants, who would see that their interests were being better served.

J.A.G. If urban life was so difficult, why did so many people come to the cities?

R.D.C. Well, it was happening all over the Western world at this time. Like most mass migrations, it was a combination of things—a push and a pull. The economics of agriculture became more difficult for the small farmer by putting less premium on labor and more on technology and capital. And this agricultural revolution was taking place in Europe at the same time. It did not so much drive established farmers from the land as make it less attractive for their children or for agricultural laborers to stay on the farm. The city, for all its difficulties, did offer opportunities that the countryside could not.

But I think that most people—and this is more of a generalization than an explanation—leave a place because they are uncomfortable where they are, and they then go to someplace else. There is some evidence that suggests that when Europeans left the countryside, it was not with a specific destination in mind. "Try Warsaw, try Berlin, try New York, try Liverpool," they seemed to say. All these cities had certain things in common, but I think the most important was that they were not the farm.

Another way of getting at this question is to look at different kinds of suggestions or encouragements that were being given at the time. On the one hand, you had the official moralists of society, who were by and large suggesting the superiority of rural life. On the other hand, you had popular literature of the Horatio Alger type, which suggested that a young person who stayed on the farm was missing the main chance. In Alger's *Bound to Rise*, for example, the boy says to his mother: "I'm going to go to the city because I want to make something of myself, and take care of you in a better way than Dad has been able to take care of you," thereby suggesting that the city is where the main chance is, where the good life can be won. Yet Alger also wrote about the superiority of rural life. It's interesting how the two kinds of ideologies conflicted with each other. Alger never implied that the young hero would always live in the city. But he could do things (make money, find different kinds of opportunities, encounter different kinds of people) that he couldn't possibly do in the countryside. Probably a great deal of the movement to the city was begun by people who didn't expect to stay in the cities all their lives.

Finally, I think that when people got into the city and encountered a different kind of life, other things took hold of them. There was a certain exhilaration in the city, economic rewards aside: the opportunity to get away from home, from the constrictions of a narrow cultural life; the chance to try different kinds of jobs. So that I hypothesize a kind of threefold process: one, the decision to leave; two, the decision to go to the city; and three, the decision to stay in the city.

J.A.G.   Can any distinction be made between why immigrants came to the cities and why native Americans in rural areas came to the cities?

R.D.C.   A little. The basic reasons were the same, but there were some special features, especially for immigrants who spoke a different language, worshiped in different kinds of churches. In a city, their chances of finding people of their own persuasion, their own dialect, even their own neighborhood were very much increased. The fact that there was a Polish church, or other Italians from Campania living on Mulberry Street, maybe even brothers or sisters or cousins, somewhat mitigated the problem of moving to an alien land. The opportunities for a post-Civil War immigrant to make a go of it in the countryside were pretty slim, especially if he didn't have a lot of capital, which very few of them did. Almost every immigrant group's leaders at one time or another tried to encourage immigrants to move out of the city, and almost without exception these enterprises were total failures.

J.A.G. What does the term "new immigration" mean? And were these so-called "new immigrants" really very different, for example, from the Germans and Irish who came into America in such large numbers in the 1840's and 1850's?

R.D.C. "New" immigration was a term used by Americans talking about immigrants, and so it's open to the possibility that the difference was as much in the eye of the beholder as it was among the immigrants. Here I take an intermediate position. When we talk about the new immigration, we're talking about the wave of immigration that crested first in the middle 1880's and then reached another big crest in the first decade of the twentieth century. Few of them were English-speaking. In the pre-Civil War wave, at least half spoke either English or an Irish version of English. Now you had not only fewer English speakers proportionately, but also a much wider range of other languages. America was still largely a Protestant country, and the new immigrants, coming as they did from continental Europe, contained a much higher percentage of Catholics and Jews. There were also, of course, sizable groups of Lutherans and other Protestants, but there were very few Protestants coming to the old-line American denominations. The new migrants seemed in that sense different.

Having made those points, I must also say that what made them "new" was not so much what they were themselves as the fact that America was new and different. It was easy to transpose the notion of newness to the immigrants themselves. Since most of them settled in the cities, they were closer together, they were more conspicuous. It's also probably true that the immigration in the post-Civil War period, at least in intention, was a more transient immigration; a lot of the immigrants came not intending to stay. (The one segment that this doesn't apply to was the Jewish immigrant, who very much intended to stay, and did.) Improvements in transportation made it feasible for immigrants to think about coming to the United States for a period and then returning. There was a time, about the turn of the century, when you could travel from Genoa to New York for about ten dollars. And that made it possible for a person to feel that if wage rates were higher in

New York than in Genoa, he could come and work for a year or two, easily pay for his transportation, and return with a sizable amount of money. That was irritating to Americans, who were willing to see America as a place where people wanted to settle, but not one to come to simply to make money and then go home. It also meant that by comparison to both the Irish and Germans of the earlier period, a much higher percentage of single men were coming. Among some groups like the Greeks, the proportion of single men was nearly 90 percent. Over the long run, families followed, but when native Americans saw colonies of single men living in boardinghouses, they concluded that they weren't immigrants at all, but simply casual laborers coming to make American money and then return. Adding these differences to the problems of the cities, you can see why there was an "immigration problem," or a concern about immigration in the late nineteenth century that I don't think ever existed in any such character before.

J.A.G.   From the native Americans' perspective, could the apparent difference be explained simply in terms of numbers—as many as seven hundred thousand a year in the 1880's, and over a million in some years in the early twentieth century?

R.D.C.   Yes, but I think it depends how you state that statistic. There probably was a higher percentage of foreign-born in America in the 1850's than at any other time in our history. But since these immigrants were more concentrated, they were more obvious. And in absolute numbers, there *were* more.

There is one other point that is concealed in the gross statistics. There were more immigrants in America in the 1850's per capita than at any other time, but later on, all their children, although legally Americans, looked like immigrants to native Americans. If you include the second generation, and it's probably reasonable to do so, the percentage of immigrants was higher in the earlier twentieth century than at any other time. That brings up the question "When does an immigrant stop being an immigrant?"

J.A.G.   That's right. Does America throughout this period continue to serve as a melting pot? Is this term "melting pot" a useful one for describing the assimilation of foreigners at any point in American history?

R.D.C.   I think that Americans would not have used the term so much (and it's used both by immigrants and native-born Americans) if something quite impressive hadn't been happening. The term was used very early. But having said that, one must not take the metaphor too literally. When you bring large numbers of people from one culture, or a set of cultures, and put them in a new one, you're going to have dramatic changes on *both* sides. The melting pot is better than another common metaphor—that America is a stomach, that no matter what was ingested it still came out America. But it's still not too helpful.

Sometimes the notion of the melting pot was used to mean that the immigrants would be melted down and become indistinguishable from the culture that existed before they came. That's like the stomach metaphor. But the host culture remained the dominant one. The problem is to find some way to describe the balance between what got changed and what got kept.

In thinking about this, the distinction made by the sociologist Milton Gordon between what he calls "cultural" and "structural" assimilation is helpful. Cultural assimilation of immigrants, he argues, involves learning the English language, acquiring a fundamental political loyalty to the United States, and, in general, accepting the values of Americans about work, progress, success, and so forth. That kind of cultural assimilation, it seems to me, was quite rapid, quite effective, even at the peak of the new immigration. Structural assimilation involves how soon an immigrant stopped thinking of himself as an immigrant, or different from the native Americans, how soon he lost the sense of "we-ness" and "they-ness." That's something that took a very long time. They may shift, as some people argue, from talking about themselves as Italians, to talking about themselves as Catholics, but the sense of different identity seems to have lasted a good while. And the attitude of the host culture is important, too. If most Americans continue to regard you and your friends as "alien," it's hard to feel like an American, however much you want to. Or take the question of intermarriage. One can acquire the English language and political Americanism, and still prefer to marry another Italian or another Swede or whatever. The kind of random intermarriage that the melting-pot notion implied still had not taken place.

And finally, there has been a disposition among people of immigrant origin to retain institutions that differed from those of the larger society, such as a German *Turnverein* or Polish *Sokol*, or a parochial school, or an ethnic neighborhood.

If this country lasts a thousand years and we don't have any more massive immigration, probably it will become structurally assimilated too. But I think a great deal of the native concern in the early twentieth century arose from the fact that, perceiving that immigrants were slow in assimilating structurally, many Americans concluded that they were not culturally assimilating. Because immigrants didn't intermarry widely, there was a feeling that they somehow were refusing to take part in American life; because they wanted to have parochial schools, they seemed somehow against the educational ethos that all the other Americans had. Actually, the fact that almost all immigrant groups supported schools meant that they were culturally assimilated and accepted the American belief in the necessity of education.

Thus, the melting-pot metaphor is useful only if you ask yourself what is being melted and what is being preserved. And then, so far I've been talking about the melting pot only as it applied to white European immigrants. When race or color are introduced, the melting-pot concept seems even less useful, because surely the experience of the Orientals and the older immigrants—the Negroes—involves a lot more reservations than I've mentioned so far.

J.A.G. Your last point suggests that the willingness of the majority to accept or to permit the melting of the immigrant was as significant as the willingness of the immigrant to melt.

R.D.C. That's very true. Most native Americans wanted the immigrant to assimilate, but with certain reservations. The Boston Brahmins were not overly delighted about intermarriage with the Irish, for example. They wanted the Irish to intermarry, but not with them. Until recently it hasn't been the easiest thing for an Irishman to get nominated for public office on the Republican ticket in Massachusetts.

J.A.G. Well, would you carry your criticism of the melting-pot concept to the point of saying that there was nothing uniquely American about the process? Would you say that America in the late nineteenth century was no more a melting pot than England was at the time of the Norman invasion?

R.D.C. Oh, no. America was much more of a melting pot than England was. It had probably the most liberal naturalization laws of any country in the Western world. America was quite an open society, and the rate of assimilation was striking. Actually, in my discussion of immigration, that's the most important and probably should have been the first thing said rather than the last!

J.A.G. You've already spoken about the effect of the social changes of the late nineteenth century on a number of social institutions. Would you now discuss the impact of these changes on some of the other major institutions of American society?

R.D.C. I'd like to begin by saying something about the impact on the church and organized religion. On the one hand, at least throughout the nineteenth and twentieth centuries, and probably before that, there has been a steady increase in church membership in this country. On the other hand, though it's harder to measure, it's also probably true that the churches' influence on the conduct of life declined steadily through the period. Churches as institutions were flourishing, but religion as a set of effective sanctions or guides to behavior became less important.

One phenomenon evident by the middle of the nineteenth century was the fragmentation of Protestantism, the continual growth and development of new sects. As the century wore on, an increasing number of Protestant religious groups achieved general respectability. More significantly, a similar attitude toward Catholics in this country developed. Catholicism, instead of being regarded as uniquely in error, a danger to the whole Protestant way of life, became thought of as a valid expression, for some people at least, of the Christian religion. The Catholic church tried to get along with and to avoid denunciations of Protestants, and Protestants tried to accommodate themselves to Catholics. A rather similar kind of development occurred in American Judaism, particularly in the reformed wing, which, by the 1880's, had pretty well shucked off any sense of separation of Judaism from what we later came to call the Judeo-Christian heritage. These churches, which had felt themselves and been felt to be outside the religious consensus, were now being brought in, both because they wished to and because the "outside" was sympathetic to them.

A second change was the response of the churches to the urban phenomenon. When you began to get really large cities, the possibility of any individual congregation or parish being coterminous with the whole population was effectively destroyed. Churches of much more specialized types appeared, each to deal with a special sector of the society: a special neighborhood, a special ethnic group, a special color, a special theological background, and so on. Urban churches began to concentrate much more on very special services; ministers became much more functionaries whose impact on the life of their people was limited to a Sunday relationship. A church became a place to go rather than something to be a member of.

The intellectual framework of religious life in America was also changing at this time. It's sometimes put too simply as a conflict of science with religion. Rather, people began to find in other forms of knowledge clues about behavior and about ways of orienting themselves, which made religion seem no longer strictly necessary. I think it was William James who said that in America we never argue with our fathers but just bid them good-by. To a certain extent, that's about what happened to a great many traditional religious tenets. People didn't so much see them as being undermined by Darwinism or geology or history applied to Biblical times, they simply found that those "scientific" truths were interesting and important to them, and they did not choose to worry about a reconciliation between traditional religious views and this new knowledge.

I would mention one further change, the developing notion that the church should speak directly to the social conditions of the new America. This was called the "Social Gospel," which is a convenient tag to define a whole range of concerns. The church should not simply preach the gospel of salvation, but should direct its energies to specific worldly problems. But this social gospel did not deeply engage the energies of most church-going Protestants or Catholics or Jews in the nineteenth and early twentieth centuries. It was a crisis within the professional class of religious leaders, it seems to me.

In the religious realm one expects to find a deep conservatism, and we have to remember that there were profoundly conservative countercurrents to these developments. One was Fundamentalism, the current of thought that began to well up in nonurban areas, and in the South, in protest against all the changes I have mentioned. Fundamentalism, as it eventually became formulated about 1911, made very specific assertions about traditional theological belief, but the dynamics behind it were much more social and cultural. At the same time, fresh outbursts of primitive religious energy occurred—Pentecostalism and other deeply emotional, deeply fervent religious outbreaks.

The "decline" of religion can also be observed in the realm of education or, to put it more broadly, the process of indoctrinating children with the values of the society. Well before the Civil War, most American Protestants had concluded that the socialization process should take place largely in public schools, in which religious values were taught but divorced from any particular denomination. The schools were, it's fair to say, nondenominational Protestant schools, public in sponsorship and control. A somewhat similar development took place in higher education in the late nineteenth and early twentieth centuries, with the formation of nondenominational public universities, and the gradual change in emphasis among colleges and universities that had been founded specifically for religious purposes toward more nondenominational, perhaps really secular, concerns.

This type of public education was not satisfactory to many Roman Catholics, to certain Lutheran groups, and to a number of other groups. These insisted that the churches themselves should superintend the education of the young. The general tendency, however, was to try to accommodate the religious content of the schools to an increasingly diverse student population. So, by the end of the nineteenth century the public school was a far less Protestant institution than it had been before.

The generation before the Civil War had concluded that at least elementary education ought to be offered to every young person who wanted it. The striking change in American educational belief and practice between the Civil War and World War I was that schooling should not simply be an opportunity for every student, but a requirement. Instead of having laws which compelled cities and communities to provide schools, there were now laws which compelled parents to send their children to school.

One must be careful not to misstate the reasons for this. Certainly the general conviction that an educated citizenry was a good thing was important, but there were other forces at work as well: the belief that the economic well-being of society depended on keeping children out of the labor market, the idea that schools were necessary instruments for the Americanization of immigrant children. Unfortunately, we don't know how successfully these purposes were met. The history of education has been written in terms of the purposes of the institutions rather than the results.

J.A.G.   Do you see a connection between this institutionalization of compulsory education and the remark you made sometime earlier in our discussion about the fragmentation of the family? Wasn't it John Dewey who suggested that the movement of citizens from the farm to the city removed children from a whole host of educational forces in rural life that had therefore to be inculcated in schools?

R.D.C.   That's right. You can either look at it as a discontent with what the family was doing, or a feeling that the family was quite incompetent, with the father away at work, and the family living in tenement houses to provide the needed education. In an urban society, the best and most diligent family in the world can't really train a child for the diverse activities of urban society. The school is going to have to do that. Sometimes it seemed almost as if the school was supposed to be a total substitute for family, church, factory, and farm. No one can think about late nineteenth-century America without thinking about the school and how enormously important an institution it was.

One other point is of interest in the development of education in the late nineteenth century: the development of public high schools. Before the Civil War the gap between the elementary school and the college was filled almost exclusively by private institutions and thus available to a very limited number of people. The new public secondary schools were conceived of during this period not primarily as feeders for the colleges, but as providing other kinds of skills which students could use in adult life. This posed a difficult theoretical question. There was general agreement that in elementary schools children should learn reading and writing and arithmetic, but it proved much more difficult to define the curriculum of these schools.

J.A.G.   What about graduate education, which really gets its start in these years? Was the development of the graduate school also a result of social change?

R.D.C.   I think it has somewhat different roots. We haven't talked much about the changes within the high culture, the intellectual world. I don't see the first development of graduate work as being immediately connected with the training of lawyers, doctors, and other professionals. That came in the twentieth century. Nineteenth-century graduate education was a response to general intellectual currents, to the internationalization of American life, to European developments.

J.A.G.   Certainly the graduate universities were *causes* of social change, and had a profound influence on the way in which the problems of the late nineteenth century were dealt with by economists and other social scientists. Was it just a coincidence that the new skills and new knowledge about how society functions were developed at exactly the time when they were needed?

R.D.C.   That's a very nice point. It's certainly true if you think about what happened to the social scientists who graduated from Johns Hopkins, and the extent to which they ended up leading muncipal reform leagues, or trying to do something about the wages of industrial workers —there must be some kind of connection there. But the immediate incentive seems to have been much more in the area of abstract knowledge and research than in application.

J.A.G.   I'd like to ask you finally about social mobility in America. Can we measure social mobility, or rather, how effectively have we measured it for this period? And was it in any way affected by industrialization, the growth of cities, and the general increase in the size and complexity of the United States?

R.D.C.   Let me respond to that by talking about two kinds of mobility: horizontal, or geographical mobility; and vertical, or social class mobility. Aside from the mobility involved in the movement from the country to the city, there was also a great deal of mobility between region and region. The possibility that a man might begin life in Boston, work in Chicago, and maybe end up on the West Coast was much more common.

As for social mobility in the usual sense, I don't think that we have now or will ever have the kind of data that will enable us to generalize with any competence. Nevertheless, I would argue for an increased social mobility in this period. With the development of really great fortunes there were possibilities of going further. Even if we admit that Andrew Carnegie was an exception, the fact that Andrew Carnegie could go from nothing to an awful lot—that says something about the inner structure of the society.

Secondly, there developed in the late nineteenth century a whole range of jobs with social status attached to them, which made possible the kind of mobility that was less available earlier; I refer to white-collar jobs. The huge increase in sales forces, the rise in the number of school teachers, the growth of the civil service, and so forth, enabled people of lower-class or lower-middle-class origin to rise. By and large, the school teachers of the late nineteenth century were recruited from among the children of blue-collar workers.

Furthermore, social mobility was both made necessary and made more dramatic by the influx of immigrants into America. The appearance of immigrants willing to do the dirty work of society made other people anxious to stop doing what immigrants were doing, but it also made stopping possible. In the mines, for example, Irish and Welsh who had been unskilled laborers in the pre-Civil War period were supervisors and foremen in the post-Civil War period. The Irish who were laying the tracks for the railroads in the 1850's and 1860's were semiskilled workers on the railroads by the 1880's and 1890's, as Poles and Italians began to do the less-skilled work. America had a great deal of social mobility, certainly in comparison with European countries at the same time.

J.A.G.   Could you suggest a half-dozen or so books that would provide a good introduction to the themes we've been discussing?

R.D.C.   Arthur Schlesinger, Sr.'s *Rise of the City* (1933), though a bit dated, raises many of the questions one ought to ask about post-Civil War America. Oscar Handlin's *The Uprooted* (1951), is an eloquent evocation of the experience of the immigrants. John Higham, in *Strangers in the Land* (1955), describes the changing reaction of native Americans to the presence of immigrants. Richard Hofstadter's *Age of Reform* (1955), develops an interesting interpretation of the causes and consequences of reform activity in the late nineteenth and early twentieth centuries. In *The Protestant Churches in Industrial America* (1949), Henry F. May categorizes the responses made to a social order undreamed of in most ministers' philosophy. And Lawrence Cremin, in *The Transformation of the School* (1961), not only illuminates the drastic change in purpose and technique of the schools between 1870 and 1920, but provides a useful summary of the major changes taking place in the high culture in this period.

C. Vann Woodward

The Negro in American Life: 1865–1918

C. VANN WOODWARD, Sterling Professor at Yale University, is one of the most highly respected members of the historical profession, having served as President of the American Historical Association, the Organization of American Historians, and the Southern Historical Association. He has won a Bancroft prize, a Syndor prize for Southern History, and a Distinguished Professor Award of the American Council of Learned Societies. Among his many important books on various aspects of the history of the South and of the Negro are *Tom Watson: Agrarian Rebel* (1938), *Reunion and Reaction: The Compromise of 1877 and the End of Reconstruction* (1951), *Origins of the New South* (1951), and *The Strange Career of Jim Crow* (1955). He is also coauthor of a widely used college text, *The National Experience* (1963). In this interview, Professor Woodward discusses the fate of the Negro after Reconstruction, the subject of some of his most original and influential research.

John. A. Garraty Professor Woodward, one common assumption about the period of the Civil War and Reconstruction is that it was a time of progress for the American Negro. Would you summarize the gains made by the black people during those years?

C. Vann Woodward I think of the era as a period of promise rather than of progress. The expectations aroused were far in excess of the fulfillment. It was a time of change, but primarily of legal change, of changes potential rather than actual. The legal foundations of slavery were of course destroyed, but not the psychological or economic foundations. The legal foundations of civil and political equality were laid down, but the enjoyment of these rights was tenuous, temporary, limited. Many of the freedmen were worse off materially than they had been under slavery. Many of the older generation of blacks never broke through the internalized psychological bondage of a servile existence, and some even sought to pass these old values on to the next generation.

This contrast between promise and reality, between the potential and the actual, has been used by cynics and conservatives to discredit Reconstruction as a stumbling collection of blunders and frauds, insincere in purpose, business-guided and futile. What the cynics have overlooked are two results of Reconstruction: the long-term significance of the constitutional and legal changes, and the genuine gains that were made to the freedmen as a direct result of the Reconstruction process.

Men still argue about the relative importance of the gains and their durability, but one of them certainly was religious freedom. There was a conscious withdrawal of Negroes from the white churches. They established their own churches, their own clergy, and this was of special importance. The leaders of the Negro churches were far more than religious leaders. They became leaders of all kinds. A second category of gains, more limited, was educational. Hundreds of schools, thousands of them for a while, were founded, and a sizable group of literate blacks began to develop. A considerable number of what were called colleges and universities were founded. Often they were mere academies, but from them evolved a great many durable colleges and universities.

J.A.G. If it is safe to assume that illiteracy was almost universal among slaves, how much progress had been made by the end of Reconstruction?

C.V.W. We don't have exact figures. Reconstruction fell between census years, and the census of 1870 was notoriously inadequate. We know the number of blacks who attended school, but not how many learned to read or write. The archives of these schools indicate that many possessed an overwhelming urge to learn, so undoubtedly many did master reading and writing. The difficulty is that some of the schools functioned only for a couple of months during the year. At least, however, some school

experience was very widespread among the freedmen. Whether it resulted in literacy is a question.

J.A.G.   Is it just a romantic myth that large numbers of the older blacks
made serious efforts to learn to read once it became legal for them
to do so?

C.V.W.   No, that was not a myth. This urge for literacy cut across the
generations. Older people wanted to read the Bible first of all. Literacy
was a social aspiration religiously motivated.

J.A.G.   What was the white reaction to the Negroes' leaving the white
churches?

C.V.W.   Many resisted it, and some churches officially fought it. Religion
was a means of control. One of the phobias of the ante-bellum era was
that Negro religious leaders might use the church subversively, and
those fears didn't end with the end of slavery.

Aside from the religious and educational advantages of freedom, the
end of slavery opened access to the professions to Negroes. They became
lawyers and doctors, for example. And they won access to public services
like transportation and to places of entertainment.

On the economic side, they did not often obtain the land that they
aspired so to own. But a black middle class of shopkeepers and preachers
and peddlers and politicians gradually emerged. It was small, but it
provided the leadership that the Negro masses needed. Reconstruction
also made political experience possible for the American Negro. The
resistance to slavery in other Western cultures often took political forms,
as in Brazil and in parts of the Caribbean region. Resistance in the South
had been not primarily political, but individual: the expression of individual discontent and frustration and resentment. During Reconstruction for the first time the Negro was acting politically. He voted, held
office, campaigned, bargained, took some small part in self-government.

I don't think this list would be complete without reference to certain
intangible, psychological gains. The black man grew in self-esteem; he
could talk back, speak for himself, resist collectively and openly, not
merely covertly and indirectly and individually. Then there was the
Negro soldier, whom other Negroes could see and share experiences with.
Guns had been a symbol of white dominance in slavery times. Blacks
had never been permitted to have weapons. Now, military service symbolized the fact that they could exercise power and authority and responsibility.

Now I'm not arguing that Reconstruction was a great success, a golden
age of Negro history. There was too much tragedy in Reconstruction
to make it anybody's golden age, white or black. Nor do I endorse the
concept of black Reconstruction. It was overwhelmingly a white Re-

construction, though this is not to disparage the Negroes' achievement. The white man was in control.

J.A.G. Among the religious or psychological gains, surely the right of legal marriage was one of the most important. Do we know anything about the durability of sexual relations among slaves, and among the former slaves after legal marriage became possible?

C.V.W. This is one of the frontiers of research in the field. Two of my students are doing some extremely interesting work with statistics and church and court records and manuscript census reports. Their research already indicates that family relationships were more enduring than was generally supposed, even in slavery times. Apparently, there was very little difference between black and white in this regard in the North before 1860. Whether that was true in the South, however, is yet to be determined.

J.A.G. Did the changes of the Reconstruction period cause any basic shift in white opinion, either in the North or in the South, about the character and the ability of the black man?

C.V.W. Let's talk about the North first. I once said that the Union fought the Civil War on borrowed moral capital. By that I meant that it committed Northern people to principles and goals that exceeded their moral resources, their capacity and will to pay the debts that they were piling up morally. The consequence was that they defaulted on their debt and went into moral bankruptcy, legalized by the Supreme Court. They have only recently begun to refund the debt. It's still mostly unpaid, of course.

Ante-bellum Northern society was thoroughly segregated on racial lines, much more segregated in the formal sense than that of the South. This situation was not changed by the Civil War. The grand moral purposes of the Civil War were an afterthought, designed to give a noble front to a power struggle. The Union had to justify the slaughter of 600,000 men (about one man was killed for every six slaves liberated) to the people. Thus, men died in the belief that they were fighting for the cause of justice and freedom, as well as union, for equality and the rights of man. The result was the depletion, instead of the accretion of moral capital. The war exhausted rather than restored the people's moral fervor, as men like Emerson and Walt Whitman were quick to point out. The professed goals of the war didn't endow the average American with moral grandeur, or destroy centuries-old racial attitudes. We are just beginning to realize how deeply embedded those attitudes were.

The work of the historians Winthrop Jordan and David Davis shows how white supremacy was used as a foundation for European identity in the New World in early colonial times. The Negro was a counter-image;

he defined what the white man was *not* going to be in the wilderness. He was not going to be savage, or sensual, or primitive, or degraded. This stereotype was as common in the northern colonies as in the southern. The South, of course, had additional incentives for building and strengthening these attitudes. And the Civil War and Reconstruction didn't eliminate or deeply change them. In many ways, they intensified white belief in race supremacy, which seemed more necessary when the discipline of slavery was removed.

J.A.G.   Then the concrete achievements that the Negro made in running his own affairs and establishing his own institutions had no effect on white opinion of his potential?

C.V.W.   It had an effect, certainly. It proved that some of the grosser conceptions of Negro inferiority had no foundation. The Negro could learn to read and write, could speak up and defend himself. But deeper attitudes were not fundamentally changed.

J.A.G.   What, then, were the motives of the Republican Radicals in insisting on the granting of legal rights to Negroes, if they still believed the Negro to be congenitally inferior?

C.V.W.   When I generalized about Northern opinion, I was talking about mass opinion; there were always exceptions, and the exceptions included many prominent Radicals. But when one speculates about motives, one tackles a very elusive and controversial question. In the last decade, a renewed sympathy for the professed aims of the Radicals has developed. The old picture was cynical and derogatory. The new one is quite the reverse. The tendency is to absolve the Radicals of selfish partisan and economic motives, and to stress their perseverance, idealism, and sincerity.

Another revisionary tendency is to point out that the extreme defense of Negro rights often cost the Radicals a great deal politically. In many parts of the North, their views were unpopular. But while the revisionists have served to correct the old picture of Radical cynicism, I don't think that they prove that the Radicals were devoid of the normal political-economic motives. It's perfectly clear that the Republican party had something to gain from the establishment of a large constituency of blacks in the South, and that in narrowly divided Northern states like Indiana, New York, and Connecticut, there was political capital to be made by securing the votes of Negroes. The Radicals identified the cause of idealism with the Republican party.

But granting even the maximum of disinterestedness and idealism on the part of the Radicals, it must be remembered that they sought to substitute Northern paternalism for the Southern type in their approach to the freedmen. Their paternalism was of a missionary sort. The planter's paternalism was a basic part of the slave society, whatever you think of it and its effect. The Northern paternalism was more shallow, and not nearly as durable. It was episodic and quickly faded away.

J.A.G.   I'm not sure that I understand the difference.

C.V.W.   The Northern paternalism was humanitarian, liberal, eighteenth-century rights-of-man paternalism. The Southern variety had little of these concepts. It was Christian but not humanitarian. Southerners were responsible, they said, for their people.

J.A.G.   You have said nothing about vindictiveness as a motive of Northern Radicals. Were they not, at least to some extent, motivated by a desire to punish the South?

C.V.W.   I think that the idea has been exaggerated. Certainly there were bitter feelings and talk of revenge, but the Radicals weren't trying essentially to debase or degrade white Southerners. No doubt some took satisfaction in the troubles of the former slaveholders. That was only human. But it's unfair to the Radicals to dismiss their motivation as that of vengeance and vindictiveness.

J.A.G.   On balance, was Reconstruction a success or a failure?

C.V.W.   In the sense of the realization of the professed aims and goals it has to be called a failure, the first great collective failure of our national (not Southern) experience. Americans have "a thing" about failure. We think of our society as successful, indomitable, ever-victorious. In coping with this failure, both Northerners and Southerners have resorted to a great deal of fancy evasion. Southerners have romanticized the "lost cause," but Northerners have treated Reconstruction with the same kind of evasiveness. One tendency has been to stress the positive gains of Reconstruction; another is to justify it in terms of the present, by pointing out that laws which we are now trying to enforce were passed at that time, and by arguing that without that period of intensive constitutional revision and law-making, recent gains would have been impossible.

Before we can arrive at a definitive assessment of this whole experience, we're going to have to move beyond the national context and take a look at comparative history. The only comparisons that are traditionally made are with the North. The important comparisons should be with other slave societies in the New World, which also went through a process of emancipation and reconstruction. How did the English, the Dutch, the French, the Portuguese, and the Spaniards make this adjustment? The United States was the only slave society that had a bloody civil war. Is that the whole story? What problems did other societies have as a result of emancipation? Until we know the answers, it's quite misleading to assume unique American depravity and failure in this field.

J.A.G.   I gather from the tone of your answer that you think comparative analyses will improve our opinion of our own Reconstruction.

C.V.W.   It will put it in a different perspective. The evidence indicates that in all postemancipation situations around the world some type of involuntary servitude followed slavery. It took various forms, and lasted for different periods, but it was always a follow-up of emancipation. The freedmen were put back to work by force, sometimes in a formalized way, as with the apprenticeship system of the British West Indies, sometimes through black codes, as in the United States. If it happened everywhere, it was not an American peculiarity.

J.A.G.   It's traditional to associate the formal ending of Reconstruction with the removal of the last federal troops from the South by President Hayes. Was this removal really very significant? After all, only a handful of soldiers were involved.

C.V.W.   One must distinguish between the symbolic and the real importance of the removals of April, 1877. By that time, the troops in Florida, South Carolina, and Louisiana were mere token units, but they were of genuine political significance. In these states two contesting governments claimed to be legitimate, one conservative and one radical. The question of which was going to prevail was unsettled until the troops were removed. As soon as they were pulled out, the radicals gave up and the conservatives took over. That would have happened sooner or later, given the political situation. The deeper significance of Hayes's withdrawal was the symbolic statement to the country and the world that the use of force to maintain Republican governments was now abandoned.

J.A.G.   I've never really understood the inconsistency of federal policy in this matter before 1877. Why were the troops removed from other Southern states sooner? Why the inconsistency?

C.V.W.   In many states, the conservative take-over was of quite a different sort. It was political. The radicals simply didn't have the votes. But in South Carolina and in Louisiana, the Republican governments had held power continuously.

J.A.G.   It's clear from President Hayes's diary and from other sources that he had received assurances from Southern leaders that the rights of Negroes would be protected after the 1877 compromise. Hayes was bitterly disappointed by the failure of this policy of conciliating white Southerners. Why did the Southerners fail to keep their promises? Had they ever intended to keep them?

C.V.W.   Here again is this elusive question of motives. It is certainly true that the Redeemers, the conservatives, assured Hayes that they would protect Negro rights. But their motives were mixed and confused. I think they were guilty of less guile than critics have charged. It's a question, for one thing, of their conception of the Negroes' rights, which differed from that of the Radicals. The governors who negotiated individually with the President—Wade Hampton of South Carolina and

Nicholas of Louisiana, both conservatives of the old order—were faithful in their own light to their promises. They handed out a remarkable amount of patronage to Negroes, and in some measure held in check local extremists. They had political reasons for so doing, since they stood to gain by Negro votes. The white supremacy element, motivated by vengeance and jealousy of the Negro, was also very resentful of upper-class conservative manipulation of the Negro vote. At the very start of the post-Reconstruction period, movements such as Martin W. Gary's South Carolina White Supremacy Party, opposed all "pampering" of the blacks. Put them in their place. Kick them out of political office. Keep them from voting.

I think we often don't realize the difference between the races in their perception of politics. To the Negro, politics was a means of gaining protection and jobs. Who had and could give those things? The conservatives. They had jobs to give, and they could, if they would, give some measure of protection. The Negroes were disappointed, mistreated, abused by the conservatives often, but the alliance was a real one, and it lasted a long time.

J.A.G. What actually happened to the Negro in the South after the end of Reconstruction? Would you trace the development of the Jim Crow pattern of social organization?

C.V.W. I've written a good deal about segregation, and I don't want to repeat myself. In general, my thesis is that formal, legalized, universal segregation was not an immediate consequence of Reconstruction, but an evolution over a period of years. Full-blown segregation appeared only very late in the century, and was not complete until the early years of the twentieth century. I have, I think, been misunderstood in advancing this description of the growth of segregation. I never claimed the period before 1890 to be a golden age of race relations. What I meant by segregation was physical separation—physical distance, not social distance, which has always been great.

Some critics have pointed out that there was widespread segregation before the Civil War in the North. This is not inconsistent with my thesis. Richard Wade, in his study of slavery in Southern cities, notes the beginnings of segregation in the cities of the South well before 1860. But at the same time he shows that racial integration, residentially and in many other ways, was far greater in the South than anywhere else in the country. John Martin is now finishing a history of residential segregation in Southern cities from 1850 to the present, and his work indicates that in most cities very few districts were segregated in the 1850's and 1860's, and that segregation was slow and gradual for a long time. The period of rapid segregation occurred in the twentieth century. In his excellent study of South Carolina developments, Joel

Williamson has pointed to local segregation laws and practices in that state. He concludes that Reconstruction itself was the time of the great physical separation of the races. But I believe the tendencies were mixed in both directions. Reconstruction brought the races into physical contact in many ways in which they had never been before. Pierre L. van den Burghe writes of two types of separation, social and physical. Social distance is that achieved by a paternalistic society, and usually physical distance varies in inverse proportion with social distance. Where social distance is established by caste or slavery, physical segregation is unnecessary.

In a competitive society, physical distance becomes a substitute for social distance. This competitive order arises in cities first, and in the North before the South. Such segregation as there was before the late nineteenth century in the South was urban—a result of an increasingly competitive society and the fading of the old paternalism. Of course, in insisting on my point about the lateness of segregation, I'm not making a value judgment about the benevolence of Southern race relations. I'm simply making a sociological observation.

J.A.G.   Might one conclude that the development of Jim Crow regulations was a sign of the progress of the Negro in the South?

C.V.W.   Yes. It is even true that this kind of "progress" produced Negroes who had a vested interest in segregation: Negro professionals and businessmen, who profited from the exclusive clientele and markets that segregation gave them.

J.A.G.   Does the development of a competitive society explain the denial of the vote to the Negro?

C.V.W.   No, that is a different question. The conservative Redeemers in the period after Reconstruction had a political interest in the Negro vote. They successfully used it and naturally protected it. They wanted to keep the Negro voting, as long as he was voting for their party. But in some states third parties made appeals to the Negro. The most notable was the Readjuster party in Virginia, which succeeded in driving the Redeemers out of power with the help of Negro votes. Later, of course, the Populists tried the same experiment. Naturally, this led to disenchantment among the conservatives with Negro suffrage.

All the defenses of Negro voting crumbled in the latter part of the nineteenth century. The start of disfranchisement occurred, however, much earlier. Ingenious ways of making voting difficult or inconvenient or embarrassing for Negroes were devised. The Negro vote was diminished a great deal before formal disfranchisement took place. But between 1890 and 1910, with the approbation of the Supreme Court, disfranchisement was made virtually complete.

J.A.G.   To what extent did the economic condition of the Southern Negro change after Reconstruction? Was the share-cropping system, which we tend to think of as a degrading form of agricultural organization, actually bad for the Negro, considering the position he started from?

C.V.W. The great aspiration of the freedman was to become a land-owner. That didn't happen, and here we are reminded of the importance of comparative history. It *did* happen in many parts of the West Indies, and it is instructive to study the consequences: the freedmen withdrew from the plantations, and the British imported coolie labor from the East Indies or China.

Many Reconstruction historians point to the fact that the freedmen were not given land as a key failure of Reconstruction. I am skeptical of that. The history of the Homestead Act shows that free land did not help white farmers very much, and it is hard to see how the black farmer would have fared even as well as the white. Even with free land, farmers needed capital, and the black man had much less of that than the white.

The most general and immediate resort was to a contract labor system. The Freedmen's Bureau was put in charge of supervising and writing labor contracts, and received a great deal of cooperation from the planters. The contract system was not successful, nor was the wage system. The planter didn't have the resources of capital and fluid funds. He'd never operated that way before, and lacked the necessary sources of credit. Furthermore, the idea of turning hard cash over to Negroes seemed to the planter a form of madness.

The upshot was the share-cropping system. This had attractions for both the white planter and the black laborer. For the planter, it meant a return to the noncash system; he didn't have to pay wages, and he had physical control over his workers. They lived on his land, in his houses, and he told them what to do. The Negroes liked the system because it gave them a semblance of independence. They lived and worked in family units. And in a fashion it associated economic reward with in-dividual direction and effort. If the share cropper made a big crop, presumably he earned more money. Of course, that often proved illusory; usually the share cropper remained in debt; he got little cash return, for it was not a cash economy.

Aside from these traditionalisms and psychological gratifications, the share-cropping system was based on the lack of capital of both planter and freedman. Out of it grew that ramshackle, incredibly inefficient, uneconomical crop-lien system. This system had many of the evils of ante-bellum slavery with none of the old virtues of planning and organiza-tion. It produced very little income for the share cropper. In place of the old system of gang labor under the direction of the overseer and driver, it substituted a one-horse, one-family, one-crop method of agriculture.

J.A.G. To what extent did Negroes migrate north between 1877 and the beginning of World War I?

C.V.W. Down to 1910, the old slave states retained 90 percent or more of the Negro population. Of these, the former Confederate states, plus Kentucky, had 85.3 percent of the Negroes in 1870 and only 2 percent less in 1910. There was, of course, a good deal of movement within the South, mainly to the cities and towns. The urban Negro population increased from about 7 percent in 1870 to over 16 percent in 1910. There was also a tendency of rural Negroes to concentrate in the so-called "black belt" of Georgia, Alabama, and Mississippi, the heart of the cotton-growing region.

Why, in view of the heavy influx of European immigration in the postwar period, didn't the Negro flock north to compete for industrial jobs? The answer is, I think, because of the European immigration. The immigrants filled the great demand for labor in those years. They took the jobs, largely unskilled, for which the Negroes would have been qualified. Being white, somewhat more literate, and without the slavery heritage and its handicaps, the European immigrants had a distinct advantage over the blacks. As hostile as was the reception given to the immigrants, the Southern Negro would undoubtedly have gotten a still more unfriendly one. An even lower status would have been assigned to him. Also, there was still a demand for Negro labor in Southern agriculture. So the Negro lacked both the pull and the push to migrate, not to mention the means.

J.A.G. Would you comment on the work of recent historians who have examined the policy of the Republican party toward the Negro in the late nineteenth century?

C.V.W. The most important work has been done by S. P. Hirshson and Vincent De Santis. They come to much the same conclusion: that the party constantly vacillated between its old hopes for the establishment of a black Republican organization in the South, and the other and different hope of establishing a respectable white Republican party. The party's first post-Reconstruction temptation was to take advantage of the white independent party revolts that broke out in nearly all the Southern states. The Republican leaders were influenced, I think, by the success of the conservative Democrats in manipulating the black vote against the white radicals, and their own despondency about winning that vote back. So they were tempted to throw in their lot with rebellious white movements, and did so notably in Virginia, where the Independents won control. But their old identification with the Southern Negro didn't entirely disappear. This can be seen in two legislative movements on behalf of the Negro that failed. One was the Blair Education Bill, which proposed a federal subsidy to education roughly proportional to the illiteracy rate in each state. The plan would have meant that the South would have gotten a disproportionate amount of the federal funds, and it gained widespread support, even among conservative Southern whites. It had a long and frustrating history in Congress. The other was the so-called Lodge Bill for the protection of the right to vote in federal elections. This was an attempt to return to the old-type Republican policy. It also was defeated, partly because of Republican maneuvers and manipulations resulting from their need of Southern votes in Congress to pass other legislation.

J.A.G. If at least a substantial segment of the Northern Republican leadership was willing to sacrifice the interests of the Southern Negro in order to build up a white Republican party in the South, why did the effort fail?

C.V.W. Their plans were defeated by the pressure of the Southern concern for white solidarity and by propaganda against Negro participation in politics. The economic program of the Republican party had a legitimate appeal in the South, particularly in the land-locked areas of the hill country. These districts needed internal improvements and industrialization—the very things that the Republicans stressed. Enclaves of Republican support existed throughout this period, but showed little tendency to spread. I think the majority of Southern whites did not feel very hospitable to the Republican economic program. Furthermore, the memories of the Civil War lingered in the South as well as in the North. The "bloody shirt" issue was quite important in retaining popular loyalty to the Democratic party.

J.A.G. Was there any substantial Northern group that worked consistently for the well-being of the Southern Negro in the latter part of the nineteenth century?

C.V.W. I've mentioned the Blair Bill and Lodge Bill as political movements which failed. Not all the Northern friends of the Negro deserted him after 1877. But the abolitionists had always been a small minority. James M. McPherson is currently studying what happened to radical sentiment in that period. He estimates that of the old abolitionists who survived, nearly half became disillusioned and drifted away from the cause, but that the rest persisted in their efforts. Of course, they were a small minority that was rapidly growing smaller. They were old people who were bucking a great tide of reaction in the country on racial issues. By the late 1880's, the vocal white friends of the Negro were indeed a tiny minority, and quite ineffectual.

The predominant attitude of educated Northerners, from whom the radicals had always recruited support, was that of E. L. Godkin, editor of the *Nation*. Godkin urged on the Negro the gospel of thrift and frugality, of chastity, morality, the Puritan ethic—plus a kind of chamber of commerce code. They wanted to make the Negro a respectable American, "usable" in an industrial society. The *Nation* very early renounced radicalism. Its most vocal editor in the late nineteenth century on the subject was Wendell Phillips Garrison, once more radical on the Negro question than his father, William Lloyd Garrison. In this period he became a conservative on the subject of Negro equality.

No voices in the North in the late 1880's and early 1890's were so outspoken, so vigorous, and so radical in behalf of Negro rights as those of three Southerners: Albion W. Tourgee, the novelist from North Carolina; George W. Cable of Louisiana; and Lewis H. Blair of Virginia. Both Cable and Blair were veterans of the Confederate Army; Tourgee was northern-born, but he had settled in the South after the Civil War. They were, of course, isolated and almost unique, representative of no substantial opinion in the South. Theirs were voices in the wilderness, a wilderness of silence, apathy, even of hostility.

J.A.G.   To what extent did Negro leaders influence the fate of black people in this period? I'd particularly like your opinion of the policies and the achievements of Booker T. Washington.

C.V.W.   About the Negro leaders other than Washington, very little is known. There are no adequate biographies of Bishop Turner, a very powerful voice in the Negro communities of the 1880's and 1890's, or of Frederick and Archibald Grimke. Little is known about the resurgence of the Back-to-Africa movement of the 1890's, which involved thousands of people, and was a pathetic and tragic experiment. The powerful leaders of the religious sects (who came closer to the mass of the Negro people than the better-known writers and intellectuals) are only shadowy figures. We don't know much about them and probably never will.

As to Booker T. Washington, there is still no biography that is anywhere near adequate, in spite of the enormous collection of his papers in the Library of Congress. He was a complex figure, in many ways a devious one. In terms of power and influence, he was second to no other Negro in American history, not even Frederick Douglass or W. E. B. Du Bois. Indeed, he was second to no Southern white figure of his time.

Washington was a leader not only of blacks but of whites, and not only of Northern whites, but of Southern whites. His leadership transcended class lines. He was middle class himself, but he influenced the working class and spoke for them. His role was that of a great intermediary. In some ways, this has been the classical role of the Negro leader; it was characteristic of the role of Martin Luther King, for example.

But there are also some remarkable similarities between Washington and the Black Nationalists of the present time, particularly in Washington's emphasis on self-help, self-respect, race pride, the importance of Negro enterprise, and also racial separatism. Of course, the separatism of Booker T. Washington was a separatism of acquiescence, not of conscious and aggressive withdrawal. Then, too, the Washington doctrine was turned to conservative rather than to radical purposes. He favored nonviolent instead of violent methods. He was an accommodationist. He never announced higher aspirations for Negroes than those he sought immediately. But he was constantly engaged in fights in the courts, and through attempts to marshal public opinion, sought to mitigate discrimination, disfranchisement, and lynching, though, of course, not with nearly the militancy that modern Negroes demand.

On segregation he was very largely acquiescent. On the surface he was very much a man of his times, an expression of his time. Underneath he was very secretive in his operations. He ran a powerful "intelligence operation," which infiltrated all the Negro movements. Wherever one developed strength, he would have an agent, often a secret agent, professing opposition to him, reporting everything that happened. Yet he had many powerful Negro intellectual defenders, T. Thomas Fortune and Kelly Miller to mention only two, who rationalized, defended, and furthered his views and protected his interests. And he had a great machine that tapped important sources of philanthropy; he had contacts with all the powerful foundations of the time and with many of their founders, such as Andrew Carnegie. His access to the seats of power, to Presidents and cabinet members, was extensive. He influenced political patronage more powerfully than anybody, black or white, in the South, and educational policy as as well.

J.A.G.   Was there really any alternative for a man like Washington to the kind of accommodationism he practiced?

C.V.W.   There was an opportunity to be more militant, and such people as Du Bois seized it and did what they could. Perhaps in the long run they accomplished more. But the avenues of power were not open to them to nearly the degree that they were to Washington. Had he adopted other policies, he would not have had the power and the money and the influence that he had.

J.A.G.   There is a tendency among Negro militants to write off Washington as an Uncle Tom. From a historical point of view, is this a reasonable judgment of him, given the depth of the prejudice against Negroes that existed in the late nineteenth century?

C.V.W.   In modern times, of course, he would certainly qualify for that epithet, but those were not modern times. Even in his own day he was not as acquiescent and supine as he's often said to have been. I notice, by the way, a renewed interest in Washington and his policies on the part of the Black Nationalists. These present-day radicals pursue different tactics, but they have the same goals that Washington had.

J.A.G.   Was the effort of Southern Populists like Tom Watson to forge a Negro–poor-white political alliance in the South based on any other motive than a wish to achieve power?

C.V.W.   I think that power is the basic motive behind all political alliances. It was the basis of anomalous alliances like that of the Southern Democrats with the Northern immigrant labor in the same period, and, for that matter, like the earlier Northern Republican alliance with the Negro freedmen. These were alliances of very disparate groups, and their purposes were to gain power. This is not to equate all examples. Some alliances, including the two I've just mentioned, were made at less cost to tradition, to folkways, to prejudices, to historical conditioning than the alliance of Southern whites and Negroes in the Populist movement. One must keep in mind how closely that alliance followed on Reconstruction, how large the Negro percentage of the Southern population was, and also the upsurge of racial feeling and exclusivism in the country at large.

To overcome the obstacles of prejudice and heritage and to form an interracial alliance in the South, the Populists had to appeal to "gut" doctrines of power and economic gain. No broad-based party can make such aims their primary ones. Politicians don't say, "Vote for us because we want power and we want economic advantage"; they say, "Vote for us because we have noble ends." That's what the Republican party said in the Reconstruction period, and the Southern Populists invoked the cause of justice and decency and human rights and equality in the same way. They attacked injustice, disfranchisement, discrimination, and lynching. How sincere they were in these idealistic, humanitarian professions is debatable. Certainly, sometimes they were sincere, and sometimes they were not. The mass of white Southern Populists remained more white and Southern than Populist. They were the same people they had always been.

The alliance quickly broke up, but not all the desertion came from the side of the whites. Many Negroes deserted their white allies, and this reflects the promises that conservatives were making to Negroes. I think that the Negro had a different perception of the Populist movement from the white man. His main objectives were protection, patronage, and jobs. Although the Populists promised those things, they were mainly interested in credit and monetary reforms, land reform, and restricting big business. The Negro was not much interested in those things. When the Populists didn't deliver on the things Negroes cared about, they lost interest, believing that they could get more from conservatives than from the radicals.

J.A.G.   Can the development early in the twentieth century of more militant Negro groups opposed to Booker T. Washington's approach, signalized by the Niagara movement and the foundation of the National Association for the Advancement of Colored People, properly be considered a part of the Progressive movement?

C.V.W. Neither in doctrine nor in motivation can the Niagara movement or the NAACP be considered characteristic of Progressivism. At no time did the Negro and his needs and the injustices he was suffering become a vital concern to Progressives. Some of them were interested in the Negro cause, but I don't think it is accurate to say that the Progressive movement was vitally concerned. The same was true of the so-called Forward-Looking movement of that time, and of the clergymen who led the Social Gospel movement. They talked of many ideals and condemned human injustices, but when it came down to cases, they did not bother with the Negroes as a group to any degree. The same was true of the Muckrakers, with the minor exception of Ray Stannard Baker, whose book, *Following the Color Line*, was published in 1908. The American Federation of Labor sponsored Jim Crow locals, or excluded Negroes from membership. Even the American Socialist party had segregationist and white-supremacy spokesmen, such as Victor Berger, Gaylord Wilshire, and H. J. Whalen. Eugene Debs was a sincere friend of the Negro, but even he had to make concessions repeatedly to anti-Negro sentiment among the Socialists.

Many leading academics and intellectuals of the period were also anti-Negro. Social scientists like Charles Cooley, Richard T. Ely, John R. Commons, and E. A. Ross were interested in and wrote about social injustice and the problems of minorities, but not about the Negro problem. Most of them manifested some racist thought, though not of the most vicious type. In the year 1907, both Henry James, the novelist, and President Charles W. Eliot of Harvard declared the warmest sympathies for Southern attitudes on the race question. Henry James has a wonderful passage describing a visit to Charleston, in which he says he understood intuitively and immediately just how Southerners felt. Eliot, in talking about segregation in colleges, remarked that "if we had the proportion of Negroes that the South has, we'd be practicing segregation too."

I use these examples to indicate that it's not quite fair to single out the Progressives for special condemnation on this question. They reflected their times. But they reflected them awfully well: they were thoroughgoing spokesmen of contemporary attitudes.

J.A.G. Why were the accomplishments of the Progressives in the area of Negro rights so limited?

C.V.W. That depends on one's interpretation of the movement. I tend to see it as more a conservative than an innovative movement, more a response to corporate needs than to popular and labor needs, and in considerable measure a reaction against the agrarian and labor radicalism of the 1880's and 1890's. In other words, it is not surprising to me that the Progressives reacted as they did to the Negro problem. In the South, which did have a strong Progressive movement, the aims of Progressivism and white supremacy proved to be thoroughly compatible. To Progressives like Charles B. Aycock of North Carolina, Hoke Smith of Georgia, and B. B. Comer of Alabama, Negro disfranchisement was a *reform:* it attacked the problem of corruption at the polls by eliminating the black voters! Similarly, in California, Hiram Johnson had no trouble reconciling his views about the Japanese and Chinese with his Progressive ideology.

In the field of foreign relations, the Progressives adopted an expansionist and imperialistic line. This led to the acquiring of territories populated by peoples of other races, and white supremacy at home was perfectly compatible with white supremacy abroad. Southerners quickly pointed this out, and Northern imperialists were quick to see the point.

The Negro problem was the great blind spot of the Progressives. The Negro was an invisible man, seen only in stereotype. Thus, the Progressive era, with all its stress on democracy, coincided with the period of the most rapid advancement of legal, formal, constitutional segregation, and the most rapid deterioration of the Negro's civil rights.

J.A.G.   What is your opinion of Theodore Roosevelt's record on the race question?

C.V.W.   Roosevelt is remembered as the man who invited Booker Washington to dinner at the White House, but I think it's significant that he never repeated this "mistake," as he called it later. He went further than any President since Rutherford B. Hayes in appeasing Southern white opinion. It is true that in his anxiety over the 1904 election he did make overtures to the Negroes of the Southern states. He appointed a Negro to a federal post in Charleston, and went so far as to close the post office in Indianola, Mississippi, because the people refused to accept the Negro postmistress. He belabored the lily-white Republicans of the South with the patronage stick. Reassured, Negro Southern bosses delivered the required delegates to the 1904 Republican convention.

Of course, Southern whites were outraged. But after the 1904 election, T.R. went to great lengths to recapture the Southern white vote. (He'd already appointed several Southern conservatives to federal office, including the grandson of Stonewall Jackson.) In 1905, he toured the South twice; he praised Robert E. Lee and the Confederacy, told Negro Southerners that the whites were their best friends, sent roses to Stonewall Jackson's widow. He had himself photographed in front of his Bullock relatives' mansion in Georgia, surrounded by a group of black "retainers," and recalled that his uncle had served in the Confederate

Navy. The whites were thoroughly charmed with this performance, the Negroes, correspondingly dismayed and disillusioned.

Roosevelt's private correspondence indicates that he was not a cynical opportunist. He was doing what he believed. In 1906, for instance, he wrote that he entirely agreed that Negroes were "altogether inferior to whites." And in his Bull Moose campaign of 1912, he went to even greater lengths than he had in his second administration to appease Southern white racism. He categorically refused to seat Negro delegates in the Bull Moose convention, and based his Southern strategy in the 1912 election on a lily-white Progressive party. In 1916, he wrote to Henry Cabot Lodge remarking on what a terrible mistake the Fifteenth Amendment had been, and saying that to restore the Negro's right to vote in the South would be to reduce the region to the level of Haiti.

J.A.G. Was there any difference between Roosevelt and Woodrow Wilson on this race question?

C.V.W. Not very much. Wilson did not—because he had no need to, I suppose—go so far as Roosevelt occasionally did to seek Negro support. It's true that Southerners played a decisive part in Wilson's preconvention campaign in 1912, and they were strongly represented in his cabinet after his election. It's also true, I think, that Wilson's Southern heritage influenced his racial ideas. But it's important to remember also that this Southern identification proved no serious handicap to his sensational rise, in both his academic and his political careers. It was, if anything, an advantage. These so-called Southern views had become American views; by the early twentieth century the American way had become the Southern way. Wilsonian policies were not drastic departures from those of Roosevelt and Taft, but rather a logical extension of them. In 1912, he promised Negro representatives "justice, executed with liberality" and absolute fair dealing. The Negroes were set up by these promises, but of course they were disappointed. The signal extension of racist policy that came in Wilson's administration was the segregation of Negro employees in Washington departments. He not only gave his official approval to this policy, but defended it as "distinctly to the advantage of the colored people themselves."

J.A.G. Many so-called "New Left" historians berate the profession for not having provided the Negro with what they call a "usable past." In part, this charge is based on the argument that white historians have either ignored, or unfairly presented, the history of the Negro in America. How much substance is there to this charge?

C.V.W. In its demand for a usable past for the Negro, I think the New Left often sounds rather like the Old Left with its effort to endow the working class with nobility, heroism, and a tradition of unrelenting resistance to the bosses and the exploiters. Such a conception of the role of the historian and the purposes of history does the Negro movement as great a disservice as it did the working-class movement.

The legitimate demand for a "new" Negro history is the result, I think, of white historians' ethnocentric self-flattery, complacency, racial chauvinism, and self-righteousness. But the resulting distortions will not be corrected by imitation of that same philosophy: by black self-flattery and chauvinism and complacency and self-righteousness. As historians have long recognized, nationalism—white, black, or any other color—is one of the worst distorters of history. This is not to deny that white historians have neglected or unfairly treated the Negro's role in American history. There are many evidences of this. For example, the South has yet to realize the extent to which its character, culture, and style of life have been shaped by Negro influences. And the whole nation has yet to realize how much of what it has compartmentalized as distinctly Southern is really national, and therefore how vitally the Negro, and slavery, and emancipation, and segregation, and discrimination have affected national history.

J.A.G. Would you explain what you meant when you said that what white historians have considered to be Southern is largely a reflection of the existence of so many Negroes in the South?

C.V.W. Well, consider how the Puritan ethic was transformed when it penetrated the South. The Negro's adjustment to slavery was absolutely central in shaping attitudes toward work and toward industry. Slaves naturally looked on work as a thing to avoid, not to encourage. With time, the white Southerner came to agree with this to the extent that he thought that work (something the Negro did) was degrading. He absorbed unconsciously attitudes which the Negro exemplified and which were the result of the institutional framework in which both white and black lived for the greater part of Southern history.

J.A.G. I believe that part of what the New Left historians are complaining about is slightly different from the point that you've made. For example, in your comments on the racial attitudes of Theodore Roosevelt and Woodrow Wilson, you painted a fairly damning picture of these two men. I think that the New Left historians would say, "Historians have presented Roosevelt and Wilson as great liberals, as reformers trying to improve the social condition of the people." In other words, they claim not merely that historians have ignored the black man and minimized his significance in the society, but that they have ignored the way the white man has treated the black man, and praised as great "liberals" men who were in fact callous to the needs and interests of the blacks. Do you think there is any justice in that argument?

C.V.W. I do. Historical estimates have often been made without taking into account liberal shortcomings in this area. Historians have been influenced by the values of the men they have been studying. They have by-passed the race question and concentrated on other issues, evaluating historical figures according to their achievement of their professed objectives and often forgetting that some of their objectives fell far short of true justice. But this has not been true of *all* historians and biographers. I think particularly of Wilson's biographer, Arthur Link, who has been quite explicit and candid about Wilson's attitudes and policies toward the Negro.

J.A.G.   This raises a larger question about the proper function of the historian. Is it the historian's job to evaluate men and movements in the light of the standards and values of our day, or is it his function to evaluate them in their own context?

C.V.W.   I don't see how the historian can pretend that he is not a man of his own time—to say, "Now, I will turn off my real personality and values and pretend that I am a Progressive of the 1900's, or a Jeffersonian of the 1800's." No one can do that. Certainly a historian should keep his judgments in proportion and admit, when he does make an estimate, that he is being influenced by his own values. To pretend that he has no other frame of reference than the people he's writing about seems to me a forced and artificial conception of the historian's role. If a modern historian tried to describe Reconstruction in the South from the viewpoint of a Southerner of the late 1860's, he would not be talking to his readers.

J.A.G.   But isn't it asking too much of the men of the past to expect them to have acted in their own times in the light of what later generations know and think? If I may use a more specific example, if one is going to judge the leading American figures of the past in terms of their attitudes toward race and to use these attitudes to form generalizations about whether they were good men or bad, liberals or conservatives, would one not immediately run into very serious distortions? The standard way of looking at Hamilton and Jefferson is to see Jefferson as representing a liberal position and Hamilton a conservative one. Yet Jefferson had a much lower opinion of the potential of Negroes than Hamilton.

C.V.W.   There are many questions involved here. I think the historian is guilty of an unhistorical view if he pretends that the people he's writing about shared his frame of reference and his values. But he has an obligation to his own age as well; he must inform his own times of the meaning of the past in terms of the present. This can readily result in distortion, and that has to be guarded against. But I don't think the historian is justified thereby in ignoring his obligations.

J.A.G.   Granted that historians have not done full justice to the role of the Negro in American history, what form should revisionism take?

What are the main areas that need to be studied in order to understand the role of the Negro better and do justice to his historical role?

C.V.W. History is an art of infinite variety: narrative and traditional, analytic and quantified, sociological and economic. All types can and should be influenced by the peculiar role of the Negro in America, among other things. The obvious debasement and subjugation resulting from white rule limited very severely the achievements and the influence of the Negro in many fields. We've had no Negro Presidents, and only lately any Negroes in high federal office. Few have achieved prominence in the fields of diplomacy, education, intellectual activities, and many others. How could it have been otherwise?

The main opportunities for Negro history lie in the direction of what one might call mass history. Analytical history will always be heavily statistical, and I would think that application of new techniques involving computer analysis will make the study of Negro mass behavior and movements much more available and much more attractive to historians. A special opportunity is in the comparative approach to history. It's obvious that one common feature of the history of all Europeans in the New World is that all of them to some degree shared the experiences of African slavery, miscegenation, emancipation, and reconstruction. Unlike the northwestern European countries with which we constantly compare ourselves, the United States is a segmented society, a society divided in races. To study the immigrant African and the relations between the races during and after slavery in the different American societies would lift American and Negro history out of the parochial, nationalistic, moralistic framework in which these subjects have been too much confined.

J.A.G. Admitting the desirability of the kind of history you suggest, is there enough evidence to write a detailed history of the Negro, especially in the United States, from his own point of view? How can anyone now discover how slaves felt, when only a handful of them could read and write and thus leave records for us to study?

C.V.W. There are obvious limitations and handicaps to the writing of Negro history. The written record is chiefly the record of what the *white* man thought. And as I have said, the Negro's achievements were small when compared to the white man's. Yet it would be wrong to attempt to compensate by exaggerating such achievements as black men have made, as historians of various minority groups have often done. The oldest minority of all, the WASP, have repeatedly exaggerated their own importance, and I don't think that the second-oldest minority, the Negroes, would benefit by imitating that example. Equally misguided would be the encouragement of biographical pursuits of ever-more-trivial figures of the past down to a level of obscurity that is ridiculous.

But it is possible to redress the balance without merely exaggerating the role of the Negro, to write scrupulously and objectively about Negroes who took part in the great themes of American history: colonization, expansion, independence, wars, immigration, urbanization. This would result in a valid redressing of the balance.

J.A.G.   What of the argument of some Negroes today that only blacks can properly write the history of the black man?

C.V.W.   This view appears to be growing; it has penetrated academic and intellectual circles. One striking example has been the fantastic attack of William Styron's novel about Nat Turner. I think one test of this "rule" would be to apply it universally: only whites could write white history, only Polynesians Polynesian history, only Russians Russian history, and so forth. It's obviously preposterous. One could next raise the question of how black a Negro historian has to be in order to qualify. Would Ralph Bunche pass such a test? He was rejected in Africa as a white man, and has lived largely in a white world. A large percentage of the Negroes of the United States, who present themselves as qualified to write black history by this standard, would be greeted with some astonishment in Latin America. They wouldn't be considered black at all.

J.A.G.   I doubt that the advocates of black history by black men would accept that last argument. They would say that what is significant is not the degree of skin pigmentation but whether or not the historian is considered black by American society. Isn't there something to the argument that only a person who has experienced the peculiar and subtle by-products of being considered a Negro in our society can really understand the problem of being black?

C.V.W.   Where would the revision of the history of slavery be without the contributions of such northern white scholars as David Davis, Eugene Genovese, and Winthrop Jordan? Where would scholarship about Negro life in America be without the work of such white foreigners as Gunnar Myrdal and Gilberto Freyre? Where would the history of Reconstruction be without the contributions of Vernon L. Wharton, a native white of Mississippi, or Joel Williamson, a native white of South Carolina, or Willie Lee Rose, a native white of Virginia? This qualification of color would eliminate, it seems to me, some of the most important and, from the Negro's own point of view, desirable contributions in this whole field.

Then another objection to applying such a color qualification is sheer recruitment. Negro historians in their thirties and forties are conspicuously few. If one has to rely on black historians, they'll be overworked;

they won't be able to do the job. That's a practical objection, but there are many others, it seems to me.

J.A.G.   How can the persistent anti-Negro attitude of the white majority in the United States be explained? Negroes have often been compared to immigrants in this connection, and yet immigrants, by the second or third generation, have been accepted into the larger society. Since there has been no significant Negro immigration into America since the first decade of the nineteenth century, why have the Negroes not been assimilated?

C.V.W.   We're only beginning to understand how deeply rooted and how universal our prejudices are. They were rooted in England nearly a century before the first cargo of Negroes was landed in Virginia in the seventeenth century. Nor is it correct to proclaim the uniqueness of Anglo-Saxon depravity in racial attitudes. Recent researchers have shown that both in their historical development and in their present relations, the white Latin-Americans have been fellow sinners. They have merely been more subtle and discriminating in their racial distinctions.

As to the comparison of the Negro with the immigrant, I once heard a prominent urban sociologist of the University of Chicago say that the Negro had really only "joined" American life in the twentieth century. I felt like pointing out that the Negro may have joined Chicago in the twentieth century, but he joined American life a long time before the great majority of Chicagoans, or their ancestors, came to this country. Of course, what the sociologist meant was that they'd only recently moved *en masse* to the cities, that they had previously been isolated, segregated in the confines of Southern life. I would insist that they'd been very much a part of Southern life, but I would not admit that they were unknown to urban life. The Negro was in New York from the beginning; there were eleven Negroes in the city in 1626, and in the eighteenth century the Negro population rarely fell below 10 percent. New Yorkers celebrated their presence variously—once in 1711 by a judicial lynching that took the lives of many Negroes, and again about 1741 when another group was executed on a conspiratory charge of little basis. One was barbecued over a slow fire for eight hours before he died.

The white immigrant, however, arrived in America under very different circumstances, color prejudices aside. He brought with him intact a culture that he cherished and preserved, with the help of his priests and his teachers and his intellectuals. And on that foundation he built a sense of identity. The African was deprived of his cultural heritage in the transportation and enslavement and acculturation to the plantation life. Anthropologists dispute this, pointing to various artifacts of African cultural heritage, but these are fragments, not comparable to what the Italians or Polish or Irish peasants brought with them to America. The Negroes' present efforts to substitute various artificial cultural identifications, such as African nationalism and Black Muslimism, are not adequate substitutes. But above all, there is the vexing question of race, which the European immigrant, even the Jew, by and large escaped. The Negro has always had this obstacle to deal with. Furthermore, the immigrant was often one of the worst offenders in the exclusion and discrimination of the Negro in the Northern slums.

J.A.G. The belief of so many white Americans that Negroes were inferior was for several centuries a self-fulfilling prophecy. If you treat the Negro in an inferior way, he will seem inferior in his behavior. But for at least a generation the psychological and sociological proof that the Negro is not inherently inferior has existed and been accepted by most educated people. Do you think that the age of prejudice will end in the foreseeable future?

C.V.W. All ages end, and ours can surely be described as an age of prejudice. When the relationship between African and English began back in the sixteenth century, these prejudices were there. The situation is changing more rapidly now than ever before, and for the better, though reactions could set in again as they did after the Civil War, for instance. In my more pessimistic moments I think it is going to happen again. I don't know. But in any event, racial prejudice is not going to pass away very swiftly. Every people who has enslaved another people has formed deep convictions about their inferiority.

Knowledge certainly affects the informed, and the knowledge of racial equality certainly pervades the thinking of educated people about the question in the way you suggest. But that's a relatively small class; this scientific evidence is not very widely shared and has not yet basically molded popular opinion. Irrational and rational fears of the Negro "menace" to one's status and place in society persist, in part because powerful elements, in science and in government and among intellectuals, have legitimately encouraged Negroes to get into the race for power and wealth. The people they must race against are in large part people who feel threatened and menaced, and who react therefore negatively toward Negro accomplishments. They want to keep Negroes out of their neighborhoods, out of their unions, out of their clubs—out. Now, I'm not so much a pessimist as to say that more enlightened attitudes won't penetrate the mass of white opinion eventually. But I don't think it's going to happen quickly.

J.A.G. What are the half-dozen or so books that you would recommend to persons interested in the subject we have been discussing? In each case, would you indicate what the particular contribution of the volume is?

C.V.W. Thomas F. Gossett, *Race: The History of an Idea in America* (1964) treats the development of racial attitudes, especially since the Civil War. John Hope Franklin, *From Slavery to Freedom: A History of Negro Americans* (1967) is the best general treatment of the subject. Joel Williamson, *After Slavery: The Negro in South Carolina During Reconstruction, 1861–1877* (1965) is a fresh and thorough history. Vernon L. Wharton, *The Negro in Mississippi, 1865–1890* (1947) revises many old notions about the freedmen. W. E. B. Du Bois, *Black Reconstruction in America, 1860–1880* (1935) is a powerful and sometimes emotional indictment of white policies. Willie Lee Rose, *Rehearsal for Reconstruction: The Port Royal Experiment* (1964) brings a reappraisal of emancipation and its consequences.

Ernest R. May

The Emergence of the
United States as a World Power

ＥRNEST R. MAY, Professor of History at Harvard and a member of the Institute of Politics in the John F. Kennedy School of Government at that university, is a specialist in diplomatic history. Among his many books are *The World War and American Isolation* (1959), *Imperial Democracy: The Emergence of the United States as a Great Power* (1961), a study of the causes and implications of the Spanish-American War, and *American Imperialism: A Speculative Essay* (1968). Professor May's work is characterized by a multiarchival approach; he sees foreign relations properly as the interaction of nations and does not look at his subject from a narrowly American point of view. In the following discussion he describes the course of America's foreign relations from the 1870's to World War I.

John A. Garraty Professor May, is the common tendency to see American foreign policy in terms of a conflict between isolationists and interventionists a useful way of approaching the subject?

Ernest R. May It is a useful distinction to make, at least for the years from the late eighteenth century to the first quarter of the twentieth century, because it describes a continuing difference of opinion between people who thought that the United States ought to function *as an example* to the world, and other people who felt that the United States ought to exert its influence *in* the world—not just as an example but by having some positive effect on other peoples and other governments. The distinction was perhaps most clear in the early nineteenth century, when, for example, Henry Clay felt that the United States ought to move into Latin America, while John Quincy Adams held that the United States ought to be just an example for the Latin Americans and not get mixed up in their affairs.

But the difference was also fairly clear in the late nineteenth century. Compare the anti-imperialist who believed that the United States ought not to run any risk of getting mixed up in international politics, and the Theodore Roosevelt type who insisted that the United States should bring its political and moral influence to bear on world affairs.

There was also a spectrum among isolationists, running from those who thought primarily in terms of moral influence to those who thought in terms of power. Some said that the nation should avoid involvement in international politics because that would increase the moral strength of the United States, and others took the same policy position, but argued that the reason was that the nation simply wasn't strong enough yet to impose its standards on other peoples.

J.A.G. Could you give me an example or two to clarify this distinction?

E.R.M. William Jennings Bryan, it seems to me, argued fairly continuously that the United States ought just to improve itself; that it ought to be observed by the rest of the world and imitated by them.

Some of the older anti-imperialists—Senator George F. Hoar of Massachusetts is a good case in point—contended, on the other hand, that if the United States ventured into European politics or acquired colonies, it would overstrain its resources. The need to have a larger navy and army and a colonial service would cost more than it could afford, and foreign crises would strain a polity already fragile because it was made up of so many potentially conflicting sections, races, and creeds.

J.A.G. How would you fit President Grover Cleveland into this analysis?

E.R.M. It's hard to put him in a category because it's hard to put anyone clearly into one. I take the examples of Bryan and Hoar because they illustrate the tendencies. Cleveland had a very pragmatic approach to the issues that came before him. He was willing to take Hawaii if it were both safe and moral to do so. He was concerned about the image of the United States. He was worried about annexing Hawaii, because he thought illicit force had been used to overthrow the native government. At the same time he sometimes felt the United States ought to show its muscle, as in the Venezuelan boundary case, where he thought Great Britain had violated the Monroe Doctrine. I think it's hard, too, to put McKinley into any one of these categories, and it's even hard to put Theodore Roosevelt in one, after he became President. The responsibility of making decisions makes it more difficult for people to be ideologically consistent.

J.A.G.   I don't mean to ask a leading question, but were there many Americans who felt that the United States had a vital interest in the European balance of power per se?

E.R.M.   No. Beginning in the late 1880's, and particularly after the Venezuelan crisis, you do, of course, find people who are talking about the importance of Anglo-American solidarity and the importance of Britain. But the argument was couched in quite different terms. They were not saying that it was important to the United States that the British position in Europe be preserved. They thought in much more general terms. Andrew Carnegie is an excellent example. He spoke of the importance of Anglo-American solidarity, but never used any language that would suggest he was thinking about a concrete American interest in the European balance of power. In 1898, an article in *The Atlantic Monthly* by former Secretary of State Richard Olney did claim that the United States had an interest in what happened in Europe and was likely to be threatened by a combination of power in Europe, but this was a rare kind of utterance.

J.A.G.   When did this point of view begin to become important?

E.R.M.   It was a very small group at best, all the way down to American intervention in the First World War.

J.A.G.   What about Roosevelt's interest in the Algeciras Conference?

E.R.M.   You have to make a distinction between the behavior of a President or an administration dealing with international problems as they arise, and the rhetoric of international relations. One of the impressive things in Howard K. Beale's *Theodore Roosevelt and America's Rise to World Power* is his demonstration that inwardly Roosevelt was thinking in terms of world power politics. But the evidence is found in his correspondence and his own private musings. The thing that strikes me is how little of it is *public* evidence—how little Beale found in Roosevelt's speeches and official statements. Roosevelt didn't say this kind of thing even in private correspondence that was likely to be seen by more than a few congressmen, or in communications with ambassadors that might be published in congressional documents. He wrote it in private letters.

J.A.G. A number of recent historians have tried to push the beginnings of American imperialism back into the 1880's and even into the 1870's. Would you describe the case that they make, and then explain your own view of this subject?

E.R.M. The argument, as I understand it, is that there was a basic change in the structure of American society after the Civil War, with a shift from an essentially agrarian base to an essentially business, commercial, industrial base. The result was a change in the dominant group and dominant set of concerns in the country. And as interest shifted from land and crops to outlets for the products of industry, businessmen, manufacturers, and bankers became more and more concerned about foreign markets, particularly as industrial production increased. The cyclical depressions in the 1870's, and particularly in the early 1890's, made them apprehensive about whether or not the domestic economy could absorb their output—whether there were enough domestic consumers for what American industry could produce. So they became more eager for foreign markets. And the argument runs that they sought, not so much colonies to provide customers, as free access to markets in other parts of the world. They were interested in obtaining island possessions, but mainly to serve as entrepôts to these markets.

That's the argument as I understand it, and there is a lot of evidence in support of it in business periodicals, in newspaper editorials, and other sources. One of the questions that I would raise about this thesis is: Can one really say that there was anything unusual about it in the late nineteenth century? The same kind of thing was said in the early nineteenth century. It's a natural thing to be said by people who've got goods to sell. In the early nineteenth century, when there was a question about whether or not Spain would be able to keep Cuba, or whether the British might take it, or whether it might apply for annexation to the United States, the same rhetoric was used, and exactly the same kinds of considerations were brought forth.

J.A.G. I suppose the real question, then, is not so much whether there was an interest in foreign markets or islands or imperialism, as what kind of priority these interests received from policy makers.

E.R.M. That's one question. I wish someone would try a comparative approach, to see if what Americans were saying about this kind of question was different from what Englishmen were saying, or Germans.

J.A.G. Do the statistics of foreign trade throw any light on this question? Do they support the new interpretation?

E.R.M. No. One of the logical weaknesses in the argument is that the people most likely to consume the things that were in oversupply in the United States were Europeans. But that isn't necessarily very important, because the same thing is true of the imperialistic European countries. Their trade, by and large, was not increasing with the areas that they were colonizing. Of course, some of the people who were most interested in this kind of development were concerned not so much about trade as about overseas investment opportunities.

J.A.G.   The difficulty I find in that line of reasoning is that in the late nineteenth century the United States was still importing capital rather than exporting it. Was there any great interest on the part of the American capitalists in investing in Asia or Latin America?

E.R.M.   No, there really wasn't much. Investors seriously involved tended to be gamblers, men on the edge of the New York financial community.

J.A.G.   If American foreign policy was not in any substantial way influenced by economic interests, what did control the formulation of policy? Was it simply partisan politics?

E.R.M.   I always lean to a political interpretation, on the simple logic that the people who make the decisions and carry them out are in the business of politics. Their primary interests are getting themselves reelected, and getting their friends elected, and conserving their positions in history. They deal with persons who have economic interests at stake, but, in a way, even there, I suspect that the motivation of the politician is political. He's judging the political weight of the man with the economic interest.

J.A.G.   If that's true, doesn't it indicate that foreign affairs were not particularly important in the late nineteenth century to Americans?

E.R.M.   Yes. That seems to me hard to challenge.

J.A.G.   Many of the younger historians are challenging it.

E.R.M.   But the range of disagreement is not all that wide. To say that relatively few people were acutely concerned about foreign affairs is a proposition that all can accept. The question then is how serious the politicians were in catering to the interest of the relatively few who were concerned about it. Consider Secretary of State James G. Blaine's Latin American policy, for example. Blaine was conscious that a very small number of people, particularly in the shipping business, were interested in improving economic relations with Latin America. Now one can argue that, as a politician, Blaine was just using the language of "Pan-Americanism" to get that small group to make contributions to his campaigns. One can also argue that these men were a good deal less important to him than the Irish were. He certainly took strong foreign policy positions very critical of the British, with no other object than to attract Irish voters. I would also guess that Blaine was himself influenced by what he saw going on in Europe, and that sometimes he was not really appealing to any particular constituency but considering his own historic position, and thinking about how his policies would look in retrospect.

J.A.G.   Is there any connection between American foreign policy in the late nineteenth century and the earlier psychological influence on American development which we call "manifest destiny"? Can one interpret the beginnings of an interest in overseas expansion as a continuation of the westward movement, and relate it to the so-called closing of the frontier in the 1890's?

E.R.M. I suspect so. "Manifest destiny" was an American tradition. To many persons, the idea of taking territory on and beyond—Hawaii, the Philippines—seemed to fit in with this tradition. One newspaper editorial in the late 1890's that I recall chided the Democrats for opposing the annexation of the Philippines by saying that they were being disloyal to the tradition of Jefferson! The notion of the disappearance of the internal frontier could strengthen the feeling that this tradition ought to be revived. However, it's easy to dispute this argument, because many who picked up the Turner frontier thesis were not advocates of extra-continental expansion.

J.A.G. How important were missionaries interested in China and other distant lands in influencing public opinion in favor of expansion? Was the moral argument that the United States had a role in Christianizing heathens influential?

E.R.M. Certainly among missionaries, and missionaries formed a quite significant group. After all, the numbers of people who were involved in missionary work were fairly large, and the amount of contact between the churches and the missionary movement was greater than it was to be later.

Probably several distinctions should be made here. One would have to do with the influence of the missionary groups on the specific steps of expansion taking place at the end of the nineteenth century. Missionaries spoke for the annexation of the Philippines in large numbers in 1898. It was a peculiarly attractive case to them, because the Philippine Islands had been exclusively Catholic, and anti-Catholicism was certainly a very strong element in Protestant missionary development. Many of them regarded Catholicism as worse that heathenism, and annexation gave them an opportunity to battle both. It's hard to dispute that missionaries had some effect on the willingness of congressmen to go along with the policy of annexation.

But by and large, I don't think the missionary influence was expansionist. It was more on the side of this exertion of moral influence. The missionaries were early advocates of the "open door" in China. They pressed the American government to oppose *any* colonization of China.

J.A.G. Does that apply to the American missionaries in Hawaii? They certainly favored annexing the islands.

E.R.M. Hawaii was a special case. It's very hard to separate the missionaries functioning in Hawaii from the rest of the American community, a very interbred group. Some of the pineapple planters were sons of missionaries who had come earlier, and the cousins of missionaries who were functioning there then. This American community feared the native majority, and the Japanese who were migrating into the islands. The Hawaiian missionaries also thought that what they stood for was better for the islands, politically, morally, and culturally. To some extent the revolution was—from their standpoint—an act of self-defense.

J.A.G.   How was the expansion of the Grant era, as reflected in the purchase of Alaska and Grant's attempt to get Santo Domingo, different from the expansion of the 1890's?

E.R.M.   The real difference that I see is in terms of the public reaction. I don't think there was a single utterance in opposition to the Alaskan purchase that was based on ideological grounds. Santo Domingo, on the other hand, seems to be exactly the kind of case that was posed by Hawaii, by the Philippines, and by Cuba, after 1898. It was a potential island possession, it required a navy to protect it; it had a substantial population; it was different ethnically and religiously from the majority of the population of the United States. And there the public reaction was largely adverse. In the 1890's, many groups supported the acquisition of Hawaii and the Philippines. The people who defended Grant's proposal did so because they were supporters of Grant, not because they thought it was wise.

J.A.G.   Did the movement for modernizing the Navy in the 1880's reflect a growing national concern for an active foreign policy?

E.R.M.   I really don't see much connection between foreign affairs and naval policy, even in the 1890's. The relationship between naval power and foreign policy, in Congress, at least, only becomes clear after 1899, when congressmen were beginning to think about the American Navy as one of the great navies, and to compare it to British and German and French navies. Earlier debates on the Navy had to do with the welfare of the iron and steel industries; the need for some kind of federal subsidy to keep the steel industry on an even keel. One of the things that struck me in reading the debates on naval appropriation bills in the 1880's was that the solid bloc favoring a new navy consisted of congressmen with shipyards in their districts and congressmen whose districts ran along the tracks of the Pennsylvania Railroad.

Of course, a few officers—Captain A. T. Mahan, Admiral Stephen Luce, and a few others at the Naval War College—argued that sea power and foreign policy were very closely connected, but outside of a very small circle that argument was not much used or heard or understood until after the Spanish-American War.

J.A.G.   Does Cleveland's belligerent stance in the Venezuela boundary crisis of 1895 indicate that he was an expansionist?

E.R.M. No, I don't think so. That was a really mystifying episode. I've never felt I understood why Cleveland and Secretary Olney took the position they did. Perhaps the two of them looked at this problem as lawyers, thought that a great power was bullying a weak little American nation and was going to take some territory from it, and that this wrong was about to be done by the British government. And they made a connection between this action and the Monroe Doctrine. Cleveland was also conscious that if he took up the issue forcefully it was more likely to help him than to hurt him politically.

J.A.G. Was there even a remote possibility that this so-called crisis could have led to war between the United States and Great Britain?

E.R.M. Oh, I think there was a real possibility of it.

J.A.G. How could Cleveland have acted on such narrow political grounds if war was even remotely possible?

E.R.M. That's one of the things I don't understand. If Cleveland and Olney had been very knowledgeable about British politics and European politics, they could have discounted the dangers, because Britain could not afford to fight the United States. But I've never seen any evidence that they were.

J.A.G. Would you explain the significance of the statement in your book *Imperial Democracy* that Cleveland's action "startled England and the United States into one another's arms"? I think that's a fascinating idea.

E.R.M. On the British side, most politicians had simply not paid much attention to the United States before 1895. The United States was there, and Englishmen had talked a good deal about Anglo-American friendship, and there was a lot of travel back and forth, and a lot of writing in England about American growth. But as a factor in international politics, the United States was ignored. The professional diplomats had a map of the world in their heads which was primarily a European map with Africa and Asia as appendages. The United States just didn't figure on that map. The contingencies that British cabinets talked about when crises occurred in Europe, the possible alliances and combinations they considered, hardly ever took the United States into account.

Then suddenly this challenge over Venezuela! The possibility of having the United States as an enemy! This bombshell forced the British government to think about what the world would look like if they found themselves in a conflict with a combination of European powers, and the United States allied itself with the foe. Recognizing the extent to which Britain would then be unable to concentrate its sea power, the extent to which it might have difficulty obtaining resources, and the trouble it might encounter in Canada, they suddenly saw the political map of the world as somewhat larger.

On the American side, just thinking about the possibility of war in the winter of 1895–96 caused a number of Americans to consider in more practical terms the Anglo-American solidarity that had long been part of after-dinner speeches in exclusive New York clubs, and to realize what a terrible thing a war would be.

J.A.G.   Turning now to the Cuban revolution and the Spanish-American War, about which you have written lucidly and at length, was there any economic argument for American intervention?

E.R.M.   Obviously, the economic interests of some Americans were involved, but by and large those who owned property in Cuba favored non-intervention. Edwin Atkins of Boston, who owned sugar properties in Cuba, was continually writing to the successive Presidents telling them why the United States should not intervene—indeed, why the United States ought to help the Spaniards restore some kind of tranquility in Cuba. Such persons stood to lose if things were shaken up there. Their concessions were from the Spanish government. They did not know how an independent government would treat them, but they did know that the war was tearing up the Cuban economy.

Similarly, the New York financial community deplored the movement for intervention as a threat to recovery from the depression of the mid-90's. The possibility of war with Spain also jeopardized the inflow of investment from Europe and the stability of the dollar.

J.A.G.   Did individuals who lined up on the interventionist side in the Venezuelan crisis take the same position in the Cuban crisis, which was going on at the same time? Cleveland, for instance, certainly took diametrically opposite positions.

E.R.M.   That question is hard to answer, because the leading group in speaking out against Cleveland on the Venezuelan crisis consisted of lawyers and philanthropists; businessmen and bankers were less visible. Whereas, on the Cuban question, businessmen and bankers played more prominent roles than lawyers and philanthropists.

J.A.G.   Why were businessmen less concerned about the disruptive effects? After all, a war with Great Britain would have had far larger effects than a war with Spain.

E.R.M.   I think they were. It's merely a difference in who takes the lead in speaking out. Partly, it's because the Cuban question was not presented as primarily a legal question. The Venezuelan question was so presented, and therefore lawyers addressed themselves to it and were listened to by businessmen.

J.A.G.   What, then, *were* the differences between these two crises?

E.R.M.   The Cuban question was much harder to handle. Even people who argued ardently that the United States ought not to meddle in Cuba because of what could happen to the American economy had nevertheless to take account of the fact that there was an enormous amount of suffering in the island and that many Americans were understandably concerned about the death and disease and hunger there. It was impossible for anybody openly to take a pro-Spanish position. Spain was "backward," a symbol of everything that Americans had revolted against in 1776, and on top of that, Catholic.

J.A.G. One of the most interesting aspects of your book *Imperial Democracy* is the way you show that the political position of the parties in Congress almost completely reversed itself after McKinley replaced Cleveland as President. Was McKinley hampered by this partisan shift? He had been closely identified with the Republican position, critical of Cleveland, yet, when he took office, he substantially adopted Cleveland's policy.

E.R.M. McKinley's main political problem was that many members of his own party had taken strong positions in favor of intervention in Cuba. They could now say, "We ought to give the new administration a breathing space," but they could not back off and say, "We were wrong, and we really ought to let the Spaniards win in Cuba." McKinley came into office conscious that some kind of deadline awaited him unless he could get rid of the issue.

J.A.G. Would you comment on McKinley's handling of the crisis between the spring of 1897 and the declaration of war in April, 1898?

E.R.M. He was in a very tough position. He had a set of priorities in which the policy that the United States pursued with regard to Cuba stood below various other concerns. As a party leader, he was worried about the preservation of his party and the maintenance of its congressional majority. He was looking toward the elections of 1898 and 1900. He saw the most important job of the administration as preventing Bryan and the Democrats from winning the presidency, which, he genuinely believed, would mean economic ruin for the country. This was more important to him than anything else. So he did not think that the United States ought to intervene in Cuba. He thought it would be best if Spanish sovereignty over the island could be preserved, and he pushed very skillfully for some kind of arrangement that would provide local autonomy for Cuba. But with the events of early 1898 and the increase in public feeling about the Cuban situation partly triggered by the *Maine* sinking, he saw that unless he came to terms with the interventionists he was going to have trouble in his own party. The issue had to be dealt with. So, reluctantly, and feeling that he was making the wrong decision in terms of the specific relationship with Cuba and Spain, he went to war.

J.A.G. Could he have prevented the war?

E.R.M. The question that has been traditionally raised is whether, in his war message to Congress, he should not have placed more stress on the concessions that the Spanish government had recently made, particularly their offer to agree to a cease fire in Cuba. His assessment of the situation in Congress made him doubt he could get away with that. Republican congressional leaders had told him that, if he did not recommend a declaration of war, they would act without his recommendation. The message that he sent in had been a result of a deal he'd made with these leaders. He had gotten them to agree to a delay, to allow Americans in Cuba time to get out. If he changed the message, he was in danger of being accused by his own party of welshing.

If the Spanish government had conceded independence for Cuba, then he could have gotten away with it. But that was highly unlikely. Furthermore, the timing had to be taken into account. The rains were about to come to Cuba; there was not going to be any dramatic change in the military situation there until the eve of the congressional elections.

J.A.G. By the way, who sank the *Maine?* Is there any reasonably clear answer to that question today?

E.R.M. No, I don't think there is. The evidence I've seen is very mixed. The most plausible explanation to me is that it was an internal defect.

J.A.G. Didn't the official American report suggest an exterior explosion?

E.R.M. Yes. There were several studies of the wreckage. The Spanish study indicated that it had been an internal explosion, the American that it had been an external explosion. But I find it hard to imagine how *anybody* could have brought it off deliberately. It seems most plausible to me that something happened on board ship. Another possibility is that there was some kind of a mine in the harbor that broke loose and just drifted against the ship. I can't imagine the Spaniards doing it deliberately.

J.A.G. An individual or a small group who were resentful of America's policy might have done it for personal reasons.

E.R.M. Perhaps. But it's a pretty complicated undertaking to blow up a warship.

J.A.G. Considering the ease with which Spain was defeated in the Spanish-American War, how can one explain the Spanish government's stubborn resistance to American pressures?

E.R.M. You have to remember the very delicate situation of the Spanish government, trying to run a country very unstably held together by a Queen Regent who was thinking about the future of her son. The most powerful single group in the country was the Army. Cuba meant the same thing to the Army that Algeria meant to the French Army in our day. They had fought a ten years' war there in the 1860's and 1870's. Their honor and prestige was engaged in the effort to overcome the rebels. The generals in Cuba had made the kind of extravagant promises that generals always make, whether it's in Algeria of Vietnam or wherever. The parallel with Algeria is a very close one. Cuba was Spain's one remaining American colony; there were Cuban deputies in the Spanish Cortes; Cuba was part of the Spanish metropolis. Many Spaniards who had made money in Cuba had come back to Spain and were important figures; there was a "Cuban group" in the Cortes which had family and business ties with the Army. The Queen Regent and her political advisers couldn't see their way safely to doing anything but continue this terribly bloody, expensive war. The Queen Regent once said to the Austrian Ambassador that if she granted Cuban independence it would mean the end of monarchy in Spain.

J.A.G. Could a parallel also be drawn between the Spanish position and the Mexican government's position in 1846 when faced with a hopeless war with the United States over the boundary of Texas?

E.R.M. There are some similarities. The difference is that the Spanish government was trapped and really had no other way of proceeding than the way in which it did. I have the utmost sympathy with those poor people in Madrid who were trying to avoid both war with the United States and revolution at home. In the Mexican case, Santa Anna was in a different situation. He had seized power and was holding it partly by exploiting anti-American feeling. It was useful to him to have trouble with the United States, for that dampened local separatism, and helped keep him personally in power.

J.A.G. How did the major European powers react to the Spanish-American crisis and to the war?

E.R.M. Each major government had concerns of one kind or another with the crisis, and then with the war. There was a sort of shared concern lest the Spanish monarchy be completely humiliated. Queen Victoria called the behavior of the Americans "shameful," and the Kaiser had similar feelings. The Kaiser was a very curious man; really a lunatic sometimes and at other times very canny. In his manic phases he would talk about the danger to the monarchical principle in an American-Spanish conflict, and the importance of European solidarity.

J.A.G. I don't quite understand. You said before that the monarchy would be threatened by *concession* to the Americans. Defeat didn't destroy the Spanish monarchy. Why did the European powers think a war between Spain and the United States would lead to a revolution in Spain?

E.R.M. Because a monarchy would be defeated and its territory taken away by a republic. The idea had been vividly expressed earlier by Metternich—that the very existence of the United States as a republic was a logical menace to monarchical stability in the world.

J.A.G. That idea persisted that late into the nineteenth century?

E.R.M. Yes.

J.A.G. The idea that a European monarch would fear a war that would damage another European monarch seems rather strange to me. They certainly fought with one another all the time. Was Spain so weak that it had simply passed out of the European power structure?

E.R.M.   Not altogether, but it was not treated as a serious force. The powers were influenced in their maneuvering only by the fact that if Spain sided with a hostile combination it might be able to close the Straits of Gibraltar. But the monarchical principle as opposed to the republican principle was important, and not merely to the monarchs. It was a terrible wrench for the Russian government to bring itself to sign an alliance with the French in the early 1890's, because France was a republic. The Czar was upbraided and criticized by numbers of individuals and groups in Russia for not preserving monarchical solidarity. It's not so terribly unlike the ideological element in contemporary international relations, the belief that communism per se is a dangerous thing.

J.A.G.   Did any of the European powers foresee in 1897 or 1898 the profound effect that the war would have on America's role in world affairs?

E.R.M.   The same kind of thing happened in continental Europe that happened in Britain at the time of the Venezuelan crisis. Numbers of European states learned suddenly that it was a bigger world than they had realized.

J.A.G.   You talk of the United States in *Imperial Democracy* as the "seventh power." Was this recognized before the results of the war became clear?

E.R.M.   Not really. There was a lot of discussion of the possibility of assistance for Spain, but less grounded on political argument about the power of the United States than on ideology. It was the military victory (its suddenness and thoroughness) and the extent of the American mobilization that caused European chancelleries to take seriously the statistics about the population and the wealth and maritime commerce and industrial power of the United States. The American action in the Philippines, an area where European powers were maneuvering and making combinations, also had a big impact. The United States was now there; it had to be taken into account in arrangements made in Asia. And so it was thereafter also thought about in connection with combinations in Africa, and in Europe itself.

J.A.G.   Do you think that the action in the Philippines was more significant in this respect than the defeat of Spain in Cuba itself?

E.R.M.   The fact of an American naval victory at that distance from the United States really inflamed the imagination of some people in Germany. Documents were circulated in the upper levels of the German government that envisaged a German-American alliance and its possible effect on the British.

J.A.G. Were American attitudes toward the rest of the world affected by this quick victory over Spain as profoundly as Europeans' attitudes toward America were?

E.R.M. They should have been, but they weren't. It's very curious. In 1898, the idea is suggested that isolation is outworn because the United States has become so powerful that it can't avoid involvement in international politics. In some of the debates about the Philippines, men argued that with its new strength and prestige, the United States could not avoid foreign entanglements.

But the question was fudged when it became a partisan issue in 1900. McKinley then said that the United States had taken over the Philippines on a temporary basis, and that the occupation was not a step toward imperialism. Bryan advocated that the United States commit itself not to dispose of the Philippines immediately, but to get rid of them at the earliest possible moment. As so often happens to issues in political campaigns, the gap between opposing views was narrowed. Thereafter, this whole line of argument practically disappeared.

Another reason for the playing down of the world-power argument was a change in the intellectual climate. Between the Grant period and the late 1890's, the relatively small number of Americans who were interested in international affairs were also, in effect, partly Europeans; they were people who traveled a lot and paid close attention to European politics. They saw prominent English Liberals, like Rosebery and Joseph Chamberlain, becoming imperialists, whereas earlier, liberalism and imperialism had appeared antithetical. At the time of the Dominican question in the Grant administration, most sophisticated and cosmopolitan Americans had felt that it was just wrong to take colonies. But then they saw heroes of theirs, men whom they aspired to imitate and who were in the mainstream of liberalism, turning toward imperialism. The idea of a liberal nation possessing colonies became more acceptable, particularly to men like Theodore Roosevelt who identified themselves with this younger generation of English statesmen.

But almost immediately after the United States became an imperial power, the Boer War broke out. Along with the complexity and horror of Philippine insurrection, with its clear evidence of Filipino opposition to American rule, the Boer War, which all identifiable young liberals in England opposed, produced a reaction against imperialism among many intellectuals, both in Europe and in the United States. Thereafter, the chief defenders of European imperialism were more clearly militarists, with whom few Americans chose to identify.

A consensus developed among people interested in international politics that the acquisition of colonies was not the right thing to do—a "liberal" state didn't acquire colonies. This explains the otherwise inexplicable fact that, after taking Hawaii and the Philippines, the United States made no more significant colonial acquisitions. We did take two pieces of territory after the turn of the century: the Canal Zone and the Virgin Islands. But the annexation of the Virgin Islands during the First World War was a special situation, based on the theory that the Germans were going to take them. The canal movement, of course, had a long background to it, and the taking of the Zone was the expedient available to Roosevelt, given the situation he found himself in.

J.A.G.   Are you suggesting that America was not an imperialist power in the first decade of the twentieth century?

E.R.M.   Only very briefly. It seems to me the United States got on the colonial band wagon at just the point when the band wagon was stopping.

But to get back to the question of American attitudes toward the rest of the world. The anti-imperialist argument against annexing the Philippines on the ground that it would involve the United States in international conflict had considerable influence, although I think it had no substance. Actually, the relationship between the United States and Japan was probably eased by the American presence in the Philippines. The conflict between the two governments over the treatment of Japanese in the United States and over China might well have been sharper, but for the Philippines. The United States government was always made a little bit more moderate, a little bit less doctrinaire, by the fact that it possessed the Philippines and was worried about their security.

J.A.G.   Can you generalize about the colonial policy of the United States after 1898?

E.R.M.   As I said before, I believe the colonialist movement died out around the turn of the century. There are several ways of looking at this subject. Some of the historians who identify themselves with the New Left would accept my generalization, but they would amplify it by saying that American strategy was to pursue markets and not to seek colonies themselves. They would claim that post-1898 policy was part of a continuum, that the acquisition of the Canal Zone, the influence that the Roosevelt, Taft, and Wilson administrations exerted in the Caribbean and Central America and Mexico, was consistent with earlier policy. The business community did not want colonial dominion, only control, for the sake of profit, trade, and investment opportunity.

I part company with them on this question, because I don't see this strategy in operation. It goes back to the central difference we were talking about earlier between the view of the politician or diplomat as essentially the tool or agent of the possessor of economic power, and the view toward which I tend to lean, that the politician was the driver, trying to keep his constituencies in line.

J.A.G. You don't see any radical difference then between American foreign policy in the 1880's and 1890's, and the policy between 1900 and 1914? The driving force, as you put it, was still essentially political?

E.R.M. There is one major difference, and it also relates to one of your earlier questions. After 1898, the sense that the United States was a world power, regarded as a potential friend or adversary by the European great powers was ever present in policy makers' minds. The Presidents, secretaries of state, their intimates, members of the Senate Foreign Relations Committee, did not think this way before 1898. After 1898, they had to do so.

Let me take a particular case by way of illustration. In 1897 there was an incident in Haiti arising out of the maltreatment of a German citizen named Lüders, who was imprisoned by the Haitian government. The Germans sent a warship, and threatened to bombard Port-au-Prince unless he was released. They made some almost outrageous demands on the Haitian government. The United States government just passed the affair by; it accepted Germany's acting this way in Haiti, even though there were rumors that it might be a pretext to annex Haiti. Presumably, had that actually happened, there would have been concern in Washington, but nobody was prepared to do anything about it in the early stage.

But when Germany pressed the Venezuelan government for payment of debts and had warships off the coast of Venezuela in 1902, or when there were rumors that German creditors in the Dominican Republic were pressing their government to take possession of that country, the situation appeared much more serious. The possibility that a European power which looked upon the United States as a potential adversary might acquire a base of operations in the Western Hemisphere was a source of deep concern. This sense of a need to take preventive strategic action in cases where there was disorder gave rise to the Roosevelt corollary to the Monroe Doctrine, the argument that the United States should act as a policeman for European powers in the Western Hemisphere so that they would not act for themselves. That attitude as much as anything else led the Roosevelt, Taft, and Wilson administrations into more positive action in the hemisphere than the administrations of the late nineteenth century were given to.

But such a policy isn't colonialism. I won't dispute that there were Americans who were interested in trade and investment opportunities in the Caribbean and Central America, and it's quite clear that these, particularly the banking houses which had floated loans that were supporting governments in Central America, were pressing the State Department to use American influence to encourage stability, to send in the Marines to prevent revolutions that might lead to the cancellation of debts or the devaluation of bonds. The Presidents were respectful of this element, realizing that if they could be accused of disregarding the economic interests of American citizens, it might cost them votes. But it seems to me to have been a more resistible influence than some others.

J.A.G.   What you are saying makes sense in that after 1900 the United States certainly had the power and the diplomatic flexibility to take almost anything it wanted in the Western Hemisphere, but didn't. But would there have been no substantial European resistance? Would the powers have stood by and allowed America to conduct an aggressively expansionist colonial policy in Central America?

E.R.M.   I can't see any reason why they would not have.

J.A.G.   That's a very important corrective to the argument which attributes an ulterior motive to every American action in Latin America.

E.R.M.   Of course, the interpretation proceeds from an assumption—that the men who were making decisions and those who were giving advice that was really listened to were acting as political animals. I do not believe that politicians as a rule think as much about the possible creative results of what they do as they think about what might happen if they don't do it. It's a poor analogy, because the stakes were so very different, but in the Cuban missile crisis the position that Secretary McNamara took was rationally quite correct: that a missile is a missile, and it really didn't matter whether it was in Cuba or on a Soviet submarine. In a strategic sense there was no real issue, but to all the political animals in the Kennedy administration the key question was: *What happens to us if people begin to say that you let the Russians do this?* To them, the more visible vulnerability was terribly important.

   The same thing operated in the case of the Dominican Republic during Theodore Roosevelt's administration. The report that the Germans might move in led the policy makers to say, in effect, "My God, if they do, what will people here say?"

J.A.G.   Would you say, then, that you agree with historians like Robert E. Osgood and George Kennan that American policy toward Asia and Latin America was based more on idealism than realism?

E.R.M.   I've never been able to use that analytical framework very happily. And I suppose the central reason is the difficulty I have in seeing a foreign-policy issue as a separate kind of rational game, and in thinking about national interests abroad that are separable from the domestic political interests of the people who are the custodians for those interests. I suppose most people would regard the clearest case for a realist-idealist division as being American policy toward China in the 1930's—an attempt to preserve the integrity of China. If you imagine the United States as a rational, unitary actor playing a game internationally, you cannot see that it had *any* interest in the preservation of China or anything to gain strategically, economically, or politically, that would not have been more easily gained through Japanese control of China. Our policy appears both idealistic and unrealistic. But if you put yourself in Franklin Roosevelt's position and consider what people at home and in Congress were going to say, then the argument that the Japanese might as well have China would be very unrealistic.

J.A.G.   Theodore Roosevelt has often been characterized as a warmonger and a wielder of the big stick while President, and yet he also won a Nobel Peace Prize. Would you comment on his impact generally on American foreign policy, both before and after he became President?

E.R.M.   Roosevelt was, like almost any man who gets to be President, a very complex personality. Certainly he did give vent before 1901, and occasionally afterward, to a kind of impulsive bellicosity. He liked to talk in the 1880's and 1890's about how war benefited civilization, and how nations were judged by their willingness to fight and their manly qualities. But as President, he was very cautious, both in domestic and in foreign affairs. He was genuinely worried about the possibility of the Germans finding a foothold in the Western Hemisphere. There was a tendency in writing about Roosevelt in the 1930's—Henry F. Pringle's biography is the best case in point—to interpret this as a neurotic manifestation of the kind of jingoism he expressed earlier, but these historians lacked a sense of what the world looked like when he was President and forgot the impact of the expansionistic nationalism of imperial Germany. The provocation of a crisis by the Krüger telegram, the apparently deliberate decision to start building a battle fleet to challenge the British, and the bellicose rhetoric of the Kaiser and the Pan-Germans led many observers to believe that Germany had almost unlimited ambitions and was willing to think about warfare at the drop of a hat.

But I have been impressed by Roosevelt's caution in dealing with Germany, and even more by his caution in approaching Far Eastern questions, and questions of the American role in Europe.

J.A.G.   What is your opinion of his behavior in the Alaska boundary controversy? Did he not ride roughshod over Canada, and put an awful lot of pressure on Great Britain over a relatively minor issue?

E.R.M.   Yes, he did, but he believed that the American position regarding the boundary was legally and morally right. He felt that the Canadians were claiming land to which they were not entitled, and that the British, for reasons of maintaining what was later to be called "the Commonwealth," were catering to Canadian wishes. But he also knew how important to the British government was American friendship, and he was therefore sure he ran no risk in taking so hard a line.

I suppose the strongest evidence that Roosevelt was a jingo as President was his naval program. Here, clearly, he was putting his domestic political position on the line. For the sake of having a larger navy he made concessions, even on some things very important to him domestically, like railroad regulation.

J.A.G.   Would you say that Roosevelt really didn't have much of a foreign policy, but dealt with foreign problems as part of his political task of staying in office?

E.R.M.   You can't really separate that kind of short-run consideration from another that nearly always works in Presidents, the question of how they are going to stand in history. Let's go back to the canal question for a moment. Roosevelt really believed that the interoceanic canal would be a monument to him, something that would be remembered as a kind of equivalent of the Louisiana Purchase. Along with everyone else, he overestimated what the effects would be on American trade.

J.A.G.   Of course there was the alternative Nicaraguan route. Wasn't there considerable support for saying: "If Colombia doesn't agree to our terms, build it in Nicaragua"? From an engineering point of view the Nicaraguan route was perfectly feasible.

E.R.M.   Not really. You've got to follow the sequence of things. The choice between Nicaragua and Panama was wide open *at the beginning.* But apparently Roosevelt, along with Senators Hanna and Spooner, was convinced by engineers that the Panama route would be both better and cheaper. They were worried about the possibility of trouble developing in the Nicaraguan route. They didn't know as much about the terrain, and they feared the possibility of earthquakes. So the choice was made for Panama, with the rider that they would go back to Nicaragua if the Panama negotiations failed. But the negotiations with Congress and the negotiations with Colombia had gone on at the same time; the senators had been shown the terms on which the treaty with Colombia would be signed, before they agreed to go along with the Panama route.

When the Colombians rejected the treaty, the situation was as follows: If the Americans went back to Nicaragua, the chances were that the Nicaraguans would ask for a great deal more money than they'd asked for before. They would be aware that the American government had no choice. Furthermore, the administration had convinced many senators and representatives that the Panama route was better; it was doubtful if a large amount of money could be gotten for the Nicaraguan project, given the disadvantages which the administration itself had disclosed about it. There seemed to be a very good chance that time would pass with *no* canal. If Roosevelt went back to Colombia and renegotiated the treaty, the treaty would not have passed the U. S. Senate. Roosevelt had advertised the great benefits that the canal would bring; he was counting on it as one of the assets of the Republican party and of his own candidacy in 1904. It looked as if it were going to be an embarrassment instead. The revolution in Panama provided a welcome solution.

J.A.G. Is there any evidence that Roosevelt actually triggered the revolution in Panama?

E.R.M. No, I don't think so. Many people have tried very hard to find evidence that he conspired with the revolutionaries, without success. He may have let it be known that he would not be averse to this happening, but any intelligent observer could have perceived that the President of the United States would probably not react adversely to a revolution in Panama at that time.

J.A.G. What is meant by the term "dollar diplomacy"?

E.R.M. In so far as it represents a unique policy, it relates to a speech of President Taft's in which he talked about the good that the dollar could do, in Latin America particularly.

The government had faced problems in the Caribbean area from the turn of the century, with frequent internal disturbances in one country or another and the attendant risk that some European power, probably Germany, would intervene. Taft himself had been involved in the negotiations for establishing a customs receivership in the Dominican Republic, and it was a messy business. Taft did not like this situation, especially the domestic risks involved in sending American troops into small Latin American countries. So he and some of the people around him conceived of dollar diplomacy as an alternative: encourage trade and economic development; political stability will follow from economic development, and with political stability there will be fewer occasions when the United States will have to intervene by force.

But to picture this as a deliberate extension of quasi-American rule into Central American countries seems to me a distortion. My impression is that, more than anything else, Taft and Secretary of State Knox were trying to avoid trouble.

J.A.G. I think everyone would agree that if the government had adopted a completely laissez-faire attitude, economic opportunities would have led many Americans to invest in Central America. To what extent did American investors in these areas act because of the American government's actions and policies? Did Taft's dollar diplomacy affect the amount of foreign investment in these countries?

E.R.M. My impression is that it really didn't. Taft and Knox were trying, both in Latin America and also in China, to encourage American bankers to invest funds, but they had very little success. The amount of substantial American investment in either Central America or China during this period was quite small. American banks did enter into a consortium for the financing of Chinese railroads at Taft's behest, but when Wilson declared, after he took office, that the government wouldn't support them, it appears that the bankers were delighted. They hadn't been enthusiastic, and this gave them an excuse for telling their European counterparts that they would take their money out.

J.A.G. Is there any indication that policy makers were subjected to pressures to take positions in diplomacy that would benefit American investors?

E.R.M. In some instances this happened, but at a very grubby level. It was not the house of Morgan that was pushing the White House. There were cases in Central America where Americans who had made chancy investments were doing their best to influence the American consuls, the people who reported to Washington on local situations. They tried to get them to say that this politician was better than another, and that if general such-and-such didn't stay in power the result would be chaos. Of course, to an extent this on occasion happened. But I don't think you can trace any pattern in it or find any significant results.

J.A.G. Woodrow Wilson's Latin American policy presents a particularly difficult problem. He was certainly very different from Roosevelt temperamentally, and he openly rejected both Roosevelt's brand of big-stick imperialism and Taft's dollar diplomacy. On the other hand, as President he does not seem to have acted very differently from either Roosevelt or Taft in Latin America. How can this be explained?

E.R.M. As to the *verbal* repudiation of the big stick and dollar diplomacy, I think any Democrat would have had to take the same general position: repudiation of the past. Everything had to be labeled "new" in those days. This was particularly true of foreign affairs, where administration policy, it seems to me, was not Wilson's, but Secretary of State Bryan's. Bryan insisted that something "new" had to be done in diplomacy. However, mixed with this was Wilson's disposition to put issues in moral terms, to elevate any course of action to a moral decision.

Actually, Bryan tended to handle Latin-American questions in very much the same way that Taft's administration had. But when the Mexican revolution became an issue, Wilson seized hold of policy. He saw important moral principles at stake, and took the view that the United States ought to exert its influence in Mexico in favor of democracy, which was being frustrated by a military dictator.

J.A.G. Are you saying that his policy was idealistic, that in this instance he ignored the total political picture which you have repeatedly suggested tends to dominate in the formulation of foreign policy?

E.R.M. I think both elements are there. When Wilson looked at the Mexican question and decided that he would withhold recognition from Huerta, a large part of his impulse was moral, a desire to achieve a noble objective. At the same time, Wilson saw this as something that would work. The tragedy of Wilson's involvement in Mexico starts right there, at the point where he was misinformed, or misinformed himself, about what the effect of American nonrecognition would be on Mexican domestic politics. He had the same kind of illusion that successively Kennedy and Johnson had about Vietnam, that for a small payment he could get a big return.

The Mexican question was not, after all, something that was just the concern of the President. The liberal periodical press paid a lot of attention to it, and it was pro-Madero and anti-Huerta. Wilson could reasonably calculate that if he adopted a hands-off attitude he was going to be severely criticized.

J.A.G. I suppose one could also argue that Wilson's Mexican policy in the long run was anything but a failure, that even though it led immediately to serious problems and bad feeling, it eventually convinced the Mexicans of America's concern for democratic values.

E.R.M. Well, this is like the question of whether taking the Philippines was a mistake; it involves so many steps along the way, comparing the consequences of what happened with the possible consequences of what did not happen. Also, one has to judge on premises that may not be unchanging. The essence of the Good Neighbor policy was precisely the kind of policy that Wilson did *not* follow toward Mexico, since it was based on the idea that it didn't matter to the United States what happened internally in Latin-American states. The tendency since about 1960 has been to be critical of that proposition and to take the view that the United States faces dangers in Latin America precisely because it has not done anything about dictatorships and domestic conditions that breed revolution there. Some people might take a kinder view of Wilson's Mexican policy than they would have twenty years ago.

J.A.G. Do you think that American imperialism was a cause of our entry into the First World War? Is it likely that the United States could have or would have stayed out of that war if it hadn't fought the Spanish-American War, had never taken any colonies, or gotten involved in manipulating the internal affairs of small countries in the Caribbean?

E.R.M. That's a very hard question to answer, because again one must try to reconstruct what might have happened. Let's imagine that the Spanish government had conceded independence to Cuba and there had been no war and no military encounter and no Philippine question.

Probably it would have been somewhat later before continental European governments began to think of the United States as a factor in international politics. Very likely there would have been less talk in Germany about naval bases in the Western Hemisphere. Maybe the antipathy toward Germany in the United States might have been less in 1914 than it was. Certainly, some of the public and governmental reaction to the German invasion of Belgium and the reports of German atrocities in Belgium was influenced by the feeling that the Germans regarded the United States as a potential enemy and were thinking of moving into the Western Hemisphere. So you can argue that there might have been a little less strong reaction against Germany at the outbreak of the war. Maybe then Wilson might have taken a slightly more tolerant view of German submarine warfare when it was launched early in 1915. And that has always seemed to me to be the crucial moment. The American government could have argued that German submarine operations did not involve matters of high policy and principle; that it would insist on compensation for any damage done, but stop short of declaring its general, legal, and moral opposition to any use of submarines.

I think it's arguable that, had the Wilson administration taken that kind of position, the German government might not have authorized unrestricted submarine operations as provocative as those resorted to in 1917. Time would probably have proved their navy people wrong in what they claimed about the potential effectiveness of submarines, and the issue might not have been drawn in 1917. But all this is pretty far-fetched. It seems to me that the greater role of the United States in world affairs resulting from the Spanish war worked rather to restrain the American government and to slow progress toward intervention, because this role influenced Wilson to think that he could be the peacemaker. Hence his various efforts to mediate. Had he not had that idea and had there not been evident public support in the United States for it, Wilson might have been inclined, and certainly public pressure would have been stronger, to take a stronger stand at an earlier point on the submarine issue.

J.A.G.   What is your view of the so-called New Left interpretation of American foreign policy?

E.R.M.   Lots of things get lumped together under that label. A certain amount of what goes by that name seems to me very hard to distinguish from a kind of history, common in the 1920's and 1930's, that has two characteristics: an emphasis on the way in which economic interests of individuals, groups, and corporations, affect government policy; and a tendency to sit in judgment on the past and to write in terms of great mistakes that have been made or villainies that have been perpetrated.

Some of this New Left history is interesting and challenging, but much of it lacks substance.

Let me take as an example, not a work on our period, but one of the best-known books of this school—Gar Alperovitz's *Atomic Diplomacy*. I think this is a very valuable book for students to read, in part because it causes them to think about the use of the atom against Japan without adopting the conventional view that we wore the white hats and the Russians wore the black hats. It's a good book for discussion. On the other hand, as an effort to re-create what happened, I think it has, to say the least, weaknesses. Alperovitz treats Truman and his advisers as villains in the way that the revisionists dealing with the First World War treated Wilson and House and Walter Hines Page as villains, reversing the kind of the thing that was being said about their virtues in the early writings on our intervention in that war.

But there is in some of the really new New Left writing an argument stemming from William Appleman Williams' work, which is challenging in quite a different way and which I think is worth a lot of thought. As I understand this very difficult, really complicated argument, it is *not* that particular groups with money at stake exerted a selfish influence on American foreign policy, but rather that American society has been pervaded by a set of business values which have been translated into the ideals that the American government professed and acted upon, idealistically abroad, realistically at home. The idea is that it is possible to create other models in which other sets of ideas—other sets of values than those of a business civilization—might have prevailed and produced a different course of conduct. Such an idea, it seems to me, is really quite different from arguments such as the old one that munitions makers and bankers promoted American intervention in World War I in order to save their profits. It seems to me that this line of thought is very much worth exploring.

J.A.G. In what way does this go beyond simply spelling out the obvious? Isn't it as though one were to say that American domestic policy has always reflected a belief in monogamy?

E.R.M. But it's worth thinking about what these beliefs are, and to be aware of them as parts of an ideology that might have been different.

J.A.G. Could you give an example of how a concentration on underlying values changes our understanding of some particular aspect of foreign relations?

E.R.M. One of the centerpieces in Williams' argument is the Open Door policy, which he says reflected and embodied a set of business values; that is, the idea that free markets were very good things, that an open market in China for the introduction of American goods, American technology, and the values associated with it was inherently desirable. This produced a kind of imperialism quite different from colonialism, one based on a conviction that the values of an industrialized, business-centered civilization were the highest values that men could have and that it was a very good thing to impose those values on a civilization like the Chinese.

J.A.G.   If it is important to call this to our attention, doesn't it imply that some of the other imperial powers had a different set of values? Was that true? We traditionally have seen the American Open Door policy toward China as in some way different from the position of the European powers. If Williams is suggesting a new way of understanding the policy, does he really get us any closer to the truth if the same or very similar commercial values were operating in European society in 1901?

E.R.M.   I think it's certainly worth inquiring whether this was so. I'm not sure that it was. We are very far behind in developing techniques for comparative history.

J.A.G.   To what extent is the New Left approach to history a reflection of a different set of underlying values on the part of the New Left historians?

E.R.M.   Surely to a large extent. It starts from the post-Cold War discovery of the ideological conflict with the communist world and a sense that perhaps the American or "free world" ideology does not embody all the good values.

J.A.G.   What do you consider the major unanswered questions about American foreign relations in the late nineteenth and early twentieth centuries?

E.R.M.   One of the questions that I think very much worth exploring in detail is the relationship between public opinion and policy. We've got a lot of evidence on this point, but there are a number of questions that it would be useful to pursue. One has to do with what the public was; who were the people who were really interested in foreign affairs, and what kinds of divisions existed among them, and how did they get to their various positions? Then there is a question which nobody has successfully dealt with: How can one connect public opinion with what happens in Washington? How do people in positions of judgment get their information about public feeling? In so far as they make calculations about public opinion, officials are apt to be concerned not with current calculations but with prospective calculations. They ask, what will be the reactions of interested groups to this choice or that choice?

Another area that is very nearly virgin territory has to do with the internal functioning of the government. Most writing about policy formation has dealt with the subject at a very high level. It has been about Presidents and secretaries of state. It is written as if everything were going through the mind of the President and he was making rational choices. Now we know that this just isn't so. Alternatives are sorted out and decisions are made at relatively lower levels of government. Presidents are presented with a relatively small range of choice, and they have to make their decisions not on the basis of a kind of courtroom analysis of the arguments in favor of one course against another, but on the basis of their relative trust of this man as opposed to that man, or of this agency as opposed to that agency. We know startlingly little about the internal working of the American government, about how the bureaucracy functions. In the diplomatic service, why is one area or one country regarded as more important than another? How do the career interests of individuals affect policy? This is an enormous area for investigation, and one that we are in a good position to start looking into because of the amount of thinking that has been done about these processes by social scientists.

J.A.G.   Does the documentary material exist in the archives to study the role of undersecretaries and other lesser bureaucrats?

E.R.M.   In some cases. It presents a research challenge to find sources also, as well as to figure out what to do with the sources. This is an area in which we're going to have to play back and forth between the present and the past, and make use of hypotheses that are founded on contemporary studies based on interview data, and see what we can read back into the past.

J.A.G.   Would that apply too to what you said about understanding public opinion?

E.R.M.   I think so. We must take hypotheses which have been built up on the kinds of evidence that we don't have for the past, like the Gallup poll, and see if such evidence as does exist fits these hypotheses.

J.A.G.   Both of these general areas that you've mentioned require at least as a start a very narrow, monographic approach, do they not?

E.R.M.   Yes. Another subject that seems to me worth exploration, and again it has to be done monographically, involves the other side of American foreign relations. We need studies of the German, French, and Russian positions toward the United States before the First World War. And also the other side of various "unequal" relationships: the Chinese view of American policy toward China from the turn of the century on, for example, and the Japanese side of the Japanese-American relationship. We know a good deal about the Japanese side from the 1920's on, but much less about the early twentieth century. And the

Latin-American side of our relationships in Latin America. We don't know very much about what was going on in these countries.

J.A.G.   Is this because the work has not been done or because American historians are not fully aware of what the historians of those countries are doing themselves?

E.R.M.   I'm not sure. Very little work has been done by the Latin Americans. As for the Japanese, some work is available, but only to those who read Japanese. For China, the picture is quite mixed because there has been some work by the Chinese Communists, but most of it is in the nature of propaganda tracts rather than serious research. Even on the European side there is really not much first-rate history. Some very good work has been done on post-World War I relationships, but very little on pre-World War I relations with the United States.

J.A.G.   Professor May, what are the books that you would recommend to persons interested in the subject we have been discussing? Would you, in each case, indicate what the particular contribution of the volume is?

E.R.M.   Most of the major topics have been subjects of several good, but somewhat different, books. On developments up to and through the annexation of the Philippines, Walter LaFeber's *The New Empire* (1963), is the best exposition of the line of argument first shadowed in William A. Williams' *Tragedy of American Diplomacy* (1959). Thomas McCormick's *China Market: America's Quest for Informal Empire, 1893–1901* (1967) follows the same line, picking up one particular thread. Marilyn B. Young's new *Rhetoric of Empire: American China Policy, 1895–1901* (1968), treats somewhat the same substance but deals much more systematically with the components of American ideology. I think it gives us a real advance in understanding.

On Theodore Roosevelt's presidential years, the best book is Howard K. Beale's *Theodore Roosevelt and America's Rise to World Power* (1956). Raymond Ethus' *Theodore Roosevelt and Japan* (1966), and Charles Neu's *Uncertain Friendship* (1967), both add significantly to understanding of the relationship with Japan. Neither Beale nor anyone else has delved into Roosevelt's Latin-American policies. The only really good book that is relevant is Dwight Miner's absorbing *Fight for the Panama Route* (1940). William Harbaugh's biography of Roosevelt, *Power and Responsibility* (1961), shows better than does Beale's book the interconnections between politics at home and abroad.

The key relationship of the pre-World War I era, that with Britain, is very carefully examined in Bradford Perkins's recent *The Great Rapprochement* (1968). The other key relationship, that with Germany, is treated adequately only in two massive volumes by Alfred Vagts, which are, unfortunately, available only in German.

Concerning intervention in World War I, I have to mention my own *World War and American Isolation*. It deals with the politics of policy making in America, Britain, and Germany. Of course, Arthur Link's biography of Wilson, with four volumes on the first four presidential years, provides a very full and carefully composed picture of all of Wilson's policies.

George E. Mowry

The Progressive Movement

GeORGE E. MOWRY is Kenan Professor of History at the University of North Carolina at Chapel Hill, and a former President of the Organization of American Historians. He has written extensively about early twentieth-century political history, his most notable volumes being *Theodore Roosevelt and the Progressive Era* (1946), *The California Progressives* (1952), a study of the socioeconomic origins of Progressive leaders which helped establish a new way of thinking about American reform movements, and *The Era of Theodore Roosevelt: 1900–1912* (1958). He has also written, among other works, *The Urban Nation: 1920–1960* (1965), and he is coauthor of a popular textbook, *A History of American Democracy* (1966). In the interview he discusses both the origins of the Progressive movement in the late nineteenth century and the character of Progressivism itself.

John A. Garraty   Professor Mowry, until recently, historians tended to see the Progressive era as a distinct period, a rather sharp break with the past. Without for the moment going into the counterargument, would you describe what seems to you unique about the first two decades of the twentieth century?

George E. Mowry   I'd rather use the word "exceptional," because the more I look at history, the less uniqueness I see. The most distinctive aspect of the period was the depth and breadth of the attempt to change American life, in every stratum of government and also in moral, ethical, and intellectual spheres of activity.

The Progressive years were on the whole prosperous years, and on the whole secure years for most American people. Eugene O'Neill's *Ah, Wilderness* comes to mind. There was no real threat to American values, at least in the eyes of most of the participants, nothing apocalyptic in the kind of reform advocated, no statements from reformers that "unless we did this and that, there will be dire consequences tomorrow."

Another thing that's quite unusual about the period is that the Progressive reformer was a moderately successful individual—whom one wouldn't expect to have been agitated by reform zeal. A whole complex of questions and queries, interesting to an historian, arise from this characteristic of the period.

J.A.G.   In this sense, were the Progressive reformers different from the abolitionists?

G.E.M.   The Progressives weren't as committed—one might say as irrational—as the abolitionists. The abolitionists talked in terms of apocalyptic visions, the Progressives about the brotherhood of man. They were like Emerson instead of like William Lloyd Garrison, if you want to make a comparison. The usual reform movement in the United States has been dominated by belly reactions, "gut" reforms. They have been reactions to poverty, to distress. But Progressives were people that one might see walking down the street in a prosperous neighborhood in almost any city or town in the United States. The Progressives' stress on ethics hasn't been common in American reform movements, either. They sought to uplift the average man across the whole spectrum of the population. Another interesting aspect of the period is the amount of structural or constitutional change that went on. In American history there have been three clusters of constitutional change: the Bill of Rights; the changes during and following the Civil War; and those of the Progressive era, when in twenty years four major amendments were added to the Constitution.

J.A.G.   Can a connection be established between the Progressive reform movements and the reform movements of the late nineteenth century?

For example, it seems to me that many of the things you've just said about the Progressives would apply to the civil service reformers.

G.E.M.   I come back to the thought that perhaps there are very few clear disjunctions in history. If one looks at the whole flow of history, there are very few sharp breaks. Even some of the more startling changes like the French and Russian Revolutions, I think, are not as disjointed from their past, not as rootless as we've often believed. Unquestionably, a good deal of the spirit of the late-nineteenth-century reformers was incorporated into the Progressive movement. Men like George William Curtis, E. L. Godkin, Carl Schurz, and Charles Francis Adams, Jr., were not essentially unlike the Progressives.

These people provided a bridge between the mid-century reformers of both the United States and England and those of the early twentieth century. Many were liberal Republicans, and the spirit behind liberal Republicanism can be traced back to the Manchester liberals in England. They also illustrate a peculiar characteristic of Progressivism, its patrician quality. Most were editors and intellectuals, and this was duplicated, I think, in the Progressive movement, which had much the same stress on the development of an educated, ethically minded elite with—although Americans have been reluctant to emphasize this—a sense of *noblesse oblige.*

These early reformers were reacting to some of the same things that a good many Progressives were reacting to. They were troubled by the newly rich in the country, by their economic, political, and moral excesses. They disliked the spoils system, the corrupt alliance between industry and politics, the crude methods which new industrialists and new politicians used, as new groups coming to power have always used, against the establishment. The opinion of Charles Francis Adams that the average businessman was something he didn't want to associate with in this life or the next could easily have been said by Theodore Roosevelt, for example. And I think that these nineteenth-century "Mugwump" reformers' opposition to the crude, more vigorous forces in the Republican party was similar to the Progressives' attitude in a good many ways.

The Progressive emphasis on the good man, the honest man, the educated man, can also be traced back to people like Godkin, Schurz, Adams, and Curtis. So I think there is a close and intimate relationship between these people and a good many Progressives.

J.A.G.   What, then, was different about the Mugwumps? You compared them to Theodore Roosevelt, but Roosevelt hated the Mugwumps and was hated by them.

G.E.M.   What distinguished the Progressive from the Mugwump was the Progressives' commitment to politics, their willingness to play the political game instead of remaining aloof. The Mugwump spirit in politics, as I see it, was governed by a sense of exclusiveness that prohibited them from doing the things that lead to political success. I see some connection between the spirit of Adlai Stevenson and these people. They would lead the cause if invited, that's very plain. But someone else must do the dirty work.

J.A.G. That certainly distinquished Roosevelt from the Mugwumps, whom he resembled in other ways quite closely.

G.E.M. Quite. And also Henry Cabot Lodge. Lodge nursed his Massachusetts constituency in a way that the Mugwumps found disgusting. The Progressive politicians were more realistic about the workings of democracy than the Mugwumps, which was the Mugwumps' English bias. They looked abroad to England, where the aristocratic class didn't have to do this sort of thing because of the quality of deference in English society, which did not exist in America in the nineteenth and early twentieth centuries.

J.A.G. Was there anything Progressive in the ideas of the popular late-nineteenth-century social reformers, such as Henry George, Edward Bellamy, and Henry Demarest Lloyd?

G.E.M. The three you've mentioned typify a good many of the intellectual strains of the Progressive movement. Henry George was an egalitarian Jeffersonian Democrat. He'd watched the California frontier eat up opportunity and land for the average man. He preferred the old, rural America to the hectic exploitation of his own times. This nostalgic element was also reflected in Progressivism, especially in the less urbanized wing derived from western Populism.

Bellamy, and George too, presage the religious or quasireligious roots of Progressivism. Historians haven't taken into account enough the religious developments of the period: the impact of Darwinism, the destruction of a good many certainties that the average citizen had had before. It's hard to understand the emphasis of so many Progressives on ethics—"carrying Christianity to the marketplace," as one of them put it—except in terms of what had happened to religious certainties because of Darwinism. The Social Gospel movement came out of the same sort of religious ferment that produced an Edward Bellamy.

Bellamy is also representative of the Christian socialistic strain in Progressivism. Eugene V. Debs was much the same sort of person as Bellamy. He didn't know too much about Marx. Probably, one of the troubles with the American Socialist party was that it was so American it couldn't be socialistic. After all, Norman Thomas was the same sort of preacher as Edward Bellamy, with much the same mission in life. Historians have often considered President McKinley's religio-ethical explanation of his decision to take the Philippines after the Spanish-American War as illustrating the hypocrisy of the man, but his attempt to use theological ethics to solve political problems could easily have been made by a Bellamy. I'm not at all sure that we ought to ridicule his statement.

Henry Demarest Lloyd illustrates another phase of Progressivism. In the first place, he was a big-city boy, a lawyer, a journalist, who very early became a champion of the worker. He represents to me the sidewalk element of the Progressive movement, and I assume that his joining the Socialist party in 1903 was indicative of his frustrations with rural Populism. Progressivism always exhibited tensions between its more agrarian-minded adherents and city people, between the middle classes and the labor unions. Lincoln Steffens, for example, traveled much the same road in the twentieth century that Lloyd traveled in the nineteenth.

J.A.G. What were the other differences between the Populists and the Progressives?

G.E.M. One of the main differences was their motivation. The Populists were distressed farmers, faced with falling prices, a tight money supply, and mortgage foreclosures. Most had an economic ache in their stomachs. The reforms they were aiming at were much like those of the Progressives, but their motivation was far different. They were more theoretical, more ideological, and more apocalyptic in their approach. Secondly, the Populists were far more nostalgic. In some instances they tried to co-operate with the labor unions, but on the whole it was a farmer movement and an attempt to go back to an older society. They were fighting new developments, whereas at least one aspect of Progressivism was an attempt to make politics coincide with new developments.

One can also differentiate Populists and Progressives by the kinds of enemies they chose. The villains of the Populists were the big bankers, the monopolists, and the urbanites. Progressive rhetoric stressed the city as a basic element in the new culture. It hoped to come to terms with the city, to make life bearable there. Their objectives also were in many ways different. The Populist objective at the individual level was to raise the price of farm goods, to curb monopoly prices, and, in general, to return America to an old egalitarian agricultural society. The instruments they used to achieve these objectives were often the same ones that the Progressives used, but the Progressives were not, on the whole, dominated by the desire to return the United States to the old farming ways.

J.A.G. It seems to me that in your answer you're steering a middle course between the interpretations of your mentor, John D. Hicks, and the modern defenders of Populism like Norman Pollack, and that of the critics of the Populists, such as Richard Hofstadter.

G.E.M. You might say that I'm a little older than Pollack and a little younger than Hicks. I see the Populists as fighting a hopeless battle in 1896, just as the farmer fought a hopeless battle against the inevitable industrialization of the country. But what Hicks pointed out was true: most of the Populist reforms were taken up by the Progressives. The so-called intellectual historians disturb me to this extent: that they go to great lengths to posit that Darwinism and all the intellectual trends of the late-nineteenth century were necessary ingredients in Progressivism. Yet farmers in Nebraska and Minnesota were doing the things that the Progressives did a long time before they had heard of any of these things. Historians often give logic to things that developed not by logic but by the necessities and ethical considerations of the time.

I'd also make this comment about some of the present views of Populism. Hicks was a small-town boy, raised in Independence, Missouri. A good many of the critics of Populism come from the big cities. As a consequence, they're imputing their city orientation to the motivations of these people. Again, I suppose I occupy middle ground because I was raised in the wintertime in Washington, D.C., and spent my summers on an Ohio farm. I try to get an understanding of the problem instead of taking sides. All of us have different angles of vision.

But I was going to make some other observations about the differences between Populism and Progressivism. One was the type of leadership. Compare, for example, Tom Watson, Ignatius Donnelly, and Jerry Simpson with Theodore Roosevelt or many of the other urban leaders of Progressivism. The former were almost a homespun class of people without too much formal education, the latter a rather sophisticated group of well-educated, well-positioned people. The quality of leadership has a lot to do with the kinds of rhetoric that came out of the movements and also with our own feelings about them.

J.A.G.   To me, two of the most interesting Progressives in relationship to the differences between Progressivism and Populism are La Follette and Bryan. I've never understood why La Follette was not a Populist, or why Bryan, given his orientation, didn't go over to Populism rather than take Populism into the Democratic party.

G.E.M.   Remember that La Follette was a university man with a university mind. He'd graduated from the University of Wisconsin and had many teachers who were conversant with what was then called "modern economics." Bryan was a product of a small religious college. But I think of Bryan more as a politician than as either a Progressive or a Populist.

J.A.G.   Most persons would agree that the Great Depression of the 1930's stimulated liberalism and reform. Yet the Depression of the 1890's seems to have held back reform for perhaps a full decade. Can you explain why this was so?

G.E.M.   My main explanation rests, I suppose, with the changes in attitudes toward social problems between 1890 and 1932. In the Depression of the 1890's, far fewer people were critically hurt than in the Great Depression, so that the would-be supporters of reform in 1930 covered a far larger spectrum of the population. Bankers and businessmen suffered as well as farmers and workingmen. Those motivated toward reform came from a far wider spectrum; because of this there was little class antagonism, at least in 1932–33.

One has also to look at the methods of the reformers of the early 1890's to understand the hostility toward reform of a significant portion of the American population. One of the characteristics was the use of violence. The willingness of labor unions and of radical agitators occasionally to use force scared a great many conservative Americans. This wasn't the case in the Depression of the 1930's. It is interesting to note that in 1932, when the Communist vote should logically have been large, it was not. Beyond this there were the methods of people defending the *status quo,* and especially their rhetoric. The American businessman and man of wealth was far more rigid ideologically in the nineties, far more willing to assume that he was utterly right, far more willing to use the police, to shoot striking laborers down. Violence led to violence. What was going on in the rest of the world was also important. The Communist movement abroad made a lot of Americans of the thirties fearful, but Soviet Communism had far less impact upon the mentality of the American upper class, I would estimate, than the Paris Commune of 1870 had on their counterparts in the 1890's.

Finally, one can't help but compare Grover Cleveland's response to depression with Herbert Hoover's. Hoover has been damned as a man of insensitivity; compared with Cleveland he was a monument of social concern. Perhaps we were as a people more European in our class loyalties in the 1880's and 1890's than we were in the 1930's.

J.A.G.   Turning now to the Progressive era itself, would you describe the so-called Progressive "type"? What were the ideas and assumptions of those political leaders who called themselves "Progressives"?

G.E.M.   The average Progressive came from old American stock, middle-class in aspirations, middle-class in education. He was what is known as a WASP today, although I don't like that term—I've never heard of a Black Anglo-Saxon Protestant!

J.A.G.   Perhaps they should be called ASPs.

G.E.M.   In any case, the "typical" Progressive was a member of an evangelical sect (with the exception of the considerable number of Jews among the Progressive leaders). Most of them had gone to college, especially the younger ones. Many were wealthy or well-to-do. By occupation, as at least my study of California indicates, they belonged to the so-called free professions: they were lawyers, teachers, newspaper owners; small entrepreneurs, men tied to a locality instead of operating over three or four states or over the whole nation. Their vision was pointed toward the locality and at the same time, by the fact of their education, they were acquainted with the rest of the world, and certainly with the rest of the United States.

Politically, they were neither conservative nor radical. A good many would have preferred to see organized labor disappear, but since it was seen as inevitable, they accepted unionization. They were deeply disturbed by the growing stratification of American society and American economic life, by the growth of trusts and monopolies, by the growing centralization of banking, by all that centralization implied for individual entrepreneurs and for free professionals. The independent newspaper editor-owner, for example, had been one of the glories of American life; he'd been one of the most articulate and respected men in his community. Now he was everywhere being swallowed up by the Hearst and Pulitzer and Scripps-Howard chains. Lawyers, at least the more independent-minded of them, feared being forced to become employees of corporations. It's interesting to note that California lawyers who became attorneys for railroads and big corporations were usually anti-Progressives, while Progressive lawyers usually came from independent law firms. Governor Hiram Johnson and his brother are excellent examples of the California Progressive lawyer of this type.

In their diagnosis of the ills of society, the Progressives believed that America was drifting away from its old democratic heritage of individualism and egalitarianism, that opportunity for the individual was being limited by both organized capital and organized labor. Their prescription was the "democratization" of both labor and capital. They exhibited a surprising amount of sympathy and understanding for the underprivileged and were inclined to do something for them. The industrial problem that many of them talked about was not only a problem of concentration, but also one of the mistreatment of women and children, and in fact of all industrial laborers. A great many Progressives were also troubled by the cities because of their unattractive qualities as places to live. They blamed most of the evils of urban life upon political machines—what they saw as the nexus between immigrant groups and the boss system. They were wrong in this, but at least they attacked the problems. There was more experimentation in city government than in any other stratum of political life.

Another aspect of the Progressive mentality was a sense of guilt on the part of those who had large fortunes. They had accumulated, or their fathers had accumulated, far more money than they should have in a democratic society, and, as a consequence, they felt impelled to do something about this—I suppose, to store up credit for themselves in their own eyes and in the eyes of the final Judge. Their humane concern with educational opportunities was also part of the Progressive mentality.

This is my general summing up of the Progressive character and ideology. It was pro capital but anti monopoly capital, with most ambiguous feelings about organized labor, and a sense that perhaps what was wrong with the American world was the dilution of the influence of people like themselves by industrialization and urbanization. It will, I suppose, irritate the New Left, but I see some of the same spirit in a good many of these Progressives that I do in New Left students who want to change society, but who are very much opposed to the bureaucracy that seems to be necessary to effect change.

J.A.G.   Were Progressives frustrated, embittered men, worried because they were losing social status, as some historians have argued?

G.E.M.   Perhaps some of them were frustrated, but few were embittered. Progressive politicians and Progressive editors and nonpolitical Progressives were in the main a very favored group of people. They came from good families, they had a good education, they had prospects that were denied most of the population. As a consequence, I don't see how they could have been embittered. Secondly, these people had great hope for the future. One of the things that comes through in the Progressive rhetoric is their optimism and their hope for the future.

As to their frustration, the younger generation in every age is frustrated, frustrated because they can't immediately take the place of the establishment. The slogan "I Want It Now!" characterizes the mentality of a certain group of present-day students, although not of the majority. Well, a good many young Progressives wanted it "now." This brings up a tentative, highly speculative idea for study: the turnover rate between generations, the problem of youth as the "historical disturber." It seems to me that most of the fuss in American life has been made by young men. I'm thinking of the Revolution, of the War of 1812 with its youthful "War Hawks," and even the Civil War. In the crisis leading to secession, as long as Webster, Calhoun, and Clay held the reins, they managed to stave off a real confrontation. But by the fact that these men had lived so long, I suspect younger leaders were frustrated, and the longer the frustration, the more emphatic the change when the oldsters finally pass on.

To apply this thesis to the Progressives, look at the Republican and Democratic parties between 1870 and 1900. Most of the successful politicians traded regularly on war loyalties. Then a younger generation arose—Roosevelt, Lodge, and others, who had no relationship to war. I think Roosevelt's lament that the Spanish-American War wasn't a great war but the only one we had, says more about the yearnings of youth and their recognition of how to get ahead in American political life than about his liking for battle. Or consider Robert La Follette. He was a regular Republican supporting McKinley in 1896 and 1900. Why did he suddenly become a great radical? I suspect largely because the existing Wisconsin Republican establishment refused to support him for governor. Radicalism was one way to get ahead. On the whole, the Progressives were young, eager, and ambitious to take the place of the older men. The Republican House and Senate were dominated by ancients. The Progressives were perhaps a frustrated generation in that sense.

J.A.G. In many respects, the achievements of the Progressives at the state and local level seem to have been more extensive than those at the national level. Is it possible to generalize about these state and local accomplishments?

G.E.M. I think so, but before I do I'd like to qualify the question. Certainly, local reformers touched the average citizen's life far more often than the reforms on the national scene, but qualitatively, railroad regulation, conservation, the Pure Food and Drug Act, the Federal Trade Commission Act, and a lot of other national measures were at least as significant. But city and state reform was extremely important. The typical large American city was perhaps the most polyglot city in the world. It was made up of sizable minorities from all over the world, and much of the native population often hadn't lived there very long. Americans didn't know how to live in a city. They were confronted in the 1890's and early 1900's with as bad an environment as existed in the United States, with high taxes, bad water, corrupt police, uncertain sewage, and inadequate fire protection.

The shocking inadequacies of the American city explain both the quantity and the quality of Progressive urban reform. Some very interesting things happened. For example, it appears paradoxical, but the Los Angeles *Times*, one of the most conservative newspapers in the United States, supported the municipal ownership of both water and electricity companies. As a consequence, Los Angeles has one of the best urban water-supply systems, and lower electrical rates than almost any city in the United States outside the Northwest, where water power is cheap.

It's more difficult to generalize about reform in the state governments. Birmingham was, after all, not too different from Detroit or Pittsburgh, but Alabama was a far different place from Utah or Ohio. Regional differences in Progressivism were far more apparent at the state than at the urban level. Reform in Wisconsin can't be easily collated with reform in Georgia under Hoke Smith; there were wide differences between Woodrow Wilson's years in New Jersey and George Norris's in Nebraska. There are, however, similarities. I can't think of a really Progressive state that didn't make some move toward democratization, toward tax reform, toward the regulation of common carriers and utilities. Social reforms such as workmen's compensation, the regulation of woman and child labor, and better schools were Progressive concerns wherever one found a manifestation of the Progressive spirit.

J.A.G. Were these accomplishments at the state and local level at all new or path-breaking?

G.E.M. Most of them were new to Americans of that generation, although isolated precedents can be found. But much was borrowed from abroad. Municipal ownership of utilities, for example, had a long history in Germany and England and in certain parts of Scandinavia. Most of the Progressives' ideas of conservation came from Europe (Gifford Pinchot went to forestry school in France and Germany). The techniques of the initiative, referendum, and recall, designed to give the public more direct control of government, were employed in Switzerland. Many progressive labor reforms had been tried in one part of the British Empire or another. Workmen's compensation goes back to Bismarck's Germany and to England. The city manager form of government was an American invention, but I can't think of many state reforms that didn't have a long ancestry somewhere.

J.A.G. Can state and local Progressivism be associated with either one of the major political parties alone?

G.E.M. No. But in most instances—and here is a characteristic peculiar to the Progressive movement—the reform element usually came from the dominant party. One almost had to be a Republican to be effective in many of the Northern states, a Democrat in many of the Southern.

J.A.G. To what extent was Progressivism nonpolitical? What sort of things did the Progressives try to do that did not require partisan political activity?

G.E.M. A great many things—women's rights, for example, and prohibition. On the state and local levels the churches, especially the social gospel wing of many denominations, supported educational reforms. Another area that was largely divorced from politics was the social settlement movement. Most of the settlement workers were women, and I think the reason why the settlement-house idea wasn't readily politicized was that professional politicians weren't used to talking to women and therefore avoided the issue. Social reforms rising from the impact of the university upon American life, those proposed by sociologists in particular, tended to be nonpolitical. The movement for prison reform, for example, was stimulated by the new science of penology. E. A. Ross's definition of sin as social instead of theological in his book, *Sin and Society*, had a great impact on Progressives. Theodore Roosevelt wrote a preface for that volume.

There are other interesting examples of this which may confound some of the New Left critics of Progressivism. The founding of the National Association for the Advancement of Colored People was an achievement of the Progressive years. The establishment and expansion of businessmen's clubs like the Lions and the Kiwanis was a phenomenon of this era. Although liberal scholars may decry their impact on national political questions, which was usually conservative in its effect, their civic activities were, and on the whole remain, fundamentally progressive.

J.A.G. At the national level, why were most of the Progressives Republicans, at least down to 1910 or 1912? Was Bryan, for example, truly a Progressive?

G.E.M. Excluding the South and the Southwest, I think your generalization is sound. An important wing of Progressivism was urban-minded and urban-centered. But the Democratic party was rural, except in New York. It wasn't until workingmen began to exert political strength through the normal party channels that the Democrats developed strength in the cities. There were also other conflicts between the dominant agrarian strain in the Democratic party and Progressivism. Many Progressives, for example, were interested in outlawing child labor, and this ran foul of the farmers' attitude toward child-labor regulation.

As for Bryan's relationship to Progressivism, he represented the Jeffersonian-Jacksonian nostalgic element of the agricultural population, which was fundamentally conservative. His whole attitude toward religion was tied with conservative values, with which the Progressives had little sympathy. His attitude toward learning—he was contemptuous, if not envious, of graduates of eastern colleges—was also out of character with the movement. Lawrence Levine's study of Bryan's later life, *Defender of the Faith,* reveals how, after World War I, he reverted to type. I believe Bryan chose to become a Democrat instead of a Populist in the 1890's largely because he had more chance of becoming President as a Democrat than as a Populist. I think he was basically a politician.

J.A.G. Would you comment on Theodore Roosevelt's relationship with the Progressive movement down to the end of his presidency?

G.E.M. One's view of Roosevelt's relationship to the Progressive movement largely depends upon one's opinion of his character. I see him as a cultivated, educated, elitist, almost a Mugwump, all through his career.

J.A.G. Then the bitterness of the Mugwumps toward Roosevelt grew out of the fact that he was so much like them?

G.E.M. That he was so much like them yet didn't join them. The most hateful enemy is the man who thinks like you but doesn't act like you.

In 1900, Roosevelt was a man in a hurry—in a hurry to take the place of the old men in the party who were running things. During his first administration after the death of McKinley, his overriding concern was to get re-elected in 1904. He recognized that the conservative leaders of the Republican party in Congress would prevent any real progressive measures from going through. This led him, in the first two or three years of his presidency, to try to make his mark in foreign policy.

J.A.G.   Was there really any possibility that Roosevelt would not have been nominated in 1904? Isn't his enormous concern difficult to explain on rational grounds?

G.E.M.   I'm not certain. He felt, until Mark Hanna died, that he was a threat. But, I suppose, if a man desires something very much he becomes supersensitive to the possibility of not getting it. Even in the midst of the campaign of 1904 he was still worrying about the possibility of losing the election to a man like Alton Parker, which is hard to understand.

But to go back to his Progressivism, one of Roosevelt's constant fears was that the Republican West would desert the party on much the same grounds that the Populist West had in the 1880's and 1890's. As a consequence, he early sensed the rising demand for reform. But he had to surmount the obstacle of conservative Republican senators like Aldrich, Spooner, and Allison, whom he well knew would not permit progressive legislation to pass. His one opportunity lay in the realm of administrative acts. This explains as much as anything the Northern Securities Case, in which he used the courts to revive the supposedly moribund Sherman Antitrust Act, and his intervention in the 1902 anthracite coal strike, actions that logically allied him with Progressives. By 1904, after the Democratic party presented him with a great boon by nominating the antediluvian Parker, he certainly thought of himself as the Progressive candidate.

This brings up an interesting speculation about Roosevelt. Had he been contending against Bryan in 1904, would he have been less Progressive in his second administration? Roosevelt was a fighter. His friend Elihu Root once called him a "berserker." When he got into a fight, he persisted until a decision had been reached. Perhaps, having taken the Progressive line and become the Progressive champion, he felt that this was his role. It might have been different if his opponent had been a reformer. But the opposition in 1904 was conservative, and so Roosevelt automatically assumed that he was the chief Progressive of the country. He also saw that a good deal of his popularity came from Progressive centers, and that a great many Republicans were leaning toward the left, bowing to the Progressive wind. Jonathan Dolliver, for example, had lived happily with the conservative Republican party of Iowa for twenty years in local politics and then in the House and Senate; he was no flaming liberal, but he was now for reform.

But above all, Roosevelt was a very ambitious man, and he had a sense of history. He knew one cannot achieve things by standing still, that without a war a President's fame is related to the amount of domestic legislation passed during his administration. In 1905–1906, I think he tried desperately to shove his party as far as he could toward reform, and he achieved a good many things, rather important things, some of them over the opposition of a very reluctant Congress. Then, in 1907, he ran foul of the sharp financial panic which many business leaders blamed, quite unreasonably, on his reforms. Instead of making him more pliable, this opposition stiffened his determination; he became far more radical, at least in talk, than he was before 1907.

I'd like to see a comparative study made of the last years of presidential administrations. I suspect that Presidents have always felt freer to recommend things in their last year. Certainly Roosevelt was a different man in his messages and in his quarrels with Congress than he had been before. He lost his sense of caution. Between his last two annual messages and the New Nationalism of his 1912 campaign for the presidency, Roosevelt didn't move much to the left.

J.A.G. Would it be correct to say that Roosevelt led and strengthened Progressivism rather than moderated or checked reformers more radical than himself?

G.E.M. I think he did both. Being a politician, he attempted to get as much reform as the Senate would permit, which was essentially the behavior of a compromiser. He balanced the muckrakers against the "malefactors of great wealth." He aimed to immobilize the far left and the far right so that the middle could move. But on the whole, compared with the Presidents who preceded him, he was very much an asset to the Progressive movement. He kept a rein on some of the more advanced Progressives, but I can't think of any President of the period who had more sympathy for Progressive reform.

J.A.G. Perhaps his real political genius was to be a compromiser and still manage to associate himself with principle and morality.

G.E.M. Yes, but he also moved the center of the Progressive movement. If you think of the precedents that Roosevelt established—the Pure Food bill, the conservation of natural resources, putting teeth in railroad regulations, government intervention into a strike not from the viewpoint of keeping peace and protecting property but of trying to arrive at a just settlement—these were quite a lot for one administration to achieve, especially considering the leadership he had to deal with in the Senate and the House. Speaker "Uncle Joe" Cannon was so narrow that he could see through the keyhole with both eyes at the same time. The Republican directorate in the Senate, headed by Nelson W. Aldrich, was antediluvian in attitude. To achieve what he did and still keep a semblance of unity in the party seems to me quite remarkable.

J.A.G.   Was Roosevelt responsible for the failures of his successor, William Howard Taft? If he had a talent approaching genius in extracting things from a reluctant Congress, his tactics in his last year seem totally unreasonable.

G.E.M.   I think so, in part. But his behavior also reflected his belief that the country was moving to the left and that his party wasn't moving fast enough. As a consequence, he made promises that his successor would have to try to carry out. But even the best of politicians in the presidential office get tired of trying to move men by persuasion.

However, his choice of Taft was a mistake. Had he been a better judge of human nature, he would have known that Taft was far less responsive and subtle a person than himself. It's amazing in American political life, if you think back, that Presidents who have personally selected their successors have usually been bad judges.

J.A.G.   Whom do you think he should have picked as his successor?

G.E.M.   That's another point. What were the alternatives? He considered Elihu Root, but I don't think Root would have been the right man. Who else might it have been? *Was* there a good man? I suppose Taft was as near as Roosevelt could get.

J.A.G.   Was Taft a Progressive as you have defined that term?

G.E.M.   It depends. Taft ran into a lot of troubles in 1909–12, troubles which showed up aspects of his character that perhaps even he didn't know were there. As an administrator under Roosevelt he was completely loyal. He did things that perhaps he would not have done had he been his own man. When he became President, he found a conflict between his loyalty to Roosevelt's policies and his loyalties to the Republican party. His own inner convictions were largely conservative. One of the interesting things about Taft was that most of his close associates were conservatives or reactionaries. He didn't like Progressives like Dolliver and La Follette. He enjoyed the company of good conservatives; they were comfortable people. He had made a lot of promises, and he did a pretty good job of keeping them until 1912.

J.A.G.   The final break between Roosevelt and Taft came over the question of how to deal with large corporations. Would you trace the development of Roosevelt's approach to the corporation question, and also explain why Taft, given his conservative instincts, was such an energetic trust-buster?

G.E.M.   There is less development in Roosevelt's view of the corporation question than historians have made out. Roosevelt was a modern man. He lived easily with the polarization of force, whether it be in nations or in cities or in industrial corporations. In the second place, he admired bigness, looked forward, instead of backward to a small America. Very early he realized the intimate relationship between big industry and all big power—naval power, diplomatic power, in fact, the power of the United States. He was interested in *controlling* power. It would have been frightful had he been a Carnegie or a Morgan. With all of that superhuman energy of his, he might have been the biggest magnate in the country. But being a politician and given his upbringing and sense of responsibility, he identified the public interest with himself and became a public servant. Given his inclinations, trust-busting was not his idea of a viable relationship between government and industry.

His attack on the Northern Securities Company under the Antitrust Act was a very special case, a perfect fit for Roosevelt's particular political situation. It won him a reputation for Progressive action and a lot of popular support. Also, he was extremely sensitive to law-breaking. The Sherman law was not being enforced, so he enforced it. But one must balance the Northern Securities case against his contemporaneous recommendation that Congress create a Commissioner of Corporations, a much more significant long-term policy. He asked Congress to give the Commissioner power even to subpoena corporate records. From that time on, again and again he stressed that trust-busting was rather silly, that once you scramble the eggs, you can't unscramble them. However, whereas J. P. Morgan, for example, wished to leave the eggs unguarded by the cook, Roosevelt would see that they were properly seasoned and prepared and served to the American public.

Taft, on the other hand, felt there was a chance to restore the old competitive conditions. He was devoted to law, and the precedents of English law certainly didn't emphasize regulation. His attitude toward life was not Roosevelt's; it was conservative in the best sense. When he became President, I think he felt that unless the big monopolies were broken up, government regulation would become inevitable and he saw regulation as leading to a huge federal bureaucracy. Secondly, Taft was a legalist. The Antitrust law was on the books; he saw it as a presidential obligation to carry out the law.

J.A.G. Does this question of regulating versus breaking up the large corporations separate Progressives into two broad types, or was the division unrelated to Progressive attitudes on other issues?

G.E.M. I think that the division is symptomatic of a mentality which comprehended most of the schisms in the Progressive movement. I can't help going back to a letter that Roosevelt wrote in 1911, describing the Progressives' attempt to unseat Taft. He called the western Progressives, among other things, "rural Tories." This attitude characterized the thinking of a   good many eastern, educated, urban-oriented Progressives. It separated men like Bryan from men like Herbert Croly, whose *Promise of American Life* (1909) argued so forcefully for the regulatory state; it even separated Roosevelt from La Follette. Roosevelt was referring to La Follette and Dolliver, and, to a degree, Hiram Johnson in California. What he was referring to specifically was their inability to accept the fact that modern industry was beyond the point of returning to the old individualism. He believed one had to substitute the power of government for competition, and this of course led him to the New Nationalism and his program of 1912. The division was also reflected in the attitudes of Progressives on foreign policy. Some favored a "Little America" policy, others saw the United States as a world power and a world determinant of power. Roosevelt, of course, took the latter position, while La Follette and some of the western Progressives supported the "little America" policy.

J.A.G.   Did the trust-busting issue divide businessmen in this same way?

G.E.M.   I think it did, and this is something that most of my generation of historians missed in writing about Progressivism. We were products of the Depression, and our mentality was shaped by a predilection to divide the country between reactionaries and progressives. We saw in past history what we wanted to see in the New Deal: the good men on one side, the bad men on the other. We put the average businessman of the Progressive era in one corner, the good people in the other—which of course was nonsense. Small businessmen on the whole hoped against hope that government regulation could be avoided; they saw most of the virtues of life wrapped around their own personalities and their own occupations. On the other hand, big businessmen split right down the middle. They didn't want antitrust, and they didn't want government regulation. But the Armstrong investigation into the New York insurance scandals in 1905 indicated to many businessmen that if they didn't have federal regulation, then the states would regulate them, and in the interest of efficiency it might be easier to live under a federal regulation. Moreover, a growing element in American business recognized that rational regulation probably was not only inevitable but also for the social good.

J.A.G.   Would you comment on the thesis of the historian Gabriel Kolko, who argues that Roosevelt was merely a spokesman for big-business interests?

G.E.M.   I don't agree with Kolko. If Roosevelt was a spokesman for big business, he was a spokesman for people whom he either didn't care for or was unconcerned with. If there was anything that Roosevelt was uninterested in, it was the operations of business and making money in that way. He didn't mind making money, but he preferred to make money in other ways than through business. Secondly, it is illogical to charge that Roosevelt was the spokesman of big business. He supported business, but what President hasn't?

J.A.G. Perhaps it would be fairer to say that Kolko sees Roosevelt as a profoundly conservative President, and the whole Progressive movement as a conservative one—an attempt to protect large corporations against what they conceived of as an attack on their efficiency.

G.E.M. If Roosevelt was overly protective of big business, it was not for business ends. He certainly saw the relationship between big business and national power. But to say that he was protective of big business for business values is something else again. Secondly, he was ready to curb business profits for social purposes, which of course most businessmen would not have agreed to voluntarily. The amount of social legislation Roosevelt favored is amazing. Had his proposals all been passed by Congress, I think business would have been as much against him as it was against Franklin D. Roosevelt in 1936.

J.A.G. Was Woodrow Wilson's New Freedom really a different approach to reform from Roosevelt's New Nationalism? Perhaps what I'm asking is: What are the continuities and discontinuities between Roosevelt's New Nationalism and Woodrow Wilson's New Freedom?

G.E.M. If one looks at Woodrow Wilson and Theodore Roosevelt in 1912, Roosevelt was the radical, Wilson the middle-of-the-road conservative. Wilson's speech accepting the presidential nomination was an extremely conservative document, praised by most conservative newspapers. He hoped to rely chiefly on free competition to achieve reform. Grover Cleveland wouldn't have taken exception to most of the things that Wilson said. What has happened is that, in the name of logic, historians have looked back at what Wilson accomplished from 1913 to 1916 and assumed this is what he promised to do in 1912.

In the first year and a half of Wilson's administration, most of the major legislation, except for the Federal Reserve Board, was pointed in the direction of the New Freedom. It was only later that Wilson went toward the New Nationalism. In fact, some of the more radical measures passed during his administration he accepted only with reluctance: the Federal Reserve Act, the highway act, federal aid to technical schools, the Adamson Railroad Act (which he accepted only when faced with a major strike).

J.A.G. When did the Progressive era end, and why did it end at that time?

G.E.M. Some historians have suggested that it ended in 1914. There is a certain amount of truth to that; both Wilson and Governor Hiram Johnson of California claimed that their programs had been accomplished by 1914. On the other hand, there was much Progressive legislation after that date. When the movement died is not a matter of date, but a matter of the psyche of reformers. The Progressive movement lasted a long time as reform movements go. And if you'll look at other reform movements, you'll find the same sort of diminution of strength over time. You ask, "Why?" One thing is quite apparent. Men get old; as they become older and more mature and less vigorous, they are concerned, I suspect, with conserving their power instead of expanding it.

Secondly, there comes a time when the radical ideas of their youth no longer appear radical. What happened to the Progressive movement around 1918 is what happened to the Liberal party in England. It had arrived at the end of "permissible" reform—permissible in the sense of what the Liberals' own loyalties would permit them to support. They became frightened of further innovations by what happened in 1918–19 —not only by the divisive issues of the peace, but by developments abroad in Russia and England, and probably more by what happened in England with the rise of the Labour party than by the Russian Revolution. Russia was "exotic"; it was not a Western country. When the British Labour party proposed the socialization of the major productive facilities of Britain and a capital tax, a great many Americans were shocked. They saw the possibility of things that they couldn't possibly accept occurring in their own country.

J.A.G. Was the New Deal a continuation or perhaps a "revival" of the Progressive movement?

G.E.M. Otis Graham's *Encore for Reform* has some rather interesting things to say about the persistent element among Progressives. There weren't too many of them with much influence, but they came from the urban element among Progressives. Furthermore, those who had been interested in social reform in the cities were more responsive to the New Deal than the type of Progressive who worried about the relationship of business and labor.

J.A.G. What is your opinion of the so-called New Left interpretation of American history as it applies to the Progressive era?

G.E.M. The New Left is obviously in favor of socialism, but also antibureaucracy and antiestablishment. Its emphasis upon individualism is a sort of combination of Emerson and Marx, if one can conceive of that. It reflects, I suppose, a paradox of the present generation of radical students that one deals with daily: presumably, they want to preserve the productiveness of modern society but destroy its social and political organization. Since the New Left historians are highly critical of corporate capitalism in the United States, the Progressive movement seems anything but radical to them. The Progressives thought they were creating a solid center of middle-class sentiment to support reform but not to support radicalism. They were a conservative force, if looked at from the left of the political stratum.

To my mind, the Progressives ought to be considered closer to the New Left than the New Deal. If anything, the Progressives stressed individual rights. They also stressed ethics; Progressivism was the last reform movement in the United States that emphasized personal ethics. The New Deal solution to most problems was to build up a federal bureaucracy and to spend money. However effective it was, it increased the power of the federal government and the bureaucracy. After a serious study of recent history, I think New Left historians would view the Progressives more charitably than they would most of the New Dealers.

J.A.G. Radical historians have criticized Wilson and Roosevelt with regard to their attitudes toward the Negro. Did the Progressive movement really do much for the underprivileged?

G.E.M. It's difficult to describe the Progressive attitude on the race question, because in large part Progressivism as I've been discussing it was a northern movement. At that time there wasn't much of a race question in the North. The Negro population in most northern cities was insignificant before World War I. Most Progressives were concerned with the problems nearest at hand.

But it is true that the Progressives were insensitive to the question of race. The Wilson administration can be charged with actually depriving the Negro of opportunities for federal employment.

But the New Left doesn't understand that certain ages in history have imposed limits beyond which men could not operate effectively. If the Progressives had broken those conventions and limits, they would have immediately ostracized themselves from their supporters and lost their usefulness as political instruments. A confrontation over the race issue in early twentieth-century America would have been deadly to reform; it would have destroyed anyone who forced it, because the sentiment of the country was absolutely opposed to real racial equality.

J.A.G. What are the half-dozen books that you would recommend to persons interested in the subject we have been discussing? In each case, would you indicate briefly what the particular contribution of the volume is?

G.E.M. Although published many years ago, *The Populist Revolt* (1931) by John D. Hicks is still the most comprehensive, sympathetic, and authoritative work on the Populists. Shorter, and thus less comprehensive than several existing biographies, John Morton Blum, *The Republican Roosevelt* (1954) is perhaps the most satisfying in its interpretation of this complex and many-faceted President.

Arthur S. Link, *Woodrow Wilson and the Progressive Era* (1954) is still unchallenged in amplitude for the Wilson period. Of the numerous more interpretive works running across the entire spectrum of post-Civil War reform movements, from the viewpoint of a variety of approaches, perhaps three are of cardinal interest: Richard Hofstadter, *The Age of Reform* (1955), Gabriel Kolko, *The Triumph of Conservatism* (1963), and Robert H. Wiebe, *The Search for Order* (1967). Hofstadter's stimulating volume bases much of the Progressive activity upon the psychic crisis of America's middle classes, inspired in part by a national revolution in status. Kolko, one of the New Left historians, argues brilliantly, if not entirely convincingly, that Progressives were really conservatives who effectively blighted all hope of a humane socialist state. Robert Wiebe, on the other hand, finds Progressivism the product of a new organizing middle class, who articulated the values and ideals necessary for the new urban, industrialized state.

Arthur S. Link

World War I

PROFESSOR Arthur S. Link has devoted most of his scholarly career to the study of Woodrow Wilson. His definitive biography, *Wilson,* five volumes of which have so far appeared (1947–65), has won many honors, including two Bancroft prizes. His edition of *The Papers of Woodrow Wilson* (1966–) will eventually run to some forty volumes. He is also the author of *Woodrow Wilson and the Progressive Era* (1954), *Wilson the Diplomatist* (1957), and many other books, including an important survey of twentieth-century history, *American Epoch* (1955). Professor Link, a former President of the Southern Historical Association, is currently Edwards Professor of American History at Princeton University. In the following interview, he discusses the causes, course, and consequences of American participation in World War I.

John A. Garraty Professor Link, when the Great War broke out in Europe in 1914, nearly all Americans believed that the United States should not become involved in it. Did this merely reflect American isolationism, or could sound arguments be made that no vital interest of the nation could be threatened by a major European war?

Arthur S. Link I should say both. American neutralism, a better term to describe American reactions than isolationism, grew from a deep-seated popular desire to avoid involvement in the ghastly carnage, but it was also the product of a century of thinking about the proper role of the United States in world affairs. At least since the Monroe Doctrine, if not before, detachment from the quarrels and controversies of Europe had been the cornerstone of American foreign policy. Neutralism was compounded first by a natural desire not to be involved in useless wars, but perhaps more importantly, of a deep-rooted conviction that the United States could play its best role in world affairs by serving as an example to the world of a peaceful nation.

Americans said a great deal about the First World War soon after its outbreak: newspapers, periodicals, books, and private letters of the time were filled with comment on the war. The great majority of Americans regretted the war and were shocked by its outbreak, but virtually all, at the outset at any rate, agreed that the United States had no vital interest in the conflict that would justify the risk of involvement.

J.A.G. Were they correct in this assumption from the perspective of the present? Did it not matter to the United States who won the war?

A.S.L. The reactions and attitudes of the people were not totally unrealistic. Most Americans assumed that the Allies were going to win the war. All American reactions have to be read in light of that assumption.

J.A.G. In his Neutrality Proclamation, President Wilson urged the public to be impartial even in thought. What did he mean? Was Wilson himself impartial in that sense?

A.S.L. All proclamations, decrees, and state papers, have to be understood in terms of the circumstances prevailing at the time they are issued. Wilson's neutrality appeal of August 17, 1914, was issued specifically in response to a suggestion from the then Counselor of the State Department, Robert Lansing, who, viewing the cacophony of voices on the American scene, urged the President to appeal to advocates of the rival alliances to exercise some degree of caution and discretion in their public utterances. I don't think that Lansing was overestimating the degree of public frenzy. There was a great deal of talk by people who were afraid of a German victory, and by German-Americans, Irish-Americans, and other champions of the Central Powers who were advocating the claims of Germany. Actually, there were a number of statements by public figures comparable to Wilson's appeal. The Federal Council of Churches of Christ in America issued a special appeal:

> The Federal Council . . . suggests to the President of the United States, in view of the attempts already made to induce this country to take sides in the present European conflict, that he appeal to the people of the United States, as lovers of their country and of humanity, that neither as individuals nor as groups do they take any action to destroy the complete and absolute neutrality of the United States. We believe that he who would attempt to drag this country into the present war not only sins against patriotism, but would destroy all hope of a speedy peace. Only as this nation remains strictly neutral can she offer mediation. If she becomes involved, there is no impartial court left to which the nations may appeal.

J.A.G.   The key word, it seems to me, in that statement is "action." It says nothing about thought. Why did Wilson ask the people not to *think* partially, which it seems to me is impossible?

A.S.L.   That's quite right, and Wilson, who was not unintelligent, certainly understood that point. What he was asking was not, I think, that the American people utterly void their minds of any thought about the war, but simply that in their thoughts they keep the interests of the United States foremost. As he put it: "The United States must be neutral in fact as well as in name during these days that are to try men's souls." The nation should "exhibit the fine poise of undisturbed judgment, the dignity of self-control, the efficiency of dispassionate action" in order to be "truly serviceable for the peace of the world." That's really all he meant.

Certainly he himself was not totally impartial, at least not at the outset. Wilson's reactions, like the reactions of his fellow countrymen, went through various stages. I'm convinced he was pro-Allied in his emotional reactions at the outset. We have much evidence of this, such as his famous conversation with the British Ambassador, Sir Cecil Spring Rice, in which he said that everything he believed in and stood for was at stake in the war. Like many Americans of his class and education, he tended to react emotionally at the outset when the Germans were threatening to win the war, but once the western front had been stabilized he had plenty of time to consider the issues of the war soberly. By the autumn of 1914, all of the major belligerents had issued various books, attempting to exonerate themselves from any blame in causing the war, and throwing the blame on their enemies. These documentary collections revealed a great deal about the immediate background of the war. Americans like Wilson were able to see that the causes of the war were extremely complex. By the late autumn of 1914, Wilson had reached a detached, fairly objective, almost scholarly view of the war. As he said on several occasions, he consistently tried to detach his own emotions from his evaluation of events.

J.A.G.   Then he meant by neutrality in thought only that one should not let one's feelings affect one's judgment?

A.S.L.   Precisely: not let one's feelings carry one away in denouncing the other side.

J.A.G.   How did various groups in the United States actually feel about the belligerents? Were many people aware, even in a general way, of the causes of the war?

A.S.L.   The answer to the first question depends in large measure upon the answer to the second. Numerous people in the United States were aware in much more than a general way of the causes of the war. The tendency of a later generation is always to assume that an earlier generation was totally ignorant of events. The United States was a great market place of ideas, a place in which all the belligerents could sell their ideological wares. Propagandists, scholars, and publicists from all the warring countries aimed a barrage of propaganda and other expository materials at the American people. One consequence of this was the quick education of thoughtful Americans.

Looking at it as an historian, I believe we have not learned a great deal about the causes of the First World War since 1914. The essential facts even then were well known. The great majority of thoughtful Americans had made up their minds about the causes of the war in October and November, 1914, and did not change very fundamentally throughout the rest of the conflict, even during the period of American participation. German-Americans tended to react with considerably more emotion than did recent immigrants from the British Isles. The great majority of Americans, while of British stock, did not feel any strong emotional attachment to Britain. In fact, the British started with a great deficit, the century-and-a-half-old tradition of hostility to Great Britain. German-Americans, on the other hand, not only defended the German cause, but supported it through bazaars, the purchase of Imperial German bonds, and contributions to the German Red Cross. The German-American community in 1914 was still an identifiable community which preserved its identity to a remarkable degree.

J.A.G.   What attitudes did the warring powers take toward the United States? Did either side show any disposition to try to enlist active American participation in the conflict?

A.S.L.   No. Both the Allies and the Central Powers took essentially the same position: that their main task was to win emotional and political sympathy. Neither the British nor the Germans attempted to enlist active American participation. The Germans were shrewd enough to know they could not obtain it. British officials consistently took the position that it would be fatal to their cause for them even to suggest American participation; any efforts to encourage it would only be counterproductive.

J.A.G.   Is there any evidence that British diplomats attempted to influence American political leaders in this direction? For example, the same kind of pressures could have been applied to the United States that were applied to Italy: some kind of *quid pro quo* could have been offered in return for participation.

A.S.L.   On a few occasions the British cautiously suggested that the United States might enter the war. At the time of the *Sussex* crisis in the spring of 1916, when Wilson was considering breaking diplomatic relations with Germany because several Americans had been injured in the torpedoeing of a French steamer, the British Foreign Secretary, Sir Edward Grey, hinted that the United States could make its best contribution to peace as a belligerent. Then, in February 1917, David Lloyd George, the new British Prime Minister, sent two personal appeals to President Wilson, urging the immediate entrance of the United States into the war on the ground that only American participation could give the war a noble, commendable rationale. These are the only occasions in which any of the belligerents suggested directly to the United States that America should enter the war.

J.A.G.   Would you describe how each side tried to influence American opinion?

A.S.L.   Both sides tried hard and were, on the whole, successful. Only a few weeks after the outbreak of the war, the British Foreign Office established an official propaganda agency, Wellington House, concerned directly with the United States, and placed in charge a member of the Canadian Parliament, Sir Gilbert Parker. Parker published direct appeals in American periodicals and distributed hundreds of tracts by British scholars and statesmen. He also sponsored lectures by Americans. Above all, Wellington House distributed the Bryce Report of 1915, the report of a commission headed by Viscount James Bryce on Germany's so-called atrocities in Belgium. Early in 1916, the British began to conclude that their propaganda effort was not succeeding, because it consisted too much of direct appeals to the American people. Thereafter, they took pains to give opportunities to American journalists to describe the British war effort.

The Germans, very much like the British, conducted a gigantic propaganda effort in the United States. This began in August, 1914, with the establishment in New York of the German Information Service. The

German effort, on the whole, was larger than the British. It took many forms. German political leaders appealed directly to the American people. American newspapers and periodicals are simply filled with these appeals. German scholarship was held in very high regard in the United States, and German scholars and religious leaders also participated in the propaganda effort by writing articles in American periodicals and by publishing tracts and pamphlets for distribution in the United States. In the summer of 1915, one of the German propagandists, Heinrich Albert, head of the German Purchasing Commission, left his briefcase on an elevated train in New York. It was picked up by an American secret service agent, and the contents were published. This tended to neutralize German propaganda, although I'm not inclined to give as much weight to the Albert exposures as most people. Americans were, after all, not simpletons. They knew that both the British and Germans were carrying on high-powered propaganda campaigns. But from the autumn of 1915 onward, the Germans used increasingly the vehicle of direct appeal.

Did propaganda have any appreciable effect on public opinion? I should say, "Yes and no." "No" because the propaganda was so immense and varied that it tended to be self-cancelling. "Yes," most emphatically, and particularly considering the difficulties of German-American relations from 1915 to 1917, the German propaganda effort was probably decisive in preserving German-American peace. We tend to discount the success of propaganda for a cause that failed. But the United States and Germany might have gone to war much earlier had it not been for the propaganda of the Germans.

German propaganda, far from being blundering, was shrewd and subtle. It appealed to American self-interest, to American idealism, to the traditional ties of friendship between the United States and Germany, to the image that Americans held of Germany as a nation of cultural, scientific, and educational achievements. Many of the conclusions regarding the effectiveness of German propaganda put forth in the 1930's were based on the assumption that the Germans never had a chance to present their point of view to the American people. This is utter nonsense. The newspapers and periodicals of the time reveal the extent, sophistication, and general excellence of German propaganda. There were no serious impediments to the propagation of the German point of view in the United States.

J.A.G. We know that the war enormously stimulated the American economy. How did this affect public attitudes toward the belligerents?

A.S.L. If I had to single out one American reaction to the war-inspired boom, it would be that the great majority of Americans had deep-rooted feelings of guilt about the prosperity the United States was experiencing at the expense of the European people. This attitude was expressed particularly after the great and bloody battles of the late autumn and early winter of 1916. Moreover, American economists and public officials were by that time growing increasingly worried by the boom. They considered it dangerous that the prosperity of the United States should depend so much upon war trade. The war was bound to come to an end, and fairly soon. What would happen to the economy then? I have seen no evidence that the stimulation of the economy had any direct effect on American attitudes toward the Allies or toward Germany. I'm not prepared to say that there were no subtle effects, but if so they are difficult to measure.

J.A.G.   I can understand that there was concern because the prosperity would have to end sometime. But what evidence is there of the sense of guilt you mentioned?

A.S.L.   Religious newspapers and periodicals discussed this question from time to time. One also gets it *sub rosa,* and occasionally in an open way, in the private correspondence of the time. I'm not suggesting that it was overwhelming. Most Americans were so busy with other things that they didn't stop to think about such matters.

J.A.G.   How did these issues affect Wilson? How much importance did he place on the economic benefits that the war was bringing to the United States?

A.S.L.   This is not easy to answer, because Wilson didn't often comment on it; one has to make deductions from other evidence. The Wilson administration was conscious that prosperity had resulted from the war trade. Wilson was eager to maintain this trade. He derived great satisfaction from the knowledge that war trade made the Allies dependent upon the United States, which meant that his own diplomatic power was growing by leaps and bounds. In any case, to suggest that war profits seriously affected United States policy is to ascribe to American leaders a Machiavellian and almost malign intention that they simply did not have. The majority of Americans would have been glad to make economic sacrifices if it would have been conducive to peace. The very notion of perpetuating the war for profit was morally repugnant not merely to Wilson but to most citizens.

J.A.G.   Would you discuss the ways in which the warring powers violated the rights of the United States on the high seas during the war?

A.S.L.   Everything depends upon one's view of the rights of neutrals in wartime. With the exception of certain well-defined practices and rights, neutral rights were in a state of controversy. Neutrals tended to take a very broad view of their rights, belligerents a narrow one. Neither was altogether wrong, because international law governing neutrality and belligerency was not well adjusted to reality.

The British attempt to control maritime commerce to their advantage expanded as the war progressed. However, the two great controverted points were evident from the outset. One was the manner of blockade: whether the British were justified in maintaining a long-range blockade by a cordon of cruisers, or whether blockade had to be an actual blockade off the coast of enemy ports. The British employed a long-range blockade, arguing that modern weapons—mines, submarines, long-range artillery—made the maintenance of a traditional blockade impossible and were a violation of international law. The other was the British view of contraband. The original British contraband lists, although somewhat limited, went beyond any definition of contraband that had been made up to that time. As the war progressed and occasion permitted, they extended the list still further to include things like food, cotton, and raw materials. Finally, in February, 1915, the British instituted a *total* blockade of the Central Powers, allegedly in retaliation against the "illegal" German submarine blockade. Everything depended upon the legal argument of how far one could legally go in exercising the right of retaliation.

The United States naturally asserted the traditional rights of neutrals to virtually unlimited free trade with all belligerents, except in absolute contraband, such as munitions. But the British had all the conventions and force of international law on their side, and were also able, pointing most devastatingly to American practice during the Civil War, to say that they were doing no more than the United States had done against the Confederacy. The Germans' violations of American rights were, in the nature of things, bound to be more limited. Indeed, before the introduction of the submarine as a commerce destroyer, it was virtually impossible for the United States and Germany to have any point of conflict, because the German Navy had been swept from the seas. The American-German controversy over neutral rights revolved about two points: the safety of American lives on belligerent or neutral passenger ships, and the safety of American ships themselves on the high seas. These points came into controversy as a result of the German submarine warfare, beginning in February, 1915. Negotiations on these points constituted the core of German-American relations from 1915 to 1917, but before January 31, 1917, the rights of American ships on the high seas was never an important matter of controversy. In 1915, as the result of the case of the *Freye*, an American sailing ship which was destroyed, the Germans reaffirmed the validity of the Prussian-American Treaty of 1778, which specified the rights of the ships of each nation during wartime.

J.A.G. Were the rights of neutrals ever really observed by major powers during war?

A.S.L. I think not.

J.A.G. Then were American officials fair in their presentation of the issue to the American people?

A.S.L. There is a difference between the assertion and defense of neutral rights. The *reservation* of these rights for adjudication after the war can be a very important thing. There's a big difference between taking this posture and belligerence. No neutral nation is obliged to give up theoretical rights during wartime. It can defend them rhetorically, and put in claims after the war is over. This is all the American government did, it seems to me. Wilson and the State Department maintained a strong, rational defense of American neutral rights, but Wilson was very particular that such defense should be of a rhetorical nature.

J.A.G. If Wilson was seriously interested in forcing the belligerents to respect American rights on the high seas, why did he not place an embargo on foreign commerce?

A.S.L. The question Wilson had to answer was whether he was going to recognize British sea power as a legitimate weapon during wartime. An even more basic question was whether he was going to be truly neutral. There may at times be good reasons why a nation should be *un*neutral, but Wilson did not think this was true in the period 1914–17. He made the fundamental decision to acknowledge British sea power. It would have been extraordinarily unneutral to have placed an embargo on all foreign trade. This would have been greatly to the detriment of the Allies and would have caused them to lose the war.

But such a policy might well have been adopted if some large political goal could be achieved by doing so. Look at it this way: defense of neutral rights is fine if one simply wishes to remain neutral. But if the objective of a power, of a *great power,* is to do more—in the case of the United States to bring the war to an end—then it will use its economic power to achieve particular ends. There would have been no reason whatsoever to put an embargo on American commerce unless the objective was the triumph of the Germans.

J.A.G. If an embargo was impolitic, why didn't Wilson prohibit American citizens from traveling on belligerent ships to avoid the loss of human life and the incidents which resulted from it?

A.S.L. Unfortunately, the question of the safety of human life on the high seas erupted in such a way that the American government could not deal with it rationally. The right of Americans to travel on belligerent passenger ships first arose when a German submarine sank the British vessel *Fabola,* killing an American, Leon Thrasher. The legal experts in the State Department were disposed to make an issue of this, but Secretary of State William J. Bryan was not, and Wilson apparently agreed with Bryan. Unfortunately for German-American relations, the sinking of the *Lusitania* on May 7, 1915, raised the issue in such a dramatic, horror-evoking form that it was difficult to deal with it sanely. Wilson did attempt to do so, and on the whole I think he succeeded, with the cooperation of the German government. Much more important was the issue of the right of American citizens to travel on belligerent merchant ships without fear of attack, which would have challenged the German right to conduct submarine warfare. That issue was never a subject of much controversy or discussion. So neutral rights boils down to one single issue—the safety of human life on unarmed passenger ships. Respect for this would in no way have damaged any vital German interest.

J.A.G. Did the large private loans that American citizens made to the Allies have any effect on American policy before 1917?

A.S.L. The only effect that the loans had on public policy before 1917 was to increase the self-confidence of the Washington government in its economic influence on the Allies. Of course there is the larger question of whether the making of these loans involved the American people in an emotional attachment and commitment to the Allied cause. But there is no evidence whatsoever that it did. The groups who made the loans were, to begin with, emotionally committed to the Allied cause. There has been a great deal of misunderstanding about the nature of these loans. The British and French governments made only one important, unsecured public loan in the United States, the $500 million Anglo-French loan of 1915. It was a disastrous failure; only $30 or $40 million were in fact bought by the public; the underwriting banks were required to take up the rest of the loan. The Allies concluded that it was simply impossible to raise large quantities of money by direct sale of their bonds in the United States.

Between August, 1915, and April, 1917, when the United States entered the war, the Allies did borrow approximately $1,800 million, but all this money was secured with high-grade American stocks and bonds owned by British and French citizens. The bankers lending this money had no fear whatsoever about repayment. But, in any event, no one believed that the British and French governments would default on their public debts. That their loans were dependent for repayment upon an Allied victory did not occur to Americans.

J.A.G. At what point did any sizable group of Americans begin to think that the United States should enter the war on the Allied side?

A.S.L. What do you mean by "sizable"? Before the spring of 1915, you could probably count the number of influential Americans who believed that the United States should enter the war on two hands. After the *Lusitania* crisis, the number increased, but it was still an extremely small group, consisting of Theodore Roosevelt, Robert Bacon of the House of Morgan, Elihu Root, Senator Henry Cabot Lodge, Augustus

P. Gardner of the House of Representatives, the son-in-law of Senator Lodge, a few American literati such as George Haven Putnam and William Dean Howells, and a few leaders in education such as John G. Hibben of Princeton. But I suspect that as late as January, 1917, you could have put all the influential Americans who favored American entry into the war into one fair-sized room.

The astounding fact, as one studies American newspapers and periodicals during this period, is the absence of any significant group that favored American participation. There's a vast difference between favoring the Allies in a general emotional way, and wanting to go to war to support their cause. It was not until the publication of the Zimmermann telegram, revealing the German plan to get Mexico to attack the United States, and the wholesale German assault against neutral as well as belligerent ships, that large numbers of Americans began to advocate war.

J.A.G. Are you sure that you're not reading the sources too literally when you say that? Certainly, there was a substantial preparedness movement in the United States before 1917. How conceivably could a man justify building up the military forces of the United States if he was not contemplating war?

A.S.L. That was easy enough to do. It depended on the type of preparedness. Most Americans, when they talked about preparedness, simply meant strengthening the defenses of the United States to prepare for some vague and ill-defined future threat. The number of people who were proposing measures that would have put the United States in a state of readiness to fight in a major European war was tiny.

J.A.G. But weren't the preparedness groups pretty solidly pro-Allies?

A.S.L. I don't think so. A great majority of preparedness advocates were neither pro-German nor pro-Allies, or if they were pro-Allies, their attachments were so vague and mild that they were of no consequence so far as policy was concerned.

J.A.G. Did Wilson's obvious desire to act as a mediator between the belligerents lead him to neglect his responsibilities toward the interests of the United States?

A.S.L. I don't think so. I suppose it could be argued that he was so desirous for mediation that he failed to press the British as strongly as he might have in defense of American rights, but I don't think that this argument would hold water. When neutral rights became a live issue in the summer of 1916, the British had already made it perfectly clear that they weren't interested in American mediation, and Wilson reverted to strict neutrality.

J.A.G. Why did Wilson hesitate so long before coming out for preparedness? If he was unwilling to accept restrictions on freedom of the seas, didn't he realize that war might be the only alternative? After all, if the United States had engaged in a more intensive preparedness program, its military contribution after entering the war would have been larger and more quickly decisive.

A.S.L. Let's get a little perspective on this. Actually, Wilson came out for what he called "reasonable preparedness" in July, 1915, only eleven months after the outbreak of the war. I think he reacted hesitantly to preserve the nation's calm and poise, and in the hope that there would be some early chance for him to mediate. His defense of freedom of the seas was mainly rhetorical and legalistic. He realized that war might be the only alternative in the event of a wholesale assault on American commerce, and the *Lusitania* crisis raised this possibility. This experience caused him to come out for preparedness.

J.A.G. Why did he finally decide to ask for a declaration of war in 1917?

A.S.L. I wish I could give a competent answer to this question, which numerous other scholars have long pondered. Wilson's first reaction to the German declaration of unlimited submarine war on January 31, 1917, was to adopt a policy of armed neutrality. He adhered to this course for about a month. Sometime between late March and early April, he concluded that armed neutrality was not a sufficient response to the German threat, and decided that full-scale belligerency was necessary. He explained his decision in letters at the time, and indeed in his war message to Congress. He said that the Germans themselves, by declaring that armed American ships that attacked submarines would be treated as pirates, had made it impossible to wage a limited war on the seas, and that in view of the Germans' position, the United States had only one recourse—all-out belligerency in defense of its maritime commerce.

Now, this was the explanation that Wilson gave publicly, but with a man whose mind was as subtle and complex as his we can be quite sure that other motivations were at work. He had lost all confidence in the integrity of the German government because of the Zimmermann telegram, with its proposed Mexican-German alliance. Wilson was a man with a high sense of personal honor. The Zimmermann telegram was certainly a very powerful force in convincing him that the German government was devoid of integrity and a criminal force in the world. Secondly, there was the simple, immediate problem of the defense of American rights on the seas. Conceivably, Wilson could have reacted to the German submarine announcement by simply withdrawing all American commerce from the seas, but such a policy would have resulted in massive loss of face. The United States would have lost whatever influence it had in the world. I don't think Wilson was himself interested in national prestige per se, but he was interested in certain great objectives, especially mediation, achievement of which could not be accomplished without prestige and influence. His desire to mediate the war caused him to act.

But the most decisive factor which caused Wilson to move toward belligerency was his conviction that the war was grinding to a stalemate, that it would be impossible for Europe to endure another year of the agony. Perhaps both sides would make one great final effort in 1917, but then both would be prepared for peace talks. He felt that the end of the war would be greatly hastened by American participation. The Germans would see the handwriting on the wall. Finally, Wilson wanted a prominent place at the peace table. His efforts at peacemaking in 1916 and early 1917 made it clear to him that American mediation was bound to be of limited effect so long as the United States remained neutral. He would rather be inside the conference room, as he put it on one occasion, than merely have his foot in the door looking in.

J.A.G. What did he mean when he said, in calling for a declaration of war, that the United States must make the world safe for democracy?

A.S.L. I wish I knew. Obviously he meant something, although one can't always take everything that a public leader says in his speeches too seriously. I think what he meant was very simple. He believed that the German government was an international criminal, devoted not merely to the expansion of German territory but also to the destruction of liberal governments in Europe and the New World. The war had become in Wilson's eyes not merely a war for territory or prestige, but also for control of Europe. If one believed that, then one purpose for American belligerency would be to make the world safe for democracy —that is, to make it safe for all liberal democratic governments.

J.A.G. Would you discuss the American mobilization effort after April, 1917?

A.S.L. The mobilization effort developed over time. Even before the United States entered the conflict, it was clear that a high degree of socialization would be necessary, but neither President Wilson nor his principal advisers realized the degree to which the war effort would have to be nationalized and centralized. Mobilization went through two major stages. The first emphasized cooperative effort, with only a slight degree of government control. The railroads, for example, were run by a voluntary committee of railroad managers. Food was conserved by voluntary efforts, organized, to be sure, by the Food Administration directed by Herbert Hoover. The production of war goods was managed mainly by cooperation through a Munitions Standard Board, later the War Industries Board. Even censorship, to a large degree, was voluntary.

Between December, 1917, and January, 1918, it seemed for a time as if the mobilization effort was collapsing. There were fuel shortages, a jam-up of railroad cars, a lack of shipping, and so on. This crisis caused a rethinking of the problem, and in January Wilson decided to institute sweeping controls, to leave nothing to the vagaries of the market place. The railroads were nationalized temporarily under the control of Secretary of the Treasury William G. McAdoo. Wilson also reorganized the War Industries Board, and gave it control over both raw materials and the production of finished products. Wages and hours, which had heretofore been subject to the supply and demand of the market place, were subject to control in the spring of 1918. The entire mobilization effort was thus centralized and made, as it turned out, spectacularly effective. Industry, labor, transportation, and other elements of the economy were mobilized for a total war within something like nine or ten months. The British had required some two-and-one-half years before they were able to mobilize effectively.

J.A.G. Were the changes in economic organization that occurred as part of the mobilization effort permanent? Is it possible, looking ahead, to see aspects of economic policy after 1918 that originated during the war?

A.S.L. Nothing a great government ever does is insignificant; nothing accomplished is ever lost for the long run. To be sure, the great mobilization machinery was dismantled with astounding speed after the Armistice, but the wartime experience had an immediate impact on public policy, to say nothing of its long-range impact. The Transportation Act of 1920, for example, was a product of wartime experience; it provided for the eventual consolidation of American railroads into six or eight great regional systems, and vastly increased the power of the Interstate Commerce Commission, not only over rates but also over the issuance of railroad securities. The United States Shipping Corporation, unable as it was to dispose of the vast merchant fleet that had been assembled or built during the war, stayed in the business all through the 1920's and 1930's. In addition, prohibition was a wartime product, a product of wartime idealism as well as the grain shortage.

However, the really lasting impact of the wartime experience was on a whole generation of young men who experienced firsthand how effective centralized direction and control could be in marshaling resources, human and material, in making a hitherto disorganized economy operate for one great common purpose. Many of the personnel and most of the program of the early New Deal were products of the experiences of 1917 and 1918. When the American people sought to wage a great war against the Depression, they turned back to the experience of the First World War, not only for programs and plans, but even for their slogans. The use of wartime language in the war on the Depression was striking.

J.A.G. Did the shift from voluntarism to coercion in Wilson's approach to the problem of running the federal government represent an increasing conviction on his part that Theodore Roosevelt's New Nationalism was correct, or was it forced upon him by practical considerations?

A.S.L.   Between 1914 and 1918, Wilson began to shift away from the New Freedom and toward the ideology of the New Nationalism. He crossed his political Rubicon in 1916, and, having done so, it was much easier for him to embrace concepts and methods of centralized regulation and control during the war.

J.A.G.   You have argued in your books on Wilson that there was considerable political expediency in his shift of position immediately before the 1916 election. In the light of what you've just said, have you changed your mind?

A.S.L.   I think I've modified my opinion considerably. In 1912, Woodrow Wilson advocated a program which he called "The New Freedom," which envisaged a reduction of tariffs, some kind of banking and currency reform, and a stronger antitrust law. This was an extremely limited program, and its limitations are seen best when it is compared to the New Nationalism, which called for comprehensive federal participation in important economic decisions through direct regulation of industry, the hours and wages of labor, and so on. Between 1913 and 1914, Wilson put his New Freedom program into legislative form. However, in 1916 he effected a very significant shift in position and came out for many measures he had previously opposed, like the Federal Rural Credits Act and the regulation of the hours of labor. Wilson did this during the campaign of 1916. The question, of course, has been the degree to which expediency influenced this shift. When I published *Woodrow Wilson and the Progressive Era* in 1954, I argued (I fear rather dogmatically and certainly unequivocally) that the main, if not the only, motivation behind the change was political, that he changed in order to attract former Progressive voters to his camp.

However, it now seems to me that Wilson had been undergoing a metamorphosis. His political thought had been changing from the autumn of 1914 onward. Experience had early revealed to him the difficulty of applying simple solutions to complex economic problems. For example, his thought about banking and currency had undergone very considerable change while the Federal Reserve Act was being hammered out in 1913. It was during discussions of the so-called "trust problem" that the inadequacy of the New Freedom approach first became apparent to him. The resources and shrewdness of the American businessman knew no limits, he began to see. It was simply impossible to define legislatively unfair trade practices or unfair competition. So he was persuaded that the proper solution lay in the establishment of a trade commission that would have power to oversee business and stop unfair competition before it reached the point of destroying competition.

Between 1914 and early 1916, Wilson's energies were virtually consumed by the war in Europe. He simply did not have time to give much attention to domestic problems. But by 1916 he had come authentically and sincerely to a much more advanced progressive position. The measures which he proposed in 1916, which so strongly resembled the kind of measures that Roosevelt had proposed in 1912, he could in all honesty and sincerity support and commit himself to.

J.A.G. Why, then, did he undertake economic demobilization so swiftly after the war?

A.S.L. That question is very difficult to answer. I think he concluded that the machinery of mobilization was so powerful that it was unsafe to permit it to exist any longer. His great fear was that conservative businessmen would gain control of the machinery, if not in the immediate future, certainly after he went out of office. Elbert Gary, President of the United States Steel Company, asked Wilson in the autumn of 1919 to permit the organization that had controlled the steel industry during the war to carry on for another six or eight months during the period of demobilization and readjustment. This would have allowed the Iron and Steel Institute to set prices and production levels. Gary was even willing to recognize the Steelworkers' Union as part of this package. Wilson absolutely refused, on the grounds that big business was trying to get control of the economy with the approval of the federal government.

J.A.G. Can Wilson be blamed for the anti-German hysteria of wartime? Could he have done more than he did to protect civil liberties and to shield innocent victims of popular prejudice from mistreatment?

A.S.L. It would be unfair to blame Wilson for the anti-German hysteria. He said over and over that the American people had no quarrel with the German people. However, he did establish the Committee on Public Information, headed by George Creel, which unquestionably contributed to anti-German hysteria by its frantic propaganda.

J.A.G. How vital was the American military contribution to the defeat of Germany? Could the Allies have won the war if the United States had merely joined in protecting the sea lanes against submarines and continued to supply large amounts of war matériel to the Allies?

A.S.L. The American military contribution was indispensable to the defeat of Germany. The Allies could not have been *defeated* so long as American goods were available, but they could not have *won* the war without the military contribution of the United States. The Germans had a preponderance in March, 1918, of about 400,000 men on the western front. By November, 1918, by the time of the Armistice, in contrast and on account of the American infusion, the Allies had a preponderance of over 600,000. This was sufficient to break the deadlock and win the war. The tremendous influx of American troops in the summer and early autumn of 1918 turned the balance. It enabled the Allies to take the offensive with great vigor, and to maintain their momentum. It was soon obvious to the Germans that the Allied offensive which began in July, 1918, was not going to end, primarily because of the almost endless supply of fresh American troops.

J.A.G.   Would you describe Wilson's plans for postwar reconstruction, and comment on his tactics in trying to carry out these plans at the Versailles Peace Conference?

A.S.L.   For Wilson, planning for postwar reconstruction meant creating the League of Nations. Through the League, he hoped to reconstruct the international order along new liberal lines, to organize an effective international agency that would preserve peace and enforce international law. It's incorrect to say that he had a program at the end of the war in any more specific sense. To this degree, Keynes was right in his *Economic Consequences of the Peace.* Aside from the idea of a League, Wilson went to Paris without any worked-out program for a peace settlement. He had done a good deal of thinking about the disposition of former German colonies, about reparations and indemnities, about new states in Central Europe, about the problem of Bolshevik Russia, and so on. But on all these matters, his thoughts were quite inchoate.

But while Wilson was quite flexible as to details, he held his one great objective clearly in view, the reconstitution of a viable international order that would have a built-in capacity for change and adjustment, and would enable liberal democracies to operate peacefully.

J.A.G.   Do you mean that from Wilson's point of view, the specific territorial and financial settlements that might grow out of the Peace Treaty were much less important than the creation of some kind of an international organization for the settlement of disputes between nations later on?

A.S.L.   Precisely. That is what he said over and over again.

J.A.G.   Well, if one can agree that this was a liberal conception, how can the great disillusionment that so many liberals experienced when they saw the terms of the Versailles Treaty be explained?

A.S.L.   Wilson was hoisted by his own petard. He went to Europe saying that he was not particularly concerned about the details of the settlement (whether this bit of territory went to this nation or to that nation), but he did of course become deeply involved in the details of the settlement, particularly over the disposition of German colonies, the question of indemnities, and the disposal of German territory in Europe. As a consequence, he inevitably also became engaged in the politics of confrontation, with the French particularly, but to a lesser degree with the British and the Italians, who had clear territorial and indemnity objectives. Much of the controversy at Paris in the first months of 1919 re-volved around the particular aspirations of the Allied governments. Wilson usually found himself fighting in isolation for a treaty of justice and reconciliation against his supposed allies. And in many cases, he had to give way. The liberal revulsion, once the terms of the Treaty were known, was a natural result of the disappointment of idealists who had placed their trust in Wilson. They had trusted him to defend the ideals set forth in the Fourteen Points, and they thought that he had let them down.

J.A.G.   Was the Treaty as bad as the liberal critics thought?

A.S.L.   No, in the context of the times, but yes, compared to the settle-ment after World War II. But on the whole, given the passions and ambi-tions of the governments involved, the Treaty of Versailles was a very good treaty. Wilson was absolutely right in saying that while it had deficiencies and injustices, it was different from any earlier international agreement because it provided the machinery for the rectification of whatever injustices and inequities it was found to contain.

Consider the reparations settlement, probably the most unjust and out-rageously unfair part of the Treaty. Precisely the adjustment that Wilson had foreseen did occur; Germany's obligations were sharply reduced in the following decade. The same is true of German membership in the League, and of naval disarmament.

J.A.G.   But was Wilson correct in putting so much reliance on the League as a device for preventing future wars? Were the citizens of any of the major powers willing to subordinate nationalism to the degree that was required under the Convenant of the League of Nations?

A.S.L.   That is a fair criticism of Wilson's *hopes*—he had no dogmatic expectations—about the League. He said over and over that any effective system of international organization would be the product of generations of experience. He thought the nations of the world would have to acquire the habits of peace gradually. I think, frankly, that we're still in the midst of this process. Who would argue now that the United Nations was a truly effective peace-keeping device? And yet, who would want to abolish it simply on the ground that it wasn't perfect?

J.A.G.   But that's a good illustration of the point I was trying to get at. The UN is a much less ambitious type of international organization than the League which Wilson envisaged.

A.S.L.   I'm not so sure about "much" less ambitious. The main difference between the League and the UN is that under the League a party to a dispute did not have veto power, whereas members of the Security Council of the United Nations do in fact have a veto. Aside from this important difference, I see no significant differences between the two organizations.

J.A.G.   Yet exactly this lack of a veto was at the heart of the American opposition to ratification of the League, wasn't it?

A.S.L.   Yes. I suppose one has to be realistic and admit that there simply was no disposition in the Western world in the 1920's or 1930's to subordinate national interests enough to make a peace-keeping organization truly effective.

J.A.G.   Should Wilson have accepted the Senate's reservations to the League of Nations Covenant?

A.S.L.   I believe that Wilson would have been well advised to accept the Lodge reservations to the Versailles Treaty. It was perfectly obvious by December, 1919, that American ratification could not be accomplished without them, whereas with them he could have won for the League of Nations a chance to succeed through American leadership. The most unfortunate aspect of his rejection of the Lodge reservations was that he thus deprived the American people of the experience of international leadership that they would have gained through membership in the League, and the League of American support.

J.A.G.   Do you think Wilson's stroke explains his stubbornness and refusal to compromise at this time?

A.S.L.   I do. A few years ago one could have argued both ways. But Dr. Edwin A. Weinstein's broad-gauged medical history of Wilson argues persuasively that his 1919 stroke was a massive one, caused by the occlusion of the main artery on the left side of his face. According to Weinstein, Wilson's behavior during Treaty fights was typical of the behavior of a person who had undergone such an experience. He became irritable, proud, defensive, rigid, dogmatic, unyielding. Wilson was different after the stroke; his refusal to compromise, his stubborn insistence upon having the whole or nothing even though he might have got two-thirds is altogether typical of a stroke victim.

J.A.G.   Should he not have resigned as President? Why didn't he do so?

A.S.L.   Weinstein argues that Wilson was *not* deranged. But neither Mrs. Wilson nor his doctor, Cary Grayson, ever honestly told Wilson the extent of his illness. He knew he'd had a stroke. But he had had a stroke in 1906, very comparable to this one, and had recovered from it quickly. Because they thought it would be conducive to his recovery, they kept telling Wilson that he was recovering rapidly. Weinstein believes that if Grayson had told Wilson the full extent of the damage he had suffered, he would have resigned.

J.A.G.   Perhaps Grayson didn't know how badly Wilson had been affected.

A.S.L.   That's entirely possible.

J.A.G.   What were the reasons for the overwhelming defeat of the Democrats in 1920?

A.S.L.   It was not just a defeat, it was a landslide; not just a tremor, an earthquake. The answer, while complex, is not obscure. The United States in 1920 was still preponderantly Republican. It was normal in those years for about 55 percent of the people to vote the Republican ticket. It took the split in the Republican party of 1912, or such unusual circumstances as prevailed in 1916 when Wilson was able to capitalize on the peace issue, to give the Democrats any chance of winning. Wilson had put a coalition together in 1916 that consisted of the regular Democratic minority, a large element among the Midwestern farmers, who swung to the Democratic camp on account of Wilson's support of the Rural Credits Act and other measures favorable to farmers, and independent and social progressives. But for one reason or another, Wilson had succeeded in alienating every important group that had backed him in 1916. The Republican farmers objected to the ceiling on the price of wheat imposed during the war, while the price of cotton was allowed to rise without price controls. Wilson had also alienated German-Americans by his conduct of the war and because of the harsh treatment of Germany in the Treaty of Versailles. The Irish-American element disliked him because he had refused to press for Irish independence of Great Britain. Social workers and independent liberals objected to his suppression of civil liberties during the war, and above all, to his Attorney General A. Mitchell Palmer's raids aimed at supposed alien radicals.

J.A.G.   What were the long-range results of the war?

A.S.L.   The results are not easy to describe because they were so complex. Momentarily, the German drive for hegemony over Europe was turned back—but of course, not decisively enough to prevent the Germans from making a second great effort at dominance twenty years later. The war seriously if not fatally weakened France and Great Britain. So lavish was their expenditure of resources that the British unwittingly set in motion processes of dissolution and disintegration within their Empire. These were not immediately apparent, but they were seen at once when British strength was put to a second test by World War II.

Another long-range result of the war was the very rapid emergence of the United States as incomparably the strongest economic power in the world. So great was the transfer of capital from Europe to America during the war that New York became not merely the leading money market, but also the major source of credit for the world. The experience of the First World War was so profound for the American people that they never got over it. Although they appeared in the 1920's to be spending a good deal of their energies repudiating policies that had been put into effect during the war, in fact, the people had had a brief glimpse of what could be achieved through economic integration and national control. They had set in motion processes in the national government that were bound to come to fruition in the 1930's, even had not the Depression occurred.

J.A.G.   How would you place Wilson in the history of the United States?

A.S.L.   Woodrow Wilson deserves to be placed among the first rank of Presidents, certainly among the first five, judged from the point of view of success and effectiveness. His proper place cannot be understood apart from his concrete achievements. On the domestic side, it's no exaggeration to say that he almost singlehandedly presided over the reordering of the federal government's relationship to the economy— that is, the policies of the federal government relating to business, industry, and finance. It's also no exaggeration to say that he laid the foundations both in theory and in policy for the superstructure of economic regulation that would be added later in the 1930's and 1940's. Even more than Theodore Roosevelt, who began the process, Woodrow Wilson was the architect of modern American economic policies.

Ironically, Wilson is coming, I think, to hold a position of equal eminence in the field of foreign affairs. I say "ironically," because his record in this area was anything but an unbroken triumph. He sought to teach the people of Latin America how to "elect good men," for example, and ended at least in Haiti and the Dominican Republic by imposing military regimes on them. Wilson tried sincerely, and I'm inclined to think desperately, to avoid involvement in the First World War. Again, obviously, he failed. He worked with incredible energy at Paris to reconstruct the international order on principles of justice and reconciliation. Again he failed. He almost gave his life in a tremendous forensic effort to persuade the American people to assume the leadership in world affairs which he said history had laid upon them. Again, in this greatest effort of his life, he failed.

And yet, looking back on this figure, undaunted, facing four square the forces of greed and imperialism, I believe that history will view him with increasing sympathy, understanding, and perhaps admiration. We are now not quite as naive as we once were in foreign affairs. We no longer expect quick and easy solutions to difficult international questions. We understand now the difficulty of the problems with which Wilson was grappling, and the reason for his so-called failures. For his failures were not altogether failures; he made a lasting contribution in educating the American people to their responsibilities in the modern, interrelated world. Perhaps it was even *necessary* for Wilson to have failed before the American people could acquire the wisdom and knowledge which they must have effectively to employ the kind of power that they dispose in the world.

J.A.G.   To what degree did Wilson change Americans' conception of the office of the President?

A.S.L. Every President since Woodrow Wilson has been an effective public and congressional leader to the degree that he has emulated Wilson's example. Not all Presidents since Wilson have consciously studied his performance, but several certainly have done so. Franklin Roosevelt, for example, studied not only Wilson's successful techniques, but also the causes of his failures. Harry Truman and John F. Kennedy also copied many of Wilson's techniques of public leadership. Wilson brought together the inherent personal and political powers of the presidency in a most striking way. He was probably the first President to utilize all the potential resources of presidential leadership—of public opinion, of his party, and in legislative matters.

J.A.G. What are the chief unanswered questions about this period in America?

A.S.L. To begin with, the whole social fabric of American life between 1910 and 1920 needs study. We have only the faintest outlines of that tapestry. It was a period of tremendous social and intellectual change. All of the great forces which produced revolutions in the 1920's were already at work: literary developments, the rapid growth of cities, the fantastically rapid change in the pattern of life that was taking place as a result of the automobile, and so on. We also know virtually nothing about reform movements which did not find expression on a national level. This period saw the culmination of a generation of reform movement on the municipal level. Little historical work has been done on this subject. The same is true for state history during this period.

Even in national and diplomatic history, much remains to be done. We have no complete account of the relations between the United States and Mexico during the Mexican Revolution. Indeed, the relations of the United States with all Latin America remain to be written for the Wilson era. The same is true even of large aspects of our European diplomacy during the period of neutrality. The recent opening of important materials in the British Foreign Office offer great new possibilities for research. And look, for example, at the Peace Conference. We have some excellent monographs on various aspects of the Versailles Conference, but it's a striking fact that we've had only one attempt at comprehensive analysis of the Conference since the publication of Paul Birdsall's *Versailles, Twenty years After* in 1941. Dozens of biographies of congressional and administration leaders remain to be written. We stand just on the threshold of historiography for the Wilsonian era. The trail has been blazed through the forest, but the definitive writing of the history of this crucial period remains to be done.

J.A.G. What are the half-dozen or so books that you would recommend to persons interested in the subject we have been discussing? In each case, would you indicate briefly what the particular contribution of the volume is?

A.S.L. I would begin with John Wells Davidson (ed.), *A Crossroads of Freedom: The 1912 Campaign Speeches of Woodrow Wilson* (1956), because it is the most reliable source for the ideology of the New Freedom. Robert E. Osgood, *Ideals and Self-Interest in America's Foreign Relations* (1953), is excellent on the impact of the war on American thinking about foreign policy. Edward H. Buehrig, *Woodrow Wilson and the Balance of Power* (1955), and Ernest R. May, *The World War and American Isolation* (1959), are both good accounts of the neutrality period, 1914–17.

Daniel R. Beaver, *Newton D. Baker and the American War Effort, 1917–1919* (1966), is the best work on American economic and military mobilization. Arno J. Mayer's *Political Origins of the New Diplomacy* (1959) and *The Politics and Diplomacy of Peacemaking* (1967) are pioneering works that set the problems of Wilsonian peacemaking in their world context, while N. Gordon Levin, Jr., *Woodrow Wilson and World Politics: America's Response to War and Revolution* (1968), focuses brilliantly on the President. I think that Paul A. Birdsall, *Versailles, Twenty Years After* (1941), remains the best brief account of the Paris Peace Conference. We have no good general work on American demobilization, but Stanley Coben, *A. Mitchell Palmer: Politician* (1963), is excellent on the Palmer raids.

Dr. Weinstein's article, referred to in this interview, will be published soon in *The Journal of American History*. It is a broad-gauged study of Wilson's medical history. Dr. Weinstein has also published "Denial of Presidential Disability: A Case Study of Woodrow Wilson," *Psychiatry*, XXX (November 1967), 376–391.

Robert K. Murray

The Twenties

ROBERT K. MURRAY, who is Professor of History at Pennsylvania State University, specializes in the social and political history of the post-World War I era. His *Red Scare: A Study in National Hysteria* (1955) is the standard work on the subject, while his *The Harding Era: Warren G. Harding and His Administration* (1969), is based on exhaustive analysis of the Harding papers and other manuscript sources. Professor Murray deals with both these subjects in the course of his discussion of the major issues of the 1920's.

John A. Garraty Professor Murray, as the decade of the 1920's recedes into the past, does it still appear to have been a distinct period in American history? If so, what were its chief characteristics?

Robert K. Murray I really don't see the 1920's as a separate unit in American history. I find too many contradictions and inconsistencies to be able to support a unity concept. Hoover, for example, doesn't seem to me to fit with Coolidge any better than he fits with Roosevelt. I personally believe that in the long run the administrations of Harding, Coolidge, and Hoover will be considered, along with the New Deal, as simply the "between the wars" period.

One basic reason why the unity concept exists is that our historical introduction to the 1920's came first from practicing journalists, such as Frederick Lewis Allen, who, looking back over ten years of frivolity and ballyhoo, saw the period as a distinguishable unit. These men artificially created the decade as a separate entity, bound on each side by the two great events of the early twentieth century—World War I and the Great Depression. Also, the decade seemed to them to be a logical unit since it divided two colossi in American history—Woodrow Wilson and Franklin Roosevelt.

When historians began at last to evaluate the period, they naturally sought unifying themes, and believed that they had found one in the economic conservatism of the era. But of even greater significance was the fact that at the time the most articulate members of the historical profession were liberally oriented; hence, when they began to search the twenties for signs of liberal continuity and couldn't find any, they were confirmed in a decision to treat the period separately. The predilections of these historians, particularly those trained in the Progressive tradition, gave them a built-in bias against the 1920's anyway. Then, after personally experiencing the Depression, they were all the more convinced that the decade was somehow unique, "illegitimate," and distasteful. Thus, rather than attempting to fit the 1920's into the mainstream of modern American history, they preferred to retain it apart. This inclination they passed on to their students, and to their students' students, creating the framework we now have.

But this situation is changing, due primarily to the activities of younger historians trained in the post-World War II era. Within their own lifetimes, these newer historians have experienced so many contradictory and awesome events that when they look back on the 1920's they do not use the same perspectives as their mentors. Present-day problems of affluence and world responsibility make the 1920's seem more relevant and less negative to them than the decade did to their predecessors.

To sum up: while I think that the 1920's are certainly worthy of study,

I do not believe that in the future they will be handled as a separate and distinct entity.

J.A.G.   Is it correct to say that the period was shaped primarily by World War I?

R.K.M.   American involvement in World War I was a definite watershed, and the war supplied the main conditioning factor for the period that followed. Subsequent economic diplomatic, social, and cultural developments in the United States were shaped by that war, from the time of Harding through that of Franklin Roosevelt.

J.A.G.   In what ways were the postwar years similar to the years immediately following the Civil War?

R.K.M.   There were many similarities, although I think there were differences too. Both were times of transition from abnormal conditions created by wartime needs, and both were marked by the necessity of finding new directions. As to specifics, both periods had problems involving demobilization and the adjustment of the economy to peacetime circumstances. Both had monetary upheavals and severe social dislocations; both suffered from laxity in morals. Industrial expansion and the growth of new industries occurred in both instances. Both experienced a conservative reaction and a tendency on the part of the general public to question further dramatic changes or drastic reforms.

J.A.G.   You used the phrase "laxity in morals." Do you accept the explanation that moral laxity results from disillusionment following the failure of the idealistic purposes of great conflicts? Or does war unleash powerful aggressive emotions which can't be turned off like a faucet?

R.K.M.   War does unleash brutal passions which cannot easily be stopped, and there has been disillusionment after every war, because wars do not really solve problems. But I think that wars produce a broader malaise than mere disillusionment or the release of passions: wars breed a willingness of the human spirit to condone whatever brutality is necessary to resolve violently what men had hoped to resolve rationally by pacific means. Wars force the human mind to accept situations in which the basic moral precepts of the human experience are breached. Every scrap of the Christian code, for example, is violated by war. As a reaction to this traumatic wartime exposure, men are likely in an immediate postwar period to continue to act in an aberrant way. In other words, a peculiar lingering reaction is produced psychologically by the use of violence as a means of establishing peace.

J.A.G.   To what extent can the troubles of the immediate postwar period be blamed on Woodrow Wilson?

R.K.M.   I'm afraid that they can be blamed to a considerable extent on Wilson. We must remember that in the last two years of his administration Wilson was a very sick man, and not entirely responsible for his actions. These last two years were frankly disastrous for the nation, since it suffered from an almost complete lack of executive leadership. But even before his illness, Wilson, confronted with the League crisis, virtually ignored postwar domestic planning. Very little was done to effect an easy transition to peace, and that, too late. Thus, postwar monetary and fiscal problems were worse than they might have been, labor unrest was more bitter than necessary. Further, Wilson's persistent and uncompromising concentration on the League question tended to skew all postwar matters into emotional rather than rational areas of response.

Wilson unnecessarily antagonized Congress in the 1919–21 period, although I'm not suggesting that Congress was blameless. In Wilson's last two years, the work of the State Department came almost to a standstill. Because of Wilson's illness, foreign ambassadors were left in limbo, some of them not being able to be fully accredited. Not only were European policy questions left unresolved, but many other diplomatic problems were hanging fire, such as the nonrecognition of Mexico, American military intervention in the Caribbean, the need for establishing firmer ties with the Middle East, and so on.

Wilson, meanwhile, was unable to handle his own official family. That Attorney General Palmer was free to operate in the highly repressive manner he did during the Red Scare was damaging both to the Wilson administration and to the nation. In this instance, lack of executive leadership permitted hatreds and prejudices to explode which might otherwise have been kept in check. I think, too, that Wilson's blindness to the farm situation piled up problems for the 1920's. He made the emergence of the Farm Bloc in Congress inevitable, for example. He also ignored prohibition. He was the first President responsible for prohibition enforcement, and his inability to put enforcement procedures on a sound basis at the very start left a problem for every succeeding President from 1920 to the time of repeal.

J.A.G. But is it correct to assign this whole catalogue of his failures to his physical decline? If he hadn't had a stroke, would none of these things have happened?

R.K.M. You're asking me for my personal opinion. Well, I think I understand Woodrow Wilson fairly well because I, too, come from a Calvinistic-Presbyterian background. Let me put it this way. Given the psychological, moralistic, and idealistic make-up of Woodrow Wilson, I believe that once he had fastened upon the League as his *primary* goal, even had he remained in full possession of his faculties, most of these other matters would have been slighted.

J.A.G. The so-called "Red Scare" of 1919–20, which you have studied intensively, was clearly one of the most disgraceful episodes in American history. How can this eruption of hysteria and repression be ex-

plained in the light of the American tradition of free speech and fair
play?

R.K.M.   First of all, there was that preconditioning process of great importance, the wartime situation. True, George Creel and his Committee
on Public Information directed vitriol against "the Hun," but it was
easily transferable to "radicals" after the Soviet Revolution. Graft onto
this the insecurity and the instability that the war produced; people *were*
bewildered and confused. Then, add the fact of deep economic antagonisms, such as labor-management disputes, resulting from the necessary
readjustments following the war, and combine these with the propaganda
of patriotic societies and the sensationalism of the press. Top it all off
with a lack of executive leadership and a few *bona fide* suspicious revolutionary events, and presto!—you have the major ingredients for the
hysteria known as the Red Scare.

J.A.G.   Could Wilson have done more to protect civil liberties during
the war than he did?

R.K.M.   Wilson was certainly aware of the dangers involved in arousing
public emotions against the German enemy to such a fever pitch. That
he could have done something to have forestalled this hatred from being
transferred and applied indiscriminately to domestic radicals, both during and after the conflict, I think, is beyond dispute. To have done so,
though, would have meant muting to some extent the propaganda effort
by which the war was fought.

J.A.G.   In describing the causes of the Red Scare, you mentioned that there
were a few real incidents of subversion. Was it possible for intelligent,
unprejudiced citizens to believe that there was a real danger of revolution in the United States in 1919?

R.K.M.   Yes, it was. It's easy to cast the average man in the role of being
a moronic dupe, yet considering the fact that newspapers bombarded
him daily with exaggerated accounts of radical subversion at home and
revolutionary communist activity abroad, it was logical for him to draw
erroneous conclusions. The bitter and violent labor disputes of the 1919–
20 period especially stirred his fears. Then, when a few bombings, radical riots, and red flag parades actually occurred, he was prepared to
believe the worst.

J.A.G.   How many real revolutionaries were there in the United States?

R.K.M.   As near as we can tell from the evidence available, there were no
more than 40,000 to 60,000 Communist party members in the country in
1919–20. Some of these had been recruited from the Socialist party; how
committed these were to communist ideology as contrasted with their
earlier proclivity for socialism is hard to say. The hard-core underground
Communist movement by 1924–25, after Palmer's raids and the passing
of the Red Scare, consisted of no more than 20,000.

J.A.G.   Is there any way to estimate how many "fellow travelers" there were? Were large elements in the labor movement influenced by Communism?

R.K.M.   I don't think that the labor movement was seriously influenced by Communism, although numerous workers were socialists. Estimates of radical sympathizers were wide-ranging. In 1920, the Justice Department put the number as high as 5 million. Undoubtedly, this figure was a distortion. Many American workmen expressed sympathy for European radical movements without necessarily thinking that they ought to be grafted onto the American environment. American Communist revolutionaries were almost totally divorced from the American labor scene and from American laborers. They had little influence really, because their frame of reference was so foreign to the American experience that even those workers who might have been beguiled by them were put off by their strange idioms and slogans.

J.A.G.   Was the severity of the Red Scare of 1919–20 exacerbated by the fact that the Russian Communists had pulled out of the war in 1917?

R.K.M.   Definitely. The Brest-Litovsk Treaty was a major cause of anti-Russian and anti-radical feeling in the United States. The Communists were not only foes of the capitalistic system, but also traitors to the common war effort.

J.A.G.   What were the motives of Attorney General A. Mitchell Palmer in the Red Scare? How could a man with his liberal record in the Progressive period have acted as he did?

R.K.M.   The interesting question involved here is: how and why does a liberal become a reactionary? Palmer was raised in an eastern Pennsylvania community which had been settled by the Welsh, Quakers, and Dutch. He was raised a Quaker. He early displayed an intense desire to succeed, graduated from high school when he was only fourteen years old, and was first in his class at Swarthmore. He was one of the most brilliant men in the area and was classified as a "comer" in Pennsylvania politics. He served several terms in Congress; but, being a Democrat in a solidly Republican state, he had to rely more on appointive rather than elective office to attain national prominence. This situation made him a maneuverer and a conspirer in politics.

He worked very hard for Wilson at the 1912 convention, was regarded by party leaders as a sound progressive, and was ultimately rewarded by Wilson by being made Attorney General. The fact that he was a pacifist caused him considerable anguish when World War I broke out. At first he opposed the war, but after the sinking of the *Lusitania* he supported the conflict, despite the fact that his wife was very critical of his action.

Later, when he began to feel that the humanitarian objectives for which the war had been fought were being vitiated by the Bolshevists, he became bitter. Meanwhile, public opinion was demanding that something be done to curb domestic radicalism. With a vacuum in the White House and with every cabinet officer free to do whatever he thought best, Palmer became the man on the spot. The Justice Department, after all, was the logical agency to fight the alleged radical menace. Then, in the summer of 1919, his own home was bombed, markedly adding to his frustration and fears. At the same time the 1920 Democratic convention was rapidly approaching, and Palmer, still seized by a desire to "succeed," suddenly grasped the radical issue as a potential springboard to the presidency. These were the major reasons why Mitchell Palmer acted as he did.

J.A.G. Did he in fact think that there was a real danger of subversion?

R.K.M. Yes. By the late fall of 1919, Palmer had convinced himself that there was a serious danger to the United States.

J.A.G. What brought the Red Scare to an end?

R.K.M. The Red Scare subsided. Unfortunately, it has never really ended. Fear of Communist subversion is still a part of the modern American scene. It subsided, first of all, because labor was soundly beaten in its postwar strikes. Then the postwar boom came, reducing fears and encouraging complacency. Furthermore, Palmer's excesses aroused opposition from moderates. Lewis Post in the Labor Department, Charles Evans Hughes, and many others spoke out against him. Two congressional investigations uncovered the true facts and examined the radical menace in a less emotional framework. The ridiculous expulsion in early 1920 of five harmless Socialists who had been legally elected to the New York Assembly caused a reaction that brought many people to their senses. Finally, when Palmer's scary prediction that May 1, 1920, was going to produce a huge radical upheaval in the United States failed to materialize, the public began to laugh, and the worst of the Red Scare was over.

President Harding deserves some credit too. His soothing nature was an emollient in the situation, as were his promises of tranquillity. Standing on his handsomely tiled front porch in Marion, Ohio, in his dark blue pants and white coat, talking about "normalcy," he was the picture of reassurance for a nervous public.

J.A.G. One of the most paradoxical developments of the twenties was the religious controversy that flared up between fundamentalists and modernists. Why, a decade after the churches had apparently come to terms with Darwinian evolution and the science of geology, could advocates of a literal interpretation of the Old Testament version of creation still find a hearing in the United States?

R.K.M. Church leaders, possessing relatively sophisticated ideas about science, are one thing; the laity is something else. At the time, *educated* ministers were aware of recent scientific and intellectual developments, but the average parishioner remained largely ignorant of such things. This was particularly true in the "Bible Belt" and on Main Street, U.S.A.; religious fundamentalism was still the dominant view. These popularly-held myths merely became manifest in the 1920's, rather than being reborn. The Scopes trial simply brought them to the surface.

In a sense, though, the Scopes trial was of great value in promoting enlightened religious ideas in the United States. We usually regard the trial as an example of bigotry and extreme ignorance, but there is another side to the coin—it was a tremendous educational experience.

J.A.G. Would you explain what you mean by that remark?

R.K.M. If the Scopes trial achieved one goal it was its exposure of the intellectual shallowness of fundamentalist beliefs. As a result of the trial, even those areas of the country where fundamentalism was relatively strong began to develop a more enlightened approach to religion. Scopes lost his case, but his lawyer, Clarence Darrow, was far more effective in defending modernism than William Jennings Bryan was in defending fundamentalism.

To explain adequately the fundamentalist controversy of the 1920's one must recognize at the outset two important factors. One was Bryan. Without the voice and support of this popular political figure the fundamentalists would not have been *that* significant. The other factor was the press. Suppose newspapers had chosen not to make the Dayton episode a three-ring circus and had concentrated instead on something else. Unquestionably, the controversy would have had a different impact. But the press, sensing what kind of material would sell papers, fed the public its own sensationalized version of God-on-trial in Tennessee. If the press had ignored the Scopes case or treated it as the minor event it really was, the fundamentalist controversy might not have existed as a subject of national concern.

J.A.G. Was there a relationship between fundamentalism and the resurgence of the Ku Klux Klan?

R.K.M. Definitely. The one tended to reinforce the other. Both movements sprang essentially from prejudice and ignorance. Both were designed to preserve the local religious and cultural *status quo*. Both had a nativist base.

J.A.G. How did the Klan of the 1920's differ from the original Ku Klux Klan of Reconstruction?

R.K.M. The Reconstruction Klan was a white, Bourbon organization designed to *reassert* local white political control. The post-World War I

Klan was a lower-middle and middle-class method of *maintaining* cultural, as well as political, control. The Reconstruction Klan was a revolutionary organization in the sense that it wanted to change conditions, to overthrow black reconstruction. The post-World War I Klan was a reactionary organization in the sense that it desired to entrench and protect white, Anglo-Saxon, Protestant dominance. The older Klan was essentially southern; the modern Klan was transregional, having great support and power in the Middle West.

The Klan of the 1920's was also far more of a "joiners" organization than the earlier body. One didn't often join the Reconstruction Klan as a social club. Many did join the modern Klan for that purpose. Furthermore, the new Klan was run on a profit basis; it was designed to make money for its leaders; ultimately it became little more than a promotional racket. But the two Klans had many similar characteristics: their common nativist and white supremacist attitudes; their secrecy and their bias; their repressive, violent techniques.

J.A.G. Is there a similarity between fundamentalists and the types who were caught up in the Red Scare?

R.K.M. Not precisely. Fundamentalism was, with some exceptions, a rural and small-town phenomenon. The Red Scare was a national phenomenon. Those caught up in the hysteria of the Red Scare were as likely to be—indeed, more likely to be—Wall Street bankers than small-town types. Both supported repressive antiradical action—the former by means of national legislation and federal activity; the latter by vigilantes who ran suspected subversives out of town. The issue of fundamentalism produced no real common bond between such diverse groups.

J.A.G. These reactionary movements provide support for the historical interpretation that the Progressive movement ended with World War I. Yet some historians, most notably Arthur S. Link, have argued that the Progressive spirit remained strong throughout the 1920's. What is your view of this question?

R.K.M. I disagree with Link, although our disagreement may hinge partially on a problem of definition. My own researches suggest that the Progressivism of the Square Deal and New Freedom variety ended with the war. Elements of Theodore Roosevelt's New Nationalism did survive, and there were vestiges of the Progressive spirit left at the local level. But taking Progressivism as it is usually defined, it *was* a casualty of the war. It is true that Robert La Follette got 4.8 million votes in 1924, but he ran a very poor third in that election. Liberal historians, looking for bridges between the New Freedom and the New Deal, may call this a sign of Progressive life. But it is questionable how many of La Follette's votes actually were "Progressives"; even if many were, his polling of only 4.8 million out of 28.6 million votes cast was by any test an eloquent witness to the bankruptcy of the Progressive movement, at least on the national level.

In this regard it is interesting to observe La Follette's position as a candidate in 1924. He spoke a great deal of nonsense; he indulged in late-nineteenth-century shibboleths and slogans which had no place in the 1920's. He talked loosely about the "Wall Street crowd" and about Easterners taking bread out of the mouths of farmers. He was not realistic, and it showed in his final vote. Any man who could seriously advocate high-priced beef on the hoof and low-priced beef on the dinner table was an economic imbecile.

Many of the old Progressive leaders did some strange things in the 1920's. Some became unabashed champions of welfare capitalism and the business system, arguing that company unions and competition-destroying trade associations were in the public interest. Observing the efficiency and the prosperity that the "enlightened" capitalist brought to the nation in the 1920's, such Progressives logically assumed that welfare capitalism was a formidable new weapon in forging solutions to all man's problems and needs. Herbert Hoover, more than any other person, symbolized the union between the Progressive humanitarian tradition and the efficient businessman of the 1920's. We can classify Hoover both as a Wilsonian humanist and as an efficiency engineer who developed and controlled the mass production system.

Much more research needs to be done on this subject, but Progressivism may actually have metamorphosed into something quite different in the 1920's than we, as historians, have been prepared to recognize.

J.A.G.   Were there reactionary elements in Progressivism?

R.K.M.   No doubt of it. Take the immigration question, for example. Many Progressives favored a highly restrictive policy and adopted a typical nativist view of "foreigners." With regard to the Negro, the story is even sadder. In general, Progressives did not attack the Negro; they simply ignored him. Politically, the black man was a nonentity in the Progressive era. The few times that Wilson took any recognition of the Negro, he behaved in a way that one would have to call racist. What gestures Theodore Roosevelt made were hardly sincere attempts to improve the lot of the black man. The Progressives, after all, were predominantly white, middle-class citizens whose views on race were no different than the national mores of the time would allow. Strangely enough, the conservative Warren Harding (who was charged with having Negro blood himself) tried to do far more for the black man than any of his Progressive predecessors.

Prohibition provides another example of the reactionary tendencies of Progressivism. Many Progressives saw prohibition as the culminating reform. Yet by all standards of individual freedom it was repressive. When Harding, Coolidge, and Hoover attempted to enforce prohibition during the 1920's, they were merely executing an earlier Progressive mandate.

J.A.G.   Do we make too much of phenomena like fundamentalism and prohibition when describing the 1920's?

R.K.M.   I think so. Our preoccupation with these occurrences stems, it seems to me, from the fact that most of the early writers on the 1920's were newspapermen who concentrated on such matters. They did so because these topics were sensational, popular, and subjects for which source material was readily available. Adequate primary material for an analytical examination of the Washington Conference, or of tax policy, or of the farm problem, would become available only later. But at the moment, the reporter-historian could speak with a certain amount of authority on these "public" phenomena. Only recently have we begun to redress the balance by delving deeply into other, less sensational, but more significant matters.

J.A.G.   Was the movement for limiting immigration as unreasonable and xenophobic in character as the Red Scare, the Klan, and fundamentalism?

R.K.M.   No, I don't think it was. There were legitimate economic, social, and political reasons for considering a policy of restriction in the 1920's. Although Professor John Higham disagrees, I feel, for example, that the emergency Per Centum Act of 1921 did ease the unemployment situation during the winter of that year. Hardships would have been even more severe had the postwar flood of immigrants been allowed to continue. That's a personal opinion, to be sure, but I use it simply as an indication that there *can* be sound economic reasons why a nation may restrict immigration at a particular time.

I don't think that immigration restriction was, or is, a moral issue, nor does it directly involve inalienable freedoms or personal rights. It is a policy matter, which, although it may be drastically affected by contemporary political trends or popular prejudices, transcends such phenomena as fundamentalism, the Klan, or Red Scares.

J.A.G.   Was it, from a rational point of view, a good idea to restrict immigration in the 1920's?

R.K.M.   In addition to the economic motivation to restrict immigration in the early part of the decade, fears were expressed by sociologists that the newer immigrants coming from southern and southeastern Europe could not be as easily acculturated as those who had come earlier from northern and northwestern Europe. Protestant ministers, meanwhile, claimed that the continuation of "American" institutions depended on retaining a Protestant orientation, and that the emergence of a predominant Catholic influence might have adverse effects on the democratic quality of American life. Those fearful of Communist subversion naturally argued that the newer immigrant was more susceptible to radicalism and represented a real and present danger.

Unquestionably, many of these arguments were spurious. Yet the newer immigrants did tend to exacerbate unfortunate conditions in the nation's metropolitan centers, especially in those areas where the nation already was experiencing its most severe problems of adjustment with respect to local government, racial and ethnic conflicts, social welfare requirements, transportation, adequate health protection, and so on. The congestion and confusion that resulted from the rapid increase in the population, and the impact of the increased flow in the 1920's of people from the countryside to the city, would almost certainly have been heightened by a greater influx of immigrants.

J.A.G. Can a similar case be made for prohibition? Did the Eighteenth Amendment reduce any of the social problems associated with drunkenness and otherwise improve society?

R.K.M. Prohibition was a "noble experiment," in the sense that it sought to reform human nature by legislative action. Prohibition did make liquor more difficult to get, and some persons who might have succumbed to alcoholism possibly did not. There was a decline in drinking among the poorer classes; among other reasons, they simply did not have the money to pay for bootlegged liquor during the 1920's. While some citizens manufactured their own, there was a decrease in consumption. Open drunkenness was indeed less apparent. The speakeasy, whatever its defects, was a decided improvement over the old saloon.

But in the long run, the drawbacks were far greater than the benefits. As a legal venture, prohibition was a failure; citizens refused to abide by it. Economically, prohibition was a flop; it diverted a legitimate business activity into underground criminal channels. As a political program, it was unsuccessful; it caused the majority party no end of trouble. And as a social experiment, it was a failure; it was supposed to end the evils of drinking; it did not.

J.A.G. Andrew Sinclair, in his recent book on prohibition, argues that if the prohibitionists had been less extreme in their demands the noble experiment might have worked, that if the law had allowed the consumption of beer and wine it might have achieved its purpose of eliminating the social evils associated with drunkenness and still allowed people the reasonable use of alcohol.

R.K.M. I agree. Andrew Mellon, Secretary of the Treasury and the cabinet officer most responsible for enforcement procedures, advocated precisely that. But he and other "moderates" ran afoul of the Anti-Saloon League and militant "drys," and were trapped by political realities. Had beer and wine been permitted legally, and had only hard liquor been stringently controlled, the Eighteenth Amendment might have survived.

J.A.G.   Turning now to economic developments, were the 1920's as prosperous as they appeared to contemporary observers?

R.K.M.   The age was not uniformly prosperous, nor was it as prosperous as it seemed to be at the time. The 1920's did see a ripening of capitalism. There was a tremendous increase in the Gross National Product. The machine-tool industry, the automobile industry, the electrical-appliance industry, the oil industry, the prepared-foods industry, the chemical industry, public utilities, and wholesale and retail trade expanded markedly.

The increase in automobile production was particularly fantastic. The number of cars in use rose from eight million in 1919 to more than twenty-three million in 1929. What this meant in the way of road building and to all the industries dependent on the motor car is obvious. It was estimated that perhaps as many as five million jobs were created directly or indirectly by the expansion of the automobile industry during the 1920's. As one commentator put it, "Give us this day our daily bread" no longer applied to the Almighty, but to Detroit. It was claimed that, by 1929, sixteen million Americans depended on the automobile in one way or another for their livelihood. In 1929, for example, that industry was consuming 75 percent of all the rubber produced in the United States and 15 percent of all steel.

The weaknesses of the economy were not so obvious. In 1929, even before the Crash, there was an average of two bank failures a day. In that same year, 40 percent of the American population was earning less than $1,500, the minimum level of subsistence. Twenty percent were making less than $1,000. There were pockets of extreme poverty in the midst of affluence. Whole areas of the economy were sick. The agricultural system was certainly not in a healthy condition during the twenties. The textile industry, the coal industry, and the railroad industry were all suffering.

In the final analysis, prosperity in the 1920's was mainly a middle-class and upper-middle-class phenomenon. If we can assume that the middle class, and especially the upper-middle class, represented the most articulate and influential elements in American society, then we can understand why prosperity seemed more pervasive than it really was. Prosperity in the 1920's was definitely concentrated at the top and in the metropolitan areas. It was largely a "corporate" prosperity.

J.A.G. Was the long-term trend toward a planned economy, which had begun in the late nineteenth century and which had been accelerated by the reforms of the Progressive period and by World War I, checked or reversed during the 1920's?

R.K.M. I cannot think offhand of any instances in which the reforms of the Progressive period were actually reversed. In most cases they were checked, although a few were extended. The truly important question is: Who controlled the major regulatory boards and agencies during the 1920's? In the Progressive era, these various commissions were populated by men who regarded business competition as preferable to cooperation, who opposed bigness for bigness' sake, and who desired to inject into the capitalistic system a degree of governmental regulatory responsibility. These men, however, never really succeeded in establishing their views as national policy before World War I stripped them of a peacetime milieu in which to apply their theories.

In the twenties, a significant change occurred. The shift to peace and to the Republicans now permitted new policy alignments; increasingly, these were formulated and executed by men unsympathetic with earlier Progressive regulatory activity. One naturally wonders what would have happened if these agencies had been able to operate under peacetime conditions for several years after their enactment in the Wilson era, before war overtook them. I'm tempted to believe that even Progressive regulators would have had to make an adjustment to the realities of the expanding American economic system, but that's only conjecture. The fact remains that peacetime precedents for many of these commissions were not set until the 1920's, at which time they were established to conform to the requirements of the corporate structure.

Whatever the outcome of the struggle between the regulators and the nonregulators, the government, contrary to superficial appearances, markedly increased its involvement in the economy during the 1920's. Through rising cooperation between government and business, government assumed an ever-expanding role. The result was a wedding of government and business in what amounted to a joint enterprise. Herbert Hoover and his Commerce Department were the prime movers behind this trend.

J.A.G. How can the election of Warren G. Harding by such a huge majority in 1920 be explained, considering his obvious limitations as a statesman?

R.K.M. Harding has been somewhat misunderstood. He has been pictured as the archetypical conservative leading the reaction that is alleged to have occurred after World War I. This is not wholly true. There are good reasons, it seems to me, why such a huge majority of the American people supported Harding in 1920. "Wilsonism," by that time, smacked of defeat and failure to many people. They related Wilsonism to a misguided venture overseas, and to turmoil, confusion, and chaos at home. To many, Wilsonism meant strikes and labor-management difficulties, and the Red Scare. In addition, there was the beginning of a severe economic depression in 1920, and many voters associated the economic distress with Wilson. Harding, meanwhile, had few enemies; he was acceptable to almost everybody. His personality was the exact opposite of Wilson's: he was a gregarious, back-slapping, friendly individual who was nonintellectual and possessed an undisciplined mind.

He appealed partly because of this fact. And, despite his excess verbiage and dreadful syntax, he made some telling speeches during the campaign. He said, "I will revise the tariff upward," and most people, including the farmer, wanted it revised upward. He said, "I am going to give business its head." Already the Red Scare proved that public opinion was behind the businessman and against labor. He said, "I am going to restore normal channels of diplomatic activity abroad," and adopted a sufficiently ambiguous stand on the League that satisfied completely an electorate which was also ambiguous about the League. Harding said, "I am going to restore efficiency and economy in government." What better time to push for economy and efficiency than after a period of high wartime and postwar taxes and expenditures?

J.A.G. Was Harding as ineffective a president as he has usually been pictured?

R.K.M. No, he was not. If one puts aside the various scandals and his known sexual immorality, and concentrates instead on his performance as chief executive, one must upgrade Harding and especially the Harding administration. Harding possessed some salutary qualities as a leader, and the total operation for which he was responsible, including the activities of Secretary of Agriculture Henry Wallace, Secretary of State Hughes, Secretary of Commerce Hoover, and Secretary of the Treasury Mellon, was anything but a failure. The Harding Papers, which have recently been made available to scholars, are eye-opening in this regard. They reveal that Harding was a hard-working, conscientious executive, aware of the nation's most pressing problems, and sometimes willing to take chances to achieve laudatory goals.

In foreign policy, for example, the Harding administration achieved a success far above the average. His personal support of the World Court was an act of moral courage. He almost single-handedly brought about the *rapprochement* with Mexico. While Secretary of State Hughes often dragged his feet on matters relating to the withdrawal of American marines from the Caribbean, Harding was extremely anxious to liquidate such military ventures. The basic story of the Washington Disarmament Conference is well known, but the Harding Papers show that it was Warren Harding who was Hughes's mainstay throughout the delicate negotiations, and that it was Harding who held the Navy admirals in line behind Hughes's disarmament plans.

On the question of German reparations and Allied war debts we discover that, although Harding did not fully understand the problem, he encouraged Hughes to take the action that led to the Dawes Plan of 1924, scaling down these obligations. I was especially surprised to find that while Hughes remained intransigent on Soviet nonrecognition, Harding, by the end of his administration, had come to the conclusion that a new departure in dealing with the U.S.S.R. was in order.

Harding's domestic policies were somewhat less successful; indeed, throughout the 1920's the Republicans badly misread the economic signs. But almost everything that has been written about Harding and the farm problem is erroneous. His papers show that the leaders of the Farm Bloc, although persistently reviling him, worked closely with him, and the Harding administration supported every one of the Farm Bloc's major proposals. There is even an indication in the Wallace-Harding correspondence that, shortly before his death, Harding was prepared to discuss the question of agricultural subsidies. In short, Harding was not as conservative, ineffective, or uninformed as he has been depicted.

J.A.G.   But how could the man you've just described have permitted the kind of moral laxity in his administration that he so obviously did? How could a man who had the good judgment to appoint Hughes and Hoover and other first-rate men have also appointed so many hacks and corruptionists as well?

R.K.M.   That can only be explained by the transplantation of an affable, easygoing man from a small-town, political environment to the White House, and by the curious dichotomies in the Harding personality. Harding was, as has sometimes been said, the most human of all of our Presidents. He could rise to great heights and fall to abysmal depths. He could see the outstanding qualities in a Hoover or Hughes, yet be personally attracted to a Fall or a Daugherty. Harding was unwilling to make moral judgments about his associates. Desperately wanting to be liked and constantly desiring companionship, Harding put friendship above reason, loyalty before ideals. He once admitted that if he had been a girl he would be in a family way all the time because he could not say no. He was right.

J.A.G.   How can the extraordinary popularity of Calvin Coolidge be explained? What is your opinion of his record as President?

R.K.M.   Well, I would classify Coolidge as the worst President of the 1920's, inferior to Hoover and Harding on virtually all counts. If there was anything politically constructive about the decade, it was Harding who started it and Hoover who picked it up. Coolidge was merely an interim caretaker.

Certainly, Coolidge was less malleable and more big-business oriented than either Harding or Hoover. In this respect, Mellon was the "villain" of the piece. The multi-millionaire occupied a different relationship to the President and to decision-making in the Coolidge administration than in either Harding's or Hoover's. Whenever Coolidge was in doubt on any subject, he sought Mellon's advice. This gave the Coolidge administration a depth of economic conservatism which neither the Harding nor the Hoover administrations possessed. Coolidge's lackluster record, together with his lazy, do-nothing qualities, mark him as one of our inferior Presidents.

As to Coolidge's popularity, one must put his accession to the presidency in its proper context. Harding had been a very popular President; there was a great outpouring of national grief when he died. When Coolidge took over, the nation was automatically sympathetic. Then, when the Harding scandals were exposed, the "establishment" did not desire to see the office of the presidency further degraded; hence there was a natural rush to build up the prestige of the office. Coolidge thus became an innocent victim as newspapers created a Coolidge myth. They took this dour Vermonter with few lively aspects to his character, and made him into something he was not. Conversely, they took qualities that in a different time and place would have been regarded as defects and made them into virtues. Journalists such as William Allen White now suddenly found Harding's easy affability "bad," and Coolidge's aloofness and parsimony "marvelous." Of course, big business regarded Coolidge as highly satisfactory, and it did everything in its power to embellish his reputation. Then, too, there was a curious affinity between Coolidge's apparent diffidence and what was so obviously a non-diffident age. The average American, reading about gangland murders and the other juicy events that were being paraded in the press, felt it somehow comforting in the midst of all these thrills to have the opposite in the White House.

J.A.G.   Do you think that Coolidge was aware of the different sides of issues and concerned with evaluating positions before coming to conclusions?

R.K.M.   As I've indicated, Coolidge was less open-minded, if that's the word, than Harding was, and even less open-minded than Hoover was. Coolidge may have been aware of two sides, but that he bothered to think much about alternatives is unlikely. I would put both Harding and Hoover above Coolidge in the quality of their perception of the nature of the political process. I would rank both of them higher than Coolidge in their understanding of what was necessary to gain political ends. Certainly as compared to Coolidge, Warren Harding was far more perspicacious with respect to congressional and party affairs, and much more knowledgeable about political behavior. Except for Mellon, the cabinet officers who served both Harding and Coolidge made no attempt to hide the fact that they found Harding the better President to work with.

J.A.G.   Did the economic prosperity of the Coolidge era have anything to do with Coolidge's conservatism and his uncritical admiration of big business?

R.K.M.   I think so. Coolidge was so much a partisan of big business that businessmen naturally adopted a buoyant and optimistic mood. This unquestionably helped fuel the economic expansion known as "the Coolidge boom." But the primary factors which made the Coolidge boom possible were really established during the Harding years. Moreover, we should not lose sight of the fact that Coolidge's disregard for the agricultural situation and for other soft spots in the economy, and his unilateral concentration on what benefited corporation interests, injured the economy in the long run.

J.A.G.   H. L. Mencken once wrote off Herbert Hoover as "a fat Coolidge." Was this a fair judgment?

R.K.M.   Hoover was by no means a fat Coolidge. Hoover never personally got along well with Coolidge, and sometimes opposed Coolidge's policies. The Vermonter, in turn, once made the statement that Hoover had given him unsolicited advice for six years—all of it bad. Hoover was intensely ambitious and industrious, more so than Coolidge. Coolidge reflected the views of finance capitalism, Hoover of industrial capitalism. Hoover was more intellectually curious; despite his saturnine personality, Hoover had a fertile mind and he was knowledgeable about many subjects.

Hoover's reputation inevitably suffered because of the Depression. Although he made that famous speech on the eve of the Great Crash about the nation soon eliminating poverty, he was worried at that very moment about stock-market conditions, and opposed the "easy money" policy that the Federal Reserve Board had applied in 1928–29. So, for a variety of reasons, including his intellectual acumen, his humanitarian instincts, his managerial ability, his administrative finesse, and the innovations which he made as Secretary of Commerce, I could never classify Hoover as a fat Coolidge.

J.A.G. Can Hoover be blamed, if not for *causing* the Great Depression, for failing to moderate its effects?

R.K.M. The Depression was bigger than Hoover, bigger than FDR. Granting, however that the Depression occurred because of myriad factors, I would certainly have to agree that Hoover's major error lay in not being willing to move fast enough and with sufficient vigor to counteract it.

Hoover, more than most people, had a comprehension of the complex and international character of the Depression; he realized that American recovery was somehow tied in with international monetary and trade rehabilitation. On the other hand, Hoover was curiously myopic with regard to the Depression's domestic manifestations. In his outmoded and old-fashioned way, he was not prepared to consider *sustained* federal activity to do something about it. He was too budget-conscious, and strove too strenuously to maintain a clear separation between the powers and functions of the local, state, and national governments. Moreover, he was dead wrong in assuming that since business had policed itself successfully during prosperity, it could police itself adequately in a period of extreme depression.

Having said this, I should add that I think Franklin Roosevelt was narrowly partisan in not offering Hoover some help in the interregnum period and in not working toward some kind of *modus operandi* to contain the crisis.

J.A.G. Recent historians have suggested that the massive shift of city voters to the Democratic party that was characteristic of the New Deal era actually began during the 1920's. What did the Democrats have to offer city dwellers in these years? Did the party provide voters with a reasonable alternative to the policies of the Republicans?

R.K.M. This is a question that requires much more research. I'm tempted to think that there was a subtle shift, at least in urban communities, to the Democratic party long before Roosevelt's victory in 1932. What appeared to be a Hoover landslide in 1928 may have been more apparent than real.

The Democrats were peculiarly inept during the 1920's. One need only observe the Democratic convention of 1924 to see what kind of trauma that party went through in trying to deal with the conflicts and divisions within its own ranks. Had the Democrats been able to adjust some of these differences earlier, they might have made a real fight out of the elections of the 1920's. Failing this, they didn't offer, in national affairs, any real alternatives to the Republicans. By the late twenties, at the local level they were beginning to do so, as J. Joseph Huthmacher suggests in his study of politics in Massachusetts. At the very close of the decade, the two parties were displaying a growing divergence on a few economic and social matters, with the Democrats at last providing the voters with some real alternatives.

To its discredit, the national Democratic party held to prohibition and immigration restriction (to name only two issues) long beyond the time when urban elements had begun to question these policies. And large Democratic city machines, while autocratic politically, had become far more tractable on most issues than the national organization. Such machines were, for example, less racist and less dominated by Anglo-Saxon elements, which automatically made them more appealing to new voters, to the poor, and especially to immigrants. This fact tended gradually to alter urban party affiliations and urban political control. I believe, too, that in the urban areas the Democratic party began to represent the only viable political organization that offered a haven to persons excluded from the middle-class prosperity of the 1920's. Thus, the Democratic party by the close of the decade began to serve as an outlet for many frustrations; people came into the party possessing a variety of complaints against the *status quo*.

J.A.G.   What were the most noticeable social changes of the decade? How was the United States different in 1929 from what it had been in 1919?

R.K.M.   Restricting my comments only to the period prior to the great crash, it seems to me that a number of important changes had occurred. First, the emancipation of women had been fully carried out by 1929; that issue simply ceased to exist. In a similar vein, comparing 1929 with 1919, the moral revolution and the revolt of the younger generation had been contained, or consummated if you prefer. The revolution was far from over, but for the moment an adjustment satisfactory to most elements in society had been made with respect to sexual-moral issues. The year 1929 marked the maturation of the United States as an urban nation. America was now an industrialized, mechanized, highly complex, and sophisticated society with an international economic prowess that outstripped its diplomacy. Electricity had become the major source of power, and the gasoline age of the automobile, truck, and airplane had arrived. By 1929, mass culture had been enthroned through the movies, the radio, and the daily newspaper.

By 1929, confidence and optimism had replaced the fear, confusion, and turmoil of 1919. In 1929, President Hoover could speak honestly of a glowing future for the American people. Business was booming; the nation seemed unified and happy; no problems seemed insurmountable. In all, this represented a marked contrast with 1919.

J.A.G.   What is you opinion of the so-called "New Left" interpretation of the 1920's?

R.K.M. I think we would be mistaken to reject the New Left out of hand; their views may give us some new perspectives on old problems. For example, they stress the fact that there is a continuity to modern American history. I personally like their implied premise that there can be no dividing of history into arbitrary periods.

Beyond this, what the New Left is saying, I think—and it requires some clairvoyance, since up to this time their methods have been sloppy and their research weak—is that the United States since the Industrial Revolution has been an expansionist, violent society which has produced for itself more than it could utilize, and that this "overproduction" has caused it to seek overseas markets and the control of natural resources. The nation, they argue, has had to move externally, whether it possessed an idealistic or moral reason for doing so or not. Industrialization, in the New Left view, has made America a "corporate state," a state dependent upon the existence of a corporation-riddled economic system with a faceless, dehumanized way of doing business. This has caused the American nation to act in an extremely aggressive manner on the world scene and promote stability, American-style, as a primary requirement. Consequently, the United States has opposed popular revolutions and engaged in repression against truly free, indigenous governments. In short, the country has customarily taken actions which are totally contrary to the ethical and moral principles which we claim to uphold.

Personally, I disagree that the United States has been as divergent in its ideals and actions as the New Left suggests, or so totally preoccupied with the needs of a corporate society. But I must admit that their argument may offer a fruitful way to re-examine American foreign policy, and can indeed help explain some of the actions which the United States has taken. Certainly, the 1920's fit neatly into the New Left thesis, because there probably never was a time when the nation more overtly, without diplomatic gobbledygook, pursued a policy of "business economic penetration" throughout the world. Harding and Hughes continued "dollar diplomacy" unabated, Coolidge strongly supported it, and Hoover was the very embodiment of that policy.

J.A.G. What are the half-dozen books that you would recommend to persons interested in the subject we have been discussing? In each case, would you indicate briefly what the particular contribution of the volume is?

R.K.M. Writings on the 1920's are now becoming so voluminous that it is extremely difficult to select such a few from among so many. However, in deference to my own tastes and in view of the various topics we have been discussing here, I would recommend the following.

For capturing the flavor and spirit of the decade, no book surpasses Frederick Lewis Allen, *Only Yesterday: An Informal History of the Nineteen-Twenties* (1931). Concentrating on the fads, fashions, and follies of the period, Allen has written not so much a history book as an historical document. Fascinating and lively, *Only Yesterday* offers a rare reading experience, even though Allen overemphasizes the superficial aspects of the era.

William E. Leuchtenburg, *The Perils of Prosperity, 1914–1932* (1958) is perhaps the most balanced interpretative account of the decade. Combining grace of style with clarity of analysis, Leuchtenburg in his book sees the 1920's as a time of transition, tension, and paradox. While charitable toward the era's mistakes, he believes that the kind of prosperity experienced in the 1920's led to the development of a politically bankrupt and shallow society which failed to meet the challenges of the modern industrial age.

In his *Republican Ascendancy, 1921–1933* (1960), John D. Hicks gives us the most up-to-date, scholarly, comprehensive, one-volume survey available. The book concentrates on politics, economics, and foreign policy, with a few side trips into the cultural and social area. Somewhat lackluster in style, it excels in factual information and possesses meaningful footnotes and an excellent bibliographical essay.

On the purely economic aspects of the 1920's, George Soule, *Prosperity Decade: From War to Depression, 1917–1929* (1947) is hard to beat. Although it is Volume VIII in the nine-volume *The Economic History of the United States* series, it stands by itself as an outstanding example of the economic historian's art. Not likely to appeal to the general reader because of its heavy use of statistical aggregates—prices, profits, currency levels, national income, output—it is still the most perceptive work we have on the nature and functioning of the expanding economy in the 1920's.

There are numerous significant specialized studies on various developments in the Roaring Decade. Among them is Norman F. Furniss, *The Fundamentalist Controversy, 1918–1931* (1954). A thorough, well-documented work, Furniss's book has as its main argument the belief that the fundamentalist movement was a threat to intellectual freedom. Using the Scopes trial as his point of departure, the author shows that fundamentalism was not wholly confined to the South or to rural areas, but existed wherever ignorance and unenlightenment flourished.

Examining another important aspect of the twenties is Andrew Sinclair, *Prohibition: The Era of Excess* (1962). This book is the first truly comprehensive scholarly account of the subject, and is the more remarkable because it was written by an Englishman. Sinclair regards prohibition as the final victory of the defenders of America's past and, with a self-confident Freudian approach, he evaluates the phenomenon by exploring literature, religious beliefs, racial theories, reform politics, medical science, crime, and urban growth. Suffering occasionally from overstatements, it still is a superb work.

William E. Leuchtenburg

The Great Depression and
the New Deal

WILLIAM E. LEUCHTENBURG, Professor of History at
Columbia University, is a specialist in twentieth-century
history. His *The Perils of Prosperity* (1958) was one of
the first major scholarly syntheses of the period of World
War I and its aftermath. His *Franklin D. Roosevelt and
the New Deal* (1963) won both a Bancroft and a Parkman
prize. He has also written *Flood Control Politics* (1953),
and he has edited a large number of volumes, including
The New Deal: A Documentary History (1968). Currently, he is at work on a book on Roosevelt's attempt
to "pack" the Supreme Court in 1937. Professor Leuchtenburg discusses the Great Depression of 1929–39 and
the domestic aspects of the New Deal era.

John A. Garraty   Professor Leuchtenburg, why did you call your history of the 1920's *The Perils of Prosperity*? Did you mean to suggest by the word "perils" not so much that the 1920's was an unsavory or dangerous period, but rather that the policies of the decade caused the Depression?

William E. Leuchtenburg   I think that was implicit in the title, and to that extent I think the title unfortunate. I tried to look at the 1920's as an entity, and to assume that the people of the time ought to be respected for their own opinions and actions. The period shouldn't be seen simply as a foreshadowing.

J.A.G.   But surely the economic policies of the 1920's were related to the Great Depression. To what extent can the Depression be blamed on the Presidents of the decade?

W.E.L.   Insofar as one accepts the thory that underconsumption explains the Depression, and I do, then one can say that the Presidents of the 1920's are to blame for operating a single-interest government—that is, a government responsive mainly to large business corporations. This led, among other unfortunate consequences, to the failure to maintain an adequate level of puchasing power on the part of workers and farmers, which left the economy with inadequate underpinnings.

J.A.G.   How significant was this in causing the collapse?

W.E.L.   This question is difficult to answer because the economic literature on the causes of the Depression is very unsatisfactory. In writing on the New Deal, I read through every volume of every economic journal of the 1930's. The question, which to an historian seems very "commonsensical," does not seem to have attracted the attention of many economists.

J.A.G.   Well, to be more specific, if Coolidge had signed the McNary-Haugen bill providing subsidies for farmers, or if the Muscle Shoals project, which has some connection with the TVA approach of the New Deal, had been adopted, is it likely that the impact of the Depression might have been moderated?

W.E.L.   I wouldn't think so. Muscle Shoals could have had no more than a modest effect, and the McNary-Haugen scheme seems to me to have been a mistake, since it was a move in the direction of economic nationalism at a time when the United States was already headed too much in that direction. It was not simply that conservative policies were followed by the Presidents, but that the progressive program was so barren. The reformers themselves were not speaking adequately to a great many of the issues.

J.A.G.   Why were the effects of the Depression as profound as they were, and why did it last as long as it did?

W.E.L.   The Depression was a watershed in American history; no explanation of the 1930's or subsequent years is satisfactory if it doesn't recognize what an enormous blow the Depression was, what a tremendous sense there was that an era was ending.

A big reason why it lasted so long was simply the lack of knowledge about the functioning of the economy and of useful statistical indicators. Much of the accepted theory was wrong-headed, and the indicators that did exist, such as the Dow-Jones stock-price averages, led policy makers in the wrong direction. Then there were long-range developments, partly affected by the Depression and partly the result of secular trends, which made it so profound and so lasting. One was the slowdown in population growth, which cut down the national market and slowed the pace of growth. Furthermore, no new industries emerged to play the role which radio and automobiles had played earlier, and which plastics, electronics, and others played later in stimulating the economy. There were also faults within the structure of the economy, such as the collapse of the banking system, which did enormous damage.

This was a worldwide depression; international repercussions bounced back and forth like a ball in a squash court. The blows to the United States' economy buffeted other countries, and the collapse of the Kreditanstalt in Austria in 1931 had deleterious effects in the United States, and so on all through the 1930's. Another fault within the American economy was the heavy burden of debt (farm mortgage indebtedness, home mortgage indebtedness), a debt structure far more burdensome than we have today. And lastly, there were the various errors of policy of both Hoover and Franklin Roosevelt.

J.A.G. With reference to the lack of sophisticated economic and social statistics and of economic knowledge generally, is it possible to defend the conservative argument of the 1920's and early 1930's that government intervention in the economy was dangerous? Perhaps laissez faire was the only viable policy, given the absence of intelligent understanding of the economy.

W.E.L. At least one can say that, whatever excuses one makes for Franklin Roosevelt for failing to undertake various experiments (for example, for failing to adopt deficit financing more vigorously), one also ought in all fairness to make for Hoover. But both Hoover and Roosevelt did have practical experiences that they might have made use of— in particular, the experience of World War I when active government intervention in the economy and increased spending resulted in national prosperity. Numbers of people were asking, if we could spend so recklessly in World War I, why couldn't we spend in the same way in this new war against depression? This argument did not persuade Hoover at all. Roosevelt was somewhat affected by it, but not enough.

J.A.G. Would you comment on President Hoover's attempts to deal with the problems of the Depression?

W.E.L. Almost every historian now recognizes that the image of Hoover as a "do-nothing" President is inaccurate. In comparison to Presidents in previous depressions, particularly Cleveland in the 1890's, Hoover broke many precedents and showed considerable willingness to have the government intervene. He stepped up public works spending, he asked businessmen to maintain wage rates, he encouraged the Federal Reserve to pursue an easy credit policy. Various subsidiaries of the Federal Farm Board purchased wheat and cotton. Within his own administration, Hoover defied the fatalism of Secretary of the Treasury Mellon and the bankers who were urging him to pursue a deflationary policy. In international affairs, he provided one of the few imaginative developments of that period in the moratorium on debts and reparations. Yet, with all that, I think that historians perhaps have overcompensated in their current view of Hoover. Perhaps, because most of them are liberal Democrats, they feel a need to lean over backwards. Whatever can be said of the wisdom of Hoover's policies in the first two years of the Depression, by 1931 clearly his policies weren't working. In the end, Hoover was pursuing policies which were not very different from those of Mellon. He makes a great deal in his *Memoirs* about his disagreement with Mellon, but essentially he was committed to budget balancing at a time of underutilization of resources, and to the gold standard. Furthermore, he was committed to voluntarism, particularly with respect to agriculture and labor.

Consider his farm policy. Despite government intervention, cotton prices fell more than a third. Huge surpluses were piling up. The head of Hoover's Federal Farm Board was advising cotton planters to plow under every third row. And the situation was getting worse. Hoover's policy had become bankrupt, and yet he had nothing to offer except more of the same. The failure of his relief policies was even more striking. He placed his main reliance not on federal action, but on local community resources. But how could a city like Toledo, where 80 percent of the working force was unemployed, possibly meet the needs of the jobless through its own resources? This truth was recognized by many of the national welfare leaders who had started out by sharing Hoover's views. A man like Allen Burns, for example, head of the Community Chest, originally opposed federal action, but by 1931 he had come around to favoring it. By 1932, the Hoover relief program was bankrupt. There was a real relief crisis in the country. Philadelphia had suspended aid. New York City had a big backlog of emergency cases. In Chicago, they were sending husbands and wives to separate relief shelters. Yet

Hoover continued to issue statements saying that the generosity of the public was adequately caring for the needy.

J.A.G. Can you suggest any explanation for his extreme rigidity? Hoover was an intelligent man, and not completely without imagination. How did he justify his insistence on private relief in the face of the fact that 80 percent of the work force in Toledo, Ohio, was unemployed?

W.E.L. That is the big puzzle about Hoover. He came to office with a reputation as a great humanitarian; he had experience with massive relief spending in Belgium, and with government intervention in the economy as head of the War Food Administration. He supported labor unions and public works spending and countercyclical actions in a time of depression as early as 1921. Yet in office he became the most extreme kind of advocate of laissez faire.

J.A.G. Do you think that his rigidity can be explained by the unreasonableness and partisan character of some of the critics of his handling of the Depression?

W.E.L. That probably had something to do with it. If you assume that there was a general fear of not maintaining a balanced budget, and of going off the gold standard, it must have seemed to him grossly unfair to rail at him for not doing what every "sensible" man knew should not be done.

One other point ought to be made. There is a "Hoover theory" which argues that the country was coming out of the Depression in the summer of 1932, and that recovery would have been achieved if it had not been for the election of Roosevelt, which produced the bank crisis and then the subsequent faulty policies of the New Deal. I'm not persuaded. Some economic indices went up in the summer of 1932, but indices had gone up earlier in the Depression only to come down again. By the fall, there was already a turndown. Moreover, I find it very hard to believe that a country which had just overwhelmingly elected Franklin Roosevelt was terrified by his assuming office. The bank crisis occurred because there was something seriously wrong with the banking structure. Even in Wall Street there were many persons who believed that the United States ought to go off gold, and who hailed Roosevelt when he did go off gold in the spring of 1933.

J.A.G. At the time of his nomination for the presidency in 1932, many liberals considered Franklin Roosevelt too conservative and something of a lightweight. What led them to these opinions?

W.E.L. One has to recognize that the kinds of issues which seem to us to have been important, particularly those centering on unemployment, were not those which many writers and politicians considered central. There were three big questions which seemed significant with respect to Roosevelt's record as Governor of New York. One was municipal corruption, the second was prohibition, and the third was the League of Nations. On all three he took positions which made him seem to be a lightweight. He seemed to be vacillating. On municipal corruption he was faced with the delicate question of what to do about Mayor Jimmy Walker of New York, a member of his own party. Liberal reformers charged him with temporizing.

Prohibition was a lively issue in 1932, and Roosevelt took a stand which satisfied neither the wets nor the drys, once more leaving the impression that he was not a forceful character. On the League of Nations issue, although he had run for Vice President in 1920 as a Wilsonian Democrat, he bowed to William Randolph Hearst in January, 1932, and indicated that he did not favor America's entrance. Once more he gave the impression of being weak.

Then, in the campaign itself, he failed to strike a clear enough note. Raymond Moley, an early member of the group of intellectuals who made up FDR's Brain Trust, tells of his horror at confronting Roosevelt with two different versions of his tariff speech, and of Roosevelt's saying, "Weave them together." Then there was that classic speech at Forbes Field in which he accused the Hoover administration of being the greatest spending administration in all our history. His ability to make a speech of that sort, at the same time that he was saying he was in favor of unemployment relief, once more left people with the impression that he was, in the phrase of a book at the time, "a gay reformer," without very much substance to him.

J.A.G. Did Roosevelt really fashion the great coalition which produced his sweeping victories of 1932 through 1944?

W.E.L. He didn't do so in 1932. Arthur Krock of *The New York Times* wrote after the election that the country was voting a national grouch, and this seems to me very likely to be true. It was a vote against Hoover rather than one for Roosevelt. By 1936, however, the coalition had emerged full-blown. We don't know enough yet about how it was put together to say how much of it was conscious on Roosevelt's part. He certainly was a political animal, and he knew that there were political benefits to be gained from "recognition." In 1936, one of the men who seconded Roosevelt's nomination was a Negro congressman. A Negro minister gave the benediction at one of the sessions of the Convention. Roosevelt gave an unusually large number of appointments to members of various ethnic groups. He worked with labor's Non-Partisan League. He was fashioning what was less a Democratic party than a New Deal party. It was built around what one writer called "the Politics of the Deed." Roosevelt could point to a series of specific benefits which had gone to specific individuals as a result of the New Deal expansion of government activity.

J.A.G.   What of the argument, advanced by Samuel Lubell and others, that especially in the cities the swing of popular support from the Republicans to the Democrats had really occurred before 1932?

W.E.L.   There was some party realignment in the 1920's. But in 1928, Al Smith was a badly beaten candidate, while in 1936 Roosevelt scored one of the greatest victories in the history of the two-party system. This shift seems to me of vastly greater importance. Roosevelt ran much better than Smith had in cities like Los Angeles, and there were many new groups he won to the Democratic party. As late as 1932, Negroes voted heavily for Hoover; they began to switch in large numbers in the 1934 congressional elections, and by 1936 they were in the Democratic column.

J.A.G.   Much has been made of Roosevelt's apparent lack of an organized plan for coping with economic problems in 1933, and of the confusion and contradictions in many of his early actions. Is this criticism entirely fair?

W.E.L.   Certainly there were contradictions, particularly in the early years of the New Deal, and conflicts among Roosevelt's advisers, with an orthodox man like Lewis Douglas, the Budget Director, opposing the policies advocated by Rexford Tugwell, who was a national planner, and between New Nationalists and the Brandeisian wing of the party represented by people like Felix Frankfurter. Secretary of State Cordell Hull pursued a policy of expanding international trade at the same time as Roosevelt was scuttling the London Economic Conference. The administration advocated supporting purchasing power and expanding productivity at the same time that it practiced restrictionism, symbolized by the famous episode of the slaughter of the little pigs in an effort to raise the price of pork. Yet despite all of this, there was more cohesion to the policies of Roosevelt than critics allow. The basic idea that Roosevelt started with was the notion that there was imbalance in the economy created by the overexpansion of the 1920's, and by the fact that a single interest—business—had control of too large a percentage of national resources. He tried to achieve a new balance by increasing purchasing power, particularly that of farmers. He was more concerned about farmers than workers, in part because of the vast extent of the rural depression. He thought that although some gains might be made in international trade, essentially recovery was going to have to be a domestic operation, achieved by building up the home market, chiefly by increasing the farmers' purchasing power.

   At the same time, the New Dealers were led both by the experience of World War I mobilization and by that of the trade associations of the 1920's, to seek recovery through greater cooperation between government and business. Although they were not out-and-out greenbackers, they favored some kind of inflation—actually, the decision to go off gold was all but inevitable. And the policies which Roosevelt followed in his first term worked out reasonably well. By 1937, the country had about gotten back to 1929 levels of output, although not of employment. No doubt, other policies would have worked better, but that judgment comes from hindsight.

J.A.G. Historians frequently speak of a first New Deal and a second New Deal. Would you discuss the differences between these two New Deals?

W.E.L. The terms "first New Deal" and "second New Deal" are not terms that I find helpful, in part because they mean different things to different historians. There are at least three different sets of meanings that historians have given to the term "the two New Deals." The first was popularized by Basil Rauch in his *History of the New Deal* (1944). He saw the shift between the two as being from Right to Left. The first New Deal, essentially conservative, was dominated by the excessive business influence in the NRA, and by a solicitude for large farmers in the AAA. The aim of the first New Deal he sees as being essentially that of recovery. The movement to the second New Deal started in 1934, and matured with the "second hundred days" of 1935, as a result of attacks on Roosevelt from the Right (the Liberty League and the United States Chamber of Commerce) and on the Left from men like Huey Long. It produced progressive measures like the Social Security Act, the Holding Company Act, and the Wagner National Labor Relations Act.

But during the "conservative" first New Deal, radical legislation like the TVA Act was passed, while during the "liberal" second New Deal the themes of the first New Deal persisted. This interpretation exaggerates the differences between the two periods. The Social Security bill, for example, was very early in the works, and was held up in part because some of the reformers wanted to refine the details of it. A second conception of the two New Deals was advanced by Eric Goldman in his book, *Rendezvous with Destiny* (1952). He sees the first New Deal as essentially New Nationalist, and the second New Deal as New Freedom. This, too, contains a certain amount of truth, but again, there are problems. For one thing, in the so-called "New Nationalist" phase in 1933, Brandeisian legislation like the Securities Act was passed. In the New Freedom period, measures that are hard to call Brandeisian, such as the Wagner Act, were enacted.

Finally, there is the version of the two New Deals developed first by Rexford Tugwell and given its largest expression by Arthur M. Schlesinger, Jr., in his volumes on *The Age of Roosevelt*. They see the two New Deals as a move from the Left to the Right. The essential characteristic of their first New Deal was a commitment to national planning and a holistic view of the economy. While the second New Deal was much more antibusiness in its rhetoric, nonetheless it was more capitalistic in substance. Here again, I find weaknesses in this kind of generalization. Tugwell did indeed believe in national planning, but it's hard to find anybody else in 1933 who did. And how can such measures as the Wagner Act or the Farm Security Administration or the National Planning Board be seriously represented as marking a shift to the Right?

J.A.G.   Were such raucous radical critics of the New Deal as Senator Huey Long, the "Radio Priest" Father Coughlin, and the Townsendites really, in your opinion, reformers?

W.E.L.   It's hard to classify Long. At the time, many considered him a fascist, and the fact that he was so benign and struck a comic pose was thought to be simply a disguise. On the other hand, one can make a case for Long as a reformer. His "Share-Our-Wealth" program went much further than anything the New Deal was countenancing. In his own Louisiana, he put through the first state income-tax law. He did a great deal to improve education, got rid of the poll tax, taxed oil companies. Yet he was hostile to the CIO, tolerated child labor, and particularly from the point of view of urban reform, was anything but forward-looking. It's probably too extreme to call him a fascist, nor was he, incidentally, a racist. But his control of the Louisiana legislature and of elections and his use of police forces all suggest a drive toward power and a contempt for parliamentary institutions. Long himself, when asked whether he ought to be categorized as being on the Left or the Right, said, "Hell, I'm *sui generis*," and let it go at that. And that may be where the historian has to leave it.

Long certainly must be taken a good deal more seriously than Father Coughlin. Most of Coughlin's emphasis revolved around the money question. One critic said that what he knew about economics, if turned to salt, wouldn't physic a chickadee. Townsend was a one-idea man, concerned only with the old-age pension movement. He shared the values of much of his following—elderly Republicans WASP elements on the decline, so that although he helped greatly in the push for social security legislation, he did not contribute a great deal more than that toward reform. And by 1937 he was so strongly opposed to Roosevelt's Supreme Court packing plan that he even neglected the old-age pension scheme.

J.A.G.   Well, are there any threads binding these extremist critics together? Did they at any stage cooperate with one another?

W.E.L.   By 1935, Long, Coughlin, and Townsend were moving toward a kind of political alliance. After Long was assassinated in September, 1935, one of his followers, Gerald L. K. Smith, joined in a very loose federation with Coughlin and some of the Townsend forces in the Union party, which ran William Lemke for the presidency in 1936. Other threads link the movements. All were distrustful of "Eastern intellectuals," and of the liberal establishment. They found their following often among the dispossessed rural poor and the urban poor who were not reached by New Deal programs. And they spoke for a politics of revenge. All heaped ridicule on the pretensions of the New Dealers, whom they thought of as spokesmen for the old order, ostensibly reformers but actually working against the interest of "the people." Long particularly used the weapon of ridicule against the New Dealers, but the other two did so as well. They were also captivated by the idea of self-generating economics, which reminds one a lot of the chain-letter craze of the 1930's. And yet despite these common themes, there was a world of difference between the Brooklyn and South Boston constituency of a Coughlin, the Deep South followers of Long, and the old folks of the West who backed Townsend. In 1936, the Union party quickly broke up in a series of squabbles among the different leaders.

J.A.G. Would it be accurate to call them neo-Populists?

W.E.L. Yes, indeed. Long came from a Populist stronghold in Louisiana, and he clearly was in the Populist tradition. Lemke corresponded regularly with "Coin" Harvey. As for the Coughlinites, Herman Kahn, the librarian at the Roosevelt Library, once said, "Scratch a mid-westerner and you find a funny money man." I think Townsend is a little harder to put in the Populist category, and, of course, these men had centers of strength, such as the Irish Catholic neighborhoods of Brooklyn, that were far removed from the old Populist heartland.

J.A.G. How did the attacks of these men influence Roosevelt's behavior?

W.E.L. He regarded them as rival political operators and sought to put them out of business or to lessen their appeal. Within Louisiana, he deliberately distributed patronage to Long's opponents. Secretary of the Interior Harold Ickes cut off relief funds in Louisiana. Roosevelt sent a whole army of agents from the Internal Revenue Bureau into New Orleans to look into what turned out to be well-founded suspicions of wrongdoing by men in Long's organization. When the Union party was organized in 1936, and when Coughlin was becoming more and more vitriolic in his denunciations of Roosevelt, the President worked very closely with members of the Catholic hierarchy to undercut him by obtaining statements that F.D.R. was not a Communist, as Coughlin charged.

The more interesting question to historians is whether Roosevelt, in the phrase of the day, was "stealing Huey's thunder"—that is to say, did Roosevelt change his program to undercut these extremists? In particular, it has been suggested that the Wealth Tax Act of 1935 was a response to Long's "Share-Our-Wealth" program, that the National Youth Administration was a response to Long's proposal to give students free college educations and free textbooks, and that the Social Security Act was a consequence of the Townsend Plan. There seems little reason to doubt that Long and Townsend influenced these developments, but the matter is not quite so simple. The Wealth Tax bill had been advocated by many others for a long time. The Social Security bill was also in the works well before the Townsend Plan had developed any national appeal.

One often hears it said that Roosevelt destroyed the appeal of these men by putting through social reforms that undercut the discontent on which they fed. There's something to this, but it ought to be noted that Townsend was much stronger *after* the passage of the Social Security Act. These men appealed to emotions that no mere statute could wipe out.

J.A.G.   In recent years, historians have pointed out that the New Deal did relatively little for underprivileged groups: Negroes, the poor, share croppers in the South. If this was so, how can the overwhelming support that these groups gave Roosevelt in the 1936 election be explained?

W.E.L.   I don't agree that the New Deal did little for these groups. The historians you refer to may be confusing the question of whether the New Deal permanently changed the social system with the question of what the government's response was to the particular crisis which these groups faced in the 1930's. In sharp contrast to the performance in the Hoover period, there was an enormous outpouring of federal relief funds. In many counties, the majority of the population was on relief. By the end of 1934, more than twenty million Americans were receiving public assistance. This seemed to a great many Americans far more impressive than the inadequacies of the relief program.

The federal government was visible in the 1930's in a way in which it had not been before. The national government came into contact with people who had never before seen it other than in the form of the postman. When I entered Cornell as a freshman in 1939, with very little money and knowing that I would have to work my way through college, the first indication I had of a federal presence was the ease with which I was able to get an NYA job, cleaning out test tubes in a laboratory. My children in Dobbs Ferry go to a high school which was built by the WPA in the 1930's. This kind of experience was multiplied all around the country. The people who faced the foreclosure of farm mortgages and who were bailed out by the national government felt an allegiance to Roosevelt and the Democratic party, despite the "inadequacies" of the New Deal.

Negro attitudes are particularly interesting, because in some respects the New Deal was not merely inadequate but even injurious to the interests of the Negro. The NRA often discriminated against Negro workers; the AAA drove some Negro share croppers and tenant farmers off the land; the TVA operated segregated facilities; the CCC refrained from setting up camps in some southern states in order to appease white southerners. How, then, does one account for the fact that the Negro executed an historic change in his political allegiance in the 1930's, one which persists to this day? Simply because the discrimination which he suffered at the hands of the New Deal was no different from what he had been suffering all along. What was *new* to him were the benefits that he received from the New Deal—such things as relief programs and low-cost housing projects. Some three hundred thousand Negro illiterates were taught to read and write under the New Deal. Federal funds went into Negro schools. Roosevelt refused to fight for civil-rights legislation, but I know no reason to suppose that his political judgment was wrong; he would not have gotten the legislation, and he would have jeopardized other reforms, some of which did benefit the Negro. Finally, there was the political appeal of the New Deal to the Negro. In addition to taking part in Democratic party affairs, large numbers of Negroes also voted in AAA and NLRB elections, even in the South.

One last point that might be made is that quite apart from any specific program, many workingmen, poor farmers, and others who felt themselves to have been neglected in the past regarded Roosevelt as their friend. They sensed that his was a humane administration, that the President cared what happened to them. Eric Goldman quotes a worker as saying that Roosevelt was the first man who had ever been in the White House who would understand that his boss was a son of a bitch. Probably without being able to explain exactly why, a lot of Americans had that sense in the 1930's.

J.A.G. Why did Roosevelt try to pack the Supreme Court in 1937?

W.E.L. Many historians argue that Roosevelt made a bad mistake in trying to pack the Court, because he never needed to do so in the first place. They stress the so-called switch in the Court, "the switch in time that saved nine," that took place between 1936 and 1937. It was once thought that when the Supreme Court handed down its decision upholding the Washington Minimum Wage case in the spring of 1937, Roosevelt's plan had produced a sharp shift from its decision against the New Work Minimum Wage law in the spring of 1936. It was then discovered that the Washington decision had been reached *prior* to Roosevelt's announcement of the Court packing plan. Hence, since the Court was going to change its mind anyway, it was said that if Roosevelt had just waited, he would have gotten all that he wanted.

A second line of argument was developed by Justice Felix Frankfurter in an article in the *University of Pennsylvania Law Review*. He stated that the Court never did switch, that the only reason that Justice Owen D. Roberts voted in the negative in the New York case was because of technical matters concerning the way the case was presented by the state of New York. This is not my view. There's no doubt at all, if you take the range of opinions from 1935 through 1937 (the Court's attitude toward the commerce clause in the Schechter and Carter cases contrasted with its view in the Jones and Laughlin case, or the Rail Pension decision contrasted with the Social Security case), that what political scientists have called a "constitutional revolution" took place.

Considering the realities that Roosevelt faced, I think he faced a real problem with the Court. After all, it had held that not even a state could enact minimum wage legislation. It had gone out of its way in the Carter coal case to deny that as large an enterprise as mining was a proper subject for congressional action under the interstate commerce clause. The Court was about to rule on the Wagner Act and the Social Security Act, and there was every reason to believe that it would hold both of these laws unconstitutional. In November, 1936, Roosevelt had been elected by an unprecedented landslide. Roosevelt had his big mandate, but what could he do with it? If the Court followed the line it had been following, it was likely that most of the major New Deal measures would be declared unconstitutional and so too would be the social legislation the President planned to recommend in his second term.

J.A.G.   What about the old adage, "The Supreme Court follows the election returns"? Isn't it likely that the Court would have changed its tune of its own accord after the 1936 election?

W.E.L.   I doubt that we'll ever have a satisfactory answer to that question, but I suppose some kind of response would have been made. Here too, however, the historian has information which the President did not have. One of the things I was struck by in going through Justice Van Devanter's papers is that he and men like himself seriously thought a Republican victory possible in 1936. Many of the justices may have thought that they were tribunes of the people, defending popular rights against an arbitrary ruler, and the Roosevelt landslide could well have brought them up short. Certainly an argument can be made that Roosevelt would have been wiser to have waited to see how the Supreme Court was going to respond to his victory, especially since he had not proposed reform of the Court during the campaign. But although it might not have been unreasonable to suppose that the Court would yield on some issues, there was no reason to predict a basic shift in attitude. Even after Roosevelt introduced his Court packing plan, almost everyone believed that he was going to lose some of the Wagner Act cases. Roosevelt also thought that he had to capitalize on his election victory at the outset. Moreover, if he waited until the Court handed down an adverse decision in the Wagner cases, he would appear to be arbitrarily attempting, by a political solution, to defy the will of the judiciary. But having said this, I must add that Roosevelt undoubtedly believed after the election that the world was his oyster, and that a few justices were not going to stand in his way. He couldn't help feeling some vindictiveness. The tone of his message suggests a desire to chastise the Court.

J.A.G.   Well then, why actually did the Court change its attitude?

W.E.L.   I would say it did so largely in response to the Court packing plan. It was beating a strategic retreat. Chief Justice Hughes in particular was a very adroit politician and also a man with a sense of the integrity of the Court as an institution; he acted in part in a self-protective way. The fact that the Court had a different line of precedents which it could follow with respect to the interpretation of the commerce clause made it relatively easy for it to change.

J.A.G.   If the Court had not changed its position while the reform bill was being discussed, would the bill have passed?

W.E.L.   It might not have passed in the form that it did, but I think that Roosevelt would have gotten at least two additional justices. Particularly if the Court had struck down the Social Security Act, the pressure for reform would have been so great that some kind of Court packing plan would undoubtedly have gone through.

J.A.G.   Is it therefore correct to say that in the Court fight Roosevelt "lost the battle but won the war"?

W.E.L.   Roosevelt himself claimed this was the case, and if you believe, as I do, that a constitutional revolution occurred in 1937, there's a lot to support his argument. Within two-and-one-half years he was able to appoint five new justices. After 1937, every piece of New Deal legislation was upheld.

On the other hand, Roosevelt lost the Court fight in that it greatly damaged his standing with Congress and within the Democratic party. It was probably the most important single event in the creation of the conservative coalition which brought the New Deal to a virtual standstill by the summer of 1938.

J.A.G.   In the last analysis, why did the New Deal fail to restore real prosperity?

W.E.L.   One has to start by saying that by the time Roosevelt took office, so much damage had been done to the economy that a massive effort was required to straighten things out. Business confidence had been shattered; the banking system was in a state of collapse; the debt structure was extremely burdensome; the loss of purchasing power was so great, the reluctance to invest so considerable that rapid recovery was unlikely.

It is true that some of the measures that Roosevelt pushed either did not contribute to recovery or actually worked in the wrong direction. The National Industrial Recovery Act probably accounted for a certain amount of re-employment, but on the whole the administration invested more energy in it than it got out of it in economic improvement. Much the same could be said about gold buying. It didn't do as much harm as its critics charged, but it represented a loss of valuable time. Probably the greatest mistake of the first term was the failure to do enough about public works and housing. The real impetus to recovery was to come from rapid, large-scale spending. This is what some of the Progressives like young Bob La Follette of Wisconsin had been pushing in the Hoover years. But throughout the New Deal, as Keynes pointed out in his famous letter to Roosevelt in 1938, the biggest single failure of policy came in this area.

Housing was particularly significant. One of the most important causes of the economic breakdown was the sharp decline in construction in the 1920's. Building continued to fall off in the 1930's. This was an area where the administration might well have done a great deal more than it did. To use Roosevelt's famous phrase, at least a "third of the nation" was ill-housed. A large-scale housing program of the sort that Britain and other countries undertook was practicable. Furthermore, not only had residential housing declined, but construction of other kinds was also down drastically. If the construction problem had been attacked in the 1930's, all kinds of beneficial results would have followed. Yet it must be repeated, for all the weaknesses of the New Deal, by 1937 the 1929 levels of production had been reached.

Then came the precipitous recession of 1937–38, the sharpest decline in our history. There are numbers of explanations for this recession, but the biggest one is that Roosevelt continued to believe in balancing the budget. By 1937 he had the budget in balance, and the recession resulted. Despite all his reforms, Roosevelt failed to move the government enough into the center of economic decision-making. Business groups suffered a loss of confidence because of the Depression and were even more unsettled by the New Deal reforms. (One of the dilemmas faced by a reform government in a capitalist system is that it sometimes is confronted with a choice between either not undertaking reforms that ought to be undertaken, or going ahead with those reforms with the knowledge that they may cause hardship by imparing business's will to invest, thus precipitating or prolonging a depression.) In 1938, Roosevelt abandoned budget-balancing and accepted the idea of massive government spending. An upturn followed once he had made that change, but not until World War II was full employment achieved.

J.A.G.   Did Roosevelt ever really learn much about modern economics and its relationship to public policy? More specifically, to what extent did his advisers try to convert him to the new Keynesian economics?

W.E.L. It has often been implied that Roosevelt was something of a dunce with respect to economics, but I think he was a lot better informed about economic matters than one has any right to expect of an American politician, who has his own special skills. He got a rather good undergraduate education in economics at Harvard, and he had a certain amount of business experience in the 1920's. His grasp of detail was truly extraordinary; numbers of people have commented on his ability to recite with remarkable precision crop prices and other economic data. So he was far from being an economic ignoramus.

The question of Keynes's influence is a more difficult one. Roosevelt appears to have disliked Keynes because of his attack on Woodrow Wilson's handling of the Versailles Conference in *The Economic Consequences of the Peace*. Keynes came to the United States in 1934, and there are conflicting views of what Roosevelt's response was. He wrote to Felix Frankfurter that he'd seen Keynes and thought him a splendid fellow. At the same time, he told Secretary of Labor Frances Perkins that all he'd gotten from Keynes was a "rigmarole of figures." The weight of evidence suggests that the Perkins version is the right one. Roosevelt was not much impressed by Keynes, nor Keynes by Roosevelt. There was, however, a group of people around Roosevelt who, by the second term, had read Keynes's *General Theory*. However, they never to my knowledge attempted to educate Roosevelt in the same way that Walter Heller gave Jack Kennedy training in the New Economics when he became President. By 1938, Roosevelt was moving more or less in a Keynesian direction, but while he may have grasped the idea that *spending* could be a good thing, he probably never grasped the concept that *deficits* were a good thing.

On this whole question, timing is of the greatest importance. If Roosevelt had followed the ideas of the most accepted professional economists when he took office, he would have done the wrong thing. Some of the things that we think of as Keynesian were not what Keynes was arguing for in 1932. The *General Theory* did not appear until 1936 —there was a relatively short time for a new administration to absorb a complex theory, especially one that seemed to fly in the face of common sense. So on the whole I'm more impressed by how responsive Roosevelt was to Keynesian doctrine than by his failure to go along with it all the way. It took the experience of World War II to persuade most people. The war proved that massive spending under the right conditions produced full employment.

J.A.G. Was Roosevelt as bad an administrator as his critics have often charged?

W.E.L.   From the point of view of the public administration theory that prevailed when he was in the White House, he was a very bad administrator. He didn't follow organization charts, and permitted all kinds of conflicts among his subordinates. He found it hard to fire people, and he frequently left men with the impression that he agreed with them when in fact he did not. (This was one of Huey Long's particular gripes. He said, "When I go to see Roosevelt he says to me, 'Fine, fine, fine.' And when my opponent goes to see him he says, 'Fine, fine, fine.' Maybe he says 'fine, fine, fine' to everybody.")

But historians give Roosevelt higher marks as an administrator. Having a low opinion of organization charts, they point out that the new agencies that he set up gave vigor and a spirit of innovation to the government which would not have been achieved under the old-line departments, and that the setting of administrators against one another brought choices between alternative policies out into the open. The airing of clashing views helped Roosevelt to decide difficult questions. But probably the greatest thing to be said in Roosevelt's favor is that he was able to attract first-rate men to Washington. That is the highest tribute that one can pay to an administrator.

J.A.G.   How closely did Roosevelt follow the complexities of New Deal programs? Was he the leader or merely the cheerleader of the New Deal?

W.E.L.   He followed some programs more closely than others, but at the high policy level, he followed most programs remarkably closely. Obviously, some things were closer to his heart than others. He could never get very interested in urban housing, but anything that had to do with conservation or the movement back to the land captured his attention. He liked to think of himself as a Georgia farmer, and he watched a whole range of agricultural questions very closely. He was terribly interested in anything that he'd been closely involved with as Governor of New York—for example, public power. In short, so far as any President can keep on top of the proliferating federal bureaucracy, Roosevelt did a pretty good job.

J.A.G.   Well, looking back on the New Deal from the perspective of today, what impact did Roosevelt make on the office of the President?

W.E.L.   This question is less easy to answer than one might suppose at first. Roosevelt was an activist President, who set a precedent for those who would follow him; the degree to which Lyndon Johnson thought of Roosevelt as a model for some of his actions is one indication of this. If you compare Roosevelt in the office with Coolidge, you immediately sense the expansion of the conception of the office. Yet to try to spell out the way he changed the office permanently is difficult. Probably, what first comes to mind is Roosevelt's performance as chief legislator, but

Theodore Roosevelt and Woodrow Wilson had both done a great deal along the same lines. However, in part because of Roosevelt's long period in office and the wealth of legislation enacted in his time, he carried on a much bigger operation than any predecessor. Under him, the presidency was so much bigger in degree that it became bigger in kind.

Roosevelt also used different instruments. I have in mind particularly the radio: his use of the fireside chat. But he also made better use of press conferences. Presidents had talked to newspapermen before, but there was a marked difference between the formal press conferences of Hoover and the free-swinging sessions that Roosevelt carried on. He always thought of himself as a veteran newspaperman because he'd been President of the *Harvard Crimson,* and he would say to reporters, "If I were you, I would write my story this way." He knew them by their first names; he obviously liked them and they liked him. He used press conferences to educate the country. He expanded the office, too, by becoming, to use Sidney Hyman's phrase, Chief Economic Engineer (something no President had ever been), and this trend led subsequently to the Full Employment Act in 1946 and the development of the Council of Economic Advisers.

Probably the main change he made in the presidency was his creation of the Executive Office of the President in 1939. He moved the Bureau of the Budget under his control at that time and a number of other agencies that were later created—the Council of Economic Advisers, the National Security Agency, for example—were added in the Truman-Eisenhower period. Many political scientists feel that this change has enabled Presidents to stay on top of the myriad of agencies and impose some kind of order on their administrations.

J.A.G.   How has the New Deal experience permanently changed American life and American society?

W.E.L.   There has been a tendency recently in writing about the New Deal to minimize the changes that were wrought, in part because so many social evils still exist. If the New Deal changed so much, how does it happen that things are still so bad? I recognize the limitations of the New Deal, including those in some areas where it might have brought change, and yet I do think of the New Deal and the Great Depression as a watershed, probably the most important episode in American history since the Civil War.

First of all, there was a vast expansion of the role of the federal government in American life. Before 1933, the federal government had made little impact on the lives of ordinary Americans. After the New Deal, it was inserting itself in a wide range of ways into the affairs of every citizen.

J.A.G.   But was it the New Deal that caused this great expansion of government activity? Hadn't the expansion been taking place steadily for decades?

W.E.L.   Yes, of course. But if you compare the status of the national government in 1932 with that in 1939, an enormous change has taken place. The expansion under Hoover, who was regarded in 1928 as a great social engineer, a man in touch with the latest developments in the social sciences, was trivial by comparison, and I would argue that if Hoover had been re-elected, we would not have had the kinds of changes that came about under the New Deal. A development related to this expansion of government was the change from voluntarism to state intervention and coercion. Instead of trying to persuade business-men to be nicer to workers, the New Deal provided penalties to make them go along with unionization.

Another big change that took place as a consequence of the Great Depression and the New Deal was in American politics. For a period of some eighty years, the Republican party had been, with certain excep-tions, the majority party in the United States. No Democrat after Franklin Pierce had entered the White House with as much as 50 percent of the vote, until Roosevelt. Yet, since 1930, the Republicans have succeeded in capturing control of Congress in only two elections. This was more simply than a change of parties. The Democratic party as recently as the candidacy of John W. Davis in 1924 had been the party of small government; under F.D.R. it became the party of big government. In 1932, the country was debating war debts, prohibition—matters of this sort. By 1936, it was talking about the Wagner Act, and public housing, and valley authorities. The whole nature of political discourse had been changed.

Another permanent effect of the New Deal was to make poverty a national concern. Of course there were areas in which the New Deal did not achieve effective social change, and there certainly was a hiatus in the Eisenhower period during which the country seemed indifferent to poverty, but Roosevelt's message, pointing out that a third of the nation was ill-housed, ill-clad, and ill-nourished, put poverty on the national agenda. Related to this was the development of public housing. Critics point out that the New Deal never did all it should have done in that field, and I share that view. Still, except during World War I, there were no national public housing projects until the 1930's. In addition, the activities of the FHA in supporting private home building were an innovation of great importance. And with respect to the welfare of the most impoverished, the sweatshop and child labor were virtually erased in the New Deal years.

One of the most important changes of the 1930's was in the status of industrial labor. To be sure, Roosevelt was often indifferent and even hostile to industrial unions at the beginning, but even in 1933 he helped establish an atmosphere conducive to unionism, and the NLRB subsequently did a lot more. In 1933, most factory workers were not unionized. Men in the mills worked without vacations; they were subject to the whims of foremen, had no job security. In the coal towns, workers faced the tyranny of the company town and the company store; they were harassed by private police. Under the Roosevelt administration, a redistribution of power between labor and capital, of the greatest significance, took place. Writers of the New Left would say that practically nothing changed in the 1930's, but few steel workers or auto workers, having lived through the decade, would agree.

Roosevelt always had a deep interest in the conservation movement, and the Tennessee Valley Authority stands forth as one of the very big achievements of these years. Grand Coulee and Bonneville transformed much of the Pacific Northwest, and think of what the Rural Electrification Administration meant to farmers. Only one in nine had electricity at the outset of the Roosevelt era; eight out of nine had it at the end. But probably most important—what distinguishes New Deal efforts from the conservation movement of the Progressive era—were developments in soil conservation: the creation of the Soil Erosion Service and the Soil Conservation Service. Here were gains that permanently changed the landscape of the United States.

Another New Deal development was the greatly increased role of intellectuals in government. They had a brief appearance, to be sure, on the state level in Wisconsin for a brief period before World War I, but not until the Brain Trust did the intimate association of the university campus and the government develop. A new administrative class arose, with a particular sense of values and ambitions and a unique power base that had not existed prior to the New Deal. Along with this came a series of new government activities, like the Federal Art Project, the Federal Theatre, and the Federal Writers Project.

If one examines the experience of the American farmer between 1932 and 1939, one is struck by the enormously increased involvement of the national government. To be sure, the Department of Agriculture had been very active since the late nineteenth century, but never so intimately concerned with the everyday life or the economic welfare of the farmer. The novelist William Faulkner once said that the Mississippi cotton farmer no longer plowed the cotton fields, he plowed the corridors of government buildings. (By the way, the developments I'm describing should not necessarily all be thought of as good. Whether intellectuals ought to be as involved in government as they are, whether the farm subsidy program has been a success, whether public housing projects are well conceived, are all debatable questions. But if the issue is whether the 1930's changed anything, the answer is self-evident.)

I ought also to mention some more subtle changes in American life unrelated to particular pieces of legislation. One was the growth of ethnic diversity. For example, nowadays one frequently sees Negroes as actors in commercials on television. There has been far too much self-congratulation on the part of white liberals because of this development. What is much more to the point is the shocking degree to which Negroes in the past were not permitted to be a visible part of the national culture. The New Deal began the process of change, although painfully inadequately. Similarly, to a remarkable degree, American society prior to the Depression was a WASP society, but during the Roosevelt administration the names of Jews, of Catholics, of members of Italian and Slavic ethnic groups became prominent. One has a sense of large numbers of groups being brought into American society and government to a degree that had not been true in the past.

I think, too, that the nature of American liberalism changed sharply in the 1930's. Aside from the great proliferation of the functions of the federal government, there was a shift of another sort. It suddenly occurred to liberals that they could *buy* reforms. Expenditures by the national government could achieve all kinds of social changes. They turned away from Poor Richard's values of thrift; they rejected the orthodoxies of the old economics. The long tradition of limitations on the power of government was broken. There was a sense of a boundless range of activities which the state could undertake. This is one of the big differences, I think, between the Hoover era and the Roosevelt era. Related to this was the end of fatalism about the business cycle. No longer did men believe that they had to wait out a depression, that somehow a depression was the judgment of a wrathful God. The New Deal created countercyclical tools. Later administrations have not always been willing to use them, but they've been there.

J.A.G.   What are the chief unanswered questions about the period that you think historians should investigate?

W.E.L.   The largest single question is, "How much social change actually took place?" This is related to the question of continuity and discontinuity. Does one see the New Deal and the Great Depression as an outgrowth of the 1920's and the Progressive era, or as being a sharp break with the past? The answers to these questions will affect our interpretation of subsequent history. How much welfare has been accorded under the Welfare State? Has social security in fact been achieved? It's often said that the Fair Labor Standards Act of 1938 was inadequate, and certainly it was. And yet admirers of the New Deal might reply, "In America you begin by establishing the principle and then you make it better. The minimum wage has been raised steadily over the years. If it is still too low, is this a fault of the New Deal or of subsequent generations?"

Historians should also look at what the range of actual possibilities were for Roosevelt instead of imposing on his period our latter-day concerns. It's often said that the Supreme Court fight and other developments cut short reform, but it's not altogether clear what Roosevelt would have advocated if it had not been for these setbacks.

And despite all the writing on the New Deal, it's remarkable how many of the big stories have yet to be told. We have no adequate histories of most of the important New Deal agencies. There is no adequate book on the NRA, for example, or TVA, or the AAA program. One of the most glaring deficiencies in our scholarship involves the story of the movement of financial control from Wall Street to Washington. How exactly did the Securities and Exchange Commission affect the operation of Wall Street?

I think, too, that we've given a great deal more attention to the New Deal than we have to the Great Depression. A lot of the social history of the Depression has yet to be written. The Depression in America ought to be looked at as an aspect of the worldwide depression.

J.A.G. What is your opinion of the New Left interpretation of the New Deal era?

W.E.L. There hasn't really been very much on it; no book sums up a New Left interpretation of the New Deal. Although the implications of the New Left approach are being heard more and more at history conventions and in articles in scholarly journals, the most sustained effort has been the essay by Barton Bernstein in *Towards a New Past*.

Actually, there is no basic distinction between the New Left and the Old Left in interpreting the New Deal. All of us who were raised in the Roosevelt era and lived through the intellectual arguments of the 1940's grappled with the Marxist critique of the New Deal. The attacks of Marxist critics were quite sharp; for instance, Stolberg and Vinton's comment that there was nothing that the New Deal had done in agriculture that an earthquake could not have done better. No New Left critic has damned the New Deal with more abandon than the old Marxists.

The main contribution of the New Left has been its emphasis on participatory democracy. This, too, is something that has interested me since I wrote on the works council movement in Germany and England in Franz Neumann's seminar. It seems to me rather curious that given this interest the New Left historians have not chosen to look at the various evidences of participatory democracy in the 1930's: the AAA production control associations and the "grass-roots democracy" of the TVA and the soil conservation and grazing districts. If they did, they would discover that experiences with participatory democracy in the 1930's, like those with the modern poverty program, often did not turn out very well.

There's something rather ironical about the New Left approach. Their main targets are the "consensus" historians who homogenized American history, and yet their own approach homogenizes American history to a far greater degree by making it appear that nothing really ever happened. Since socialism was not attained, they seem to suggest, no other development really had much significance. In short, they are interested less in what happened in the 1930's than in what did not happen—the triumph of socialism.

I took part in a panel on the Left and the New Deal with Arthur M. Schlesinger, Jr., and Irving Howe a couple of years ago. One of the members of the audience was Roosevelt's former adviser, Ben Cohen. Cohen got up and chided all three of us gently, saying that we were talking about the ardent New Dealers and forgetting that this was also the administration of conservatives like Cordell Hull and the banker Jesse Jones. No adequate history of the 1930's can overlook the fact not merely that Roosevelt had to contend with the Jesse Joneses, but also that the great majority of ordinary people rejected extreme solutions to the problems of the day. New Left historians accuse their predecessors of being elitists who deny the virtues of participatory democracy, and yet they don't know what to make of the fact that the mass of citizens in the 1930's did not support radical movements and were enthusiastic about Roosevelt. They're left with the rather lame (and incidentally elitist) explanation that the masses simply did not know what was good for them and were swept away by Rooseveltian rhetoric.

J.A.G.   What are the half-dozen or so books that you would recommend to persons interested in the subject we have been discussing? In each case would you indicate briefly what the particular contribution of the volume is?

The most important study, of course, is Arthur M. Schlesinger, Jr.'s *The Age of Roosevelt* (1957–60), a three-volume synthesis by an historian who is sympathetic to the New Deal. Probably the best critique from a conservative viewpoint is still Raymond Moley's *After Seven Years* (1939). The major biography is Frank Freidel's, also in three volumes (1952–56), which carries through the 1932 election. The most discerning memoir is Frances Perkins' *The Roosevelt I Knew* (1956). James Mac-Gregor Burns's *Roosevelt: The Lion and the Fox* (1956) is a lively political biography which claims that F.D.R. missed an opportunity for party realignment, and Rexford G. Tugwell's *The Democratic Roosevelt* (1957) examines the period from the viewpoint of a social planner. Especially good on economic aspects are John M. Blum's *From the*

Morgenthau Diaries (3 volumes, 1959–1969) and Ellis Hawley's *The New Deal and the Problem of Monopoly* (1966). There is no adequate history of the Depression, but Irving Bernstein's *The Lean Years* (1960) is helpful on the early years. However, a small list of titles does not begin to suggest the great number of first-rate monographs now available on the New Deal.

Robert H. Ferrell

The United States in World Affairs: 1918–1941

Among students of American diplomacy between the two world wars, Professor Robert H. Ferrell of Indiana University ranks as one of the most productive and provocative. His *Peace in Their Time: The Origins of the Kellogg-Briand Pact* (1952) and his *American Diplomacy in the Great Depression: Hoover–Stimson Foreign Policy, 1929–1933* (1957) are each marked by solid scholarship and lively, colorful writing. Professor Ferrell is also editor of the series *The American Secretaries of State and Their Diplomacy*, to which he has personally contributed studies of Secretaries Frank B. Kellogg (1963), Henry L. Stimson (1963), and George C. Marshall (1967). He is also the author of an important textbook, *American Diplomacy: A History* (1959), and, with Howard H. Quint, he has edited *The Talkative President: The Off-the-Record Press Conferences of Calvin Coolidge* (1964). As the interview reveals, Professor Ferrell has some highly original and stimulating things to say about post-World War I foreign relations and the men who made and carried out American policy.

John A. Garraty Professor Ferrell, how did World War I affect the average American's conception of the role that the United States should play in world affairs?

Robert H. Ferrell I think it affected it adversely. Around the turn of the century and perhaps until 1914, there was a good deal of uncollected idealism in the United States, but unfortunately this idealism then came to nothing during the First World War. People misconstrued the events of the war and the purposes of the European allies, and rather quickly decided that the American war effort was not going to solve European problems. In fact, this idealism came to less than nothing because it turned into a dislike of Europe and anything that came from Europe.

One could almost argue that if the United States had not gotten into the First World War it might have done some things more constructive for the peace of Europe. It might have involved itself with the political problems of Europe that were the essential problems, and perhaps helped to solve them. Instead, we produced a series of advices and programs which the Europeans didn't need, but sometimes took simply to please us.

J.A.G. I'm not sure I understand what you mean by European political problems.

R.H.F. Europe's problems were problems of power—of boundaries, of economic relations, of using force to preserve peace. Americans didn't want to touch these problems after 1918.

J.A.G. Was this attitude a product of the war itself, or of the controversy over the Versailles Treaty and American entry into the League of Nations?

R.H.F. Mainly of the war. The Versailles Treaty, its rejection by the Senate, the problems of President Wilson—these things have engaged historians, and of course they engaged the American people, but I think it was the experience of two million American troops in France, this mass tourism if you will, that disillusioned the nation about Europe. It had never happened before—the generality of Americans going to Europe. Previously, only the Boston and New York upper crust traveled in Europe, and they saw a very special part of Europe. Suddenly, two million soldiers from all over the country, Captain Harry Truman of Missouri being one of them, saw another, and in a sense the worst, part of Europe. This was not a pleasant experience.

J.A.G. What role do you think that Wilson's idealism played in this reaction? Did his setting of exalted goals for the United States which could not be achieved influence it?

R.H.F. It's rather easy to point out Wilson's mistakes now. I think historians have especially enjoyed doing so because Wilson was himself an historian. He pitched his rhetoric too high. But one could argue that, if it were possible to erase Wilson from the equation, it might not have made much difference.

J.A.G. You say that the experience of American soldiers in Europe made them anti-European?

R.H.F. This is evident in whatever correspondence of the 1920's one picks up. The generality of manuscript collections in the Library of Congress bear testimony to it. Dislike of Europe is a common theme in all of this material.

J.A.G. Do you mean letters written by men who had served in the Army?

R.H.F. Yes. I could start with my own father, and move from there rather easily to statements by Harry Truman—the short section in his memoirs about life in his battery, for example.

J.A.G. How did this differ from the "traditional" suspicion of European standards of morals and society that one finds in American writings as far back as those of Thomas Jefferson?

R.H.F. That's a good question. Jefferson saw France in the 1780's, and he never forgot it; if before he wrote that cities were sores on the body politic, after that he was sure they were. But there was an exaggeration of American criticism in the 1920's, a perhaps deeper conviction and certainly a more widespread one.

J.A.G. Is the historian's strategy of dividing Americans into interventionists and isolationists useful for understanding American policy between the two world wars?

R.H.F. This strategy of putting people either into one category or the other has its advantages. We cannot know or describe everything and show all its complexities, so we have to shear off some of the truth, I suppose, as we try to describe the past. Yet having said that categories are useful, I think we must be especially careful of the word "interventionist." There were no interventionists in the sense in which we use that word today. Most so-called interventionists in the 1920's merely wished to apply moral force to the problems of Europe. Some might have been willing to use real force in the Far East (provided it wasn't very much force). But in Europe no one was ready to use military power or even economic influence. A few kind expressions together with much free advice (we like to give advice to Europeans), this was how these interventionists hoped to solve the problems of Europe. They were not willing to get into the problems of the balance of power in Europe, which essentially was the problem of Germany. They liked to think that the Germans had turned over a new leaf when they set up the Weimar Republic; the very fact of establishing the republic seemed sufficient, and we thought we had done something at that point and really didn't need to do any more. And I don't think intervention ran beyond advice-giving after that.

J.A.G. Are you saying, in effect, that *everyone* in America was an isolationist?

R.H.F. It would be better to say that there was a spectrum of isolationism. At one end stood those who believed that the less one had to do with Europe the better; on the other, those willing to join the League of Nations and particularly to participate in its various humanitarian projects. The interventionists of the 1920's and 1930's might now properly be called isolationists.

J.A.G. I'm not sure I understand.

R.H.F. I think that most Americans were, by present-day standards, isolationists.

J.A.G. If everyone was by modern standards isolationist, how, then, can one distinguish between isolationists like Senators Hiram Johnson and William E. Borah, and "isolationists" like Secretary of State Charles Evans Hughes?

R.H.F. Borah is perhaps the most interesting and maybe even the most representative man of the period. He was essentially negative. He always had some great proposal that he was about to advance, but he never quite advanced it. Meanwhile he enjoyed himself taking apart the going notions of the moment. For example, he was in favor of a league but not *that* league; he was in favor of *a* world court, but not the court which was proposed by the League of Nations.

Secretary of State Charles Evans Hughes was, I think, mainly a legalist. He contributed little beyond advancing the disarmament conference of 1921–22. One could argue that his secretaryship was not his most important public service.

J.A.G. Some Americans in the 1920's wanted the United States to join the League of Nations, others were opposed. Some favored joining the World Court, others were opposed. Were these divisions simply ad hoc reactions to particular situations? Was there no underlying difference of world view? If not, how can the two positions be defined?

R.H.F. I suppose that having quibbled over words, I would argue that it's not very helpful to try to create new words. We might just as well live with the words "isolationist" and "interventionist," understanding that they had a meaning which is not our present-day meaning.

J.A.G. Was the League of Nations in your judgment a good idea? Was the world, and especially the United States, ready for international cooperation to the extent that the League called for?

R.H.F. I think that it's entirely possible that if we had joined the League of Nations the League might have been the worse for it. Let me explain.

J.A.G. I wish you would!

R.H.F. The basic problem of Europe after the war was Germany, and a basic tension existed between the French and the British with regard to

Germany. The British, to reduce their position to a street phrase, argued that if one were nice to the Germans they would be nice to you. The French believed that the best way to handle the Germans was to put the lid on them and let them live with some of their problems. I think that if we had gotten into the League we would have sided with the British. This, then, would have given the Germans a latitude in European affairs which in fact they only obtained in the 1930's. I would contend, and perhaps this is an anti-German view, that the Germans were so embittered by their loss of the First World War that the success of Hitler or someone similar to him was only a matter of time, and that in retrospect the best policy toward Germany was to contain Germany, forcefully if necessary. If the United States had joined the League we would have had a Hitler a decade sooner.

J.A.G. To what degree was American foreign policy between the two wars influenced by domestic political considerations?

R.H.F. I think that the politicians of the 1920's and 1930's, when they turned to questions of foreign policy, rather accurately reflected the feelings of the American people, except that, being uncertain about what women's suffrage would mean, they gave a little bit more weight and credence to the opinions of such people as Carrie Chapman Catt and other women peace leaders than their real influence deserved. Apart from that exaggeration, I think that politics generally reflected, almost mirror-like, the state of opinion in this country on foreign affairs. I see little evidence that politicians made points in foreign policy for partisan political purposes.

J.A.G. Did economic interests influence the shape of foreign policy?

R.H.F. The question of the influence of economics on politics has been much debated. The Great Depression focused the attention of Americans on economic problems as never before in their history, and it became popular to attribute economic purposes to all sorts of actions which may not have been economic in purpose at all. Misapplying the feelings of the 1930's to the mood of the 1920's inspired a number of historical interpretations about the concern of the government for economic interests in foreign policy. Some historians insisted that Herbert Hoover turned the Department of Commerce into a machine for soliciting business abroad. They pointed out that the first commercial attachés were appointed in this period, whereas earlier the support that the State Department gave to foreign commerce had been desultory and almost completely unorganized. One can grant this and yet say that the political purposes of the government were not much expressed through economic pressures. I don't think that people do large things for economic reasons, although they often do small things that way. I certainly don't see our policy abroad as being shaped by economics. There was, for example, much talk in the 1930's about the economic aspects of our policy in Latin America, notably in Nicaragua. But the major American investments in Latin America were in Cuba and Mexico. Only a few million American dollars were invested in Nicaragua. The revolution of the later 1920's in Nicaragua, which admittedly involved several thousand American marines, had almost nothing to do with economics. It resulted from the well-intentioned effort of Nicaraguans and of the United States to rid the government of the awful political alternation which had been tearing the country apart ever since the nineteenth century. I've seen some correspondence in Sate Department files which indicates that the presidency of Nicaragua was sold for $30,000 in 1925–26. In that sense it was an economic arrangement, but I don't think there was anything more to it.

J.A.G.   Was the Washington disarmament conference in 1921 a diplomatic triumph for the United States?

R.H.F.   The Washington Conference, considering what it did for the navies of Britain, the United States, and Japan, was, I think, a considerable success. Not only did it establish a reasonable ratio for the navies of the three great naval powers, but it coupled this with political arrangements in the Far East. It brought Japan to a kind of judgment after fifteen or twenty years, during which the Japanese had been able to operate rather freely in the Far East. The Japanese had moved against the Chinese in 1894, and against the Russians ten years later. They had taken the German colonies in China in 1914. It was impossible to stop this expansion while the war was going on. That was the purpose of the Washington Conference. It was a marvelous combination of bringing Japan to account and achieving some helpful limitation in the number of battleships and aircraft carriers. Of course, the arrangement collapsed in the 1930's, beginning with the London Conference in 1930. But in the context of the problems of the 1920's, I think it was quite a successful conference. (One could even argue that it was the only successful disarament conference we've ever participated in.)

J.A.G.   It has been said in criticism of the settlement that the naval ratio agreement misled the American people, that while it gave the United States a larger navy than Japan, the particular 5:3 ratio assured Japanese domination of the Western Pacific—that in effect we were surrendering the Philippines to Japan any time the Japanese really wanted to take them. What is your opinion of this line of reasoning?

R.H.F.   It's true that the Philippines were vulnerable, but not as a result of the Washington disarmament conference. They were vulnerable from the moment we took them in 1898. The files of the War Department are full of references to the fact that the American position in the Philippines was indefensible. This was a well-known fact before the First World War. The 5:3 ratio made no difference.

J.A.G.   Professor Ferrell, you have written an important book on the Kellogg-Briand Pact of 1928. Will you explain why this toothless attempt to outlaw war seemed so important to many people at that time?

R.H.F.   After the First World War the American people were tired of involvement in Europe. In writing about this period most historians use Harding's invented word "normalcy." I suppose it's as good as any. Using this word, one can say that Americans chose to enjoy life. After all, they had a higher standard of living than any people had ever had up to that time. Nonetheless, there was considerable feeling that somehow we had not done what we should. Many Americans thought that while the Europeans were fooling with the League of Nations and generally pursuing their own rivalries (which the United States should of course keep out of), their country had some responsibility which it was not undertaking.

Much unformed peace sentiment in this country was attaching itself to what I would say in retrospect were foolish ideas, such as the World Court, and arbitration and conciliation treaties. This sentiment gathered in 1927–28 to support the proposal, first made by Aristide Briand of France and then shrewdly amended by the State Department, which we call the Kellogg-Briand Pact.

Secretary of State Kellogg, who started the whole thing as a maneuver against Briand, came to think that what he was doing was of very large importance. President Coolidge was always lukewarm to the proposal, but he probably felt that it wouldn't hurt anyone and that he could go back to his fishing in the Black Hills.

Kellogg had for a short time the support of the almost united peace sentiment of the United States: the educators, the preachers, the League of Nations people. But six months after ratification of the treaty came the stock-market crash, whereupon Americans turned to other, perhaps more important, thoughts. In one sense, however, it really was a great treaty for its time because it marked the first serious American effort, apart from the intervention in the world war, to amend the policies and perhaps the future of Europe.

J.A.G.   Why did Kellogg think the treaty so important?

R.H.F.   Frank B. Kellogg was a man whom many contemporaries made fun of. He had been defeated for re-election to the Senate in 1922 by a dentist named Hendrik Shipstead. It was said, perhaps correctly, that Coolidge had been nice to Kellogg, first sending him as American Ambassador to England and then making him Secretary of State, largely because Kellogg had been nice to Coolidge when Coolidge was only a Vice President and when other Senators weren't paying much attention to him. Kellogg did not have a college education. He did not understand the mysteries of the French language. When he saw the phrase "M. Briand," he didn't know that "M." stood for "Monsieur." He used to go to a hairdresser in Washington to get his hair curled, and he was very proud of one lock of hair, which showed prominently in all his photographs. I suppose he thought he was a great man.

But Kellogg was a man of many fine qualities. He was not merely a good lawyer; he had been President of the American Bar Association in 1912. In the Progressive era he had been *the* trust buster. He had, after all, sued the Standard Oil Company, and he had won. He knew not merely the law but the workings of American politics. Coolidge appointed him, I think, because Kellogg's views were largely those of Coolidge.

Why, then, did he go for such a fatuous proposition as the Kellogg Pact? I think he did so because of his age—he was over seventy—and his desire for greatness, for the public approbation which, in fact, came to him. I think that's the answer, but I want to add hastily that in many ways he *was* a great man.

J.A.G. You said earlier that the idea of the United States participating in the World Court was "foolish." Why do you think so?

R.H.F. The World Court was largely an American proposition. It was the reigning idea of American international lawyers, and it was pushed by Elihu Root, who had a large part in its establishment when the protocol was drawn up in 1920. But it was not important for the peace of the world. It could not apply to the grand political problems of Europe, or even those of the Far East or Latin America. It could apply only to disputes over tiny islands or small minorities, or boundaries of a minor nature. I would argue that it was not worth the intense concentration which the peace people gave to it, and which American lawyers gave to it, and even American politicians.

J.A.G. Do you mean that opposition to the Court rose out of a misapprehension of its importance? That people were opposed to it because they thought it was more important than it in fact was?

R.H.F. Yes and no. The same misconception which focused attention on it produced the enormous concentration of nit-picking by critics. Actually, the Senate accepted the Court with five conditions, which the other members refused to accept until Elihu Root went to Europe in 1929 and persuaded them to do so. Whereupon the Senate turned the protocol down. But with or without conditions, the Court was never important. I understand that even today it has practically no business.

J.A.G.   Would you discuss American policy toward Latin America between the wars? Was there any significant change in the policies pursued by the United States?

R.H.F.   I think there was a break, but not until the 1930's. As soon as the World War broke out it was clear that whatever influence Germany or any other possible enemy nation might have in Latin America was going to be finished by the war. Thus imperialism was no longer necessary. But during the 1920's withdrawal was slow. A nation cannot easily pull out of a complex situation merely because involvement is no longer necessary.

Policy was no longer based on strategic considerations. In the best sense of American national ideals, efforts to be helpful, to move Latin-American nations along what seemed the road to good international behavior, were attempted. And of course these nations, realizing that the old strategic purpose and its implied tool, military force, no longer existed, took advantage of the situation.

The policy of the country was benign and well-wishing, but it was impossible to pull the plug and walk out. In 1928 Hughes told the Latin Americans as much in a speech—which he, in retrospect, thought the greatest act of his career. During a conference at Havana, Hughes said that the United States would not stand by while Americans were, as he put it, "butchered in the jungle." His remark was almost the last defense of intervention, whether for the purpose of imperialism or "protective" imperialism, or simply for maintaining a sort of missionary policy in Latin America. In December of 1928, President-elect Hoover toured Latin America and made all sorts of declarations of nonintervention. (In some of these speeches he used the phrase "good neighbor," and later claimed that he was the inventor of the "Good Neighbor Policy" rather than Franklin Roosevelt.) The government early understood how times had changed after 1917–18, and wanted to pull out but couldn't do so easily.

J.A.G.   The United States certainly has vital strategic interests in the Caribbean area, interests which have repeatedly appeared to be threatened, most recently in the Cuban missile crisis of 1962. Looking back at the whole period since the Spanish-American War, could an argument be made that we should have been more frankly imperialistic? Would the United States, and perhaps even the Caribbean nations, have been better off if, after 1898, we had taken the entire Caribbean area directly into our orbit?

R.H.F.   One can make a very good argument in favor of that. It has sometimes been made in the case of Nicaragua, where the United States intervened just enough to maintain order. This intervention was somewhat analogous to British activities in Egypt, where the British worked through the Egyptian bureaucracy and all the institutions of the Turkish rule. In India, on the other hand, they made major changes and their impact was much more constructive. If we had taken over the government of Nicaragua, more constructive results might have occurred. And the same principle may be applied to Cuba, to the Dominican Republic and, in view of the horrible regime there now, to Haiti. This is partly retrospective. Probably I'm suggesting what at the time was an impossible policy. But perhaps we should have done it.

J.A.G. What is your opinion of the record in foreign relations of the post-World War Presidents, Harding and Coolidge?

R.H.F. Harding's reputation is in the throes of re-evaluation because of the discovery after many years of his papers, but when the re-evaluation is completed we may not know a great deal more than what we do now. Harding was not greatly interested in foreign affairs. I don't think he had any feeling for Europe at all. He was basically a small-town Ohioan —a person who liked to talk, who enjoyed the hustings, who liked to get out and, as he put it, "bloviate." Foreign affairs were outside his understanding. It has been said that he was in safe hands because of his Secretary of State, Charles Evans Hughes. However, his own lack of initiative in foreign affairs I think limited Hughes, who, being a man of conservative instincts, usually hesitated to move very far because he knew that he would have to take Harding with him. So Harding's impress on foreign affairs was virtually nil.

Coolidge, however, deserves much more credit than historians have given him, both in domestic and foreign policy. He did not advance any large policies beyond supporting Kellogg in the Kellogg-Briand Pact. His one personal essay was the Geneva naval conference in 1927, which ran for a few weeks in the summer and turned to nothing, and in fact embittered Coolidge about Europeans.

But if Coolidge was not much more adventuresome than Harding, he did understand the problems of the day. I think Coolidge was an intelligent man and well versed in European problems. He was not much of a letter writer; therefore, it's difficult to find out what Coolidge thought about things. But there is one place where his opinions have been recorded—his press conferences. These were meetings with the Washington Press Corps, a group of perhaps a half-dozen persons in those days. He referred to these reporters as "pupils," and he would lecture them as a teacher lectures to a class. Whatever he said was not quotable unless he gave express permission. Verbatim transcripts of the conferences show that Coolidge expressed his views on all sorts of subjects in great detail, presumably without notes. I find extraordinary his knowledge of domestic and foreign affairs, judging from these transcripts.

Coolidge also had a feeling for how far one could go in foreign affairs without raising domestic complications. He was a man of great good judgment. He has always been credited as being a funny man. He was witty, but I think the wit really showed the keenness of his intellect. He doled out his humor in a sort of Vermont way that always had a purpose, and it showed, I think, the acuteness of his mind. He realized that for Europe the latter 1920's were a much better era than the early 1920's. It looked as though postwar European problems were on the way to solution. Germany was recovering and apparently peaceable. In Italy, Mussolini at that time did not seem the malign creature he later became —he appeared to be confining his attention to such things as clearing up the Roman streets and trying to solve the traffic problem. Coolidge, viewing Europe in this Indian summer of its life, felt that it wasn't necessary to be much concerned with the Continent.

He certainly had a wonderful sense of knowing when to do nothing, which is not a typical American attribute. He assumed that many problems would solve themselves without action. This was his attitude in domestic affairs and likewise in foreign affairs. Maybe he was right with regard to the Europe of his time. It was the Depression that turned everything askew, and this, of course, he did not anticipate. But then even John Maynard Keynes himself, the great economist of the 1930's, had no idea of the importance of the Depression until well into the 1930's.

J.A.G.   The first occasion when the question of acting to stop the aggression which eventually led to World War II came up was the Manchurian incident of 1931. What did the United States government do at that time and why?

R.H.F.   Many publicists at the time, and many historians later, called the actions of the United States in the Manchurian crisis a turning point— that's the phrase they liked—in the course of world affairs. The usual argument is that if the United States had faced up to the Japanese more quickly, with force or the threat of force rather than with words, the Second World War would not have occurred. The contention is that the failure to stop the Japanese was a great object lesson to Hitler, who came into power a year and a half later, and to Mussolini, already in power and becoming dangerous. Mussolini then tried his "experiment" in Ethiopia, which met with no large objection, and then Hitler, seeing Japan and Italy so successful in their aggression, proceeded to capitalize on the situation in 1938.

If this argument is correct, one can contend that the United States perhaps touched off a series of events which led to war in Europe in 1939 and eventually to Pearl Harbor. But I think that this was not quite the case. Some people argued at the time that it was possible to divorce the problems of the Far East from those of Europe; many more contended that any unresisted aggression was likely to affect Europe. The usual way of describing the situation was to say that anyone who thought that you could isolate aggression was being unrealistic and even stupid. But I believe that the problems of Manchuria, which the Japanese, in their own way, were trying to solve in 1931–33, were not much connected to the problems of Europe, and that if the United States had better understood Japanese and Chinese affairs at the time, and had sensed what the mood of both of those governments in the early 1930's was, it might have made an arrangement in Manchuria that would have been quite acceptable for the Far East and would have had no repercussions in Europe. The tendency to equate the Far East and its problems with the problems of Europe was in this instance unfortunate.

Next, let us talk about what the United States did. Our policy, as we can now see from the documents of the State Department, the diary of Secretary of State Henry L. Stimson, and other papers, is clear enough. It passed through stages. When the incident occurred, the reaction of the American government was extremely cautious. There was a feeling that we ought to find out what was actually going on, to give the Japanese a chance to save face—to control their troops, was the way Stimson put it—and to bring the situation into the control of the Tokyo government rather than that of the supposedly mad militarists in Manchuria. This point of view lasted for several weeks. The government then attempted a rather difficult diplomatic maneuver, sending Charles G. Dawes to Paris to push the League of Nations Council, to which of course the United States did not belong, into some sort of action. Dawes failed, at least partly because he offered no specific plan for action, and the League merely sent an investigating commission, which it eventually persuaded the Japanese to accept. The investigating commission contained an unofficial American member, Major General Frank R. McCoy. The assumption was that the Japanese would not move any more troops into Manchuria while the commission was in the Far East.

This Lytton Commission was appointed in early December of 1931, and did not report until the following October. Meanwhile, with the consent—or at least the tacit support—of the government in Tokyo, Japanese troops in Manchuria continued to advance. This led the American government to adopt a new policy. On January 7, 1932, Secretary Stimson announced what became known as the Stimson Doctrine: The United States would not admit the legality of any situation *de facto* or any treaty or agreement set up in violation of existing treaties and affecting China.

No sooner had we announced this doctrine than the Japanese began to attack Shanghai. Our policy then moved into a fourth stage, signalized by the publication of the so-called Borah letter on February 24, 1932. This was a blunt restatement of the traditional American position toward the Far East, established in the Open Door notes at the turn of the century: There must be no violations of the "territorial integrity" of China.

Finally, there was a fifth American policy shift, an effort to get Japan "convicted" in the League of Nations, to prove to the world through the vote of the League that the Japanese had done something they shouldn't have done in Manchuria.

Stimson, being a lawyer, thought that this would have great effect upon the Japanese. Instead, it led only to a scene in the League of Nations. When the League made its judgment, the Japanese simply stood up and walked out. (The chief Japanese spokesman, Matsuoka, said that as Christ had been crucified on the Cross, so was Japan being crucified by the League of Nations. When Matsuoka passed through the United States en route to Tokyo, he told a reporter that this was not quite the case. The nations of the world, he said, had taught Japan poker, in the course of which tuition they themselves had picked up most of the chips. But after they had gotten most of the chips they pronounced the game immoral and took up contract bridge.)

I think that our policy was for the time not a bad policy, but it was not effective. When one finds that having done several things yields no result, I suppose one always wishes that he hadn't done anything at all. It's clear now that nothing short of military force would have stopped the Japanese, and this was politically impossible in the United States in the midst of the Depression. It was almost impossible ten years later in 1941. After all, it took an outright attack upon American territory to bring the United States into the war.

This being the case, it was perhaps a mistake to have done anything, but as for the accusation that by allowing the Japanese to go ahead in Manchuria, we insured the success of Hitler—that's merely foolish. Europe had its own problems, which were not related immediately or even very remotely to the problems of the Far East. Manchuria itself was a very special situation. It was possible for certain Japanese actions to take place in the Far East without having any effect upon Europe. One could even argue that a man like Hitler would have done what he did no matter what the world had done about Manchuria.

J.A.G.   You said that it was politically impossible for the United States to use force in 1931–32 against Japan. Public opinion in America would not have countenanced that. Did the political situation change in any way when superficially similar situations developed in Europe, beginning with the Ethiopian crisis?

R.H.F.   In the Manchurian crisis, the government of the United States acted with almost no reliable information. In fact, the details of all of Japan's policy are just beginning to come out now, as Japanese scholars are working through the archives. We didn't know why the Japanese acted the way they did. But with regard to European affairs, of course the purposes of Hitler and Mussolini and the causes of their actions were fairly well known. Nevertheless, from the Ethiopian crisis through the Austrian and Czechoslovakian and Polish debacles, the Americans showed even less willingness to act, even in terms of giving advice, than they had displayed during the Manchurian affair.

I'm not altogether sure why this was so. Perhaps the intense popular fear and dislike of European politics was responsible, perhaps the feeling that events had already passed beyond any control of the United States. It may have been a comfortable belief that the British and French could take care of the Germans in event of war. But the fact is that, as European politics cascaded into war, the United States did almost nothing.

J.A.G.   Wasn't the American neutrality legislation in effect a policy related to events in Europe?

R.H.F.   I suppose so, in the sense that dislike of European politics was formalized in these neutrality pronouncements. To have a "policy" of neutrality, no matter what, is, in effect, to have no policy.

J.A.G.   Are you saying that in the Manchurian situation, where our national interest was relatively uninvolved, we had a positive policy, but that in the European crises, where our interests were much greater, we had no policy?

R.H.F.   Yes. That sounds like a paradox and perhaps it is, but of course it would have been safer to intervene in the Far East, since after all the situation didn't have the possibility of turning on us—we thought. There's a dictum attributed to Mahan which seems—whether Mahan actually said it or not—to characterize aptly our policy at the turn of the century: In Europe, abstention; in the Far East, co-operation (presumably with the British); in Latin America, dominance.

J.A.G.   Did the European powers react more forcefully against the aggression of Italy and Germany, considering how much more directly they were threatened, than they had against Japan in Manchuria?

R.H.F.   In considering the actions of the European powers, one comes back to the conflict between the British and the French over Germany. In the 1920's, the French policy prevailed because the French were more active in the League of Nations, but in the 1930's, perhaps tired of trying to contain Germany, France surrendered leadership to Britain—at the wrong time, as we now see it. The differences between the French and the British enabled the Germans to operate very shrewdly. The willingness of the British to give in to Hitler's early importunities was particularly unfortunate. It is wrong to say that the United States started the chain of events which led to 1939 by its reaction to the Manchurian crisis; it is much more accurate to say that the British began it in 1935 by making a naval arrangement with the Germans in direct violation of the Treaty of Versailles. This apparently convinced Hitler that anything he did short of war itself was likely to get the consent of the British and thereby the reluctant consent of the French. It was a most unfortunate thing. If there was one single event in the 1930's that opened the floodgates to Nazism, as Churchill put it, it was the Anglo-German naval agreement of 1935.

J.A.G.   What is your opinion of Herbert Hoover's performance in foreign policy?

R.H.F.   Hoover, a distinctly different personality from his two predecessors, was equally interesting. He has done himself a disservice by publishing the three volumes of memoirs, which he wrote on odd occasions after he left the presidency. There is an inflexibility in the memoirs, a waspishness which could not possibly raise his historical reputation. But the Hoover of 1929–33 was a man of large qualities, and the man best prepared for the presidency, one might argue, since John Quincy Adams.

J.A.G.   And also equally as unsuccessful a President as Adams?

R.H.F.   Equally unsuccessful, yes, and perhaps for the same reasons. Many comparisons can be made between Hoover and Adams. Hoover worked very hard. It was said that he worked about eighteen hours a day, and this is probably no exaggeration. He turned his attention to all sorts of details of the government. He was a very efficient person. He installed a telephone switchboard in the White House, and it was his custom to keep in close touch with the leading officers of the government. Any official could expect at almost any time of the working day to have the phone ring and hear the White House operator saying that the President was on the wire, whereupon President Hoover would come on with some comment or question. Of course, this often did more harm than good, because it brought Hoover into all sorts of situations which he should not, I think, have entered.

This was probably Hoover's worst mistake as President: failure to delegate authority. (Coolidge, incidentally, was a master at delegating authority.) Hoover had to do things himself. His penchant for detail hurt his presidential performance greatly. Cordell Hull once said that Hoover was a person of great vision: "He could see a mare's nest farther than any other living politician." With all of his qualities of mind (he was a very intelligent man) and with all of his experience not merely in American domestic politics but also in foreign affairs, he failed as President. He couldn't deal with novelties when they suddenly came upon him. The Great Depression was of course his greatest failure, but he failed also in foreign relations because he lacked the appreciation of Europe that his wide travels might have been expected to give him. He had a profound dislike of foreigners, particularly Frenchmen, but also, I think, of Europeans generally. He referred to Frenchmen, incidentally, as "frogs," the World War I term. I think it was his experience with the financial problems of Belgian relief, and then at the peace conference, that led him to this position. His experience before the war abroad, I might add, was largely in Asia, not so much in Europe.

J.A.G.   He was in Europe during most of the war, however.

R.H.F.   Right, but he emerged from the peace conference feeling that the Europeans had tried to do us in. I think he believed firmly in that old cliché, "Americans always win wars and lose peace conferences."

At any rate, when Hoover turned to foreign affairs he didn't seem to have much imagination. He would "carry forward," as he liked to put it, the policies of his predecessors. He continued efforts toward disarmament; he continued especially the idea of naval conferences. Beyond this he did not go. He did allow himself to be talked into the moratorium on international debts, and when that became an item of possible political importance he rather carefully attached his name to it. Yet this Hoover moratorium was essentially a negative policy, a policy of dealing with problems that had appeared prior to his administration and that were not solved simply by delaying them.

J.A.G.   Would you comment now on President Franklin D. Roosevelt's conduct of foreign relations?

R.H.F.   Roosevelt was in office for a little more than three terms, and while it's usually not profitable to discuss a President's actions in the framework of his terms of office, it so happened that his first term coincided with the period of preparation in European aggression. From 1933 to 1937, while the politics of Europe were moving in ways which hardly inspired confidence, there was still some hope that the peace of 1919 might prevail. In that period Roosevelt did almost nothing in foreign affairs other than to set on foot officially a policy toward Latin America which had been well in force prior to his accession. Most historians pick that phrase "Good Neighbor" out of his inaugural address, but it was just a chance remark; the expression, as Arthur P. Whitaker has shown, was used as far back as the early nineteenth century. It was just a piece of guff of a sort which was often expressed about Latin America. He did not really have an active policy even toward Latin America. It was the passive policy of nonintervention which had become feasible after the First World War. The first Roosevelt administration was not a time in which he made any sort of international reputation. If anything, his reputation went down after his action at the London Economic Conference in 1933, which was a completely irresponsible piece of diplomacy.

Beginning in 1937, Roosevelt took a stiff position toward Japan's resumption of the Far Eastern war. Later, at least verbally, he began to stand against Hitler when Hitler went first into Austria and then into Czechoslovakia and elsewhere. But, until the summer of 1940, his policy was not much more than verbal. Only with the destroyers-for-bases deal with Great Britain, which, while not of enormous aid to the Allies in itself, promised large assistance, did he begin to move seriously against Germany. It's possible, in fact, to argue that, until 1937, and perhaps even through 1939, Roosevelt's German policy was largely like that of Great Britain.

One can sense even before the election of 1940 that Roosevelt had decided that as President he simply had to move into the European arena. Then—and historians have long pointed this out—with the Lend-Lease Act in the spring of 1941, he came down unmistakably on the side of the democracies. This was a very large business, the Lend-Lease Act, clearly the most important act of foreign relations of his administration down to American entrance into the war. And he followed Lend-Lease with a policy which, although pursued surreptitiously, was almost equally important: the business of convoying ships to Great Britain.

That convoying is an interesting phase of Roosevelt's handling of foreign relations. It showed him, it seems to me, at his very worst as a President. As James MacGregor Burns has pointed out in his biography of Roosevelt, *The Lion and the Fox*, when F.D.R. was pursuing a great idea or a great purpose, he was almost irresistible, a wonderfully attractive national leader. But when the going was difficult, he was tempted to move sideways and become, as Burns puts it, the fox rather than the lion. The convoy issue brought out his worst qualities. There is no question at all that Charles A. Beard was correct in calling his policy deliberately deceptive. In *President Roosevelt and the Coming of the War* Beard brought together the almost extraordinary assertions of Roosevelt in the summer and early fall of 1941 about convoying. Roosevelt decided he had to convoy Lend-Lease materials, otherwise they would simply be sunk in the Atlantic by German submarines. But he didn't know how to get public support for convoying without lying about it. So he lied. He invented something which he called a "patrol," which was, he told the American people, something quite different from convoying. He said that a convoy and a patrol were analogous to a horse and a cow; they were two different animals, even if people wanted to think they were the same animal.

This particular example of press-conference pleasantry or joshing, at which he was a master, was a piece of misrepresentation, to put it mildly. He followed this up with a series of other deceptions, the most notable of which was his description of the attack by German submarines on the destroyer *Greer* in the early autumn of 1941. The *Greer* had been pursuing a submarine and broadcasting the submarine's position. It was only in desperation that the submarine launched a torpedo or two at the destroyer. Nonetheless, Roosevelt then went on the radio. In this broadcast, which it almost hurts to read, he said that the *Greer* was carrying the mail to Iceland. He added some more irrelevancies and misrepresentations and then announced that he'd given the Navy orders to sink all German submarines on sight. It was, I think, the worst act of his twelve-odd years as President.

It may be that if Roosevelt had told the American people what he was doing they would not have supported him. But I like to think that on a great issue such as convoying, they would have gone along had Roosevelt set all the facts before them.

J.A.G. Much criticism has been leveled by historians at the neutrality legislation of the 1930's. Can anything good be said about this legislation?

R.H.F. I suppose, in view of our experience in the First World War and all the criticism that was leveled at Wilson because of his decision to stand firm for the right of Americans to travel abroad belligerent vessels, the legislation of twenty years later made sense. It was better to define what the American choice, if there was one, on neutral rights should be.

I suppose the legislation did, as historians have said, apprise the European powers of just where we intended not to defend our rights. This is the result of any sort of definition. And one can argue that we did ourselves a disservice by being too plain.

But I suppose I'm hedging. Perhaps I should merely say that I don't know whether any good results flowed from the Neutrality Acts. There was an inevitability about this legislation. It has usually been ascribed to the investigations of the Nye Committee of 1934–36 into the causes of the First World War. I think that even had Nye not held those hearings, only part of which concerned the neutrality issue, some kind of definition was almost certain to come as soon as war threatened to erupt in Europe.

Some historians have argued that Wilson chose to defend the right of Americans to travel on belligerent vessels because he knew or sensed that this policy sooner or later would get the United States into conflict, which they presume he desired. I don't think that's true at all. Wilson took what to his generation seemed the common-sense view of the situation. He naturally interpreted the rights of Americans as broadly as he could, and in view of the fact that there had never before been a submarine issue, he did what one would have expected him to do.

J.A.G. If there was a certain inevitability about the neutrality legislation, and if Roosevelt, after 1939, was convinced that the national interest required active intervention in the war, doesn't that throw certain doubts on your estimate of the effectiveness of a more candid policy with regard to convoying? Wasn't the risk of candor enormous?

R.H.F.   I'm not sure. It's true that Roosevelt desired to see the United States in the war, and was, by any detached view of the situation, more certain to get his way by doing what he did.

J.A.G.   In other words, then, given the strong public sentiment for neutrality, a disingenuous policy was almost necessary.

R.H.F.   Perhaps.

J.A.G.   Do you feel that the Nye investigation had a large effect on the man-in-the-street's feeling about European entanglements, or did it simply reinforce attitudes that were already very strong?

R.H.F.   I'm sure the Nye investigation reinforced attitudes which already were strong. The investigation actually didn't turn up as much sensational evidence about war profiteering and "merchants of death," as Nye claimed.

J.A.G.   When Roosevelt began to change his mind about intervening in the war, what sort of people agreed with him?

R.H.F.   It is difficult to generalize, but persons who had traveled in Europe and who followed European affairs closely were the ones who took alarm, and many—those who had not tended to hold to the old attitudes—favored intervention.

Consider, as an example of the latter type, Senator Borah. He was Chairman of the Senate Foreign Relations Committee from 1924 to 1933 and the leading Republican spokesman on foreign affairs thereafter. He had never been outside the United States, not even to Canada or Latin America, not to mention Europe. He once said that he had intended several times to go abroad and he had applied for a passport once or twice, but something of importance had come up and he had not been able to go. So his knowledge of European affairs first-hand was nil. But ignorance did not prevent him from holding forth on the national interests and values of all the nations of the world he'd never seen.

J.A.G.   Did partisanship have much to do with public attitudes? Does the fact that Roosevelt was a Democrat explain why the Republican party seemed to be more isolationist than the Democratic in the 1930's?

R.H.F.   Some wits said that the Pacific was the Republican ocean and the Atlantic the Democratic one, that the Republicans had been in power when we took an interest in the Far East at the turn of the century and the Democrats when we went to war in Europe in 1917. I suppose the personality of Roosevelt, dominating the Democratic party, drove most of the isolationists out of that party, or at least put them off in a corner. And I suppose the need to oppose Roosevelt drove some Republican rhetoricians to statements which, when the chips were down, they were not prepared to back up. (During the election campaign of 1940,

Wendell Willkie made a statement almost akin to Roosevelt's famous statement about not sending "our boys" into a "foreign" war. When he was asked about it later, he said it was simply a piece of campaign rhetoric, and dismissed it.) There were, though, many die-hard isolationists, such as former President Hoover, in the Republican party of 1940.

J.A.G.   In what ways were the pressures that drew the United States into World War II different from those that led to American entry into the First World War?

R.H.F.   I think that historians now generally agree that it was Wilson's defense of neutral rights that led us into the first war. In the Second World War, American entrance resulted, I think beyond question, from the hard line that the administration and the American people took toward the Japanese. The administration was not willing to allow Japan to expand in China, and the public backed it up. On November 26, 1941, the very day on which the Japanese attack fleet sailed for Pearl Harbor, Secretary of State Cordell Hull sent a note to the Japanese which virtually asked them to get out of China entirely, an impossibility considering their involvement there, which went back to 1894. This policy brought the Japanese to the decision to attack Pearl Harbor.

Of course, Roosevelt's measures in support of the French and British had won a good deal of popular approval; if there was not a complete support for his policy toward Europe, there was at least no chance of our supporting Hitler. Once the war with Japan began, it was a foregone conclusion that we would fight against Hitler too, and he settled the question by declaring war on us.

J.A.G.   If Japan had not attacked Pearl Harbor, is it possible that we would *never* have entered the war in Europe?

R.H.F.   I think it's entirely possible that we would not have gotten into the war until perhaps 1943, and perhaps we might have stayed out altogether. It's an interesting question, because had we not been dragged in by the debacle of Pearl Harbor, all of 1942 would have gone by without the sort of mobilization which we needed to exert our strength in Europe, and if we had entered in 1943 we would not have had any effective forces available until 1945. By that time, the Russians probably would have rolled back the Germans—perhaps somewhat slower than in fact they did, but nonetheless, they would have kept their juggernaut going, and they would have gone all the way to Gibraltar and taken over all of Europe, and presumably the British Isles with it. We would have been mobilized by that time, but it would have been too late to save Europe.

J.A.G.   In other words, in your estimation the Germans would have lost whether we went into the war or not?

R.H.F. I think they could not have won against the Russians in view of what we know did happen. After all, up until 1944 and the invasion of France, the great bulk of the fighting was between the Russians and the Germans, and by that time the Russians clearly were rolling the Germans back. The Germans just didn't have the population to stand against the Russians.

J.A.G. The question of Pearl Harbor is, of course, very controversial. Did Roosevelt want the Japanese to attack some American interest directly so that the question of getting into the war would solve itself?

R.H.F. Charles C. Tansill, who was a writer of quality on nineteenth-century American foreign policy, wrote a book, *Back Door to War*, which had as its theme the notion that Roosevelt, unable to open the front door to war, then tried with the back door. He took on the Japanese, who were not as clever as the Germans, and he maneuvered them into starting a war with the United States.

This is an ingenious but unbelievable thesis. For example, the cost of this "maneuvering" was the Pacific fleet. Roosevelt's great interest in and love of the Navy, demonstrated by the many naval mementos at the Roosevelt Library in Hyde Park, suggest that he would have been the last person to sacrifice the Navy even for a supposedly great end. Furthermore, any kind of a plot would have involved many persons, and someone would surely have let something out of the bag. I might add that those who accept the "back door" theory have never been able to find any concrete documentary evidence. All they have is circumstantial evidence, which in itself is quite interesting.

J.A.G. Well, of course there is a difference between saying that Roosevelt wanted Pearl Harbor attacked and saying that he wanted to create a situation where Japan would attack somewhere so that the United States could enter the war.

R.H.F. If you put the case that way, I think it's quite true that Roosevelt was ready for an attack by the Japanese somewhere. The first place he thought that they might attack was Malaya; the second place, Thailand; the third place, the Dutch East Indies; the fourth place, the Philippines; and the fifth—Pearl Harbor. The situation was like that of President Polk in the Mexican War. Polk was glad the Mexicans attacked, because he wanted war. I think Roosevelt by December, 1941, was convinced that the Japanese had to be put down—that it was impossible to try to prop the British up in Europe while the British Empire was disintegrating in the Far East. Secretary Hull's note of November 26 to the Japanese was itself an apt expression of Roosevelt's feeling: Japan had just gone too far. The administration was ready for a Japanese war, and perhaps even invited one.

J.A.G. I still think that you're skirting around Tansill's argument. The

American people were reluctant to get into a fighting war. If the Japanese had attacked Malaya or Thailand as you indicate Roosevelt expected, would it not still have been extremely difficult to get Congress to declare war? Whereas an attack on *American* territory would, as it did, solve Roosevelt's "problem."

R.H.F.   The fact that they chose Pearl Harbor was not the first nor was it to be the last Japanese stupidity. They did it in a fit of logic. They figured that the Pearl Harbor fleet represented the largest and most dangerous force in the Far East that was hostile to them. They felt it had to be eliminated. It was a marvelous piece of logic, but it was very bad politics, because, as you say, even had there been an attack on the Philippines, Roosevelt would have had a devil of a time persuading Congress to declare war. But I think that by late 1941 Roosevelt was willing to go to the Congress and ask for war, even if it did not involve American territory. The fact is that the Japanese, with extraordinary foolishness, bailed him out by attacking Pearl Harbor.

J.A.G.   Can responsibility for the defeat at Pearl Harbor be laid on the shoulders of anyone "higher up" than the commanders on the scene, Admiral Kimmel and General Short?

R.H.F.   Some years ago I wrote an article appraising the literature of Pearl Harbor, in which I defended Admiral Kimmel, who was still living. I sent a copy of the article to Kimmel, and the old man wrote back a rather primitively typed and spelled letter, in which he reiterated his feeling that the blame for the destruction of the fleet rested, as he put it, in Washington. He believed this, so far as I know, down until the time of his death. His book, *Admiral Kimmel's Story,* did not receive good reviews, but what is important is that he pointed out, cleverly— and, I believe, truthfully—that Pearl Harbor was indefensible in 1941; that his predecessor, Admiral Richardson, had told Roosevelt this, and that Roosevelt had fired Richardson as a result. Kimmel was doing his best to make the place defensible, but almost no American position in the Pacific was defensible in December, 1941. It was Kimmel's bad fortune that the Japanese chose Pearl Harbor.

General MacArthur in Manila was much more culpable than the commanders in Pearl Harbor because MacArthur had several hours of warning and, despite this warning, lost his touted B–17 bombers, which were sitting on the ground. MacArthur, in a rather undignified manner, passed the blame to subordinates, and the question of responsibility was fudged, but it was not fudged at Pearl Harbor. Kimmel and Short were virtually forced into retirement. It was a disgraceful episode, and General Marshall later admitted manfully that he bore some of the responsibility for what had happened. Roosevelt never did admit to any responsibility. I feel very sorry for Kimmel. I think the responsibility ran all up and down the chain of command, and it probably reached well beyond that, into Congress, and probably to the American people.

J.A.G.   Do you have any thoughts about the breaking of the Japanese code, and the extraction of information about the Japanese plans for Pearl Harbor?

R.H.F.   Failure to use this intelligence at the time of Pearl Harbor was one of the great intelligence failures of the United States. The direct result was the creation of the Central Intelligence Agency six years later. After we got into the war, the Army and Navy repaired that mistake by winning at Midway an intelligence victory by using the code. The military later shot down Admiral Yamamoto through this same code. Indeed, we read Japanese messages down until the end of the war. But on the initial occasion when the code should have been used, we failed miserably.

J.A.G.   How is Roosevelt's place in history affected by his performance as a diplomat during the war? For example, he is said to have had a penchant for personal diplomacy. Would you comment on his relationships with the great foreign leaders with whom he dealt, Churchill and Stalin?

R.H.F.   Roosevelt's relations with these two men, Churchill and Stalin, were complex. When he first met Stalin at Teheran, he simply tried to impress his personality upon Stalin. The American war effort had not produced much of consequence in Europe as yet. There being no large, current issues between the two countries, it was a fairly successful meeting.

But at Yalta, when things got more concrete, the President found that he could not get altogether what he wanted from Stalin. He had to give on some things, and it doesn't seem that the good personal relations established at Teheran produced anything of moment. It would be difficult to show that Stalin gave in to the American President just because of any personal aura which Roosevelt created at either of these meetings.

His relations with Churchill, while still not yet entirely clear, were fascinating. Someone should write a book entitled *Roosevelt and Churchill*. They were, despite superficial cordiality, in the main uneasy relations. Churchill was too great a man, too properly calculating of the interests of Great Britain, to allow personal feelings to obtrude when he dealt with Roosevelt. He had to put up with a great deal from Mr. Roosevelt. Roosevelt liked to twit him about India and about the British Empire, and he liked to give him advice on all kinds of subjects on which Churchill was in fact much more experienced. Churchill was himself an advice giver of some note, and when he had to take advice from Roosevelt, it must have been one of the most difficult experiences of his career. But advice he did take, and he seems to have been very careful not to say anything personal about Roosevelt. This was one of the great marks of Churchill's quality as a statesman.

As the war progressed, and as the American contribution became larger and larger, Roosevelt liked to put himself in the position of mediating between the British and the Russians. This Churchill detested, as well he might have. But he didn't say anything, in order to preserve the friendship, which of course was the right thing to do.

J.A.G. Do you think that Roosevelt was too reliant on personal relationships?

R.H.F. I suppose so. The differences between the Americans and the Russians were potentially so large that no amount of personal glossing could have covered them. Roosevelt might have had more success had he allowed some of these problems to come up more quickly and then dealt with them. He followed a policy in itself quite supportable, that larger diplomatic questions ought to be postponed until the end of the war. Victory was the important thing. But it might have been better to have allowed some of those disagreements to emerge in 1943–44. Whether we could have then used our army in 1944 to counter some of the Russian demands, I'm not so certain, but at least the disagreements would have been out in the open. Then, perhaps, the postwar disillusion would have been less intense.

J.A.G. What were Roosevelt's hopes or intentions for a settlement after the war?

R.H.F. Roosevelt did not have a philosophical mind. He liked to deal with concrete problems. He felt that the problems of peace were essentially postwar. He felt also that the American troops would be withdrawn from Europe and probably that we could not do much about postwar Europe.

J.A.G. Was American foreign policy from 1918 to 1945 realistic or idealistic, in the sense that these terms have been used by historians like Robert Osgood and George Kennan?

R.H.F. Ever since George Kennan published his remarkable book *American Diplomacy* in 1951, students have been talking about realism and idealism, and splitting these philosophical hairs. Robert Osgood, in a less well-known but equally important book, has made the same point about idealism and realism. But I think both of these works obscure the realities of foreign policy. All life is a combination of ideals and interests. To paraphrase Jefferson—we are all realists, we are all idealists. One simply cannot separate these things.

If one looks at the history of American policy in the twentieth century, it is possible to argue that there has on occasion been more ideal than interest in foreign policy, that only since World War II has American policy displayed a reasonable combination of ideals and interests, a bringing together of power and diplomacy. It is foolish to ask: "Are we realists or idealists?" Where I disagree with both Kennan and Osgood is that I think we have to be both, whereas they think we should be, as they put it, realists. If one deals with the American public, one has to talk in ideals. There have to be doctrines. Except for John Kennedy, every President since Roosevelt has had a doctrine—the Truman doctrine, the Eisenhower doctrine.

J.A.G. What is your view of the so-called "revisionist" school of diplomatic historians?

R.H.F. One of my revered teachers, Harry Rudin, said years ago—and it's a point I like to remember—that we are all, as historians, revisionists, that we have to separate what happened from what people thought happened, and that the thought often gets quite remote from the actuality. The revisionists of the historiography of the First World War performed a useful task when they pointed out that what the nations said in 1914 and before was not always what they were doing. The publication of the documents in the 1920's, first by the Germans and then by the other leading powers, gave historians a field day, and they rewrote the history of the First World War. Their history was not always completely, shall we say, realistic, but it certainly showed aspects that contemporaries never even imagined had existed. But the fact that revisionists proved useful in regard to the First World War was picked up by a group with different purposes with regard to the Second World War. These people were in essence Roosevelt haters, determined to show that Roosevelt not merely moved the country toward socialism, but also took it into an unnecessary war. These revisionists have merely obscured the historical record.

J.A.G. What is your opinion of the "New Left" interpretation of the diplomatic history of this period?

R.H.F. The New Left writers, most of them comparatively young men, are also revisionists, and in the sense that all history is revision I think we need these new interpretations or investigations. In so far as the New Left has looked at foreign policy, they have read the present, especially the problem of Vietnam, into the past. They are concerned mainly with the mistakes of American policy. They believe that the prime mistake was getting out of tune with the Russians in 1945–46. Gar Alperovitz, for example, in his book *Atomic Diplomacy*, argues that the Americans dropped the two atomic bombs on the Japanese not to destroy two supposedly military targets and hasten the end of the war in the Far East, but to overawe the Russians and gain leverage in the postwar era.

Alperovitz makes a good case. He writes well. He moves easily in his discussion from point to point. But when he leaves the evidence and presents his conclusion, one discovers that the evidence has not quite proved his point, which is actually unprovable, at least from the research materials presently available.

But I would like to make a general point about the New Left history as it applies to twentieth-century subjects. There has been a great proliferation of historical materials available for research. There has been an enormous keeping of records. We have so many documents that it is impossible to read them all. The young historian just coming out of graduate school, terribly anxious for a book, or at least an article, wanting something which will advance his fortune in the profession—a profession which is bouncing in terms of income and possibilities for promotion—the young historian, having been told by his graduate teachers that he must have an idea or thesis, and having learned also that it is possible to plunge into the morass of research materials and come out with something resembling support of almost any thesis, can put together a rather convincing, or at least plausible, argument which may not have much relation to history as it happened. I won't say that one can prove anything by documents presently available. But most of the documentary sources are opinions. If one takes the opinions on the side which he wishes to support, he can put together an argument.

I think that the New Left, worried about America's moral stature and distrusting the present government, has produced literature based largely on this type of use of source material.

J.A.G. That raises a very interesting question. Even if we accept what you say about the motivation of the New Left historians, how can the historian of modern foreign relations deal with the unreadably large body of conflicting evidence? What can the honest historian do if he cannot truly master the sources and yet still wishes to be objective?

R.H.F. It's absolutely true that the historian cannot read all the sources. I've had the experience of sitting down with great masses of State Department files and trying to sort out what seems to be repetitive or trivial from the materials that seem to be the heart of controversy. I don't have any solid advice in this regard. There isn't much that one can say, other than to ask the historian always to be willing to change his mind, to try to use common sense toward the material. One must always ask himself how close he is getting to the truth, and whether he has seen what *appears* to be the most important information. I think the New Left has instead tried to score points, set up their objectives, and then simply move flippantly into the archives for support.

J.A.G. What are the half-dozen or so books that you would recommend to persons interested in the subject we have been discussing? In each case, would you indicate briefly what the particular contribution of the book is?

R.H.F.   For the secretaries of state in the interwar years there are several able books. Merlo J. Pusey, *Charles Evans Hughes* (1951) is clearly favorable to its subject, as one might have expected when Hughes in his great old age gave Pusey considerable assistance through interviews and by looking up items in his files. Nonetheless, Pusey is an able writer and these two volumes are delightful history.

For Kellogg, the best book is by L. Ethan Ellis, *Frank B. Kellogg and American Foreign Relations* (1961), a much more critical account than Pusey's *Hughes*, indeed verging on the contemporary description of Kellogg as "Nervous Nellie."

Two opposing views of Stimson appear in Richard N. Current, *Secretary Stimson: A Study in Statecraft* (1954), who sees Stimson as wearing a look of "bored martyrdom" (to use the telling phrase of Drew Pearson), and Elting E. Morison, *Turmoil and Tradition: A Study in the Life and Times of Henry L. Stimson* (1960), which is an authorized life and times, beautifully written.

Julius W. Pratt, *Cordell Hull* (1964), is the best accounting of Hull, although this statesman has not inspired many books; Pratt's judgments are acute and trustworthy.

The involutions of prewar diplomacy appear in William L. Langer and S. Everett Gleason, *The Challenge to Isolation: 1937–40* (1952), and *The Undeclared War: 1940–41* (1953). The Council on Foreign Relations sponsored these volumes to prevent false revisionism of prewar and wartime diplomacy, but the industrious authors encountered a mountain of documentary materials and were able to finish their task only for the years 1937–41. Published some years ago, their account remains the best available.

For the war era, see Samuel Eliot Morison, *Strategy and Compromise* (1958), a short little volume that shows the compromises between the British and Americans in the business of defeating Hitler; and William L. Neumann, *After Victory: Churchill, Roosevelt, Stalin and the Making of the Peace* (1967), on how the "grand alliance," as Churchill described it, fell apart.

Richard W. Leopold

The United States in World Affairs 1941–1968

ICHARD W. LEOPOLD, William Smith Mason Professor of American History at Northwestern University, began his career as a specialist in social history, his biography of the reformer *Robert Dale Owen* (1940) winning the Dunning prize of the American Historical Association. Since World War II, however, he had worked in the field of American foreign relations. His books include *Elihu Root and the Conservative Tradition* (1954) and a highly regarded textbook, *The Growth of American Foreign Policy: A History* (1962). The following interview, dealing as it does with so many controversial issues, gives full scope to Professor Leopold's outstanding qualities as a historian—fairness, sound judgment, and a broad view of his subject.

John A. Garraty Professor Leopold, to most Americans the discord that developed so quickly between the United States and the Soviet Union after World War II came as a considerable shock. Why had Americans expected American-Russian relations to be friendly, considering their long history of hostility to Communism and the well-known character of the Stalin regime?

Richard W. Leopold To answer this question we must put ourselves back into the mood of 1941–45. Those who lived through the period after Pearl Harbor were immensely impressed by and even indebted to the Russians for their part in staving off the Nazi threat to American interests. Moreover, not every American was well versed in the history of Soviet-American relations; many did not know nearly as much about the character of the Stalin regime as Americans know today. Certainly, the details of the purges of 1936–37 were not fully appreciated. But even if these had been fully understood, given the nature of the war and their admiration for the character of the Soviet Army, the great majority of Americans were prepared to hope for the best. Also, most Americans fell into the same trap which had claimed Franklin Roosevelt as a victim. They were so eager to cooperate with the Russians that cooperation became an end in itself.

I do not think we know all we ought to know, and perhaps we never will, about Roosevelt's innermost thoughts. But the available evidence is overwhelming that Roosevelt put too much faith in his powers of persuasion with regard to Stalin. He was prepared, at least through Yalta, to overlook Stalin's past history and hope for the best. But I do not think we will ever really know how firm was his conviction that we could get along with the Soviets in the postwar world. A change may have taken place after Yalta. This is suggested in his letters to Churchill and in his talks with General Marshall.

Then there is another factor that perhaps has not been sufficiently explained. Most Americans probably had their eyes mainly on the war in Europe. The landings in Normandy were a much more dramatic and understandable operation, for example, than the return to the Philippines. But with the end of the war in Europe, a major shift of interest took place. Thus, things which seem clear in the minds of historians today, and which *may* have been reasonably clear in the minds of some of the leaders at the time, were not fully appreciated by the public. For example, I have no independent recollection of what was going on in Rumania or Bulgaria as the Russians were settling the Soviet system on that area. But I suppose the shock would have come, no matter what had been the nature of the postwar world. After every war there is bound to be some turn, some reaction, some discord among the victors.

Separating the popular from the governmental level, I think that not only wartime propaganda, but also wartime facts (the valiant Red Army hurling back the invader) explain the friendly attitude of Americans toward the U.S.S.R. As for those in government, it depends upon who is talking. The *Memoirs* of Cordell Hull and Robert E. Sherwood's *Roosevelt and Hopkins* give the impression, because of the activities of Hull and Hopkins, of a high degree of Russo-American cordiality. On the other hand, the account of Admiral Standley, who was Ambassador to the Soviet Union, suggest that the good will was not so great after all.

J.A.G.   Perhaps the answer is that Americans wanted so much to have good relations with Russia that they convinced themselves that they were going to.

R.W.L.   I would accept that, but I would put it, perhaps, that Americans were so eager to win the war, and win it quickly, that they were prepared to sup with the devil to achieve that end. Eagerness for good relations was a substitute for a realistic appraisal.

J.A.G.   How well did Roosevelt prepare for the peacemaking during the war? Would you compare his performance with that of Woodrow Wilson during World War I?

R.W.L.   If membership in a new United Nations was one goal of peacemaking, Roosevelt certainly prepared for peace during the war. And in this respect he profited from the lessons of history, that is, from Wilson's experience. You can go right down the line: he maintained better relations with Congress, gave more publicity to the type of international organization he had in mind, committed the legislative branch *in advance* to at least the general principle, maintained better communications with cobelligerents. With regard to some of the deeper problems of preparing for peacemaking, such as foreseeing what the shape of postwar Europe would be and what obligations we would assume in the Pacific, again I think he did better than Wilson, though probably his marks would not be as high as on the issue of the UN.

J.A.G.   What is your over-all evaluation of Roosevelt as a diplomatist?

R.W.L.   In the early years, he was so concerned with domestic affairs that he let Secretary of State Cordell Hull control several areas of foreign policy, although in such matters as the ill-fated London Economic Conference of 1933, the decision to build up the Navy, and the recognition of Russia, Roosevelt, not Hull, made the big decisions. The most important foreign policy issue of the thirties concerned the Neutrality Acts. If Roosevelt's purpose in choosing Hull to be Secretary of State was his influence on Capitol Hill, it seems to me that Hull failed when this influence was most needed; but in any case Roosevelt did not handle the neutrality problem very well. Some writers say that he had no choice but to bow to the anti-interventionist sentiment of the day. Perhaps. But through the campaign of 1936 and even as late as 1938 he showed little courage in trying to combat the trend.

Between 1939 and 1941, however, I think he did a good job. The big question mark is how well he handled the Japanese issue. Some critics argue that the decision to go ahead with economic sanctions in July, 1941, prevented a peaceful solution. That seems highly unlikely, but we do have to consider the possibility that a policy of delay would have given the military those extra few months that they wanted to prepare the Pacific defenses. I personally think the Japanese were determined that if they had not gotten what they wanted by the end of 1941, they were not going to wait longer. This leads to a different question: Should Roosevelt have given them what they wanted? I am inclined to think that no real accord was possible between the desires of the Japanese and the desires of the United States. Yet perhaps no concessions were made to Japan mainly because Roosevelt was puzzled and uncertain; beset by arguments from one side and another, he merely let events take their course.

As to his performance in wartime, if diplomacy includes his keeping the wartime coalition together and winning the war in the quickest possible time with the smallest loss of lives, he did a superb job. If one argues that this policy won the war but lost the peace, then it behooves us to ask what he should have done differently. A negotiated peace with Germany would have been impossible at any time before 1945. What he could do about Central and Eastern Europe depended on the military picture, and nothing that he could have done by military means would have kept the Red Army out of Eastern Europe. Even if the Allied armies had reached Berlin or Prague before the Russians—Prague was within the realm of possibility, I do not think Berlin was—what would we have done after we got there? My own feeling is that the war against Japan would have still loomed so large that Roosevelt would have been unwilling to risk a break with the Russians over that region.

Looking at diplomatic skill in the sense of old-fashioned note-writing and negotiation, I suppose Roosevelt, because of his very personal approach, and the gap that he often created between himself and the State Department because of his improvising, would not rank as a great diplomatist. But as a coordinator of foreign and military policy at a critical moment, I think he deserves pretty high marks.

J.A.G. The conference of Roosevelt, Churchill, and Stalin at Yalta has been one of the most hotly debated subjects of all American history. What is your opinion of the decisions made at Yalta?

R.W.L. Given the situation as it existed in January and February, 1945, the decisions made at Yalta were about as good as the United States could have hoped for. By "under the circumstances" I do not mean to give any credence to the argument that Roosevelt was not in command of his senses. His health was declining, but there is no evidence that his mental faculties had failed. So far as Europe was concerned, Roosevelt got very little other than paper promises, but it is hard to see how anyone could have gotten more. With regard to East Asia, my feeling is that Yalta was a stand-off. Undoubtedly the Russians obtained certain promises from Roosevelt, but they could have gained the same advantages without promises. All Roosevelt did was put his stamp of approval on something that they might have otherwise have had to do unilaterally. In February, 1945, every important American military leader, including General MacArthur, felt that Russian military assistance was indispensable to bring the war in Asia to a swift conclusion with a minimum loss of life. Of course almost all of these military leaders changed their minds within three or four months; by June and July they felt that they could defeat Japan reasonably quickly without Russian help, thanks to the submarine campaign and the B–29 fire bombings— and this without considering the atomic bomb.

J.A.G. Did either Roosevelt or Stalin outmaneuver the other, or was the Yalta settlement in your opinion a reasonable compromise?

R.W.L. The settlement was a reasonable compromise. The difficulty about Yalta that has bothered many historians—aside from the fact that the situation changed very quickly—was that Roosevelt tried to use Stalin to gang up on Churchill. The extreme secrecy surrounding the conference has also annoyed them. Certain decisions could have seen the light of day a little sooner. When the terms of the Yalta Agreement leaked out after Roosevelt's death, the suspicion was created that there was perhaps more there that had not leaked out. Personally, I do not believe we are likely to learn more about Yalta from the American side, but from the Russian side—like everything else in this period—there is a lot more that could be known. Whether we will ever know it is another question.

J.A.G. You mentioned the fact that the Russians made certain promises (about Poland and other areas in Eastern Europe) which they did not keep. Is it a fair criticism of the American position that we did not anticipate that the Russians would not keep their promises?

R.W.L. Some Americans were shocked at the Russians' blatant disregard of these promises, but there is no evidence that the people who actually dealt with the Russians were sure that everything they promised would come to be. They knew that they were gambling. One can sense this in the growing urgency of what Averell Harriman and George Kennan were cabling from Moscow. By the spring of 1945, they knew with certainty that the gamble had been lost. So it is wrong to suggest that American diplomats were naïve about the Yalta agreements.

There is a generation gap between historians who were old enough to be aware of these things and those who came of academic age in the mid-1950's. The older group tends to say, "We had no alternative. If the war was to be won, we had to run these risks." The younger ones do not readily accept this argument. They feel that there *was* an alternative. But I have not seen anybody who has given a plausible account of what we should have done differently.

J.A.G. What about the Potsdam Agreement? Given the evidence available at that time of Russian hostility, does the division of Berlin and its isolation in the center of Russian-controlled East Germany appear to have been a good idea?

R.W.L. I do not think that the division of Berlin, or more particularly its isolation, was a good idea at any time. But it was not Potsdam that was perhaps important but the decision Truman made before the conference to pull American troops back into the American Zone. Churchill urged delay until more assurances could be gained from Russia, especially about Poland. Churchill was very reluctant to let the Soviets take over Poland. But again, we must remember that the eyes of the Americans were on the war with Japan.

J.A.G. To what extent were political factors as distinct from purely military ones responsible for the decision to drop the atom bomb on Hiroshima?

R.W.L. I see very few other than the military. Whether the military decision was a wise one is another question.

J.A.G. Critics contend that the bomb was dropped to add to the diplomatic prestige of the United States vis-à-vis Russia, by demonstrating the enormous power of this weapon.

R.W.L. This view is popular, but what do we have in the way of historical evidence to go on? A good deal depends on Truman's own *Memoirs*. These important volumes have never been subjected to rigorous historical analysis. When they came out they had great value. They were not great memoirs; as a matter of fact, the organization and the writing was pretty poor. But they contained documentary materials not then available. When Truman writes, however, "I talked to Molotov in a way in which he'd never been talked to before," I must confess as an historian I am not prepared to believe it. Obviously we are not likely to get our hands on Molotov's dispatch to Moscow on what was said to him and how he reacted; but there is every reason to believe that, given the time at which Truman wrote these memoirs, his recollections, as distinct from the documents he quoted, would tend toward a hard line.

With regard to the dropping of the bomb, my guess is that the vital influences were those of Stimson and Marshall, and I do not believe that either was concerned with brandishing the new weapon to gain prestige, or to discourage the Russians from making further advances in Central or Eastern Europe. Wisely or unwisely, they were concentrating on getting on with the war.

J.A.G. Does the dropping of the bomb appear to have aided or hindered the course of world peace?

R.W.L. I do not think there is any doubt that if those who made the decision knew what we know now, the bomb would not have been dropped. I do not want to get into the question of whether it aided or hindered the cause of world peace. It has been a sin in the minds of many people, Americans and otherwise, that the United States has had to live with. The wonder is that relations with Japan have been as good as they have been in spite of it.

The evidence is overwhelming that the war would have come to a close very quickly—that the Japanese Army on the mainland was not a substantial force, that the firebomb raids had done as much damage as the atomic bomb was going to do, that the Japanese had practically lost the will to resist. No, I cannot really believe that the bomb aided the cause of peace. In all probability it shortened the war, but not by very much.

J.A.G. What is the most likely explanation of why the Soviet Union refused to accept the Baruch plan for the control of atomic energy?

R.W.L. When a historian tries to explain why the Soviet government did or did not do something in this period, he is on pretty marshy ground. We can only guess. One factor, I imagine, was simple pride; another, plain fear; another, the expectation that Russia would be able to develop its own nuclear capability. In the minds of the Russians, the Baruch plan would have also, I think, undermined their position in the United Nations on the question of the great veto power. If they accepted abandonment of the veto in one area, they feared they might be pressed to abandon it someplace else. And finally, it is likely that at least some Russian leaders felt you just don't make this kind of agreement with the capitalists. They saw the Baruch plan as a capitalist plot.

J.A.G. Did the Russian rejection of the Baruch plan influence American attitudes toward the U.S.S.R.? To the average citizen, the plan seemed eminently reasonable.

R.W.L. Perhaps on the popular level, but not on the governmental level.

J.A.G. Can an argument be made that the American position on the control of atomic energy should have been more liberal? Should we have proposed, for example, international control without a close check on atomic research?

R.W.L. The argument could be made, but I am inclined to think that this was beyond the realm of practicality. The atomic monopoly was genuinely approved of by Americans across the board.

J.A.G. Would you compare the UN with the League of Nations? Has the UN proved a useful instrument for the maintenance of peace?

R.W.L. It is fairly evident that Roosevelt tried to profit from the lessons of history. The United Nations Charter was much more like the League Covenant with the Lodge Reservations than like the Covenant itself. There was a realization on all sides that the big powers were to call the tune, and that unless the Big Three could agree, the organization was not going to work. Whether or not it is true, as some historians charge, that the United Nations was oversold to the American people, Americans did believe that the United Nations was necessary. Therefore, the government tried to find a way around the Russian veto, to reduce the power of the Security Council and to increase that of the General Assembly—at least until the General Assembly became so large as to be practically unmanageable. Yet the United Nations has played an important role in keeping the peace, although obviously it is not perfect. It has not had the power that many Americans felt it would in 1945.

J.A.G. Could the UN have been given more power, considering the atmosphere of the time of its creation?

R.W.L. I do not think there was any way in which the organization could have been made to function better in the face of dissent by one of the larger powers. Neither the United States nor Russia was prepared to give up certain safeguards.

J.A.G. What exactly was the policy of containment? Did it evolve out of the Truman Doctrine of supporting anti-Communist forces in Greece, or was the Truman Doctrine the first application of an already determined policy of checking Communist expansion?

R.W.L. The policy of containment was an attempt to prevent the further spread of Russian power in Western Europe, and the spread of Communist-dominated elements throughout the world. Now, I do not think it began that way. The early exponents of containment disagreed among themselves as to how far it would go. But if we take the Truman Doctrine, the statements as formulated by George F. Kennan in 1947, Walter Lippmann's dissents therefrom, the Marshall Plan, the European Economic Recovery Act, the mutual defense assistance acts, and the North Atlantic Treaty, they all fit into a general pattern which I am prepared to call "containment."

I do not think that George F. Kennan actually formulated the policy, but then I do not think anybody actually formulated it. The Truman Doctrine as stated was a rather open-ended and unwise policy if one took it, as some did, as an ironclad promise to oppose Communist expansion everywhere. I cannot believe that Truman or his advisers intended it to be so. Kennan argues in his *Memoirs* that his famous "X" article in *Foreign Affairs* created the false impression that there should be a heavy stress on military containment, but I am inclined to quarrel with him and anyone else who reads back into these early policy statements too comprehensive and generalized intentions. It is clear that in 1947 Kennan was unhappy with the wide-ranging implications of the Truman Doctrine, but it is also clear that few people in the government desired to apply the Doctrine immediately anywhere, except in Greece and Turkey and perhaps in Eastern Europe generally.

J.A.G.   There was no sense that it would be applied in Asia?

R.W.L.   I find no persuasive evidence to that effect. The statement by Truman in his 1947 message to the Congress was a response to a crisis, defined as a general policy, but not fully thought through. In the early part of 1947, the Russians seemed to have withdrawn from China. The Chinese Civil War had not blown up, though it was perfectly clear that there would soon be a full-scale conflict there. So I do not think that either Truman or his advisers thought of applying the Truman Doctrine to East Asia. China aside, the situation in Japan was in good control at the moment. The United States had not signed a peace treaty, but they had frozen the Russians out. The situation in Korea was frustrating, but no one could foresee the dangerous situation that was to develop there in another two-and-one-half years.

With regard to the Middle East, the focus was on Palestine, the emergence of Israel. There was no great fear that Russia was going to move immediately into that area. There was, perhaps, an unjustified hope that even if they did, England, France, and the United States, working in unity, would be strong enough to keep them out.

J.A.G.   If I understand you correctly, the concept of containment was seen by its formulators as applying to Europe, and only to Europe?

R.W.L.   Yes. The question within the question was: Was containment to be by military or economic means? Looking at our military capability in the Mediterranean at this time, short of using nuclear weapons there was none. We sent a certain number of naval vessels into that area, but purely as a demonstration. So the basic approach had to be economic.

J.A.G.   Was the Marshall Plan directed at Russia, or at the frustration of Russian ambitions, or primarily at its ostensible objective— the rehabilitation of Western Europe?

R.W.L.   This question is difficult to answer, because we do not have the necessary documentary evidence. The State Department has published no special volumes, such as those released in the past fifteen years on Yalta and Potsdam. There have been some very useful memoirs, but George Marshall and his plan remain fairly inscrutable. My guess is that the Marshall Plan was seen as an *answer* to the Russians. I do not really think that Marshall or Truman expected the Russians to participate fully in it. For the record, inviting them to cooperate was a good grandstand play which just might tempt them. But the Plan was primarily intended to strengthen Western Europe by making its economy more viable.

J.A.G. From the American point of view, what was the purpose of the North Atlantic Treaty Organization? Was it designed for actual military purposes—that is, to defend Europe against Russia—or to boost European morale and encourage cooperation among the Western European nations themselves?

R.W.L. I am sure that both motives entered in, but the latter was more basic. With regard to the military purpose, that was going to take some time accomplishing. When the North Atlantic Treaty was signed in April, 1949, the American atomic monopoly still existed. How much warning our government had as to Russian capabilities (the first Russian atomic device was exploded in September) I do not know. But it was going to be some time before the United States could put a substantial number of troops in Europe. American military planning, so far as it existed, still envisaged defending Europe with manned bombers and probably nuclear weapons. Many American leaders regarded NATO as having great symbolical value as proof of our determination to be concerned with the stability and peace of Europe. Whether that determination could have made good in any military sense in the foreseeable future was less important—we had committed ourselves to accept alliances and to be bound by them. This may have been more important than the North Atlantic Treaty Organization itself.

J.A.G. Turning now to Asia, did the United States mishandle its relations with China during and after World War II? Would a different policy perhaps have prevented the Communists from gaining control of China after the war?

R.W.L. I do not think that our wartime China policy was mishandled, in the sense that it led to the downfall of the Nationalists and the triumph of the Communists. That we made particular mistakes I think probably is true. But I do not see—given the nature of the enemy, the nature of the attack—that much more could have been done to make China a more important element in the war. It was just bad luck that the war ended with the lines of battle where they were. This, as much as anything else, enabled the Chinese Communists to mark out for themselves areas of China in which they were dominant.

J.A.G.   Could the United States have brought more pressure on Chiang Kai-shek during or immediately after the war to institute a more enlightened regime in his own country, and thus perhaps have changed the attitudes of the mass of the Chinese people toward the Communists?

R.W.L.   I do not think so. We have never been very successful in bringing pressure on people, whether they live under a dictatorship or a democracy. Chiang, aside from his own conviction that he was following the best path, was not going to move because he felt that we would never go so far as to destroy him. There is a school of thought that says that the real lost opportunity was the failure to build up the third force in China—something between Chiang and the Communists. I do not believe that the elements for that third force were very large. The situation had polarized between the Nationalists and the Communists. It would have been nice if we could have persuaded Chiang to do this or that, but it would be easy to exaggerate the effects of the reforms that might have been made. No Nationalist policy would have affected those areas occupied by Japan, and these the Communists pretty much controlled after the war.

J.A.G.   Can an argument be made that when the Civil War erupted in China we supported the wrong side?

R.W.L.   If by the "wrong" side you mean the side that eventually won, I do not see how we could have been on that side. The options available to the United States were either doing what we did, which was essentially a policy of drift, or deciding that our national interests were so threatened by a Communist triumph that, like Chiang Kai-shek or not, we had to plunge in on his side. That was not within the bounds of practicality. Public opinion aside, our military capability by 1947 was pretty weak.

J.A.G.   But if our actual policy was to drift, would we perhaps not have been better off if we had declared our neutrality?

R.W.L.   That assumes that somehow we would have antagonized the Communists less by official neutrality. I am inclined to doubt whether it would have made much difference one way or the other. The time to have acted in that way was in the winter of 1949–50, when the Communists had driven Chiang from the mainland.

J.A.G.   Why didn't the United States adopt the old-fashioned policy of recognizing the Communist regime as the *de facto* government of China?

R.W.L.   It was impossible for domestic reasons for the United States immediately to recognize Red China the way the Russians did, and indeed the way the British were to do a month or so afterward. Public opinion was too much against it. It is within the realm of possibility that if there had been no invasion of South Korea, and if domestic anti-Communism had not become so unbearable, Truman would have recognized the Chinese Communists before he went out of office. But the Korean War foreclosed the possibility. Furthermore, the Chinese Communists' reaction to British recognition was not encouraging. Recognition, however, was still an open question until June, 1950.

J.A.G. Could any American policy, other than the one actually adopted, have prevented the Korean War?

R.W.L. That depends on what you mean. It is conceivable that if we had been willing as early as 1946 to accept a protectorate over all of Korea, war would have been avoided. But after 1947, the answer is No. I very much doubt that, by withdrawing our troops from South Korea, we encouraged the North Koreans to invade, or that Acheson's address before the National Press Club drawing a "perimeter" and leaving Korea outside tempted the Communists. I suppose if we had known what was coming, Acheson would have reworded his speech, but it is fairly clear, at least in retrospect, that he was not writing off Korea. He was simply saying that there were some areas which the United States and the United States alone would assume responsibility for. In other areas, all of the free nations so-called would assume that responsibility. I do not think the withdrawing of American troops made a great deal of difference, either.

J.A.G. Putting aside the anti-civil-libertarian, demagogic aspects of the behavior of Senator Joseph R. McCarthy, was there any substance to his charge that American security procedures were inadequate and that the Soviet Union had profited enormously from information obtained from American traitors?

R.W.L. There was substance to this charge. The word "enormously" is something we cannot be sure of, and, whether the informers were "traitors" or not might be another qualification. But there is little doubt that the information that Klaus Fuchs obtained about the atomic experiments in New Mexico was important. While McCarthy and some of his cohorts were riding a wave of certain disappointments and frustrations, there was some substance to the "security risk" issue. Yet no nation has been free of security leaks.

J.A.G. Granted that perfect security is impossible, what criticisms of the Truman security policy can be made?

R.W.L. I do not have any easy answer to that. Perhaps he was more trusting than he should have been, or less suspicious of the Russians. He had, I suppose, little excuse for not being more cautious, because whatever Americans may have thought about the possibility of meaningful collaboration and cooperation, the Soviet conspiratorial apparatus was surely sufficiently well known.

J.A.G.   What is your evaluation of John Foster Dulles as Secretary of State? How did his policy and his management of the State Department differ from that of the Democratic Secretaries who preceded him in the postwar period?

R.W.L.   One is struck by how essentially similar the Eisenhower-Dulles policy was to that of their predecessors. I find it hard to reach a final judgment on Dulles. I do not care for his sloganeering and his callous attitude toward some of the Foreign Service officers who had been under attack by McCarthy. Dulles was so impressed (or depressed) by what had happened to Secretary of State Acheson, when he fell out with the legislative branch, that he was determined above all else to avoid that problem. "Demoralization" may be too strong a word, but certainly the deterioration of morale within the State Department during his term of office was very great, and in part owing to his unwillingness to stand up for subordinates who were under fire.

Yet Dulles was a man of considerable ability. I once watched him at a press conference, and he came through in a way I had not expected. He had a sense of history, which would endear him to any historian. The parallel with Woodrow Wilson, which is often drawn, is worth noting. Both were eloquent, both felt that they could carry the ball single-handedly. All the familiar aspects of Wilson's Presbyterianism were present in Dulles. In general, I expect that the historians of the future will rate Dulles a little more highly than we do today. The Dulles of 1958 was not the Dulles of 1953; he did not remain rigid. Then, too, consider his China policy. Here was a man who was a hard-liner, presumably a devotee of Chiang Kai-shek, a bitter opponent of the Communists. Yet, while he held office, the situation did not change very much. Far from unleashing Chiang, Dulles leashed him. Given the rather fluid situation in the mid-fifties, this may turn out to have been a stabilizing force. But I do not claim to see any long-run gain resulting from Dulles' China policy. I do not think he would ever have come round to the recognition of the Red government.

As to how his management of the State Department differed from his predecessors', we tend to forget that it was Acheson who made the decision to rearm Germany. Dulles, of course, with his friendship for the German leader, Konrad Adenauer, cemented this, but the policy was not very different. I dare say that Dulles shows up at his worst in his personalizing the men with whom he had to deal: his great affection for Adenauer, his suspicion of and dislike of Prime Minister Anthony Eden, and so on. The common assumption that Dulles was unfettered as Secretary of State, that he was the man who was directing foreign policy and that President Eisenhower deferred to him and let him do what he wanted, is, however, unfounded. Rightly or wrongly, Eisenhower felt it was wise to build up Dulles, and defer to him. Instead of making a report to the nation, he would have Dulles make the report. But Eisenhower himself controlled basic policy.

J.A.G.   Do you think that Dulles' weaknesses were more those of style than of policy?

R.W.L.   His weaknesses were partly those of a man carried away by his own rhetoric, but he also had exaggerated faith in his ability to handle people and situations. His sense of timing was not always the best.

J.A.G.   Did he not fail to pay proper attention to the significance of the death of Stalin and the policy changes which Khrushchev instituted in Russia?

R.W.L.   I think this is a legitimate criticism. He dragged his feet on a number of issues with the Russians. He was reluctant, for instance, to hold the Geneva Conference of 1955. What makes me hesitate here is the question of how many other diplomats would have been more flexible on that issue. George Kennan would argue that *he* would have been more flexible, but I do not know how differently Acheson would have behaved. With regard to the death of Stalin, I think we are perhaps the victims of hindsight. It took people quite a while to understand what was going on in Russia. Then there is the whole question of military strategy and defense policy. Flexibility was not the order of the day in the Eisenhower defense policy, which stressed economy—"more bang for the buck."

J.A.G.   Didn't this represent a considerable change in policy?

R.W.L.   Yes, to the extent that Dulles said he wanted no more Koreas. But I just do not know what the implications of the Truman-Acheson policy would have been. They ended their administration with a military build-up. It is clear that Dulles put renewed emphasis on the Strategic Air Command—on a reliance, that is, upon nuclear weapons. But at no time during his tenure did he come close to using them. The landing in Lebanon, for example, employed conventional methods.

J.A.G.   If I may push my question a little further, if one wished to argue that Dulles did not react to changing realities very rapidly, couldn't one stress the lack of realism in his talk about "massive retaliation" after the Russian development of the hydrogen bomb?

R.W.L.   Yes, but with one qualification: he believed in going to the brink, not over the brink. He really meant what he said: If the enemy is convinced we are willing to do something, he won't. There was an element of the gambler in Dulles, although of course the stakes were much too high to be bearable.

J.A.G. When we talked about the containment policy, you suggested that when the idea was first advanced, no one had really thought it through as a global policy. I think it's fair to say that in Dulles' day, containment was a global policy clearly. Was Dulles responsible for this, and for applying containment to Asia?

R.W.L. This brings us into the realm of alliances and regional understandings. Acheson tried, in his closing months as Secretary of State, to build up some Middle Eastern alliance, but he did not complete the work. Dulles certainly saw containment as global in nature, but apparently he felt that the shadow was more important than the substance. He was too intelligent a person to think he could fool people by saying that the Southeast Asia Treaty Organization (SEATO) was another NATO. His argument here was that SEATO, not NATO in a military sense, would get at the problem of Communist subversion in the area. The Baghdad Pact, which became CENTO in 1959, was pretty much a farce, but even here Dulles felt that *some* form of opposition to Communist advancement was essential.

J.A.G. What changes in foreign policy were made by President Kennedy?

R.W.L. Certainly he desired to make changes, in the sense that he wished to be more accommodating, to try harder to reach some understanding with the Russians without putting ourselves in a position of being supplicants or weaklings. In addition, Secretary Dean Rusk came to the State Department convinced that Dulles had let administration of the Department go to pot, especially by being absent from Washington too much. He thought the place for the Secretary of State was in Washington. Kennedy also believed there should be important changes in Latin-American policy, and he favored changes in defense policy, particularly the idea of relying on conventional weapons to take care of "brush-fire" wars.

Well, Rusk was not able to carry out his desire to stay stationary, and I am not sure that the morale of the State Department was very much improved as a result of his tenure. (It was Kennedy, not Rusk, who made State Department people feel uncomfortable. Kennedy distrusted professional diplomats, and relied on many bright outsiders like McGeorge Bundy and Arthur M. Schlesinger, Jr.) But in most areas, the policy of the Kennedy regime was pretty similar to what it had been under Eisenhower and Dulles. My guess is that historians looking back twenty-five years from now will conclude that Kennedy made few substantial changes. Depending on your affections and affiliations, you may speculate that there would have been more changes if he had lived.

J.A.G. Can Kennedy's blunder in the Bay of Pigs affair in Cuba be written off as the result of the inexperience of the new administration?

R.W.L. I do not think I would use the word "inexperience." My explanation of the Bay of Pigs is, first of all, that the thing had already started; the danger of calling it off, both internationally and domestically, appeared greater than pursuing it. Secondly, the government was using a new technique, one I hope it will never use again, in allowing the CIA to undertake an operation for which it was not equipped.

J.A.G. That was also a decision of the Eisenhower administration, was it not?

R.W.L. Yes, and it would have been difficult for domestic reasons to have continued the operation by taking it out of the hands of the CIA in the three or four months before it was scheduled to come off. Finally, there was a perhaps understandable tendency to drift. Not being quite sure what to do, Kennedy let things go on until they reached the point of no return.

J.A.G. Do you think that the Russians decided to install missiles in Cuba because of the Bay of Pigs affair?

R.W.L. Undoubtedly, Khrushchev was not prepared for the response that he got when the United States learned about the missiles. But whether his bad judgment resulted from an underevaluation of Kennedy's nerve based on the President's Bay of Pigs performance or some superficial conclusion he drew after their meeting in Vienna, or whether there were pressures he did not feel he could resist within the Communist world is unclear.

J.A.G. It has been suggested that Kennedy took a dreadful and unnecessary risk in forcing a confrontation in the missile crisis, because Russia already possessed the capacity to strike American cities with nuclear weapons without Cuban bases. What is your opinion of this reasoning?

R.W.L. Once it became known that the missiles were there, the pressures to do something were so overwhelming that Kennedy could not ignore them. To have done nothing, especially in the light of the Bay of Pigs, would have completely destroyed confidence, in many quarters, in his nerve and his will.

J.A.G. The difficulty with that argument is that by forcing the confrontation, he was putting the Russians in exactly the same position.

R.W.L. Well, I think that is correct. But I am sure he hoped to find some face-saving out for Khrushchev. I do not believe we are ever going to know fully what went on in the Kremlin.

J.A.G. In the long history of the conflict in Vietnam, where did the United States go wrong? Was there any specific point at which the nation became committed to actions that were not in the national interest?

R.W.L. I do not know exactly where to place the turning point where we moved beyond what we had originally intended. Various commentators have located it anywhere from the summer of 1962 to the fall of Diem in November, 1963, to the Tonkin Gulf episode in August, 1964, and to the expansion of the bombing into North Vietnam in February, 1965. The real error was not in going against our national interests at some point, but in assuming that the forces at our disposal were capable of affecting the outcome in a decisive way. We were powerful enough to prevent a military defeat, but we failed in the effort to prop up the South Vietnamese regime. It was also a blunder to believe that somehow we could solve the problem by bombing the North. This has done more to alienate world opinion than anything else. Of course, if the bombing had succeeded, it would have been seen differently. But it did not succeed.

J.A.G.   Is there any evidence that when the first American military advisers were sent into Vietnam the government was determined not to lose South Vietnam?

R.W.L.   I am not sure, but my guess is No. Kennedy made frequent statements during the summer and fall of 1963 to the effect that the United States could not win the war for the South Vietnamese. Yet I believe he meant they must *win* it themselves; I do not think he thought defeat possible.

J.A.G.   But doesn't this suggest that critics of President Johnson are in error when they suggest that he changed American policy in Vietnam? He changed tactics of course, but did he change policy?

R.W.L.   There is indeed a school of thought which blames Kennedy for what happened, and I think the critics of President Johnson are unfair in putting so much emphasis on the comparison between his policy and Kennedy's.

J.A.G.   Even under Eisenhower, if at some point there had been a real, immediate danger of North Vietnam overrunning South Vietnam, would not an equally large-scale American response have been likely?

R.W.L.   I think so. Note what the Eisenhower administration was prepared to do in Laos. They were not prepared to accept a basic change there in late 1960.

J.A.G.   Is there any truth to the argument that American policy toward Asia, Africa, and Latin America is imperialistic in its purposes?

R.W.L.   What do you mean by "imperialistic"?

J.A.G.   Well, a policy designed to exert influence in these areas for the benefit of the United States, even at the expense of the well-being of the local people.

R.W.L.   I would assume that policymakers believe there is no conflict between the two. Take our policy in Latin America. They would say that it is to the interest of all concerned to have better trade relations, for us to invest money to help build up local industry, to keep Communism out.

Of course, there are certain areas in the world where we have conflicting interests. We had *no* African policy down to about 1960; but since then we have been trying to balance our interest in keeping the Atlantic allies together, even though they were colonial powers, and our concern for encouraging the orderly development of the new, independent African nations. But I am not sure I would want to call American policy "imperialistic" in purpose, except for the still-latent tendency to regard the Caribbean area as our special province.

J.A.G. What criticisms would you make of our policy toward the underdeveloped areas of the world?

R.W.L. Since 1945 we have been dealing with areas about which we are not well informed. We too readily assume that solutions that work in situations with which we are familiar can be applied to areas where things are different. This explains in part our difficulties in Vietnam, and we have certainly demonstrated a total lack of understanding of what makes Laotians, for example, tick. How many experts on Africa did the State Department have in 1960 when the Congo crisis erupted? Further, our besetting sin ever since our imperialist venture in 1898 has been the belief that money and sanitation and things of that sort are what "natives" (as we used to call them) want. Very often they do not want them at all, probably even less than Aguinaldo and his followers in the Philippines did in 1898. It is hard for Americans to understand minuscule states.

J.A.G. Can a case be made for the argument that our whole policy of aiding underdeveloped countries is merely an aspect of the Cold War? Is our governing motive resistance to Russian ambitions rather than a desire to help in the social and economic development of these areas?

R.W.L. I would not go so far as to call it the sole aim, but I would not deny that it is important. Like so many things, it is hard to draw an exact line between our conviction that stability in these countries is good for them and good for us, and our belief that stability and prosperity will prevent them from going Communist. But I also believe the American people have felt a sense of responsibility of leadership in the world. I would not want to say that this was the primary consideration, but it is amazing how long Congress was willing to support a huge foreign aid program. I do not think this was solely a matter of competition with the Soviet Union. There has been an acceptance of the responsibility of power, and a willingness to pay the price. Having said this, however, I still think that anticipating the Russians and promoting the stability of underdeveloped nations so that Communism will not thrive in them has played a major part in our foreign relations.

J.A.G. What is your opinion of current American policy toward Western Europe?

R.W.L. In the last few years, we have needlessly neglected what many believe to be our primary focus of concern, Western Europe. This has been accentuated by the change in France, especially De Gaulle's hostile attitude toward NATO. Many students of foreign policy believe that the time has come for a fresh look at NATO. Yet this cannot be done while the nation is so heavily committed in Vietnam, and so deeply divided over Vietnam.

J.A.G. Was De Gaulle's policy toward the United States based on an actual conflict between American and French objectives in Western Europe, or did it simply reflect an old man's memory of how he was treated by Franklin Roosevelt during World War II?

R.W.L. The General had a sense of history, and sometimes he thought he was history itself. But it went much deeper than his memory of how he was treated during World War II. What he saw was less a conflict of interest than a conflict of roles. De Gaulle was convinced that France had a role to play in the world and that it could not play that role while the United States is as active as it has been. His desire, I think, was less to oppose the United States than to free the way for France. On the other hand, I must say that there were times when I found it difficult to stand and to understand him!

J.A.G. Looking at American policy toward Europe more generally, I think it's fair to say that the average American would assume that there are no significant conflicts of interest between the United States and the Western European democracies. Putting General De Gaulle and his personality aside, are there any conflicts of interest between the United States and its allies in Europe?

R.W.L. In the broadest sense I think not, now that France is much resigned to no longer being a great colonial power. The conflicts are in method, and the manner in which common interests are pursued. These range from the role the United States should play in the economic life of Western Europe to the role that France might play in a conflict between Russia and the United States. And, of course, De Gaulle believed that he knew the answer to the Vietnamese problem, and it is not one that we are likely to want to follow.

J.A.G. Is there any significance to the fact that our relations with our major World War II enemies, Japan and Germany, are more cordial than our relations with most of our World War II allies?

R.W.L. Toward Japan we have a certain proprietary pride in the way that nation adjusted to defeat under our control. Also it became perfectly clear what Japan meant to us in a military sense at the time of the Korean War. All the talk about the "privileged sanctuary" that the North Koreans and Chinese had in Manchuria appears foolish considering the privileged sanctuary we had in Japan. What advantage would there have been for us in not cooperating with Japan in the postwar world, particularly after 1949? It would not have made sense. The German question is more difficult, and I must say that every once in a while, as when I listened to Kennedy's speech in Berlin, when he said, to tumultuous applause, "*Ich bin ein Berliner*," I have to pinch myself. But then I belong to the generation which regards June 1940, when the Germans launched their great assault that almost conquered Europe, as one of the most decisive dates in history.

J.A.G. But it is true that since 1945 there hasn't been any major disagreement between West Germany and the United States, whereas with all the other Western European countries we have had rather serious disagreements. Is it simply that Germany is more dependent on us? To put the question more broadly, is not the degree of anti-American feeling in Europe inversely proportional to the degree of anti-American feeling there in 1944?

R.W.L. With the British, down to 1956, there was certainly a potential conflict because of Britain's interests in the colonial world. We disagreed with England over what to do about Indochina in 1954, about Suez in 1956. Since then we have not had much difficulty with the British. I suppose what caused much of the difficulty with the British throughout this period was the belief held by certain segments of our population that the British were going socialist. Certainly the Germans did not cause us any "trouble" on *that* score. The Germans seem to have been the perfect example of capitalism at work!

J.A.G. And the Japanese too.

R.W.L. The Japanese too. The French situation has been a lot more complicated. Roosevelt was the first to criticize French postwar colonial plans. India might have become a source of Anglo-American conflict, but British Indian policy was not comparable to French policy in Algeria, for example.

J.A.G. Can those who currently argue that the United States is overcommitted in Southeast Asia and elsewhere in the world be properly called "neo-isolationists"?

R.W.L. I do not think the word "isolationist" means *anything* anymore. Those who say we are overcommitted are not isolationists. Senator Fulbright does not want to tear up the North Atlantic Alliance; I do not hear him saying that we have no important stake in Western Europe.

Those who are charged with neo-isolationism because of their position on Vietnam are "Europe firsters." Furthermore, those who say that we ought to spend more money on our cities and perhaps a little less in some area of the globe are not indulging in neo-isolationism.

J.A.G.   What is your opinion of the work of the so-called "New Left" historians?

R.W.L.   The point of departure here is an obvious one: as historians, we are all somewhat the children of the age in which we have grown up. We reflect our own experiences in our writing. I would be the last to deny that events in twentieth-century history have affected my own thinking and approach to foreign policy. But several things bother me about New Left writing on foreign policy. What bothers me most is the assumption that somehow, taking a position is more important than the documentary foundation on which the position rests and the thoroughness of the research. What is important to the New Left is to expose and to say something new. Now, to some extent, we have been through this before, though I must say that the so-called revisionists— men like Harry Elmer Barnes who criticized American foreign policy in the 1920's and 1930's—at least made an attempt to deal with the traditional documents. But some of those who pass as oracles of the New Left devote little effort to the sort of research we expect of historians. If the materials are not available—all right, we can accept that. But then they should be a little more modest and a little less sweeping in their judgments. A second attitude of the New Left that bothers me is its intolerance—the assumption that these matters are not susceptible to doubt.

Then, finally, there has been a tendency for New Left writers who are interested in intellectual history to get themselves involved in matters of foreign policy, which is really outside their professional competence. Thus, much of the writing by the New Left which passes for diplomatic history is interesting primarily in terms of the intellectual currents of our day; it is not persuasive as the history of foreign policy.

J.A.G.   Do you see any benefit at all that has resulted from the re-examination of American foreign policy in the twentieth century by New Left writers?

R.W.L.   I am sympathetic to a good deal of what Hans Morgenthau has written about American foreign policy, though he is not a devotee of the New Left. Morgenthau has been a good influence if only because he has made some of us go back and rethink some of the conclusions we perhaps arrived at too easily, in the light of his criticisms. But here again, some of his generalizations about American foreign policy in the nineteenth and early twentieth centuries are not going to stand up because they do not rest upon sufficient historical research. Yet I think and hope that the writings of the New Left will have a healthy effect by stimulating discussion. If only they could escape their intolerance. I do not see how one can be a good historian without being a little more understanding of the people of past ages, and of historians who have written about them.

J.A.G. What are the half-dozen books that you would recommend to persons interested in the subject we have been discussing? In each case, would you indicate what the particular contribution of the volume is?

R.W.L. It is not very purposeful to recommend six books which would interest persons concerned with the subject I have been discussing without making clear the basis of my selection. I have omitted all meritorious textbooks, which are often the most valuable source of information on recent American foreign policy, largely because the statements above reflect the conclusions I reached in my own survey of American foreign policy. I have also omitted all monographs and specialized studies in order to make room for works that take a broader approach. Finally, I have not sought to identify the most scholarly books in the field, but rather to list titles that are readily available (most of them being in paperback) and of moderate length and of current interest.

Walter LaFeber, *America, Russia, and the Cold War, 1945–1966* (1967) is a perceptive summary, broadly conceived and tightly written, of the period under discussion. I have listed it first because the author's emphasis and conclusions sometimes differ from my own.

Seyom Brown, *The Faces of Power: Constancy and Change in United States Foreign Policy from Truman to Johnson* (1968) provides a useful comparison of the broad goals of the first four postwar Presidents, enabling the reader to judge the elements of continuity and those of discontinuity in American foreign policy.

Louis J. Halle, *The Cold War as History* (1967) is the most detached and least polemical of the many works that have recently appeared on this subject. It has the advantage of being written by a man who was once active on the Policy Planning Staff of the Department of State and who has now turned his attention to the history of American foreign policy.

Fred Greene, *U. S. Policy and the Security of Asia* (1968) is particularly useful because it discusses East Asia, Southeast Asia, and South Asia, along with a very careful examination of problems involving arms control and the proliferation of nuclear weapons.

Richard J. Barnet and Marcus G. Raskin, *After Twenty Years: The Decline of NATO and the Search for a New Policy in Europe* (1965) is a readable and analytical account of the development of our policy in Europe.

Hans J. Morgenthau, *A New Foreign Policy for the United States*

1969) is the latest full-scale treatment of a veteran analyst and constructive critic of American foreign policy. The author argues for an abandonment of those policies which served the Republic well in the half decade after the end of the war but which are now sorely in need of revision.

Robert L. Heilbroner

Economic Change: 1941–1968

ROBERT L. HEILBRONER, Professor of Economics at the New School for Social Research, is a scholar who has long been recognized for his ability to combine the mastery of complex ideas about economic theory with a lucid prose style; his books have been both critical successes and best-sellers. He is best known for *The Worldly Philosophers* (1953), a history of economic theory. Among his many other books are *The Future as History* (1959), *The Making of Economic Society* (1962), and *The Limits of American Capitalism* (1967). Professor Heilbroner, although trained as an economist, is steeped in the history of the United States and uses his knowledge of our past experience effectively to help explain the current state of the economy.

John A. Garraty   Professor Heilbroner, every historian who has studied the economic growth of the United States has been impressed by the rapidity and dynamism of its development. Broadly speaking, what were the reasons for this growth?

Robert L. Heilbroner   Well, to begin with, America has a self-selected population, literate, skilled, and enterprising, and a continent with an extraordinary abundance of resources. It's a bit of an exaggeration, but America did spring fully formed from the brow of Athena—at least so far as its developmental potential was concerned. Within a very short space of time the colonies, which began from scratch, enjoyed a higher level of real wages than the mother country.

By 1800, America was already a very prosperous nation. One couldn't say it was the most prosperous in the world so far as the upper classes were concerned. For them, it was much more pleasant to live in Europe. But for the lower classes and the farming classes, America was a far superior place.

A couple of accidents of history, mainly having to do with the Revolution and the Napoleonic Wars, further speeded growth. Up to about 1814, America was on its way to becoming a tremendously successful New Zealand. But the Revolutionary War and then the Embargo made it clear that the price of a purely agrarian economy was dependence on Europe. After the War of 1812, even Jefferson, who formerly had regarded cities and workshops as the breeding places of every vice, realized that America had to make its own manufactures. The whole country turned toward industrialism, and proceeded over the next three decades to create, more or less as an act of conscious national policy, the underpinnings for industrialization; so that by the Civil War the nation was, so far as industrialization was concerned, ready to go.

J.A.G.   In what way was the experience of Latin America different from that of North America? Wasn't the same selective process going on among Spaniards and Portuguese who went to the New World, and weren't the resources there? Why didn't industry develop in Latin America in the nineteenth century?

R.L.H.   I stumble for an answer, but several factors probably were involved. One was climate. It appears to me a plausible conjecture, based on the distribution of wealth around the globe, that it's very hard to build dynamic economic societies in the tropics. It has only recently come again to the fore among economists (although the idea was discovered in the sixteenth century), but productivity depends in great part on plain hard work. There is a very interesting article in the *American Economic Review* by Harvey Leibenstein, "Allocational Efficiency vs. X-Efficiency," which points out that it's very hard to explain the differences of efficiency among economic systems only in terms of the standard explanations of economics. One has to assume that some workers, firms, or countries simply do not approach what economists call the "production possibility frontier," where presumably all right-minded entrepreneurs dwell. A hot, disease-bearing climate doesn't help a man get to the production possibility frontier.

Then there is the matter of cultural differences. Of course, the trouble with ascribing things to culture is that it involves you in a nonfalsifiable hypothesis. But when you line up the countries of the world according to per-capita living standards and examine their religious affiliations, the Protestant ones are on top. America was a Protestant country and Latin America was not. I can see historians giving me dirty looks at the suggestion that Catholic cultures weren't also "enterprising." They were, after all, the great trading centers of Genoa and Venice. But in trying to answer your difficult question, this is a *possibility.* The colonizers of Latin America brought over the attitudes of the grandee, which were very far from those of the entrepreneur.

J.A.G.   One characteristic of American history, at least since the late nineteenth century, has been an increased regulation and control of the economy by the government: federal, state and local. During the same period, there has been a corresponding development of economic theory from the so-called New Economists of the 1880's, through the institutionalists and on to the Keynesians and neo-Keynesians. Have the politicians been influenced by these economic theorists? How well has public policy reflected that current state of economic knowledge?

R.L.H.   I think that economics has followed politics rather than politics economics. As political leaders discovered problems like the trusts, or the regulation of railroads, economists got interested in those problems. It was not until the Great Depression that economics began to lead to public policy. Before the Depression, economics was an epiphenomenon —it just floated on the surface. On the whole, economists were rationalizers, apologists, or, at most, general social critics. With the rise of the New Deal, however, the reverse feedback from economic theory into policy began, very hesitantly at first. Now, of course, economists have become almost as sacrosanct as businessmen used to be.

J.A.G.   But certainly in the late nineteenth century businessmen were parroting the ideas of the classical economists.

R.L.H.   I would make a distinction between ideology and practice. I don't think that economists shaped national policy, with the possible exception of the tariff, until the New Deal. They were not the initiators. When it came to the formulation of the ideology of the period, the justification of the social system itself, then, of course, the economists played a role. Economists have always been somewhat like theologians. In the works of Adam Smith (largely distorted) or John Stuart Mill (carefully edited), Americans found all sorts of rationalizations and justifications for their policies as businessmen. Today, by an ironical twist, economists certainly do not formulate the ideology of the period, but they *are* creators of policy.

J.A.G. How effective were the attempts of the federal government between the 1880's and the First World War to shape and control the American economy?

R.L.H. First of all, there was the tariff. How effective was the tariff? Who knows? My feeling is that alterations in the allocation of resources resulting from the tariff were insignificant. The other thing that the government did was to regulate the railroads, and to supervise—that's probably a better word than "regulate"—some other industries affecting the public interest. This too was of little significance. In fact, in *The Triumph of Conservatism*, Gabriel Kolko suggests that the effort of the government to do this, which appeared to be antibusiness, really answered very well the needs of a section of the business world which was alarmed at the unsettled competitive state of the market and which therefore pushed for regulation or supervision as a means of preventing the constant undercutting and whittling away of the power of the large corporations. Actually, I've often thought that if there had been no government regulation of business up to World War I, the difference wouldn't have been very great.

J.A.G. If the First World War was a turning point in this connection, how did it affect the American economy?

R.L.H. Unlike the Civil War, it was extremely propitious for growth. The Civil War, an unmechanized war, had only a small direct effect on capital formation or industrial production, but the First World War had an enormous effect. (I should add that a great many fortunes were made in the Civil War, which helped give rise to the spurt of industrialization in the late 1860's and 1870's.) More important, in the First World War the government intervened in economic planning for the first time. Although this planning apparatus was *ad hoc* and quickly dismantled— being regarded by many as a kind of flirtation with the devil—it marked a basic change in the relationship of the state and business. The state suddenly assumed an organizational role, not merely a supervisory or regulatory one. The changes were not permanent, but the blueprints remained, so the second time it was easier to do than the first time.

J.A.G. The Harding-Coolidge-Hoover era is usually seen as a time when businessmen had great influence on government policies. Did the actions of the government in this period really benefit the businessman?

R.L.H. What actions? This was really the last era of laissez faire. There was a considerable amount of government regulatory activity, but it was certainly an era of "high-jinx" finance, merger activities, and the like.

Insofar as the absence of restrictive policies permitted this carnival to go on, government policy aided business in the short run, but since these policies resulted eventually in economic collapse, or at least made the collapse worse than it might have been if therapeutic action had been taken earlier, in the long run it hurt business. But as I said earlier, before the New Deal era, government policy didn't matter much. There were powerful forces making for a boom in the twenties. In retrospect, it was a very curious boom, with many evidences of disequilibrium (unemployment, technological displacement, weakness in foreign trade). In addition, a shift of the income distribution toward the top 5 percent occurred, so that the prosperity was a very lopsided one.

The government played such a small role that all one can say is that capitalism at that time followed its inherent characteristics to nearly disastrous conclusions.

J.A.G.   Did the lack of activity of the government in the late 1920's exacerbate the Depression?

R.L.H.   I'm impressed by two possible interpretations of the Depression. One of them is John K. Galbraith's, and the other Milton Friedman's. (You couldn't have two more disparate viewers.) Galbraith puts great store on the flimsy banking structure. When the banks went down, he argues, they brought down, like a house of cards, an extraordinary superstructure of credit, and this was a tremendous factor in diffusing and lengthening the Depression. The government might have done something about the banking system in the twenties, but only within limits established by the realities. It was not empowered, in law, or in public acquiescence, to effectuate the kind of regulation that would have avoided the banking collapse.

Friedman's explanation is that once the Depression broke out it was terribly worsened by the activities of the Federal Reserve, which did just the wrong things to counter it. The "Fed" tightened credit when it should have loosened it, and loosened it when it should have tightened it. It refused to take strong action against stock-market speculation to begin with, and then, when the Depression broke, became so concerned about liquidity and solvency that it tightened restrictions. But there is little indication that a different government might have done better. There really wasn't a very clear understanding of the relationship between monetary policy and economic activity in general.

J.A.G.   To what extent did the New Deal succeed in coping with the Depression?

R.L.H.   It is hard to give a simple answer. It did some essential things, and failed to do others. For example, it rescued some people who were virtually at the edge of starvation. Yet, when World War II came, there were still some nine million unemployed. It restored national morale. Yet it did not succeed in restoring national economic health. It invited many overdue reforms. But it did not basically alter the system—as witness our deep problems today. In the immediate terms of the 1930's, it did not end the Depression. There was some recovery, but the recovery was sluggish, and the economy did not get back to the trend line of growth from the 1870 period through 1929 until the Second World War.

There were many reasons for all these failures. The New Deal strained the American consensus; it thrust the nation over the established boundaries of what had been regarded as the American Business Creed, and brought about, as everybody knows, a tremendous polarization of attitudes between labor and capital. Ideally, what Roosevelt should have done was expand the scale of many of his policies. The economy required expenditure programs running in the tens of billions. In the climate of the times that was impossible—in those days expenditures of $1 and $2 billions were regarded as virtually socialistic. Hence the New Deal was doomed to fail.

J.A.G. Were economists suggesting in the 1930's the kind of action that we now consider necessary in that kind of situation?

R.L.H. When the Depression broke out, no one really knew what to do about it. Economists were intellectually unprepared. When I studied economics in college in 1936, we used one of the best textbooks of the time, written by a man who was later to be one of the foremost exponents of Keynes. There was almost no mention in it of National Income, then called "the National Dividend." The nearest we came to modern economics was the chapter on business cycles, which discussed the up and downs of *prices*. There was almost no discussion of the ups and downs of *output* or *employment*.

J.A.G. Doesn't this suggest that Roosevelt's attitude of saying, in effect, "We must experiment," made much more sense than Hoover's? Perhaps critics have concentrated too much on what was wrong with what Hoover proposed, instead of pointing up his arrogance in thinking that he knew what to do.

R.L.H. Hoover was a slave to his received wisdom, while Roosevelt had his full share of the American characteristic of pragmatism. Roosevelt campaigned in 1932 for a balanced budget! I'm sure he sincerely believed that was the proper policy.

In any case, the government approached the Depression in a state of extraordinary unpreparedness. We didn't know how to disaggregate the economy. It wasn't until the vocabulary of income-investment-consumption and national income emerged that it became possible to know what to do. FDR's government had to live through this period of concept formation, until economists began to see that the key lay in expenditure, and that fiscal policy was crucial.

Roosevelt didn't understand Keynesian economics, but he understood the practical need for government unemployment programs—a Keynesian idea. He also accepted the advice of bankers like Marriner Eccles, that a public debt wasn't a disaster. I daresay that he didn't understand as well as President Kennedy what was really meant by the term "public debt." After all, this is a complicated subject; we don't teach it to freshmen now until their tenth week!

J.A.G.   Has the experience of the Depression and the application of the economic theories that grew out of the study of the Depression made it impossible to have another depression of the severity and duration experienced in the 1930's?

R.L.H.   I think so. First of all, the dangerous credit structure of the thirties doesn't exist any longer. Federal Deposit Insurance, margin requirements on the stock market, the prohibition against pyramiding holding companies—these things make the "domino effect" of failure much less likely. Secondly, the monetary management of the economy is much more sophisticated, and the mistakes that the Federal Reserve made in those days are not apt to be repeated. Thirdly, there is a wider public acceptance of the inextricable presence of the government, and of the need for the government to "do something" in bad times. All sorts of things can be done today that would have been unthinkable in Roosevelt's day. One hears very little these days about the unbalanced budget. Few people understand it, really, it is a sophisticated concept, and it can easily rouse popular fears. But people have somehow gulped and swallowed the fact that the "new economics" is right. For these reasons a prolonged depression is very unlikely.

J.A.G.   Did World War II have a different kind of impact on the economy from the First World War?

R.L.H.   It had one enormously different impact; it broke out in a period of underutilization and underemployment, so that its first effect was to bring the economy into a state of full employment. It also produced an extraordinary burst of production, and although the government took close to half the national output—a far larger proportion than in World War I—total output nevertheless rose so much that standards of living increased during the war, rather than declined. The other difference is that in the Second World War there was far more planning, a function of the degree of industrialization and the interdependence of an economy. During the First World War, the United States was still largely an agricultural country. In the Second World War, it was basically industrial. Industrial planning involves a multitude of interconnections. If you plan to change one part, you have to plan to change a lot of other parts to fit into the altered whole.

J.A.G. What are the major changes that have been taken place in the economy since World War II?

R.L.H. The big change has been an altered relationship between government and business. It wasn't until the 1950's that the responsibility of government to act as a balance wheel in the economy was formally recognized. In the 1920's, business recognized the legitimacy of government functions only in foreign affairs. No businessman today suggests that the government has no business spending money for social and economic purposes, or no business regulating business.

J.A.G. Was this change simply the product of businessmen's wartime experience, or did the fact that under Eisenhower the Republicans had control of the regulatory machinery make their conversion possible?

R.L.H. Mostly the former. There is always, in history, a lag between fact and the recognition of fact. The change in the role of government has come about through many "forces" which nobody could control: urbanization, population growth, the industrial process, new popular aspirations, and so on. Government—local, state, and federal—intervened in response to hard problems that had no other way of being handled. But for decades its right to do so was under contest. Gradually, this changed. Government's role, of course, is still increasing: vis-à-vis poverty, for example. Whenever new areas are explored, the legitimacy of the government to act is never immediately acknowledged by all.

J.A.G. Looking at the modern economy and some of its problems, first of all, do you think that corporate giantism is inevitable?

R.L.H. Yes, I do, if by "inevitable" you mean the product of forces over which we have no control. Technology and the driving competitive spirit of business produce it. Technology, especially the technology of information retrieval, makes it possible to increase the size of efficient operations almost without limit. The role of present-day competition is a curious one. Despite the much-advertised growth of managerialism, with its change in emphasis from acquisition to administration, managers are still plenty acquisitive, and very interested in growing for growth's sake alone. The acquisitive spirit, added to the technological possibilities, produces giantism. The counter forces to giantism are two: economic inefficiency (the limits beyond which it becomes unprofitable to grow), and public policy. Public policy has so far been exerted *within* industries. It is considered very important to maintain the rough balance of power that exists in the automobile industry and the steel industry, for example. The burst of recent mergers of the conglomerate kind is raising the question of whether public policy should be applied to check the type of growth that goes across industry boundaries.

J.A.G.   Do you believe the tendency to form conglomerates is in the national interest?

R.L.H.   I'm of two minds about it. J. K. Galbraith got off a wonderful line in *American Capitalism,* when he said that the attorneys of the Justice Department, searching for violations of the antitrust laws, visit the same plants as do the representatives of the Commerce Department, when showing distinguished foreign visitors our finest industrial enterprises. Big business brings amenities of no inconsiderable amount. For someone who has suffered the vicissitudes of the competitive market, to enter the calm waters of a megalopoly is great. It's much nicer to be a worker in a big, air-conditioned, fluorescent-lit, fringe-benefited plant, than in a crummy little plant; the big corporations do bring significant social benefits. At the same time, of course, they increase business power. I'm one who would like to see business power bounded, and who believes that we have not yet arrived at a very satisfactory division of social responsibility as between the public and private sector. The degree of power possessed by the public sphere is not yet large enough.

But I confess myself to be uncertain about this terribly important question. It depends on the direction in which one thinks American capitalism is going. Are we going to live in the future under corporate capitalism, or are we moving toward a more socially responsible planned society? I would like the motion to be toward a planned society, and the rise of the great corporations appears to me to be a countermovement away from the general direction of wider social responsibility. But many disagree. Many see in the great corporation itself an instrument of planning. Certainly, the managerial echelons are becoming much more socially aware and flexible. Perhaps a compromise between private and public power is possible that was not possible in the 1920's.

J.A.G.   Regarding the conglomerates, aren't most of the things that are socially desirable about large corporations, such as fluorescent lighting, air conditioning, and fringe benefits, unrelated to the question of whether large corporations combine with other large corporations in different fields? From a national perspective, what possible benefits do conglomerates produce? How does the society as a whole benefit from the combination of large corporations engaged in manufacturing diverse products?

R.L.H.   First of all, conglomerates, by buying up smaller businesses are spreading "the amenities." Secondly, the conglomerate corporation conceives of itself as a means of allocating capital. Heads of conglomerates don't see themselves as operational managers of a dozen businesses, but as central boards for the allocation of capital who can transfer capital from less to more productive or efficient elements of the combined businesses. If this is so, greater social efficiency results and economists must applaud.

The other side, of course, is whether all this bureaucracy is a fair exchange for the amenities, and whether these gigantic organizations which Adolph Berle compares to nation states serve the national interest. The trouble is that it's very difficult in our day to describe what you want. In the 1930's, liberals and radicals wanted the nationalization of industry. Today, the bloom is off that rose to a large extent. Would we gain public well being by nationalizing General Electric or General Motors? It is not clear. We would have the same self-serving bureaucracy in charge; it would only be a public bureaucracy rather than a private one, and maybe even harder to control.

Our society, in which technology is rampant and productivity is rising, is entering a new era of social organization. It has its own natural impetus toward bigness, but how that bigness is to be controlled is unclear. More and more the idea of the market as the ultimate controller gains repute. The conglomerates are still subject as private corporations to the pressures of product selection and product rejection by society, and this exercises some over-all control on their economic operations. The sticky part comes in the political sphere. Does the rise of great conglomerates mean that businessmen now occupy a position of too great importance in society? If society ought to devote huge resources to education, the cities, and the race problem, will the rise of conglomerates and of associated business power interfere?

J.A.G. Are modern labor unions becoming obsolete? Do they actually function in the public interest?

R.L.H. Labor unions grew up essentially to answer the needs of the unprotected individual in the large plant. That function is still maintained, but to a lesser degree in that corporations have become so personnel-relations conscious that in a good many instances they would doubtless continue to have adequate grievance mechanisms even if the union disappeared. When it comes to fighting over wages, which is still a central issue, of course the union is still a very powerful device. Unions help workers get good wages. They may ease the anonymity problem somewhat as well, although they're terribly bureaucratized. Attendance at labor-union meetings is usually very low, even in the most progressive unions like the Auto Workers.

The public interest question is difficult. In the 1930's we tended to identify the industrial worker with the public. Today this is much less true, first of all because the industrial worker is better off, secondly because employment has been shifting into the service trades, and not least, because the industrial unions, having won power, have impinged on other groups very strongly.

Of course it has always been true that a strike might affect the public interest adversely. At any time, a group of strategically placed workers could bring society practically to a halt. But as the economy becomes more complex, more groups have this power. What perhaps sharpens the issue is affluence, which makes strikes easier for workers to sustain over long periods than in the past. Then there is the eroding influence of affluence on social cohesion. It can be argued that industrial society depends on the existence of a large body of workers who *must* offer themselves for jobs they don't particularly like in order to survive. People are forced to work by hunger. When individuals don't get hungry because they have bank accounts or because they can go on welfare, the question arises, what control mechanism can be substituted? The answer is, the deliberate pressure of social control of one kind or another: despotic, or democratic, or however.

When more and more people are in a position to defy want and to sustain this defiance for a very long period of time, social collapse threatens. I am not an alarmist about this question, but I see it as an endemic problem of our society. And there has been very little discussion of what control mechanisms might be employed to hold together a society in which want was no longer a basis of social control.

J.A.G.   Does automation threaten to produce mass unemployment?

R.L.H.   Most economists do not regard automation as anything particularly alarming; they see it as a continuation of the process of mechanization and technological change which has brought particularistic disturbances, but which has been fundamentally beneficial to society. Mechanization in the past has brought about a shift of labor from one broad area of occupation to another—from the farm into the factory, and then from factory into the office. Between 1800 and today, a society built on an agricultural base has been turned into one built on an industrial base. However, the proportion of the work force that is engaged in manufacturing has, over the last half century and more, been very stable. During the single greatest era of expansion of manufactured products that the world has ever known, technology has advanced sufficiently rapidly so as to hold the demand for labor to a constant percentage of the work force.

In effect, labor has gone off the farm into manufacturing and has passed into still another sector of the economy, one that has acted as a great sponge to absorb the labor force. This sponge has been that congeries of occupations called the service professions, trade, the government, and so on.

What interests me about automation—and I must underline the fact that this is a hypothesis—is that it represents a new direction for technology. If automation were just the introduction of more machinery into manufacturing, I would agree with the economists that it is only a continuation of the trend of the past. Putting a computer into an automobile factory is not inherently any more labor-displacing than putting an overhead conveyor system in. But the introduction of computers and other machinery *into the service sector* is another matter. Technology has now reached a degree of flexibility that makes it possible for it to perform tasks that formerly required a high degree of brainwork (checking, comparing, calculating, as distinct from pushing, carrying, or cutting). This may add a serious dimension to the employment problem, for it might exert the same squeeze on service employment that it has exercised in the past on the manufacturing or agricultural sectors.

Where will the people who used to be absorbed into this expanding sponge of service occupations go? Perhaps into public or quasi-public activities—the hospitals, the supply of city services, the schools, nursing homes. But note that these employment-creating activities have as their common denominator the fact that they are largely funded through public means. If that's so, then automation implies the necessity for shunting new funds into the public sector.

It is possible, of course, that the new techniques will in the end attract labor rather than displace it. If machines can do bookkeeping for small companies, it may help establish more small companies. If men can use machines to keep the books in a dry-cleaning establishment, more men may set up as dry-cleaners. I don't think so, but I wouldn't want to rule it out as a possibility. But my hunch is that automation will displace labor in the service industries and will add pressure for enlarging the public sector.

Another possibility is that as the steady pressure of technology continues, we will avoid mass unemployment by adjusting, as we have in the past, to shorter work weeks. This will bring a qualitative change to life: four-day weekends and two-month vacations will make life different, and probably better, although it will also open new problems about the uses of leisure, even the purpose of life.

J.A.G. Can modern capitalism function efficiently without the artificial diversion of a large portion of its output into economically sterile war production?

R.L.H. Modern capitalism is a social mechanism that, among other things, generates extraordinary quantities of profits, and it is not easy to find means to invest this profit. Companies are always looking around for places to use their money, which accounts, I believe, for the enormous migration of American capital abroad. Now, one of the places in which capital can be used, a place with an absolutely insatiable demand for capital, is the military sector. It would simply be blind to deny this, although it's not quite the same thing as saying that military expenditures are essential to the existence of capitalism. Before World War II, the military was always the stepchild of the government, except for a little flurry around World War I, and business had very little interest in the military sector, which it regarded as a nuisance, and certainly not as a major source of enterprise or investment. Since World War II and the Cold War and the change in the conception of American power from isolationism to what is essentially a kind of imperialist view, there has certainly developed a combined political and economic impetus toward the creation of a war industry. Companies like North American Aviation or General Dynamics wouldn't exist without the military sector. Yet companies like General Motors are very little affected by military demands; they sell only a fraction of their output to the government. They would be more relieved by the diminution of the tax burden if the military establishment were dismantled than they would be penalized by the loss of orders.

It's hard to say whether the interest of business in military production ever becomes controlling in political activity. A number of historians and economists have argued both sides of this question. I would say that big business largely acquiesces in the judgment of the military, or at least sees no reason to oppose its judgment. Why should it? Military expenditure is a considerable source of profits. But I also believe that a strong impetus toward war spending comes from an ideologically fixated congressional element that strengthens and promotes the "military-industrial complex" independently, without, or anyway not because of business pressures. Not that I think these congressmen are pawns of the military. They have their own "middle-class" position which is xenophobic and aggressive, and very strongly anticommunist. They exercise a strategic position of power that helps to create and fortify this massive military sector.

J.A.G. What would happen to the economy if so much of our productive energies were not being diverted into war production?

R.L.H. There's a theoretical answer and a political answer to your question. The theoretical answer is very simple. Of course capitalism would survive, but it would require much larger investments in the public sector than now exist. The spontaneous demands of the public for private goods will not keep the economy running at full tilt. William James used to talk about the moral equivalent of war. I'm talking about the economic equivalent of war production.

But this is the solution in theory. Whether or not it can be done in practice is problematical. Would the prevailing beliefs of businessmen and congressmen permit a $100 billion national budget for education, welfare, cities, roads, and so on? *Maybe.* Could we generate enough public peacetime demand without forcing the government to compete with private industry? I think this is possible. Take the cities. I see no reason why public corporations funded by the government could not rebuild Pittsburgh or Detroit or New York by tendering bids to private companies who would do the actual work.

The problem is, essentially, one of ideology and political awareness. A neo-Marxist would disagree with my hopeful diagnosis. He would maintain that capitalist interests will not tolerate such an invasion of their precincts. I believe that the big corporations could easily make their peace with it simply because it would be profitable.

J.A.G. Doesn't the fundamental difficulty lie in the fact that given modern technology, we can make goods faster than we can consume them?

R.L.H. I think that's a misconception. Actually, what you mean is that we have a very high level of productivity. There are a number of ways of adjusting to this. It is perfectly true that we may produce more automobiles than the country can buy. If that is the case, General Motors will have to make something else. Can you have a flood of *all* goods? That's not so easy to imagine. If we did, we could cut the work week to 20 hours instead of 40. The specter of overproduction is valid as applied to individual industries, but I do not believe we can yet overproduce goods as a whole. There's still obviously an enormous demand for goods in America. The average family gets along on $7,000 or $8,000. I've never heard a man who makes three times that complaining that he couldn't use his $25,000. When income rises, demands shift from the goods that pour off assembly lines to goods that are characterized by services. You go to a good lawyer if you're in trouble, to a more expensive doctor, take more expensive vacations. Hence we can expect a very rich society to produce proportionately fewer goods and more services.

J.A.G. Assuming the soundness of Keynesian theories about controlling and directing the economy, are these ideas feasible in a democracy like the United States?

R.L.H. That depends on whether or not public guidance to the economy is acceptable to business and to other groups. American business can't be described just in terms of the great corporations. There are twelve million enterprises in this country, and although the economic weight they swing is minuscule compared with the weight swung by the thousand biggest corporations, the political weight is very considerable. Small businessmen vote; they dominate the small communities. Small business has not "bought" either the economics of unbalanced budgets, or the philosophy of a guided economy. This explains the reluctance of Congress to take the necessary steps to implement Keynes's theories—that is, to adopt a flexible tax policy.

When all is said and done, the level of public expenditures is a national choice that is made every four years. But to make the system work—as the New Economics has it, to fine-tune the economy—requires the power to change tax levels frequently. What is clearly needed to make modern macroeconomics effective is a discretionary tax policy, controlled by the President. In the fullness of time we'll probably get this, but we haven't got it now.

J.A.G. The idea of allowing the Executive to control the purse is antithetical to the whole tradition of English and American democracy.

R.L.H. Of course. But the Executive does control the purse, let's not kid ourselves. It's a bounded control, but it infringes upon traditional divisions of power. Modern economics still hasn't found full popular acceptance. But, in general, the uneducated public, albeit uneasily, allows the economists to control policy. Of course there's always the lurking danger that one day the people will say, "No, you can't unbalance the budget because it's wrong." Lots of congressmen still say this. One pins one's hope, as always, on this frail reed called education.

J.A.G. Is the United States today an imperialist nation? Does modern American capitalism profit by exploiting other parts of the world? Does it exert strong influences on other nations without regard for the desires of their people?

R.L.H. We are certainly an imperialist nation in one sense: we have shown a willingness to send military forces abroad. Whether we're an imperialist nation in the Marxian sense is a more difficult question. Is there a force that impels American corporations to send their money to underdeveloped areas, the force being the inability to find adequate investment opportunities for profits at home? Perhaps. Then the question is: When the money goes to Brazil, say, or Mexico, does it dominate the local economy? Again, perhaps. The position of foreign capital in the "backward" nations is much less secure today than it used to be. These countries aren't supine colonies any more.

Exactly what American capital *does* in these countries is hard to say. Most of the governments in Latin America are conservative, loath to push very hard for fundamental changes in the structure of landownership or in various social areas. This conservative tendency is acceptable to American corporations because it means they're not pushed very hard. I am sure that American corporations help these governments to stay in power. But I do not think it's very likely that we would go to war "to defend Standard Oil."

American capitalism feels threatened today in much the same way that the English aristocracy felt threatened by the French Revolution. Forces are at work in the world which call into question the premises on which capitalistic society is built. It is hardly surprising that those who are the most direct beneficiaries of capitalism feel personally jeopardized, and bend policy to whatever extent they can to mute or block those forces.

J.A.G. Leaving aside ideological and moral considerations, how different is modern American capitalism from the economic system of Russia?

R.L.H. Of course there are similarities; they are both industrial systems, both characterized by large enterprises, with all the managerial problems associated with bureaucracies, and so on. But there are striking differences. Russia is still essentially agricultural in terms of its "labor" force, nearly half of which is on the farm. America is industrial: only one in twenty of its labor force is a farmer. The American economy is essentially guided by the marketplace. In the Russian economy the central guiding force is still a plan.

Both the planning system and the market system have important shortcomings. The market system is marvelous for achieving internal efficiency, but it's disastrous in terms of achieving certain kinds of allocations, as witness conditions in our cities, the coexistence of poverty and riches, and so on. The Russian economy is just the opposite. What cries out to be done there is to introduce flexibility and efficiency; the system is unbelievably inflexible and inefficient. The convergence thesis —the idea that each of the two systems is borrowing certain features from the other—has nothing to do with ideology. Neither side will be undone in this process. But that there is a degree of structural convergence is beyond dispute.

J.A.G. What are the half-dozen or so books that you would recommend to persons interested in the subject we have been discussing? In each case, would you indicate briefly what the main contribution of the volume is?

R.L.H. Stuart Bruchey, *The Roots of American Economic Growth* (1965) is an eclectic (in the best sense of the word) survey and pronouncement on the complex question of how American economic growth began and what sustained it. Thomas Cochran and William Miller, *The Age of Enterprise* (1961) is a very well-written general economic history concentrating on the rise of industrial America. Gabriel Kolko, *The Triumph of Conservatism* (1963) is a controversial but extremely interesting analysis of the role of big business in the rise of government regulation of business. Then J. K. Galbraith, *The Great Crash* (1955) a little book, less well-known than many of the author's works, presents a cogent analysis of the causes of the Great Depression and the chances for the recurrence of such a catastrophe. Finally, Robert Averitt, *The Dual Economy* (1968) is a short, original, and important description and analysis of the size and operational significance of the big corporation in the American economy today.

Arthur M. Schlesinger, Jr.

Political and Social Change: 1941–1968

ARTHUR M. SCHLESINGER JR., Albert Schweitzer Professor of Humanities at the City University of New York, is one of the most prolific, highly regarded, and controversial of all American historians. He has won Pulitzer prizes for both history and biography, along with a Parkman prize, a Bancroft prize, a National Book Award, and the gold medal of the National Institute of Arts and Letters. The popular enthusiasm generated by his work is attested to by the fact that several of his books have been selections of the Book of the Month Club. Among his many historical works, *The Age of Jackson* (1945), *The Age of Roosevelt* (three volumes to date, 1957–60), and *A Thousand Days: John F. Kennedy in the White House* (1965) are the best known. Professor Schlesinger has also, however, maintained a continuing interest in politics and public affairs, having served as a special assistant to President Kennedy and written extensively about current politics. Thus the interview brings out his talents both as a historian and as a commentator on contemporary affairs; he discusses domestic history since World War II and also comments shrewdly on the present state of the nation.

John A. Garraty Professor Schlesinger, it has often been said that the domestic reforms which we call the New Deal ended because of the need to focus national energies on the international crises that led to World War II, but it is also a kind of historical cliché that the war itself was a powerful instrument for domestic reform. Would you comment generally on the political and social effects of.the war on the United States?

Arthur M. Schlesinger, Jr. The coming of the war did mark the end of social reform in the legislative sense; indeed, following the congressional elections of 1938, a coalition of Southern Democrats and conservative Republicans in the House of Representatives blocked nearly all progressive social legislation for nearly a quarter of a century. But the war did not quite mean the end of the New Deal, because the executive branch could still pursue reform goals. And the war was certainly a force for social reform, if in most cases only by indirection. Legislation which had a reform character could be passed when it was alleged to serve wartime purposes. Generally, the primary motive was effective war mobilization, although a certain amount of reform could be smuggled into the war effort, as in the case of the attempt to distribute war contracts to small business. There was, for example, a movement toward equalization of income. This was not done in the interests of economic equality, but in the interests of "equality of sacrifice" in the war effort.

Consider the establishment of the Fair Employment Practices Commission. To head off a threatened march on Washington organized by the black union leader A. Philip Randolph in 1941, Roosevelt agreed to the establishment of a wartime FEPC. Though its powers were not extensive, it did open the way for Negroes to move into war employment. The need for more labor in defense industries provided the pretext for the FEPC. In a larger sense, however, the fact that we were at war against a nation committed to the doctrine of the master race raised a question that had long been ignored by most Americans. How could we send men to kill and die abroad if we continued to cling to a doctrine of the master race at home? How could Americans fight and die for Roosevelt's Four Freedoms elsewhere in the world, and not extend them to Alabama and Mississippi? The war provided a new stimulus to the American conscience, a new awareness of the black problem. The beginnings were made of the desegregation of the armed forces. Black leaders were given a kind of bargaining responsibility as representatives of the black community. In short, Negro Americans improved their position during the Second World War, both through the political recognition they received because of national war aims, and because of the economic opportunities created by war mobilization.

On the other hand, various New Deal agencies like the WPA were terminated; the Farm Security Administration was eviscerated; one after another, the social reform agencies were brought to an end. Still, war-time agencies such as the War Production Board and the Office of Price Administration were ordinarily run by people with a sense of responsibility not only to war production, but also to the general structure of society.

One other fact should be noted: the extent to which the war stimulated internal migration and accelerated the flight of both blacks and poor whites from the countryside to the cities. This produced a marked change in American society.

J.A.G. Every major American war has produced profound social and economic, and often political, changes. Can you strike a balance about World War II, as compared with earlier wars, as to the changes accomplished?

A.M.S. Compared to the First World War, the effects of the Second World War were greater and more lasting. It was seen, I believe correctly, as a fundamental struggle between democracy and fascism. For this reason, there was a high degree of idealism involved in the war. Though much of it was dissipated in the process, enough remained to postpone the quick domestic reaction that followed the First World War. The 80th Congress, which was elected in 1946, was a right-wing Congress, but it did not attempt to revise the structure of legislation produced by the New Deal. Truman was re-elected in 1948, and immediately set forth a program which carried forward the New Deal in many ways. The sharp wave of postwar reaction—the equivalent of the Red scare following the First World War—did not come until 1950.

J.A.G. Why did conservatives make so little effort when they did regain power to do away with the social and economic changes of the New Deal?

A.M.S. In most cases, they discovered that they'd grown to accept the new social structure erected by the New Deal. They realized that the Roosevelt reforms had been good for the country and that it would be hard to reverse them. Not only had these reforms attained very widespread popular acceptance, but one result of the New Deal was the creation of a large bureaucracy, and bureacracies always have a great capacity to resist change. Just as the federal bureaucracy in 1961 resisted the efforts of the Kennedy administration to change policy in a liberal direction, so in 1953 it resisted the efforts of the Eisenhower administration to change policy in a conservative direction.

Furthermore, accepting something is a good deal easier than starting it. Conservatives can be defined, in American history, as men who stand firmly on the liberal position of the preceding generation. This is the essence of what happened in the 1950's. But they were very much opposed to further innovation, and therefore successfully blocked most of the attempts at extending the New Deal.

J.A.G. Putting aside his role in international relations, how would you rate Truman as a President? He certainly considered himself a disciple of Franklin Roosevelt. In what ways was he different from Roosevelt as a political leader, and as a chief executive?

A.M.S. Truman was an authentic disciple of Roosevelt; his Fair Deal was an effort to consolidate, systematize, and extend the New Deal. As an executive, he was much more orderly than Roosevelt. He lacked Roosevelt's relish for confused, competitive administrative situations, as well as his capacity to manage people of diverse ideas and conflicting personalities. Truman's government was organized in a much tighter way, and his program was less internally contradictory than Roosevelt's. Of course, the country was not nearly in the state of emergency that it was in Roosevelt's time. Truman was not under pressure to do a lot of things at once. On the other hand, because the situation seemed less urgent, he had great difficulty in getting Congress to go along with anything he wanted to do in domestic affairs.

Yet, in spite of that, Truman drew up what has been generally recognized as the agenda for liberal action for some time to come. His Civil Rights Commission of 1946 established civil rights as a national peacetime issue. Roosevelt may have made it an issue during the war, but primarily in the guise of mobilizing American labor for war purposes rather than as a fulfillment of the rights to which Negro Americans are entitled as American citizens. Similarly, Oscar Ewing's plan for medical care, although still not enacted, led to the Kennedy-Johnson Medicare Plan. Truman's Secretary of Agriculture Brannan made an effort to get at the farm problem by shifting the emphasis from the support of prices to the support of income—again a very fertile idea, that has only been applied in a limited way. Truman tried in these ways to round out and push forward the New Deal program. He did so with much less fire, much less eloquence. The people around him were less dramatic; the times were not nearly so propitious for domestic reform.

His Fair Deal came to frustration also because of Truman's weaknesses. As Elmer Davis used to say, Truman was good on the big things and bad on the small ones; his tolerance of improper behavior by men in his administration, the exposure of scandals in various departments, and so on, tarnished and further complicated the prospects of the Fair Deal.

J.A.G. Did Truman really change his times through his own personality or ideas, or was he merely a product of the particular circumstances in which he happened to be President?

A.M.S. He was a continuator, and continuators often perform useful functions. Truman could not have existed without Roosevelt, just as Van Buren and Polk could not have existed without Jackson, or, in modern India, as Shastri could not have existed without Nehru. I do not think he made any great contributions so far as domestic policy is concerned through his own force of personality or his own vision. Foreign policy, of course, is another matter.

J.A.G. Most historians, I think, would agree that Eisenhower was something less than a first-rate President, and that his conception of the proper role of the President was extremely limited. What is your particular estimate of his inadequacies? Were they entirely personal? Can a case be made for the argument that during the 1950's the times conspired against effective presidential leadership and serious domestic reform?

A.M.S. I think Eisenhower symbolized and expressed a national desire for repose. Any activist President would have encountered great difficulties in the 1950's. My father has argued that there has been a rhythm between periods of activism and periods of passivity in American affairs. The fifties were certainly a time when the cycle was in a phase of quiescence. If Adlai Stevenson had been elected in 1952, he probably would have encountered the same frustration that Truman encountered in trying to pursue an activist policy. Eisenhower unquestionably suited the national mood.

On the other hand, looking back, it's perfectly clear that we could not afford a do-nothing presidency in the fifties, at least in domestic affairs. One reason for the intense internal crisis in which America finds itself today is surely the failure of the national government in the 1950's. If Eisenhower had moved on the question of racial justice, on the problems of the cities and of poverty, much of the bitterness in the nation today might have been avoided. The Supreme Court gave a hint in 1954 with the School Desegregation case, but Eisenhower ignored that. Indeed, he rather resented the Supreme Court's raising the issue, and acted on civil rights only when forced to. Similarly, the problems of the cities were much more manageable then. Had he begun to recognize things that might be done, the urban crisis might now be much less acute.

So these were wasted years, wasted as a result of Eisenhower's conception of the presidency—what Theodore Roosevelt called the "Buchanan-Taft" conception—the view that the President should not play a large role in initiating legislation. Eisenhower couldn't altogether stick to that conception because it is an impossible one. He was forced into a more active stance on many occasions. Nonetheless, this was his theory.

J.A.G. You have written extensively about the Kennedy administration, both as an historian and as an eyewitness. Have recent events, particularly the assassination of Robert Kennedy, added to or modified your judgment of John F. Kennedy's impact on American politics?

A.M.S. I would say that events have strengthened my impressions. The one thing Kennedy most deeply believed in was the existence of a deep reserve of idealism in the American people. He was a very unsentimental politician. He did not think idealism could be invoked by sentimental means. But he was persuaded that Americans cared about something other than the scramble for money and selfish fulfillment, that there would be tremendous response to a call to achieve some larger purpose, particularly among the young. He recognized the strength of vested interests. At times he perhaps overreacted to the existence of these interests. But he had a basic conviction that America was about something else and that if we could find ways of releasing this idealism and giving it expression, we could, as he said in 1960, "get the country moving again." This was something which Robert Kennedy also believed, possibly even more keenly.

The reaction to the deaths of John and Robert Kennedy suggests the character of a problem which they both were tackling: each murder produced a period of extraordinary national mourning, followed by a rather quick return to business as usual on the part of the country. Our easy capacity to revert to things as they were, the shortness of the national memory, is a problem with which the Kennedys were struggling, and which others will struggle with. We've now murdered not only the Kennedy brothers, but Dr. Martin Luther King and a number of other prominent Americans, and, in spite of all the orgies of remorse and sorrow, we still do not have, for example, effective gun-control legislation.

J.A.G. Have the tragic circumstances of the assassinations tended to make Americans overestimate the significance of the Kennedy family in politics?

A.M.S. It's impossible to say. I think that both Kennedys were very exceptional political leaders. They were both men of great intelligence and deep conviction, who combined idealism with a shrewd and realistic understanding of politics. John Kennedy once described himself as an idealist without illusions. The capacity to unite realism and idealism is a very powerful thing. I believe that in any case, they would have had a tremendous impact on America.

J.A.G. Is there any possible connection between the particular qualities of the Kennedy brothers and the fact that they were killed?

A.M.S. There are those who suggest that the Kennedys, coming from a wealthy family, being good-looking, having excellent educations, beautiful wives, and so on, were natural targets of envy, whom resentful, frustrated, alienated, embittered, ruthless men would be tempted to kill. Yet there have been many leaders for whom those things were also true who have not been murdered. The one thing which distinguishes the series of political murders we've had in this country in the 1960's is that with the single exception of the American-Nazi leader, George Lincoln Rockwell, the victims have been on the left. I know no way to explain this except to suggest that there is something about the atmosphere in the United States in the 1960's which legitimatizes a resort to violence. In the 1930's, despite the sharpness of the internal conflicts, despite the great unemployment, despite the violent personal hatred of F.D.R. (perhaps unmatched in the annals of President-hating), there was no attempt on Roosevelt's life while he was President.

J.A.G. Kennedy made heavy use in government service of intellectuals and scholars such as yourself. Was his policy actually a very novel one, or does it merely seem novel because it contrasted so sharply with that of Eisenhower before him, and Johnson after him?

A.M.S. In a sense, I think it was novel. Obviously, other Presidents, particularly F.D.R., had drawn on academics and intellectuals. But F.D.R. used them mostly for advice; he rarely gave them administrative responsibility, or if they held government jobs, these were not particularly connected with their intellectual experience. The historian W. E. Dodd was sent to Germany as ambassador, but this cannot be compared with Kennedy's sending Edwin O. Reischauer to Japan or John Kenneth Galbraith to India. Kennedy went further than any preceding President in systematically giving intellectuals positions of administrative power.

He was responding to a situation which is going to have increasing force. Even President Nixon has drawn on the academic community. Kennedy happened to like intellectuals and enjoy their company. Nixon, I imagine, does not. But the circumstances of the presidency in an age of high technology—the complex nature of the problems he faces and the solutions he must seek—will require political authority to draw increasingly from the intellectual community. Kennedy anticipated this, encouraged it, and enjoyed it.

J.A.G. Did Kennedy have any other insights into the changing character of the American political system, and particularly into the proper role and function of the presidency in that system?

A.M.S. He was a strong, conscious exponent of the activist theory of the presidency. He wanted to redeem the office from the passivity which had enveloped it in the Eisenhower years. He modeled himself on Presidents like the two Roosevelts. In his administrative method he did not go as far as Franklin Roosevelt in the cultivation of competition, but he was far more informal and free-wheeling than either his immediate predecessor or his successor. He was particularly concerned never to become a prisoner of a single structure of information, as Johnson did, for example, on Vietnam. Like Roosevelt, he was prepared to get information from all sorts of sources.

J.A.G.   You have spoken and written persuasively about the right and duty of intellectuals to participate in government, rather than to remain on the sidelines as critics and evaluators. But what about the impact of politics on intellectuals? Did Kennedy's concern for the intellect have any appreciable effect on American culture?

A.M.S.   There is no single role for intellectuals. Their roles will vary according to their temperaments. Some will be participants, some will be critics, some will be denouncers. The important thing is to maintain a spectrum of opinion in the intellectual community. Those who enjoy being close to power should be encouraged; it would be disastrous to have a government without intellectuals. On the other hand, those who are temperamentally disposed to exhortation or detachment or denunciation should be encouraged too; it would be terrible if all the intellectuals became accomplices of power. I do not personally think it a mistake for intellectuals to serve an administration whose general purposes they approve, or to make the compromises which are inevitable in the democratic process. Any form of involvement requires compromise; indeed, compromise is the essence of democracy; and it is possible to compromise in practical legislative or executive situations without abandoning one's basic convictions. Participation in the national government seems to me far less compromising and corrupting than participation in some tight and dogmatic body like, say, the Communist party. But if intellectuals go into politics, they should learn something about it; one of the troubles of so many intellectuals with political opinions is that they have no knowledge of what they're talking about.

The Kennedy administration stimulated the intellectual and artistic community by giving it appropriate recognition. During the Eisenhower period, the national government conveyed the impression that intellectuals were second- or third-class figures, if not in some sense un-American. Kennedy believed that the life of the mind was close to the center of what America was all about. In various ways, some of them ceremonial and symbolic, he tried to make this point.

Beyond that, in certain of his own convictions and actions he set in motion processes of revaluation. For example, consider the stimulus he gave to thinking about foreign affairs in his American University speech, the first statement by a Western leader of the exhaustion of the old concepts of the Cold War. He encouraged Americans to postulate a world of diversity, to recognize that America was neither omnipotent nor omniscient. A lot of people were thinking along the same lines, but K   · ᵃᵗ in motion that attitude toward America's relation in the
˚ ᵈ the limitationist school.

J.A.G. Was Lyndon Johnson's role in history like Truman's in the sense, to use your phrase, that he could not have existed had Kennedy not existed first, in the same way that Truman couldn't have existed without Roosevelt?

A.M.S. In a certain sense that's so, but there were pathetic developments in the Johnson presidency which distinguish it from Truman's. In a loyal, dowdy, tough-minded way, Truman carried forward the main Roosevelt impulses in both domestic and foreign policy. Johnson certainly carried forward the Kennedy impulse in domestic policy: the Great Society was a new face on Kennedy's New Frontier. The irony of Johnson is that, having started out so promisingly, he allowed his domestic program to be derailed by his obsession with the war in Vietnam, an obsession which increasingly monopolized not only his own attention but the resources and concern of the country. It's ironic, because in national affairs Johnson had experience, knowledge, and sound instincts. In foreign affairs, his knowledge was scant, his ideas rigid and simplistic.

J.A.G. In reading your volumes on Franklin Roosevelt, I was repeatedly struck by the extent to which the job of President had become, even in the 1930's, so complex that Roosevelt appeared to have little to do with the shaping of legislation. If anything, this seems even more apparent in your account of the "thousand days" of John F. Kennedy. Has the role of the federal government become so complicated that any President, despite the enormous power at his disposal, is not really any longer capable of running the country?

A.M.S. Certainly, the task of the President is infinitely greater than it used to be. It never was an easy job, but when Andrew Jackson was President, the population of the United States was about twenty million, hardly more than the population of the state of New York today. It was not until 1857 that Congress, with great munificence, passed a law giving President Buchanan a staff—a secretary, a messenger, and a steward. Up to this point, the Presidents had to run the government ordinarily by drafting relatives, most often nephews, to write their letters and run errands for them. It was not until Theodore Roosevelt's administration that the presidential offices were moved out of the residential part of the White House into the new West Wing. The Government Reorganization Act of 1939 created a White House staff—half-a-dozen special assistants whom the President could use as he desired. After the war, the President acquired the Council of Economic Advisers and the National Security Council as further means of control.

A reasonably hard-working, bright President with sufficient energy can, through these mechanisms, maintain control over the *major* issues which confront him. But in any enterprise so vast and multifarious as the United States government, many small things go on which the President knows little about. Robert Kennedy one day said to me as he was looking through some of the papers left by J.F.K., "I thought I was closer to my brother than anyone else. I thought he talked over with me most of the things he was involved in. But I'm absolutely astonished at the number of things he was doing that I didn't know anything about."

I don't know what alternative there is. Some political scientists have suggested a plural presidency. Others have suggested having a couple of deputy Vice Presidents, one for domestic affairs and one for foreign. In practice, Eisenhower did that with Sherman Adams and John Foster Dulles. I can't conceive of any President—except one like Eisenhower—who would wish to delegate decision-making in any basic way. We've had two kinds of Presidents: those who like to make decisions and those who don't. Each type designs an administrative structure to suit his purposes. One reason why Roosevelt was pleased with overlapping jurisdictions and competing delegations of authority was that he wanted to make sure that the important issues were brought to him to decide.

Kennedy liked making decisions. The job of the White House staff was to alert him of impending crises before they came to him through the normal channels of government. Cabinet members naturally like to preserve as much power as they can for themselves, if they're any good. Also, they don't want to bother the President or worry him. This may deny the President information or decisions necessary to him. Kennedy wanted to know about things before they happened, and he used the White House staff to make sure he did.

J.A.G.   Nevertheless, the cumulative impact of your description of the various actions of the government during the New Deal suggests, at least to me, that Roosevelt had little to do with much of what went on. Have your researches increased or decreased your sense of Roosevelt's responsibility for the New Deal?

A.M.S.   It's true that there has been a tendency in writing about the New Deal to exaggerate Roosevelt's personal contributions and to understate the contribution of others, especially of the Congress. A number of the important actions of the Roosevelt administration, such as the Wagner Labor Relations Act, were really products of congressional initiative. But this does not mean that the decisions which determined the directions of policy were not made by Roosevelt, or that his aides did not carefully control and supervise the drafting and movement of New Deal legislation.

The personal role of the President varies. There are only so many hours in a day, and part of them have to be spent in seeing people and so on. The President's use of time is influenced very much by the crises of the moment and by the bent of his own preoccupation. For example, even in the depths of the Depression, Roosevelt, since he was interested in it, kept close tabs on the Navy. He had a consuming interest in the conservation of natural resources, and kept working it into all sorts of other things, such as unemployment relief. Curiosity and personal interests are great things for Presidents.

J.A.G. What is your opinion of the so-called "New Left" interpretation of recent political history?

A.M.S. I'm in favor of reinterpreting things; I think revisionism is a good idea. It forces everyone to take a fresh look at problems. The New Left has done a good job in calling attention to neglected areas of American history. We should have done much more work in the past about Negro history, and the New Left has certainly stimulated that. I'm not unhappy about the New Left approach to the Jacksonian period, because I find that their attack on the consensus and entrepreneurial interpretations defends some of the points I made in *The Age of Jackson*.

As far as the period we are talking about is concerned, I'm less impressed by the work of the New Left. The problem of the origins of the Cold War, for example, is more complicated than was once assumed, but I do not share the New Left view that it was a result of American aggression against a benign Soviet Union bent on getting along with the rest of the world. The effort to portray Truman as a villain is not to my mind convincing. Oddly enough, this general approach indicts Roosevelt as well as Truman, and in a curious way connects with the old revisionists like Charles Tansill and Charles A. Beard. The New Left historians feel that Roosevelt wanted to force World War II on Japan, and provoked the attack on Pearl Harbor; that American foreign policy since the Open Door has been at all times at the service of American economic interests. I have never understood how F.D.R., for example, could be in his foreign policy the passive instrument of those same businessmen with whom he was fighting so savagely over domestic policy; but this is what the New Left historians would have us believe.

J.A.G. What about the New Left view of Roosevelt and Truman as being reactionaries in domestic affairs?

A.M.S. Obviously, that view was not shared by the powerful economic interests of the thirties and forties! And this New Left proposition reveals a pervading weakness of the New Left, in historical analysis as well as in political action. They are chronically indifferent to or contemptuous of the political realities which leaders in the real world—especially in a democratic system—have to face. They complain because Roosevelt and Truman did not take steps which would have been politically infeasible. I do not pretend the judgment is always easy. I must confess

I used to have arguments with President Kennedy about such matters. He felt that there were greater limits on what he could do than I felt there were. Yet one has to admit the possibility that Presidents may know more about politics than their special assistants. Perhaps that is one reason why Presidents are Presidents and their special assistants are only special assistants. A historian must suppose either that a President did not want to achieve an objective, or that, if he did want to achieve it, the situation looked more complex and intractable to him than it does to the historian in retrospect.

J.A.G.   It is a cliché that we live in a dynamic age. Would you summarize what seem to you the most significant social changes that have occurred since the Second World War?

A.M.S.   I would say that some of the following ought to be included. Certainly the Negro revolution—it has been so long and shamefully delayed. The population explosion in the years after the war is also basic in what has happened to American society. The urban problem—"the crisis of the cities"—is still another: the crowding and disintegration of cities, and the changed relation between the cities and the suburbs. In recent years, the problem of the young has emerged in a way rather different from ever before. And the development of electronic media has colored American life in ways in which we can only begin to perceive. The identification of poverty as an issue is another thing, as is the shift from a production to a service economy, and the new importance in this highly specialized economy of education and what John Kenneth Galbraith calls the "technostructure." Beyond all this, we must look forward to a society where, before too long, many people will spend more of their lives at leisure than at labor. Already, people are entering the labor market later, working shorter hours, taking longer vacations, retiring earlier, and living longer. One question for the future will be whether our society makes wise or wasteful use of this unprecedented amount of free time.

J.A.G.   How actually has life changed for the average American Negro since the war?

A.M.S.   Life has improved for the average Negro, in the South and in the North. He has a better opportunity for employment, for political participation, for education. And the improvement in the situation of the Negro has quite naturally increased his sense of grievance and bitterness. As Tocqueville pointed out long ago, ills acquiesced in and thought beyond the possibility of change can be accepted, but the same ills become intolerable when change appears possible. There is no puzzle for the historian in the fact that the objective improvement in the conditions of black Americans has been accompanied by an increasing sense of injustice and alienation. A concept which sociologists, with their usual literary felicity, have called "relative deprivation" works in this case.

J.A.G.   The new militancy of Negroes is, as you say, perfectly understandable, but what of its effectiveness?

A.M.S.   Given the complacency of the white community, I do not believe that black Americans would have gotten anywhere without militancy. If blacks had remained meek and submissive and invisible, white America would have done damned little about them. If violence becomes irrational and obsessive and excessive, white America has first itself to blame. When the blacks decided to organize and become militant, they forced white Americans to consider the problems. They awakened the white conscience, and they awakened white fears. The civil rights movement has resulted from this combination of circumstances. Of course, many white liberals worked for civil rights for a long time, and they played an indispensable role.

But conceding that militancy from a black viewpoint has been useful and that every ghetto riot probably increases the disposition of public authority to do justice to black America, may not militancy be carried to such an extreme as to provoke a dangerous reaction? Does the Black Power movement help or hurt the Negroes? A debate is going on within the black community as to the relative merits of integration and separation. This has been very distressing to liberals of my generation, who believe that civil rights means integration. I have talked to a number of black friends about this, and I'm beginning to see the problem more clearly. Is black separatism a temporary stage or an ultimate goal? A strong and rather persuasive case can be made that the present rhetoric of integration implies total acceptance of white values, and therefore is demoralizing for the Negro; and that genuine integration will be impossible unless it's *preceded* by separatism, because integration will be meaningless unless it takes place from a base of racial equality. Thus a period of black separatism may be essential to restore the Negro's sense of identity. From this viewpoint, Black Power may become an indispensable transition. Indeed, there is a strong argument for giving blacks their own communities, their own schools, their own police forces. In effect, that's what happened with white immigrants around the year 1900 in Boston. The Yankees decided that they would let the Irish run the city.

But there are also those who argue for separatism as the final objective. Roy Innes, for example, of the Congress of Racial Equality, says he wants a black republic, based on a federation of black communities throughout the country, which would exist geographically inside the United States but would be absolutely separate from it. My own guess is that Innes is putting us on, and that his real purpose is to stimulate Negro morale. Probably, in the short run, black separatism could be a useful means of achieving the ends of integration.

J.A.G. Is the white majority prepared to accept black separatism on these terms?

A.M.S. I don't think the white community is very much aware of this problem. Even white intellectuals have only recently begun dimly to perceive the intensity of black feelings. The separatist impulse may give some whites a temporary sense of relief. It would mean, for example, an end of school bussing, of all legislated forms of desegregation. Presumably, the black separatists couldn't care less about open housing. I should be very sorry to see a general cessation of the struggle for open housing and desegregated schools. But, in the short run, this may be the direction in which things will move.

J.A.G. Is the poverty problem in the United States primarily a racial problem?

A.M.S. I don't think it is primarily a racial problem except in the largest cities. In fact, there are probably more white Americans living in poverty than there are black. The evolution of the poverty problem is very curious. For a long time, so many Americans were so poor that it was not a problem which seemed likely to yield to specific measures. Then came the Depression, and it was impossible to distinguish between unemployment and chronic poverty. After the war, there was (at least among liberal Democrats) a general faith in aggregate approaches to economic problems. The Keynesian policy of compensatory spending was expected to produce so much economic activity that the problems of poverty would disappear. But it became evident in the 1950's that there was a structural dimension to poverty: some people had been poor so long and were so demoralized that they accepted poverty as a permanent condition. The ambitious immigrants of the 1890's and the resentful unemployed of the 1930's regarded poverty as a burden they were determined to throw off, but for people in the Appalachian area, in Mississippi, on Indian reservations, and so on, poverty was a way of life. This kind of poverty finally became separated out from the general problems of unemployment.

J.A.G. How can the fruits of our enormously productive society be more equitably distributed?

A.M.S. One mechanism of income redistribution is taxation. The form of transfer may be by payments to individuals, as through social security or unemployment compensation, or by transfers of public services, like education or medical care. Obviously, people don't like to be taxed, and the heaviest taxing of the very rich wouldn't yield very much more in the way of effective income redistribution anyway. There is also the question of whether increasing taxation beyond a certain level would not reduce incentive, and therefore the capacity for producing wealth, although I am skeptical about that because other motives than money-making are involved in the process.

Our society, based on private ownership, has not yet gone to the point of providing everyone with an adequate income. Various proposals have been made to remedy this situation: one, currently fashionable, is the negative income tax; another, the concept of the government as the "employer of last resort." I favor the second, because I think the government could provide useful employment of many kinds and it would be better for people to get their income by doing something than as a handout from the government.

J.A.G. Is the inequitable distribution of wealth more the result of the structure of our institutions or of the selfishness of those who presently control the wealth?

A.M.S. It's a result of both. Selfishness preserves the structure which causes the inequity.

J.A.G. So many of our social problems today seem to be urban problems. Is this a new trend in American history?

A.M.S. As Carl Bridenbaugh and Richard Wade have made clear, urban problems have been with us for as long as we have had cities, but since about 1920, more Americans have been living in cities than in the countryside, and thus the urban problem has intensified. The decline of the cities has been partly a consequence of the flight to the suburbs. One of the interesting things about the 1968 election is that for the first time a suburban boss, Spiro T. Agnew, got on a national ticket.

But as the problems of the cities have intensified, municipal leadership has improved. In the 1880's, James Bryce described municipal government as the great failure of the American system. And as late as the 1930's, when I was in college, courses in municipal government were regarded as the end—no one was interested in urban government. One of the most astonishing and hopeful recent signs has been the extraordinary revival of interest in municipal government. Today, at Harvard, courses in municipal government are the most popular ones in the Government Department. Since the Second World War there has been an extraordinary flow of talent into city government, starting with such postwar mayors as Joe Clark in Philadelphia and Hubert Humphrey in Minneapolis, and going through people like Carl Stokes in Cleveland today, or John Lindsay in New York. The level of municipal government is better today than it has ever been in United States history. Bright students want to work for city governments rather than state or even the federal government. So while the problems of the cities have grown worse, the quality of the attack mounted against these problems has improved.

J.A.G.   But what is there about urban life that produces so many enormous social difficulties?

A.M.S.   The attractions of urban life are obvious: excitement, diversity, and so on. One of the problems we face in the cities today is that we're not going to solve the urban crisis until we do something about reconstructing the countryside. The city is attractive, hectic, diverting, and it also offers more opportunities for able people. On the other hand, you can't breathe the air or drink the water. Cities are also constantly at the mercy of strikes of one sort or another. In New York in recent times we have been deprived of taxis, of newspapers, of schools, of garbage collection, of the subways—there has been a constant series of interruptions of the rhythm of life. And quite apart from that, there is the consolidation of ghettos where people pay extortionate rents, higher prices at the grocery, and live in misery.

These problems were manageable only when people accepted bad social conditions as their fate. The future of the cities depends on their relationship, I think, to the federal government. In the past, normal relations have been between Washington and the governors. In the future, the vital relationship will be increasingly between Washington and the mayors. City government is where the action is.

J.A.G.   But what is the root of the problems of urban life? Is it simply that a high concentration of individuals, each going his own way, produces social friction?

A.M.S.   That's part of it, but it is also the impersonality of city life. The title of David Riesman's book, *The Lonely Crowd*, epitomizes the isolation that exists in our jammed cities, and this isolation is a great source of social disquietude. Also, the cities very sharply present the contrast between poverty and wealth. And they separate their inhabitants from nature. Cities give everyone a basic case of the jitters. One is always late and always under pressure, and there's never available the relaxation which a walk along the beach or a stroll through the woods provides.

J.A.G.   But why is there so much concern *today* about the problems of urban life? As you said, urban government is undoubtedly better than it was in the 1880's, and, bad as they are, urban sanitation, housing, and any of the other aspects of the urban problem that one might mention are not as serious as they were in the late nineteenth century. Why, therefore, are we so deeply concerned about urban problems? Why are they so critical now?

A.M.S.   Because our expectations are so much higher, especially the expectations of ethnic minorities. They want full access to the opportunities and amenities of American life. Since municipal services are so much better than they ever were before, the disadvantaged are legitimately irritated because they are not as good as they could be.

Moreover, the impersonality of the city, the separation between worker and employer, between producer and consumer make city dwellers feel both alone and irresponsible. They are not involved with their neighbors as they would be in a small town. Furthermore, many of the rich and responsible citizens who in other times might have had a sense of concern about the community no longer live in the city. They work there, but they go off to some suburb in the evening.

J.A.G.   But you said that urban government is attracting a higher type of person now than it used to.

A.M.S.   It certainly is on the administrative side. Graduates of the Harvard Law School rejoice in the chance of going to work for John Lindsay. For sociologists, political scientists, and to a lesser degree economists, city government has become increasingly attractive. And many young lawyers feel they have more scope and opportunity in city government than they would have if they were to work in the national bureaucracy.

J.A.G.   You mentioned the problem of the population explosion as one of the major social changes of our times. Is there a direct danger that the United States will suffer from overpopulation, say, in the next hundred years?

A.M.S.   I don't suppose so, but since the end of the Second World War the increase in the population of the United States has been equal to the total population a century ago. There is going to be a constant pressure on public and private facilities, particularly in the area of communication and transport, but also in education, where we've always faced the dilemma of trying to maintain a system of mass education and at the same time preserve high standards.

J.A.G.   Would you comment on the changing character of this larger American population? How is the changing structure of our population affecting American civilization?

A.M.S.   Well, for one thing, the country has an increasing portion of young people, and also a lot more old people than ever before, as a result of medical advances. In a sense, the population is more homogeneous, at least insofar as the white population is concerned, but the black and Puerto Rican tendencies toward self-affirmation are going to replace the European immigrants as sources of strain within the national community.

J.A.G.   Can you explain the existence of racial prejudice in our society? Isn't it inevitable, given the clear evidence that there are no fundamental intellectual and moral differences between the races, that the so-called race problem will disappear?

A.M.S. I suppose that there is always a tendency for people to group together against people who are different—who speak a different language, or have different customs, or whose skin is a different color. We have come to understand that human nature is not necessarily benign. Along with man's capacity for good exists a great capacity for resentment and aggression and destruction. Add to that the particular American experience—after all, as a people we began by killing red men and enslaving black men—and this helps explain our conditioned reflexes of contempt for people of other colors. This is only gradually being overcome; no amount of scientific demonstration that there are no differences between ethnic groups is going to be immediately convincing. Whatever the sources of the differences, whether biological or social or whatever, there obviously are differences among races, just as there are differences between people from Maine and people from Texas.

J.A.G. But differences don't necessarily have pejorative implications.

A.M.S. Of course not. In the long run, I would imagine, the resolution of the racial problem will come through intermarriage. It is hopeful to see the extent to which, among the young, a mixed couple is no longer the rarity it was a few years ago.

J.A.G. Another of the social changes which you mentioned was the electronic revolution. Would you discuss the various ways in which computers, television, and other electronic devices have changed our society?

A.M.S. We're going through an extraordinarily important change—the second phase of the industrial revolution. The first industrial revolution was a mechanical revolution, and the second is electronic. Whether expressing itself in computers or in the informational media, it is going to change our lives in really fundamental ways.

On this, one has to acknowledge an indebtedness to Marshall McLuhan who, with all the nonsense with which he adorns his arguments, has made some basic points. The mechanical world (which he would regard as an extension of typographical culture) tends to see experience at a distance and in logical sequence. The electronic world is one in which everything happens at once.

J.A.G. What has been the effect of television on politics?

A.M.S. Television is an unsparing medium; it's hard to fake on it. I don't believe that it requires candidates to be more photogenic. If we had made the 1968 election a beauty contest, I doubt any of the successful presidential candidates would have come out near the top. But television requires a certain coolness. The most effective candidate in the last election among the aspirants for the nominations was probably Senator McCarthy. He was often disappointing to people who came to hear him in person, but he came over very effectively on television.

Television has had one manifest defect, and that is to shorten the length of political speeches. In the old days, men drove fifty miles in a buggy to hear Bob La Follette; they would have been chagrined if La Follette had talked less than three hours. When the radio came along, it cut down political speeches, first to an hour, and then to forty-five minutes, and then to thirty minutes. In television they're cut essentially to fifteen minutes, and often to one-minute spots. It's difficult to have an organized and thoughtful discussion of issues when you're only speaking for fifteen minutes.

J.A.G.   Is that a result of the cost of television time, or does it reflect a general lowering of standards in the attempt to reach a mass audience?

A.M.S.   I think more the second, although the first is also a factor. Television encourages a decay in one's span of attention. Many find it hard to concentrate when someone is speaking for very long. But television has also increased the sense of mass participation in politics. In the old days, there were a series of mediating institutions between candidate and voter—the political machine, the trade union, the farm organization, the ethnic group. These middlemen interpreted the wishes of their constituencies to the politician, and rallied their constituencies if the politician cooperated. The electronic media have dissolved this middle layer in politics. People no longer depend on mediating agencies in making their political decisions. They make their decisions on the basis of what they themselves see on television, and the ultimate effect is direct confrontation between the candidate and the electorate.

J.A.G.   Does this mean the end of political parties?

A.M.S.   Not of parties, but of political organizations in the traditional sense. The old-time political machine is about dead anyway. It exists only in a few backwaters like Chicago; I suggested recently to a Chicago friend that the Daley machine ought to be put in the Museum of Natural History, to which he retorted that it should be in the Museum of Mechanical Arts because, after all, it is a machine. But the old-style machines are dying. The trade unions, as far as politics is concerned, are letterhead organizations. They can't really deliver the labor vote. Farm organizations and ethnic organizations no longer have their old power. Voters make their own judgments on the basis of what they see every night on TV, and register their judgments vicariously every week through the polls of George Gallup and Lou Harris.

In the 1968 election, Hubert Humphrey was the candidate of the traditional agencies of politics, very probably the last one. The group which knows best how to organize the electronic age are the young. Eugene McCarthy, whose personal style was much more congenial to the electronic media, was able to make an alliance with youth. McCarthy carried his conception of the new politics to the point where he doesn't think parties are very important. But obviously there will have to be parties to serve as signposts indicating alternatives and direction. Yet political organizations will take new forms—they'll be very different from the Daley organization in Chicago.

J.A.G.   What about the economic effects of the electronic revolution, particularly automation?

A.M.S.   Some economists believe that we've already reached the point where automation is destroying more jobs than it creates, but the recent National Commission on Technology, Automation and Economic Progress was rather more optimistic on that point. What is happening is a shift in the character of the economy. More people are now engaged in the provision of services than in the production of goods. This means a change in the character of the labor force: a decrease in the proportion of people engaged in production and an increase in the amount of "white-collar" employment, especially in the professional and technical groups. These groups now constitute the fastest-growing segment of the labor force.

J.A.G.   Everyone agrees that education is a good thing, and it's obvious that more and more Americans are getting more and more education. Why, then, is there so much dissatisfaction with our educational system?

A.M.S.   There are so many reasons for the dissatisfaction that it's hard to sort them out. One of the basic problems is that we have a commitment to mass education, even mass *higher* education. As a consequence, it is difficult to maintain standards of quality. If universities are going to be mere extensions of high schools, can they do the kind of job that university education has done in the past? There's also the serious question whether it's worthwhile for everybody to have a college education. A college education has become important not so much for the training of the mind as for obtaining social status.

I think college students feel dissatisfied less because of the impersonality of the system—the fact that they seldom meet any professors and see them only in large lecture courses—than because they feel it absolutely intolerable to continue under regulations which were drawn up when colleges were boys' academies and which deny them any kind of rational role. I see no reason why all sorts of problems like student discipline, student housing, and so on, should not be confided to students, and why students should not have an important and organic consultative role in questions of curriculum and other aspects of university administration. The student demand for participation seems to me legitimate; and if the university does not make way for rational forms of participation, less rational forms will be forced on it.

J.A.G.   Why is it so difficult for individuals to feel that they can exert any influence on the course of events in our times? Why does our society seem less democratic in so many ways than it did a generation ago?

A.M.S.   Sensitive individuals have always felt relatively impotent in society; our increasing sense of impotence is due in part to the fact that the sense of individuality is probably more widespread today than ever before. The range of individual choice, for example, has never been so great. Yet, as the individual develops a keener sense of his own individuality, he also becomes more conscious of threats to his sense of individuality. Here the Tocqueville point applies again; once men feel a sense of power, they no longer acquiesce in powerlessness as the normal condition of life.

The contemporary sense of impotence is also due in part to the domination of the high-technology society by great organizations—organizations of government, of industry, of labor, of education. A sense of powerlessness consequently pervades all industrial societies. Every particular person, of course, thinks that his own group is uniquely powerless: the intellectual, the academic, the radical, the Negro, the businessman, the lawyer, the government official, and the John Bircher. But this is part of the universal feeling that somehow the institutions of modern life have become impervious to influence. The distinctive struggle of our age is the individual's attempt to affirm and verify his own sense of identity. And, since the young are the most resistant to the discipline of the great organizations, it is hardly surprising that the form the struggle between the individual and the structure takes in many countries is the revolt of the student against the university.

At the same time, though, that modern industrial society builds a host of great organizations, it builds an enormous educational establishment to man those organizations—and this establishment also generates skeptics who subvert and challenge the organizations. The very necessities of modern life that create the organizations also create a countervailing force: the more people are educated, the more they are inclined toward independent and critical thought.

We need a new social contract which will redefine the balance of force between the individual and the organization. Because organizations are necessary to industrial society, they have been able to get away with a lot. Opposition to "the organization" is heresy. The momentum of the organization is to create its own ethos—its own meaning, purpose, and truth. But the war between the individual and the organization is only just beginning, and I do not think the resources of the individual have been exhausted. In the political field, for example, in spite of everything, escalation of the war in Vietnam was stopped, negotiations were begun, Johnson was forced out. It's a continuing struggle, and there's no reason for defeatism.

J.A.G.   I know that prediction is not the historian's proper function, but would you try to suggest in a general way the directions in which you think our society is moving?

A.M.S. We are going through a period of crisis, a crisis produced not by the decline or decay of our institutions, but rather by the rapidity of their change. One aspect of this is the shift from a mechanical to an electronic society, another the shift from a racist to an equalitarian society. These changes, coming at a time of accelerating technical change and continuing population growth, greatly strain our institutions. I think that the next few years are going to be a rather edgy period. Whether we can hold the country together will depend very much on the resources of our political leadership. It is not inconceivable that in the next years there may be guerrilla fighting in our cities, an increasing breakdown of municipal institutions and facilities, and, in general, deep and savage dissension within our country. But if we can get through the next few years, we may, because of the extraordinary possibilities created by electronics, move in the direction of a society marked by increasing levels of education, material well-being, and leisure, a society perhaps marked by a division between a small minority of hard-working managers and a large majority of hard-playing hedonists.

I do not suggest that this would be a better society. John Locke once said that all the world was America, meaning that America was the original state of nature out of which the social contract came. From time to time I have the awful feeling that we can reverse Locke and say that all the world will be California, that life in Los Angeles is a portent of our future. But I don't have any crystal ball. I think there are both great possibilities and great hazards in this new age we are entering. I am sure, however, that the future will involve considerable re-evaluation of American institutions, and of the axioms on which we have operated as a people in the past.

J.A.G. What are the half-dozen or so books that you would recommend to persons interested in the subject we have been discussing? In each case, would you indicate briefly what the particular contribution of the volume is?

A.M.S. I would begin by mentioning Emerson, Tocqueville, and William James. I think they got the point of this country better than any other writers; and, though they were writing about a different America, what they said still applies in astonishing and illuminating ways to contemporary America.

Among more recent writers, I would suggest J. K. Galbraith—*The New Industrial State* (1967), *The Affluent Society* (1958), and *American Capitalism: The Concept of Countervailing Power* (1962)—because of the brilliant diagnosis in these books of the pressures and perplexities of advanced industrial society. David Riesman and his collaborators in *The Lonely Crowd* (1950) made some stimulating guesses about the impact of this society on the formation of character. Kenneth Keniston perceptively discussed the alienation of the young in American society in *The Uncommitted* (1965) and *Young Radicals* (1968). Michael Harrington's *The Other America* (1963), placed the problem of poverty on the national conscience. Kenneth Clark's *Dark Ghetto* (1967) offers an excellent introduction to the problems of racial justice along, of course, with Gunnar Myrdal's *An American Dilemma* (1944). And I suppose one must add Marshall McLuhan, *The Gutenberg Galaxy* (1962) or *Understanding Media* (1964) with the caution not to let the nonsense obscure the insight.

Alfred Kazin

A Century of Realism
in American Literature

ALFRED KAZIN, Distinguished Professor of English at the
State University of New York at Stony Brook, is known
in and out of the academic world as one of the most
sensitive and thoughtful of our literary critics. In addition
to *On Native Grounds: An Interpretation of Modern
American Prose Literature* (1942), he has published two
volumes of criticism: *The Inmost Leaf* (1955) and *Contemporaries* (1962), and he has edited the works of William
Blake, F. Scott Fitzgerald, Theodore Dreiser, and other
writers. He is also the author of two autobiographical
volumes, *A Walker in the City* (1951) and *Starting Out
in the Thirties* (1965). In this interview he traces the history of the American novel from the time of Twain,
Howells, and Henry James to the present day.

John A. Garraty Professor Kazin, why do you choose as the topic for our discussion "a century" of realism rather than, say, one hundred and fifty or even two hundred years?

Alfred Kazin The American novel, as a realistic form, began just about one hundred years ago, when men like Henry James and William Dean Howells, who were very much influenced by European novelists, suddenly began to write realistically about American society. The novel as a form really began around that time. I don't mean that there weren't novels before, but they were really what used to be called the "romance." Melville, Cooper, and Hawthorne were romanticists, properly speaking.

The major difference between James and Howells, on the one hand, and people like Hawthorne and Cooper and Poe is, first of all, that James and Howells thought that the novel was the greatest possible literary form. They were full of admiration for the great European novelists, especially Balzac (the master of them all), but also Tolstoy and Dostoevski, and they believed that modern society in all its aspects was the proper subject of the writer. The word "realism," though it can be very confusing, had to do with this concern for reality in fiction. James and Howells didn't like to use the word. Only late in his career did Howells speak of the necessity of being a realist, and James hardly ever did. But they were both thinking of reality in this sense of the word, and today Saul Bellow, Norman Mailer, James Jones, Louis Auchincloss and many other depictors of modern American society have the same point of view. But in the romantic fiction that was published before the Civil War—in Poe's hallucinated stories, in Hawthorne's guilt-ridden, fear-filled characters, and of course in Melville's great, apocalyptic novel *Moby Dick*, the approach is quite different. One gets the lonely individual, very much concerned with his physical fate, in a world ridden by demons and ghosts and ancestral symbols, as in Hawthorne, or with religious problems, as in Melville. Only with James and Howells, roughly one hundred years ago, did this marvelous sense of the world as a place that can be accepted for itself alone begin to appear.

With the new taste for realism in literature came an appreciation of realism in painting and drawing. It is no accident that the art which Henry James all his life loved more than any other was painting. It was allied also to the novelists' sense that Europe provided the natural environment for a writer. The American writer who went abroad came to see himself as a detached spectator of American life. When he came back, he was changed.

The new realism was allied also to the influence of magazines. Writers like Poe and Hawthorne had made a living (if you can call it a living), by writing for magazines, and, in fact, much of their best work was in the form of short fiction. Suddenly, magazines like *The Atlantic*

Monthly, which had been founded before the Civil War, became extraordinarily hospitable to a new kind of realistic short story. There was a very clear-cut beginning to this trend. It began when William Dean Howells became assistant editor of *The Atlantic* and met Henry James. They discovered how much they had in common, and they discovered, too, that they could take on the whole of American society as a literary project. They felt themselves part of a movement.

Another aspect of realism was that for the first time a certain kind of American woman became the principal character in novels. *Daisy Miller* (1878) depicted a type of woman who hadn't appeared in American fiction, or in American life, before. Almost a century later, when the freedom and the vitality of women is one of the clearest examples of what has happened to American society, it's a fact of some interest to look back and realize that James's awareness of this "new" woman is pretty much what distinguishes him as a novelist. When James saw the young American girl sitting on the piazza of the Grand Union Hotel in Saratoga Springs, surrounded by her parents and possible suitors, she stood out for the same reason that she stood out for Henry Adams: in a society full of rather tiresome money-getters, she was a symbol of culture and refinement and the only person who seemed to be interested in beauty per se. This is what Henry Adams meant when he said, in his *Education,* that he never knew an American woman who wasn't better than her husband. Winslow Homer expressed this point of view in a different medium in his paintings of the young American girls walking in their flowing summer gowns on the cliffs of Newport, holding up their parasols as feminine insignia. Of course, the other side of this is that the audience for the novels of James and Howells and other writers was very much an audience of women. This is still true, to my knowledge. I almost never see a man carrying a book unless it is a textbook or income-tax guide, whereas women still do carry novels and best-sellers. The feminization of culture seemed to James of very great importance. Women were his readers; women were his main characters; women were the principal new content which attracted the interest of writers like Howells and James, and even Mark Twain, though what they did with women in their books was something else again.

J.A.G.   Would you distinguish more clearly between what you call the realistic novel and the "romance" of earlier times? Weren't there large realistic elements in a book like *Moby Dick?*

A.K.   The difference is that a realistic novel like James's *The Portrait of a Lady,* or Twain's *Huckleberry Finn,* or Howells' *The Rise of Silas Lapham,* is a realistic novel all the time. There is a concentration on one tone, on one form. Although people like Mark Twain were to depart from this (Twain was nothing if not inconsistent), the realists were trying to describe manners and mores in the European sense; whereas *Moby Dick*, which began as a realistic description of whaling, was completely transformed through what Melville himself called a "hideous metaphysical allegory." It becomes in turn an epic poem, a play; there is suddenly a whole set of characters brought from every country in the world, who are never seen again after their brief appearance on the stage; there is a kind of exalted romantic dialogue between these characters; there's a long soliloquy—the most important part of the book in my opinion—in the great chapters on the whiteness of the whale and on Moby Dick itself. Like an epic poem, *Moby Dick* is held together entirely by the *thinking* of the narrator rather than by the narrator as a "camera eye."

Realism has always been the very essence of literature. One of the greatest books I know of on literature is Erich Auerbach's *Mimesis*. Auerbach shows how, starting with the Gospels, the effort to depict characteristics and characters plainly has always meant realistic detail as compared to the frigid and formal patterns of classical literature. But realism as a movement didn't really begin until the middle classes began to claim literature as their own, and until the middle class became interesting to writers. We associate its origin with England and Germany in the eighteenth century.

J.A.G. Why did it begin relatively late in America, the completely middle-class society?

A.K. The best American writers before the Civil War—Emerson, Poe, Thoreau, Hawthorne—were haunted by religion, driven almost crazy by the problems of the Protestant soul trying to reach God by words alone. American literature before the Civil War is really a church of the Word. It consists almost entirely of great exalted flights of the soul trying to reach some metaphysical base. Suddenly, after the war, this changed. Twain, James, and Howells were not interested in religion. They were a sharp departure from their parents. Henry James the elder was a Swedenborgian and a great religious philosopher. Howells' father was also a Swedenborgian, and Mark Twain's father, as far as we know anything about him, was a Calvinist. But in the next generation there was a complete absence of interest in religion.

Now the primary thing about the novel as a realistic form, not as a romance, has always been the fact that, no matter what the personal religion of the writer, he doesn't allow religious orthodoxy to shape his work. He describes religion realistically. What Mark Twain said about the Southern writer George Washington Cable is still true. He said he couldn't understand how Cable, whom he liked and with whom he went on lecture trips, could spend his time worrying about God. It seemed to him absolute nonsense. And Twain's attitude was typical of the skepticism of his generation.

I think it's fair to say that religion in the formal sense has never been of less interest to writers than in our time. There is something about writing realistic fiction that makes it impossible to view religion as anything but another aspect of human experience. It is obvious, too, that this movement was related to developments at that time in psychology and philosophy, with the work of Henry's brother, William James, and later on of John Dewey, as well as to the growing awareness of what was happening in the late nineteenth century to big cities.

However—and this point is not often mentioned—the early realistic writers, despite their interest in women, displayed very little of the European realists' concern with sexuality in their books. What Henry Adams said about Henry James is in a sense true of all of them: James knew nothing about women except the outside. Of course, James never had a wife, but Howells and Twain were married, and they were nonetheless very careful not to touch on any vital aspect of human passion.

J.A.G.   Isn't that related to the fact that American culture was really a subdivision of British culture, and that the period we're talking about was the height of the Victorian age? Were English writers of stature dealing with sexuality at this time?

A.K.   The so-called Victorian attitude toward sex was really a very temporary interlude in the English literary tradition of healthy licentiousness. The eighteenth-century English novelists were extremely frank and even bawdy in this respect, and even Dickens, when he came over here, made a point of shocking Americans by saying, for example, that he didn't want his sons to be virgins when they were married. The American attitude toward sexuality was peculiarly American in this period, because of the actual roughness of American society. The literary class was very genteel and very careful; I'm often fascinated by the self-conscious gentility of Howells and James and even of Mark Twain. All of them wrote exquisitely; they were all marvelous stylists. But they were all rather goody-goody when it came to literary culture. Their air of superior refinement was their way of getting away from the roughness of the American experience more than anything else. This was fundamental. The American novel today has certainly gone to the other extreme, but the early realists felt themselves to be a part of that small Brahmin class, even Mark Twain, the self-educated printer and frontiersman. And as a result, their work displays a certain tendency to elegance quite different from the aristocratic quality of English fiction in this period. Of course, the English had a much more complex society to describe. The American experience was peculiarly narrow in this sense. That was one of the reasons why James went to England, why he started writing novels about English society.

J.A.G. I think Twain fits into your construct less neatly than Howells or James. To what extent did the local-color interests of Twain and other writers of lesser stature contribute to the development of the new realism? Certainly, the local-colorists were trying to describe reality.

A.K. Local color has always been important in American fiction. We can see this right now, for example, in the use of the big-city environment by writers like Norman Mailer and Saul Bellow. It's always a response to an earlier experience in which the writer sees literary possibilities. Mark Twain had a fantastic career. He rose from great poverty and a provincial background to a position of incredible cultural leadership. When he was living in Hartford and hobnobbing with Standard Oil millionaires and Republican politicos, when he had become a colossal figure in American folklore and was constantly being quoted, he became aware of what he had lived through. Then he began to write things like *Life on the Mississippi* and *Huckleberry Finn*. Local-color writers are always either gentlemen who could observe the local "peasants" from outside, or people responding to earlier experiences which suddenly have become very important. Bellow and Mailer became very conscious of certain aspects of life in New York City or Chicago at exactly the point when they themselves moved away from this sort of environment.

Most of the local-color writing in America in the late nineteenth century was simply dialect humor. It was a way of patronizing people and regions. Kenneth Lynn pointed out a long time ago the logic of the South, where there was a great sense of class differentiation and where the people on the top felt very superior to the average poor white. There the local-color school flourished. If you look at *Tom Sawyer*, apart from all the sentiment that has collected around it over the years, you will realize that Twain was patronizing the world he was describing, and *Huckleberry Finn*, which is, of course, an extraordinary book, is in this sense no different.

J.A.G. Was not Mark Twain also different from the other realists in that he was particularly unsuccessful in dealing with female characters?

A.K. That is true. Twain idealized women; the only "real" woman in his work is Roxy in *Pudd'nhead Wilson*, a Negro woman, interestingly enough. Almost all the others are little golden-haired lasses in school, like Becky in *Tom Sawyer*. Twain wrote about the Mississippi, but he never for a moment talked about the whores and cardsharps who flourished in the river towns and on the river boats. One would never guess from his writing the kind of life that went on in those places. But I think this was because he felt himself to be a cultural arbiter, that he had to set a certain tone. All the early realists were too conscious of women as their audience. Take the case of *Daisy Miller,* one of the most hilarious episodes in American fiction. Daisy Miller was the young American girl who, in Rome and in Venice, did not understand that respectable young European women did not go about in society by themselves or in the company of slightly dubious Italians. Her frankness, freshness, and directness—all the things that made her stand out as a character—cost her her life. She allowed an Italian adventurer to take her to the Colosseum at night and as a result caught her death of cold. Quite properly, she died for her "sins," the fate she deserved after doing a thing like that.

Now James had a problem about women: he could only write about them as objects to be looked at. There's a very feminine side to James's fiction which makes him, I think, proportionately valuable as a writer, as a depictor. But the point is that when *Daisy Miller* came out, it created a storm. American women—the audience—were outraged by James's treatment of Daisy. No American girl would do a thing like that! Daisy was an insult to American womanhood. This, by the way, was one of the reasons why James eventually left America. He was insulted by women in the streets of Boston because of his "immoral" fiction. Although it is very amusing to think of James as an immoral novelist, in fact he was the only novelist of this period who hinted at the depths of sexual passion. He was obsessed with the sexual question, though he was too genteel or too inexperienced to write about it frankly. People recognized this, and the result was that some women had a lasting suspicion about James. This is ironic, because James's greatest novels— *The Portrait of a Lady, The Ambassadors, The Wings of the Dove, The Golden Bowl*—are all famous for their "good" heroines.

Then, of course, there is the thesis which Van Wyck Brooks got rapped on the knuckles for stating, in *The Ordeal of Mark Twain,* that Twain's wife edited his manuscripts and took out the cuss words and everything remotely sexual. Brooks's point was that Mark Twain, victim of his own drive for success, had become too domesticated. Brooks's thesis has been proved over and over again, and only recently Justin Kaplan's acclaimed *Mr. Clemens and Mark Twain* showed just what a divided man Twain was.

J.A.G.   You have described the differences between the American realists and the Europeans, such as Balzac. Would you comment on their similarities?

A.K.   James and Howells—James particularly—considered Balzac simply *the* greatest novelist that Europe had ever produced. They felt that he could create his splendid imaginative world only because of the great variety of classes in Europe and because of the conflict between the aristocracy and the emerging middle classes. They were trying to show that these class differences could in some way be suggested even in America. Since the whole epic of industrial capitalism dealt with the upward struggle of the middle classes—described by Dickens in *Bleak House,* and Balzac in *Père Goriot*—James and Howells tried to find this in American life, too. It was far more difficult because there was less variety in America. When Howells tries to describe a Boston aristocrat in *The Rise of Silas Lapham,* he produced an elegant but pretty sterile character.

The Americans were similar to the Europeans also in that they found a large public for fiction, based chiefly on the new importance of magazines. The magazines that Poe wrote for tended to be fly-by-night affairs. But James and Howells made a lot of money from their books. What they did was to serialize their novels, month after month, in the great magazines, both here and in England, exactly as the great European novelists did. Dickens eventually created his own magazine; Dostoevski wrote almost all his greatest novels for Russian magazines. But all these writers had to be very careful for just that reason: they simply couldn't afford to offend the magazine audience.

J.A.G. If the realists were so popular, how can the continued enormous success of romantic gush in the 1870's, 80's, and 90's be explained?

A.K. There are always several reading audiences at the same time. More trash is published today than ever before in the history of civilization, but there is also a fantastic dissemination of good books. But more particularly, the very prosperity which inspired realists like James and Howells, the national sense of stability and confidence, also produced a desire to ape the English aristocracy. And on the other hand, the South, which not only lost the war but also its self-confidence, became addicted more than ever before to the romances of Sir Walter Scott.

J.A.G. How did "naturalistic" writers like Theodore Dreiser, Stephen Crane, and Frank Norris differ from James and Howells and Twain? Did their work develop logically out of that of the older generation of realists?

A.K. Crane, Dreiser, and Norris were all born within a few months of one another, and two of them, Norris and Crane, died at a very young age. (Actually, I don't take Norris seriously except as a literary symptom.) Crane and Dreiser fascinate me because they were both extremely gifted but very different. Dreiser was clumsy and verbose, but he wrote very powerfully. Crane was one of the most amazing geniuses we've ever produced. The 1890's represent the great watershed of American history, not only in fiction but in politics—the beginning of open class struggles, of open polarization in American life. A cocky, disparaging attitude toward the bourgeois experience developed; the ethos of the middle class had been exploded. Many of the younger writers were much more cynical, much less hidebound by genteel conventions. Can you imagine Henry James going as a correspondent to the Greco-Turkish War as Crane did? Or having the kind of experience that Dreiser did when he was taken in by a prostitute in Evansville, Indiana, who happened to be his brother Paul's mistress? Or having the concern with money that Crane had all his life and which made Dreiser, as a young man, steal from the laundry for which he worked? The writers of the 1890's represented a tougher, harsher, crueler world. Take Crane's fascination with war. Everybody knows that he wrote *The Red Badge of Courage* before he ever saw a battle. Yet many Civil War veterans thought that he had been at Chancellorsville. Crane saw the life of America as war, the life of the world as war.

Crane was the son of a Methodist minister; he grew up in a religious Christian home. His mother was a pillar of the Women's Christian Temperance Union. Yet, coming from this respectable, almost traditional kind of American background, Crane found himself always looking at things with a beady eye, finding objects of derision in American institutions. When he came to New York as a newspaper reporter and began to observe the misery and degradation of slum life, he was intoxicated by the literary possibilities of this kind of world. Compare Crane on New York in the 1890's with what William Dean Howells was writing about the East Side! Howells was a very decent man. He was a utopian socialist. He was properly dismayed by the fate of Jewish immigrants living in East-Side tenements. But he regarded this as something with which he had no personal relationship. He felt rather disgusted by the slum dwellers, although he rose above his disgust like a true gentleman. Crane, on the contrary, was delighted with the life of the Bowery. He was fascinated by what used to be called "fallen women"; he defended prostitutes who were being shaken down by the police so vigorously that the police persecuted him and wouldn't give him any peace. Unlike James and Howells, Dreiser and Crane both were seriously concerned with low life.

They also had very strong feelings about religion. Dreiser, the first important American writer who was not a Protestant, reacted bitterly against the Catholic church in which he was raised. He hated orthodox religion and conventional morality. The literary historians make too much of what is called naturalism as a style. It was wholly a social-human question: these writers were a new class of people, they were at war with middle-class values. Crane lived with an extraordinarily vivid and courageous woman, Cora, who in Jacksonville, Florida, kept a whorehouse. They lived in England because they couldn't have that kind of relationship in the United States.

J.A.G. I know that Howells appreciated and aided some of the naturalist writers. What about Henry James?

A.K. Even Howells didn't like all of them. He was a very generous critic, a great supporter of all new fiction. But there were severe limitations to his appreciation. He thought *Maggie*, Stephen Crane's first book, wonderful, but he did not like *The Red Badge of Courage* for reasons I'm not sure I understand entirely. I think the fact that in *Maggie* the young girl becomes a prostitute and eventually commits suicide must have pleased his moral sense. But in *The Red Badge of Courage*, a masterpiece written in letters of fire, the underlying depiction of the violence of war apparently distressed Howells' peaceful soul.

Howells didn't like Dreiser at all. Despite his importance, Dreiser is still one of the most neglected figures in American literature. All sorts of literary professors are still afraid of him. But in his own time, Dreiser was treated with the most incredible contempt and hostility by the literary establishment. They always, of course, complained about his bad writing, though they didn't seem to mind it when they read other things. In fact, it was his attitude toward society that they didn't like, his conviction that there wasn't, fundamentally, any real design to life. James and Howells, after all, were profoundly ethical writers. At the end of James's novels there is always a subtle victory for the human conscience. Goodness wins out, as in *The Wings of the Dove* or in *The Golden Bowl*. These books are, in a sense, religious allegories. But in Crane, and especially in Dreiser, there is a strong feeling that there is no design, no meaning. They keep themselves separate from anything they are describing. With them the human being is getting more and more difficult to reach and describe intimately; there are nothing like the marvelous close-ups which you get in James's novels. In Crane and Dreiser, the world is pretty much a cold world. People are described as if they are far off. This coldness toward the world, toward human beings, becomes the limiting fact in American fiction later on.

J.A.G. How can this be reconciled with what you said about Crane's warmth, his reaction to poverty and vice on the Bowery?

A.K. I didn't say he was warm, I said he was interested. When I spoke of distance in the fiction of Crane and Dreiser, I meant their sense that what they were writing about was far removed from them. We can see the same thing in our own lives. We write about politics and power and the people around us, but we feel ourselves to be engulfed by too many people, too many problems, too many pressures. We are more detached; the world has become more complex, more overwhelming. Crane was interested in writing about the Bowery for literary and artistic reasons. He regarded the people on the Bowery as aesthetic facts. He was fascinated by the new opportunity, the new material he found there. His concern for prostitutes reflected only his rejection of his father's morality. That's why he liked being a police reporter. He liked to hobnob with criminals, precisely because it was a way of shocking the people he'd lived with before. Nothing delighted him more than to feel he was a scapegrace, in some way a naughty fellow. But he wasn't warm. He didn't care a hang about Dora Clark, the famous prostitute he defended. He just hated the police, and was outraged because he thought that they were being mean to her. As a matter of fact, Crane was very much what used to be called a womanizer. He had no feeling of closeness to Bowery bums; he felt that these people were all helpless.

As we know from Crane's most famous story, one of the greatest stories in the world, "The Open Boat," a description of what he went through in a dinghy after the *Commodore,* the ship he was taking from Florida, blew up in the water, he was interested in getting at the facts of experience. Sitting in this dinghy, freezing and starving and expecting at any moment to be drowned, he observed everything with a cold, clear eye. That shocked readers, too; he was able to write about things with merciless detachment.

After all, that is what makes the novelist. No matter how warm he may feel about people, fundamentally he's a professional. The professional eye is an extraordinary thing in such writers; it gives them a kind of chilling expertise in describing things which would involve other people emotionally.

J.A.G.   The difficulty with that statement to me is that it removes the writer from the society he's a part of.

A.K.   I guess I didn't put that very clearly. Professionalism in any field has nothing to do with one's own emotions. Any historian who's studying a subject may be personally involved with it in terms of memory or sympathy, but he tries to get at the facts as far as he understands them. No one, to this day, has given us a better picture of the transformation of American life in the 1890's than Crane did, in *Maggie,* in *George's Mother,* and even in "The Open Boat," precisely because he saw clearly what was happening. To use a modern example, I happen to admire Norman Mailer's book on the Pentagon, *The Armies of the Night,* very much. I think it's the best thing that has been written about the political atmosphere in which we've been living since the Vietnam War started. His book seems to me a triumph of detachment and involvement at the same time.

J.A.G.   Were all the early realists gifted with this combination of detachment and insight?

A.K.   I think so. James and Howells in their earlier work show very clearly what a great age of confidence the 1870's and 1880's were for the people they were writing about: the Northern middle classes who went to Saratoga and Newport and lived in the best of all possible worlds. Then, bit by bit, one sees in their work a growing anxiety. Howells became a socialist; he grew more and more resentful of the crassness of American society, the exploitation of the poor, the brutality of American corporations. James became more and more struck by the corruption of society, in England and this country. His analysis took the form of sexual allegory—the attempt to get money through marriage or the betrayal of adultery became symbols in his work of the corruption of society as a whole.

James was disillusioned with his society, but a good writer always is. The mood of anxiety and bitterness which many Americans feel right now certain American novelists felt as early as the 1920's—F. Scott Fitzgerald, for instance. *The Great Gatsby* is one of the great American social novels. *The Great Gatsby, Tender Is the Night,* and the unfinished novel about Hollywood, *The Last Tycoon,* were all immensely prophetic documents as well as beautiful novels. Nowadays we teach them to undergraduates, and say, "You see, that's American life." But in the 1920's one couldn't have said this so easily, though it was already true. In the 1890's, Dreiser and Crane saw things which many a smug American wouldn't see for thirty or forty years.

J.A.G.   How were novelists influenced by World War I?

A.K.   The basic thing about the First World War and American novelists was that so many of them got into it. When relatively few Americans were actually in the Army, Hemingway, Faulkner, Fitzgerald, and many others were in the war. They found in the war a great sense of adventure. Hemingway was so eager to get into it that he enlisted as an ambulance volunteer. He was on the Italian front long before America entered the war. At the very beginning, many writers felt that this was their chance to get to Europe, to participate in things. All the wonderful works of fiction of the World War—Dos Passos's *1919,* Hemingway's *A Farewell to Arms,* even the first novel of Faulkner, *Soldiers Pay,* can be described conventionally as tales of disillusionment, but actually they are tales of adventure. These writers had a great sense of buoyant confidence; this was their moment. You can see in *1919* and in Hemingway's stories the great sense of freshness and adventure. They were free of American provincialism; they were free of their parents. (Many were young enough to have to worry about parents.) Above all, they had that literary desire to participate in extreme experience.

Later on, of course, when they came back and began to write these novels, it is easy to describe them as disillusioned, but I think the disillusionment was less important than the early sense of romantic adventure. They were quite impersonal about this. The war was for them a way of getting involved in a very big way. Take, for example, one of the great works of American literature, *The Enormous Room,* by the poet E. E. Cummings. When Cummings went to Europe as an ambulance driver, he was utterly cynical about the French. He refused to say that the Germans were terrible, which the French authorities wanted him to, and because of a critical letter his friend Slater Brown had been writing they both were arrested. Out of this experience came that marvelous book, one of the first great books about the concentration-camp world. But when you read *The Enormous Room* now, the thing that strikes you is how fresh it is. It's full of energy. I've just reread the whole of Dos Passos's famous trilogy, *U.S.A.* The parts about the war are a constant record of carousal—of drinking, love-making, roaring through the streets of Paris and elsewhere. Dos Passos obviously had a great time.

J.A.G.   When did disillusionment begin to affect their fiction, and why?

A.K.   When they began to look at the world after the Versailles Treaty and especially when they began to look at the leadership we were getting under Harding and Coolidge, they felt, understandably, that an awful lot of people had died for nothing. Actually, "disillusioned" is not the correct word here, though it is a word which I have used, along with everybody else. I don't think they had many illusions to begin with. What they did have was a sense of romantic contrast. In Dos Passos's *U.S.A.,* one sees the career of certain young Americans who were very successful in the Army bureaucracy in Paris; when they came back, and as a result of their being spoiled by having been close to power, they became corrupt figures in the advertising industry. The contrast makes the book so sharp and bitter.

I think the greatest thing ever written about the First World War by an American is the prose-poem in *U.S.A.* called "The Body of an American," which depicts in a most sardonic and savage way the finding and burial of the Unknown Soldier. It portrays the unctuous hypocrisy of the government in picking out to honor one corpse from among so many. But the point is that it is also an attempt to describe the physical ecstasy of war, both the danger which is an ecstasy and the sense of annihilation, triumphing over danger, and then the losing oneself in it. That's why *The Red Badge of Courage* is such a great book; it describes war as if it were a sexual encounter.

Of course, Hemingway's *A Farewell to Arms* is very sentimental and romantic about this kind of experience. But then Hemingway always was sentimental, as well as the most self-centered of all American novelists. He was a brilliant lyricist, but he could never write a really fine novel. He captured perfectly one level of the physical experience of war because he was perhaps the most wounded writer of our time. He suffered a whole series of wounds and catastrophes in the war, and he described them with physical immediacy.

J.A.G.   You once wrote that Hemingway "brought a major art to a minor vision of life." Would you elaborate on this thought?

A.K.   Well, I'll take the word "major" away; Hemingway produced an *original* art. He was one of the great painters of prose, a writer of extraordinary freshness. The early stories have a directness and a lyric vibration which is absolutely incomparable. He was the most original stylist of his period. The "minor vision of art," of course, resulted from his self-centeredness. Hemingway's career is depressing because he could only return to early experiences. He was very much preoccupied with his own wounds, and with an image of himself as a virile male which obviously derived from a very great anxiety. He was an original rather than a great writer.

Disillusionment is clearest in Faulkner's early work. Faulkner had volunteered for the Royal Air Force before America entered the war; he was overeager to get involved, and he had some bad experiences in those rickety, primitive planes of 1916. His early work is not as interesting as Hemingway's or Fitzgerald's, however. Yet he developed in the 1920's a whole series of truly Balzacian novels—perhaps the only Balzacian novels in American fiction—about a whole region, the South. He was able to do this because of his marvelous sense of contrast between the popular image of the South and the reality. Of course, he had, unlike the Northern writers, many different groups to write about. No other American novelist had such a range of types and classes to choose from—the aristocracy, the low peasant class, and the Negroes and Indians. This gave his work the human contrast and differentiation that didn't exist in St. Paul, Minnesota, or Oak Park, Illinois.

J.A.G.   Certainly, any other Southern novelist, of whom there were many, would have had the same opportunity.

A.K.   Mississippi was and is special because it was so poor, because it was so full of illusion. It had been a frontier territory for a long time. In *The Bear*, one of the greatest stories ever written, when Faulkner describes the wilderness and the hunting, you realize that a physical frontier still existed, and the effect is fantastic. There was also tremendous provincialism in Mississippi, and of course the excess of Negroes over whites created for the whites an atmosphere of danger, hostility, and tension. Faulkner also evokes the feeling, oddly enough, of being close to the Middle West, which in many ways allies Faulkner to Mark Twain and also to contemporaries of his own like Dos Passos and Sinclair Lewis.

J.A.G.   It seems to me you're attributing Faulkner's greatness exclusively to the environment he lived in.

A.K.   Not at all! I'm saying that he seized upon that environment. But no one could write about the wild, wonderful world of race passion that Faulkner describes in *Light in August* if he lived in Richmond, Virginia. Mississippi didn't create Faulkner. Faulkner had the talent to seize upon what he had around him.

J.A.G.   Which of the other writers of the 1920's seem to you important?

A.K.   I think that Sinclair Lewis was a very important writer. He was a brilliant satirist and social critic, but above all, he had, like H. L. Mencken, a very strong sense of values, a very solid point of view. In his best books—*Main Street* and *Babbitt*—but even in *Dodsworth*, he presented a dissection of American materialism and cultural sterility. Only after the Depression, when Lewis lost that sharp-edged point of view, did he stop being interesting as a writer. Lewis is easy to under-estimate; his achievement is very hard to pin down. He had an enormous influence on the American mind. Indeed, many of these novelists of the 1920's had great impact on their society. Dos Passos, Hemingway, Lewis, and Fitzgerald became creators of a new language, of a whole new vision of society. They made readers aware of two different cultures in America: the middle-class culture, which was satirized so bitingly by Lewis, and the "ideal" culture of the intelligentsia. And to a degree they changed how readers looked at these cultures and thus the cultures themselves. Henry James was widely read and influential in that sense, but he did not shape the beliefs and attitudes of readers the way Lewis, a lesser writer surely, shaped them.

J.A.G.   Why was this so?

A.K.   Because the characteristic point of view of James and of Howells was ethical. James's greatest stories were about individual conscience winning over social institutions. But the characteristic note of Lewis's fiction was his sardonic, subversive feeling about American mores, which was easy for the reader to catch. It requires a very delicate kind of imaginative sympathy to read James's *Portrait of a Lady*, for example, and feel that a basic problem of American society is being described. One must identify completely with Isabel Archer, which takes some doing, to recognize the complex and subtle moral world in which she's involved. But when Lewis describes Babbitt in his office, fumbling over the writing of a letter and having a secretary finally write it herself, when Lewis portrays the American businessman as essentially an inefficient parasite, almost any American can recognize the type. Very simply, Lewis dealt with social patterns, social fables—with *groups*. Even Fitzgerald, who was in many ways the most exquisite American novelist after James, was concerned with group behavior, whereas the only group portrayed by James was the American elect.

J.A.G.   It still seems to me that you're making more of Lewis than he deserves to have made of him.

A.K.   I don't think I am. Lewis is a very much underrated writer. One of the things that fascinates me about any kind of writing is what makes it last. Fitzgerald said that his aim as a writer was to get that into his prose which would make people read it like Braille. That's a marvelous figure. The difference between a good writer and a not-so-good writer is simply that with the good writer you're always aware of the immediate, tactile thing you are reading. No matter when you read *Babbitt* you're aware of a whole world (a physical world, a social world, a human world) which is terribly real. Of course, it is very much a caricature, but caricature, after all, is one of the great elements of art. Why should caricature be less successful in a Lewis novel than in a Hogarth painting?

Again and again, looking back upon these writers of the twenties, I see that Faulkner, Fitzgerald, Lewis, Dos Passos, and Hemingway each did something quite remarkable. None of them was like anybody else. There has never been anyone remotely like Sinclair Lewis. That is true also of the romantic Fitzgerald, of the utterly idiosyncratic Faulkner, of Hemingway. Or consider Dos Passos. Today, no critic takes him seriously. But read *U.S.A.* There is nothing remotely resembling Dos Passos's method, his tone, his color, his vocabulary. He is absolutely his own man. And that, of course, is a great thing.

J.A.G.   Why did so many of these writers of the 1920's deteriorate in their later careers?

A.K.   Well, remember Fitzgerald's great remark, that there are no second acts in American life. If anything, deterioration is the rule rather than the exception. American writers are famous for early brilliance, and then for petering out. Ever since Mark Twain, the successful American novelist has also become a celebrity, a prima donna, and in a way an economic royalist. Mark Twain was a rich man; Lewis and Hemingway and others became very rich through their work. Successful American novelists have a peculiar relation with the public, very much like that of a movie star. They tend to become too much concerned with fame. Hemingway became so interested in reaching a big audience that after a while he couldn't write at all.

J.A.G.   How about Faulkner?

A.K.   Faulkner did not wear out, but one reason was that he didn't live in a big city. Remember also that Faulkner did not become successful until relatively late in his career. Unlike Hemingway and Fitzgerald, both of them great best-sellers, Faulkner did not catch on with the public. He was able to withstand success because he didn't have any for a long time.

F. Scott Fitzgerald, from the moment he published his first book, *This Side of Paradise,* was a great celebrity. He conducted his love affair with his wife, which is a very tragic story, in public. He felt he had to make a lot of money. When he couldn't make it writing novels, he wrote short stories for *The Saturday Evening Post,* being paid $5,000 or $6,000 for a story he would turn out in two or three days. But he never had enough money or enough praise. So he began to drink heavily. (Liquor, by the way, was a problem for all these writers.)

J.A.G.   How did the Great Depression affect American writers?

A.K.   The influence of the 1920's lasted pretty much until the middle 1930's, when the experimental, *avant-garde* side of the 20's petered out. As to the Depression itself, it produced some good novelists, like James T. Farrell, Richard Wright, and Nathanael West, whose *Miss Lonelyhearts* is important. But many writers got caught up in ideological issues which in general lessened their artistic achievements. Only a very great writer like Faulkner was able to withstand the pressure of constant political criticizing. Properly speaking, the American novelist didn't get back to himself, as an independent creator, until after World War II. By and large, the 1930's was a period in which many writers sacrificed their individuality, became more conscious of society than of themselves.

J.A.G.   What about the Great Depression as a subject for novelists?

A.K.   John Steinbeck's *The Grapes of Wrath* is a very good social novel; it communicates perfectly the sense of outrage that this rich country should produce a whole mass of people forced to wander the roads looking for food and shelter. Then James T. Farrell's *Studs Lonigan* trilogy provides an accurate, intense, savage picture of the narrowness of Irish Catholic life in Chicago. Farrell's bitterness as an intellectual and as a socialist against what he felt to be his own distorted upbringing comes through of course, but the most valuable side of the book is the sense of the group, the clan, that Farrell transmits. These novels are really about gangs, not about individuals. They reveal the clash of groups and forces.

J.A.G.   If World War I was the greatest political event of the early twentieth century, wasn't the Great Depression the most important socio-economic event of the era? Did it not have an impact on literature comparable to that of World War I?

A.K.   No. The reason why the First World War produced such a brilliant body of American novelists and books was that the writers were all upper-middle class; the war for them was a great chance of breaking with their backgrounds. What the Depression did for American literature was to awaken literary recognition on the part of people from the immigrant groups in the big cities. The typical writer of the 1920's was someone from a "good family," like Cummings, whose father was a

Unitarian minister; Hemingway, whose father was a doctor; Dos Passos, whose father was a lawyer. The typical writer of the 1930's, however, was someone like Richard Wright, whose father was a tenant farmer; Ralph Ellison, whose father was a poor Negro in Oklahoma; John Steinbeck, who worked as a bricklayer.

The Depression era saw a remarkable coming-of-age of Jewish, Negro, and Irish writers. (Dreiser was the first important American writer who was not a Protestant and not, properly speaking, middle class.) Middle-class attitudes had absolutely dominated American fiction. Suddenly this changed. In literature, nothing is more important than childhood: that's when the vital social experiences that shape us all occur. With the middle-class writer, life provides a sense of balance and poise and subtlety, but it does not provide the direct assault of harsh experience which is so important. After the Depression and World War II, there suddenly burst forth a passionate, brilliant school of writers—Jewish, Negro, Irish—who became perhaps the dominant force in contemporary American literary experience.

The Depression and the Second World War were intimately related; after all, the Depression did not end until war broke out. And these events shaped a whole generation of writers. Saul Bellow and Ralph Ellison, for instance, both came of age during the Depression, and were in their late twenties when we entered the war. Their points of view were shaped by the social experience of the New Deal. I myself was a reporter during the war both here and in England, and the thing that always moved me most was to recognize that even in the Army and Navy people were trying to teach recruits some respect for the new social legislation. I remember at the Great Lakes Naval Training Camp I encountered a class of Negroes, all of them illiterate, who were being taught to read and write by a young lieutenant from a wealthy Wisconsin family. It took the war to bring this about, just as it took the war to help end segregation in the Army. Class relationships changed, and class is always a great element in the history of the novel.

Yet the Second World War did not produce many great novels, and for very clear reasons. The middle-class writers of the twenties went from protected, sheltered homes—from a world still full of the belief in American destiny—to the shattering experiences of the war. But the people of my generation who went to the war from the Depression had no illusions. The war seemed to us neither just nor unjust, but merely a horrible necessity. It also follows that the people who wrote after the second war were not middle class, not interested in forms the way Hemingway and Dos Passos were, not as sophisticated artistically, and not very often as original. Steinbeck wrote one or two quite good books, but he was not as interesting a writer as Hemingway or Dos Passos.

There is nothing in the least original artistically in *The Grapes of Wrath;* it is simply a true, forceful book. No new forms were developed. Norman Mailer's first book, *The Naked and the Dead,* was modeled on Dos Passos and Hemingway. It was not in the least original, though it's a good book.

J.A.G. Do you mean that modern conditions do not provide a favorable environment for creative writers?

A.K. That is, I suppose, the most important question one can ask about the current literary situation. Novelists, of course, enjoy living well and having money, but they cannot keep from feeling morally and intellectually that things are wrong with our society. There is a contradiction between the enormous wealth and splendor of American life and the sense of anxiety, of something fundamentally immoral going on in our society today. A lot of people are able to delude themselves that they are living in the best of all possible worlds, but the novelist, if he's a real writer, senses that things are not right. A writer like Saul Bellow, for example, whom I think very highly of, is a very successful American. He has a position of great honor and he certainly enjoys all the fruits of living in our intoxicating century. Yet his work is full of the most terrible sense of grief, of guilt, of foreboding. Why is this? Because in this privileged world human relationships are deteriorating. Bellow is aware, I would assume, that we have a civilization but not a culture, a society without standards.

Twentieth-century America has produced some of the most extraordinary capacities for unhappiness the world has ever seen. And the best novelists have called the score properly on what is happening. The novel as a literary creation deals with the human soul in *active* relationships, and these are enough to make one despair sometimes. The easy confidence which Americans were supposed to feel has quite departed. I don't know anyone who doesn't live with a sense of anxiety and foreboding because of the violent animosities of our time. And this is where the modern novel really succeeds—in describing human beings and their capacity for destruction.

J.A.G. It seems to me you're contradicting what you said before. If a very successful writer like Saul Bellow continues to be moved by the human candition, why did writers like Hemingway and Fitzgerald lose their power when they achieved popular recognition and material prosperity?

A.K. No. I didn't mean that I pretend to understand why successful writers have sometimes petered out. The connection I was making was much more a psychological one. I am saying, in effect, that a man can live morally and psychologically in several traditions at the same time. He can be a child of prosperity and a child of despair, as Mark Twain was; he can enjoy the physical world very much, but also recognize that something about the very nature of modern society makes for great destructiveness. This awareness of man's destructiveness has become more intense as a result of the Second World War. You cannot kill thirty million people and then expect that the world will go back to normal and that sensitive writers will say, "Life is great." A novelist like Bellow who comes from a poor Jewish family in Chicago obviously gets a great kick out of being successful, out of being admired. But in his heart, he feels that the world is a pretty dismal place. There is no contradiction between these two things.

J.A.G.   The other contemporary novelist you said you particularly admired was Norman Mailer. How does his work reflect the problems of our age?

A.K.   Mailer is an extraordinarily talented man. He has a very muscular, combative kind of talent, and he completely understands and rejoices in the popular side of American life. In what I think is his best book, *The Armies of the Night,* he says that he even felt a sneaking sympathy for the federal marshals in Washington opposing the pickets (of whom he was one), because he recognized in them the same comic, sardonic talent which he had found among the men he had known in the Army.

J.A.G.   Is he like Crane in this respect?

A.K.   Very much so. He has a great passion for what happens in the street, in crowds. At the same time, of course, Mailer is also a very interesting ideologist. More than any other good novelist that I can think of, he openly declared after the war that the next chapter in the American imagination would have to deal with a whole new attitude toward sex. His point was that white, middle-class men had deprived themselves of certain fundamental qualities of passion. In a famous essay called "The White Negro," he compared the active, strong, reckless quality of the Negro, who as a kind of outlaw in American society had to gain his way by forceful means, with the timid and obedient white, middle-class American.

As a novelist, Mailer has been extremely erratic. He has shown himself to be almost uninterested in finishing books properly. But I think he is an original, in many ways the most original, American novelist since Scott Fitzgerald. He reminds me always of Crane and Fitzgerald. He's very sophisticated, but very passionate, very strong, and he also has an extraordinary sense of mischief. The best thing about Mailer is that he has recognized that in our time a strong talent is in fact subversive. He has social intelligence of a very prophetic kind.

When Mailer was in the Army during the war, and later when he became interested in the things which led him to write books like *An American Dream,* he recognized that the big thing that was happening in American life was a new attitude to sexuality. This of course relates to what we were talking about earlier: James's treatment of women. James was launched as a novelist by his sense of what one might call the feminine interest, the recognition that women were the audience, that women were the main characters in the middle-class story. What Mailer is saying one hundred years later is that now the male has to be emancipated from capitalism, and from the whole sense of being simply a citizen, a faithful father and worker. Mailer believes that there is a tremendous emotional force in American men which most of them don't allow themselves to use. And the great thing about Mailer as a writer is that he tries to put this energy into his work.

J.A.G.   Are there other contemporary writers that you think will be read one hundred years from now?

A.K.   The writer most likely to endure, in my opinion, is both a European and an American, Vladimir Nabokov. Nabokov is, first of all, a man of stupefying talent. He is original, independent, so much his own man in every way, and he has extraordinary resources of language. I don't admire his social views. He would like to go back to the eighteenth century, which is a little difficult. I don't think he is always a very nice man; he has tremendous contempt. But as one knows from his most famous novel, *Lolita*, and from his best novel, *Pale Fire*, Nabokov is a man of extraordinary authenticity. For him living still consists in deciphering, inch by inch and moment by moment, what things are really like. None of the great political ideologies of our time mean a damn thing to him; all he cares about is looking at life as it is.

He's a European, obviously, and yet he's American, too. America has helped to bring him out. *Lolita* was a product of his American experience, and so was that charming little book called *Pnin*, about a Russian *emigré* scholar. So is *Pale Fire*, a still obscure, ambiguous, but wholly fascinating book. In Nabokov, the line of the 1920's has never quite died out. He is plainly the heir of James Joyce, who has been, of course, the greatest influence on twentieth-century fiction. His being an *emigré* has preserved in him a kind of independence which the American writers of our time have lost by being too attentive to society.

In a funny sort of way, Nabokov's very remoteness, his haughty indifference, has given him a tremendous advantage. Writing does not exhaust him. Ralph Ellison has published one book, *Invisible Man*. Ellison is a very good writer, and *Invisible Man* is a marvelously inventive and original book, but one feels that it took all of Negro history to produce that book. A lot of Jewish and Negro writers who have been through the mill tend not to be very productive; it's as though it has taken all their resources to produce one book. Moreover, it takes great cosmopolitan experience, great knowledge of the world, to produce many great novels. Nabokov knows the world. He has lived in Russia, Germany, France, England, America; he now lives in Switzerland. He's not provincial. Whereas one feels, with all due respect to their experiences, many writers from the minorities have had only minority experience, and therefore they are much more limited.

Someone once asked Henry James whether he preferred *Madame Bovary* or *Anna Karenina*. He said, sputtering with amazement, "Why, *Anna Karenina*, of course. *Madame Bovary* is the story of a sordid little adultery in a provincial French town, but *Anna Karenina* deals with the highest Russian aristocracy." He was right in the sense that the world of *Anna Karenina* was a very big world. If you care about human experience, and a novelist certainly must, there is a lot to be said for being born into the upper classes and for knowing the world as widely as possible.

J.A.G. What are the half-dozen or so books that you would recommend to persons interested in the subject we have been discussing? In each case, would you indicate briefly what the particular contribution of the volume is?

A.K. The best general book I know of on the American novel is Richard Chase, *The American Novel and Its Tradition* (1957). Chase had an extraordinary sensible, detached, comprehensive understanding of this subject. On the earlier part of the century under study, I recommend Henry James's keen essays on fiction in general, usefully collected by Leon Edel into *The Future of the Novel* (1956). The essays in interpretation collected by Mark Shorer on Sinclair Lewis, by Irving Howe on Sherwood Anderson, by R. P. Warren on William Faulkner, by Leon Edel on Henry James, are all in the Prentice-Hall series of collected critical essays on famous writers, and are very useful. I can also recommend the many new "critical" editions of Crane's *The Red Badge of Courage*, Theodore Dreiser's *Sister Carrie*, Scott Fitzgerald's *The Great Gatsby*, as well as similar editions of earlier books like *Huckleberry Finn* and *The Portrait of a Lady*.

David M. Potter

Interpreting American History

D AVID M. POTTER, who is Coe Professor of History at Stanford University, is primarily a specialist in the Civil War era, but his interests encompass the whole span of American history. In addition to such works as *Lincoln and His Party in the Secession Crisis* (1942), *The Lincoln Theme and American National Historiography* (1948), *The South and the Sectional Crisis* (1968), and a soon-to-be-published two-volume study of the events leading up to the Civil War, he has written on subjects as varied as the exploration of the West, Nathan Hale, Huey Long, the importance of television, and numerous histori-ographical topics. A continuing interest has been his con-cern for the nature of the "American character" and the forces that have shaped it over time. His book, *People of Plenty: Economic Abundance and the American Char-acter* (1954), has proved to be one of the most influential treatments of this subject written in the twentieth cen-tury. In this concluding discussion, Professor Potter talks about *People of Plenty* and the attempts of earlier historians to discern what is unique and important in the American experience.

John A. Garraty Professor Potter, your book *People of Plenty* has been one of the most widely discussed and influential recent attempts to put the whole course of American history into a single framework. Would you briefly summarize the thesis of this work?

David M. Potter I was trying to develop the argument that when historians had studied American values they had given too much emphasis to ideology and perhaps not enough to the conditions that were formative in American life. It seemed to me that one of the most distinctive and widespread of these conditions had been physical abundance, and in a great many different forms. One could think of abundance in terms of cheap, fertile land, or in terms of the high productivity of the American economic system, or of a demand for labor which was conducive to high wages. The economist sees abundance in terms of the gross national product; perhaps for the layman the most familiar concept is the famous "American Standard of Living." But these are all aspects of the same thing.

I believed that this abundance had had widespread effects upon American values, sometimes in what seemed paradoxical or contradictory ways. Certainly, it was basic to much of what we call American materialism, what Washington Irving called the "worship of the almighty dollar." But it also contributed to the American belief that social advantages can and ought to be extended to the whole population. Abundance both whetted competitive acquisitiveness and also made possible the fulfillment of democratic ideals which would have remained abstractions if they could not have been fulfilled. Abundance made possible the realization of the expectations which democratic ideology promised.

J.A.G. You said that abundance worked in paradoxical ways. Could you illustrate that?

D.M.P. The opportunity that existed here for men to acquire property accentuated the drive of acquisitiveness. Wealth became a measure of the standing of an individual in a community. Yet I think it was always coupled with the idea that this opportunity made possible more latitude for the development of the potentialities of more people, which I regard as a very essential part of the democratic concept. It is evident, for instance, in the rapid development of public education in the United States. We could afford this education, first at the primary level and eventually at the level of college. We have a vastly greater proportion of our population in colleges and universities than any other country.

J.A.G. Isn't there a contradiction between the American's concern for material goods and his belief in education?

D.M.P. The materialistic emphasis caused Americans to put a heavier stress upopn vocational education as a means toward gaining wealth, but idealism led some rich men to use their fortunes idealistically in the support of liberal education. Many American fortunes have been diverted to such public services as medical research, education, and the like. American attitudes toward poverty reflect another sharp paradox, and *People of Plenty* has been criticized for its failure to take poverty into account.

The criticism is in some ways justified. If I were rewriting it I would give more explicit attention to it. But I would not qualify my argument very much. Problems of poverty in American life have been the problems of disadvantaged minorities in an affluent society. The advantages of affluence are held tantalizingly in front of the poor in a way that makes their failure to enjoy these advantages especially frustrating. But modern poverty leaves the poor, who are now in a minority, in a more helpless position politically than in the old days when the majority of people were *relatively* poor. Through political action they might then command electoral majorities to implement some of their desires.

J.A.G. Is the poverty problem as we think of it in the United States merely a euphemism for the Negro problem?

D.M.P. It might be called the problem of the minorities and not simply of the Negroes. American Indians clearly are very badly off, and so are a great many Mexican Americans and other minority groups. But a great many old-stock, white Americans, especially those in Appalachia, live in a deplorably bad condition too.

J.A.G. Would you explain how you developed the basic thesis of *People of Plenty?*

D.M.P. Well, one can never be certain how one gets hold of a thesis. But I think I was influenced partly by a reaction to what seemed to me the prevailing attitude that there was a certain superior virtue in American ideas. The phrase was current after World War II that the United States was a "freedom-loving nation," and this implied that some nations didn't love freedom as much as they should, that while we were, so to speak, "monogamous" in our love of freedom, perhaps other nations were polygamous. I felt that nations generally, like people, have the kind of ideals which they can afford, and that we had had the good fortune to be able to afford some rather expensive ideals, more because of our condition than because of our character. I know I was influenced by the generalizations of other historians and I suppose especially by some of Frederick Jackson Turner's ideas about the impact of the frontier. But by Turner's own admission, the frontier was a diminishing influence in American life after 1890. According to his analysis, some of the older attitudes should have become attenuated after 1890, and I was not sure that they had. Turner had seen abundance too much in the form of free land; he had been rather oblivious of other forms of economic opportunity which had freed many Americans to develop their potentialities.

It struck me, for example, that one thing which had done a great deal to emancipate American women was the opportunity for employment in business which resulted from technological changes, such as the typewriter, the telephone, and the elaboration of office functions. The city became, if we use Turner's term, the "safety valve" for the American woman. I doubt that emancipation of women was promoted by frontier conditions at all. There was a saying, in fact, that the frontier was great for men and dogs but hell on horses and women!

J.A.G. Would you comment on some of the older general views or syntheses that have been devised by American historians? For example, what were the underlying assumptions that George Bancroft, who was probably the first serious generalizer about America, made in his *History of the United States?* What did he see that was unique about America?

D.M.P. Bancroft's ideas now seem outdated, but certain of his attitudes or points of view have really had a very lasting perservation, as the psychologists say. He wrote in the framework of a religious belief that was more literal than modern religion. He claimed that American history was dictated and guided by Providence, that the working out of American destiny was a fulfillment of a Divine Plan. Of course, now that we think of history in secular terms, that concept hardly communicates at all. But implicit in the thought that America was somehow distinctive, that it had a special destiny, was a concept of American exceptionalism. And it seems to me that whether Bancroft was responsible for it or whether he merely participated in something that was general, the concept of exceptionalism has always been a very strong element in American historical writing. Of course *People of Plenty* reflects this preoccupation, and indeed might be criticized as reflecting it too strongly or too literally.

J.A.G. Isn't it possible that when Bancroft saw America as the child of destiny he was looking at the same facts about American development that you were treating in *People of Plenty,* and translating them into religious rather than material terms?

D.M.P. As you state it, it seems to me that one could make a very strong case that the essences are the same, but the form in which Bancroft stated them was very different: the bounty which Providence had awarded to the Chosen People.

J.A.G. What sort of sources did Bancroft draw upon? How does his work stand up, aside from the interpretation that he gave to the events he described?

D.M.P. Bancroft's research approximates modern standards to a degree that is surprising, when one thinks of how dated his ideas seem. Edmund

S. Morgan, a close student of much of the material that Bancroft used, regards Bancroft as first-rate in constructing history from sources—a historian whose work deserves attention even today.

J.A.G. Historians have certainly come round full circle to his general view that British "oppression" was the major cause of the Revolution.

D.M.P. They have indeed.

J.A.G. Aside from Bancroft's belief that there was something very exceptional and unique about America, is there anything else in his work that has affected the way in which later historians have looked at the history of the United States?

D.M.P. Bancroft was certainly one of the first writers to stress the democratic theme. He was convinced of the validity of the democratic ideal and of its thematic importance in American development. Possibly, he set the tone for a great deal of other historical writing. He was, also, of course, an active Democrat. I suppose one might think of him as a Jacksonian counterpart of Arthur Schlesinger, Jr., who is both an important historian and a Democratic political figure.

But I have another thought about the doctrine of American exceptionalism. It is a fundamental part of Frederick Jackson Turner's frontier thesis, and one of the things that gave Turner's thesis a very special appeal. He emphasized this, and the historical profession responded to it almost with unanimity for nearly a generation.

J.A.G. Is there anything uniquely American about emphasizing the exceptionalism or special quality of a nation's history? Don't historians of other nations do more or less the same thing? The Whig historians in England certainly saw something very special about English history, did they not? And for that matter, don't German and French historians do so too?

D.M.P. I believe that is true, although I don't know that anyone has ever made a systematic comparison of the intensity with which historians have emphasized what they believe to be the distinctive features of their own nationality. But it's clear enough, as you say, that French and German and English historians are full of the same sort of rhetoric about distinctive character and unique values.

It has always interested me that zoologists give all forms of life both a generic name and a specific name. They use the generic name to focus upon similarities between the unique object that they are looking at and comparable objects. And by the specific name they emphasize the distinctiveness or uniqueness of the particular strain or variety that they are dealing with. This technique is a constant reminder to the zoologist to think of both similarities and of differences, to maintain some sort of balance. Now, there are zoologists who emphasize similarities—they're known as "lumpers." They put all sorts of varieties into one genus.

There are others who are known as "splitters," because they put closely related forms into separate generic categories. But historians don't have any way of doing this, no way comparable to the binominal names used in zoology. They sometimes exaggerate terribly very marginal differences without being reminded of how marginal these differences are, while at other times they generalize recklessly about the common qualities of groups.

J.A.G. The extreme form of the historical "splitter," I suppose, is the biographer.

D.M.P. It is true that biographies almost inevitably put too much emphasis on the role played by the individual that they are dealing with and minimize the role of the other people he interacted with. The biographer who treats his subject as a hero or as a villain is like the historian who treats a nation as one with a very special destiny.

J.A.G. How did the Civil War influence the writing of American history?

D.M.P. The fact that the Civil War was the great trauma in the American experience has led historians to exaggerate it as a great divide, winding up of the problems of the early republic, introducing those of modern society. This took the form of regarding the war as settling the question of whether the United States was a pluralistic body of states, or a single American nation, and led to the oversimplification that before the Civil War America was an agrarian republic and after the war it was an industrial nation. It also caused historians to treat emancipation in terms that now seem entirely too simple. The termination of slavery was regarded by a whole generation of historians as somehow also ending the problem of race relations. It became a kind of convention in textbooks to discuss the slavery controversy, emancipation, and Reconstruction, and then ignore all further questions about race, not allowing for the fact that while slavery had been sectional, racism had been national, and racial problems had continued in a very acute form.

Another thing about the Civil War is that when it was over, the North and the South had to be psychologically reunited. It was by no means a foregone conclusion that they would be, but by the beginning of the twentieth century that reunion had been pretty effectively accomplished. I think that the Civil War created a very important psychological need for healing sectional divergences, and that this led to a reaffirmation and perhaps an even heavier emphasis upon American nationalism. The key figure, historiographically, was James Ford Rhodes, who, while maintaining scholarly standards, was clearly concerned to avoid making his history one of vindication and indictment and to try to make it something that would be acceptable to southern Americans and northern Americans alike. While Rhodes insisted that slavery was the cause of the war, he was careful to say that the South was not exclusively responsible for slavery, and he blamed the North for what were then regarded as the mistakes of Reconstruction.

Another concept of that time which was useful to historians emphasizing the national theme was the idea that the conflict was "irrepressible." If it was irrepressible, no one could be blamed for having failed to repress it. No one need look for villains, if the Civil War was the result of blind forces which no one could control.

J.A.G.   You're suggesting that historians ignored or rationalized the meaning of the Civil War in order to preserve their belief that America had a divine destiny, in Bancroft's terminology. What about your own "people of plenty" thesis? Does the war provide evidence that abundance has been the primary force in the American experience?

D.M.P.   I'm not certain. I wouldn't want to be dogmatic about abundance explaining every historical situation. But one way of looking at the Civil War is this. Northern society had developed a system based upon the mobility of labor, the flexibility and adaptability of the economy, and rapid technological change. This produced high wages, a high standard of living, public education, and the fulfillment of the potentialities of the individual. One of the things that made it work was the fact that a market had been created that would fuel a highly productive economy. It was very important to have a large body of consumers at a fairly high standard of living.

I don't think this was consciously recognized at the time, but the South was lagging in this respect. Slave labor was largely immobile and restricted to agricultural pursuits; it received no wages and only a subsistence living; it did not have the capacity to consume at a level that would provide much stimulus to the national economy. The Southern economy was not responsive to technological change. Not to disparage the importance of the moral issue of slavery for a moment, I think there was a feeling that the South ought to be drawn into the dynamics of the American system; that it ought to do its part to gear up the economy; that it was resisting the system and must not be permitted to do so.

J.A.G.   How did the introduction of German scholarly methods of research and writing in the late nineteenth century affect the writing of American history and the training of American historians?

D.M.P.   I suppose that there are a good many people in the profession who take a more affirmative view of the contribution of the German school than I do. It certainly had a profound value in teaching American historians standards of rigor and precision in research. David Levin, in his book *The Romantic Historians*, has shown that most American historical writing really was literature rather than the carefully formulated results of research prior to the impact of the German universities upon eager young American graduate students. German methods certainly corrected some of the romantic excesses and subjectivism of earlier American historians.

But we paid a high price for precision—the illusion that we had arrived at a scientific accuracy that transcended human error. It led to the foolish dogma that if the historian accumulated and validated data and laid it out in chronological sequence, the facts would reveal their own meaning, and the historian was exempted from responsibility for interpreting the facts. Interpretation tended to be driven underground, expressed in indirect or unconscious form, as unstated assumptions. The Germanic school inhibited the development of historical theory, and the profession still suffers from this.

The social scientist asks a question and looks for enough data to answer it. The historian sometimes feels that his job is to examine data and state what it is, without ever having asked what question this data relates to and what answer it provides to the question.

J.A.G. Can that really be blamed on the German scientific school? The intellectual roots of all the social sciences in the United States are Germanic. Can you explain why the other social sciences stress the formulation of hypotheses and the development of logical, theoretical methods of study, whereas so many historians insist that history is just a spewing forth of facts?

D.M.P. Perhaps I am being too harsh toward the German school. But one thing that surely must have happened is that the other social sciences have dealt more with quantitative matters. The necessities of quantification have forced them to examine their theory. One cannot count all the sociological facts, all the economic facts, or generalize safely from a single sociological or economic item. Therefore, the social scientist was compelled to develop a technique for generalizing from systematically selected data. But a historian could regard the record of a single military commander, or a single head of state as a unique phenomenon, and to that extent evade the questions of generalization and of the interpretation of quantiative data.

J.A.G. Was it merely a coincidence that Frederick Jackson Turner advanced his frontier hypothesis at the very time that the so-called frontier was disappearing in the 1890's?

D.M.P. I doubt if it was entirely a coincidence. Turner was both a historian reacting against the German school and a Wisconsin boy reacting against the New England monopoly on learning. He was also a romantic in an age when realism was beginning to assert itself. His treatment of the frontier reflects all these things—the denial of the unique importance of New England and of the Teutonic antecedents of the American experience and the romanticization of the frontiersman.

It's curious that Turner insisted that democracy came out of the American forest but also idealized the frontiersman, who, you might say, destroyed the American forest.

J.A.G.   Turner's thesis has had an enormous influence, but it has also been subject to a great deal of criticism by modern historians, including yourself. What is the current historical opinion of the role of the frontier?

D.M.P.   The idea that the experience of wrestling with physical hardships, rather than with social problems, left a mark upon those who participated in the basis of Turner's concept of frontier individualism. To him, individualism was not so much the quality of the person who differs from his fellows and exercises dissent, but the quality of self-reliance. Some interpretations of the American character have suffered from this ambiguity in the term "individualism." On the frontier, the conditions of life were very demanding. They tended to force men into the same mold rather than allowing them to develop their potentialities entirely according to their intrinsic talents. Richard Hofstadter's *Anti-Intellectualism in American Life* is, in a way, a comment on the continuing influence of the frontier: emphasis upon stamina, accompanied by a distrust of intellectual virtuosity or cleverness. Frontier life led people to exaggerate the importance of brute strength and to underestimate the merits of innovation and originality.

J.A.G.   What is true of the Turner thesis is also true of the point of view of the so-called progressive historians, men such as Charles A. Beard and Vernon L. Parrington. Was the Beardian variety of history as much related to the times as Turner's?

D.M.P.   Beardian history can be related to its era possibly more directly. Beard's *Economic Interpretation of the Constitution* was written at the high tide of progressivism. Progressivism emphasized a certain kind of democracy, and Beard saw American history in terms of conflicts over democracy. He can certainly be criticized for projecting the democracy of 1913 backward to 1787. Beard and Parrington tended to read American history as a conflict between conservatives and democrats, the children of light against the children of darkness—a typical progressive view.

J.A.G.   To what extent were historians like Beard merely American disciples of Karl Marx? *An Economic Interpretation of the Constitution* put great emphasis on economic interest as a motivating or directing force in history.

D.M.P.   When people talk about the question of Beard as a Marxian, the problem that is always in the back of my mind is whether or not they are construing Marxism in restrictive terms. Americans have tended to link Marxism with the ideas of Lenin, with the Russian Revolution, with the Russian Communist party. But Marxism is very much broader than those particular manifestations. Directly or indirectly, Beard certainly accepted some of the concepts of Marx, such as the idea that economic interest is a basic factor in the political process.

J.A.G. Do you see in Beard's view of American history the Marxian emphasis on conflict between the proletarian and the capitalist?

D.M.P. No, I don't. It seems to me that he saw history in terms of economic conflict, but not in the simplistic terms of a capitalist-proletarian polarity. But again I feel that Marxism is a very ambivalent word. Beard took a middle-class point of view. He was not at all concerned with any sort of proletarian dominance in the society. But he was highly critical of industrial capitalism, and I think that ran through his writing pretty consistently.

J.A.G. How did the alienation of intellectuals from the prevailing values of the Harding-Coolidge-Hoover era affect the interpretation of American history?

D.M.P. I wonder if the primary effect was not to cause historians to search for what might be called an American alternative to industrial capitalism. A small body of radicals were prepared to subscribe to the Marxian alternative, but most Americans hesitated to accept that rather drastic solution. They were looking for something in the American tradition, and they found it in the concept of agrarianism, and particularly in the figure of Thomas Jefferson. Here again Beard was important, in that he drew the antithesis between agrarianism and industrialism with vigor and simplicity.

J.A.G. Was the effect of the Great Depression of the 1930's on historical writing any different?

D.M.P. Only in the sense that in the 1920's the protest was against what appeared to be a successful system which many people disliked in spite of its success. The Depression brought many historians to the view that it was not even a successful system. The New Deal is often presented to students with the question, was it a revolution or a reform movement? This has always seemed to me a rather indirect way of asking whether it was within the American tradition. Its advocates appear to have a kind of psychological compulsion to argue that it was, its opponents that it was not, instead of looking at what it accomplished.

J.A.G. Why didn't the Marxian view of history find a wider acceptance in the 1930's, since it provided a tailor-made explanation of the failure of capitalism, and since many historians thought that capitalism was failing?

D.M.P. The notion that economic success was the coefficient of an individual's own endeavor had been so rooted into American beliefs that it persisted even in the face of the traumas of 1931–32, and before there was time for deep-seated changes in values, Franklin D. Roosevelt had come forward with a program that said the system could be made to work again. The readiness with which people accepted the New Deal is indicative of their reluctance to give up their old beliefs. Of course, another way of putting this is to say that Americans rejected the idea of a class society in the European sense. Furthermore, I think the Marxist historians in America were really not first-rate minds.

J.A.G.   The post-World War II period gave rise to what is called the "consensus school" of history. Would you describe the assumptions of the consensus historians?

D.M.P.   What John Higham meant when he coined the term "consensus school" was that these historians took the view that agreements, the shared ideas of Americans, were more significant in our past than the conflicts, the issues over which they had been at odds with one another. Of the older historians, Parrington had emphasized ideological conflict; Turner, geographical; Beard, economic. These men had treated almost all the episodes of American history as examples of conflict, and they carried some of these examples to almost comic lengths. The consensus historians, of whom Louis Hartz may be regarded as typical, say that the American experience had been within the framework of liberalism, based upon the common acceptance of the ideas of John Locke. Daniel J. Boorstin, whose approach is more pragmatic, argues that there has been a surprising lack of deep issues in American politics, that the major political parties have offered voters a very narrow range of alternatives. Factors of agreement have been much more important than factors of disagreement.

J.A.G.   If I may return to your analysis of the role of abundance in America, you pointed out that in our day abundance is possible for everyone. Could the awareness of this fact have influenced consensus historians to conclude that there were no underlying economic conflicts in America?

D.M.P.   Perhaps. I am reminded of the sociologists' concept of "significant others," the idea that each person in his own visualization of society tends to include certain components, and tends to be oblivious of other components. For a long time, for example, we were quite oblivious of the Negro component in American society. We simply screened it out of our mental picture of the society. I wonder if the period of the 1940's wasn't a time when we had a particularly limited view. The "significant others" were mostly white middle-class Americans. What has happened since then is partly that we have changed our concept of the "significant others," and thus obtained a little broader and less bland visualization of society.

J.A.G.   I think the use of the word "bland" is particularly significant in

understanding the consensus psychology. Do you think that the blandness of American politics in the Eisenhower era might have had something to do with this? Were the consensus historians reading back that
blandness into earlier periods?

D.M.P. There certainly have been many important conflicts in American
history, but for some reason the consensus historians have tended to
manipulate their views so that they didn't see them: the revolutionary
experience, the Civil War, many ethnic and religious conflicts, and so on,
as Richard Hofstadter has recently pointed out.

J.A.G. In your zoological terminology, they are generic historians rather
than specific historians?

D.M.P. They are, indeed. In the case of Hartz, it seems to me he adopted
an ideological emphasis that enabled him to overlook things that didn't
fit in with his thesis. One can argue that there was a basic ideological
agreement between the supporters of the Confederacy and the supporters
of the Union during the Civil War. Both were committed to certain
principles of constitutional government. But I think that Hartz did not
allow for the fact that men can hold to the same ideological principle
and yet fight bitterly about the construction they place upon it. Harmony
is not entirely a coefficient of ideological agreement.

J.A.G. What do consensus historians mean by the term "status politics"?

D.M.P. What they mean is that men's opinions are sometimes governed
by their psychological insecurities; that psychological needs replace economic needs as a focus of conflict; and, especially, that in times of rapid
social change, groups whose social standing is somehow threatened by
the change react against it because of their anxiety about their standing.
They usually express this anxiety, the argument runs, in indirect terms,
as if they were concerned about policy questions. The analysis of status
rivalry is rendered more difficult by the fact that its expression is cryptic
or indirect.

J.A.G. Would you give an example of how the status argument has been
employed to explain a particular group of Americans?

D.M.P. It has been suggested that the clergy dominated colonial New
England, but that as society became more secularized and as wealth
came to be more important the clergy felt threatened. They expressed
this by becoming active in reform movements. Their motivation was
sometimes not really concern for the objects of reform, but a kind of
self-assertion. The argument has been made, for example, as an explanation of New England abolitionism.

Richard Hofstadter has done as much as anyone to make the concept
of status politics familiar to the historical profession. He has argued
that the Progressive movement illustrates the process. Progressivism

had what he calls a reform side and a sour side. Reformers were concerned with social betterment, but they were also people of "Main Street" America who felt threatened by the big city and the great corporations. That reaction manifested itself, for instance, in the antitrust movement, but also in the prohibition movement and in hostility to immigration. In short, there was an indiscriminate hostility toward and mistrust of anything that was not part of the familiar environment of small-town America. It took the form of constructive reform in connection with some issues, and rather repressive attitudes in connection with other issues.

J.A.G.   Is not this explanation of reform movements almost essential, given the consensus point of view? If there are no basic differences or major conflicts in society, reformers must have some obscure, nonrational motive for complaining?

D.M.P.   At least the concept of status politics lends itself well to the ideas of consensus historians. However, the interpretation presents problems. Hofstadter argues that in bad times conflict is likely to be genuine, but in times of prosperity conflicts are likely to be more related to status anxieties. He may be correct, but it requires an extremely conscientious and expert historian to choose judiciously which analysis to apply. The status motivation implies a degree of psychic anxiety bordering upon fantasy or even paranoia. Since these are not qualities which we admire, an analysis in terms of these qualities is inherently disparaging. On the other hand, if one analyzes a man's policies with the assumption that his issues are real, this inherently creates a presumption in his favor. It lends itself to the view that he is concerned with a meaningful problem and that his goals are public-spirited. If one is free to employ either approach, the option gives biased historians an opportunity to put the stamp of approval or disapproval on a particular historical policy, not by analyzing its merits but by choosing which form of analysis to apply.

J.A.G.   Do you think that historians who have used this status concept have misused it in the way you suggest?

D.M.P.   I'm speaking more of a potential danger. The trouble is that either explanation is a blanket explanation. One could pick out certain abolitionists and make a very strong case that they were badly maladjusted persons. Their behavior would be compatible with the status-politics analysis. But many of the abolitionists were men with long-range views and sustained devotion to the cause of freedom; they were apparently not motivated by psychological problems of their own. Similarly, some injustice has been done to the Populists by the application of the status-politics interpretation. That is not to say that the Populists were utterly devoid of status motivation.

J.A.G. What is your opinion of the historical technique of trying to understand the underlying character of a movement by collecting data about the lives and social backgrounds of a large number of people who can be identified with the movement and generalizing on the basis of their collective biographies?

D.M.P. With the tendencies of historical study being what they are, and the new techniques for quantification being what they are, we will certainly see more of this kind of study. Thomas Cochran's *Railroad Leaders* and Otis Graham's study of the attitudes of Progressives toward the New Deal are excellent examples of what can be done along this line.

But it can be a pretty tenuous approach at times. A study which examines the social, educational, occupational, and economic status of conservative Republicans, as contrasted with liberal Republicans during the Progressive period, and finds a difference primarily in the age level of the two groups, is not historically very enlightening.

J.A.G. Do you consider yourself a member of the consensus school of history?

D.M.P. I think John Higham suggested that perhaps I was. I don't reject this suggestion, nor do I really claim membership in the club. I fall back on what I said about the zoologists—the lumpers and the splitters. There are some circumstances in which the historian must ask himself: "Do the points of difference predominate or the points of agreement?" He ought to treat his subject according to the specific answer to this question. He ought not to have a philosophical commitment one way or the other.

For a large part of American history I think that the points of agreement have been underestimated by historians. The consensus historians performed a useful service by offering their view as a corrective. But that doesn't mean that their views have any philosophical superiority over other views.

J.A.G. Do you think that the young "New Left" historians really make up a school of history?

D.M.P. Most of the historical schools of the past were united by positive or affirmative convictions—for instance, the Progressive historians by the belief that social betterment was possible and that democracy was a particularly effective way to advance it. The writers of the New Left that I'm familiar with seem to share negative rather than positive views. They are convinced that the American past was discreditable, and that we need to break with that past. They reject the view of the past of most historians, even historians who have disagreed with one another within the limits we've been talking about. So if negative points of agreement are significant, I think these give a certain coherence to the New Left.

Otherwise, I would be hard pressed to make a case for there being much agreement among them.

J.A.G. What do they mean when they claim that older historians have not given them a "usable past"?

D.M.P. Well, the term "usable past" has two quite different connotations. In one sense a "usable past" means a realistic, functional recognition of that part of the past which helps us to understand living questions. Such a past might not be psychologically satisfying at all, but it would be germane. In another sense, the term means a past that is psychologically satisfying, one that gives sanction to some predetermined ideology, or massages the ego.

It seems to me that the latter is subjective, and while nothing is wholly objective, the first is a good bit closer to being objective. I'm afraid that certain vociferous members of the New Left, when they speak of a "usable past," actually want a sanction for their particular points of view, a historical record that will be compatible with their own system of values. That's a very different thing from what historical relativists mean when they argue that historians ought to write about things which are germane to what we are concerned with today, and not about matters which have no current relevance and are merely antiquarian.

J.A.G. Can you think of a particular case that illustrates these two approaches?

D.M.P. Well, let me try. Take the question of slave discontent. To begin with, there were apologists of the Southern system who denied that there was any slave discontent. In due course, a reaction developed there, which produced a realistic recognition that there was discontent that expressed itself in various forms: slaves could run away; they could sublimate their aggressions and turn them to acts of injury against one another rather than against their masters; they could resist individually or revolt collectively. All analyses which recognized slave discontent were in a sense germane to reality.

An example of the historians who have used the past in this sense would be Eugene Genovese, who faces realistically the fact that there was a great deal more slave rebellion in Latin America than in the southern states. Genovese is a Marxist and, it is safe to say, concerned to show that slavery was evil and that American slaves were discontented with their lot. But he does not seek to "prove" that slaves in the United States were rebellious. Instead, he examines the full range of psychological forms in which slave discontent found expression.

On the other hand, Herbert Aptheker, with the same personal point of view, has a dogma which makes it impossible for him to admit that American slaves were not overtly rebellious. He has therefore, in his

American Negro Slave Revolts, dredged up every scrap of evidence of slave resistance in the record, and has, I think, extracted the utmost he can from every such scrap to create a picture of constant seething potential slave rebellion. It seems to me that he is engaging in seeking a past that would be "usable" in the sense of being compatible with his ideology, whereas Genovese is looking for a realistic analysis of a phenomenon that is germane to the problems of American Negroes, past and present.

J.A.G. When the New Left historians complain of the lack of a "usable past," don't they also mean that historians have ignored aspects of history that didn't suit their particular prejudices or interests? For example, they claim that there has been little interest in the study of poverty, and they condemn older historians for not writing about the poor, for not investigating what it was like to be poor, say, at the time of the American Revolution or at other periods in our history.

D.M.P. I accept that, but I think that among those who complain of the neglect of important questions, there is a difference between those who really want a realistic, functional exposure of the relevant data and those who want a psychological sanction and an ideological confirmation for their own preconceptions, arrived at a priori and not by deriving it from the historical record.

J.A.G. Is it *possible* to write a history of the poor? Is it possible to write the history of the slaves' discontent? Do the necessary records exist, or is the history of the inarticulate masses of the past lost simply because of their inarticulateness?

D.M.P. Inarticulateness is certainly a limiting factor upon what one can do, and often one has to work from scraps. American historians are not accustomed to doing that. But when one thinks of what medieval historians have done with limited scraps of evidence, it is clear that we ought not to abandon the effort. Medievalists have shown what can be accomplished by drawing inferences carefully from fragmentary evidence. And we have information of various sorts, both about the poor and about the slaves, that gives historians something substantive to deal with.

J.A.G. What is your view of the current concern for giving more emphasis to the history of the Negro in America? Can the role of the Negro in American life be given more attention without simply exaggerating it?

D.M.P. Perhaps this is not a direct response to the question, but I do feel that the emphasis is likely to be misplaced. It is a mistake to use the historical record as a device to supply a sense of identity and dignity for the blacks by providing them with fake heroes. I wish that the treatment of Negro history could be given a place proportionate to its importance, which is substantial, by an effort to cope with the difficult problems you mentioned a moment ago, the study of the inarticulate masses. It is important to examine the way slavery removed the enslaved from their culture as no other people who came to America were torn away from their culture. This is vital for understanding the obstacles that American Negroes in the twentieth century have to live with. If history could "visualize" these conditions, it would be performing a far more valuable service than by contriving a heroic record from a distortion of the evidence. The point is that American Negroes were denied the *opportunity* to make heroic records for themselves, to participate in the successes and achievements of their fellow Americans. The historical emphasis ought to be upon that denial rather than upon the pretense that somehow they overcame all obstacles.

J.A.G.   In this sense, history is indeed amoral, isn't it? As historians, we seek to discover and record what happened.

D.M.P.   I suppose I agree, though I think that there is a moral value in recognizing how circumstances enhance or limit human potentialities. The historian should be mindful of the moral implications of that fact.

J.A.G.   We have been talking about many enormous historical generalizations. How do historians go about formulating generalizations?

D.M.P.   There is some difference between the theory by which they go about forming generalizations and their practice. And this may be one of the crucial problems of historical study. Theoretically, historians claim that they approach a body of data with as few presuppositions as possible, examine the data, and formulate tentative hypotheses, perhaps, and then try to confirm these hypotheses by more intensive study of the data.

But the traditional belief that the mere accumulation of data and the arrangement of data in chronological sequence would explain itself—that is, lead to a generalization—has inhibited historians from theorizing about the actual nature of generalization. It is virtually impossible to put data into a pattern without implying some meaning to that data. Unstated, implicit assumptions run through all historical writing that purports to contain no generalizations. It is much better for the historian to recognize and define his assumptions. If he does that, he is more likely to modify them when the data undermines them than if he has not formulated them in his own mind.

J.A.G.   But where can his assumptions come from, except from previous study of the data?

D.M.P.   Admittedly, it is often hard to tell whether a writer gets his history from his policy or his policy from his history. That encapsulates the problem. One can start with a point of view, for instance, about the qualities of human nature, draw inferences from that about the form that a political system ought to take, and then rationalize these inferences through an historical presentation. The historical interpretation is really derived from the assumptions instead of the generalizations being derived from the presentation.

For instance, James Madison argues in the *Federalist Papers* that, because of the nature of factions in society, a system of checks and balances is desirable. The historian can take such an assumption, which is, after all, a psychological assumption about human nature, and he can interpret the history of the early state constitutions and the federal Constitution in a way that would suggest that he is vindicating Madison on the basis of historical experience rather than on the basis of his political theory.

J.A.G. Well, Madison's assumptions are fairly clearly stated, or at least can be easily inferred from his writings. What you are expressing concern about is that historians don't make their assumptions as clear as Madison did, even to themselves. But if history has to be based on assumptions and if assumptions are essentially subjective, does this mean that there cannot be any such thing as a definitive history of anything?

D.M.P. I believe the real question is: "Can historical interpretation be shaped by the historian's data and not by his subjective presuppositions?" I think the answer to that is Yes. All the time we see historians starting out with presuppositions about the particular topics which they are investigating, and changing those presuppositions as their investigations proceed. The *discipline* of history involves learning to curb the subjective impulse to believe what one prefers to believe. It may be impossible to eliminate wishful thinking, but a good historian can discipline his wishful thinking and thus limit the range of error. That's what we have to aim at, not the elimination of error, but the reduction of the range of error.

J.A.G. Does what you've been saying mean that history is not a science at all?

D.M.P. The word "science" is a little like the word "definitive." "Science" implies exact knowledge, just as "definitive" implies the last word. One hesitates to believe that a historian will ever say the last word or that he will ever reach a degree of exactness that is absolutely precise. But if by science you mean a body of material and a way of dealing with it which will reduce the range of error or uncertainty, it seems to me that history has some claims to being regarded as a science.

J.A.G. If so much depends on the assumptions that historians make, does this in turn mean that, since they assume things about human nature and human society, they must be psychologists, and perhaps even philosophers in order to write first-rate history?

D.M.P. I'm prone to think that it does. The English historian E. H. Carr speaks of the fact that, in evaluating the past, the historian has to evaluate policies in the past in the light of available alternative policies, just as a statesman has to shape policy in the present in the light of available alternatives. The judgment of the historian has to be rather like the judgment of a man who is engaged in policy decisions, because although he knows what resulted from the course that was taken, he does not know what would have resulted from the courses that were not taken.

J.A.G. In your opinion, what are the interesting historical problems of our own day?

D.M.P. Historians place their bets in different ways, but I believe we will see a good deal more comparative history. I think we also need to restudy many questions with more careful attention to problems on which the social sciences can throw light, such as the question of whether ethnic affiliation or interest groups or ideals are most important in determining which political party a person supports.

J.A.G. Are we training young historians properly for these tasks?

D.M.P. I'm afraid that there's a good deal of confusion in graduate history faculties about what their mission really is. They continue to demand knowledge of a huge body of fact and bibliography, and along with that they indirectly put pressure on students to be more aware of the social sciences. I feel that we should sacrifice some of our demands for content and put a greater emphasis upon the mastery of technique and concepts.

J.A.G. Do you mean that students should be required to specialize in narrower fields, or rather that the amount of factual and bibliographical information that they should be expected to have should be reduced?

D.M.P. I think most doctoral candidates are afraid to take their examinations until they have at their command a very large supply of what is called factual information and bibliographical information. Training ought to be restructured in a way that would minimize attention to factual information and place more stress upon the capacity of the student to handle problems that involve subtle concepts and the weighing of one type of consideration against another.

J.A.G. But doesn't this run into the problem that we are not only training students to be historians but also to be teachers? As teachers, don't they need to have a solid knowledge of fact and bibliography?

D.M.P. I think they do, and of course here I'm talking about changes in emphasis. I wouldn't want to throw out all "content," and I don't think "concepts" are any good unless they're tested against data. But just as a matter of emphasis, I believe that I will stick to my guns. I would rather bet on a student who had a first-rate understanding of the nature of historical forces to work up the story for his classes, than on a man who knew the story to work up an understanding of the nature of the historical forces.

J.A.G.   What are the half-dozen or so books that you would recommend to persons interested in the subject we have been discussing? In each case, would you indicate briefly what the particular contribution of the volume is?

D.M.P.   Let me begin by mentioning two outstanding treatments which approach historical interpretation by way of historiography. One of these, I think I can safely say, is the best general discussion of the subject, namely John Higham's sections on "The Historical Profession," "Theory," and "American History," in Higham, Kreiger, and Gilbert's *History* (1965). The other pertains to the whole range of American history, though its detailed focus is on a limited segment. This is Richard Hofstadter, *The Progressive Historians: Turner, Beard, Parrington* (1968).

On the relationship between the past as it happened and as it has been perceived by historians—that is, on the process by which the raw data of the past is converted into one man's ordered reconstruction of the past—there are three titles which I regard as especially outstanding. One of these, by now a classic, is Marc Bloch's *The Historian's Craft* (1964); another is E. H. Carr's excellent *What Is History?* (1962); the third is J. H. Hexter, *Reappraisals in History* (1961), which shows unusual realism in dealing with the historian's everyday practice.

Another title which I think should be on a list of this kind, Professor Garraty, is your own book on *The Nature of Biography* (1957). This thoughtful and wide-ranging study of the materials, methods, and problems of biography extends over a broad segment of the spectrum of history.

Of course, one of the major concerns of modern historical study is to make use of the concepts and methods of the social sciences insofar as they may be relevant to historical study. There is a good generalized treatment of the potentialities of the social sciences for history in the Social Science Research Council's Bulletin Number 64, *The Social Sciences in Historical Study* (1954). Another treatment, somewhat more concrete in suggesting specific modes of application of the social sciences, is Thomas C. Cochran's *The Inner Revolution: Essays on the Social Sciences in History* (1964). Also, Edward N. Saveth has edited a highly useful collection of essays, *American History and the Social Sciences* (1964).

On the practice and problems of generalization in history, one should consult the collection of essays edited by Louis Gottschalk on *Generalization in the Writing of History* (1963).

Finally, though we have been discussing practice rather than theory and interpretation, and generalization rather than philosophy, let me remark that a very fine introduction to the philosophical side of the subject is a collection of essays, edited by the late Hans Meyerhoff, *The Philosophy of History in Our Time* (1959).